The Luckless Girl

The Luckless Girl

Published by The Conrad Press Ltd. in the United Kingdom 2022

Tel: +44(0)1227 472 874
www.theconradpress.com
info@theconradpress.com

ISBN 978-1-914913-76-1

Copyright © Michael Coy, 2022

The moral right of Michael Coy to be identified as author of this work has been asserted in accordance with the Copyright, Designs and Patents Act 1988.

All rights reserved.

Printed and bound in Great Britain by Clays Ltd, Elcograf S.p.A

Typesetting and cover design by The Book Typesetters
www.thebooktypesetters.com

Cover drawing by Elaine Moore
www.elainemoore.info
blosseymoore@gmail.com

The Conrad Press logo was designed by Maria Priestley.

The Luckless Girl

Michael Coy

Ben poco ama colui che ancora può esprimere,
a parole, quanto ami.

To my wonderful siblings, who have helped me so much.

Introduction

A true story

In the city of Rome, on the evening of 2 January 1698, a 35-year-old man stabbed to death his 17-year-old wife and also killed her parents.

What follows is the story of the teenage wife.

Pompilia was born in the year 1680 in obscure circumstances (this will be important later in the story). Guido, the husband, was a minor Tuscan aristocrat. We need to bear in mind that this was long before Italian Unification, and to a Roman a Tuscan was a foreigner – and vice versa.

It seems barbaric to us that Guido (arrested hours after the stabbing) should admit everything, then go on to plead 'honoris causa' – in effect, 'I killed her for the sake of my honour, and am therefore entitled to a merely nominal punishment.'

Pompilia's Predicament

It also seems strange to us, in the 21st century, that parents would tell a 13-year-old child, 'we've selected a husband for you, and you're marrying him today.' But that is precisely what happened.

In September 1693 the Comparini (Pompilia's parents, Pietro and Violante) negotiated a marriage contract with Guido and his brother. Pietro Comparini followed no profession and appears to have lived off his investments. His wife Violante was a snob and found the idea of marrying into the aristocracy irresistible. Guido, for his part, needed a wife. In his 30's and a failure (he had not managed to secure the patronage of some powerful cardinal), he was the only Franceschini brother who had not taken full holy orders. In order to keep the family house and farms in Arezzo, it fell upon him to produce an heir.

It doesn't surprise us that a marriage founded on such a transactional basis might fail, even if marriage as a business strategy was then the norm. Perhaps we should be mildly surprised that it lasted four years.

By a curious stipulation of the marriage contract, Pompilia, Pietro and Violante were to uproot and move from Rome to Arezzo. The Comparini were dyed-in-the-wool Romans, who do not seem to have spent any time previously outside their native city. Guido's widowed mother Beatrice was (as we shall see) not much of a hostess. The notion that the Comparini and the Franceschini could all live together in harmony under the same roof seems unlikely – and so it proved.

The Franceschini were impoverished. Whatever dreams Violante had of living in a 'palazzo' were quickly dashed by the reality. The house was not in good repair, and arriving in December, the Comparini found conditions Spartan to put it mildly. Added to this, Pietro was by habit a frequenter of taverns. The code by which Arezzo's 'quality' lived made drinking in taverns an unforgiveable sin. Two headstrong women, each accustomed to getting her own way – Violante and Beatrice – were bound to clash. In short, by Easter, the Comparini were packing up and heading back to Rome.

But Pompilia had to stay. She was Guido's wife and therefore, in effect, his property. She must remain in Arezzo. Thus began a period of three years which proved a living hell for the teenage girl. Not only was she a constant reminder to the Franceschini of the hated Comparini (now back in Rome), but she was proving rather tardy in providing the male son which was her 'obligation'.

There is no question that Guido bullied his wife physically. At one point, he even held a pistol to her head. What could Pompilia do? Divorce was not an option. There were no women's refuges, no social services. Two or three times, she literally ran into the Bishop's Palace and (on another occasion) into the office of the Civil Governor. A girl in her mid-teens could not be expected to understand the social dynamics of Arezzo, but the two magnates (temporal and spiritual) to whom she turned for protection were members of the same class and faction as Guido. After holding out for hours on the stairs of the

Bishop's Palace, Pompilia had to give up and return to her husband.

Just a quick mention of the 'Duomo' and the 'Pieve'. Arezzo has many churches, but is dominated (even today) by the two big ones. The Cathedral or *'Duomo'* is a gloomy Gothic pile at the top of the hill. In the 17th century, it was attended by the conservative faction (Bishop Marchetti and Governor Marzi-Medici being prominent members). Guido's family, the Franceschini, were part of the 'Duomo Set'. The *Chiesa di Santa Maria della Pieve* stands on the main street, the *Borgo Maestro* (today, the *Corso d'Italia*). In Pompilia's day its congregation constituted Arezzo's liberal opposition.

Like millions of women before and since, Pompilia probably resigned herself to an unhappy existence. Lacking economic means or even opportunity, there was little else she could do. Under the moral code of her place and time, it was unthinkable for a woman to travel alone, so she couldn't just flee to Rome.

Then two things happened.

First, Guido took his wife to the opera. We know very little about when or where, or even why. Probably, it was the 'done thing' for someone of his class to attend this kind of event. Two canons of the Pieve seem to have been fooling around in the auditorium before the opera began, and one of them threw some sweets ('*confetti*') into Pompilia's lap. Guido had a jealous fit. As we shall see, Guido was not one to challenge other men – Pompilia bore the brunt of his anger over an incident that she neither provoked nor controlled.

Second, she realized in the spring of 1697 that she was pregnant. She must have reached a decision that her child would never be subject to the Franceschini regime. She decided to escape.

Giuseppe Caponsacchi

One of the two canons who misbehaved at the opera was Giuseppe Caponsacchi. In his early twenties, he was attached to the Pieve church.

His religious duties do not seem to have been onerous. He had not taken full Holy Orders. Like many other young aristocrats in Arezzo, he spent his abundant free time drinking, street-fighting and chasing women. He knew Guido, naturally, and was even a visitor at the Franceschini home in the *Borgo de'Cenci*.

Pompilia at some point came to the conclusion that Caponsacchi was the man to help her. At first, he resisted. Why ruffle the calm of the provincial pond where he swam so contentedly? However, by April 1697 Pompilia and Caponsacchi were making plans to run away to Rome.

The obvious explanation is that they became lovers. One of the beauties of Pompilia's story is, we simply don't know. There is evidence pointing to an affair, but there is also plenty to suggest that Caponsacchi acted from the motives of a noble-spirited rescuer.

The Barretts of Wimpole Street

In 1845, Elizabeth Barrett was in a bad situation. Her eccentric father had forbidden her to marry, or even to meet men socially. She had serious health problems. And she was no longer young.

But Elizabeth was a poet. She had built up an international reputation, despite being a recluse who lived and worked in one room. Robert Browning came to see her, and to talk poet to poet.

At the time, Browning was less well-known than Elizabeth, though of course he was to become a literary giant of the Victorian era. He and Elizabeth fell in love.

What was to be done?

Browning devised a daring plan. He would have the banns read at a church around the corner and on the appointed day he and Elizabeth would marry. Of course, her father would disinherit her, but the lovers could escape to Florence and live there.

And that's exactly what happened.

For many years, Browning had a favourite print in a frame on his desk. It shows Andromeda, chained to a rock, threatened by death, but with Perseus on his way to help. In real life, Browning was Elizabeth's Perseus.

The Old Square Yellow Book

In the summer of 1860, Robert Browning was strolling through the centre of Florence when he happened upon a bookstall. He bought a book for a few coppers, not even knowing what it was.

He wrote subsequently about this experience, so we can trace his precise route as he walked back to the apartment and Elizabeth. He started to read his new book. By the time he reached the *Trinità* Bridge, he understood that this strange bundle of documents, some handwritten, some printed, was in fact a barrister's brief. He had purchased a set of papers from a Roman murder trial, undertaken 162 years earlier – the murder trial of Guido Franceschini.

It took Browning more than a decade to turn this source material into his masterpiece – 'The Ring and the Book'. It lent itself beautifully to his 'dramatic monologue' technique, by which various characters tell the story, each speaker seeing events from a limited perspective, and revealing as much about himself as he tells us about the overall situation.

The Elopement

At the very end of May, 1697, everything was in place. Caponsacchi had let it be known around Arezzo that he had to go to Rome on business, and he had arranged with Agostino Chimato, landlord of the *'Canale'* tavern, to borrow a calash – a simple horse-drawn carriage.

Pompilia slipped a sleeping-draught into the bedtime drinks of Guido and his mother, and escaped. Whether Caponsacchi came to the *Borgo de'Cenci* or met her en route is not entirely clear. At any rate, they made it to the *San Clemente* Gate without being challenged by The Watch. They clambered over the collapsed *Torrión* (a bastion in the city wall) and rendezvoused with the calash and its driver, 'Venerino'.

Venerino took them as far as *Camoscia* (now called '*Camucha*'), 20 kilometres south of Arezzo. There, they transferred to another vehicle at a coaching inn and pressed on towards Rome.

Today, by car, the Arezzo-Rome journey can be accomplished comfortably in a couple of hours. Back then, on unsurfaced roads in vehicles without suspension, it took a bone-jarring three days. The fugitives had agreed to make directly for Rome without stopping, but at Castelnuovo di Porto (only 30 km from central Rome) Pompilia could bear it no longer, and asked for a brief stop.

Guido, meanwhile, had woken up to find his wife and her possessions gone. He quickly figured out what had happened, and knew she must be heading for Rome. He set off on horseback and made good time.

It was at Castelnuovo that Guido caught up with Pompilia and Caponsacchi. One might have expected an indignant husband (given the manners of the time) to attack both his wife and her companion. Guido didn't do that. He called out The Watch, and initiated a lawsuit against each of them, alleging adultery – a capital offence back then. The trial did not take place immediately. Pompilia and Caponsacchi passed the summer in custody in Castelnuovo, and stood trial in September.

The verdicts are baffling.

No finding of any kind was made in respect of Pompilia. Caponsacchi seems to have been found guilty (it's questionable), but was sentenced to the mildest of punishments – he was transferred from the Pieve to the city of Civitavecchia, 30km from Rome, for three years. The Court appears to have taken an extremely enlightened view of the couple's behaviour. Pompilia was sent to a convent in Rome, the cost of her upkeep to be paid by Guido, and when that didn't work out she was allowed to live with her parents in her childhood home. This smacks more of protecting her from Guido than of any notion of punishing her.

The *Dénouement*

Pompilia gave birth to her son, Caetano, in the late autumn of 1697. She never saw Caponsacchi again.

Guido seems to have been bitterly disappointed by the light sentences handed down by the Roman court and by what he regarded as the pollution of his blood.

Violante, Pompilia's mother, was not a woman to be trifled with. She had been badly treated by the Franceschini during her three months in Arezzo. She was minded to exact revenge – and she knew just exactly how to do it.

Pompilia was not her natural daughter. She had tricked her husband back in 1680 by faking a pregnancy and buying a baby from a poor woman named Corona.

It just so happened that the Pope – Innocent XII – was declaring a jubilee year. Anyone who made a clean breast of old sins would win an indulgence, and have time in Purgatory erased from their record. The announcement that Pompilia had been born in the gutter to unknown parents would devastate Guido. He had hitched himself to an utter nobody. Not only would he be a laughing-stock in Arezzo – but any future offspring would be a corruption of the Franceschini line. Of course, Violante would have to reveal to her husband Pietro that she had been deceiving him about their 'daughter' for close on two decades – but she calculated (correctly) that she could manage that situation.

The trigger was probably the birth of Caetano. If Pompilia's baby was Caponsacchi's child, Guido was utterly humiliated. If the child was his own, his bloodline was permanently compromised. Guido hired four accomplices in December 1697, and set off for Rome.

The five men stayed at Paolo's vineyard at Ponte Milvio. The omens were not good. Abate Paolo – Guido's bother and mentor – had recently run away. Whether this was out of shame at having lost his position with the Knights of Malta, or because he knew what Guido was about to do, and wanted to create an alibi, we will never know. Guido and his gang stayed at the very modest vineyard with very basic amenities while the plan matured. Crucially, Guido omitted to buy permits for horses. When the assassins needed to escape after the murders, they would have to do so on foot.

On 2 January they killed Pietro and Violante at the family home in the Via Vittoria, and mortally wounded Pompilia. The Roman *sbirri* (rudimentary police) had little trouble following and capturing them. Pompilia lived on for four more days, and was able to name Guido as her assailant. He died on the scaffold some six weeks later.

Treves, Gest and Corrigan

Friend of both Thomas Hardy and the Elephant Man, Sir Frederick Treves saved the life of King Edward VII in 1902. More importantly for our present purpose, he became fascinated by the story of Pompilia and in about 1910 made a literary and photographic record of her and her elopement.[1] He took, or caused to be taken, photographs of key locations in the Pompilia tragedy which might otherwise be difficult to identify today.

One repeated criticism of Browning's poem is that he treated the trial lawyers with a flippancy that the real individuals did not deserve. Judge John Gest of Philadelphia certainly thought so,[2] and a century ago he set about putting the record straight. He assembled a library of medieval Italian legal texts, and wrote an indispensible book on the law as it was applied in Guido's case.

Browning knew nothing about Violante's bid to get revenge on Guido. In the 1940s, a Canadian scholar was rummaging in an old library in Cortona when she discovered a bundle of invaluable documents which explain the dowry lawsuit.[3] She was able to establish that Pietro Comparini went far beyond forgiving his wife for her deception. He launched a lawsuit in which he denied owing

---

[1] *The Country of the Ring and the Book*, F. Treves, Cassell London 1913
[2] *The Old Yellow Book: Source of Robert Browning's 'The Ring & the Book'*, J.M. Gest, Chipman Boston 1925
[3] *Curious Annals*, B. Corrigan, University of Toronto Press, 1956

anything to Guido in respect of unpaid dowry contributions (if Pompilia was not his daughter, how could he be liable?) The case collapsed when all the principals died in early 1698 (Pietro, Violante, Pompilia and Guido), but Beatrice Corrigan's 'find' is precious: Pietro had half-a-dozen statements sworn out by midwives, wetnurses &c., so we have a reasonably complete picture of what Violante did.

Comments on the Present Poem

The *novella* was a literary genre very much in vogue in 17th-century Italy. Many of these works were hand-written. The idea was to take a sensational story, work it up into a text, then read it 'live' in salons and at literary soirées. Several of the stories included here ('The Countess of Cellant', 'Nay, Guiltiness Will Speak') are based on *novelle*.

In one of the Middle Ages' seminal works, *The Golden Legend*, a Genoese Bishop (Jacopo de Voragine) tells the story of how the Tree of Knowledge in the Garden of Eden gave rise to the Cross on which Jesus Christ was crucified. Arezzo's outstanding art treasure is the frescoed chancel of the church of San Francesco, where Piero della Francesca painted in episodic fashion the salient details of the story. They appear here as one of two *leitmotivs* running through the poem.

The other *leitmotiv* is the Congress of the Wits. Popes from the Renaissance to the 20th century, being also temporal princes, were keen to exercise censorship. Anything approaching free speech or dissemination of liberal ideas had to be stamped out ruthlessly. Roman acuity is difficult to suppress, and the populace selected six ancient statues dotted about the city and dubbed them the 'talking statues', or the 'Congress of the Wits'. Satirical and scandalous poems would appear, hung around the statues' necks. The tradition continues today. Here, Abate Luigi and his friends intervene at regular intervals to make their caustic remarks.

Anyone who has ever read a barrister's brief will have noticed how it has passed through various hands before now, and along the way it has acquired extraneous and anonymous documents of questionable relevance to the matter in hand. I have sought to replicate this by imagining that unknown individuals of a literary bent have 'owned' this bundle of documents over the centuries, and have dropped into the brief unsigned poems tending to comment on the action.

Michael Coy

Ronda, Spain   April, 2022

Contents

TO THE READER	26
Perseus and Andromeda	27
Euphuistic Sonnet	27
Stray Leaves	28
A DEPLORABLE HISTORY Being a novella written by Cardinal Fabrizio Spada	29
STRAY LEAVES: GUIDO FRANCESCHINI, BY A NEIGHBOUR	32
STRAY LEAVES: A CULINARY METAPHOR	36
STRAY LEAVES: DOCTOR BARTOLOMEO ALBERGOTTI RECOUNTS A NIGHT AT THE OPERA	39
AGOSTINO 'CANALE' CHIMATO, LANDLORD OF AN AREZZO TAVERN, ENTERTAINS HIS CUSTOMERS	40
STRAY LEAVES: THE DUOMO AND THE PIEVE	46
A DEPLORABLE HISTORY (CONTINUED)	48
A LETTER WRITTEN BY THE COUNTESS FRANCESCA POMPILIA FRANCESCHINI TO HER PUTATIVE PARENTS IN ROME, FROM A PRISON CELL IN CASTENUOVO	54
A DEPLORABLE HISTORY (RESUMED)	55
STRAY LEAVES: THE ROSE AND THE CROSS	59
THE CONGRESS OF THE WITS: (1)	62
TABLE TALK	64
THE OFFENDING OCTAVES	67
DEPOSITION OF COUNTESS FRANCESCA POMPILIA FRANCESCHINI IN THE PROCESSUS FUGAE	68
DEPOSITION OF CANON GIUSEPPE CAPONSACCHI IN THE PROCESSUS FUGAE	74
THE ROMANCE OF THE ROSE, being a tale told by Giuseppe Caponsacchi	85
L'INGANNO FELICE	102
REX JUDAEORUM, RES JUDICATA, Being a Tale Told by Jacopo, the Yardman at the Castelnuovo Inn	126
FATHER URBANO ROMANO REMEMBERS POMPILIA	128
THE DREAM OF THE ROOD, Being the Dream of Francesca Pompilia, as She Related it to Father Urbano Romano	129

LETTER OF CIVIL GOVERNOR VINCENZO MARZI-MEDICI TO ABATE PAOLO FRANCESCHINI, 2 AUGUST 1694.	141
STRAY LEAVES: TELLING TALES	144
THAT NICE DECISION OF DOLABELLA'S, Being a Tale Told by Governor Vicente Marzi-Medici to His Brethren, I Forzatti, during a convocatorio at the Horse Inn	145
THE HISTORY OF THE TRUE CROSS (1)	146
HALF-ROME	153
STRAY LEAVES: Pompilia and Her Priest	159
THE OTHER HALF-ROME	164
STRAY LEAVES: HONORIS CAUSA	172
TERTIUM QUID	172
STRAY LEAVES: APOLLO AND DAPHNE	174
STRAY LEAVES: UP AT THE VILLA	177
THE WELL AND THE HEAD, Being a Cluster of Tales told by Cardinal Fabrizio Spada at the Dinner Table in the Villa Farnesina	180
The Tunnel and the Obelisk	188
STRAY LEAVES: RUTH AND BOAZ	199
THE HISTORY OF THE TRUE CROSS: (2) The Death of Adam	201
STRAY LEAVES: THE HART AT BAY	205
THE CONGRESS OF THE WITS	206
STRAY LEAVES: WHO KNOWS?	208
LA PUTTA ONORATA	208
Light Denied (1)	214
SLEEPLESS IN SIENA, Being a Tale told by Pietro Ottoboni, His Account of a Play He Once saw at a Fairground	218
STRAY LEAVES: I ADORE AN ESPINELA!	222
EVIDENCE OF MARIA MARGHARITA CONTENTI, SWORN PURSUANT TO A LAWSUIT IN THE EPISCOPAL COURT OF AREZZO, AN ACTION WHICH WAS SUBSEQUENTLY DISCONTINUED	240
STRAY LEAVES: THE LOVE OF FATE	241
STRAY LEAVES: THE FATE OF LOVE	242
STRAY LEAVES: POMPILIA'S PORTALS	243
CONSENTING ADULTS, Being a Tale told by Maria Margharita Contenti	247

THE HISTORY OF THE TRUE CROSS	256
STRAY LEAVES: 'As fragrant as …'	258
STRAY LEAVES: THE ARRANGEMENT OF THE FRESCOES	261
STRAY LEAVES: 'Like any journeyman …'	262
QUELLE STESSE PAROLE!, Being the Recounting, by Tertium Quid, of an Opera he Once saw)	263
STRAY LEAVES: A FUNCTIONING DRUNK	266
STRAY LEAVES: WANTING THE SHAFT ON	267
STRAY LEAVES: VESTI LA GIUBBA	269
STRAY LEAVES: RAGAZZE, O PAGLIACCI?	270
STRAY LEAVES: A DRUNK-SHUNNING FUNK	272
STRAY LEAVES: SHAFTING THE WANTON	273
TWO ANONYMOUS PAMPHLETS: ONE IN SUPPORT OF GUIDO FRANCESCHINI, ONE AGAINST HIM	274
PRIMUS STUDIORUM DUX	295
I DREAMT I DWELT IN MARBLE HALLS, Being a Tale related by Cristina Paperozzi	297
THE BROWNING VERSION	304
TO A MOLINIST	305
IL PASTOR FIDO, Being a tale told by Giacinto Arcangeli, Procurator of the Poor)	306
STRAY LEAVES: 'Our human curse …'	306
STRAY LEAVES: 'The cause, we later find …'	307
STRAY LEAVES: 'What is there to be feared of …?'	335
STRAY LEAVES: PISA SONNET	347
STRAY LEAVES: ON TWO JUXTAPOSED COLUMNS IN THE CHURCH OF SANTA MARIA IN COSMEDIN, ROME	356
WRITTEN STATEMENT OF DONNA COSTANZA DONATO, PREPARED FOR THE PROCESSUS FUGAE	358
THE CONGRESS OF THE WITS: (3) Madama Lucrezia	361
THE HISTORY OF THE TRUE CROSS: (4) Burying the Wood	362
ROSINA IN THE OVEN, Being a Tale related by Agnese Santa Olivieri	363
LO SPOSO DELUSO, Being a Tale told by Giovanni-Battista Mucha	374
THE SLEEP OF SORROW AND THE DREAM OF JOY, Being various Scraps of Verse discovered among the Papers of Massimo	

Taparelli, Count d'Azeglio, after his Death	390
SAN CLEMENTE GATE	392
DOCTOR ANTONIO LAMPARELLI, PROCURATOR OF THE POOR, DEFENDS CANON GIUSEPPE CAPONSACCHI AT THE PROCESSUS FUGAE	393
THE COUNTESS OF CELLANT, Being a Tale told by Fra Angelo Celestino	398
MEN MAY DIE OF IMAGINATION	406
LA SALTA DE LA CONTESSA, Being a Tale told by Gregorio Guillichini	406
THE LUCKLESS GIRL	417
A STRANGE DISDAIN, Being a Tale told by Donna Costanza Donato of Arezzo	418
THREE SONNETS IN WHICH ARE ENCAPSULATED THE 366 POEMS OF PETRARCH'S 'CANZONE'	422
THE CONGRESS OF THE WITS: (4) Il Babuino	423
THE VANITY OF HUMAN WISHES	425
THE HISTORY OF THE TRUE CROSS: (5) The Recognition and Testing of the True Cross	425
ATTESTATION OF FRA CELESTINO ANGELO DI SANTA ANNA, BAREFOOT AUGUSTINIAN PRIEST, TO BE ACCEPTED WITHOUT DEMUR, INASMUCH AS HE GAVE CORPOREAL AND SPIRITUAL SUCCOUR TO THE CONTESSA FRANCESCA POMPILIA FRANCESCHINI, EVEN TO HER DEATH: WHEREIN HE SPEAKS OF HER GOODNESS, AND HER DECLARATION THAT SHE NEVER ONCE VIOLATED HER CONJUGAL FAITH	427
PRIVATE LETTER FROM GIOVANNI BATTISTA MUCHA, SOMETIME APPRENTICE TO THE APOTHECARY G.B. GUITENS, WRITTEN IN HIS OLD AGE, CONCERNING HIS ATTENDANCE ON THE COUNTESS POMPILIA FRANCESCHINI DURING HER FINAL AGONY	429
WE, THE UNDERSIGNED, BEING INTERROGATED FOR THE TRUTH, HAVE MADE FULL AND UNQUESTIONED STATEMENT ON OUR OATH, THAT WE WERE PRESENT AND ASSISTED AT THE LAST ILLNESS FROM WHICH	

FRANCESCA POMPILIA, WIFE OF GUIDO FRANCESCHINI, DIED.	432
STATEMENT OF DONNA ALLEGRA BORRI, SWORN PURSUANT TO A LAWSUIT IN THE EPISCOPAL COURT OF AREZZO, AN ACTION WHICH WAS SUBSEQUENTLY DISCONTINUED	433
THE SPANISH HARPSICHORD TEACHER	439
THE CARDINAL POINTS (1)	459
TESTIMONY OF JACOPO DI CESANO IN THE PROCESSUS FUGAE, SUMMER 1697	461
MARRIAGE ON EARTH, Being a Tale told by Allegra Borri	464
THE CONGRESS OF THE WITS:	504
THE HISTORY OF THE TRUE CROSS:	506
LA GAZZA LADRA, Being a Tale told by Angelica Battista	507
STRAY LEAVES: PADDY STOPPED AT EMPOLI	509
STRAY LEAVES: BRIDGET THE FIDGET	509
STRAY LEAVES: HATE-PLOUGH	514
EL VIOLINCELLO DEL CARDENAL, IN WHICH BOTTINI'S INVESTIGATORS REACH OUT TO CARDINAL PIETRO OTTOBONI, CURRENT CURATE OF THE CHURCH WHERE POMPILIA WAS CHRISTENED, MARRIED AND IS BURIED	519
CELLINI'S CRUCIFIX	526
A TRAVELLER ARRIVES IN AREZZO	530
GREGORY THE GREAT	531
STRAY LEAVES: A STRIDENT PHILOSOPHY	534
NO HEAVIER SIN, Being a Tale told by Half-Rome	543
STRAY LEAVES: THE TRUMP OF DOOM	544
THE MAGNANIMITY OF SCIPIO, Being A Tale told by Antonio Lamparelli	553
FORTUNE'S FROWNING FACE, Being a Tale told by Caterina Fiori	556
STRAY LEAVES: TURNING-POINT	559
STRAY LEAVES: LOCHABER NO MORE	561
THE HISTORY OF THE TRUE CROSS:	566
ADELAIDE, Being a Tale told by Francesco Gambi	566

THE GATHERER OF SOLES, Being a Tale told by Desiderio Spreti	574
BELLINDA AND THE MONSTER, Being a Tale told by Urbano Romano	580
A BUNDLE OF LOVE LETTERS, ALLEGED TO HAVE PASSED BETWEEN THE COUNTESS POMPILIA AND THE CANON CAPONSACCHI	597
STRAY LEAVES: URBANO ROMANO	610
LIVISTROS AND RODAMNE, Being an Attempt at a Novella, but Clearly no More than a Fragment, Composed by The Other Half-Rome	615
THE CONGRESS OF THE WITS:	620
OPENING SUBMISSION OF DOCTOR GIACINTO ARCANGELI, PROCURATOR OF THE POOR, IN DEFENCE OF GUIDO FRANCESCHINI AND CONFEDERATES AT THEIR TRIAL FOR HOMICIDE	621
STRAY LEAVES: DULCIA VENENA	624
STRAY LEAVES: PLUMA AGGRAVANTES	637
STRAY LEAVES: DE RAPTU HELENAE	640
SUBMISSION OF DOCTOR FRANCESCO GAMBI, PROCURATOR OF THE FISC, IN THE PROSECUTION OF COUNT GUIDO FRANCESCHINI AND HIS ASSOCIATES	656
DURING A LUNCHEON ADJOURNMENT, GIOVANNI BATTISTA BOTTINI, ADVOCATE OF THE FISC, FINALISES HIS FORENSIC STRATEGY	659
STRAY LEAVES: IN A SPANISH CLOISTER	667
STRAY LEAVES: A GAME AT CHESS	672
THE HISTORY OF THE TRUE CROSS: (8) The Battle of Nineveh	674
STRAY LEAVES: THE BATTLE OF BENEVENTO	674
FEDERIGO'S FALCON, Being a Tale found among the Posthumous Papers of Massimo d'Azeglio	675
THE CASTLE OF OTRANTO, Being a Tale told by Giovanni Battista Bottini	677
STRAY LEAVES: IN DREAMS	705
STRAY LEAVES: THE STATESMAN AND THE PLACEMAN	711
FRANCESCO ROSSI, DETTO 'VENERINO', RELATES HIS	

STORY TO THE REGULARS OF AREZZO'S CANALE INN	713
STRAY LEAVES: THE ELUSIVE CANON	718
LA MONTEJAQUEÑA, Being a Tale told by Venerino	726
THE HISTORY OF THE TRUE CROSS: (9) The Exhaltation of the Cross	727
NAY, GUILTINESS WILL SPEAK, Being a Tale told by Alessandro Baldeschi	728
STRAY LEAVES; OF WIVES AND KNIVES	738
STRAY LEAVES: THE FAVOUR AND THE BLADE	740
STRAY LEAVES: HONI SOIT QUI MAL Y PENSE	741
TRIAL AND DEATH OF COUNT GUIDO FRANCESCHINI AND HIS COMPANIONS FOR THE IMPIOUS MURDER OF PIETRO COMPARINI, HIS WIFE, AND DAUGHTER: WHICH LAMENTABLE SLAUGHTER OCCURRED DURING THE PONTIFICATE OF INNOCENT XII.	749
THE CARDINAL POINTS (2)	769
THE FIRST DRAFT OF WHAT APPEARS TO BE A PROPOSED NOVELLA, FOUND AMONG THE PAPERS OF CARDINAL FABRIZIO SPADA	770
STRAY LEAVES: VERANILLO DE MEMBRILLO	772
SAINT MARTIN'S SUMMER	773
DOCTOR ANTONIO LAMPARELLI, PROCURATOR OF THE POOR, PETITIONS THE COURT TO RESTORE THE GOOD NAME OF COUNTESS FRANCESCA POMPILIA FRENCESCHINI, DECEASED	780
STRAY LEAVES: COUP DE FOUDRE	786
ON FRIDAY 18 DECEMBER 1772, BEING THE 25TH BIRTHDAY OF GAETANO FRANCESCHINI (UNDER ROMAN LAW THE DATE OF HIS ADULTHOOD), THE AFOREMENTIONED RECEIVES THIS LETTER FROM DOMENICO TIGHETTI (OF SACRED MEMORY)	789
ROSA TROVATELLA, OR THE GIRL WHO FED JESUS, Being a Tale told by Bishop Marchetti of Arezzo	792
LOS ENAMORADOS DE ANTEQUERA, Being a Poem that Giovanna Boba learned as a Child, and now recites	797
IL MULINELLO, Being the Story of Rimini, as related by Doctor	

Bartolomeo Albergotti	803
STRAY LEAVES: MY MASTERY OF HISTORY	803
ON 9 SEPTEMBER,1698, IN THE EIGHTH YEAR OF THE PONTIFICATE ON INNOCENT XII, IN ADMINISTRATIVE BUILDINGS ATTACHED TO THE BASILICA OF SANTA CROCE IN GERUSALEMME, THE MOST ILLUSTRIOUS AND REVEREND MARCANTONIO VENTURINI, DEPUTY GOVERNOR OF ROME WHO HOLDS THE CRIMINAL BENCH, GIVES JUDGMENT IN THE MATTER OF TIGHETTI VERSUS THE CONVERTITES	807
TO THE READER	814
Glossary of Foreign-Language Terms	815

> non la conobbe mentre l'ebbe:
> conobbil'io, ch'a pianger qui rimase

> I maintain that whenever any writer, poet or not,
> selects a subject, he should, before he writes about
> it, take some pains to acquire sufficient knowledge

> m'insegnavate come l'uom s'etterna

> the conscious mind is an ordered township with weird
> caverns beneath

> di grazia la renda à chi gliene porge

> the point is not that such-and-such was done on earth:
> the point is that, before such-and-such could be done on
> earth, this other, more important, primary thing had to
> be brought to pass within the labyrinth that we all know
> and visit in our dreams

> Percioche l'arte del depingere è dignissima
> veramente de gli animi liberali

> just as law from deeds may rise,
> when deeds are evil, justice dies

> diverse
> beltà, vini diversi. Io vo' gustar
> quanto più posso dell'opra divina!

> ad rosem per crucem, ad crucem per rosam

> sieti raccomandato il mio Tesoro
> nel qua lio vivo ancora, e più non cheggio

> stories as mere stories had the strongest
> fascination for him

> Id con Dios que, a fe de hidalgo,
> haré todo buen oficio,
> si con la Duquesa valgo.

> Peut-être n'est-elle norte qu'en apparence,
> suivant la coutume des philosophes, qui
> font semblant de morir en un lieu, & se
> transplantent en un autre.

> sanctum est vetus omne poëma

> Multiplicity does no more than illustrate an underlying unity.

TO THE READER

The wind is just about to fill your sails.
The poetry that fills me with disgust
is flimsy. I want something that's robust.
We've theatre, opera and ancient tales:
you'll find terrific triumphs, famous fails,
and how ambition lands us in the dust.
Great princes and events are here discussed,
plus Gina Lollobrigidas, Gareth Bales,
some alpha, beta, gamma, delta males.
Go bleat of orthodoxy if you must –
my motto is, Samantha Fox or bust.
We'll lie in palaces and airless gaols,
meet outlaws to compare with Josey Wales:
the bad gets slighted, and the good prevails.

Perseus and Andromeda

She forms the upright axis of the work.
She's naked, vulnerable, deathly white.
The chains set in the rock have bound her tight,
and something vile is stirring in the murk.
The reptile menaces, the fetters irk:
when waves inevitably reach her height,
she'll drown. She has no chance of fight or flight.
Though water overwhelms and dragons lurk,
the thing is not yet hopeless. Help's at hand.
A decent man, unselfish, handsome, brave,
is hurrying towards her on the strand,
his strength derived from words his brethren gave –
the finest act to self, to understand:
the noblest to another is to save.

Euphuistic Sonnet

In Italy (in sixteen ninety-eight)
our actors played their Drama of the Knives
(defeated longings and imagined wrongs
(he murdered for the honour she forsook,
did not anticípate the torture-tongs
(the husband and his bravos brought to book,
to die by rope and blade (in all, ten lives
cut short before their time) since Law deprives
the perpetrator of the thing he took)

attached excessive weight to parlour-songs:
each perfumed letter forged each dagger hook)
composed the solstice where our lay belongs)
the age-old tale of ill-matched men and wives,
the tragicomedy of love and hate.

Stray Leaves

You've never read a legal brief? You'd know
how random documents can interleave
your proper papers, managing to weave
into the texture, mingle with the flow,
establish squatters' privileges, though
they're alien to your purpose. How they cleave,
or where they came from, you can scarce conceive.
It's just as if a snow-white portico
of perfect pillars in November rain
allowed the wayward wind one whim, to sow
deciduous debris like some ochre bane,
to wreck its regularity. Disdain
at fertile Nature's feckless overflow
is not the way. Leaf-litter helps us grow.

THE DYING CENTURY IS BLEEDING OUT.
                A starless winter solstice ushers in
through streets of Rome as black as Indian ink
the thinnest drizzle.
              Nobody's about.
One creaking lantern's intermittent wink
reflects in puddles, miserable as sin.
It's sixteen ninety-seven. Run-off pours
expectorating from a drainpipe spout
to pool uneasily in sullen clay.
All decent citizens are safe indoors
with logs a-glowing in the kitchen range.
But Guido Franceschini's in the street.
A corner shadow like a velvet cloak
slants down across his breast. Imagined wrongs
are stinging him. Their damp unwholesome heat
an antidote to sleet – has quite deranged him.
When the *Ave*'s three lugubrious dongs
have soaked into the spongy swamp of night,

he gives the signal.
                With his Tuscan toughs,
his ragged beard a dripping stalactite,
he crosses to the so-familiar door
and hammers with the pommel of his knife.
Pompilia, his pretty teenage wife,
and both her ageing parents are inside.

They chose to open? Then they'd never more
enjoy a crisp and even Christmastide.
Yes, Guido's here to kill them. 'Who's out there?'
Pietro's bulk is inches off. The stair
groans audibly beneath the old boy's weight.
'I'm Caponsacchi's man. I've brought this note.'
The fox and vixen, fast within their lair,
need only say the hour is far too late,
or query whether Caponsacchi wrote…
but chains are chimed, arthritic bolts are drawn.
The knife will soon be seeking out the throat,
and life will ebb away before the dawn.

A DEPLORABLE HISTORY
Being a novella written by Cardinal Fabrizio Spada

Suppose a wealthy prelate writes a book
('*novella*', as they termed it, way back when).
You read it 'hand-wrought', as it left his pen.
It's table entertainment. When you cook
for forty, you can puff your 'look'
by having someone read it. (There are men
who make a living doing that.) Again,
some salon Solon, hallway Habakkuk
will thrill assembled sybarites with 'facts'
extracted from some lurid recent crime
(forget the Letters, whack them with the Acts!)

There was a market for these true-crime tracts,
a gruesome love of grabbling through grime
(can we despise them, from our point in time?

MY NAME? FABRIZIANO (SURNAME, Spada)
(just think of me as Innocent's Grand Vizier).
I'm like a running footman (only busier!)
I see the horses shod, and stock the larder,
in moments of repose indulge my ardour
for tales of lovers cozened and deceived
or condennati rope-stretched or reprieved:
novelle which are nothing, niente, nada.
My tale? Malevolenza, ipocrisia:
a child of madre, nonni, all bereaved
(I'm looking at that daub of Artemisia,
with Jael's avenging tent-peg). Interleaved
are scraps of nonsense, editings, excisia
which turned up unacknowledged, lost, ungrieved.

A WEDDING! FIT OCCASION, no, to dance?
A jig, for joyful soles to hit the bricks?
Well, no. A rainstorm sets a sombre tone.
The bride's a child, the groom is thirty-six
(foreboding? Feeling faint, by any chance?)
We're in the year of sixteen ninety-three,
just off the *Corso* (yes, the Holy See,
and Innocent the Twelfth is on the throne).
The thirteen-year-old wife (you look askance?)
provides the needed dowry, may advance
the noble cause by, when the seeds are sown,
obliging with an heir. The perfect mix!
Here, vulgar cash, there, aristocracy
that's worn a little threadbare (truth be known,
they're on their uppers). This contrived romance
has fewer hopes of floating than a stone
encased in concrete. Incrementally

the girl will come to comprehend her fix,
and see that others, through their tiresome tricks,
have marked her for a curious destiny.

The Comparini? Middling kind of folk.
Not rich, exactly. Certainly not poor!
The kind who put their cash in bricks and mortar.
You couldn't call them young (Pietro's stroke
has slowed him down). Their prospects scanty,
they've kept the wolves who slaver at the door
from getting in. And best, they have a daughter,
an asset to be bartered as a whore.
You think that harsh? You don't know Violante!
They live in quite a decent sort of quarter,
north central Rome, tall town house, lower floor
let out (a tailor and a hardware store).
The girl is thirteen (think of 'lamb' and 'slaughter'),
a beauty *abbastanza abbagliante*.
A pig should not be purchased at a poke,
as someone pointed out (it could be Dante).
The use of mirrors (and a little smoke),
the loading of each rift with *ersatz* ore,
will cozen some buffoon to come and court her
and we'll not suffer by it. Up the ante!

Enter our heroine. Her name's Pompilia.
Teenager with big eyes and long, long lashes –
quite staggering, the beauty she became!
(Though no-one spoke back then of paedophilia,
it doesn't mean they didn't play the game).
Her prudent parents feared financial crashes.
Pietro walks her up and down the *Corso*
(prefers it to the *Spagna*, which is hillier)
and through the square of *Popolo*, just the same
as in her childhood, save her slender torso
is corseted more tightly. Pietro's lame

(he's hobbling like always, only more so).
Expected now to show that shapely *dorso*,
Francesca (that's Pompilia's other name)
was taught (by Mother) how to dart out flashes
from eyes behind a fan. What could feel sillier?
Her father's foes are looking to the Law, so
we can't afford the luxury of shame!
She traipses through the Triton Fountain's splashes,
a jotting in her parents' marginalia.

STRAY LEAVES: GUIDO FRANCESCHINI, BY A NEIGHBOUR

The syndrome that describes him
is defined as 'Little Man':
he toadies when he has to,
and he'll bully where he can.
Too old to go a-courting,
he wears his fringe too long;
though I've thought a lot about him,
I can't sift him to the bran.

There's something in his make-up
that always gets it wrong;
his hose is always wrinkled
and his doublet's far too long.
Rosselli wrecked his reason
on the day he broke his nose.
He's scrawny and uncomely,
and you'd lose him in a throng.

His beard's too thick and wiry
in the patches where it grows,
his voice is harsh and scratchy,
with the timbre of a crow's,

and when the Lord gave brains out,
he wasn't in the queue.
His legs are thin and bandy
(I refer you to the hose.)

One thing above all others
is unalterably true.
There's nothing on this planet
he won't take exception to.
He's got it in his noddle
that he's somehow 'better than',
and he'll look to be offended,
doesn't matter what you do.

THERE'S NOTHING IN THE WORLD TO RIVAL ROME.
Here, human-hewn *prodigi* interlace
with smiling Nature in a fond embrace.
Broad boulevards and slender obelisks
align, combine in patterns. You'd rebel?
An impish breeze, to tease the fountain, whisks
fine droplets free of shield and sheath and shell;
a line of pines which bristles like a comb
can almost seem to crown each man-made dome.
You think Rome heaven? All the rest seems hell!
Arezzo is another kind of nome.
Another class of creature calls this home.
You'll find no functionaries, favourites, fiscs.
You want the news? The women at the well
will tell you of the latest-named disgrace.
The gates all close at *Pieve*'s evening bell.
The only urgency, evading risks
of social impropriety, a race
to scamper to your final resting-place
without provoking scandal, losing face.

And thus they sealed their tawdry business deal
and Guido got Pompilia, plus the bonds
(potentially, that is: 'one-third up front').
One can't help thinking, 'big fish, little ponds':
why move the Comparini to Arezzo?
By what hallucination did they feel
that somehow, someone waving magic wands
could make it work out well? (We're not there yet, so
let's pause to analyse this zone-change zeal,
a sort of 'why-go-Tuscan?' intermezzo).
The Franceschini focus, let's be blunt,
was, 'as things stand, we're wallowing in debt, so
what can we lose? Invite them. Take a punt.'
But Romans aren't convincing vagabonds.
Do aretines have ginger? Cochineal?
Barolo, bisi? Will we have to hunt
for somewhere decent for our evening meal?
For Violante, won't this Tuscan stunt
(where she won't rule the roost) soon lose appeal?
How long before the Roman rump absconds?

A street so narrow, you can touch both sides
at once (they say the neighbour is a *putta*),
is where the Franceschini tribe resides
(not quite the spot for spoiling teenage brides!)
The saying, *non il pane, ma il sorgo,*
decidedly applies. Like rotting teeth,
the slow-subsiding houses of the borgo
(all peeling paint and dislocated gutter)
enshroud the passage like an ivy wreath.
It's once-were-rich above, still-poor beneath!
So, in *de Cenci* alleyway he hides,
unlikely Leonidas with his Gorgo,
from creditors, the broken-batoned shutter
his observation-post. *Smorto, sporgo,*
the sullen spider-with-no-web presides,

preoccupied with what he may bequeath
to future Franceschini; heard to mutter
'we'll see how far my honour and the law go.
I'll hang on here, *sebbene si accorgo,*
I could be in the *Maestro* in ten strides.'

Accustomed to long habit of control,
could Violante canter to the rein,
or would she gravitate to 'leader role'?
We know the answer. Monna Beatrice
would brook no rival. Guido's mother owned
the Franceschini franchise: more than this,
(a source of insults) Pietro, wont to stroll
the *Borgo Maestro*, seeking grape and grain,
was classed a drunkard. Beatrice, enthroned
as moral arbitrix, could hardly miss!
Angelica (the servant) carried coal
(since this was winter) to her prejudice,
up to the room where Violante groaned.
But Beatrice, imperious chatelaine,
chastised her and forbade it. Avarice,
or 'bourgeois-are-beneath-me' high disdain?
Relations now severely under strain,
complaints and accusations dragged and droned,
and weapons, openly, were being honed,
as 'both your houses' reached the precipice.

The pair were, in effect, trapped in their room.
Pietro found himself, one night, locked out.
When Violante sallied from the 'tomb'
to help him, she wound up in trouble's way.
The door was locked against them, not a doubt.
A neighbour had to improvise as host.
If Pietro headed tavernwards, to boast
of how Rome's glamour crushed Arezzo grey,
he knew he'd have an afternoon (at most)

before (once more enveloped by the gloom)
he'd have to face the jibes and join the fray.
For Sunday lunch, inevitably, roast:
the only quarter granted Pietro's gout
was watering the wine down. What about
a balanced diet? In would come the tray:
five adults were expected to consume
the innards, gizzard, sinuses and snout.
Poor Pietro couldn't chew, and lived on toast.
The Romans washed their hands on Lady's Day
and left for Rome, devising Guido's doom.

STRAY LEAVES: A CULINARY METAPHOR

A gastronomic grande-oeuvre, your goal?
You'll find that 'good enough is good enough''ll
serve perfectly sufficiently to muffle
the meanest miff. The best of herd or shoal
will, if you tweak and tease, caress, cajole,
surrender up its soul without a scuffle.
But as regards the tantalising truffle,
your best bet? Merely smear it round the bowl!
Far better, serve the sizzle than the steak!
Resist the all-too-pressing urge to bung
in Molinism, Darwinism, Jung.
Thus, for your poor befuddled reader's sake,
you'll get the essence if you ask the question,
instead of serving instant indigestion!

THE HOLY FATHER MAKES A JUBILEE.
Can Violante use the situation?
You bet she can. She gets down on one knee:
Pompilia wasn't – hadn't been – her child.
Not ever. With these words, outrageous, wild,
she shattered Pietro's world. Her *cavatina*

had earned for her a papal dispensation,
or so she claimed. A loss of bearings keener,
her husband never felt. The impropriety
was not the point – the man had been beguiled,
unmanned, deceived – and stood to be reviled.
But then, new thoughts dispelled his perturbation
and (though disgusted) with demeanour mild
he spoke forbearingly of Jesse's Tree.
Yes, Violante has to be obscener
than any enemy – and there's the key!
'Unto my wayward wife I'm reconciled.
Though forced to take this fierce humiliation,
we're heading, thankfully, for our *Paulina*.
They think themselves aggressive? We are meaner!'

Now Paolo. Guido's brother, five years older,
a priest of hairless head and piercing eye.
A contemplative thinker (some say sly),
who calculates more often than opines.
Too sleek and fox-like to be termed as 'hearty',
is none the less a social butterfly.
Though not averse to penning well-turned lines,
he captures what is meant by 'office-holder',
too much the climber to be truly arty.
Long fingers brushing lint from surplice shoulder,
that body, ever dressed up to the nines,
was far too frangible for work. Help dress his vines?
In all sincerity, he'd rather die.
His family he treated like a party,
a cause to further. Paolo was a moulder,
especially of Guido. All *castrati*
(like Orphanotrouphos) display the signs
of sibling sublimation. Aretines
(still less, these ill-disposed *illuminati*)
can never conquer Rome. One wonders why.

The Countess Franceschini's now her name.
Francesca (or Pompilia) (call her both!)
feels utterly abandoned, isolated.
Deserted by the Comparini pair
(her parents), she's a kind of Roman Ruth.
Expected to produce a viable heir,
she's tolerated as a breeding-mare
(but that's not happening, either). Bifurcated
her loyalties – the land from whence she came,
and this weird husband – breathing Tuscan air,
but dreaming still of Rome. Their coin is blame,
demand for change of state that's never sated.
There's so much turns upon that marriage oath!
The lamp that burns atop the Bishop's stair
is constant, steady, ever shines the same
when glimpsed on leaving Mass. She's always loath
to lose it from her sight. She knows she's hated.
So bright the light, so intricate the frame!
It's Rome to her, deliverance awaited,
still far away – but Rome will come with growth.

When Violante publishes the news,
there's nothing in Arezzo save abhorrence!
It's worse than have dealings with the Jews!
Like being on the gridiron with Saint Lawrence!
Pompilia is the offspring of some slut!
We've been polluted by a dirty ruse!
They've fobbed us off with offal from the stews!
We're branded with the infamy of Cain!
Our ancient house, polluted by 'profane'!
How dare that little Roman strumpet strut
among us? Now the dowry might be cut!
Enough to spark a fever in the brain!
She's made herself a target for disdain
and getting the come-uppance that she warrants.
To have a wife incorrigibly foreign's

unbearable enough – she's pretty, but
the sanctity of wedlock, social glue's
imperilled by this succubus. Such smut!
An in-house bastard goes against the grain.
How *can* one ever show one's face in Florence?

Giuseppe Caponsacchi, hero-priest,
a young man handsome, resolute and brave:
God put him on this earth to slay the Beast.
He's looking for a heroine to save,
but doesn't know it yet. He still belongs
to this provincial town, still sings its songs,
regards himself encompassed by his vows.
He stands beneath the *Pieve*'s architrave,
whose seasons, with their ploughs and sows and cows,
prescribe him from the cradle to the grave.
But life is so much more than heres-and-nows!
A hero must get on with righting wrongs:
if life's a banquet, welcome to the feast!
Arezzo can provide the cause you crave,
Pompilia the purpose to espouse!
Your life is the *impasto*, she's the yeast!
Suppose the town's awash with tattling tongues:
what's that to you? Arezzo's thoughtless throngs
have never yet alarmed you in the least.
Let's see what one sad countess might arouse!

STRAY LEAVES: DOCTOR BARTOLOMEO ALBERGOTTI RECOUNTS A NIGHT AT THE OPERA

Oh, just a bit of horseplay, nothing more,
of little consequence, correctly weighed,
and not a thing by which to set great store.
We went to see Sartorio's *'L'Adelaide'*.

Immense offence was taken, I'm afraid.
Before the first-act *settine* was displayed,
Two popular young canons held the floor.
It was December, sixteen ninety-four.

An aretine tradition, tossing sweets
(our word, *'confetti'*). Yes, it's slightly dotty.
The town's young men dispense the treats
to every pretty girl (you now say, 'hottie').
They improvise crude verses, called *strambotti*
(as when I wooed Signora Albergotti).
Count Guido and his wife were in the seats
reserved for 'quality' (social elites).

The canons, were they flirting? Who can say?
Confetti landed in Francesca's lap.
She looked at Caponsacchi in dismay,
and Guido's glare was like a thunderclap.
Francesca, now a rabbit in a trap,
could only fidget with a shoulder strap.
I'd call the culprit Conti, any day.
The truffles, truly, came from Conti's tray.

AGOSTINO 'CANALE' CHIMATO, LANDLORD OF AN AREZZO TAVERN, ENTERTAINS HIS CUSTOMERS

My name is Chimato.
Though brought up in Prato,
I've long made Arezzo my home.
They call me 'Canale';
I serve malt and barley,
provider of cider and foam.

You'd welcome The Story?
It gets kind of gory,
though I wasn't present for that.
So, pin back your ears!
(Would you like some more beers?)
Just listen, and hang up your hat.

The town was astonished!
He'd long been admonished
(providing no olives or heir)
his pretty young consort
(there's really just *one* sort)
arriving with parents to spare!

Those strange Franceschini
are not Guillichini –
begrudgers, and somewhat morose.
Opinion is smothered
by Beatrice, the mother
(but Porzia is very verbose!)

They came in December,
I clearly remember,
and stirred up a fuss around town.
We don't like outsiders
(but, adding some riders)
it's better than *nowt* going down!

For nobles, it rankles
like chains round their ankles:
the servants, incessantly stealing!
But grimmer by far,
when they head for a bar,
the secrets they're keenly revealing!

Maliciously-hearted,
the rumours got started,
with murmurs of mismatch in bed.
Il faut avoir bonnes,
but you know ten-to-one,
the source of the stuff that was said!

They say that he hit her
(she didn't seem bitter,
but anxious to blend and conform).
You know when you've seen them
what passes between them
(it wasn't especially warm!)

One thing that's important
I'll tell you (but oughtn't),
is Guido's decisive defeat.
Deprived of his posse
(he only had Rossi),
he got beaten up in the street.

One Noffi Rosselli
(no quoter of Shelley!),
a man who could lift up a horse,
had words near the *Pieve*:
when matters got heavy,
resorted to physical force.

To thus take a hiding
(with populace chiding)
destroyed Guido's standing with men.
It certainly changed him –
I'd say, it deranged him –
was never the same man again.

Oh, one took a lease on
tenuta with bees on,
the reason relations got rough
or one sold a sorel,
which led to a quarrel –
so, honey and money and stuff.

He strapped on a dagger,
developed a swagger,
cruised taverns where toughs tend to sup
Count Guido's now boozing?
We found it amusing!
A posture he couldn't keep up.

Aggressively puny,
he looked like a loony,
a creature from *opera buffa*.
He bullied his women –
a town house with *him* in
was certainly hellish to suffer!

The view of our gentry
is quite elementary
(Arezzo's a very small town):
if you drink at an inn,
you're committing a sin,
and you're dragging the neighbourhood down.

The visiting Romans
are blind to the omens,
and (saving your graces) transgress:
when Old Man Comparini
arrived on he scene, he
did pub crawls, and couldn't care less!

Least said, soonest mended.
His hosts were offended,
and let their opinion be known.
It's live and let live,
but in them there's no give:
they nagged like a dog with a bone.

Since the time of the Gracchi,
than Priest Caponsacchi
there's never been equal or peer:
all muscles and curls
(such a magnet for girls!),
and he knew how to handle his beer!

And his partner in crime,
just like lemon and lime,
was one Conti (a canon, as well).
How they flirted and fooled!
There's no question, they ruled.
They were friendly – and funny as hell!

Caponsacchi (Giuseppe),
a bit of a 'preppy',
was born of the very best stock.
And Conti had, too,
blood impeccably blue –
the pair were the pick of the flock.

Not a thought in their heads
but *ragazze* and beds –
oh, what it is to be young!
They were clerics, it's true,
but from my point of view,
what's life, but a song to be sung?

Our little *teatro*
(Andrea del Sarto
should have been there to depict it!)
saw the toss of a truffle
which led to a scuffle
(before Seppe launched it, he licked it!)

That's when bad went to worse.
It was almost perverse,
the way that he'd snub her and slight her.
To whom could she turn,
faced with lack of concern
on the part of both chamber and mitre?

We all have our dreams,
and who cares how it seems,
the home-life that humans contrive?
Put your pride on the shelf.
keep your hands to yourself
I won't have you hurting your wives.

When you close your front door,
you're your wife's guarantor,
you're supposed to look after your clan.
You are making her cower
because you hold the power?
Don't ever claim you're a man.

From Marzi-Medici,
all pompous and preachy,
to Bishop Marchetti she went.
And far from assist her,
they abruptly dismissed her
(they'd given up mercy for Lent!)

Although Conti felt sorry,
il 'fare lo gnorri'
was all he was able to do:
his ties to the others
(that wife of his brother's)
prevented him helping her, too.

To try a new tack, he
approached Caponsacchi,
a decent and resolute man.
Reluctant at first,
soon he jumped in headfirst,
and that's how the friendship began.

They clearly grew closer.
Were lovers? Don't know, sir!
The poor girl was out on a limb.
Abandoned, *in breve*,
il duomo per pieve,
I think, to get closer to him.

STRAY LEAVES: THE DUOMO AND THE PIEVE

Cathedrals have a way of holding sway,
albeit be they barns, devoid of colour.
It's hard to picture something gaunter, duller
than this one in Arezzo. Tuscans say
the House of God should be attractive, gay
(ma no secondo Misanthropic Mullah,
our bishop, sullen sacerdotal Sulla!),
a place where paint and light and plaster play.

Our Pieve is a church to top your list.
Internally, just fifty shades of grey,

but how the outside dances! We, the people
(no bishops here – we're strictly populist)
are more than willing, Stranger, to display
our apse and archivault, our stoop and steeple!

AFFECTION? ATTRACTION?
She had to take action.
She would have been killed if she'd stayed.
Some say Caponsacchi
was merely her lackey,
the one man who wasn't afraid.

A lady, you'll own,
couldn't travel alone.
She needed a man to assist her.
He knew she was lonely.
It may have been only
protection of brother, for sister.

He came to this bar –
standing right where you are –
to say they were making a dash.
We plotted and planned
and then, shaking his hand,
I told him to take my calash.

My man Venerino –
see his sexy *codino!* –
my teamster, my seamster, pot-washer,
abandoned the topers
to help the elopers,
and drove them as far as Camoscia.

You know how it ended.
Had Seppe defended
that girl to the death (and he would!) ...

But he couldn't be there –
wasn't even aware –
on that night of confusion and blood.

I'm getting upset, so
I'll stick to Arezzo,
where something unpleasant occurred.
A death unexpected –
foul play undetected –
but nobody's saying a word.

Giuseppe's friend Conti:
say what you want, he
was hearty and vigorous, still:
the town idolised him,
but someone despised him
sufficiently fiercely to kill.

His sister says fever,
But I don't believe her
(the trial was running in Rome).
For helping Pompilia
atenti i gigli, or
keep well away from your home!

A DEPLORABLE HISTORY (CONTINUED)

Pompilia has suffered at his hands.
Three years have passed. Three lonely, frightened years.
Some forty months have sunk into the sands.
It's sixteen ninety-seven, Eastertime,
and *Pieve* bells inform her, by their chime,
that Christ's dark Passion ominously nears
its climax. Now she knows there is a child.
She won't remain here, roared at and reviled,

when this new life relies on her. A crime?
To run away from this? She understands
so clearly now, at last is reconciled
to destiny. Suppose she disappears:
who fares the worse for it? There's now a prime
objective: there's a baby who demands
a world where no-one's frightened or defiled.
Her life is not her own. Guillermo's leers,
the scowls of Beatrice, Guido's throbbing glands,
the hurt and the humiliation, piled
upon her, are receding. No more tears!
There's new life now – a glimpse of the sublime.

And why is Caponsacchi on the cart?
Three stories that are being put about …
the first, he'll get her marriage set aside
and wed her for himself. This one you doubt?
The Church is stern but flexible, you'll recall:
divorce is frowned upon by the devout,
but ways and means exist. You don't abide
(the Church, I mean) millennia without
a little nimbleness. If someone lied,
or lacked maturity … why, there's a start!
We're talking sacerdotal suicide,
but what of that? In matters of the heart,
all's one. Some say that, once within the wall,
he's planning permanently to install
her as his mistress. That sounds pretty smart.
Metropolises, worldly-wise and wide,
accommodate whatever may befall
without so much as blinking. These apart,
unload her there, and Seppe's safely out,
and free of bawl and gall and caterwaul!

With no police to speak of, nothing's checked
or monitored. You have no safety net.

What does a woman do, if under threat?
Proud agencies of state, which intersect
to guarantee well-being? No, not yet.
For worried women, what's the better bet?
Whichever way they leap brings consequences.
What if the thing unravels? Leave no chink.
Abusive husband drives you to the brink –
it still behoves you to be circumspect.
You have no stockpile, standing or defences
and can't afford to take leave of your senses.
Arezzo *sbirri*, uninclined to wink
at *officer,-it's-not-the-way-you-think*,
maintain a keen *qui vive*. Just once ill-met,
disaster must ensue, the dinghy sink.
Your heart sinks (now) each time the door-knob tenses.
The only (although golden) recompense is,
you get away for good, you resurrect:
you're safe in Rome. He's powerless to object.

With Caponsacchi solidly onboard
(he's passing through the *borgo* day by day,
and signalling to her), she feels her fate
is finally unfolding – but the wait
is what weighs heaviest. Last night, *he* lay
beside her in the blackness, snoring, sweaty,
but she, surveying all that she's endured,
could not condemn this Franceschini horde.
Instead, she thought of San Clemente Gate
and open roads. Canale's cabriolet
will soon be ready, carefully procured
by her protector. Coins and *braccioletti*
are set aside – small things of silver plate
and sentimental portent, *fazzoletti*,
some fans and flounces a *fanciulla* might afford,
all stashed and waiting for the fateful date:
it can't be long, now, till they're underway,

and hurtling Rome-ward, passing strange *distretti*.
A part of her feels petulant and petty –
and guilt can be a monster to allay.

The opiate she added to their wine
has done its work. Her warders, deep asleep,
will find in time she drugged them unawares.
She rises, dresses. Things she wants to keep
(this pretty petticoat of Lucca lace,
that blouson, with the dainty ship design)
would take too long to fold. She has to sweep
her life's belongings – she wants none of theirs –
into a box in place of travel case.
It's time to venture out onto the stairs,
to kiss her fingers, touch the Virgin's shrine
(no chance just now to offer any prayers
beyond a lisped Hail-Mary-full-of-grace)
then gingerly pull back the bolt, to face
the crisis. Wont to whimper at its spine,
the door this time is silent. Eglantine
aroma, and cold air. A sudden leap
at heart – he's here! Now for the cautious creep.
The Via Sacra (fewer people!) There's
the Wall, the Gate … beyond them, endless space!

The San Clemente Gate, of course, is locked:
all decent aretines are long abed.
Giuseppe gestures noiselessly – 'this way!'
The man's a diamond! Resourceful, brave,
he doesn't flinch to find the exit blocked,
but strikes out for the *Torrion* instead:
he doesn't know the meaning of dismay!
The wall's impassable to mortals, save
just here. Some *condottiere*'s cannon knocked
the tower to pieces, years ago. Let's tread
with caution through the rubble's disarray!

Behind, the town sleeps, silent as the grave.
Clear! Venerino, pony-tailed, besmocked,
sits waiting for us, as Canale said.
Let's climb aboard, get moving. Why delay?
At last, the opportunity we craved!
Tomorrow when he wakes up, he'll be shocked
to learn the little lass he thought he'd wed
finessed his hand and planned fresh tricks to play –
a perfect partner, but a useless slave!

Elated, *certo*, but sedated, numbed,
like swimming underwater, as in dreams.
The darkness crowds our cabin, through the night.
Camoscia slips behind. A change of teams?
Perhaps I dozed a while. The carriage seems
unlike it was. The horses' footfalls drummed
more fiercely *poco fa* – or my mistake?
My saviour doesn't feel fatigue. Its bite
is quite unknown to him. He meets extremes
with equanimity. Is this the break
of daylight? That must be Cortona. Shake
me, please, as soon as Trasimeno Lake
appears. But elsewhere, someone falls awake.
His godforsaken eyes and glued-up, gummed.
Hard morning light which, uninvited, streams
across the bedroom, strives to blind him quite.
An aeolian harp is being strummed
inside his stress-torn head. So, black is white:
the depth of her depravity is plumbed.
Someone will die for this. She's taken flight.

Two days and nights, no time to eat or rest:
the constant anguish of the prey pursued:
beyond each hill that's climbed, another crest!
With each exhausting mile, the trial's renewed!
We'll know we're safe at Popolo's palimpsest

but, though we've crossed the Papal States frontier,
(now choked with dust, now sodden to the skin)
it never seems to us we're getting near.
I find I'm always glancing to the rear
(the fabled shark's foreshadowed by its fin).
At Castelnuovo, there's a wayside inn.
They pause to change the horses, forage food.
Pompilia's resting upstairs, fully-dressed.
Giuseppe's working with the wagoneer
out in the yard. His bread is left unchewed.
Someone's approaching, riding like the wind.
Into the lamplight, man and horse appear.
It's Guido, by his straggle-bearded chin.
'Whatever you've imagined, or construed,
I'll answer you.' But Guido shirks the test!

Preferring not to prod the proud young priest,
the cuckold didn't come on like a man,
insist on satisfaction. Guido ran
to fetch the watch. Adultery's a crime,
a capital offence: in double-quick time,
credentials were presented, palms were greased,
and Guido placed reliance in the Law
(for, after all, what is 'position' for?)
But *in flagrante* – shouldn't that be yeast
to raise the dough of dudgeon? Go, at least,
confront the harlot, up in her divan!
They pinion Caponsacchi (Guido can
attack him now – but doesn't.) *Sbirri* climb
the stairs and bring Pompilia. She, released
a moment, runs and manages to draw
her saviour's sword and lunges at the craw
of Guido (someone here's got *palle*!) I'm
unsure why they restrained her. Thus began
processus fugae. Tawdry love-nest, or
heroic rescue? Slime? A thing sublime?

A LETTER WRITTEN BY THE COUNTESS FRANCESCA POMPILIA FRANCESCHINI TO HER PUTATIVE PARENTS IN ROME, FROM A PRISON CELL IN CASTENUOVO

Dear Father, I'm in prison in this town.
My time is limited, in which to tell
what happened. I will try to write it down

(you didn't think I'd learned to write and spell,
and didn't think those other letters mine).
I'm in a Castelnuovo prison cell,

with just one patch of wall where light can shine.
My husband has alleged adultery –
some things have happened, largely clandestine –

but Papi, can you come and rescue me?
The gentleman who helped me to escape
has also been detained. Both I and he

are innocent. (And bring my velvet cape!)
He knows the Guillichini – they're related.
And now he's got himself into this scrape

on my account. My husband really hated
and despised me, and his loathing
(with blows and kicks and insults, unabated)

was growing wilder, fiercer. There was no thing
that I could do to please or palliate him.
(I'm desperate for clean and cosy clothing.)

My friend, who's of the Pieve, said verbatim:
'My duty is to save you.' See? He's virtuous!
And when you meet him, you'll congratulate him.

The duomo crowd – this isn't about churches.
Suspicions that my husband housed aren't true.
My life was valued less than one hour's purchase.

You know he's violent, what he can do.
You saw the things he did, the words he said,
so none of this will come as something new.

To simply keep on living – yes, I fled.
I made the choice – indeed, I had no other.
If I'd stayed in Arezzo, I'd be dead.

I love the one who squired me like a brother.
The one who brings this letter is a friend.
And give my salutations, please, to Mother.

I kiss you, dearest Papi, and commend
my welfare to your care. (See? I can write!)
And now they're telling me I have to end …

A DEPLORABLE HISTORY (RESUMED)

So Guido had the runaways detained,
and then returned to Tuscany. In Florence
he made his plans to have them executed.
Transferred to Rome, the prisoners were kept
in *Via Giulia* (papal prisons), chained
and *incomunicado*. Had the warrants
been Tuscan ones, it really would have suited
Guido better. Same offence, except
on Tuscan soil, advantage would be gained:
defendants who were classified as 'foreigns'
would get short shrift. In court, they would be hooted,
derided, and their case would not be prepped
by buckshee lawyers. But the plaintiff deigned

to come upon the culprits where the torrents
of chauvinist abuse would now be muted.
All summer long, the goddess Justice slept,
but in September, Guido's smugness waned
to learn Pompilia had, to his abhorrence,
escaped all punishment. The convoluted
opinion of the court was, she'd be 'stepped'!

What do I mean by that? Well, simply this:
they found no case – therefore, no punishment!
They couldn't put her back in Guido's hands,
and so they found a worthy edifice
(a convent for depraved and fallen girls)
in which to lodge her. Caponsacchi lands
a stiffer penalty: not innocent,
but as the judges' reasoning unfurls,
not very guilty either. Where he's sent,
Civitavecchia (as go reprimands)
is three years' loss of fun – a bit like Lent.
And when they bring the news from Aix to Ghent,
the blood in Guido's ears starts pumping, swirls
as if he's drunk: one thing he understands
is, he's been cheated, served a Judas Kiss.
'She needs beheading! Give her silks and pearls?
Not I! I'll take some men to Rome,' he's heard to hiss.
He gathers four unedifying churls
and, as they talk, his vengeance plan expands.
Count Franceschini's reached the precipice.

The final straw that broke the camel's back –
that's how, for Guido, strikes this worst of news
to mark the sombre autumn equinox.
'They've freed her! By some underhanded ruse
the mother-vixen, leader of the pack
(no doubt with full connivance of the jews),
has slipped her daughter through another crack!

Pompilia's pregnant. So, the changeling fox
would play her mother's game. The worse her loss!
A curate's offspring, sired on gutter dross!
In Ponte Milvio, we've a rustic shack
(the same where Constantine received The Cross):
my boys can bed in that bucolic box.
Enough of open, ordered, orthodox –
I've undergone too many shameful shocks!
She needs to understand who is the boss.
For quality she doesn't give a toss?
I'd like to see that doxy disabused.
The lads will help acquaint her with my views.
The time has come to mount my own attack.'

Pugnale genovese – vicious thing!
It's nothing but a spike with bristling spines.
Of mankind's diabolical designs,
it ranks the worst. Disgusting when inserted,
it rips the body badly coming out.
Such weapons are what Guido wants to bring.
'Conventicle''s one law he's set to flout
(five burly men in an unlawful gathering):
a second's carrying lethal arms about.
Rome doesn't like to see its laws subverted,
but Guido's visit blithely undermines
the Sacred Constitution. He's concerted
with four gruff bravoes (his assassins' ring)
to leave the Comparini in no doubt
(when daggers flash, and blood begins to spout)
who's in the right. His scheme is on the wing.
His wife's the one who drugged him and deserted
the matrimonial home, so now the lines
are drawn. With logic palsied and perverted,
he smiles upon his dagger's curling tines.

A pinched and drizzly January night,
and Gambassini's acting as observer;
he's looking both ways (it's the Feast of Janus)
as Guido creeps along the Via Vittoria.
The moment has arrived. Each acolyte
(if Guido's Nero, Santi's surely Nerva,
for none of these is Scipio Africanus)
is at his post when, posing as a courier,
the hapless husband gratifies his spite.
Directness never was his strength. The swerver,
inept at vengeance, latter-day Uranus,
bangs on the door in feverish euphoria.
It's Violante's voice, still out of sight,
which detonates his homicidal fervour.
He stabs her in the face. His crazed hyenas
are cutting Pietro down. Santi is gorier
than even his leader. Still, the daggers bite!
Now Guido shows his wife his Genoese 'curver':
what went before was shocking. This is heinous.
Pompilia is butchered. *Lei di santa memoria* ...

There's only one direction now to run
to get away from carnage and confusion:
the sense of vindication, having won,
is strangely not as strong as one expected:
the open country now, in place of strife,
is what is needed. Safety in seclusion!
But Guido, true to character, neglected
to buy a permit. Inns and taverns shun
demands for horses. Neither knock nor knife
is fruitful. And the highway, once elected,
proves difficult. Disheartened and dejected,
the troupe is terminating its intrusion:
the trudge to Tuscany has now begun –
but refuge in Arezzo? False illusion!
The slaughter in Vittoria's been detected,

and rumours of five ruffians are rife:
pursuit and capture rapidly directed:
proofs and prayers provided in profusion!
But what of Guido's violated wife?
Against all odds, she's clinging, still, to life!

STRAY LEAVES: THE ROSE AND THE CROSS

The metaphor of suffering and loss,
of yesteryears and ill-remembered snows,
of cornfields compromised by carrion crows,
a solitary regal albatross,
the thudding dithyramb of thanatos,
thematic death-mask such as seldom shows
without invoking threnodies and throes,
the Other Side, the Bride of Abydos.
But through the ribs of ruin, beauty grows.
The kernel, our internal nature, knows
la vie, la morte, sont guidées par les noces
chymiques; the Bacchanal of Being flows.
Supposing that which mortals may suppose,
our quest is not the glimmer, but the gloss.

They're apprehended just before the dawn
in squalid circumstances near Merluzza
where, blood-encrusted, filthy and forlorn,
they're found by their pursuers, worn-out, sleeping
like ferrets in a nest, together heaping.
Since Guido is the leader of the five,
assassin now, not merely wife-abuser,
he's pinioned like a cutpurse. His accuser,
returning him to Rome for safer-keeping
(of knife – not life – and liberty deprived),
informs him what the latest scraps of news are,

but doesn't even try to hide his scorn.
'The corpses of the Comparini, loser,
will lie in San Lorenzo, terribly torn.'
Then Guido's question. 'How did you contrive
involvement of us five? Why come a-creeping
along this empty highway? What might spawn
suspicion? Which deduction served to drive
you to us?' Dread awareness started seeping:
'What's that you say? Pompilia's still *alive?*'

Hunching forward on a stranger's arm,
Pompilia can neither sit nor lie.
Internal organs lacerated, broken,
she sees the open wound we call the sky.
Within the bedroom, not a word is spoken
by any of the ten attending men.
Oblivion engulfs her. Now and then
resurfacing to consciousness again,
she whispers listlessly and, by and by,
remaining preternaturally calm,
she finds herself alternatively woken
and overcome by slumber's blessed balm,
impossible to live, yet hard to die:
apologetic, unassuming, shy,
this wreckage of a wronged and ruined wren
knows, when she's lucid, what this must betoken,
but signals no resentment or alarm.
Around her faces, motionless and oaken,
observe the fine frail form, the harrowing harm,
and ponder petulance beyond their ken.

A man may kill the girlfriend-daughter-sister
(and wife, for sure!) who tramples on his honour.
A girl who's not an armour-clad resister
will bring her husband's righteous wrath upon her
for messing with some marriage-marring mister.

In Gubbio or Grosseto, she's a goner!
All Tuscan totty's minx if not Madonna:
your choice is, you're *donnaccia* or you're *nonna* –
so woe betide the bride if someone kissed her!
God help her if she gets the *bella vista*!
It's what he's going to offer to the judge.
He doesn't know it yet, but it's a *fallo* –
he's now got Marlowe's 'mercenary drudge'
who's up all night, exhausting precious tallow,
but does he really think this court will budge?
Forensically, he's fundamentally fallow.
He's shown himself a shameless old *sciacallo*,
Especially since he killed *ex intervallo*.
No matter how his lawyers fuss and fudge,
he murdered three. He's wallowing in sludge!

Il Palazetto Turci was my spot
to watch if he'd die well, or if he'd not
(I spared myself the gallows' grim gavotte!)
Our sordid Samson in his garish Gaza –
I'd say he did alright (he prayed a lot,
if that's an indicator!) Who knows what
is stretching out before us, once we're dead.
I'm not convinced a God rewards each waiter,
or if a hell awaits both trull and traitor.
As tumbrils trundled past us, people said
he braved alike the barracker and baiter
the *hoi polloi*, the heckler and hater.
Well, Guido's gone. *È nella sua casa.*
He did the thing he did, and for it, bled.
We'll leave him and his bravoes in the *piazza*.
Let's talk of something happier instead.
Our consciousness is just a *tabula rasa*.
There's word come from Farnese. Seems he has a
banquet in his *loggia* a little later.
So, off to *Farnesina* to get fed!

THE CONGRESS OF THE WITS: (1)

The Congress of the Wits

Six characters are lurking round the city.
These wasters haven't anything to do
but chew the fat (there's lots of fat to chew!)
They form a form of Public Watch Committee,
and get involved in all the nitty-gritty;
they'll scathe and satirise no matter who!
(You'd think, to look at them, they won't say boo!)
They're made of marble. Don't expect their pity.

Since Mona Lisa, down to Monica Vitti,
they've corruscated those who (in their view)
are undermining Roman social glue.
They may compose a devastating ditty,
or hum a hymn that's wholly hissy-fitty,
but (as has been suggested hitherto)
these petrified pundits paddle their own canoe.
When worse than withering, at least they're witty!

Abate Luigi

I'd like to say a word for Guido's brother,
Abate Paolo, he who's much-maligned.
It seems that, taking one thing with another,
he's got himself in quite an awful bind.
(I'm leaning on the wall of Sant' Andrea,
and don't believe I've ever yet felt gayer!)
He left (one hears it said) with pockets lined,
but Roman rumours really are unkind!

To run away from Beatrice (that's the mother)
– a course to which I'd find myself inclined! –
is fair enough. A tendency to smother

with parsimonious pedantry combined!
You'd never label Paolo 'dragon-slayer',
and Beatrice wants a lodger who's a payer.
To live in *Borgo Cenci* – what a grind,
apart from have your mother rob you blind!

It seems the Knights relieved him of his duty
(don't listen if they tell you he resigned!)
Administered The Order of the Boot, he
received it in his brotherly behind!
To start anew for such a nerd nay-sayer
was asking him to climb a Himalaya.
One wonders on what luxuries he dined,
This veteran work-shirker. Bacon rind?

We've heard from sources close to the *arguti*,
forsaking Italy for pastures new,
unbendingly, incorrigibly snooty,
he walked the planet like the Wandering Jew –
a sort of latter-day Giordano Bruno,
responsible for solely *numero uno*.
With Guido written off (what else is new?)
he took to paddling his own canoe.

One hears the Franceschini's home-grown beauty,
the one and only Porzia (sibling, too)
had cooked up something definitely fruity –
and Conti kicked the bucket, right on cue!
Jejune, or jealous? Jezebel, or Juno?
Let's ask her brother Paolo, 'what do *you* know?'
I call my piece, the Blaming of the Shrew:
poor Conti bit off more than he could chew.

TABLE TALK

I Forzati

Academies are certain to endorse
enormous dinners. Arezzo's 'I Forzati'
(think small-town, ill-informed illuminati)
have hired the humble inn that's called The Horse
(the upstairs room). To give their banquet sauce,
They've picked a Roman theme – The Cincinnati –
a glorified unbuttoned toga-party!
We join them as they taste the starter-course.
Their honoured guest, Giovanni M. Marchetti
(the local bishop) finds all pig-outs peachy.
This epicure, Spinoza of Spaghetti,
the Plato of the Plate, this human leech, he
has never paid a soldo (thinks it petty).
Veni et comedi, ergo vici.

The Bishop Relaxes

The year is seventeen hundred (then four more), a
long while since Spada, sbirri, spose, Spreti:
the bishop's role inglorious, and yet he
can talk of it with effortless bravura.
He punctuates each Pinot-sodden sura
with tantalizing tidbit, tempting truffle,
regales us with his Resurrection Shuffle,
discoursing at The Horse fuori le mura.
It hardly matters if this fat-arsed Fuhrer
grows garrulous or positively preachy.
No need tonight for disciplined demurrer:
the Keepers of the Flame (Marzi-Medici,
for one!) are all around him and, perforce,
the wine is talking (wine, and not remorse).

Table Talk

Whenever we dig statues from the ground
(have any of you seen Laocoon?
– a thing to write a monograph upon!)
whenever ancient hypocausts are found,
we see that we're descended from the best.

Arezzo's amphitheatre – case in point!
Menander moves me, makes me meditate:
I ponder Plautus and tergiversate
on Terence, individually, joint,
whatever – and the past is repossessed!

So, Porzia got the Franceschini raised.
They're in the foremost rank of Tuscan 'quality'.
She's not the one for jollity, frivolity,
but don't you think she really should be praised?
For her it's family first – and no mistake!

Arezzo needn't hover in the wings.
We've Petrarch – we can step onto the stage!
The sonnets are, in Europe, all the rage
(but who would ever read the bloody things?)
You *have* to try the fish-and-fennel cake!

Vasari – there's a man! *Gonfaloniere,*
with property and money, civic pride.
Utility and beauty coincide
in Giorgio's *loggia,* spacious, gracious, airy
the place to taste your slow *vermutti scuri*.

The architect is useful, gets things done.
The poet is equivocal, contrary,
a paper-plagued inconsequential fairy.

It's men I want around me. Giorgio's one.
I like solidity, not sound and fury!

Although you know I'm native aretine,
I'll pass on *la batalla delle chiese,*
but say, in passing, Conti was too lazy
(oh, don't you find the goose surpassing fine?)
and Caponsacchi far too fixed on pleasure.

I hope you know the latter has resigned.
Civitavecchia may have sobered him up.
To the *Duomo* Faction, raise your cup!
It's been so long since *I Forzati* dined.
The Lent thing's tiresome, but we've got its measure.

Don't mention San Francesco's frescoes, please.
They draw the raw unlettered turnip-workers,
the shoeless, clueless, pewless narthex-lurkers,
and *senza sapienza* sienese.
The scriptures, told in pictures? How absurd!

Sure, 'let the little children come to me',
and many don't know how to read and write,
but are we there to gratify their sight?
It smacks to me of rank idolatry.
The Lord is not The Vision – He's The Word!

That wife of Guido came to me, it's true.
The brother of that other one attacked
young Girolamo Franceschini, cracked
the latter's skull. That's why the wretched crew
behaves so oddly. That one's just as bad.

And as for Conti, what is left to say?
Robust and healthy. Easy-going. Liked.
The whisper is, the spikenard was spiked!

What heaven gives, it yet may take away.
A reasonable man. It's very sad.

So Guido beat her – I reply, so what?
The day you give the slut your second name,
it's no-one's business. Fill me up – the same!
I'm sure she asked for everything she got.
And why's a loving chiding so distressing?

My sermon will be Matthew, seven-three.
No, not for me – I find this Easter Lamb
quite indigestible – it's how I am.
Where's Duty found? In Deuteronomy!
I'll bolt this back before I give The Blessing.

THE OFFENDING OCTAVES

How I'd love to be your slip!
What I'd give, if I could get
closer to you than your sweat,
cling to bosom, belly, hip!
The well is where I'd love to sip,
cover you, protect you, pet
you, maybe even leave you wet!),
last to leave you when you strip.

Oh to be your *sottogonna*!
Feel the beating of your heart,
easing into every part!
See me swell with sense of honour!
Chè Vittoria, chè Colonna!
Learn you like a work of art,
all your hills and valleys chart!
Let me wrap you, *Gentildonna*!

Non me interessa peste!
I could be your second skin,
gathering your soft bits in,
snugging botty, hugging chesty,
nuzzling your naughty nesty,
from your ankles to your chin,
holding on through thick and thin,
if I were once your *sottoveste!*

DEPOSITION OF COUNTESS FRANCESCA POMPILIA FRANCESCHINI IN THE *PROCESSUS FUGAE*

The Countess Franceschini is my name,
a married woman, sixteen years of age:
transplanted to Arezzo, fled the same.
Confronted by my husband's violent rage,
this bird escaped the not-so-gilded cage.
They made me marry him three years before.
We moved away from Rome – but, at that stage,
we weren't quite man and wife. You'd push for more?
There wasn't any physical rapport.

December of that year, we left our home –
my father, mother, me – as per the deal.
I'd never set my foot outside of Rome,
but from the marriage contract no appeal
was possible. Though others stamped the seal,
I was the one who had to live it out.
The Franceschini, jaded but genteel,
dirt-poor, inured to serving hoof and snout,
engulfed us in a drab and drafty drought.

They treated us like filth – they really did.
My parents ran the gauntlet of abuse:

I felt myself a kind of *tertium quid*,
unable to defend them, not much use,
until the day that they made hay, broke loose
and headed Romewards once again. But I,
my husband's chattel, neck still in the noose,
had no-one (and had nowhere I could fly).
The only chance of ransom was, to die.

The time dragged by – elapsed, perhaps, a year.
It seemed as if I couldn't have a child –
was met each morn with insult, grimace, sneer.
'The Countess Franceschini' I was styled,
in truth a lonely teenager, reviled
because I couldn't spawn an heir. The line
(the fault was mine) had been defiled,
my contribution poisonous, malign:
the family would wither on the vine.

    * * * *

WELL, if the Court is curious
about what was injurious
in terms of life and limb,
the Court should put to him,
'why permanently furious?'

The *loggia* on the townhouse roof
provides, I think, sufficient proof
of Guido's state of mind,
his need to be unkind,
inventing outrage on the hoof.

I went up there to take the air,
but guess who scrambled up the stair!
'Ay! Adultery!' he cried:

I, desultory, replied,
'Can you see lovers anywhere?'

Apart from dragonfly or dove,
the *loggia* lay too far above
the level of the street
for glimpses indiscreet,
so how much less, illicit love!

If Canon Conti came to visit,
I was put though such a quiz, it
was easier to stay
in bedrooms, well away:
that's hardly normal, is it?

He termed my reticence a 'trick'
and, diligent with whip or stick,
he wasn't slow to punish
(or in his words, 'admonish')
unless I answered, double-quick!

The sweets that landed on my knees
appear to have destroyed his ease:
he yelled, his face dark red,
a gun held to my head,
'here's what I do with tramps like these!'

We're talking of the early days,
just after the *confetti* phase,
when he would shout aloud
(albeit in a crowd),
'Let Caponsacchi mend his ways!'

* * * *

A WEAKLING GETS INSULTED IN THE STREET.
How purge himself of his humiliation?
At home, he's got a scapegoat called 'the wife'.
He's had to swallow pride, lose face, retreat?
In every village, city, county, nation,
the selfsame syndrome shows itself. It's rife.
He says she's clearly guilty of deceit:
the judge decides there must be expiation.
His easy target's currency? Her life.

He'd drown me in the Tiber, or the Arno,
and if I tried to flee beyond his reach, he
would find me, and he'd torture me for spite.
The talking classes term it *abusano*,
but what do they achieve by getting preachy?
Instead of curbing it, they just incite
a worsening. I went to Fra Romano,
but like the Bishop and Marzi-Medici,
he didn't lift a finger (save to write!)

* * * *

THE CANON CONTI? UNDER PORZIA'S THUMB.
I liked him, and I also liked to tease him.
At times, a sudden passion seemed to seize him:
a girl knows how to throw a man a crumb,
to lead him by the nose, make him succumb.
I'd tell him how I loved him. That would please him.
But then my husband suddenly decrees him
persona non plus grata. He'd become
an enemy. *Cognato* was, in sum,
excluded from my presence. I felt numb.
I reasoned with my husband, to appease him,
but all my protestations landed dumb.
Of all the depths that jealousy could plumb,
this was the worst – but *dis aliter visum*.

My thoughts on Caponsacchi? What a man!
Your worships might regard it rather quaint
that I, approaching motherhood, should paint
a priest in primal colours, but I can!
For every woman, since the world began
(I choose my adjectives with due restraint)
our first-rank fantasy is to acquaint
ourselves with one who'll dominate the clan!
The Canon's more ferocious than he's faint
(he's glorious crusader more than saint!)
I have no criticisms, other than
the cool aloofness which can sometimes taint
his otherwise fine features. That complaint
aside, he's perfect. Others, also-ran!

Cross-Examination Transcript

And have you ever posted here to Rome,
while you were in Arezzo, ever sent,
any kind of written document?
The witness is reminded, she's on oath.
Well, yes …
        So, you confess!
… but what I meant …
To Franceschini? Comparini? Whom?
I sent some things to either – that is, both.
The Via Vittoria always was my home.
I'm thinking of a note that might have gone
to Paolo, your *cognato* –
        More than one.
The Countess's admission will be noted.
Please go on.
        My husband was insistent –
It wasn't my idea to write to him –
I mean, to Paolo. We were rather distant.
I wouldn't class myself as his devoted

sister-in-law. He seemed so old, so grim.
My point is, that you wrote.
                        I sent a note
or two ...
            Signoria, I'll now quote –
... but he's the one who set it down in pencil.
He wrote it all, and made me trace the letters.
I inked it over, following his stencil.
My husband wasn't open to discussion.
A girl of fourteen doesn't balk her betters!
For all it meant to me, it might be Russian.
I wonder if the witness may be shown
this item. Tell me, Countess, will you own
that you composed it?
                   Sorry. I can't say.
'*Signor Cognato*', and you've signed it, there.
Your authorship, as plain as night and day!
It could be, but I'm not prepared to swear.
Not even when it's down in black and white?
I couldn't then, and – here and now – can't write.
The Castelnuovo inventory, please.
Belongings listed here – you say they're yours?
I do.
        Record it! Noted – she agrees.
How can you say this list is on all fours
with things found on you?
                       It just seems to me
quite logical. Who's going to mislead –
The inventory's accurate. Concede!
I'd do it, sir. If only I could read.

DEPOSITION OF CANON GIUSEPPE CAPONSACCHI IN THE *PROCESSUS FUGAE*

I'll tell the story. Something in our blood
responds to narrative. The viscerae
accept what, otherwise (not understood)
would fail to fly, would crash in misery.

A tale of failure, sure. But I believe
that in our defects lies our certain glory,
since failings drive all change and thus achieve
our spiritual growth, and … very well, the story.

Arezzo is my home, my native town,
and mine a family of standing there.
At nineteen years I donned the canon's gown
(you see my crown, denuded of vain hair).

I lived there like a baby in the womb,
my duties light, protected by the walls
that hem Arezzo in. We don't need room
when life is vegetal. But heaven calls

when least anticipated. Canon Conti,
my friend and kinsman, clearly must have known –
I must have told him – *traversar' il ponte*
can turn on tiny things – I'd come alone

to Rome. I'd business here. He bears no blame
if, chatting with the chaplain or the dean, he
divulged my plans and, mentioning my name,
induced the same to reach the Franceschini.

I knew the co-accused, but only slightly.
Arezzo's 'quality' are all related.
I wouldn't say I saw her daily, nightly,
but all our lives were closely integrated.

A supper here, a wedding-banquet yonder –
she was around, as I was (so were many!)
and, though I hear her termed my 'co-absconder',
she didn't rank among our *indigeni*.

I was astonished when I got her note.
She said that I was now the only one!
Her husband aimed to kill her (so she wrote)
and swore by Mark and Matthew, Luke and John

that saving her was now my Christian duty.
Yet nothing could be farther from my mind:
I'll grant that I was conscious of her beauty,
but this was perilous. So I declined.

Her notes kept coming, thick as autumn leaves
that strew the streamlets down in Vallombrosa.
The learned Fiscal calls us 'thick as thieves',
but he and I assuredly are closer

than I could ever be with her. What next?
The truth seeps out beneath the ikonostasis:
Count Guido read a letter, and was vexed –
and some would say (and do!), not without basis .

A husband surely has a serious grouse
if once his spouse makes plans to run away
with someone else. Commotion in that house
convinced me that the Countess couldn't stay.

I heard from servants what she underwent!
Count Guido and his brothers bullied her
and threatened her with firearms. All this meant
her life was forfeit. I must rescue her.

A Sunday, end of April, was the day.
I notified the Countess. I would wait
with coach and horses. We'd be on our way,
if first she met me at Saint Clement's Gate.

'Far better after midnight. Safer still,
come by the *Via Sacra,* as it's lined
with convents. There, no busy-bodies will
observe you. And leave everything behind.'

As *Sant'Annunziata* chimed out 'one',
she came around the corner. She seemed shocked
or dazed. Her face was deathly white. Upon
discovering the city gate was locked,

she looked like she might faint. We had to grope
along the wall. The masonry had crumbled
and could be scaled, some distance up the slope.
Her sobbing stabbed the darkness as she fumbled

behind me. When we crossed the broken tower,
I had to hold her – carry her, more or less.
Her heart was pumping with alarming power:
I felt it through the fabric of her dress.

Free of the wall, I led her by the hand
(so not to lose her in the ink-black night).
We found Canale's carriage, horsed and manned,
and off we went. The first thing to get right

was, find the road to Rome: to circumvent
Arezzo's walls (and this, without a moon),
and strike out for Camoscia. As we went,
I saw (these things are wholly opportune)

a silhouette that touched me to the core:
the *Pieve* campanile against the sky –
and then I couldn't see it any more.
It seemed to me an ominous goodbye.

We only met one vehicle that night,
a carriage heading back the way we'd come:
my fair companion suffered such a fright,
her terror bordered on delirium.

'I know that woman!' Once the moment passed,
she settled into something – if not calm,
then close to stable. Driving hard and fast,
and conscious of (behind us) looming harm,

we hardly paused for food or change of horses
and sped on, arrow-straight, towards our goal.
Hard-pressed, commanding very few resources,
we pressed ahead. The effort took its toll.

Three dusks, two dawns engulfed us in a blur
of passing farms and draughty courtyards: my
unique concern was trying to care for her,
too tired to sleep, and too depressed to cry.

We got to Castelnuovo Tuesday night.
The husband came upon me in the yard.
I was ready – eager – for the fight,
but he felt otherwise, and called the guard.

And that's the tale. I understand there may
be questions on specific points of fact,
and I will meet them squarely. Ask away.
There's nothing I would sidestep or retract.

If Giambattista Conti played a part
in these events, it was a minor one,
though his involvement, from the very start,
was what the larger issues turned upon.

He had a way of not quite being involved,
yet at the heart of things. Immensely petty,
he strikes me as a puzzle unresolved.
Profoundly shallow. As with the *confetti* !

At Carnival, he grabbed a mandolin,
and he and I were in the theatre pit,
lampooning audience members coming in
for no good reason (save the fun of it!),

and throwing sweetmeats to the pretty girls.
It hit me with the impact of a slap –
I'm watching Conti grinning, as he hurls
a fistful: landing in the Countess' lap,

the sweets attract her husband's jealous eye –
and Guido takes me for the perpetrator!
I was entirely blameless – that's no lie.
Count Guido is a legendary hater,

and set his face against me from that point
while Conti, in his long-accustomed role,
was conscious that the time was out of joint.
This salmon, always swimming centre-shoal,

was brother-in-law to Porzia, Guido's sister.
Though Conti knows the Franceschini pole
is toxic, he's a passive non-resister,
an easer, pleaser to his very soul.

He knew about my plans to visit Rome
and probably – I don't attribute malice –
discussed it in the Franceschini home.
Regarding Porzia (she of poisoned chalice),

I always thought of them as chalk and cheese.
Pompilia was passive, yet appealing,
while Porzia's aspects, the reverse of these,
included interfering, double-dealing:

the one attracted men like moths to light,
surrendering their swords without a fight:
the other never could, try as she might.
You don't know women if you rule out spite!

Pompilia's swept along by people, things,
she doesn't understand, but's never beaten,
and Porzia, operating, pulling strings,
is trapped in bitterness she cannot sweeten.

The one thing that I know that Porzia knew
was how her maid, Maria, moved between us,
conveying notes and messages. It's true,
but she was not the Harbinger of Venus.

Indeed, the letters. Let me mention those.
Before I do, I must set out one fact:
I'm not a leaf, borne whence the river flows,
I am a man – and, being a man, must act.

(Waiting on a miracle will not do.)
You'd hear about the letters. So. The first
communication I was party to
was utterly spontaneous, unrehearsed.

The maid Maria (Porzia's servant) caught
my sleeve just by the *Canto* – that's *de' Bacci*,
where the Caponsacchi townhouse … (I ought
to bear in mind your knowledge may be patchy.

Arezzo's not as famous as I think.)
It was a hasty letter in a hand
I didn't recognise. Expensive ink.
It puzzled me immensely as I scanned.

Some woman knew about my coming trip
and begged me to escort her when I left
for Rome. I couldn't guess the authorship.
You'd hardly class the lettering as deft.

I didn't know the maid. It wasn't signed.
I just ignored it. In the following days,
Borgo de' Cenci (where I often dined)
resolved the mystery. I was amazed.

The Franceschini house lay in that street
(I'd been there many times). As I passed by,
to my surprise, a note fell at my feet.
Pompilia, without explaining why,

implored my help in getting her to Rome.
Another time, she waited on the stair
('if once more I could see Saint Peter's dome!')
The door was open. She was standing there,

as if she knew I'd pass. We'd never talked
before. I said I couldn't get involved,
or rather, didn't choose to. On I walked.
However, this young woman was resolved

to have me help her. Notes came thick and fast.
Her 'winning way''s her most outstanding trait:
I tried to keep my distance, but at last
I couldn't feel indifferent to her fate.

A certain neighbour with an axe to grind
obtained a note which, lowered to the street,
escaped my grasp. I was appalled to find
she'd shown it to Count Guido, short and sweet.

Imagine our position! I could bear
with equanimity the settled scores,
but yet was all too painfully aware
of what she'd have to face, behind closed doors.

The servant told me what went on inside.
We shouldn't intervene 'tween man and wife,
but I could not stand by. She could have died!
My obligation was to save her life.

Apart from such events as mentioned here,
Pompilia and I have never spoken.
And contrary to how it may appear,
we've traded neither *billet-doux* nor token.

Her letters? I destroyed them. Not from guilt.
I didn't know the scope of Porzia's net, so
I feared they compromised her to the hilt,
and burned them all, before we left Arezzo.

The *sbirri* searched me when we were detained,
and subsequently countless times. It's clear
that if some damning evidence remained,
we'd hear of it. Of that I have no fear.

Who wrote the letters? Ah, the physical act!
Who knows? I'd never seen the Countess' hand.
The sentences were chopped about and hacked,
but sometimes primitivity is ... planned.

If I were shown the writing, I would know it.
The letters are authentic, one infers?
Wait – Porzia's pertinacious, Paolo a poet –
that there be writing doesn't make it *hers*.

Some people use their servants as their scribes,
while others bolster evidence that's slight.
Despite the innuendos and the jibes,
I don't know if Pompilia can write.

You use the term, 'love-letters'. I'm appalled.
Present the case against me, but reflect:
no evidence identifies who scrawled
those notes. The Countess, modest and correct

(you see her here, before you) gave no cause
for denigration. Fleeing for her life,
this dignified young woman broke no laws
and has not sinned, as citizen or wife.

I did indeed. I wrote a letter, yes.
Its purpose? Just to tell her I agreed,
that I would help her. No man would do less.
It simply said, 'So be it. Let's proceed.'

I'm shown a letter with no date, unsigned,
beginning, '*Adorata mia Signora,
vorrei sapere* ...' Style-wise, quite refined,
if that's the stuff you like. My words are poorer,

or rather, much more virile. Yes, the letters
are somewhat similar to mine, but mine it's not.
I'm not effeminate. My idle betters
have endless leisure time in which to jot

Jugurthine this, or Jeremiad that,
but I don't play those games. An active man,
I write in language unadorned and flat,
as dry and dusty as a harmattan.

Another letter? '*Amatissima mía,
Signora, Io ricevo* ...' Not my writing.
Pretentious, silly, *raccogleticcia*.
dismissable on one initial sighting.

Maria Margherita? '*La Contenti*'?
Well, what about her? What is there to tell?
If I recounted rumours (and there's plenty!),
you'd class her as a denizen of hell.

Her house stands opposite the Franceschini.
'Her door is always open', as they say:
she thinks of men as bloodless *burattini*:
they're welcome, yes, but then they have to pay.

I know her, yes, like everyone in town,
but blame's a thing I'm tardy to apportion.
I'll merely say her skin's an even brown.
She's not above *ricatto* or extortion,

and when she got her hands on Porzia's note
(I mean, Pompilia's), she went to Guido.
And, though she has the morals of a goat,
I'm sure her reason wasn't his libido.

The room at Castelnuovo? There's an inn.
A posting-house. Arriving there at length,
the only option left was booking in.
Pompilia simply didn't have the strength.

The Tuesday night before the first of May,
we'd one short ride to safety, to our goal,
but she implored me urgently to stay.
She'd rest, she said, or offer up her soul.

The room they gave us had two separate beds.
They made up one for her. I sought the yard
to supervise the change of thoroughbreds
(my little joke) and mount a kind of guard.

No clothing was removed – to that I swear.
I didn't want avoidable delay.
The room was hers. In no sense did we 'share'.
At best, I'd get her rested, and away.

Down in the yard and hitching up the team,
I heard a rider coming down the road.
As I recount it now, it's like a dream –
the darkness, hearing how the hoofbeats slowed,

and knowing this could not now turn out well.
If only we'd gone on, an hour or two!
We'd be secure, inside the citadel!
The man dismounted and stepped into view.

I said, 'Count Guido, here you see a man,
and what I've done, was for the Countess' sake.
I'll answer you in any way I can.'
But that was not the course he chose to take.

No further questions? Then, my final word:
some men there are who simply do their duty,
no matter how outlandish or absurd.
And mine will always be to champion beauty.

THE ROMANCE OF THE ROSE, being a tale told by Giuseppe Caponsacchi

The Pentateuch unites the Jew,
the Jesuit and the Shi'a.
What makes a crackpot hack and hew
his ghastly Galatea?
What is the thing you wish you knew,
would make you gladder, freer?
Can Love ennoble? Is it true,
amor es alegría?
Did Alighieri misconstrue
the pertinence of Pia?
Is 'gush' a goal we'd best pursue?
Mere onomatopoeia?
Though chicks may chide, they'll guide us to
the Sacredest Idea.

As in my prison cell I lay
bemoaning my confinement,
though shut off from the light of day
I learned my life's assignment.

Though sap is sweet, the spikes are hard –
cosí is aloe vera.
Though *she* was just across the yard,
I couldn't see or hear her.

Her pretty face to me gave grace,
and herein I aver
I use my talent and this space,
returning grace to her.

Deep Thought had never been my friend,
but now the songs of thrushes
brought meditations, nights on end,
to blight my bed of rushes.

And that is when The Dream occurred,
one night of summer thunder.
My eyes were opened to The Word,
my breast was filled with wonder.

Beyond my bars the lightning flashed,
too many bursts to number:
against my walls the hailstones dashed,
the enemies of slumber.

But rules there are that guide these things
despite their random-seeming,
and sleep arrived on see-through wings,
and then I fell to dreaming.

Two butterflies played in silent braid
as Heaven's azure awning
benignly splayed o'er grange and glade
on this, the Perfect Morning.

My clothes seemed, like my style of hair,
when I was five years younger.
I, tall and fair, without a care,
felt neither pain nor hunger.

There is a word I've read (or heard)
– a weather word – 'attempre',
or 'all is perfect'. Nothing stirred.
Ahead of me hung 'SEMPRE',

A single sign above a gate,
that gate set in a wall:
both were constructed tall and straight,
with 'SEMPRE' over all.

An artifice in Nature's face,
this month of Florial:
a quadrilateral, campo-placed,
like the Escorial.

I walked beside the wall a stretch.
Carved figures, set in niches
(and every one an ugly wretch),
impressed me as pastiches.

A devil here, a tyrant there,
a Nimrod and a Nero,
and everywhere a hideous stare,
no Halcyon or Hero.

A hundred faults adorned these vaults,
like Old Age, Sorrow, Felony:
the frieze is long, and hardly halts:
Pope-Holiness with Villainy.

The Young love Love, and God above
forgives the very flirtiest:
we courteous are conscious of
the Love that makes us courteous.

Each face glared down with hideous frown
and plaques like 'WRATH' or 'SIN'.
I guessed this outer face might crown
great beauty, safe within.

The singing birds were proof enough
that all was peace inside,
for nothing untoward or rough
could in that place abide.

I walked the walls – they formed a square,
five hundred cubits long
on every side, and no point where
the birds were not in song.

No gate found I except the first,
and promptly I returned:
to be in scent and song immersed
was that for which I yearned!

The gate creaked open at my knock.
The calmness I could summon
was not enough to hide my shock –
there stood a lovely woman!

The way was open; I beheld
the whitest-ever dress:
the wearer said, as though compelled,
'My name is Idleness.'

This Idleness had whiteness pure
to dazzle any dove:
unoccupied politeness, sure,
will often lead to love.

Her hair was blonde and nicely tressed,
with braids cascading down:
a row of roses on her breast
set off her gorgeous gown.

When complimented on her looks,
she smiled and told me, 'I'm
not interested in old books:
for love, you need free time.'

The reader asks, 'What is the use
of abstruse tales, to me?'
The poet says, 'what seems diffuse
is really unity'.

One son inherits: one becomes
a captain, while another
is born to pick a dowry's plums,
but what befalls the brother

who, down the line, gets nothing fine?
He's stranded in the lurch!
His folks are rich, but he's consigned
to idle in the church!

We landless knights, we just destroy,
build nothing in our lives
condemned to find our only joy
pursuing others' wives.

We strolled together, at our ease,
and everywhere we went,
the nutmegs and the apple trees
beguiled me with their scent.

'I'll take you to Spassolo now,'
suggested my young friend.
She eased aside a cherry bough –
what poet ever penned

the sight which charmed my startled eyes,
before me in the hollow?
All shapely waists and sprightly thighs,
impossible to follow!

Spassolo was a striking youth,
upon a cedar throne.
Nothing vulgar or uncouth
could here be ever known

within this bourne, beneath this tree.
Here, dancing, music, mirth
and beautiful young company –
the riches of this earth –

combined in flawless harmony.
Spassolo, gentle king,
made signal to a woman. She
prepared herself to sing.

Exquisite accents, *comme une ange*,
expressive, eloquent:
her song was called a *rotrouenge*,
and this is how it went:

*Je suis Marie,
je suis de France.
J'en ai besoin,
je recommence:
L'air est doux,
le jour est bon,
et je retourne
d'Avignon:
je me sens triste,
je dis pourquoi.
Je suis une femme
(c'est mon envoi)
si amoureuse
mon oriflamme
ma bannière
autrefois fougueuse,
n'est plus chère.*

*Mon âme est las:
si tu as aimé
tu comprendras.*

Some female dancers took the floor,
and they were 'fetis, smale':
a woman came to me: she wore
a long and languid veil.

Her eyes were blue, her lips were red:
she called herself 'Raffina'.
The grace in all she did and said
suggests a ballerina.

'The women here are all like me,'
she said in conversation:
'all beautiful, benign and free,
the essence of temptation.'

The God of Love was stalking me!
I, unaware of him,
Thought of my love, and could but see
perfection in each limb.

Are you surprised I speak of Love
as if it were a thing,
and not some Being from above,
beyond imagining?

Love, virus-like, has mere potential.
But when it enters us,
it takes on life, is consequential:
we give it animus.

Five arrows of a bitter bow,
Like Openness, Fair-Seeming:
but made of gold, I'd have you know:
Simplicity was gleaming!

The other two which ran me through
were Company and Beauty:
we lovers who, attentive to
these barbs, fulfill our duty.

A helot now to Love was I,
without hope of assistance:
and spotted, with a fevered eye,
a rosebud in the distance.

I'd gone from jape to drunken scrape,
accustomed to carousal,
but when I saw that gorgeous shape,
I felt my first arousal.

Invited to the house, I saw
the rosebud at close quarters:
and lost all tender feeling for
Arezzo's surly daughters!

The modesty, the downcast eyes,
just multiplied the feeling:
here was my gold: I'd found a prize
that merited the stealing!

Echo and Narcissus

It's odd how, in mythology, The Curse
on women, not the guilty ones, descends.
To punish Echo, Juno makes amends
for quite a harmless jape with something worse:
and thus the gods our errors reimburse!
She must repeat, with strangers or with friends,
the words with which the other's sentence ends,
and can't her proper sentiments rehearse.
Narcissus's reflection in the pool
prompts 'Come together!', but the puffed-up fool
takes umbrage at the unintended drone.
She would have been the best he'd ever known!
How many men, unthinking, end up cruel!
How many women pine away, alone!

SINCE FRAUENDIENST WILL HAVE ITS DAY
in all humility
we men accept that we, not they,
must bend the beggar's knee.

La Donna Fugata

This is a tale of spite and blood,
the victim one Sibilla:
Charybdis being spinsterhood,
her marriage proved her Scylla.

A child and father, hand in hand,
explore their city's squares:
was happiness, however planned,
as absolute as theirs?

But men and women aren't the same,
they 'sup from separate bowls':
and some there are who know no shame
in furtherance of goals.

The Esquiline's awash with bricks,
the Pincian is wooded:
your putative progenatrix,
ineffably cold-blooded,

is casting nets and casting lots.
Sibilla, you are frail,
for moneypots use honeypots
to climb the social scale.

What is a husband? How acquired?
What is the woman's role?
How literally is she sired?
Where lies the axis-pole?

Was Naples just a Piedmont shill,
a latter-day Bithynia?
A conscious act of sovereign will,
or conquered by Sardinia?

You call him upper-middle-class,
I see a mowing ape.
Vous dites 'l'amour', je vois la chasse:
thus marriage shades to rape.

She's torn from latin epigrams,
and sonnets sentimental
(the trashing of a young girl's dams
is hardly incremental!)

These violators of the lambs
in every sense ungentle,
whose humour turns on ewes and rams,
are semi-oriental.

Her father was the culprit's boss.
A tricky situation,
but his the triumph, hers the loss.
He raped her at her station.

So all that she had counted on
must now perforce miscarry:
the perpetrator is the one
who condescends to marry.

Our violence remains our shame,
too atavistic, grim:
the victims always say the same –
'I now belong to him.'58

He whisks you to some fly-blown town
where you are classed as 'foreign'
They see you as some kind of clown
as if you wore a sporran.

The man was marred by puerile pettiness.
Incredible! One day, she had been shopping.
Froth at his jealous mouth, his red eyes popping,
he ripped to shreds her newly-purchased dress.
That was the day she truly recognised
that all was lost, and something in her died.
He was an evil, vast, primordial tide:
and she was, in his presence, paralysed.

She loved the arts, but even an allusion
to notions satisfying or delightful
would wreak a change in him to something frightful.
He jumped each time to some absurd conclusion,
about her seeking extra-marital mollities.
Her self-esteem drained thus into the sands,
her innocence wrought by this tyrant's hands
into a nest (at best) of lame frivolities.

His fears and urges reached a form of fusion,
impelling him to claim he saw as rightful,
and she could not discern as low and spiteful:
hermetic was his cachet of illusion.
No longer did she long for long-lost jollities,
or contemplate her fate: no taking stands,
no speaking out, resisting his demands:
no individual impulses or qualities.

'I don't want denigration in the press,
or prison time,' he went on, hardly stopping
for inhalation, casually dropping
a hint at something no sane man could guess.
His hateful eyes dilated, over-sized,
he tried to reprimand, to scold, to chide:
'I need you to consider suicide,
and then you will be properly chastised.'

A peasant's son, when young I sought
to join the bourgeoisie
but on me dawned the lethal thought
they're not as bright as me.

The small town's ways to her uncouth,
their idiom, a warren:
to them she seemed a ghostly youth,
unconscionably foreign.

She watched each schism come and go,
like Etna's last eruption:
by staying silent, came to know
the town's inbred corruption.

A woman's fame remains fair game,
especially a stranger.
She's innocent? It's all the same
when snouts go in the manger.

Two sects contended for her name,
against and pro-Sibilla:
each keen to whitewash or defame,
each with an armed flotilla.

She stayed at home, and let them vie
without her interruption.
She'd learnt how they were driven by
hypocrisy, corruption.

The family adopts a role
too often deleterious
the husband's sister, inbred troll,
both frosty and imperious.

To show herself by verses moved
she, all too plainly zealous,
when faced by young-and-pretty proved
inordinately jealous.

This woman's husband's brother paid
Sibilla close attention
and forms of gallantry displayed
indelicate to mention:

his compliments, ineptly planned,
were inauthentic, phony,
but once offend a woman, and
beware the canellone!

He acted like he was 'her man',
as if he'd been enlisted:
as if they'd hatched some kind of plan
where no accord existed,

to locals, her 'chevalier'.
This led them to infer
That this was how the land now lay,
with '*droits pour son seigneur*'.

The truth slips out, notorious,
when men are in their cups:
when what we hear's uproarious,
the Devil also sups!

Though blind or deaf or homeless, he
would rather shag her maid:
an error of diplomacy
for which he later paid.

With nothing concrete said or done,
yet planted in her head,
it ended sooner than begun:
the brother-in-law was dead!

She wondered if it could have been:
could love have burgeoned, though
she'd hardly known him, sight unseen:
but now she'd never know.

The Doctor was another chance
to find the love she sought,
but nothing came of that romance,
and hope died down to nought.

The husband's mother, haughty, cold,
each morning more demented,
in widow-garments, shabby, old
and vaguely camphor-scented.

the ruined house her fermament,
her less-than-nimble brain
bequeathed her face its permanent
expression of disdain.

It constituted an escape
if only for an hour
with sleepy maid and satin cape
to sit there and devour

the San Francesco fresco show
transported in the silence
by flags and bodies, ebb and flow,
cartoon-like unreal violence.

In Rome once more, she stood before
'Prometheus' by Rosa.
Far from offended by the gore,
she felt it drew her closer.

Her loneliness she understood:
we have an inner fire,
and men were fodder, merely wood
to fuel her funeral pyre.

Could she be someone's Beatrice?
Could she be someone's Laura?
poetic muse, *inspiratice*?
To look back in angora?

She turned to face her inner drought
to suffer on her own
just for her son, she'd see it out
unloved, unmourned, unknown.

Back then, men kept their women blind:
her elders were her betters:
her satisfaction was confined
to windows and to letters.

The husband, mother, brother, all,
aware they couldn't 'heal' her,
afraid of what might yet befall,
decided to conceal her.

Though free to move around the house,
she couldn't enter spaces
where windows let her, thought her spouse,
look out on handsome faces.

A figure passing slowly by
whom sentries don't discover
occasionally caught her eye
Is this Sibilla's lover?

Men sniffed around her scent, of course,
as men are wont to do,
but in a land with no divorce
what was it leading to?

we city-dwellers never think
in terms of tilth or tillage
does this one-horse burg offer drink?
It's just another village.

An adolescent cannot grow
to be a wife and mother
if adults she's allowed to know
are ugly to each other.

Though not content, Sibilla passed
her calmest years in Rome:
it is, no matter what our caste,
to Europeans home.

She knew she'd lost all chance to thrive,
or save her reputation:
the only way to stay alive
was passive resignation.

Her son her only ally, though
naive, uncomprehending:
this lonely road, she had to know,
could have no happy ending.

She'll count on no-one but her son,
a baby not yet grown,
she'll tread the path so ill-begun
and do so all alone.

L'INGANNO FELICE

1. *Brief to Counsel*

We heartily wish counsel luck with this!
As far as we can judge, our client seeks
to drop his daughter (without prejudice
to the undying love of which he speaks).
The fourteen-year-old's living in Arezzo,
and married. (She's been told of nothing yet, so
we have to tread with caution.) Counsel knows
the way a normal lawsuit kind of goes:

one party doesn't want to pay the other,
and tries to wriggle out of obligations.
The centre of this tempest is the mother,
who's keen to shaft the aretine relations.
You catch a lizard? All to no avail.
It skitters off, you're left with just its tail.
The mother's mode of offering no quarter
is, lizard-like, to jettison her daughter.

(Or *are* they mother-daughter?) Here's the thing:
we're arguing no bond of blood exists.
One Pietro Comparini wants to bring
an action of non-fatherhood, insists
Pompilia's not his offspring. In support,
Violante will aver in open court
that she deceived her husband – nay, the world –
and have her far-fetched fakery unfurled.

'I love my daughter, but she isn't mine.'
Pietro palmed her off on Guido, who
(we're sorry, Counsel, but it's serpentine
or labyrinthine – either word will do!)
is standing on the contract. By its terms,
Pietro owes a dowry, but he squirms
and sheds his former skin. 'I here divest:
dixit uxor, filia non est!'

What lunacy possessed them? Who can say?
The bargain was, the couple stipulated
(we always throw our happiness away!)
they *must* live in Arezzo. They translated
from Rome to Tuscany, lock stock and barrel,
pets, potted plants, possessions and apparel.
The Tuscan, to the Roman, is a Turk:
this radical uprooting couldn't work.

Two women in one kitchen never serves,
but Violante plus the chatelaine
of Casa Franceschini? That deserves
a ring of Dante's Hades. Mother Hen
against the local dowager means war!
Result? The Comparini headed for
their former home in Rome. Fate unforeseen!
a Roman rout to rank with Trasimene!

But Violante's never low for long:
Antaeus-like, draws succour from bare earth:
you knock her down, she rises twice as strong!
Her rivals' ranking rests on noble birth –
so use their strength against them! Undermine
their standing with opinion aretine:
if, by the self-same stroke, the dowry's shed …
this harpy always finds the thing you dread!

The Jubilee of Innocent falls pat.
Old sins will be forgiven, if confessed.
Thus, Violante's meek *Magnificat* –
her simple soul's the purest palimpsest.
Pompilia's not her daughter – never was.
The thing was all a set-up, staged because
an heir was needed. Better to come clean.
Oh, by the way – these revelations mean

there never was a marriage. Simple fact!
Since we've no daughter to be married off,
there can't be any dowry to contract.
The pigs can take their snouts out of our trough.
By canon law you're notwithstanding married?
If all your aspirations have miscarried,
what's that to us? No matter how you splutter,
you've hitched yourself to garbage from the gutter!

(We're sure that Counsel shares our sense of fun.
With fickleness like Alcibiades,
our task, establishing the scam was done,
means *we* must prove *our* client's *mala fides*!
Lest Counsel thinks our brief a plot from Plautus,
we promise him our clients will exhort us
to take it all the way – right to the Curia!
Nemo me lacessit ex Etruria.)

2. Testimony of Violante Peruzzi

I'll try to be candid, and not to meander.
It was 'seventy-nine when I first met Angiola.
I tell you sincerely (and swear in all candour)
there's no Francis Xavier without a Loyola!

I hope you don't think that I'm pointing the finger,
but Angiola Biondi provoked the upheaval:
the day that I first sent a servant to bring her,
I named her 'Angiola-Beyond-Good-and-Evil'!

The seeker of bribe and below-stairs backhander,
a muse of the stews with the soul of a stroller,
she puts herself out as professional pandar,
her character solid as warm gorgonzola!

I told her I wanted a baby – a 'ringer'.
She called it 'recycling', and 'rugrat retrieval'.
And that's when I trapped both my tits in the wringer –
I opened my soul to that blood-sucking weevil!

I told her my secret, and begged 'Don't disclose it!'
I asked her to swear by Our Mother, the Virgin,
the chastest of promises (that's why I chose it!)
Angiola was willing. She needed no urging.

At not far off fifty, as well as I wore it,
too old to bear children (although I concealed it),
my money was short of an heir to ensure it:
an off-the-peg offspring both signed it and sealed it!

I said, you're the only *amica* who knows it.
She told me to start with the swelling and purging,
and vowed on her virtue she'd never expose it,
but things have a way of eventually emerging,

including the baby. The world thinks I bore it,
Angiola excepted. She really big-dealed it,
and guarding the secret, she totally swore it –
then, needless to say, she completely revealed it!

I couldn't have kids of my own. That could never be.
My best bet was one of those put-upon mums,
downtrodden and hopeless. You see them in every
malodorous stairwell in all the worst slums.

Angiola the midwife took on my assignment
and sought out a victim, like any good bawd.
She certainly knew what 'unlimited wine' meant,
and supped from deception's umbilical cord.

Some poor woman's child was my permanent reverie:
my baby would get something better than crumbs!
I sent my assistant to trawl through Trastevere,
saying 'Squeeze some poor sucker until she succumbs!'

And meanwhile one's task was to get in alignment
with pregnancy's programme: one couldn't afford
the slightest mistake over faking confinement:
clad in more padding than our old harpsichord!

She finally spotted a prey with potential,
a desperate mother-to-be who conceded
a far better life for the child was essential:
the fee was agreed, and the arguments heeded.

My previous pregnancies all had been wrecks,
so Pietro accepted, this time, from the start.
Miscarriages came from a surfeit of sex
protecting the baby meant sleeping apart.

'The mode is commercial, the code confidential:
the die has been cast and the sow has been seeded.
The only thing now is to hope that the wench'll
adhere to the bargain – and we'll have succeeded!'

Contractions and contracts and last-minute checks,
and I had accomplished the wish of my heart
(with wringing of hands, if not wringing of necks)
if not quite by nature, then surely by art.

I fashioned a 'tummy' by tying a cushion
and, feigning a fad of fastidious eating,
I took to my bed and forestalled all discussion.
Then, just as we stood on the verge of completing,

a flurry of obstacle-problems began.
Too late in the evening, her waters first broke.
Her sister had started opposing our plan.
What could we do if she chose to revoke?

The following morning my screaming and pushing
was due to commence. Would they see I was cheating?
Could we get through it without repercussions?
Which was the better – insisting? Entreating?

My husband was literally carrying the can:
I sent him for charcoal, then chick-peas to soak:
he had to be absent. They brought in a man
who pulled out a baby from under his cloak!

You never get everything. It was a girl!
The messenger brought a container of blood
(from a lamb, I believe) and he gave it a swirl:
it had started to clot, and it wasn't much good.

The afterbirth, too, had arrived from the 'source'
(to add authenticity), wrapped in a shawl.
I (smearing the infant) was retching, perforce
for the blood smelt disgusting, and I was appalled.

She didn't get hairbands in mother-of-pearl
(we hadn't prepared quite as well as we should):
the one piece of fabric we had to unfurl
must serve her as nightdress, *camisa* and hood.

The murmurs she uttered seemed stifled and hoarse,
but plainly, this child had the power to enthrall.
The lamb's blood was stinking, the textile was coarse –
'Francesca', however, wasn't crying at all.

Angiola said 'Scream, for the sake of the neighbours,'
so that's what I did, then she rolled up her sleeves:
'I'm fetching a witness to bear out your labours.
If one woman sees it, the public believes.'

The wife of our tenant came up for the 'birth'.
She climbed on the mattress, to brace me behind.
Giovanna 'La Boba', for all that it's worth,
was there for the pantomime (must have been blind!)

There weren't any fireworks. No piping or tabors.
The mightiest thing that a woman achieves
deserves to be feted with dancing on sabres,
but none of that happened. A few lusty heaves,

and there stood the midwife, all girdle and girth,
with child and placenta (umbilicus entwined),
a scene which now strikes me an object of mirth,
a farce – *'Gl'Ingannati'*, but not so refined.

Giovanna alerted the family facing,
and Barbara came with her favourite hen
(the bird had no clue it would soon need replacing,
would never be strutting the alley again!)

Angiola got busy and kindled the fire.
Whatever she fancied, she'd only to ask:
with things that were mine, I would gladly supply her:
she settled at last on an ell of damask.

The hen was dispatched after turbulent chasing:
We've not had such fun since I've never known when!
The baby got lots of coo-cooing, embracing,
and all that goes on in the absence of men.

We dined on the hen, when removed from her pyre,
but still there remained one unenviable task –
permitting Pietro's paternal desire
(but after concealing the blood-bearing flask!)

I stayed, from that day, in my own private quarter.
My wish had been granted – I now had a daughter!
(She'd been someone else's, it's true – but I'd bought her!
Do chickens and lambs disagree with their slaughter?)

3. *Deposition of Giovanna Boba*

My name? Giovanna Boba,
I'm thirty-eight years old.
This all happened years ago,
fifteen (I think) all told.

It feels like it was summer,
going by length of day,
but I just can't remember.
The month? I couldn't say.

We were five young women,
counting *La Oliviere*,
preoccupied with living,
born in the *quartiere*.

I lived below Violante
with husband Giovanni.
Pietro knew the girls, and he
labelled us, *'i zanni'*.

We were on the ground floor,
the others lived on top.
The Comparini's tenants,
we ran a tailor's shop.

We never talked of personal things
(just recipes and weather).
I've no idea if Pietro and
Violante slept together.

Fifteen years ago (I know,
because my second daughter
was born in early summer)
the talk of all the quarter

was Violante's body, and
its obvious additions.
But fat or flat, it didn't
awaken my suspicions.

Sometimes women put on weight,
and there are several ways
to make their clothing comfortable,
like letting out their stays.

Corsetry adjustment is
a tricky job to do,
and far beyond Violante, as
anyone who knew

the woman would attest: what's more,
Violante was a snob.
She wouldn't soil her dainty hands
with such a menial job.

My husband was the obvious choice
for any work like that –
he wouldn't ask for payment, and
we lived below their flat.

She knew us and she came to us
with many a tailor-task,
but this is one was never done –
because she didn't ask.

Petronilla's known to me.
I'd say she was a friend.
The Comparini's servant? Well,
that really would depend

on what you say a servant is.
Ventura (that's her man)
was full-time, livery and all.
A wife does what she can.

I saw her going up the stairs,
I saw her coming out.
She wasn't there for buying shares,
of that I have no doubt.

When Violante needed help
(a cleaner or a nanny),
She'd give the work to girls she knew,
her favourites, *'i zanni'*.

Who made the beds, I couldn't say.
Don't think I ever knew it.
Could Petronilla take it on?
Don't know who else would do it.

The day the baby came, they called
for me to help them out.
The midwife was a friend of mine,
and knew I'd be about.

To tread those carpets felt so nice!
(I'm used to naked board).
We crossed the salon, where they have
that yellow harpsichord.

Violante's boudoir's on that floor,
but difficult to find.
The midwife said, 'climb on the bed,
and brace her from behind.'

Violante's tall and I'm quite small,
and when the baby came
I didn't see the birth at all,
blocked by the mother's frame.

It seemed routine. By that I mean,
the baby didn't cry
(it's not unknown). One thing alone –
the blood was rather dry.

Well, when the child comes gushing out,
it's very wet and red,
but this had stains all grainy, brown,
around its downy head.

Across the *strada* lives a man,
the Cardinal's *nostromo*.
They told me, 'summon, if you can,
Signora Majordomo'.

So, yelling from the window-frame,
I captured her attention.
Marquese, maid, no-one displayed
the slightest condescension:

we're women all and, short or tall,
we feel our pulses quicken
to greet new life. The steward's wife
regaled us with a chicken.

But dainty ladies aren't like us.
They don't do dirt, or force.
Who killed and plucked and cooked the bird?
Her servant did, of course!

What do I think? There was a stink
of something more than gory.
Brunetta didn't look at all
like either *genitore*.

I slept with Violante till
a week or more went by.
The baby needed feeding, and
her breasts (of course) were dry.

My mother taught me many things
you'll never read in books,
like 'folks who sit in garden swings
should first inspect the hooks:

only fools leave cherry pies
unguarded near a glutton:
and lambs aren't born (I tell no lies)
to antequated mutton.'

4. Deposition of Petronilla Feure

Events align in patterns – who knows how?
It happened on the corner of Vittoria.
L'astuzia della donna è notoria.
Just sixteen years old then, past thirty now,
I'm more inured to urine than euphoria.
It happened on the corner of Vittoria:
events align in patterns – who knows how?

I'm on this farce's margins, you'll allow.
My name is Petronilla, surname Feure, a
much imposed-on mother. *Santa gloria!*
Events align in patterns – who knows how?
It happened on the corner of Vittoria.
L'astuzia della donna è notoria.

What validates vulgarity? Bravura!
Her scruples might be best described as scanty,
but when it comes to cunning, she's Bramante!
Her plan required (a) mother, (b) procurer,
and *she* could call on both. *She* (Violante)
had scruples which are best described as scanty.
What validates vulgarity? Bravura!

Assured, and fazed by nothing (nothing surer),
she worked us like a puppeteer. *Avanti!*
A star performance, down to *boccheggiante*.
What validates vulgarity? Bravura!
Her scruples might be best described as scanty,
but when it comes to cunning, she's Bramante!

Fiori, Caterina? I don't know.
Giovanna Boba is a friend of mine.
If Pietro's Pantaloon, she's Columbine.
I sometimes do odd jobs, beat carpets, throw
the Comparini washing on my line.
Giovanna Boba is a friend of mine,
but as for Caterina, I don't know.

Does Violante sleep with Pietro? No.
If he's the Pincian, she's the Esquiline.
Not separate beds, but floors (to put it fine).
Fiori, Caterina? I don't know.
Giovanna Boba is a friend of mine.
If Pietro's Pantaloon, she's Columbine.

With Violante, everything's dramatic.
A ducker-diver-diva-temptress-lurer,
she hates it straight – she must have *coloratura*.
We servants know of quarters in her attic,
but she's got places shadier, obscurer:
she hates it straight – she must have *coloratura*:
with Violante, everything's dramatic.

Our pay arrangements border on erratic.
My husband is her footman (name, Ventura)
and, like Saint Paul, he's all *fuori le mura*.
With Violante, everything's dramatic:
a ducker-diver-diva-temptress-lurer,
she hates it straight – she must have *coloratura*.

I wasn't fooled by Violante's faking,
her belly, sometimes rounder, sometimes flatter,
proof positive of perjury. Pure patter!
There wasn't any danger of mistaking
(we women chew the fat in catty chatter)

her belly – sometimes rounder, sometimes flatter!
I wasn't fooled by Violante's faking.

Her waters (not her word) were not for breaking.
The former were a phantom, and the latter
provided gossip on a golden platter:
I wasn't fooled by Violante's faking!
Her belly, sometimes rounder, sometimes flatter,
Proof positive of perjury. Pure patter!

Giovanna's husband called. Its time had come.
When I arrived, the baby had been born.
A chicken, partly-plucked, looked so forlorn!
Our physicality – is that our sum?
We mark the day we spark, the day we spawn.
When I arrived, the baby had been born.
The chicken's neck was wrung. Its time had come.

Right from the start, we're starting to succumb.
Those drapes were gaping open, so long drawn!
And there it lay, foreshortened, shivering, shorn.
Pompilia Francesca's time had come.
Not here, for certain, but she had been born.
The chicken, partly-plucked, looked so forlorn!

5. *The Testimony of Agnese Santa Olivieri*

The Feast Day of Mount Carmel. I was twenty –
so, fifteen years ago. I'd just had Tina.
While strolling in the *Stradale Paolina*,
I met La Bracchiera – *buona gente!*

Her husband was beside her. We'd been dining
at *Casa Guidi*, somewhere of that ilk.
My breasts were aching – I was full of milk!
Though life was hard, the summer sun was shining,

and we were young and strong. July's patina
lit up the frontage of *Gli Innocenti*.
We weren't exactly in the Lap of Plenty,
so – meeting her – I couldn't have been keener

to tap her for some work. I wouldn't bilk
at working as a cleaner (though inclining
towards a wetnurse post: with some refining,
I'd drop the scullery slops for salon silk!)

We stood there chatting. Underneath his cloak,
the husband showed he had a newborn child!
I swear the little sweetheart sort of smiled!
That's when the midwife's verbal waters broke.

'I'll tell you something, but you have to give your word:
you're seeing here a wealthy woman's ruse.
She needs a wetnurse – how can she refuse?
She's not lactating. What has just occurred

is something quite outlandish, wholly wild.'
Her eyes were bright with anger as she spoke.
Said I, 'Is this some kind of cruel joke?
She said, 'The natural mother's reconciled

to sacrifice. She's poor, must choose to lose
her little sweetheart (isn't life absurd?)
to give her something better – in a word,
a life not spoiled by toil. I blame the Jews!'

We said goodnight, but not without a chuckle.
This was my opportunity! So, happily
(for once ignoring scavengers and *scapoli*),
we followed them to see with whom they'd truckle.

We passed along the Street of the Gorilla,
to find which was the home of the *famiglia*.
(I'd taken quite a liking to the *figlia!*)
Just then, as we could see the Egyptian pillar,

the husband crossed the street. Close by the chapel, he
knocked at a door. Fate turns upon a knuckle!
The rest is history. I came to suckle
right here – this very house, *Orti di Napoli* !

And so did both Giovanna, Petronilla.
The child was christened Francesca Pompilia
(I have her medal in my memorabilia).
And now I hear she's married. What a killer!

6. *The Testimony of Caterina Fiori*

The most important players are all dead.
That's what I told him, seven weeks ago,
when summoned to his presence, 'I must know,'
he started (he was lying ill in bed),
'about your sister.' 'I had three,' I said.
'Did any have a baby – yes, or no?'
I looked directly at him, speaking low
and even: 'All were mothers.' Patent dread
was rising in his visage. 'Miss Fiori,
Quindic' estati fa – a baby?' 'Yes.'
'So: male, or female?' 'Heaven chose to bless
my sister with a daughter.' Needing more, he
was yet reluctant to pursue the story.
He gave a bitter sigh, then on he pressed.

'I think you know I'm Doctor Comparini,
the husband of Violante over there.' Her
discomfort was profound, nor did he spare her:
as far as it was possible to glean, he

was knowingly prolonging her distress.
'Your niece's midwife – perinatal carer –
what was her name?' 'Angiola Bracchiera.'
'Just so,' he said. 'I'm sure I could have guessed.'
Then, glancing at his wife as if to dare her
to chance a gambit in this game of chess
he said, 'Miss Fiori couldn't have been fairer.
Just one last question. Was the child forsaken?'
'You know she was. You paid to have her taken!'
'Perhaps,' he frowned, 'it worked out for the best.'

I'm fifty-five years old, but prior to this,
when these events were fresh and in the making,
my age was forty. This concerns the taking
of newborn infants who (lest you dismiss
my words too lightly, mark my emphasis!)
are prey to callous rich folk, fixed on faking
a money-trap, untroubled that they're breaking
the bonds of God-bestowed maternal bliss.
I fought for her ferociously, believing
that money never rescues, it devours –
but then my sister stopped me. She said, grieving,
'I want my child, by dint of others' powers,
to rise above this wretched life of ours,'
and blessed the little daughter that was leaving.

My sister passed away six years ago.
A country woman, raised in Canapina,
Corona lost her husband suddenly, and so
she came here with her twelve-year-old, Cristina.
They had to move to Rome – they had no means.
I asked her was she pregnant (women know
the secret goings-on behind the scenes!)
At last, she said the yeast was in the dough.
She always called it, *il miracolo,*
and seemed oblivious to all my fears:

it hadn't even started (yet) to show,
and he'd been dead – well, even walls have ears!
Corona had no time for neighbours' sneers –
'Don't do the calculations: watch me grow!'

My very own *comare*, named Agnese,
was present at the birth. She'll tell you straight.
'It's all so long ago, it's all so hazy',
is what they try to say – at any rate,
it's not for me! The victims were my sister
and newborn niece. That midwife had the cheek
to take the child away – you think I'd not resist her?
I've never been accused of being meek.
Corona held the baby, blessed her, kissed her:
She told me, 'don't'. That's when the lightning struck.
The child was lost to us. That sly *sofista*,
Angiola, often asks me, 'Are you crazy?
She'll live a life that's pampered, easy, lazy:
if only every baby had such luck!'

Busy in my home with routine tasks
(a year had passed since Cecca's give-away),
I heard Corona call me. 'Sister, come!'
I found her sitting at the window-sill
and staring at the street. 'That's Cecca's father!'
(Our pet-name for Corona's daughter, Cecca,
was taken from 'Francesca'.) There he strolled,
along the street below. He seemed so old!
I'd pictured him a rabid family-wrecker,
but now he seemed quite feeble – rather,
a gentle, harmless man. Mistrustful still,
I studied this Pietro. I felt numb!
No ogre, this. His waistline seemed to say,
here was a favourer of food and flasks!

A lad named Paolo Grande fell downstairs.
His sister asked me (she's the one who shares
our passageway) to go with her to 'theirs',
to visit him. 'The Comparini lair's
where he's recovering, between the squares
of Popolo and Spagna.' Unawares,
she'd given me the answer to my prayers!
'I'll come and see how well your brother fares!'
They were the most hospitable of pairs.
They'd no idea who I was – but who cares?
Deceit's allowable in such affairs.
That Violante's good at setting snares,
but I'd outwitted her! She talked of heirs
and stocks and shares (but not of brooding mares!)

The house was nicely painted, finely tiled,
with ornaments and nick-nacks everywhere.
There's nothing I'd imagined could prepare
me for it. Oh, those carpets, thickly-piled!
But really, it was all about the child.
I went because I can't resist a dare,
but seeing her was more than I could bear –
one glimpse and I was instantly beguiled!
She had my sister's nose and curly hair,
the darkest, most enormous, almond eyes!
That caramel complexion, jaunty air!
Those perfect limbs, albeit pixie-size!
She crossed her legs so daintily. Right there,
I knew the child was special. She's the prize!

How many years elapsed? Say, four or five.
The midwife showed her (when Corona pressed)
the dame-school where her daughter might be found.
My sister (unbeknown to me) contrived
to wait near the *Babuino*, hang around,
anticipating that she might be blessed

and pass a moment, have her patience crowned
by Cecca's hugs and kisses. Desperate lest
the 'parents' may discover and deprive,
she lingered on the recreation-ground,
by turns exhilarated and distressed,
to press that tiny toddler to her chest
(her only reason left to stay alive).

I saw them once in Popolo, by the way.
The year was eighty-six, to be exact.
I didn't challenge them – not out of tact,
but 'rightness', as Corona used to say.
A perfect evening near the end of May –
they looked so good together – she, compact
and 'gypsy', he, ungainly, breeches slacked.
They, holding hands and chattering away,
so clearly loved each other! Such a day,
with ochre evening sunlight on the cracked
facade of Luther's church, stood firm as fact,
and breeze-teased fountains growing beards of spray,
and toddlers scattering pigeons as they play,
how else could someone reasonably react?

7. *Testimony of Cristina Paperozzi*

It's twenty-seven now I am,
twelve back then, and so
the time you want to ask about
was fifteen years ago.

My name is Paperozzi, and
Corona was my mother.
I am her eldest daughter, and
Pompilia's the other.

I've never known her by that name.
To me, she's always 'Cecca'.
It makes no sense, the ornaments
with which they try to deck her.

I was a pupil of the school
that Cecca, too, attended:
I was sixteen, she was four
when my attendance ended.

My mother couldn't pay the fee
(she was a part-time cleaner).
The school was near Pietro's home,
the street that's called Paolina.

I knew, of course, where Cecca lived:
I saw her come and go.
The dame-school kids live cheek-by-jowl,
there's nothing they don't know.

My mother died some years ago.
You'd know the circumstance?
What killed her was sheer poverty.
She never stood a chance.

We moved here from the countryside
when I was twelve years old,
because she was 'expecting'. Yes,
I know it. I was told.

She said I had the right to know,
since this affected me:
she planned to give the child away –
the reason? Poverty.

The Monte Santo feast-day eve
is when the baby came.
A midwife organised it all –
I don't recall her name.

She took the baby that same night,
with quite a little hoard –
the afterbirth, for what it's worth,
and umbilical cord.

I know the baby was a girl.
The thing was plain to see.
The midwife said, 'Oh for a boy!
How better that would be!'

The afterbirth lay in a bowl,
the cord was wrapped around it.
My mother showed it all to me,
but left it where she found it.

When Caterina saw the child,
she wanted it to stay.
She argued with the midwife, but
the babe was whisked away.

She argued, blood is always blood,
and babies don't have 'owners'.
This Caterina is my aunt,
a sister of Corona's.

The midwife said, 'a golden thread
now leads her from this squalor.
She'll bathe in milk and sleep in silk:
her father is a scholar.'

She couldn't tell us who they were,
but both were wildly wealthy.
The child would grow, and learn and know,
refined and strong and healthy.

She promised tidings in due course,
but (just for now) deferred them.
I learned these details from the source,
for I was there, and heard them.

The midwife later kept her word
(he scholar and his spouse
lived near the *Greci),* took us there
and pointed out the house.

My mother tracked a wetnurse down,
and turned up at her home
(to see that child, she would have filed
through every slum in Rome!)

Her eyes were bright when, late that night,
she came into my quarter.
At last she spoke, an almost-choke:
'I held my little daughter!'

I once asked Cecca why she was
unlike *altri bambini.*
She said, 'I am the daughter of
Pietro Comparini.'

My mother was obsessed with her.
She waited at the door
before school, and then after school
she'd hang around some more.

I think of her, and must infer
emotional enslavement:
I see them now, just as they were:
she's hugging Cecca, Cecca her:
and mother's tears, without demur
are splashing on the pavement.

REX JUDAEORUM, RES JUDICATA, Being a Tale Told by Jacopo, the Yardman at the Castelnuovo Inn

Two prostitutes appeared before the King,
to ask if he would settle their dispute
(of simpler and much fairer times I sing,
when citizens could ask for anything,
push personal appeals – the whole bang shoot!)

Said one, we've got a problem that's acute.
The ruling which we really want to wring
from you is more than massive – it's a beaut!
We share a house. We're girls of ill repute.
There are no men (save such as trade may bring).

I've given birth (I'm still recovering!)
and three days later, this whore followed suit,
but hers has died. At home, you couldn't swing
a cat, and accidental smothering
(in course of sleep) is all we can impute.

But then she chose to go the crafty route.
What kind of woman falls to cozening,
and changes babies? Has the nerve to loot
another's infant? What immoral brute
would swap the dead one, like a costume ring?

When daylight came, I started suckling
(but that the child was dead, could not refute).
Conclusions are not things to which I spring
and, after scrupulous examining,
believed the bitch had switched them. Ain't that cute?

That living child is mine, you prostitute!
The scrap of life to which you seek to cling,
so tenuous, so vulnerable, minute,
is closed to you, taboo, forbidden fruit.
Parental claim? Pathetic posturing!

The other mother, goaded by this sting,
responded like a cobra to the flute:
her tongue flicked out, but, far from staying mute,
spewed all the accusations she could fling.
Confusion in the court was absolute.

The Prince appeared inscrutable (or bored?)
and tarried for a moment, lost in thought:
at length, he barked an order – 'Fetch a sword.'
Commands of kings can scarcely be ignored:
the logical result? A blade was brought.

'I love the spare morality of sport,
whereby each ambiguity is cured.
Just cleave the child in two (let's keep it short).
Give half to each, and they can quit my court.
And thus is equilibrium restored.

By way of compensation or reward,
each mother's offered monetary support.
One hundred shekels from the palace hoard,
for any inconvenience endured.
Oh, please don't thank me – I'm the modest sort.'

One mother pondered: 'That's a lesson taught!
One baby lost is nothing untoward –
they're easier to come by than a wart.
A hundred's always handier than nought!
I'm happy to initial the accord.'

But still one tart, continuing distraught,
declared the king's decision deeply flawed.
'I won't consent to butchery! I fought
to give him life. For once, I can't be bought.
Just bung my baby to that blousy bawd.'

The monarch was amused, instead of floored.
'That's how authentic mothers may be caught!
Here is a wealth no money can afford.
I now return the woman to her ward,
bambino to madonna, as I ought.'

The Sword of Damocles hangs by a string,
but when the arbiter is this astute,
despite the danger, ever dangling,
the ultimate disposal is not moot.
With Justice joyful, Wisdom on the wing,
a King that's even cleverer than Canute,
sincerely, Solomon, take our salute!

FATHER URBANO ROMANO REMEMBERS POMPILIA

I loved a girl I hardly even know.
(It's complicated, since I am a priest.)
Our sense of intimacy was increased
by secret feelings, whispered sweet and low
in sessions of confession, and although
our friendship faltered – no, it failed, it ceased –

in early April at the Easter feast,
the pain remains. I'm glad to undergo
a silent suffering I'm sure redeems
my sharp shortcomings. Gifting me her trust,
she voiced her deepest fears, revealed her dreams,
and nothing intimate went undiscussed.
She glowed with grace, though placed between extremes,
and he who tells it differently, blasphemes.

THE DREAM OF THE ROOD, Being the Dream of Francesca Pompilia, as She Related it to Father Urbano Romano

I found myself in space
which had no up or down,
a dark and shapeless waste
in which I feared I'd drown.
Swirling on the border
where chaos threatens order –
appalling place to be!
No-one to ease the strain,
no-one to hear me groan:
shouted out in vain,
so utterly alone:
no companion creature,
or life-sustaining feature
to help or comfort me!

Then, suddenly at ease,
and treading *terra firma*,
where aromatic trees
and tinkling rivers murmur
I knew that I'd been saved.
Pleasant paths, unpaved,
led off into the shade.

At last I reached a clearing
and met with a surprise:
for there, in easy hearing,
before my very eyes
were, sitting at a trestle,
engrossed and trying to wrestle
with something partly-made,

my parents! They were sewing.
Although they sat quite near me,
I knew (my knack of knowing!)
that they would never hear me.
By now, the clouds were breaking:
the doll that they were making
(I plainly saw it now)
was scooped up by my mother.
To my useless dismay,
each leaning on the other,
my parents hobbled away.
The rain was hammering hard.
My path to them was barred,
I can't explain quite how.

I went into the woods
in search of refuge. There,
in capuchin-like hoods
around an open square,
a squad of stolid *sbirri*,
disconsolate and dreary,
were dancing in the rain.
I asked them if they knew
what dangers lay before me:
this melancholy crew
decided to ignore me.
They chose to twirl and trot

their waterlogged gavotte
and treat me with disdain.

I took to the trees again,
regardless of direction.
And that's the moment when
a fragment of perfection
a brightly-coloured bird
bobbed and skipped and whirred
a little way ahead.
It seemed to know its way
and, in its liquid song,
it seemed to want to say,
'I'm helping you along!'
So, in a better mood,
with confidence renewed,
I followed where it led.

It settled on a limb
which, up close, became an axe!
Its shaft was smooth and trim:
With enthusiastic whacks
I felled a tree with ease:
after twenty-plus of these,
a circular stockade
had started taking form.
The rain had died away,
the sun was bright and warm.
My ring of tree-poles lay
erect and strong and true
beneath a sky of blue
in a clear and open glade.

A hut in which to sleep
proved simple to construct.
When a spring began to leap,

I was grateful for my luck!
It bubbled from the ground
with a most enchanting sound,
clear, sweet water at my feet!
My dress had once been white:
the skirt and lacey train
were now a dreadful sight,
but it didn't long remain
in situ on my back!
Like some goddess of Iraq,
I was 'naked as a neat'!

My little bird stopped by
to bring a length of vine:
to hang my dress to dry,
I improvised a line.
It fluttered high above,
like a wing-extended dove,
curiously cruciform.
My nudity was fun,
and free of guilt or shame:
I gloried in the sun,
no-one to blab or blame:
innocent as a nun
enjoying the exposure
within my new enclosure,
completely safe and warm.

White clouds were sliding past:
the breeze grew stiff and strong:
a shroud before the mast,
my dress pulled us along.
Round as a bishops's belly
and pale as Lamparelli,
it billowed like a sail.
My stockade started rolling,

and seemed to gather pace,
a force beyond controlling
obliging us to race:
the dress, as taut as timber,
yet elegant and limber,
was bending with the gale.

Now snakes were all around me,
glistening, obscene:
(who fathoms how they found me?)
coiling, sickly green,
obliging me to feel
I really must conceal
my naked innocence.
The ugliest serpent there
reared upright! To observe
his matted facial hair
and spastic spinal curve
disgusted me. The brute
was somehow taking root
and swelling. In a sense,

he'd now become a tower
like *la Mangia* of Siena:
he starts to toll the hour.
Quello che impenna,
insufferably chiming,
continues swelling, climbing,
to where my dress is draped.
Intimidatingly,
the tendril arms of Time
were crowding, suffocating me,
like Ariosto's rhyme.
An instant thunder-storm:
my wedding-dress transformed,
took on a dagger-shape.

It hung there in the sky,
above us and ahead,
appearing to defy
all natural law. Instead,
it floated without weight,
kept vertically straight,
and moved along with us.
No knife was ever made
so vilely: its serration,
side-spines along the blade,
to make the laceration
intolerably severe,
to slash and gash and shear
with every single thrust.

My body was on show
for those disgusting snakes
to leer at lustfully, and so
I used the frequent breaks
between each lightning crack
to move towards the shack
and find a thing to don.
The snakes were all around.
I felt my soul recoiling
at every thrashing mound
of filthy reptiles, soiling
my beautiful stockade.
Still, progress had been made:
I had an *abito* on.

I climbed the mast, because
the knife offended me.
My sole intention was,
that gross obscenity
should not continue flying.
But, just as I was trying,

the *sbirri* crowded me,
all arms and uniforms,
and I was pinioned fast:
like octopii in swarms
they milled around and massed:
the knife was lost from sight.
That's when another fright
dislodged me from the tree!

We, tipping from the earth
as over a waterfall
(the trauma of our birth,
which we can all recall),
we plunged into a space
which bore no hint or trace
of things that humans know.
Down, down we fell, for hours.
And now we're on some rocks:
a red horizon glowers.
The thousand natural shocks
(unnatural is better!)
to which our flesh is debtor
admonished me to go.

'We have to reach the light,'
I offered to the *sbirri*
but, hard as anthracite,
with faces bloated, weary,
they swore they would not move.
'But how, then, to improve?'
My question faded, bootless.
This dark gigantic cavern
(no walls or ceiling seen)
was like Canale's tavern,
but not like it: I mean …
some kind of premonition …

I understood my mission.
To sit here would be fruitless.

I struck out for the glow,
the point which seemed to me
the place of promise, though
I had to cross a sea
of frozen waves. And when
I stood on rock again,
a storm of fire rained down.
The balls of living flame
did little harm, except
(to my recurring shame)
my nun's apparel crept
in ruins to my feet,
my nudity complete
without my modest gown.

I have always wanted
more than life allotted me.
Obviously daunted,
in case somebody spotted me,
but certain of my cause,
I strode towards the jaws
of that great citadel.
The fortress up ahead
wasn't hard to find.
In front, a sky of red,
the Evening Star behind.
I saw the mighty gate,
but had to hesitate:
before me opened Hell!

Across me (right to left)
a torrent, fast and fierce,
was surging through a cleft,

as if it sought to pierce
the mantle of the earth:
but progress has its worth,
so I was not dismayed.
Some people choose the Church
to puff their plans, or pride.
I've never had to search:
my wellspring is inside.
I clearly understood
I had to cross this flood,
and set out unafraid.

That's when I found the Tree,
all shrivelled and uprooted.
Its female form, to me,
could hardly be disputed:
as if the coursing lymph
of a sorely-harrassed nymph
had frozen into sap.
The Tree was plainly dead,
but not at all undone.
I marvelled at the spread
of runners – they'd begun
to reach and feel around.
Its heartwood was still sound.
To sail across the gap

I took a length of bark,
a raft on which to ride
and, limber as a shark,
I reached the other side.
The gateway yawned around me –
its grandeur almost drowned me
as I went walking in.
It hardly need be said
that, naked still and friendless,

I felt a sense of dread
in halls all tall and endless,
but all along I knew
that not to see it through
would be a mortal sin.

A woman on a throne
in this malignant Mecca
– apparently unknown –
cried, 'Won't you kiss me, *Cecca*?'
At this, I felt confused:
the nickname that she'd used
had mighty connotations.
My memories were scanty,
but once I'd had a mother
(I don't mean Violante,
but rather someone other).
And now I understood
that she and this one could
be (somehow) my relations.

'*Sorella*,' she addressed me,
'why have you sought me out?
You hate me? You detest me?
What is this about?'
Something in my blood
assured me that I should
in some way recognize her.
'I neither loathe nor fear you,'
I answered to her face.
'I wouldn't have come near you,
had things not taken place
which I could scarce control.'
I saw into her soul,
and I could not despise her.

'And when will you go home?'
'As soon as I'm permitted.'
'Arezzo, then? Or Rome?'
'The one to which I'm fitted.'
'One answer, and you're free:
You'll have your liberty.'
'And what if I should fail?'
'Why, then we both stay here,
until the End of Days.'
I (strangely) felt no fear,
and met her steady gaze.
'You haven't asked my name.'
'To me, it's all the same.'
I saw her features quail.

'Well then, your question. Ask.'
My confidence unnerved her
(my aim, to set the task,
not be the one who served her).
'Where can God be found?
In sea, or sky, or ground?
A thing no mortal knows.'
It's curious to relate:
I felt no trace of doubt,
nor did I hesitate.
The answer just came out.
'Where upright intersects
with crossbar, one expects
to find Perennial Rose'.

And then I saw it all,
as in a living *tableau*:
my wedding, in a squall:
a fire, Abate Paolo
destroying all his books:
myself, on tenterhooks,

the night that I escaped,
opening the window frame
to let in fresh, clean air,
a lord pronounce 'No blame!',
at a table, smooth and bare:
then Caponsacchi came
(a bald patch in his hair),
and *cap-a-pe* be-caped:

without a jot of shame,
embarrassment, despair,
we played the mating game,
we coupled, then and there.
It wasn't like before –
I was a happy whore –
like something had begun.
Then off we went together,
our path was plain and clear:
ahead, the summer weather,
behind, all drab and drear.
I knew myself indebted
to The Cross, now silhouetted
in the Portal of the Sun.

Nothing Doing

The rich and influential help their friends.
This is, and was, and always will be so.
Medici wants his chum in Rome to know
he's bent on tending Franceschini ends.
Vincenzo tells us more than he intends:
he mentions Porzia's name, as if to show
that Guido's wife is basking in the glow
of 'decent' women's friendship. Dividends
will flow. But why is she the sine qua non?
What role in this production might she play?

What denouement could she insist upon?
Weak leaders never want to seize the day.
The crucial moment happens, then it's gone:
decision cedes, deferring to delay.

LETTER OF CIVIL GOVERNOR VINCENZO MARZI-MEDICI TO ABATE PAOLO FRANCESCHINI, 2 AUGUST 1694.

My most illustrious, reverent and serene
beloved Master, whom I live to serve,
      I felt I had to act
         (in furtherance of our pact)
to stave off scandal – which is to conserve
your noble house's majesty and mien.

That Violante woman was obscene.
She had the sheer unmitigated nerve
      and utter lack of tact
         to denigrate, detract
your pious mother's every urge and *oeuvre*,
to countermand her with especial spleen.

To save the day, I had to intervene.
I told the Comparini they deserve
      (would undergo, in fact)
         to be imprisoned, wracked.
I gave an ultimatum, to preserve
the best of order. Any unforeseen

convulsion or commotion, as between
themselves and your dear mother, any swerve
      or effort to impact
         what should remain intact

our civic peace – one failure to observe
my stern command –they knew what that would mean!

If anything, the Comparini male
was even worse. Incontinently drunk
        by night as well as day,
          and snoring where he lay
in lowly taverns, in a booze-fed funk,
he was a type to make a Stoic quail.

His only quest in life was quaffing ale.
Your brother had the patience of a monk
        to let the loser stay.
          Reprove him as he may,
He couldn't win. The barfly always slunk
Canale-wards, since Satan will prevail

despite our noblest efforts. Men are frail,
but some more frail than others, and have sunk
        to such a sinning way
          that even our dismay
can't shame them. Scripture they regard as bunk,
and fine admonishments are doomed to fail.

Pietro was a punk, beyond the pale,
disposed to drinking swill and eating junk.
        But sinners have to pay,
          and Pietro's feet of clay
led finally to a packing of the trunk.
His choice of home was, Rome or Arezzo's jail.

Francesca or Pompilia (the name
eludes me) had a pattern of repeated
        behaviour. She would sprint
          (divulging not a hint

of what was coming), Holy Mass completed,
towards the Bishop's Palace, with the aim

of occupying portions of the same.
In words both immature and overheated,
      the silly little bint
        would pass a lengthy stint
in corridors or stairwells, always treated
with cool forbearance. She was there to claim

a species of asylum, and to shame
her long-enduring husband. She was greeted
      with courtesy like flint.
        The bishop's clerk, by dint
of standing orders, damped-down and defeated
the bluster based on blackguardry and blame.

The parents put her up to play this game!
Their arrogant, ill-thought-out and conceited
      attempt to cause a rift
        received the shortest shrift.
The daughter, unsuccessful and unseated,
went home again, more meekly than she came.

Comportment both more humble and more tame
have been her recent record. One has meted
      approval for this shift.
        Her modesty and thrift
(all former indiscretions now deleted)
are earning, in Arezzo, rightful fame.

My counsel, always, is 'procrastinate'.
We'll see how she develops, how she grows.
      Perhaps one day we'll list her
        a favourite of your sister.

Before she can be counted one of those,
my strong advice is simply, watch and wait.

Analogy? The San Clemente Gate
through which the San Sepolcro traffic flows
      is dust and noise and fretting,
      but as the sun is setting
the wooden shutters, like great eyelids, close,
and all again is silent and sedate.

STRAY LEAVES: TELLING TALES

The stories that we tell are two-edged things.
Medici serves the nobles as their skivvy,
ashamed he's not a soldier, just a 'civvy'.
He hopes to hawk poetic offerings
to lend his social status golden wings.
How raise a rumpus? Trumpet a tantivy?
He'll tout a tale of Titus' (Good old Livy!)
The trouble is, the canto which he sings
won't bring us anything on Dolabella.
Recitals ring of caliphates and kings,
but could the speaker be the real novella?
Our human psyche wells from hidden springs:
perhaps our trifling tales and twitterings
are not about the subject, but the teller.

THAT NICE DECISION OF DOLABELLA'S,
Being a Tale Told by Governor Vicente Marzi-Medici to His Brethren, *I Forzatti*, during a convocatorio at the Horse Inn

A woman of classical Smyrna
(I'm tempted to say, a slow learner)
   killed husband and son
   and cried, 'Punishment? None!'
(She might as well climb Annapurna!)

Reluctant (one hopes) to disparage,
one senses a risk of miscarriage:
   the husband had slain
   (to the woman's great pain)
her son from a previous marriage.

Like something from *Barnaby Rudge,*
the woman had luck with her judge:
   though blood had been spilt,
   she evaded her guilt
(forensically known as a fudge).

The magistrate of the *favela*
(one Publius C. Dolabella),
   bemused by the case,
   would far rather have faced
a sandwich of pure salmonella.

She'd felt justifiable rage,
but how could a judge (in that age)
   acquit her of murder?
   What could be absurder?
(There's social unrest to assuage!)

The crisis before him was chronic,
but Dolly came up with a tonic –
   let's send her to Greece:
   it's a blessed release!
(ironically, she was Ionic!)

The elders who sat on the hill
were legends of wisdom and skill,
   but how best to decide?
   Though two victims had died,
the moll's mitigation was brill!

The case was disposed of. Here's how.
'The court is adjourned. Stand and bow.
   We'll all reconvene
   on October eighteen
one hundred and ten years from now.'

THE HISTORY OF THE TRUE CROSS (1)

The Maiming of the Jew

Who wouldn't love that medieval art?
Those images, bewitchingly barbaric,
whose blood-lust grips us like a sauce tartarique
which, meeting mundane matter, may impart
a piquancy that's tantalizing, tart,
can make 'prosaic' appear almost Pindaric.
Those epicures who luncheon at the Garrick
would take this votive violence to heart!
One calls to mind a book in Barcelona
in which a martyrdom is illustrated.
One Quiriacus, Bishop of Ancona
is sliced by a saw that's seriously serrated.

A nut-to-navel cartilage-and-boner,
that's one incision hardly understated!

Helena in the Holy-Land

The fiercest zealot is the born-again.
Back when the world was freshly Constantined,
and folks weren't quite so empathy-inclined,
the sword was much, much mightier than the pen
and Helena, the Empress-Mother, when
this shit went down, betook herself to find
the Cross of Christ with singleness of mind,
a laser-guided-missile-mother-hen.
Establishing a beach-head in Terre Sainte,
polluting every pocket like a cancer,
and not about to take 'no' for an answer,
more like the Unabomber than U Thant,
she sought out a semitic sycophant,
and Judas thus became her Sancho Panza.

HELENA'S IN JERUSALEM
and Helena's the Boss.
She'll break 'em or bamboozle 'em,
but somehow get that Cross.

A local Jew named Judas
(not *that* one, but no better)
said 'Christians will denude us
of the spirit and the letter

of all the laws of Zion;
they're meting out Masada.
It's one to keep an eye on –
so, *no digamos nada*!'

So Helena said 'Burn the Jews.
They'll none of them be missed.'
An offer they could not refuse!
Less willing to resist,

they served up Judas to the Queen.
'He'll tell you where it's hidden.
If not, we'll intervene!'
– and Judas did as bidden.

She wanted Golgotha, and Jesus' Tree.
He said he didn't know
of any place where that might be.
'Three hundred years ago,

when the Man from Galilee
endured His crown of thorns,
it's all (to me) a mystery:
I hadn't yet been born.'

'You'll hold this line, adamantine,
as long as you have breath?'
(for thus spoke Helena) 'That's fine.
I'll starve your ass to death.'

She put him in a sheer-walled pit
and told him, with a grin,
'You spill the beans, and out you git.
If not, we fill it in.'

If he betrays his ancient ways,
here's money, wine and food.
He'll reappraise, or down he stays:
'So what's your problem, dude?'

A week it took, but he forsook
the Talmud and the Torah.
Up was he pulled, and wrapped in wool.
He looked back in angora:

'I will not rue, regret, review,
regard myself askew:
just take the cue, break the taboo –
do what you gotta do.'

To Calvary he led the crew,
along the Via Crucis:
they told him he's an okay Jew:
some Hebrews have their uses.

The Venue of the Skull achieved,
Judas felt a change:
the fragrance that he now perceived
was wonderfully strange:

he clapped his hands and beat his chest,
'Sweet Jesus! My reward
is, I accept You! I am blessed!
My Saviour and my Lord!'

(It's set in prose which all may gloze
that wolves can change their fur.
We must suppose that's how it goes,
and miracles occur.)

A temple squatted on the spot,
deformis et obscoenus:
the *dominatrix* of the plot,
the heathen goddess Venus.

But Helena was unabashed,
impervious to dismay.
She simply had the temple trashed,
the rubble dragged away.

First one in the trench was Judas.
As a good man should,
he wanted to achieve the kudos
of being first to strike on wood.

Three crosses found deep in the ground
like busts of Amphitriton:
we know now, it's the Calvary mound –
but which cross is the right one?

Said Helena, 'Await a sign.
Your work is passing zealous,
but as to which one is divine,
the Lord is sure to tell us.'

It happened that a funeral pyre
came wailing by, just then:
the Empress asked, 'Do you desire
to have him back again?'

Each cross was placed against the head
of him who was deceased,
the third one touched – he who'd been dead
was suddenly released!

The young man rose and talked and walked,
a-blinking in the sun:
but Satan, who behind him stalked,
cried, 'What has Judas done?'

'Judas! Don't we have a deal?
You're meant to bring me souls!
The other Judas was for real.
Please focus on your goals!'

But Judas now renounced his kin
and stigmatised the Demon.
'I slough the skin of those in sin
like Madoff, Maxwell, Lehman.'

'Oh, is that so? Well, waddya know?'
(said Satan, super-sarcastic):
'I've got a bro named Giulio,
who'll dish out something drastic!'

They guided Judas to a font
and named him 'Quiriacus',
as every Jew must surely want,
baptised his heathen carcass.

Our tale is told, but we would share
a footnote to our story
(but nervous readers, please beware –
it gets a little gory).

Since Quiriacus lived in grace,
a model of sobriety,
his reputation rose apace,
and all admired his piety.

The bread and wine, once made divine,
were nectar and ambrosia
to one who, at the Supper Shrine,
assumed the Bishop's crozier.

But Quiriacus had a foe
named Julian the Apostate,
who wanted to destroy him so!
(Think slugs and iron phosphate.)

The Emperor gave a stern command
to put the bishop in fetters,
and amputate his writing hand,
to stop him sending letters.

'Why thank you,' Quiriacus quipped.
'Once, synangogues employed me
to crank out anti-Christian script.
That hand has long annoyed me.'

His mouth was filled with molten lead,
his body seared with fire.
'To stop the suffering,' Julian said,
'just say Christ was a liar.'

Another pit was being prepared,
and other trouble brewing.
The Bishop, neither stressed nor scared,
said, 'Sorry, nothing doing.'

The pit was filled with poison snakes,
to work obispicide:
for Quiriacus, no great shakes –
they bit him, and *they* died!

With boiling oil his torturers toiled
(the cost, we'd scarcely guess at).
He shuffled off this mortal coil.
In pacem, requiescat.

Take courage, Christian! If that
is how a *Jew* behaved
(*mea anima magnificat!*)
then why can't *you* be saved?

HALF-ROME

He's quite the knight, 'le roi des raconteurs'.
A captive audience which promptly purrs
and solvent patrons, his prerequisites.
He entertains the table where he sits
with what he likes to call his 'greatest hits'
(annoyingly, His Worship terms them 'skits'),
The truth of which he avidly avers.
(They cling to counts and cardinals like burrs,
these men who live by living by their wits.)
His regular employment? None, of course.
He's singing for his supper, as befits
his tabloid tales of drinking and divorce,
which rest on dark sarcasm for their force.
He calls himself 'The Secondary Source'.

HOW NOT TO RUN A FAMILY: HERE'S A GUIDE.
My story centres on uxoricide,
but if you add cadavers supplementary,
you'll find that, needlessly, ten people died.
A middle-aged man selects a teenage bride.
He calls himself a count with all the pride
of weaklings, but he's really rural gentry.
He moves the girl, plus parents, to his home
in Tuscany (the in-laws are from Rome).
The mutual-suspicion point of entry
grows gravely worse when living cheek-by-jowl.
The differences are glaring, elementary:
At first they manifest in slur and scowl,

but soon the guests, fatigued of foreign loam,
shake off Arezzo dust, throw in the towel.
A cockerel turned up with a stiffer comb,
a jackanapes in motley polychrome
who laid the love on with a tricksy trowel.
The brother Girolamo, sleepless owl,
declared himself Pompilia's saturnine sentry.

The priestly Paolo, brother of the groom,
was out to seal an iron-clad Pact of Steel.
The father of the bride felt far less zeal:
all gout and doubt, all rheum and imposthume,
he sensed he'd sent his daughter to her doom.
What do they call it? 'Castle of Otrante'?
For Tuscan Franceschini? Business deal.
They spent, to rent an adolescent womb.
Display your crimson banner, dye your plume
in horribly expensive cochineal,
and have your tomb configured by Bramante:
It hardly helps you if you're upper-crust –
all human enterprise just dies in dust,
and who has said it better than our Dante?
you'll never garner *petit-bourgeois* trust.
Display your paintings, mount your forebear's bust:
all well and zealous, *ma irrilevante*.
Abate Paolo knew that he'd been 'sussed'.
Unswerving on observance, *tutti santi*,
he couldn't keep it on an even keel.

The parents (*soi-disants*), already old,
decided that a marriage was a must.
Financial fortunes had begun to falter
and what are daughters for, but to be sold?
(Some wed their own *cognate*, for the gold!)
Pompilia, then, a plump young partridge, trussed,
was primped and pimped, and peddled at the altar.

The mother, Violante, full of tricks,
presumed to put one over on the hicks:
though lucre was agreeable, her lust
could not be sated by a juncture, just:
gentility was what she tilted at. Behold!
A trek to far Etruria was discussed,
and thus the Comparini hit the bricks
and crossed the Rubicon. Once in the sticks,
they found the case considerably altered:
instead of mansions, minks and Knights of Malta,
they'd yoked themselves to yahoos. This was Yalta,
with rancid rations, desultorily doled.
Our Roman candles? Wax, with wilted wicks!

The 'Franceschini Foison' was a scam.
To get a cash injection's why they'd wed!
Half-drowning in the direst of dire straits,
their table bore the paltriest of plates,
the cellar measly wine (but mostly water).
They called it 'self-denial', forwent fêtes,
observed one minor rite – the Sunday Slaughter –
divided up and shared a newborn lamb.
One might pull out the snout, or the aorta!
They weren't like us (the fabulously-fed
Farnese) – Arno trout, then Parma ham –
their guest-list was far shabbier …and shorter.
Young blades have always blustered, often bled:
they'll slide a spike where angels fear to tread,
and this accounts for Girolamo's head.
The Comparini 'took it on the lam',
like rats up drainpipes, to the Papal States,
and shuffled off the Franceschini sham,
but left the daughter (after all, he'd bought her).
What happened next is better left unsaid …

Once safe in Rome, what action did they take?
Violante, who defines the term 'astute',
did something which seemed decent, but was cute:
declared Pompilia a total fake!
The consort of a count she may be, but
in truth she was the offspring of a slut!
With lowered eyes and trembling trepidation
she told Arezzo and the Tuscan nation
(her target audience) her drone-like drake
was no progenitor. For honour's sake?
Oh, please! First motive: burning indignation.
Those eighteen weeks of dire humiliation
in Guido's house were ulcers in her gut.
The second motive: clinging to the loot!
The dowry contract mentions Guido's cut,
but if she's not their child, the point is moot!
The final motive, love of titillation.
Like Irish peasants dancing at a wake,
the duty of discretion doesn't suit:
their mouths, the one thing they could not keep shut!

The bee in Guido's bonnet was the dowry.
Increasingly frustrated, thwarted, bitter,
he watched the Comparini dish the dirt,
extend the litigation (meant to fritter
the Franceschini's last remaining cowrie).
Pompilia was close, the parents distal –
so, whom to bully? It's as clear as crystal.
Another thing: they'd bargained on a litter,
the brood of heirs on which they'd bet their shirt –
but nothing came. More blame! A world of hurt!
(It's Guido who lacked bullets in his pistol.
She had a baby soon enough.) You titter,
but here we have the diastole and systole –
those old detractions, hurled at bits of skirt –
she's barren, and she's just a whorish *houri*.

Maghrebi, Mayan, Merovingian, Maori,
wherever there are men, those men assert
(in language one would hardly class as flowery)
'the girl's a worthless flirt'. Thus stallions skitter.
The stamen fears, and so insults, the pistil.

If Canon Conti wasn't very brave,
at least he felt affinity enough
to comprehend her crisis, try to save
the wretched girl. The impetus he gave
turned out to be the stave that stopped the slide.
(Perhaps his motive needs to be explored.)
The family was willing to confide
in him, at least at first. Did he behave
as caring relative – or had he scored?
Pompilia parishioner – or bit of fluff?
The damaged Girolamo and his sword
had reached a point that could not be ignored.
But there was Caponsacchi, young and tough:
the trick would be in luring him aboard.
Since Conti couldn't risk the reckless ride,
he'd help her with the preparation stuff
then shuffle unobtrusively aside.
The hapless Conti, affable and bluff,
perhaps a fool, can not be called a knave.
Would Caponsacchi take things in his stride?

He surely would. He swallowed Conti's bait
unhesitatingly and unperplexed,
his acts informed by decency, not hate.
Pompilia left the house with personal things,
to meet her hero at Clemente Gate.
They barreled Romewards at an urgent pace.
Despite the flight on unremitting wings
(not quite the profile of romantic flings),
Their bolt for safety turned into a race.

Some hours behind, the husband joined the chase,
but (yet again) Count Guido's hopes were hexed
(like one who clings too long to apron strings).
On Tuesday — there's some doubt about the date —
pursuer pounced on prey ... but, promptly vexed,
did Guido draw his weapon? Fulminate?
Of course not. To preserve the carapace
of honour, legal muscles must be flexed.
Refusing fight, embraced his own disgrace.
Then Paolo fled — the worst of sunderings!
He knew, for certain, what was coming next.

High summer passed, while (fast in separate cells)
Pompilia and her priest perspired ... and waited.
September made its bow. Their trial (at last!)
— adultery the charge — was celebrated.
Decisions often prove more eloquent
in terms of what is done, not what is stated.
The Franceschini family were aghast!
With Caponsacchi merely rusticated,
never did an equinox contrast
more starkly with the thing anticipated.
Civitavecchia isn't Bath and Wells,
and even less a bed of asphodels,
but neither is it capital punishment.
Pompilia, no guilt attached, was sent
to *Le Scalette* (lesser of two hells,
compared with time with Franceschini spent!)
To Guido this injustice was so vast,
he wanted to invoke the Council of Trent,
and so he cast the nastiest of spells:
resentment is a cruel iconoclast.

STRAY LEAVES: Pompilia and Her Priest

Pompilia was passive, he was brash, assertive:
he had authentic dash, her style was furtive.
For him, life was a feast, for her, a test:
the sun swells in the east, sinks in the west.
Each time he took the street, his poise increased:
she stayed at home, and thought herself the least.
His physicality, majestic, massive:
she petite and precious, pretty, passive.
The street was his domain, hers was the nest:
he slayed her beast, she gave his life its quest.
He was disposed to pioneer, propose:
her role in life was managing her loss.
The cross gives tragic context to the rose:
the rose bestows distinction on the cross.

WHEN JACKALS SEEK TO KILL, they run in packs.
Afraid to strike alone, the curs combine,
for vulpine values are not leonine,
and courage plays no part in sneak attacks.
So, Guido trawled his peasants and retainers
(who, in their ignorance, defer to 'betters')
and found four fools whom, hardly men of letters,
we wouldn't be far wrong to brand no-brainers.
They struck out for the Bridge of Constantine,
supposing that thereby they'd leave no tracks.
Their lodging was the wretchedest of shacks,
where Paolo's plot produced a paltry wine.
These gurriers weren't the gamest of go-getters
and didn't have the trustiest of trainers:
if Guido thought these losers could be gainers,
he'd soon be disabused. These feckless fretters
killed with a will, then withered down like wax.
When tested, Guido's aiders and abettors

proved nothing more than turncoats and complainers:
as fit for purpose as a Paolo vine.

THIS IS THE BARRENEST OF SOLSTICES.
A holey hovel and a bed of ferns,
no way to kill the time, but sit and brood.
Everything about it turns out wrong.
All aching joints and nostrums, plasters, poultices:
long days around a cheerless copper urn,
no wood to start a fire for warmth or food.
The Master's trotting out the same old song,
rehearsing yet again his worst injustices,
he doesn't want to, or he can't, discern
the listless turnip lying there, half-chewed.
If I had known, I wouldn't have come along.
He'll seize on any nonsense, if it bolsters his
obsession. He's a man who cannot learn.
Our beans remain uncooked, our stew unbrewed:
you fail to feed your men, don't say you're strong.
A word for this? I'd say, autolysis.
The vines are waterlogged. Their stalks won't burn.
When earth is granite-hard and gannet-hued,
no food. But still the starving starlings throng.

A dream arrived, disturbing Guido's sleep.
When darkness falls and water barrels freeze,
a troubled man has nowhere he can hide.
Preoccupations cramp him by degrees
(what was that talk of Care's unravelled sleeve?)
Unpleasant visions, like a cloud of bees,
oppressed his head. He'd feel the pallet heave,
then find himself on surly slopes so steep,
he had to scramble up on hands and knees.
No place to shelter on this mountainside.
No goats, no sheep – and, notably, no trees.
The hilltop took forever to achieve,

to meet a sight no devil could conceive –
Pompilia was hanging, crucified!
He saw two drops of blood and water seep
reluctantly from lesions in her side.
He watched her spirit leave her as she died –
she'd proved a bride impossible to keep –
the seemly thing, it seemed, would be to weep –
but though he cried inside, he couldn't grieve.

With Christmas passed, they're handing out the spikes,
with savage barbs which suit the brutes' dysphoria.
(Pascuale said he'd never seen the likes.)
There'd be no horses, ornamental brasses,
nor any kind of ride – not even asses!
This latter had emerged as quite a shock:
what's not quite normal (nay, completely crass) is,
the Master hadn't known to purchase passes
for hiring Roman horses. *Santa gloria!*
The in-and-out would be laborious hikes.
The plan was, once they'd found the *Via Vittoria*,
for Santi and the Count to go and knock
and, when they heard the turning of the lock,
unveil upon the victims vicious strikes,
each driving home his dagger to the stock
(*il grande capitano*, Frenchy pikes!
As glorious as Lepanto, only gorier!)
and leave the wife *de benedetta memoria*.
The getaway? They'd run around the block,
then find an inn, for raising of the glasses!

Black night has crept in on the empty square:
Babuino fountain – so, we're almost there!
With hoods and caps pulled low against the sleet,
the younger thugs stand lookout in the street:
a bang on Pietro's door – now for the cheat!
The enemy are close now, unaware,

about to be confronted in their lair!
'Who knocks?' 'It's Caponsacchi!' And the snare
works perfectly! Violante, first to greet,
is first to die. The overture's complete!
In febrile satisfaction, flay her face,
repay those strong resentments, so long nursed!
Pietro now, and wants to pray for grace –
afraid of Hell – fell him – so much the worse!
You always ran to judgment: run there cursed!
The garden door – of course! The bitch has burst
out through it. There's the kitchen – give her chase!
We might have guarded it, if we'd been versed
in half the subterfuge this tribe embraced.
So get her. Let's exterminate the race!

Pompilia paid no heed to where she fled.
In just a nightdress, through the starless black,
she heard the *Greci*'s unmistakeable chimes:
her bare feet felt the sandy path which led
to where the locksmith lived, but there the track
confused her. Better gain the house, instead!
She turned, and heard blood-curdling Tuscan calls:
'She's got behind us! Come on – double back!'
The kitchen candle, through the backdoor crack,
conducted her to where the lattice climbs.
She scurried past pure horror in sheer dread,
the corpses of her parents in the hall,
half-slipping on her mother's blood-soaked shawl,
then up the narrow staircase: there to crawl
in desperation underneath her bed.
Her blood and hair, today, still stain the wall:
unwarranted, the ugliest of crimes:
they'd breached her abdomen some twenty times.
'We're finished now,' the husband Guido said:
'To Ponte Milvio!', leaving her for dead.

And yet she wasn't dead – at least, not yet.
And, even as her life-force ebbed away,
she managed, fitfully, to think and talk.
She told investigators of the crew
that Guido'd brought to aid him, and abet
the murders. More: she knew where they would stay
and – even more – she said they'd have to walk:
they'd argued bitterly as they withdrew.
Patrizi and his *sbirri* retinue,
as keen and clear-eyed as the kestrel hawk,
apprised of Paolo's *finca*, drew their net
around the Ponte Milvio. Disarray
and bloodstains, and a slew of damning clues
they found, but not the felons. 'Neighbours say
they left an hour ago. On foot. That way!'
We owe Patrizi an enormous debt.
He and his *sbirri* took the consular fork
and came upon the killers. Blood was let.
The Captain's arm was cut, nor did he balk,
but fell to the infection which accrued.

The party stopped at Milvio, riding back.
There, Guido underwent an inquisition,
with full notes taken, in his brother's shack.
When Gudio asked, 'What makes you think that I've
got anything to do with murder missions?',
they said, 'Pompilia told us.' 'She's alive?'
The Count had not imagined this. Amazed,
he proved to be the first of all the five
to make admissions. How could she survive?
Santi sneered, and Blasio's blushes blazed.
They trussed each prisoner like a saddlepack,
both peer and peasant, in the prone position,
with Guido gibbering like a man half-crazed,
and on Patrizi's word the Romeward drive
began. In Rome, the riff-raff's bloodlust raised,

the church of San Lorenzo, decked in black,
received poor Pietro (cheated of contrition)
and Violante (robbed of recognition
by every plunging thrust and slashing hack).
Pompilia would linger four more days.

THE OTHER HALF-ROME

The city boasts a billion bars and inns
where gatherings of countrymen and friends
occur. Just where the Quirinal descends
and thoroughfare 'Dataria' begins,
a tavern bears the name, 'Forgive My Sins'.
Its clients' conversation largely tends
to talk of scandal-tracts and current trends.
The wine is aretine, from Tuscan skins.
Our speaker specialises in 'discorso'
and propping-up the bar in Luccan locals:
reads Roman screeds, repeating them as vocals
(while micro-managing the best morceaux).
At home in Borgomaestro as in Corso,
he drinks for free by fascinating yokels.

GOLD SOVEREIGNS URGE MORE KEENLY THAN LIBIDOS:
the plan was surely Paolo's, more than Guido's.
You didn't know him: one long losing streak –
so shabby, shaggy, gloomy, stupid. Weak.
It all begins in circumstances ... 'shady'
is not too strong a word. It seems a 'lady'
required the making of a wig in Rome
(evading taxes payable at home!)
And who should prove her un-mercurial fetcher?
Why, Guido. Who's the Tuscan *spendereccia*?
One hears the sister mentioned. Maybe so.
If *my* wife bought a wig, I know I'd know!

He asks the gossips in the *parruchiera*
if they know of any Sue or Sarah …

WE'LL SUMMARISE THE NEXT PART. GUIDO WANTS
a dowry (not a wife) and duly haunts
those idle joints whose lubricant is chatter.
Her looks? Her age? It really doesn't matter.

Paolo's Despair Regarding Guido

Abate Paolo turned a verse or two.
Had social glibness. Knew to bow and smile.
Had Lucian and Lycurgus reconciled.
Wrote latin and vernacular, and knew
that Gormless Guido simply wouldn't do.
He lacked the lush lounge-lizard's languid style.
The shadow of the Pieve's campanile
went with him everywhere, and people drew
the obvious conclusion. Talentless,
Galumphing Guido simply had to marry.
A family so fine, in such distress,
placed all its hopes on hitch-up. He must carry
the cumbersome casato, must say 'yes':
since duns were pressing them, he shouldn't tarry!

A GIRL'S SUGGESTED. FATHER'S FAR FROM SURE,
but Mother's blinded by that lordly lure.
The dad is trad and wants an inventory –
the mother swallows whole the brothers' story –
a vineyard here, a benefice out there,
majestic mansion in a spacious square –
in every other circumstance, the mother
can separate one fiddle from another
but (just this once) is roasted on the hob.
Her weakness is, she's such a total snob!
Abate Paolo crowded them. He said,

we'll wed an Albergotti girl instead.
The fall-down, if the truth be known, was not
some form of furtive Franceschini plot,
but failing to foresee a flat farrago.
What kind of man emboldens a virago?
The mother married-off the child (they say)
behind Pietro's back. Life has a way
of sharing out the chagrín. No-one knew
(Arezzo's small) what they were coming to!
I blame Pietro. Had the man no sense?
Surrendering his manly competence?
A husband's never such an utter fool
as when he gives his wife the right to rule.
His only daughter's wedding was concealed:
He should have known the cart had lost a wheel!

Beatrice Versus Violante

What kind of couple settles in Arezzo?
(It's sure that no-one heeded Guido's wishes!)
Pompilia's mother, headstrong and ambitious,
decided on the Tuscan intermezzo,
and Guido's clan was weltering in debt, so
Beatrice ('haughty and officious')
was, like her offspring, fiercely avaricious.
They struck the deal. It yet would make them fret so!
Should Romans think Etruria exotic?
(A fancy I have never yet allowed!)
One kitchen with two women is chaotic,
especially when entrambi are despotic!
Violante went up north unholy, proud:
returned just four months later, wholly cowed!

THERE'S CAUSING WOUNDS, but then there's rubbing salt.
Violante thought the whole thing Pietro's fault,
though she contrived it while his back was turned.

So, what had Violante's efforts earned?
A daughter badly married, far from home
(she wasn't free to just return to Rome,
as they were): an alliance with these yokels
(as Romans, they thought little of the locals)
and residence in this, a foreign land
whose ways they couldn't (*wouldn't*) understand:
in penury that went against the grain,
and hosts whose boast was undisguised disdain.
So, back to Rome the Comparini went,
the daughter stayed. A failed experiment.
Enough of hicks, and living in the sticks –
but Violante wasn't out of tricks.
The dowry hadn't yet been handed over,
so guess who launched out on a *Vita Nuova* –
Signora Comparini. Did you see
the scope for hurting their heredity,
the damage to their precious reputation
incumbent in one little revelation?
You didn't spot the plot-point, like you're Dante?
Well that's because you're not a Violante.
'The girl's not mine, we found her in the gutter.
She's not champagne, not even bread-and-butter.
You thought you'd plucked a rose, but grabbed a thistle:
no dowry due, so you can go and whistle!'
A suit before the Roman Sacred College,
to force the Comparini to acknowledge
Pompilia as their daughter: ill conceived,
for what (if anything) could be achieved?
And anyway, with law, you might not win.
The wisest course was simply giving in,
but Guido wasn't wise. He promptly found
(as in most things) he just kept losing ground.
He won the lawsuit – yes, but what of that?
The docket was unhelpful, stating flat
that 'Pietro had a daughter'. Getting gold

was quite another matter. Flabby, old,
Pietro had a cranium plenty nimble!
The Franceschini didn't get a thimble
worth of wealth. Far better to have lost.
Pietro lumbered Guido with the costs!
You'll notice in this tale, the men aren't men.
Both Paolo-Priest and Guido lost again.
They prosecuted those who had eloped,
but didn't get the deal for which they'd hoped.
For Caponsacchi, punishment was mean –
Civitavecchia – have you ever been?
But Guido had expected death by hanging,
and didn't even hear a cell door clanging!
The worst of all, Pompilia's was petty –
ensconced inside the convent, *Le Scalette*,
where Guido couldn't touch her, night and day.
The Franceschini even had to pay!

Guido's Horrible Dilemma

What, then, of Guido? Conscious he'd been gulled,
he saw there was no cash. At worst, he'd thought her
a bearer of five heirs (that's why he'd bought her –
in part at least) but if he now annulled
this hollow sham, the dowry would be pulled
beyond his reach (you can't say she's no daughter,
and still expect that you'll collect). No quarter!
When rabbits start to eat the wheat, they're culled.
This man and wife were now like oil and water,
and Guido's grievances grew as he mulled
the harm he'd do Pompilia if he caught her.
His sense of decency was, doubtless, dulled,
the slippery slope inclining down to slaughter.
Oh, just to swipe this knife through her aorta!

LET'S TURN NOW TO POMPILIA THE BEAUTY.
She's flirty to a fault (cosí fan tutti!)
More sinned against than sinning, goes the phrase:
just think of how she spent those thousand days!
The bullying, the sullying, the stress –
can one small child endure all that duress?
The bishop simply blanked her. No joy there.
The governor provoked her to despair
with attitudes and platitudes, no action:
iscritto of the Franceschini faction!
The wretched girl had none to take her part
(a tempting metaphor – 'the hounds and hart'!)
She went to Conti as a decent man,
but he was not inclined to carry the can.

The Unfortunate Canon Conti

The canon was that ever-open door
of which we're always hearing. Always genial,
respectful of the rich and of the poor,
committed sins, of course – but only venial.
No man, in brief, was ever quite so liked.
His brother married (so you know the score)
that Porzia Franceschini, thereby hiked
the Conti status to 'genteel'. Before,
they'd been the middling sort that you ignore.
But someone hated Conti to the core
(and someone clever, no bucolic boor).
We'll never hear his chaff-like chuckle more.
Whoever wished him ill, it wasn't a menial.
One wonders if his moscatel was spiked.

HE WOULD HAVE LOVED TO HELP, needless to say,
but his position ... there's another way ...
his colleague Caponsacchi, as it happened,
had business down in Rome, could fill the gap, and

a woman who was hoping for protection
could hardly make a luckier election ...
Since women are far weaker than us men,
and lack our moral certainty — why then,
they've had to cultivate another art,
the skill of conquering the lion's heart.
They work on us in ways we scarcely see,
manipulating manly decency.
No question — yes, Pompilia used the lure,
but did she stoop to anything impure?
I hope not! I think Caponsacchi acted
from duty — just as chivalry exacted!
And so they fled ... but things came to a head
at Castelnuovo. Wishing Guido dead,
she went at him with Caponsacchi's *spada*.
Some say, she should have lunged a little harder!
He'd followed them on horseback, hours behind,
and caught them at the posting-inn, to find ...
whatever thing he found. She'd used a sword,
and Guido was convinced he couldn't afford
a confrontation. And you'll find that's why
he rode to the *commune*, to apply
for writs against elopement. A true-bred man
would rather kill, or bleed his life out, than
require the law to do his dirty work
(the very thing a man must never shirk).

The Absconded Abbot

We know why Guido couldn't help but falter:
he was a coward. That's quite clear, at least.
What overcame his brother, though (the priest)?
In little more than months, the Men of Malta
had cut away his cruel contractual halter.
Was Paolo sacked for something, or released?
His tight control of Guido suddenly ceased.

He vanished – never knelt at any altar
in Italy again. Swamped by the scandal?
The Franceschini name, too hot to handle?
Or had his hand in 'things to come' increased?
He shook Rome's dust from sacerdotal sandal
because he was a victim, or a vandal?
Anathema to murder – or the yeast?

ONCE GUIDO HAD NO GUIDE, all bets were off
(look what happens when we opt to quaff
with commoners!) He chose a ragged crew
(who had their plans to murder Guido, too!)
How *could* it turn out well? Enough to say,
they butchered and were captured in one day.
They landed in the Pope's New Prisons, where
a few short weeks before had lodged the pair
of lovers (or elopers). Can a man
who thinks his wife's unfaithful plot and plan
her death, and still escape the fateful axe?
The Pope thought, no. He didn't read the facts!
Violante, with her lust for silken blouses,
and padded harpsichords, and well-born spouses,
must take her share of blame. But all the same,
the Franceschini don't escape the frame.
Whatever bile the others' guile arouses,
Montecchi, Capuletti – play the game!
It's family. A plague on both your houses!
Your wife is young, I think? What would you do
if once you found you had a partner who
described your manly edicts 'interference',
and started taking pride in her appearance?

STRAY LEAVES: HONORIS CAUSA

Let's say that it's okay to slit the throat
of wife or daughter on a jealous whim.
Suppose, in throes of is-it-me-or-him,
you butcher her as if she were a goat
[for, after all, you'll get the jury's vote:
you couldn't help but tear her limb from limb.
She proved a puta (choose your synonym)].
The risk of reckoning remains remote.

But how can you be certain of your facts?
A severed head's a fairly final thing
and shouldn't be decided on the wing.
You misinterpreted her blameless acts?
Your only witness afterwards retracts?
How can a man keep track of everything?

TERTIUM QUID

The Aesthete

A stroll around the Gallery Borghese –
such gorgeous art! The gardens – so ornate!
Our talker's brought a young man on a 'date'.
Prepared to offer certain works his praise, he
resembles aesthetes harping on Scorsese
or maybe denigrating Heaven's Gate
in Greenwich Village cafés. By 'debate',
he means a monologue. His views are hazy,
but vehemently held. Four years ago
a Tuscan noble killed a woman-child.
The subject raised, our Roman Oscar Wilde
insists on showing how he's in the know.

His tale is self-regarding, artful, styled,
like Molière (too soon for Marivaux!)

Whose was her baby? (Think of lackeys.)
Caponsacchi's!
How to gauge Pompilia's head?
When she fled!
Ask yourself, why head for Rome,
pregnant by your legal sire?
She admired the Canon's spire,
thought her spouse an ugly gnome.

Wedlock's a commercial deed –
we're agreed?
Thus is Gertrude queen and whore
in Elsinore.
Paolo has to take the blame.
Guido didn't know or care:
marriage? Neither here nor there.
Let's not put him in the frame.

Adjective to sum him up:
arse-licked pup.
No-one could exude more gloom,
this side the tomb.
Porzia ruled the roost at home.
Fancying a fine new wig,
sent him on that shopping gig
(when Guido lived in Rome).

'Hets' go for the gentle touch
far too much:
women view sweet words and wine
as lack of spine.
Always have the upper hand.
Once they're checked, they show respect –

read the Treaty of Utrecht!
Husbands have to take command.

STRAY LEAVES: APOLLO AND DAPHNE

What's happening is clearly understood.
Apollo has one hand around her waist,
one predator, one quarry, interlaced.
He's coming up behind her (which is good),
but she's a tree (two lovers, getting wood!)
She'd rather change her state than be disgraced,
preferring to be chaste than to be chased.
She's choosing abstinence, above her blood.

Is love a trauma, to be undergone?
Arousal something ugly, to be faced?
Should Nature's process be looked down upon?
The carnal act, a tactless lapse of taste?
Or might the thing be ardently embraced?
We, formless fragments, merging in The One?

PIETRO WAS NO KIND OF FOOL.
He was cool!
'You're some sort of landed heir?
Show me where!'
Farms they held by feudal right?
'Let me see a written list.
He'd the chutzpah to insist
'Set it down in black and white.'

Violante took the view
(as women do)
that marrying-up was simply swell –
what the hell?
Moving to Arezzo, too –

social betterment, expansion!
Living in a proper mansion!
This was progress, through and through!

Paolo emphasised the farms,
twisted arms,
made the Romans sign and seal –
closed the deal.
Love and happiness – who cares?
Comparini money's good
(in addition, Guido could
set about producing heirs).

Pietro chose to abdicate,
sealed his fate:
Violante took the reins,
which explains
reckless choices rashly taken,
plans abandoned, once begun,
people getting nothing done,
rudderless their navigation.

Take, for instance, Beatrice:avarice
(plus exerting tight control)
was her goal.
Sharing sheets with such a shrew
didn't work, and never could have:
taking hits they never should have,
if they'd only thought it through.

Comparini called a halt.
Did the fault
fall on Violante's head?
No! Instead,
poor Pietro caught the blame.
All the neighbours were appalled.

This is why the wife was called,
'she who had no shred of shame'.

What was Guido, then, to do?
Not a clue!
If the marriage was annulled,
he'd been gulled!
These annulments sometimes fail.
He'd have Comparini for
the future – worse – for ever more!
That's a plight beyond the pale.

There again, suppose he won?
That's no fun!
Annulment means, in simple prose,
the dowry goes!
Guido's gambit really worked …
Comparini, mum and dad,
designated! Guido had
to pay the costs. It really irked!

Meanwhile, what about Pompilia,
la figlia ?
Weepily she went, and wanty,
to Conti.
Bishop, Governor, *tutti* passed.
Conti also felt embarrassed,
packed off Helen to her Paris:
so to Caponsacchi, last!

Caponsacchi wasn't keen.
Could it mean
she'd do something he might rue?
(Women do!)
Moved at last by Christian pity,
he embraced her hare-brained scheme,

set out as if in a dream,
bound for the Eternal City.

Castelnuovo, dangerous dawn:
fear and scorn
tempted her to run him through:
Guido knew,
though he hadn't been impaled,
fighting was beyond his strength
(missing by a thumb-nail's length,
she had thrust, and only just failed!)

So he took his case to law.
Fatal flaw!
He who hands it to the courts
but resorts
to private vengeance, digs a grave
in which his rights will be interred:
every gesture, every word
waves away the things he'd save.

STRAY LEAVES: UP AT THE VILLA

Do you like mosaics . about gladiators?
You find Caravaggio . sexier than Titian?
Might 'a mere shag' be . your guiding ambition?
What about scarlet . for clerical gaiters?
You'd rather have conquerors? . Or cleave to creators?
You're turned on by torsos? . Prefer erudition?
Kindly expound on . your chosen position.
Have you tried leering . at handsome young waiters?

Love can be sacred, . but also profane,
and playing it straight . is a bit of a strain.
Charybdis is tempting, . but so too is Scylla:

The grape, you'll approve, . as against the grain?
Beer's for the boorish, . so let's sip champagne:
come kill a Sunday, friend, . up at the villa!

Paolo had to pay a price
for the vice
of speaking well while meaning ill –
bitter pill!
Trough-entitled was his snout,
this scion of the sinecure:
now he'd learn the word 'unsure':
the Knights of Malta kicked him out!

Who decided on the kill?
Lacking skill,
Guido seems unlikely, though
quid pro quo,
hurt him and he hits you back.
Paolo may have spawned the mission,
splitting off, to dodge suspicion –
might have engineered the sack!

Missing Paolo's guiding hand
to command,
Guido badly overshot –
lost the plot –
error followed on mistake.
Santi filled the vacuum. He
bossed his boss, but couldn't be
the adult who applied the brake.

Quite the opposite, in fact!
Fools attract
lowly felons, feckless scum
who become
their masters' masters. On arrest,

Santi said he'd always planned
to murder Guido out of hand.
Think of it – the thug confessed!

Chained where victims used to be
(irony!),
prisons of Pope Pignatelli
(*carcele*),
saddled with the selfsame hell
the felons foot the fetid floor
Pompilia trod, six months before –
perhaps the selfsame cell!

Pignatelli didn't flinch:
'beheading!'
This completes the final inch
I'm threading.
What's that clanging, down below?
Nones, ringing from the *Greci*?
Evidence is somewhat sketchy.
Luther's church in *Popolo*?

That's our sign for recreation.
Salvation!
What will ward off dehydration?
Libation!
There again – enchanting chime!
Next week, off to see The Torso.
As for now, let's to the *Corso*,
there to make the most of time.

THE WELL AND THE HEAD, Being a Cluster of Tales told by Cardinal Fabrizio Spada at the Dinner Table in the Villa Farnesina

Why's he sitting on that well?
What's he up to? Who can tell?
Scribbling some roman à clef
that's gonna blow the world away?
Writing – a gratuitous act!
What is fiction? What is fact?
What is 'is', and what is not so?
Rimani cheto sul tuo pozzo!

At the Pozzo di Tofano

Of course we mount a collar, brick or stone,
but wells, above all else, are natural things,
just places where the water simply springs.
Well, 'just' is not quite fair. For Greasy Joan,
and millions like her, willy-nilly thrown
upon the daily grind of sitherings,
of scaldings, scourings, scrubbings, skewerings,
the well's a way to tell you're not alone.

We castigate a sonnet for its rhyme.
'A misplaced alexandrine – what a crime!'
This puts the hobbyhorse before the cart:
the superstructure never was the art.
There's more than metre makes it not-quite-prose:
it's that which gurgles, surges, overflows!

The Well and the Head

A story was told
in Arezzo of old
of a man and a wife, and a bed:

and the aretines tell
of a travertine well,
and a carving – The Saracen's Head.

What remained of a statue
was sporting a hat you
would never see Christians wear.
Entirely embarrassing,
'twas known as 'The Saracen'
because of its long, plaited hair.

The well was polygonal,
quite deep and quite big, and all
the women employed it for washing.
They gossiped of men
(it's the way of the hen)
as they fell to their joking and joshing.

One woman was better
(let's meet her – she's Cheta)
at banter than all of the others.
None ever mistook her
(for she was a looker)
among all the sisters and mothers.

Her husband Tofano
was known through Valdarno
for his deep understanding of wine.
There was no imbiber
this side of the Tiber
with palate a fraction so fine.

Tofano was jealous!
The grapes on his trellis
could never grow nearly as green.
He watched over Cheta –

indeed, wouldn't let her
go out without causing a scene.

She tired of his chiding
and started deriding
Tofano's performance in bed.
He looked to his laurels?
Not hardly! The moral's
'a hurt man grows curter, instead'.

So Cheta found reason
whatever the season
to take herself out of the house.
Behaviour unfructive
– nay, counterproductive! –
thus parted a man from his spouse.

The breeze can be 'British'
(unhelpfully skittish)
in the upper environs of town.
When Cheta washed linen,
she hit upon pinnin'
her drying delectables down.

For textiles thus tented
she shrewdly invented
a use for the Saracen's Cranium:
it sat on her satin!
(They hardly do that in
Hyele, still less Herculaneum!)

The vintage was pressed
and no doubt you've guessed,
Tofano was into libation.
Was Cheta aware

that libation plus err
amounted to her liberation?

She certainly was!
We know this because
(as Tofi would one day discover),
pursuing a course
that's akin to divorce,
Chetina had taken a lover!

When topping him up
she loaded his cup,
and then doubled-up on the dose,
for to deceive
'twas better to leave
Tofano at home, comatose!

How crafty was Cheta!
She managed things better
with partner pacifically plastered,
since rendered supine
and befuddled with wine,
he then was most easily mastered!

Her trick with the booze
(we must give her her dues)
was proving a provident saviour:
repeated each day,
it was well on the way
to becoming a course of behaviour!

Tofano may drool
but he wasn't a fool:
and suspicion is stronger than stupor.
He kept rolling his eyes,

but began to devise
a pitfall in which he could scoop her!

The ambush was this:
He would 'go on the piss',
and into a coma would fall,
allow her to think
he was drowning in drink,
while in fact downing nothing at all.

'She will get indiscreet
and head into the street,
to continue whatever she's doing.
But I will be conscious
and, prudent as Pontius,
I'll prove her a prozzie. She's ruined!'

The evening began
with them, woman and man,
cracking a bottle once more.
And Cheta's one thought,
'any minute he ought
to be rolling around on the floor.'

Pretending to sup
as she freshened his cup,
she waited for Bacchus to bite
(she supposed if she feigned
that she, too, might get brained,
he might put up less of a fight).

I swear on my oath
that the pair of them, both
sat there cursing and slurring their words:
at the owl's eerie call

they had emptied in all
a bottle and maybe two-thirds.

She sure played the part
of a drink-sodden fart
with an art that no tart could invent:
Tofano, too, acted:
when she was distracted,
straight into the plantpot it went!

You'd think they got drunk
with the thirst of a monk
and the cash of a customs comptroller,
but the whole thing was feigned
and they staidly remained
as sober as Savonarola.

The moment arrived
when Cheta contrived
to head for a date with her lover.
Her movements were deft:
how quickly she left!
How quickly did Toffi recover!

Clear-minded and able
(*not* under the table!),
he muttered, 'my wife is a whore!'
No umm-ing or ahh-ing –
he set about barring
the shutters, and locking the door.

But on Cheta's return
she was vexed to discern
that all access was roundly denied her.
She felt with her feet

(it was dark in the street)
for the well that was somewhere beside her.

By now oriented,
she prudently prevented
all risk of her toppling in.
So, now for Tofano,
that dollop of guano!
Hostilities now could begin!

She shouted and yelled,
and her volume so swelled
that they surely could hear her in Rome.
By what earthly right
did he think that he might
prevent her from entering her home?

He then called her a slut
and he kept the door shut,
saying 'Go back to where you have been!'
Her tongue was now loose,
and she hurled such abuse
that she added new depths to 'obscene'!

But Toffi held fast:
she was not getting past
the barricades he had erected.
If home was what mattered,
then why had she shattered
the marital calm, and defected?

Her patience wore thin.
'If you don't let me in,
I'll jump in the well here, and drown!'
With the Saracen's Head

in her two hands, she said,
'I mean it!' and dropped the thing down.

Had Cheta been rash?
The almighty splash
was something an orca would cherish!
Tofano believed
(he was easily deceived)
that she'd leapt, and was certain to perish.

He burst through the door
like a lecherous boar
in pursuit of an in-season sow,
but his anguish was real –
who can help how they feel? –
he loved her, and realised it now!

As he felt for the well
(it was darker than hell)
'My darling, my own one!' he cried.
But quite unobserved,
right around him she swerved,
slipping quickly and slickly inside.

The door once more slammed,
and Tofano was damned!
Her guile had negated his labours.
Their roles were reversed!
(But that's not the worst:
the noise had awoken the neighbours!

The alley was filling,
the multitude milling,
and second by second expanding:
with giving up wine

Tofano was fine,
but couldn't risk losing his standing.

He quickly thought better
of fighting with Cheta.
The worm on the hook always squirms!
The couple conversed
and the neighbours dispersed –
and Cheta secured better terms!

They dropped all pretenses
and mended their fences.
It shows that you never can tell.
They lived and loved long
and it never went wrong –
and the head still remains in the well!

The Tunnel and the Obelisk

1. A Question of Calibration

Each heroine is like Lavinia
(che la storia non sia scherzosa)
and, whether grenadier or grocer,
albeit muscular or skinnier,
the hero hurts her. Drawing closer
(the plot's unwaveringly linear),
he seeks commitment from his *sposa:*
incapable of saying 'no, sir',
she pays the price. Come to Sardinia,
the pretty port that's known as Bosa.

Protagonists like Captain Bresca,
of character without a stain,
are fairly rare (to have a brain

is rarer still!) From Wales to Huesca,
bearing cargoes, grape or grain
(but not a mariner *chi pesca*),
frequenter of the Spanish Main,
as far as one can ascertain,
renowned in Rimini (Francesca
by-her-jealous-husband-slain

Polenta flourished in those parts,
the one whose looks made Dante faint)
our Captain journeyed. With restraint
he watched his compass, checked his charts:
his cautious character was free from taint.
Master of the maritime arts,
he was a sort of secular saint
and, curious of all that's quaint,
he heard men's words and read their hearts:
for knowledge laboured, *sans* complaint.

Ashore in Bosa Bresca went
one morning in the month of May,
to take a 'captain's holiday',
a term of art simply meant
he'd things to buy, and bills to pay.
Before a single *sou* was spent,
as through the town he made his way
something led his gaze astray:
a clock, just like the one in Ghent!
The man-made marvel made his day.

Extraordinary stroke of luck!
While foraging for fruit and flour
beneath the shadow of the tower,
Bresca heard – the great bell struck,
to signify the current hour!
A fellow of uncommon pluck,

his habit was to scan and scour,
all novel knowledge to devour.
His duty he would never shuck,
but (if it lay within his power)

he'd tease it out, he'd pin it down:
an explanation he'd procure:
how can anyone be sure
(in such an isolated town)
the time is accurate and pure?
And with a fine forensic frown
He made a promise to endure
Enquiry's sirens' bright allure:
in quest of truth, he'd swim or drown,
and find (no matter how obscure)

the holy grail of certainty.
How *could* they know their clock was right?
What rhyme or reason could they cite?
He swore before he took to sea
he'd solve the puzzle, nail it quite.
What could the Bosans' answer be?
Whether complex, whether trite,
on this he vowed he'd shed some light:
what laws of logic guarantee
the town hall ticker's *Wirklichkeit*?

He asked around. He asked some more,
and out of his investigation
there now emerged an explanation:
like what occurred in Elsinore,
the focal point of concentration
must be the castle. Every store,
every bar or wayside station
offered up corroboration:

at the mystery's murky core
lay a lame elucidation.

A cannon on the castle heights
(it's on the seaside esplanade)
was centrepiece of a parade,
the daily military rites
(rarely cancelled or delayed):
a junior officer recites
a prayer, and brandishes his blade.
The order's never disobeyed.
at noon precisely, someone lights
the cannon's fuse. The whole brigade

salutes the weapon as it roars.
Pikes are hoisted, banners raised.
Saints are cited, prelates praised,
then everyone returns indoors.
Ears are ringing, eyes are dazed.
Captain Bresca now explores
the cannon angle: he's amazed!
Who made the judgment, as it blazed,
that noon had come? The tale ignores
the pressing question (quaintly phrased)

quis custodiet ipsos custodes?
Who oversees the overseers?
Who controls the guys with spears?
Who minds the store? Who holds the keys?
How guard ourselves from buccaneers?
How to soothe concerns like these?
The castle looms. As Bresca nears,
he knows he has to ease these fears.
He'll seek to wheedle, try to tease
the secret from the fusileers.

As Bresca pounded up the slope,
he couldn't hinder or retard
a morbid thought – far less discard
one notion which dispelled all hope –
suppose the clock (oh, this was hard!)
and cannon ... as he tried to grope
for answers, he attained the yard.
The handsome captain of the guard
produced a brassbound telescope.
'To fix the hour, I just regard

the clock below. It tells me twelve.'
So there it was. No more to say.
The answer was as plain as day.
The captain snapped his polished helve
upon itself, and walked away.
If we burrow, if we delve,
as like as not we bring dismay
upon ourselves. Why join the fray?
This is a problem made to shelve.
We're none the wiser. Fade to grey.

He who strives to learn from life'll
only find that things ain't so.
Clock and cannon, *quid pro quo*,
celebrate or silence, stifle,
can mere Man affect the flow?
Telescopes provide an eyeful:
wisdom they can not bestow.
All the indicators show,
we can't command the blandest trifle.
We don't know what we think we know!

2. Of Popes and Ropes

Dead-centre of St. Peter's Square
there stands a slab of granite –
but why should it be stranded there,
of all points on this planet?

The obelisk is very old
(as if you'd even doubt it!)
The legend has been often told –
why, Pliny wrote about it!

A thousand years or more it stood
in ancient Heliopolis,
respected by the great and good,
and worshipped by the populace.

From source to mouth, an epic trip
(like Phoebus in his chariot):
they planned and built a special ship –
the only way to carry it!

In Alexandria's heart it rose,
magnificent and solemn,
logos-lapis juxtaposed –
both library and column.

But just as Ra succumbed to death
when Dionysus dawned,
so Athens went the way of Seth
when Jupiter was spawned.

Caligula the kleptophile
just could not leave it be:
the Tiber dispossessed the Nile.
The column crossed the sea.

He raised it in a special place,
in Nero's great arena:
the centrepiece of every race,
the high point of the *spina*.

As fifteen hundred years went by,
this was the only stone
that stayed upright to touch the sky,
imperious and alone.

Religions faded, empires fell,
whole cultures lived and died.
A new regime began to swell
along the column's side.

Here may have stood some sylvan wood
or temple of Demeter,
but martyrs' blood had earned for Good
a precinct for Saint Peter.

The first cathedral had to go:
a better was required.
Bramante, Michelangelo
and other brains were hired.

By fifteen sixty, more or less,
Saint Peter's had been finished.
The column, to the pope's distress,
now seemed obscured, diminished.

An emblem, then, of papal pride,
and such it was to prove –
but out in front, not down the side!
The giant had to move.

Two hundred horse, five thousand men,
to pull in one direction:
the granite could be great again –
a rocky resurrection!

Force, load and stress were hard to judge.
The column mustn't crack.
Four hundred tons are hard to budge –
but now, no turning back!

Tall wooden scaffolds filled the square,
quite blocking out the sun.
The public came to stand and stare
(in those days, that was fun!)

To set it upright was the aim,
and slot it in its plinth:
and hence the mighty scaffold frame,
a wooden labyrinth!

The rule of silence Sixtus willed
came with a weighty warner:
he got his architect to build
a gallows in the corner!

The strain was taken: backs were braced:
the wait was tantalising!
As horses sweated, pulses raced,
the obelisk was rising!

A gasp went round – what was that sound?
Astonishing! Dismaying!
The column lurched towards the ground –
the leader ropes were fraying!

Strands were snapping, failure loomed,
and time was growing shorter:
out from the crowd, a lone voice boomed –
'Douse the ropes with water!'

Buckets filled. Like soldiers drilled,
the workers leapt to action.
The column's downward droop was stilled,
to widespread satisfaction.

Since hemp, when wetted, must contract,
the threatened ropes grew tauter.
But who had seen the need to act?
Whose voice had called for water?

The man they should immortalise
in bold *vernice fresca*
is someone we all recognise –
our old friend, Captain Bresca!

An old sea hand would understand
the way to work with ropes,
and now he's known throughout the land,
the favourite of popes!

He broke the silence, wasn't hanged.
In fact, his act was feted.
Te Deums sounded, church bells clanged:
the city celebrated!

When Sixtus told him, 'name your price',
he said, 'we have two farms:
my family would think it nice
to ply the pope with palms.'

The column complements the dome,
its odyssey is done,
adorning Rome far from its home,
the city of the sun.

The Vatican, down to this day,
when holy week arrives
puts Bresca's palm-fronds on display:
he's still in all our lives!

3. *The Finger of Fate*

Our voyage concludes where the journey began,
in western Sardinia, in Bosa.
An under-age girl weds a middle-aged man.
You find that familiar? Draw closer.

We've heard of the castle that stands on the hill
in a spot undeniably fine,
its ruins surviving haphazardly still,
in a foam of hibiscus and pine.

The castle was once a magnificent sight,
and known by the name 'Malaspina'.
a symbol to all of the pride and the might
dell'isola della sardina.

A Marquess's seat was the castle, replete
with its soldiers and courtiers and servants:
on Sunday they all would process down the street,
en route to religious observance.

Marchese Malfatto was head of the clan
which sported the name Spino Secco.
He marched to the church at the head of the van,
and (at first) he was cheered to the echo.

Ostensibly open, approachable, kind,
in matters of charity zealous,
Malfatto was merciless, wilfully blind,
possessive and ruthlessly jealous.

In order that heirs might be duly supplied,
he sought out a marital client.
What features were foremost in sorting a bride?
She ought to be young and compliant.

It often transpires that these knights of the shires
will opt for a laundress or cleaner:
Malfatto's desires ran to buckets and byres –
his choice was the fair Ziromina.

This very young girl was an undersized pearl,
a beauty perforce immature:
her manner, however, would charm any churl:
deportment entirely demure.

But decency has a destructive effect,
is seen as a threat by the bully:
he'll act to detract, to destroy all respect,
to blacken, to smear and to sully.

He couldn't regard her as partner or peer,
his instinct to rope-in the foal,
displaying his strength to dissemble his fear,
concealing his cracks with control.

She prayed every day in the town's square-cut kirk,
her husband's anxiety firing,
provoking a physiological quirk:
the Marquess had started perspiring!

The garrison guard, forming up in the yard,
would march her to church (ie, screen her).
Her beauty was barred: none may even regard
hermetically-sealed Ziromina.

STRAY LEAVES: RUTH AND BOAZ

When 'big' men marry women half their age,
is dominance their primary objective,
or are they being sexually selective?
Why put a sparrow in a gilded cage?
What makes a silverback a gynophage?
Perhaps it's all a question of perspective:
to anyone who's reasonably reflective,
there's many a Menelaus strides the stage.

The man, mature and mighty, lantern-jawed,
adopts a child. His posture is protective.
The overlord confuses 'ward' and 'bawd'?
Analysis leads swiftly to invective:
they're drawn to it because they are defective.
Abusers aren't imperious. They're flawed.

MALFATTO (AT BEST, still severely depressed),
restricted his Ruth to this runnel:
unduly obsessed and unable to rest,
began excavating a tunnel.

The thing was complete. Now, instead of the street,
she could go to and fro underground.
It was wholly discreet: of her face and her feet
not one man would have sighting or sound.

But when jealousy bites, paranoia excites
suspicions no tunnel can quell.
Resentments and slights filled the Marquis's nights,
and he suffered the torments of hell,

for a fanciful sting (so the poets all sing)
bestows far more woes than a true.
Demanding she bring him the nuptial ring,
he informed her their marriage was through.

For once in her life, his unfortunate wife
rejected Malfatto's command:
emotions were rife, and a pearl-handled knife
emerged in the Marquis's hand.

He killed her, of course – and believed that, perforce,
the wedding ring must be reclaimed.
With no hint of remorse, this most violent divorce
resulted in Mina being maimed:

reluctant to linger, he hacked off her finger
and ordered her body interred,
no service, no singer. The lackeys must sling her
in a ditch without snitching a word.

The saints love a martyr, and the sinner's *sudata*
(the sign of his guilty distress),
like sacred *stigmata*, besmirched him *pro-rata*,
compelling the felon to 'fess'.

Her mother and father arrived from Magomadas,
their presence no pleasant surprise!
Malfatto would rather be elsewhere: a lather
of sweat was besetting his eyes.

Forgetting in wrath what he'd wrapped in his cloth,
he pulled it for mopping his brow:
as a flame draws a moth, he hadn't been loth
to butcher their daughter, but now,

the finger was spilt – and its angle of tilt
left prospects of sidestepping slim:
the Marquis's guilt proven up to the hilt –
for the finger was pointing at him!

THE HISTORY OF THE TRUE CROSS: (2) The Death of Adam

Bacci & Bicci

The hour has come (again!) to get ekphrastic.
Suppose we take a year (say, fourteen-fifty),
the place Arezzo, and someone has a gift he
is anxious to bestow, enthusiastic
to beautify a site ecclesiastic:
this Mister Bacci is extremely shifty.
Aware of all the innocents he's stiffed, he
believes a dodge draconian and drastic
is what's required. The chancel of St. Francis
could use a lick of paint. Let's get dynastic.
To cleanse the clan's black souls, I'll swipe my plastic,
and use my usufruct. Thus cash enhances,
embellishes the world. Bacci finances,
and Bicci paints. Solution onomastic!

Bicci & Bacci

Some people think in numbers (Fibonacci?):
a well-respected painter such as Bicci
who's not quite Major League (think Lionel Ritchie)

will give you stuff that's superficial, catchy
and even nice (The Shadows did 'Apache'),
but now the monks are growing rather twitchy.
The work is cold, conventional – nay, kitschy.
If someone else could only start from scratch, he
might save the chancel, bring a fresher vision.
Art's just a number-crunch to Mister Bacci,
a pitch from which you trade, like Saatchi and Saatchi.
We'll trade our pitcher, take the tough decision,
and bring in Piero. Resumé? Well, patchy –
but suddenly, two worlds are in collision!

The Day the Middle Ages Died

The finished thing, Arezzo's lasting glory,
creeps up on superstition, unawares.
Here is the moment when man's reason dares!
You don't need narrative to tell a story.
You'd burn eccentrics in *Campo de'Fiori*?
The sex of angels? You're just splitting hairs.
God's use of counterfactuals? Who cares?
The Whore of Babylon is merely hoary.
Euclidian circles, oblongs, angles, squares,
thematic theorems in matching pairs:
the Milvian Bridge offsets the Battle of Nineveh
(as clearly of-its-time as 'Mrs. Miniver'):
the Queen of Sheba reasons, and exhumes,
as Helena lifts Hebrews out of tombs.

The Death of Adam

There's always both: the sacred and profane.
The right tends to the former, left the latter.
The weak side's earthbound, ugly, heavy matter,
where even Mankind's Father's on the wane.
However, there's The Tree. In spite of Cain,

No matter how we sever, sunder, scatter,
salvation's handed to us on a platter.
If Adam died, he didn't die in vain.
Seed enters through the orifice, and sprouts.
Our molecules don't die, they just regroup.
Death? Birth, marriage? – Jumping through the hoop.
Each individual is racked by doubts,
but tranquil tropes just complete the loop.
Eternity is mere primordial soup.

NINE PANELS (IF WE DROP THE 'ANNUNCIATION',
the evil fruit of nepotism, simony
and other ills), a far-from straight narration,
obscure events, abstruse concatenation,
distractions in the shape of sundry women he
encountered on sabbatical in Rimini,
all render this improbable creation
a triumph, and an ultimate salvation.

The prose of Voragine in painted version,
the 'Legend' occupies a narrow chancel
(*L'Annonce Faite à Marie* is an incursion,
unfortunate Franciscan forced insertion).
The knowledge that he's blown his whole advance'll
incense the monks, in whom the urge to cancel
is teetering on the verge. This style ('Albertian')
is one to which they've formed a stern aversion.

The Mantuan church. The *Malatestiano*.
The Florentine *Novella*. Pienza's *duomo*.
In all the cities watered by the Arno,
as far afield as Fiesole or Fano,
between the lakes of Trasimene and Como,
they're crazy for Alberti, *galant'huomo*.
*Le cognoscente, tutti, impiegano
il dolce nuovo stile albertiano.*

And Piero della Francesca is a fan.
Here, frozen in one moment, we can trace
the perfect printout – nothing other than
the crystallizing of Alberti's plan!
Fine drawing. Elements which interlace.
The whole achieved with understated grace.
And art that's richer, since its simple span
has freed it up. Man's measure now is Man!

Old Adam is now dying. Seth decides
to ask for Heaven's help. An angel shows
him where The Garden is, and then confides:
'Seek out the Tree of Knowledge, which provides
for Man's prosperity. Whatever grows
out of its seeds will do great deeds, for those
are fruits of Heaven.' Adam's life subsides.
Seth's reappearance barely coincides

with father's final moments. On his tongue
the son inserts the seeds of knowledge. Seth
observes that shoots and tendrils, vital, young,
are now cascading from his mouth. Among
the mourners, heartbreak at their father's death
combines with something else. His dying breath
is not an end. A greater life has sprung
from what he was. The wonder spreads among

the mourning relatives. One daughter's scream
(who's left to doubt Piero's on a mission?)
prefigures crucifixion. It's a scheme
so radical as almost to blaspheme
against accepted norms of composition!
The left-to-right and up-and-down rendition
resembles Jesus' Cross and, beam by beam,
sets out to re-invent – and thus redeem.

The horizontal planes are plain as day.
Above there's no corruption, static sky.
Below, commotion. Catastrophic clay
convulses creatures. Caught in passion-play,
condemned from cradle to their dying cry
to struggle, ail and fail, decline and die,
they dance their barren ballet of decay.
Like cinders in the wind, they're blown away.

But don't forget the vertical. The tree
luxuriates and dominates the scene.
Piero plies with due humility
Alberti's strictures. Note the symmetry –
the fluted column where the mobled queen
reveres the timber, or the neat machine
for pulling Jews from trenches – could it be,
that middle-line divider helps us see?

STRAY LEAVES: THE HART AT BAY

I can't help loving complicated things.
The lamp that hangs atop the Bishop's stairs
enchants me! All those little coloured squares
which catch the daylight as it creaks and swings,
those patterned apertures and openings!
It comforted me, as I mumbled prayers,
to trace its angles. Somehow, unawares,
I drew new strength from it – developed wings!

That image etched on glass – the Hart at Bay!
I watched the westering sun, that long spring day,
ineffably passing, face by face
towards its perigee. To my dismay,
I understood the gods have feet of clay –
but also knew that pain could be embraced.

THE CONGRESS OF THE WITS

(2) Pasquino

I'm the Prince of Parione,
blisterer of all baloney:
flayer of the false and phony,
Brutus down to Berlusconi.

Excoriating crook and crony,
ardentest of all *Arguti*,
I've made mockery my duty,
put the moan in acrimony.

When the Cardinal first found me
he decided to bedeck
my one good leg and wasted neck:
in folds of crimson he begowned me.

A poet and a wit to boot,
he stuck couplets to my torso:
from *Quo Vadis* to the *Corso*,
satirists soon followed suit!

On the Feast-day of Saint Mark,
near the vernal equinox,
people cried, 'The statue mocks!
His teeth are sharper than a shark!'

In a fit of faith-based fervour
Carafa coughed cash-for-beauty:
Filippino painted *putti*
in the church 'Above Minerva'

To the latter-day observer,
Carafa's *Annunciation*

seems the height of ostentation,
like he's Nero – maybe Nerva.

Fastidious, exquisite taste,
fawner over faultless forms:
cruel enforcer of all norms –
disagree, he'll lay you waste!

Stigmata this side, that side stocks:
freeing classical remains
paired with clapping plebs in chains:
therein lies the paradox.

Followers of Father Knox,
Rienzo, Bruno, Catiline
(those who just won't toe the line)
will never see a ballot-box.

Venerino earned a boat,
rematore for the Pope,
Boethius received the rope,
for what one said and what one wrote.

Pomponio was resolute
and silence was his firm position:
they sent him to the Inquisition!
Speaking, writing, standing mute:

can't we have a point of view?
If we say that something's true,
the Church attacks with rack and screw:
so what are we supposed to do?

STRAY LEAVES: WHO KNOWS?

Was Caponsacchi just a bar-room brawler,
or was he Mister Darcy, Colin Firth-y?
Should 'Cap' have been a Blackpool bingo-caller,
or interviewed by Krishnan Guru-Murthy?

And Guido – was he blandly noble-birthy,
or just a hapless, worthless bottom-feeder?
You judge him ignorant, or grounded, earthy?
(If only he'd been seven inches taller!)

Pompilia: a saint? The slut of sluts?
Romantic? Realistic point of view?
There's plenty that corroborates, rebuts.
You have the evidence. It's up to you.

The beauty of it is, we'll never know.
Your inner core will tell you where to go.

LA PUTTA ONORATA

We never know how things will balance out.
To take a step, with one clear end in mind,
is really nothing more than groping blind.
Steered course? Perforce, mere blundering about?
Pietro, poised to have the final shout
in little litigation, thinks to find
the telling testimony. Intertwined,
the stripling cedes dominion to the stout:
Angelica the maid, three years before,
as part of Pietro's petty stratagem,
gave written evidence, attested, swore
to dire domestic doings. Apothegm:

before you wade through gore, think what's in store.
Your servant's tittle-tattle can condemn.

THE HEIGHT OF SUMMER, sixteen ninety-four.
Repelling Guido's plaint is paramount.
That hindsight has a twenty-twenty count
is often proffered but, beyond the lore,
Angelica's account will prove pure ore
when future prosecutors come to mount
a murder case. Let's drink, then, from the fount.
Let's look behind closed Franceschini doors.
It doesn't make an edifying story.
As true as Trasimene, the water's peaty,
but one thing's clear – Pompilia's *genitori*
were badly used. *Parenti acquisiti*
fell subject to an aretine furore,
inimical to anguish or entreaty.

ANGELICA BATTISTA IS MY NAME,
my village Castelluccio, and my age –
I've reached, as people say, a 'certain stage':
zitella never more, now hatted dame.
Unable to return from whence we came
(I'm thirty-five!), with grief we can't assuage,
the sage among us recognise the same.

I count myself a cut-price *Columbina*,
supporting role, a carrier of notes.
I leave the arias to smoother throats,
have never been a sexpot steal-the-scener.
The girl of breeding, she's the *ragazzina*.
I'm happy as the helper-on with coats,
unworried if my neighbour's grass is greener.

My youngest had attained her second year:
it therefore must have been three winters since.

I disregarded cautionings and hints,
and took the offered work. My overseer
was Donna Beatrice. Lurking in the rear
was one named Porzia. (I was not convinced
that she was family – it wasn't clear.)

The Franceschini household? Let me see …
ten Christian souls we were, as I recall,
six quality, four serving-folk in all.
Count Guido was the head (officially),
but who thought much of him? For sure, not me!
He didn't wield authority. Not tall,
his arrogance was plain as plain could be.

Yes, Beatrice was the one who ruled the roost.
She gave commands, admonished, punished, sacked.
The *Borgo Cenci* house was Beatrice. Fact.
The day that Guido's bride was introduced,
a kind of open violence was loosed.
The bride was chided. Qualities she lacked
were pointed out, and *faux-pas* reproduced.

Pompilia, the little Roman bride,
had brought her parents with her. Big mistake!
They took the torture for their daughter's sake.
Refused, abused, insulted and denied,
they lived a nightmare no-one could abide:
but even saintly fortitude can break!
War was declared, and flared Arezzo-wide.

Pompilia – as fragile as a rose,
so innocent, so shabbily reviled!
The family (as fierce as she was mild)
reproached her for a role she never chose.
Those liquid eyes, that lovely button nose!

It's easy to forget she was a child,
a wren surrounded by a flock of crows.

Of Beatrice, I've nothing good to say.
Her one true pleasure, breaking others' wills
(that's those below her – Beatrice' keenest quills
were kept for weak dependants, captive prey):
she shared no laughter, shunned the light of day,
her talk, rehearsal of imagined ills,
her world a dungeon of unchanging grey.

Then Girolamo, brother. What a brute!
An animal devoid of Christian soul,
oft apprehended by the night patrol,
defended by his mother, destitute
of grace or learning, heaping disrepute
on what was sacred, Girolamo's goal
was, spoliation of forbidden fruit.

I thought it odd, when I was taken on,
that in-laws could be under Guido's roof.
They say that eating is the pudding's proof
and, come spring equinox, the pair was gone.
Poor Violante! Penned-in, put upon,
she furnished furtive warp to Guido's woof.
By hurting her, he'd crossed his Rubicon.

She made me promise ('she' is Beatrice now)
the very day I started in that house
that neither Violante nor her spouse
would get my help. I took a solemn vow
(with crosses on my breast and lips and brow)
that I would not so much a lift a louse
from Violante's head, and not allow

the slightest blandishment they might exude
to cozen me from my allotted task.
Whatever boon the Romans sought to ask,
whatever innocent solicitude,
and with whatever vehemence renewed,
my countenance must stay a stony mask.
(This proved impossible, with what ensued!)

A 'palace' has high ceilings, draughty halls,
and owners in a state of penury.
The Comparini, in the depth of January,
lay whimpering in their room. Pietro's falls
and bitter chill (Violante in two shawls!)
provoked my rescue-action. 'Le ceneri'
('the ashes') – that's when Beatrice threatened me –

another of those Franceschini brawls.
Appalled, and full of pity for the pair,
I took warm ashes from my attic brazier
– of little use, I know, but as we say
in Castelluccio, 'something's something'. There,
I tried to warm their grate. Had I been lazier,
I might still be in Tuscany today.

The Franceschini fortunes came unglued.
(If truth be told, the genie fled the flask
some years before.) The curtains, though damask,
were threadbare now, where countless moths had chewed.
Denuded of all comfort, brooding, rude,
the draughty domicile prepared for Pasch
in something like senescent solitude.

These folks were broke. Without a fake *piastre*.
They'd hoped the marriage-mart might do the trick.
Pilasters, so imposing? Painted brick.
Behind the marble, all was lath-and-plaster,

a dread that one more dun would deal disaster.
They needed cash-infusion, pretty quick!
'Love solves all problems' – thus spake Zoroaster.

The one in Rome – that's Paolo – was a monk:
apart from pocket-pence, parochial perk,
he brought no money in. The others? Work?
They couldn't. Or they wouldn't. When not drunk,
or into aimless melancholy sunk,
the one named Girolamo, like a Turk,
around his houkah huddled, in a funk.

Their meanness – circumstance? Malignant growth?
The question often occupies my mind.
Irreparably poor, or just unkind?
Now, looking back, I see a bit of both.
But spite's a mighty impulse, on my oath,
and no-one guards the cheese and serves the rind
unless the reason's savagery (or sloth).

First, winter solstice, terror of the old.
Exceptionally harsh it was, that year.
A mixture of embarrassment and fear
confined them to that room. The aching cold
inflicted on them sufferings untold.
I couldn't help – but couldn't help but hear
the wretched sobbing. Once a day I doled

the cooling cinders of the kitchen fire
to give their hearth a hint of being 'warm',
some smuggled scrap inside my uniform
(whatever kitchen cut-offs I'd acquire
(she called me 'pelican', for I'd aspire
to feed them with my blood, against the norm)
would hardly keep a silverfish alive.

More help, I found beyond me to contrive.
The Franceschini listened at the door,
each member taking turns and keeping score.
My orders were to stultify, deprive,
and do whatever else I could to drive
the Comparini from us. What a chore!
To push the *invitati* from the hive!

Light Denied (1)

I well recall one dark and rainy night
when Pietro came in from the cold and damp.
I hurried to the staircase with a lamp,
to aid the ageing fellow's ailing sight.
But Guido snatched my lantern – what a fright!
He snarled, 'You're siding with this drunken tramp?
So now we know – you're in the other camp!'
At that, extinguishing the lantern light,
he left old Pietro stranded on the stairs.
Discourtesy, alone, is never right,
but when you have the upper hand, your might
should not be slily used for setting snares,
but that was Guido: at the scala height,
his helpless prey endangered, unawares.

THE NEW YEAR BROUGHT MORE GRIEF, instead of less.
Another darkened staircase – Pietro fell,
and passed three weeks bedridden, quite unwell.
I wept in sympathy, I must confess,
to witness such oppression, such distress:
my tears resounded like a funeral knell.
Whose part I took was not so hard to guess.

To 'pitch me out the window' if I switched
was Guido's constant menace. He'd got hitched,

and still the Franceschini weren't enriched –
in some inchoate way, they felt bewitched.
With Caponsacchi 'cut' and Conti 'ditched',
it had to fall on someone. Beatrice bitched
that I would always be 'the one that snitched'.

There's nothing quite as beautiful as wood
(a case impossible to overstate):
from granadine guitar to garden gate,
it brings us nothing harmful, only good.
A hissing log to glow, and warm the blood,
was snatched by Beatrice from the couple's grate,
and all of us who saw it, understood:

the Franceschini's only pole is hate.
She saddled them with pain, because she could.
(If Yahweh loves us, why inflict The Flood?)
No room to riddle, or equivocate.
What once had been suspicion, now seemed straight:
we had no future in this neighbourhood,
and even now we may have left it late.

When Guido slapped me, that proclaimed the end.
Pietro said he'd offered me a place –
that's when I caught it – twice – across the face.
How low are people willing to descend?
It marked the nadir of an ugly trend.
One blow – who knows? But how explain a brace?
Arezzo was behind me, Rome my friend.

Two further incidents will make it plain.
One offers linen when a woman cries,
a fine material to dry her eyes.
But Beatrice, with autocrat disdain,
presented us with hemp. Aggressive, vain,

she has a talent to antagonise.
Her narcissism goes against the grain.

The other thing involved an antique sword.
They'd locked me in the cellar. Since the womb,
the brother, Girolamo – we assume –
had been indoctrinated by the horde.
When Violante, properly, explored
my absence, 'Giro' chased her to her room.
I later saw the door-frame, gouged and scored.

One sucking-lamb would have to last the week.
A Sunday's share, cooked rare, the hinter quarter
(the wine diluted down to coloured water).
On Monday, liver, lungs and maybe cheek,
thereafter innards, now as tough as teak,
the head served up with un-ironic *hauteur*.
And this routine by no means was unique.

Just think of Pietro, huddled in that bed,
his only barrier against the biting cold.
His gums were tender (sixty-five years old!)
and, masticating mutton, often bled.
By Candlemas, severely underfed,
he lived on tea indifferently doled,
sustaining life by sucking slabs of bread.

On days he found the strength to rise and dress,
he'd sally forth (since provender was patchy,
to say the least, at home) to *Canto Bacci*
to offer his opinions and *largesse*
in a friendly tavern named the Olive Press,
where fun flowed freely and the songs were catchy.
The Franceschini's feelings? You can guess!

If indignation was their strongest suit,
their loathing of all public taverns seemed
a kind of mania. 'You're a brute!' they screamed,
'frequenting hostelries of ill-repute,
the lair of highwayman and prostitute!'
Against the family's standing he'd blasphemed:
this cancer must be ripped out by the root!

One chilly night in March, the abcess burst.
Returning home, Pietro was quite shocked
to find the *Borgo Cenci* door was locked:
at first, far from alarmed, he merely cursed,
but then began to bargain for the worst.
He called for Violante. Then he knocked.
Despite the freezing fingers that he nursed,

the door remained unanswered. Time went by.
Eventually, Violante came.
She opened up the threshold, crossed the same.
'You're banging on the doorjamb, husband. Why?'
'They locked me out. I think I'm going to die!'
Some unknown Franceschini (shame on shame!)
re-slammed the door. Beneath an icy sky,

the couple shivered, cast out on the street.
A neighbour's light comes on. They shout, *'Soccorri!'*
They're let into the home of Doctor Borri,
who offers them an improvised retreat.
Salvation! Oh, such decency! Such heat!
It's then that I became additional quarry.
The Franceschini had to be discreet,

and couldn't have this scandal, this disgrace.
Since I was 'one of them', I had to go.
Right there, right then. In hail or snow.
I found a bed at Albergotti's place.

Propriety forced Pietro to retrace
his steps back to Canale. A new low!
There now seemed nothing they would not debase.

And so to Rome. The Comparini's part
I took with relish. Tuscany's behind.
The Franceschini, cruel, embittered, blind,
will see no more of me. It's hard to start
afresh, agreed, to clamber on the cart.
I only know that here, I've ease of mind:
your home is where you know repose of heart.

Angelica's account is hard to parse.
An honest tale in which we can confide?
Or are we being taken for a ride?
Though evidence is relatively sparse,
her version of the Franceschini farce
(unless she's playing for the other side)
appears to be an honourable guide –
or is she kissing Comparini arse?
Perhaps her deposition states the truth.
She seems authentic. What she has to say
suggests the Franceschini were uncouth:
is she exacting vengeance, tooth for tooth?
A simple fact that will not go away –
Angelica was in Pietro's pay.

SLEEPLESS IN SIENA, Being a Tale told by Pietro Ottoboni, His Account of a Play He Once saw at a Fairground

The art of comedy's a sacred thing,
as fresh and precious in its gift of bliss
as when a worshipped one's initial kiss
transports us first. Like Fragonard, we swing

to Lena Horne's delightful rites of spring
on wings of wonder. No analysis
can pull apart a pleasure pure as this.
We humans laugh as nightingales might sing.
We're told to think creators must be serious,
but humour's both unruly and imperious,
and ridicule's the boy-god's sharpest dart.
We laugh and learn, but lifeless lead-weights weary us,
for dreariness is deadly, deleterious:
thank heaven for the comedy of art.

THE CORNER'S CALLED, 'the Cross of the Travails',
where three streets meet, hard by the Merchants' *Loggia*.
Though there are districts definitely dodgier,
the solitary Columbina quails:
she's seeking out a balcony with rails.
Committed to her mission as a servant,
her motivation's somewhat less than fervent:
but when she sets her mind, she never fails.

Despite the darkness, she can just discern
eight brackets on the Banchi side. That's it!
This is the balcony, the details fit.
She's found the house, and now her one concern,
to drop the note off neatly, and return.
Where to lodge her mistress' loving chit?
Detecting neither letterbox nor slit,
she feels around for amphora or urn

in which to stuff the message. Who's up there?
He's on the balcony – it's Arlecchino!
That's Graziano's handyman, *facchino*.
Though he and Columbina are a 'pair',
you'd hardly guess it. Coming down the stair,
he thinks he's sex on legs (but what does *he* know?)

They're working on a plan, *loro trucchino*,
to get a couple married. Gulls, beware!

(A word on Columbina's condescension:
young Arlecchino hopes to 'vault the fence',
to marry his beloved Bini, hence
his paltry income's causing apprehension.
About to flout annuity or pension?
That has to wait. He's got more time than sense.
The clown is pulling down pathetic pence –
a woeful wage, all said, to wed a wench on!)

Like servants everywhere, they're working late
without reward. Orazio and Aurelia,
the posh young lovers, really should be steelier,
confront their fathers, forge their future fate.
What can retainers do? Commiserate
together? Arlecchino, touchy-feelier,
is blocked by Columbina's red camellia,
in check, and mated, by his so-called mate.

'Let's get them married, then we'll get some sleep,'
is Chini's bright suggestion. Yes, but how?
Their fathers won't permit it, won't allow
the youngsters to associate. They're cheap,
like rich folks always are. They want to reap
that dowry windfall, want to milk the sow.
The lovers, then, pursuant to their vow,
are wooing through their servants, who must keep

nocturnal vigil, back and forth with notes.
Since Arlecchino's mind has turned to marriage,
the street being bare (not yet an open garage!)
he feels emboldened. She on whom he dotes
is right there, with him. Paucity of groats
can hardly matter, can it? Dire miscarriage!

Each word's an invitation to disparage,
each foray, one more blaze to burn his boats!

He's recently been spotted with Brighella,
the chambermaid of whom he's rather fond,
so Columbina answers, 'How's your blonde?'
Why grasp at something anodyne to tell her?
Why try to tap-dance, when your tarantella's
so swiftly swatted? Bini can't be conned.
The purest she-piranha in the pond
mauls men's *menzognas* like they're mortadela.

Who spilled the *faggioli*? Women know.
They have done, since the human race began.
Best change the subject! What, then, is the plan?
How end the ceaseless, peaceless, to-and-fro?
When challenged, Queenie Bini's good to go:
'The short way to manipulate a man
is, use his strength against him, rather than
confront him openly. We'll offer dough.'

'I think I spot a weakness in the scheme,'
advances Arlecchino, 'in as much
as we can't give a guilder, going Dutch!'
He sees arise in Bini's eyes a gleam
of triumph. 'Who needs 'have' when we can 'seem' ?'
Cheeseparing parents safely in her clutch,
she smiles contentedly. That feline touch
as much as guarantees the winning team.

'He'll meet your girl tomorrow, as agreed,'
says Arlecchino. 'Time for bed, my sweet.'
The other doesn't even miss a beat:
'But not with you, buffoon. It's sleep I need.'
With that, she's gone. He watches her recede,
engulfed in darkness: knowing well defeat

is just a form of love, surveys the street:
suppose her stratagem just might succeed?

* * * *

STRAY LEAVES: I ADORE AN ESPINELA!

I adore an espinela!
Think of elegance and flair
(Ginger Rogers, Fred Astaire):
from the attic to the cellar,
it's got energy to spare!
Strictly ruled, though never square,
redolent of 'vita bella',
redondillas, pair by pair,
for the ear and eye to share
(not ideal for Helen Keller!)

Progeny of Don Vicente
(sometime citizen of Ronda),
rhythmic rhyming anaconda
aprendido de repente,
it's a prodigy to ponder.
If you stay or should you wander
out among the irredente,
nothing's better or 'beyonder'
(Cary Grant meets Henry Fonda!)
Task me two, I'll turn you twenty!

Chini's feeling rather lonesome
in the dark and silent street,
and his misery's complete:
once again he's on his ownsome.
Nearby doorlock clicks – repeat –
Pantalone, dour, discreet,

born to bore, inclined to drone some,
sallies forth. How very neat!
'Guvnor! Just the man I'd meet!'
(Chini's confidence has grown some!)

'Arlecchino? What the devil –
don't you know it's five a.m.?'
Paragon of poise and phlegm,
Chini answers, 'On the level!
I've done nothing you'd condemn!'
(Hem and haw, then haw and hem,
fingers trace the doorjamb's bevel):
'I've learned something touching *them*.
When divulged, this little gem
is bound to make a father revel.

Something's happened – something funny.'
Pantalone's not impressed:
thumbs in braces, chin on chest,
'I'm not forking any money.'
(Feathering another's nest
is not a Pantalonefest.)
'Someone's prospects just got sunny.
Now's the moment to invest.'
(Once the pheasant plumps its crest,
Chini ladles on the honey.)

'Graziano's got a Dante.'
'What's a Dante?' 'I don't know.
Worth a prince's ransom, though.
Secret mission. Facts are scanty.
First edition. Buy it low,
sell it high – the guy's a pro.'
'What am I – some dilettante?'
'Never, Master – no, no, no!

Sow it early, watch it grow.'
Pantalone's off. *Avanti!*

* * * *

ARLECCHINO'S FURTHERING THE PLAN
that Columbina hatched. He'd best update her,
to keep the wires uncrossed – but he's a man,
and doesn't see why this can't wait till later.

An hour or two of sleep is needed now
– but soft! Orazio's approaching. Is that him?
It surely is. That handsome, furrowed brow –
he's such a fine young man ... but rather dim.

'Good heavens, Arlecchino! You as well?
I can't believe the schedule that you keep.
I'm banished from Aurelia. I'm in hell!
You lucky servants – nothing spoils your sleep!

Have you had women problems in your life?
I'm sorry – you and women – that's absurd!'
'Young master, you will soon be man and wife.
A plan's afoot – big secret – mum's the word.'

Orazio's bewildered. Off he goes,
conversing with himself in muted mutters.
The street returns once more to sweet repose,
unbroken save for gurgling in the gutters.

'So many people, out before it's day,'
thinks Arlecchino. 'This is like the Corso,'
(his pride is Rome, where once he trod the clay)
'as busy as Babuino – only more so.'

That's when he hears another pair of feet
come flopping on the flags. 'If he were faster,
it could be Pantalone. That's the beat
of Doctor Graziano. Morning, Master!'

'You don't have work to do, young Arlecchino?
What do I pay you for? You just abuse
my kindness.' 'Morning prayer, Sant' Agostino.
And I've acquired some interesting news.'

We know that Chini's knowledge borders scanty,
though he believes he's up there with Masaccio.
He pointed Pantalone straight at Dante,
but now his bullshit battens on Boccaccio.

His aim? Convince his boss that Pantalone
has suddenly grown rich. The only problem?
The liars' path is difficult and stony,
and lies they've strewn will soon rise up to nobble 'em.

* * * *

EVERYTHING'S IN CHAOS
in the merchant's living-room.
The maid is tying ribbons
on Aurelia's costume,
as busy with the hairgrips
as Brighella with the broom.

Before the full-length mirror
Aurelia risks a twirl:
now Pantalone's anxious –
'Not finished sweeping, girl?'
No answer from Brighella
beyond a surly curl,

tossed back from blondie's forehead
as Brighella mutters, 'Heh.'
Explosions of emotion
have never been her way:
just 'heh' (or 'hah' when angry)
is all she's known to say.

'He'll be here any minute,'
says the father to the daughter,
'the Captain wants a quick one:
he's soon to cross the water.'
'A quick one what?' Aurelia
feels fetters fasten, fraughter.

'It's time you took a husband –
I really think you oughta.'
'I'm going to wed Orazio!'
(this with impressive *hauteur*),
but Pantalone presses
(he's thinking bricks and mortar).

'You're sort of an investment,'
(he is trying to talk flowery)
'and when you're good and married,
that's when I collect the dowry.'
Aurelia bears the aspect
of a pugilistic Maori.

The doorbell! He's arriving!
Columbina's in a tizzy:
concealing pins and ribbons
is enough to keep her busy:
Brighella sees the Captain –
'He's not impressive, is he?'

Aurelia's insulted.
She feels that she's been conned:
before she'll wed this midget,
she'll probably abscond.
Brighella's mouth hangs open
(well, after all, she's blonde).

The new arrival, bowing,
announces he's Spaccone.
His legs are short and spindly,
and not a little bony:
between them one could gallop
a fairly portly pony.

'Warrior by profession,
and hero, some avow,
I've fought in every action
from Malta to Macao:
the Achilles of Ancona
is what they call me now.'

An unimpressed Aurelia
ignores the bragging brute:
his lies are quite outlandish,
and easy to refute:
but mutters Columbina,
'I think he's rather cute!'

Spaccone waves a bottle
with overweening motion:
'These means at my disposal
will win your full devotion.
No resistance can withstand
my Universal Potion!'

'Like Hrunting or Colada,
this sword is known to fable!'
(He sets the potion bottle
adroitly on the table.)
To draw and sheathe the weapon, though,
he isn't fully able:

Between the hilt and scabbard
he traps his finger (fore),
and when he sees it's bleeding
he runs out through the door,
vociferous in panic
(he's terrified of gore).

Brighella helps Aurelia
by carrying her train:
the daughter's in a tantrum
of dander and disdain:
she's heading for her boudoir,
and there she will remain.

* * * *

AND THAT LEAVES COLUMBINA, Pantalone:
the latter never flatter or distraughter.
They say no man's an island (*vide* Coney),
but he's alone in woe. 'I thought he'd bought her!'
And thus unfolds, when grief was never keener,
('My daughter! Oh my ducats! Oh my daughter!')
an opportunity for Columbina.

'You've heard of Graziano's acquisition?'
'Yes, Arlecchino mentioned it this morning.
He said it was a pristine first edition.'
Columbina sees a chasm yawning:
she doesn't have a clue what Chini said:

(he might, at least, have given her some warning!)
So, how to fumble forward? Where to tread?

'He said it was …?' 'Some medieval macho
composed a book of poems.' (There's her clue!)
'*Decamerone*, written by Boccaccio.'
(She has to sound authentic, follow through.)
'He bought it for mere coppers, now he's wealthy…'
(will Pantalone nibble?) '… well-to-do…
his credit rating's looking very healthy …'

'You say he's making money from a *book*?'
'It's worth a fortune, if it's ever sold.'
(She feels the minnow mumble at the hook.)
'Don Pantalone, may I be so bold?
Orazio – that's Graziano's son –
would make a fine *genero*, and there's gold
which, if you're quick, is waiting to be won!'

'Yes, young Orazio – what a splendid choice!
My favoured option. Said it all along.
Spaccone was…' (at this, he drops his voice)
'…an also-ran. Unquestionably wrong.'
'I'll talk to Graziano,' says the maid,
who – careful not to openly rejoice –
takes pleasure in a plan so ably laid.

* * * *

Middleway between their houses,
in the *Via de Città*,
see the fathers – there they are,
dealing dowries, spinning spouses.

Pantalone, Graziano,
in a corner somewhat murky

are engrossed in talking turkey.
It's a circus. (Think 'Fred Karno'.)

Fairly rarely for this *milieu*
(that's the *Loggia dei Mercanti*)
dunderheads discussing Dante –
can you think of anything sillier?

Like a star of straight-faced poker,
feinting this way, feigning that,
sumo wrestlers on the mat;
Pantalone plays his joker.

'Word is out of newfound treasure,
would-be wedlock's panacea …'
Graziano (no idea)
moves to get the other's measure:

'Yes, I'm fully in the picture,'
(which he isn't, by a mile).
Each man gives a knowing smile.
Merchants mind one single stricture:

Enemies will maul all meekness:
never show them any weakness.
Obfuscation and obliqueness!
Make them taste your tough-as-teakness!

Consequently, neither party
wants to give the game away:
all is bluffing, all display.
Avid avarice apart, he

doesn't dare to seem a dunce:
can't afford to let the other

take advantage, has to smother
any hint of ignorance.

Each, serenely as a swan,
nods and says, 'exactly so!'
Feet are flailing down below!
Neither knows what's going on.

Columbina happens by:
what this wealth is, whence it came,
whom to credit, whom to blame,
maybe she can clarify.

Fathers grilling Bini closely
don't get much by way of answers:
she, most dexterous of dancers,
knows that vomiting verbosely

hollow claims or bald assertions
leads to trouble. Better far
keep the lid tight on the jar,
notwithstanding all coercions.

Columbina, *à propos*
of treacherous interrogation,
sloughs off self-incrimination:
best response is, 'I don't know'.

Spaniards call it *cuento chino* –
rambling, shapeless, aimless tale,
such as makes one's lawyer quail –
look who's coming – Arlecchino!

Arlecchino Gives the Game Away

A useful watchword is, 'beware of blurtings'.
Proficient though you be in paltry patter,
there's peril lurking in the cheeriest chatter.
Forget your 'settled stories' and your 'certains':
no plight is quite as trite as inadvertence.
There's true blue self-assurance, there's grey matter,
the first abundant when you lack the latter.
What starts in stagecraft, often ends in curtains!
Inhabitant of Shalimar or shanty?
You hail from Aldershot, or Alicante?
Your prospects pivot on a proper noun.
Improvidence, from Ypres to Ypsilanti,
can bring the superstructure crashing down.
'Boccaccio' was the word – but he said 'Dante'.

THE FATHERS ARE FURIOUS!
The pretext is spurious,
but both of them hurry to leave.
And Bini tells Chini
by stealing the scene, he
unravelled a finely-wrought sleeve.

'Unless you know *tutto*,
You *figlio di putto*,
You never should open your mouth.
You painted us liars,
and what now transpires
(in short) is, our plan's heading south!'

She strides from the *loggia*.
You'd think Enver Hoxxa
had conquered imperial Rome!
For Chini it's painful,

but she's so disdainful,
he'd better not follow her home.

He ponders his failings.
A glance through the railings
distracts him with total surprise.
'There's Captain Spaccone,
that bargain-store phony:
I'm hardly believing my eyes!'

He's dressed for a wedding
and seems to be heading
towards Pantalone's abode.
This abject Achilles
is carrying lilies –
he's ringing the bell – 'Well, I'm blowed!'

She's cleaning and dusting.
'It's my fault for trusting
a half-wit in such situations.'
And, like Palestrina,
our poor Columbina
is conjuring lush lamentations.

'I don't know who *that* is.'
She peers through the lattice.
'The Captain is coming to court!'
She opens, he enters:
her point-of-view centres
on the *mazzo* he happens to sport.

His manner seems altered:
his speech, shy and faltered:
the brashness and bluster is gone.
He holds out the lilies:

it gives her the willies:
the warrior seems careworn and wan.

'My mistress will love them!'
His face looms above them:
his eyes are impressively blue.
'They're not for Aurelia,
Ophelia or Celia.'
His voice drops down low. 'They're for you.'

* * * *

IT'S MORNING IN THE SQUARE.
Accoutred in his best is Pantalone,
and at his side, none other but Spaccone:
a justice of the peace (corrupted crony)
is with them, waiting there.

The word is getting round.
Since six o'clock, the rumours have been spreading.
Senese citizens have started heading
towards the Mangia Tower. There'll be a wedding
upon this very ground.

Now, Graziano shows.
Apologising, straightening his hat,
he has no inkling where Orazio's at,
but offers up a clinquant caveat
in irreproachable prose.

And now here comes the bride!
Her wedding veil, cascading to her waist,
obscures (for now, at least) her bashful face:
that she looks lovely, lilies matching lace,
can hardly be denied.

Spaccone takes his stand
beside his wife-to-be. The judge begins
by buffing-up his shoes against his shins.
'If anybody knows of any sins …'
(impediments unplanned

are anything but sparse
in weddings of a comical conception.
To interrupt the nuptials – and reception! –
is customary. This one's no exception:
it's, after all, a farce!)

It's Arlecchino. 'Halt!'
Unsteady on his feet and ill at ease.
'Has anyone seen Columbina, please?'
Such odd comportment might suggest that he's
been at the single malt.

The justice of the peace
is not amused. 'Buffoon, be on your way!
I want to get this done with no delay.
You'd spoil my second spousal of the day?
I'll summon the police!'

Now Pantalone bristles:
'You married others, earlier? Then the fee
will need revising. Are you on a spree?'
The tee-drive of this wedding seems to be
careering for the thistles!

'We need to concentrate,'
the judge observes. He asks for yes or no,
both bride and groom affirm. Rings on, just so.
'Well then, you're married. Sorry, have to go.
I'm running awfully late.'

'Aurelia, lift your veil!'
Spaccone grows in stature, swells with pride:
the moment has arrived to kiss the bride:
but Graziano's eyes are saucer-wide,
and Pantalone's pale.

The judge has not gone far.
His curiosity aroused by gasps,
he turns as Pantalone groans and grasps
his purse-strings to his heart, like poison asps
(which, in a sense, they are).

Now Graziano speaks.
'But you – you're Columbina!' (to the bride):
'The knot has not – is not – *can* not be tied!
Malfeasance! Matrimony misapplied!'
But such critiques

do not impress the judge.
'The holy sacrament has been performed,
and hymeneal hyssop duly warmed.
The spousal citadel can not be stormed.
From this I will not budge.'

He shows a secret pouch
behind his jacket. 'Using your resources,
employ a lawyer. We know what divorce is.
Through any fact, we'll drive a coach and horses.
For this (if paid), I'll vouch.'

Poor Pantalone pauses:
put silver in that pouch? Yet one more cost!
What remedy? The Rubicon's been crossed!
Such pain, to sponsor what's already lost –
the wretchedest of causes.

The money changes hands.
'Did I hear 'Columbina'? That's unreal!
opines the judge. 'A basis for appeal!'
and Pantalone, sweating, starts to feel
his throbbing glands.

'I married her today.
The ceremony happened hours ago.
The boy was called – what was it? – ends in 'o',
and I presided – so I ought to know.'
There's general dismay!

'Sir, do you see my son?'
asks Graziano. 'Father, – it was me!'
Incredulous, all eyes now turn to see
Orazio and Aurelia – can it be?
'The future has begun!'

What can the stripling mean?
They turn to Columbina: 'Explanation?'
But she just smiles in triumph. Consternation!
It's now a sticky social situation,
and causing quite a scene!

'For what it may be worth,'
(this from Aurelia) 'Father, you're absurd.
It's time for younger voices to be heard.
The values you have stood for, in a word,
are passing from the earth.'

'I married him this morning,
dressed up as Columbina, for disguise.'
'And I, Orazio, Arlecchino-wise.'
Poor Pantalone! Right before his eyes,
the gates of hell are yawning.

Those eyes roll in his head.
The thin legs wobble, balance is unsound:
the blood inside his ears begins to pound:
precipitately, Panti hits the ground:
indeed, he might be dead!

'Aren't you an erstwhile Proctor?'
(The Faculty of Medicine at Pisa).
To Graziano, Chini puts this teaser.
'At least, that's what you said. Go to it, geezer!
Do something. You're a doctor!'

He *is* a man of science:
for decades, though, he's blithely port-and-sherried,
and all ambition Chaeron long since ferried
to where the Hypocratic Oath lies buried
(just like his clients).

Oh, Columbina's quick!
The slickest and most dexterous of motions
(collection-boxes weaving through devotions
might spring to mind): out comes the queen of potions!
She doesn't miss a trick!

The 'doctor' squirts the juice,
and Pantalone instantly revives.
The cat can reckon on eight further lives,
albeit that his skin is pocked with hives,
and his complexion puce.

'God bless you, friend and brother!
See how your saving sapience is applauded.
Accept my silver! Sorry something sordid
is all I give, but you must be rewarded.
There'll never be another!'

The merchant was too rash.
That surfeit of emotion having passed,
Don Pantalone's once again aghast:
this has to be the first time (and the last!)
he parts with all his cash.

The doctor is immersed
in new emotions, close akin to wonder:
he didn't mess it up, he didn't blunder:
the guy's not dead, or even going under
(so that's another first!)

Aurelia now states
that Columbina, 'though a working girl,
is better than the rest of us. This pearl,
no matter how our strategies unfurl,
controls our fates!'

This, everyone applauds.
Whatever enmity there's been is quite forgotten.
They're off to celebrate, so put the pot on!
Their outer clothes are silk, their inner, cotton
and everyone wears leather soles to trot on –
they've all that life affords!

But what of Arlecchino?
While Bini's ruse has everyone confused,
he understands. His love has been abused.
He's not the first, in failure, to have mused
unhappily on *destino*.

A friendless Nova Scotian
could not feel more unwelcome in the pack.
He gestures to his 'ex', 'what did I lack?'
She tosses him the bottle, winking back –
it's Bini's lucky lotion!

That girl across the square …
the skirt, he knows … familiar floral pattern.
It's her – it has to be! The sexy slattern!
Who could mistake that slouching child of Saturn,
one shoulder bare?

Those golden curls – Brighella!
The button nose, the long, cascading hair …
those sleepy eyes, that fetching *derrière* –
You never triumph if you never dare.
Oh well – *la vita è bella!*

The others have all gone.
He's cut adrift, to languish in the rear.
Towards the buxom blonde he starts to steer
and reaching up, behind each bristling ear
he dabs the potion on.

EVIDENCE OF MARIA MARGHARITA CONTENTI, SWORN PURSUANT TO A LAWSUIT IN THE EPISCOPAL COURT OF AREZZO, AN ACTION WHICH WAS SUBSEQUENTLY DISCONTINUED

They call me '*La Pallina*'.
Pompilia lived across from me
(unwelcome, that proximity!)
She greeted me, '*vicina*'.

She came in dead of winter.
They moved here from the Holy See
(her parents, too, chose Tuscany).
The thing was sure to splinter.

Three months the set-up lasted.
Da solstice *fino* equinox,
too many shoals, too many shocks:
the thing was swiftly blasted.

Alarms and altercations.
Farm animals from hostile flocks
are never quartered in one box.
Two clans, two plans – two nations.

She ran off three years after.
That she should go, I'm not averse:
to flee is bad, to stay is worse:
my own reaction? Laughter.

STRAY LEAVES: THE LOVE OF FATE

Directed by the lodestone in the nose,
untrammelled by a thing as slight as thought,
we steer towards the goal ('that which we ought'),
uninfluenced by poetry or prose.
What's challenged or contested, always grows.
No matter how the lesser folk exhort,
we cleave towards the plan, so finely wrought,
inherent in the petals of the rose.
Surprisingly inimical to loss,
We recognise the call, and know to go.
The fire is welcome, since it sears the dross,
and Ocean's cool ablutions go to show
that stasis is inferior to flow.
And so we seek the shadow of the cross.

STRAY LEAVES: THE FATE OF LOVE

The supernatural can never die
(but neither can it live). We've got to find
some function of our all-too-mortal mind
which offers us assistance with the 'Why?'
Is love self-interest, or altruism?
If love means anything, what does it mean?
The brutal urging of the selfish gene?
A fusion, or a fundamental schism?
Or could it be, we're dormant marionettes,
who dance (albeit briefly) when the breeze
excites our strings? The moonwind, as it frets,
conveys foreknowledge of our own demise,
but still we thrill to feel our thrumming nets,
which moan in chorus as they take the tease.

THE ONE TO START WITH HAS TO BE POMPILIA.
Like me, she was diminutive in size,
but more reserved. Not overly familiar.
You couldn't miss her big, dark eyes.
She had an act with men – I'd call her 'girly'.
Her hair was thick and long (but mine's more curly).

I don't think anyone would call us friends.
We knew each other, rubbed along, were neighbours –
but were we enemies? Well, that depends.
We sometimes – how to put it? – drew our sabres,
but nothing serious. Just irks and itches.
If ever you've owned dogs, you'll know. Two bitches!

A man like all men, Caponsacchi's weak.
With her he underwent a role-reversal.
Pompilia's unrepeatable, unique:
however, she is also universal.

You wonder why good women fall for rakes?
Whatever blunders are, they're not mistakes.

I hadn't any doubt that she would leave.
The only question was the how and when.
Some people just exist, but some achieve:
we'll never see the like of her again.
She knew, for her, these walls were there to scale:
Arezzo was the belly of the whale.

You've heard of firesticks? These are household things.
They're wooden. One's a cup, and one's a shaft.
The pole goes in the cup. For kindlings,
you swivel it and, as the cup is chafed,
the friction causes flame. Because I knew it,
one day I taught Francesca how to do it.

I'll tell you why she chose to run away.
(Don't ask for evidence, but women know.)
Towards the end of April, early May,
her pregnancy could hardly help but show.
The problem was, she knew she'd been defiled:
the embryo was Caponsacchi's child.

STRAY LEAVES: POMPILIA'S PORTALS

For humble mortals, wombs are safe and warm,
but stasis, by its nature, has to close.
The rain is cold which presages the storm,
and yet we're liberated by its throes.
Her belly-of-the-whale was not the end:
she threw the portal open, windows wide,
and chose to meet the future with her friend,
electing for the long and lonely ride.

At Castelnuovo, sbirris' oriflammes
accompanied the culling of the lambs,
but if you see an ending as a birth,
you'll have no fear of barriers or dams.
The wood of Santa Croce judged her worth,
and wood's the noblest element of earth.

COUNT GUIDO'S TINY, won't require much room.
Just weak and mean and stupid. Need another?
The feeblest men have never left the womb,
and Guido is the minion of his mother.
Domestic violence? As we've all supposed,
it's how a coward wins when doors are closed.

Opine on Canon Conti? 'Course I can.
Adventurers need help along the way.
I used to tell him, 'You're the Medicine-Man!'
Support and comfort if you went astray,
the first to offer up the fatted calf,
he lacked ebullience on his own behalf.

The sister, Porzia? Not a lot of grins!
A scowler, an ill-wisher, truth be told.
Pompilia was her opposite (said twins),
albeit one was young, the other old.
Though sometimes seen at evensong together,
they differed as a fetter does a feather.

I don't know who said character is fate,
but that's a fact. Regarding Guillichini
(called, jokingly, 'Gregorio the Great'),
he's bottled up – but isn't quite a genie.
It's true he tried to threaten me, but then
I've never felt beholden to mere men.

You sense when men are weak (at least, I do):
Gregorio shows it when he stamps his feet,
and Guido's brother Girolamo, too,
defines the point where fear and bluster meet.
You'll meet with guides and helpers as you go,
and sentries, too. And this was always so.

That dreams have meanings, I'm inclined to doubt,
but one I've had repeatedly of late
has got me thinking. As I sallied out
from Borgo de' Cenci, the Castro was in spate,
its waters clear, but gushing mightily,
it weighed on me that it was vitally

important that I reach San Spirito gate
(such missions aren't uncommon in a dream):
a woman on the bank said, 'Use that crate –
its wood will carry you across the stream.'
The box was lying abandoned in the grass,
and struck me (with regard to my impasse)

as likely to convey me over the swell.
The wood felt smooth and sturdy to my hand,
so off we set. What energy propelled
me, I can't even start to understand,
but this was such an easy, breezy ride,
in seconds we had reached the other side.

I found myself inside a box-hedge maze,
at first attractive, soon a place of fear.
A sinister sensation of malaise
swept through the angular alleys, so severe.
Awareness of direction somehow blunted,
I felt a consciousness of being hunted.

Pompilia's cognata up ahead,
the selfsame Porzia, standing on a plinth,
unspooling, Ariadne-like, a thread,
began to guide me through the labyrinth.
I reached a rosebush, knowing I was safe.
And there it ends. So why do questions chafe?

Who grew the rosebush, 'That-Which-I-Deserve'?
Whence came the welcome crate, named 'Help-Me-Cross'?
And what of Porzia's unaccustomed verve?
I can't account for these. I'm at a loss.
I've thoughts around me which I can't escape:
all norms conform to predetermined shape.

And so to Caponsacchi. He's the key.
So tall, athletic, handsome and amusing –
so many girls – it's all the same to me!
With whom you fall in love is not your choosing.
He used to stand here on this threshold stone,
and we would talk for hours, we two alone.

Afraid of no-one, carefree, light of heart,
he passed along the alley all the time,
so popular, and yet a man apart,
a curate ready with a ribald rhyme.
His glances at the Franceschini house
said everything – he'd noticed Guido's spouse.

Sant' Agostino is my parish church:
the Pieve's for the fashionable set.
However, I conducted my research:
a message here, and there a tête-à-tête
is how they worked it. Rather than confess,
Giuseppe came to see me less and less.

Relationships can sometimes grow remote,
then flare again – but one day, in the street,
I saw him stooping, picking up a note –
and then my misery was quite complete.
The billet-doux (one marvels at her skill)
had fallen from a Franceschini sill.

Adultery is such a sordid crime!
An April midnight, looking at her door,
and hearing Agostino start to chime,
I saw him coming out, and his amour
was lingering on the doorstep. Not a doubt.
The scarlet woman, seeing her lover out!

They say 'dishonest woman', meaning me?
More honest than the gentry, that's for sure.
They pay you compliments and feel your knee,
then afterwards traduce you as a whore.
Here's what I say to every gossip-monger:
Let's see what you do when you're faced with hunger!

I hear that Caponsacchi might return.
Depend upon it, that will not occur.
Milk's no longer milk, once in the churn.
Horizons have expanded, thanks to her,
and in Civita Vecchia, he's got room.
Yes, Canon Caponsacchi's left the womb.

CONSENTING ADULTS, Being a Tale told by Maria Margharita Contenti

Have we evolved since Sohrab slaughtered Rustum?
   What is the law? Its moral provenance
derives from what? From holy books? From custom?
   What are the wellsprings of good governance?

It's vested in a state? A tribe? A town?
   Can we be bound by laws we don't endorse?
Who may create them? Who may strike them down?
   Does law depend on force, or on the Bourse?
Is law a geyser of the people's will,
   emotion of the moment? Something more?
Its purpose to enable, or prevent?
   Can states (which we create) decide to kill
us? Disregard their citizens' consent?
   Say what's okay behind the bedroom door?

SOME YEARS AGO, the town of Prato
underwent a major change:
no more nobles' *obbligato* !
Emerging merchants, now estranged

from parasitic upper crust,
tired of 'breeding outranks brains'
and predisposed to readjust,
were set on reaping social gains.

A member of the merchant class,
charming, cheerful, 'chopsy', chipper,
famous for her sexy arse,
was Monna Filippa, known as 'Pippa'.

Pippa's beauty was transcendent:
she, owner of a first-class brain,
witty, pretty, independent,
treated sexists with disdain.

Her husband (not a man of action),
blue of blood and languid, lazy,
scion of Alberti's faction,
was a noble Pugliesi.

Friends had formed the firm impression
that Pippa, cards played close to chest,
flawless model of discretion,
had another interest.

Husband's moniker? Rinaldo.
Not a bad or spiteful man,
saw his marriage *(che spavaldo!)*
as a kind of business plan.

They'd been in love for quite a while
(that's Lazzarino and our girl):
she saw no need to reconcile
her one-row-knit with one-row-purl.

And who knows if Rinaldo knew?
Could anyone be that naive?
She didn't hide it from his view:
in fact, she wore it on her sleeve.

At last, they almost came to blows:
the husband caught her in his bed,
'red-handed', as the saying goes
(Rinaldo's, though, remained un-red!)

We've heard this kind of tale before.
The cuckold calls his wife a whore:
he rants revenge, but won't do more,
implores the law to fend off gore.

'Let me tell you, *bella donna*,
retribution now awaits:
you have compromised my honour:
I will call the magistrates!'

(Here's a note for legal students:
feudal *fueros* still contrive
through *pratese* jurisprudence
that cheating wives be burned alive.)

It strikes us as a little harsh:
the detriment is oft applied
– marooning Pia in the marsh –
uniquely to the distaff side.

The woman taken in adultery
must hit the flames, can't get to heaven:
a cruelty no way desultory,
and not at all John eight, eleven.

Would Rinaldo go to law?
Damn his wife to lethal pain?
Was this such a final straw?
Who could be so inhumane?

A nobleman must guard his honour.
Rinaldo's off to see His Grace.
Scratch 'belladona', insert 'goner'.
He'll let her burn to save his face.

Filippa also has a choice:
pack her bags and run away,
or give her deepest feelings voice.
Pippa opts to speak – and stay!

'Never will I disavow it.
This is love, not mere caprice.
Whether magistrates allow it
or they don't, I'll say my piece!'

Viscount Achille Alberti
(tiny specs on tip of nose)
hears the clock strike seven-thirty
(violet waistcoat, lilac hose).

He's been listening to Rinaldo
(stifled yawn, adjusted cuff):
random phrases – '*sangue caldo*' –
and he's listened quite enough.

'Don't you see, my dear young fellow?
Burning people – bit extreme.
Think of me as *tuo fratello* –
let's devise a wiser scheme.'

Stiffs obsess on retribution
(losers overdose on claims):
this one's set on prosecution,
shipping Pippa to the flames.

Ser Achille's sigh is stoic.
This is how all cuckolds are.
Spite's unsightly, unheroic –
'Why am I the *podestà*?'

Now Rinaldo's blood is rising.
'I'm not saying please endorse it –
law's not there for analysing –
I just want you to enforce it!'

Meanwhile, opposite *Carceri*,
Pippa throws aside discretion
(women in love are pretty scary)
and leaves the house. Her self-possession

oozes out of every pore.
A thoroughbred adorned with blinders,
through the pack our heroine tore,
oblivious of left-behinders.

Other-people's-business-minders,
massed in front of Pippa's door,
gossip-swappers, scandal-finders
sensed a crest, a settled score.

Striding down by San Francesco,
followed by the moiling masses,
(not today, Gerini's fresco!)
proud and peerless, Pippa passes.

Turning into Ricasoli,
She appears Pretoria-bound:
but, keeping to the pavement wholly,
eyes ahead, she covers ground

with undismayed determination,
throwing one dismissive glance
towards the seat of legislation
where, by curious circumstance,

her husband and the *podestá*
stand at the window, looking down.
'How many citizens there are!'
observes the latter, with a frown.

Ever onward Pippa surges,
followed by chaotic crowd:
into the square the mob emerges,
agitated, lively, loud.

'Cathedral of the *collegiata* –
outside pulpit – perfect spot!
Stephen being the model martyr,
I'll speak from here – I'm hot to trot!'

In the street (now named Mazzoni)
following behind the crush
the Viscount walks with his *jabroni*,
attains the square just as a hush

descends upon the multitude.
'That's Pippa in the pulpit, sir!',
Rinaldo squawks. The dismal dude
can guess what's coming. 'Shackle her!

Don't let her speak! She'll sway the mood!
She'll syllogise, deduce, infer!
Cap her rapping, or we're screwed!
Grab her, sling her ass in stir!'

Noble Achille Alberti,
posh and pampered though he be,
draws the line at deeds so dirty:
Pippa keeps her liberty.

Rostrum marble, milky-mellow,
glistens in the Tuscan light:
the masterpiece of Donatello
emphasises Pippa's height.

What is law? And who can make it?
Barons? Bishops? Bull, or bill?
Whichever way you want to take it,
law must be the people's will.

Our loyalty flows up the ladder,
gaberdine to ermine gown?
Beneficence descends the adder,
lordly largesse trickling down?

No, I say. The people matter.
Power is ours, and our consent
is more than mere *anathemata:*
law is more than just cement.

The men among you may have noted,
I'm a woman. Can't you see?
Disenfranchised, never voted.
Can the law apply to me?

What are humans? Eggs and sperm!
Peer or peasant, that's your measure.
Overlords should serve a term,
and serve it at the people's pleasure!'

The Viscount, both perturbed and pained
to hear *le gratin*'s new bedeviller,
though reluctant, feels constrained
to interrupt the lovely leveller.

'My dear,' began the *podestá,*
I am that very overlord
of which you speak, and here we are:
can't we cobble some accord?

A potent plaint has just been laid.
Your partner here, a proud Pugliese,
said his bed has been betrayed:
the details are a little hazy.

You're innocent, unless you speak:
soonest mended, least words said:
it's all forgotten in a week!
Don't you fret your pretty head.

Oftentimes, the judge's art
is skating round a toxic truth:
let's you and I now step apart
and find ourselves a cosy booth …'

But women are no longer 'birds',
passive decor, babes for bathing.
Impervious to flirty words,
Pippa answers, tart and scathing:

'The Prato Provost, I presume?
In prune and purple – I'm impressed!
It all falls pat – it's you to whom
my previous comments were addressed!

Yes, I sleep with Lazzarino,
as I have done from the first.
I have found my Papageno –
immolate me! Do your worst!'

Now the Viscount's in a pickle.
Conscious of the captious crowd,
notorious for being fickle,
so he offers, beetle-browed:

'What you say is food for thought.
You have moved us, roused our pity:
I'll refer this, as I ought,
to a new select committee.'

Pippa wasn't having that.
Nothing short of vindication
would do the trick. She told him flat,
the time had passed for vacillation.

'The law's a plain abomination –
where apter, than the Prato forum,
to change it, now, by acclamation?
(I'm fairly sure we've got a quorum!)

Tell us, citizens, your view:
should the burning statute stand?'
The human chorus swiftly grew,
magnificent, imperious, grand,

and there the law was scrubbed away
like dead leaves in a summer storm.
Worker bees are 'everyday',
but heaven help you when they swarm!

No-one now reads turgid prose
of futile suits, conflicting claims,
but every child in Prato knows
how Monna Pippa skipped the flames!

THE HISTORY OF THE TRUE CROSS:

(3) The Arrival of the Queen of Sheba

It's fluted composite, foreshortened horse.
It's binary. It's either this or that.
The mountains: brown, irregular and matte,
and strangely lifeless, sporting neither gorse
nor heather. Idle retinue, perforce.
The loggia: rectilinear and flat.

The human flow of halterneck and hat
serves only as a sort of satin sauce,
enlivening the lateral intercourse.
Within, a meeting to be ogled at:
without, the feckless courtiers wait. And chat.
A woman kneels (in rapture, or remorse?)
Inside the loggia – wedding, or divorce?
We need to read, to heed the samizdat.

Queen? Of Sheba? Where is that?
Pretty favoured, well-manured,
hasn't somehow quite endured:
Sonny Bono meets Sadat.

Solomon had wealthy friends
(Buddy Rich, Lorenzo Semple)
for whom he chose to build a temple:
he had means and they had ends.

Master passes to apprentice
secrets arcane, esoteric:
Cocteau (Jean) and Satie (Erik),
Semple, Dino de Laurentis.

Tree of Adam – what a sight!
We want something recherché.
Sweep the bloody thing away.
Useless juiceless stalagmite!

For his temple, in his pride,
Solomon removed the Tree
(impious, this iniquity!)
Cultures sometimes will collide.

Rabbis' faces, slapped by palms:
shrugging shoulders, rolling eyes,

'Who suggested Solly's wise?
Does this yutz not read the Psalms?'

Hundred eighteen, twenty-two:
'Paltry is your pantheon!
I will raise my temple on
that which mortal men eschew.'

(Those who steer by other tracts,
namely of the christian cult,
may with benefit consult
four-eleven *bis*, of Acts.)

Solly told his men to fell
Adam's monumental tree,
then with all celerity
conceal it in a well.

Thus the temple was erected,
as the prophets had foretold –
lots of cubits, lots of gold –
while the timber, thus rejected,

went to serve a humbler scheme.
Trodden down by beast and man,
Adam's heirloom formed a span
thrown across a narrow stream.

STRAY LEAVES: 'As fragrant as …'

As fragrant as the lone anemone,
semitic sovereign of Arabia Felix
(so, subject to the selfsame double helix),
epitome of all that's cute and femin-y,
the Queen of Sheba settled on a subtle

diplomacy termed 'distaff' (that is, 'shuttle'),
a go-between between Gath and Gethsemane:
thus Solomon received his Yemeni enemy.
She came to Israel. The Desert Vixen,
resolving on resistance and rebuttal,
brought riches in her train. The Foxy Fixer
(best thought of as a Neolithic Nixon),
seducing Solly, set her stall to scuttle
his policy – impressive, for a shiksa!

A Dream of a Stream

'Who is more famous than Sheba,
but stupider than an amoeba?
> *Un hijo de puta*
> discovered by Scooter –
the answer, of course, Justin Bieber!'

With riddles as lame-ass as this
she journeyed across the abyss.
> Throughout the Hejaz
> she was marketed as
the Mesopotamian Miss.

While sleeping, the Desert's Own Daughter
pre-emptively dreamt of sweet water,
> but couldn't work out
> what it all was about
(for her skull was the Emptiest Quarter).

She dreamt she was crossing a river
and the Great-Pass-to-Paradise-Giver
> said the log that she trod
> was her short-cut to God.
And us normal-type Joes? We're chopped liver?

The rich and the famous get tips,
are warned of commodity dips:
>they lounge by their pools
>while, incalcitrant mules,
our sole motivation is, whips.

When Sheba arrived at the Jordan,
she gave a command, *una orden:*
>'I'm crossing this quag,
>so procure me a log,
to act as a bridge I can ford on.'

Her acolytes foraged, and found
on a parcel of derelict ground
>the arbor of Adam.
>They said to her, 'Madam,
It's old, but surprisingly sound.'

And once she had crossed it, she knew:
the log was her throw-away clue:
>she knelt down and prayed.
>Boy, was Solly dismayed!
(These tales need a Sinister Jew).

He knew what the timber was worth:
by averting a Nazareth birth,
>which meant chucking the bole
>in a dirty great hole,
and concealing it deep in the earth,

he could prop up his Hebrew regime.
But Solomon's underhand scheme
>couldn't ever prevail
>(not in *this* kind of tale!)
In the face of a Sheba-type dream.

STRAY LEAVES: THE ARRANGEMENT OF THE FRESCOES

Its symmetry is perfect, as you see.
Two pound-the-pagan battles, left and right:
inside, two angels, strange celestial light.
Above, contingencies of cavity –
the Cross is buried, Judas is set free
to leave his torture-hole. The appetite
of women occupies the selfsame height:
while Helena proves authenticity,
the Queen of Sheba's praying to some wood.
Two higher panels mark the first and last:
the death of Adam leaves his tribe aghast,
Heraclius brings the Cross back to the 'hood.
The crewmen have restored the vessel's mast,
and all accords with scripture, as it should.

THOUGH CARVED IN MARBLE, it's alive with anthers,
the virile model of the axle-tree.
A column sprouts luxurious acanthus,
and separates two scenes hermetically:
left privacy, right public policy.
In each, there's something someone must anoint:
the right side imitates a matrimony.
Beyond the forest (trees and columns, joint),
left, horse and log suggest a vanishing-point.

The Queen of Sheba, leaning on her dream,
reveres the Holy Cross. Well, lucky her.
She's wealthy, so ... (forgive the *ethymeme*).
The great, without enticement, won't concur.
We shabby nobodies? We need the spur.
If God would lure us to Him, why the cheat?
Beneath the poor man's saddle place a burr,

while smoothing out the path for the elite?
Salvation's easy in the VIP suite.

Apparently, she'd never yet seen glass.
She thought the crystal floor some kind of pond,
and hitched her skirts to cross it. What an ass!
King Solomon decided he's been conned:
Reflection showed him, she was no true blonde!
Still, disinclined a cute behind to dump,
he promised half the world to the *demi-monde*.
Our 'betters' are not better (Donald Trump!):
a pity-shag, what's that? A Mercy Humppe.

The architecture's 'composite': *id est*,
Corinthian, but liberally dosed
with scrollery – full-on Ionicfest!
What would have been a rough-chopped wooden post
a while ago, has grown the chops to boast
a stylobate, and even egg-and-dart!
That baby gets the breast who screams the most,
and what starts late, may more adroitly start:
thus Carl Zeiss (Jena) slides to Seyss-Inquart.

STRAY LEAVES: 'Like any journeyman …'

Like any journeyman Annunciation
(there's one available for us to check),
we have a horizontal double-deck.
It's systemized, relentless segregation,
apartheid for the two parts of creation.
The Sheba woman interrupts her trek
to pray before a log – but what the heck?
She's wholly holy, hence the demarcation.
The layout seems unnaturally wide.
Why separate the super from the natural?

While Solomon gets serious inside,
the Queen is kneeling in the scrubby mattoral.
They pose, disposed to take it in their stride,
but why divide your tribe along the lateral?

QUELLE STESSE PAROLE!, Being the Recounting, by Tertium Quid, of an Opera he Once saw)

A YOUNG WIFE STABBED TO DEATH? YOU'VE HEARD THE STORY?
Discourage me, unnerve me, disincline,
convince me to withhold the puncture-line:
assail me with your cries of 'Basta! Fuori!'

Non mi regale con i tuoi fiori
if you suspect my motives are malign.
It's inexhaustible, this murder-mine!
Si puó? Si puó? Signore, signori!

It's strange how all our stories intertwine.
Take this one: it's a nido di memorie,
where jealousy and violence combine.
The unities (sono ventitre le ore)
are scrupulously followed and, in fine,
we're witnessing another Columbine.

THE AFTERNOON IS CLOSE AND WARM,
the villagers are in good form:
September, and the harvest's in –
so now the drama can begin!
An hour until the troupe arrives:
their play, 'The Comedy of Knives':
the strollers visit all the towns,
dressed as people, dressed as clowns.
Out at sea, a coming storm,

a sinner contemplating sin,
unsettles husbands (more so, wives!)
and stains the skyline with its frowns.

Word has travelled fast from Dattoli
(where the troupe was playing latterly):
there never yet was matter headier
than this concupiscent *commedia*.
The parish priest, biretta'd, shaven,
is sitting like a perfumed raven,
unable, though predicting ills,
to go against collective wills.
No-one here's read Lady Chatterley:
these are peasants, slower, steadier.
But still, the curate's careful (craven!)
Calabrian Vespers have pulled quills!

Dancers, actors, acrobats!
Baggy trousers, floppy hats!
They weren't born to swing a scythe,
pay a toll or weigh a tithe.
Not for them the horny hand,
tied to tilling leaden land.
They will never need to chew
on millet bread or turnip stew.
Red carnation, blue cravatte,
body supple, spirit blithe,
seguiriya, sarabande,
then tomorrow pastures new.

Here's Canio, the alpha male,
not young these days, but hearty, hale.
And in the baggage cart is Nedda:
she's a lifelong *palco*-treader,
and also Canio's wife. Behind
comes Tonio, the lonely kind.

Beppe is the sort you need,
the villain or romantic lead,
can harness horse or knock in nail:
Saladin or sawdust-spreader,
his repertoire is unconfined:
authentic strolling-actor breed.

Now Nedda, ready to step down,
takes Tonio, the solemn clown,
by hand – but Canio brushes off
the help – no snout in Canio's trough
is viewed with equanimity.
He's not prepared to let things be,
until the village diplomats
suggest adjourning to the vats
of Serafino's bar to drown
ill-humour. He agrees to quaff
away displays of enmity,
but reaches only for two hats –

that's his and Beppe's. Off they go,
but in the act of doing so,
Canio knows folks have their fun:
the naughty gauntlet must be run.
'You've left her with her fancy man?
It's not a very big divan!'
Canio's manner's plainly gruff,
but even this is not enough
to stem the jokes. 'I'll have you know,'
he tells them, 'when your prank and pun
are spent, not since the world began
has any man dared steal my stuff.'

STRAY LEAVES: A FUNCTIONING DRUNK

Let no-one doubt that Canio's in control!
A true-born leader, that's how he's perceived,
relaxed-but-ready, square-jawed, rolled-up-sleeved.
Protagonist his predetermined role,
in pole position (emphasis on pole!),
the sort who, should he feel himself aggrieved,
turns vicious. Preternaturally peeved,
not unacquainted with libation bowl
(or arma bianca, so the clown alleges),
as blunt as basalt, brittle as obsidian,
he might at last have passed his high meridian.
Look closely, and he's frayed around the edges.
His pack, who've started driving in the wedges,
will turn to Baal-Berith on the death of Gideon.

As Canio makes the tavern sign,
his wife unfurls her washing-line.
She likes to run a tidy ship:
scoops up some boots, and grabs a whip.
There's clothes to wash and carts to park.
The show is starting after dark:
before the setting of the sun,
a thousand labours must be done.
Secluded by a shady pine,
young Nedda strips down to her slip
while Tonio, the circling shark,
detects her scent and starts his run.

It isn't something Nedda planned,
but still the horse whip's in her hand:
repelled with yells and blows and curses,
the clown backs down, slinks off and nurses
his injured pride, while Nedda preens.
She's not abashed by any means,

but waiting for her lover, Silvio.
Like Guido at the Ponte Milvio,
She knows the next step must be planned.
She has her project, like all Circes,
and wants it crowned, like Danish queens.
She wonders if it won't or will be. Oh!

He's here! It's Nedda's fancy man:
they head straight for the caravan.
He's not the one to wear a mitre:
strictly lover, not a fighter,
Silvio has no need for knives.
A worshipper of others' wives,
his skill subsists in whispered charms.
He claims no right to carry arms.
Part-time lover, also-ran,
Silvio's an overnighter;
he ducks, he dives (and even thrives!)
on fire escapes and smoke alarms.

STRAY LEAVES: WANTING THE SHAFT ON

I think I'll name your thingy 'Solomon':
the Queen of Sheba really liked his wood.
I love it when I get your column 'on' –
it's all to do with stimulus and blood.

I serve you in two offices, like Taft.
The other? No, he's never understood.
Good skippers keep a watch-out, fore and aft:
I know he'd like to, not so sure he could!

I'm built for seamen. Such a nimble craft,
impressive hold for such a shallow draft,
and very steerable at either end

(one thing that he will never comprehend).
You want to move me? Make me feel the waft
of wanton winds, and see my sails extend!

BUT TONIO IS STILL AROUND.
His aspirations ran aground –
The lash still stings, as does the slight
(there's no impulsion quite like spite!)
He peeps in at the window-frame
(some must spectate, not play the game)
and knows the very thing to do:
he'll go tell Canio, stir the stew!
So Tonio the horsewhipped hound
is still, it seems, inclined to bite:
and off he slinks to name and shame,
to bluster up a ballyhoo.

Incensed by insult to his honour,
declaring Silvio a 'goner',
the husband comes to trap the *beau*
but, quick to come, not slow to go,
the latter's in the wind. You see,
a valid exit strategy
(as many husbands may discover)
adorns the toolbox of the lover.
As Canio heaps abuse upon her,
'Per sempre tua io sarò!'
calls Nedda in fidelity.
And though her man may push and shove her,

she'll not give up her lover's name,
or give a hint from where he came,
not even when she sees the knife.
Yes, Canio can take her life,
but can't control her. This *impasse*,
this morbid marital morass,

is halted (or at least postponed)
by Beppe. 'Would you have her stoned?
Who'd play Aurelia? Is your aim
to greet the fans, or beat your wife?
If you can't command the lass,
hang it – have her chaperoned!'

An oft-observed phenomenon!
Since Beppe is the only one
whom Canio respects enough
to swallow such a blunt rebuff,
the knife is sheathed, and quelled the storm.
'We have a drama to perform!'
Frills are fondled, feathers teased,
cheeks are powdered, swords are seized.
Tonio entones the antiphon,
declaiming cantos off the cuff.
Lanterns flare, mosquitos swarm:
but one man's hurt has not been eased.

STRAY LEAVES: VESTI LA GIUBBA

What might it mean, to say that I'm a man?
This dignity, this thing I think I feel,
is it ephemeral, or is it something real?
I sense I've suffered since the world began.
Her show of fondness was no deeper than
this gaudy paste of grease and cochineal.
I'm sick of acting, sick of this ordeal.
Is there no better universal plan?
Teeth and talons serve to gash and tear.
To merely live, all life must stalk, ensnare
and slaughter others, lower in the chain.
I gave the best in me, and met disdain.

Condemned to look for love, we find despair,
and this I know – but why must there be pain?

STRAY LEAVES: RAGAZZE, O PAGLIACCI?

The lavish lips, exaggerated eyes
are painted on an hour before we meet you.
The art lies in our impact, when we greet you.
You see emotion, but it's enterprise:
The punter gets the treatment while he buys,
but not for long. The trick is to repeat you:
to suck your proteins out, and then excrete you.
There's nothing real about us – colour, size,
emotions. All prosthetics, patches, dyes.
Before we pull you down, we overheat you:
distraction is our tactic to defeat you.
You'd blame chameleons for their disguise?
Go rail at Nature. We're designed to cheat you.
The static smile, laconic laugh, are lies.

* * * *

IT SEEMS THE ENTIRE VILLAGE CAME!
Now Nedda, who has changed her name
(she's 'Columbina'), being handy,
is in the audience, selling candy.
Silvio is sitting there:
she shrugs him off, whispers 'beware!'
A buttock touched, but Nedda's gone –
a joke, a smile, and then move on –
she treats the punters all the same.
Rustic, raunchy, rowdy, randy –
she's self-assured, she doesn't care –
but will there be a denouement?

A hush descends: the lights go down:
a prologue by the gloomy clown.
The curtain parts: as still as stone
sits Columbina, all alone.
The song she sings, *My World is Grey*,
explains her husband is away,
but is she sad? It's hard to tell:
she sings, he's probably raising hell:
some unknown friends, some unknown town.
She mentions the 'domestic throne',
perhaps a subtle way to say
that life at home has not gone well.

Taddeo/Tonio now arrives.
(He always tries it on with wives,
but *'professione'* – I profess –
is bringing Taddeo scant success).
His strategy, to play the fool,
earns Columbina's ridicule.
He tries for pity, plays forlorn,
but this engenders only scorn.
We know the nagging urge which drives
our menfolk to such sad excess,
but isn't *mente* meant to rule?
(Were it true, so few'd be born!)

Who's at the window cavity?
A paragon of *suaveté*!
It's Arlecchino, Bini's lover,
not too happy to discover
that Taddeo's with Columbina.
This more recent intervener
resolves to kick the other out:
it swiftly turns into a rout.
Somewhat partial to depravity
(not the clown's, she loves the shover:

forbidden grass is always greener),
the girl leaves none in any doubt:

'Io per sempre sarò tua!'
She's now impaled on Canio's skewer:
explanation's for the birds.
'Name of God! The selfsame words
you used on me, this afternoon!
You've sinned again – how opportune!
Who's your lover? What's his name?
Who's the author of my shame?'
Dragging marriage through the sewer
seems unwise, but what's absurd is
Canio's baying at the moon.
He knows he's done the very same!

The audience, not used to dramas,
sees Canio in clown's pyjamas
and swallows the illusion, whole,
so Nedda tries to stay in role:
Columbinas-Pagliaccos,
faithless women, angry machos
(just like Carmen-Don José,
it can only end one way).
While the goatherds and the farmers
pass around libation bowl
and masticate their salt pistachios,
plaint is obfuscating play.

STRAY LEAVES: A DRUNK-SHUNNING FUNK

That you revolt me, should be clear by now.
A settling of accounts is overdue.
You've proved that alcohol can loosen glue.

I've shown my disenchantment, you'll allow,
and fired so many shots across your bow,
that I'm impossible to misconstrue.
I see you now as something I outgrew.
My furrow's found a bright new shiny plough.

I'll always hate the odour of stale beer,
a stink which is preponderantly yours.
It seems to issue from your very pores.
You've often sneered at warnings. 'Insincere',
you've called my threats to leave – but never fear:
You're going to learn how women settle scores.

Since Beppe is the only one
that others can depend upon,
they turn to him to stop this trouble.
He's surging forward on the double
when Tonio blocks his path. 'So bold?
You know the drama must unfold.'
And, stranded on the makeshift stage,
two tiny lovebirds in a cage,
all hint of artifice forgone,
are scrambling through their private rubble.
The marionets, their fate foretold,
can neither deal nor disengage.

STRAY LEAVES: SHAFTING THE WANTON

One tendency that's underestimated
is men's recourse to violence when thwarted.
Their sense of mastery is oft inflated,
false feelings of entitlement distorted.

The penis and the dagger are related,
two things to which we've endlessly resorted.

If women's fate is being penetrated,
'eviscerated' means the same as 'courted'?

This thing called honour – what exactly is it?
And how's it salved by wiping out her life?
When lack of satisfaction comes to visit,
are men then meant to meet it with the knife?
The steel's the hard one (irony exquisite!)
but which one gets inserted in the wife?

A SUDDEN BLADE GLINTS IN THE LIGHTS,
and scribes an arc. The metal bites.
A frozen moment of confusion –
is this concrete, or illusion?
A sweeping frisson of misgiving –
her posture isn't like the living.
A *tableau-vivant*, stark and splendid –
disbelief remains suspended
in the temple of delights.
Some would talk of hard intrusion,
others of a brutal shivving.
Someone shouts, 'Our revels now are ended!'

TWO ANONYMOUS PAMPHLETS: ONE IN SUPPORT OF GUIDO FRANCESCHINI, ONE AGAINST HIM

WE HOLD IN AWE OUR GRECOS AND OUR GOYAS,
but all true artists have the common touch.
On pamphleteers we may not ponder much:
they're agitators, anarchists, annoyers.
Yet all our Scrooges, Sancho Panzas, Sawyers
were incubated in a humble clutch.
We'll turn away from tattle-tales as such,
though noble thinkers, standing like sequoias,

like hangers-on in seedy hotel foyers,
will pass on Belgian beer and opt for Dutch.
'Colloquial' can serve us as a crutch!
A steak may taste divine, but sometimes soya's
the better fare for unaware … (what? voyeurs?)
Who wrote the pamphlets? Could it be … the lawyers?

Tricks and Deceit

(Pro-Guido)

Count Guido cheated no-one. If at all,
deception worked to harm him. He's the dupe!
The Comparini had the bare-faced gall
to put Pompilia forward – that's to stoop
to palpable dishonesty. They offered
the tawdry progeny of urban gutters
as if a free-born lady. Pure and utter
fraud – Guido could not help but be appalled!
His noble line, untainted since The Fall,
has now been tarnished. In his social group
he meets with mockery, must face the scoffers,
his reputation wrecked. Amid the mutters,
what scrap of restitution has been proffered?
What treasure can the innocent recoup?

And how, at any rate, could these things matter?
Pietro, disappointed? He was lax:
he could have cut a deal much sleeker, fatter.
One side's not guilty if the other lacks
a basic business acumen. Take pains!
Investigate the others. Stir some dust!
Pietro took the inventory on trust,
relied on word-of-mouth and idle chatter.
Suppose a party's good at covering tracks:
suppose the other party is nonplussed:

one loses and the other therefore gains –
that's just the law of life. Is that not just?

(Against Guido)

So. Guido Franceschini lied – that's all.
He lied in writing, setting out his stall
when trying to snare Pompilia; deflected,
defrauded, double-crossed, deceived! Denied
his obvious poverty. He tried to hide
the truth because his object was to hit on
the Comparini – steal the dowry – sit on
the nest-egg offered by his teenage bride.
The rent rolls of Arezzo, once inspected,
show Guido doesn't own those things, as written.
He signed a deed the day his father died,
renouncing the estate (it's so moth-bitten,
who'd ever want it?) Guido is so small,
it's hard to credit how he once projected
himself as some grandee, grandly connected.

He's minor gentry, sprung from sorel seed.
Although betrayal is his constant rant, he
is less the floundering flower, more choking weed.
His treachery it was that raised the ante,
his motives were the vilest – hate and greed.
Just one defence he mounts, *honoris causa*,
but Guido has no honour. Like a dowser
who works a fairground audience, his lure
was always false: his motive, just to skewer
some innocent. This ragged rabble-rouser
inflicted on that child, his wife, the sewer
of public scandal so that he could plead
the dowry should be his. That's Guido's creed:
assert your silver's solid when it's scanty.
You can't hold down a job? Hence, *dilettante*!

Complain, coerce and cavil, *senza pausa*,
and when all fails, your scruffy sinecure,
one scrofulous orchard, overgrown, obscure,
is trotted out – a title! People heed
the magic of bend-sinister-azure,
defer to aristocracy, concede.
He took his bride to Tuscany to house her
(her parents also) solely to ensure
their isolation. Where their friends were fewer,
proportionally greater was their need.
And if they died of grief? Then he would trouser
the Comparini treasure. Fate decreed,
however, that he'd clash with Violante!
As outwardly serene as *Omnisanti*,
so matronly, so amiable, demure,
she sure garrotted Guido, made him bleed,
and showed us what he is – a hollow reed.

The Character of Pietro Comparini

(Pro-Guido)

So far from being a gentleman of wealth
was Pietro Comparini, you would scoff.
So parlous was the rogue's pecuniary health,
he'd dropped about as low as one can get,
and stayed afloat by trickery and stealth.
His burnt-out bonds were woebegone, and debt
encumbered them, destroyed liquidity.
Pietro, though, had settled in the trough.
He didn't have the self-respect to fret,
so totally devoid of dignity
had he become. Now all he did was quaff,
and live off handouts from the Holy See.

(Against Guido)

To cover up their own malodorous shame,
the Franceschini blackened Pietro's name.
When first it sees a snake, a packhorse shies,
since Nature gives it wit to recognise
its mortal enemy. Pietro, wise
to fictive fortunes, addled alibis,
soon figured out the Franceschini game:
they had to nullify him, burying in blame
the only one who saw with open eyes.
Pietro was a guppy, not a shark,
and so their strategy was cruelly stark –
they vilified, detracted and accused,
to keep the Comparini in the dark.
But Pietro's bite was fiercer than his bark
and, on emerging fully disabused,
unable to prevent the match, refused
to truckle with the crooks. Instead, he used
his greatest gift, his own God-given guile,
and Pietro's arrows always found their mark.

The Character of Abate Paolo Franceschini

(Pro-Guido)

Since Guido's brother was a man of peace,
he suffered much from Pietro's machinations.
Inflated claims (on both sides) he reproved,
being an honest man, an ordained priest.
Unable to endure humiliations
cascading down from Pietro with no cease,
this holy man was ultimately driven
to flee from these misfortunes and frustrations.
Pietro was the Devil, forked and hooved,
and further degradation seemed a given.

Accordingly, the Abbot upped and moved:
what Paolo needed badly was release.

(Against Guido)

Abate Paolo wasn't ever drawn
to play a pivotal part against his will.
He was the operation's brain in Rome
and pulled the strings with diabolic skill.
Chastise his brother? Hardly! He abetted,
he coaxed, advised, incentivised and petted,
was always there to help prepare the kill.
Think: what would Guido be if he were shorn
of Paolo's guidance? Just a neutered gnome,
aimless, frameless, feckless and forlorn.
One thing that bears the mark of Paolo's quill –
that 'special hearing', under Peter's Dome –
it never had a chance of happening. Still,
it reeks of the Arezzo grievance-mill,
that sense of 'we're-entitled,-you're-indebted',
conviction that they're to the manor born,
the instinct both to bluster and to fawn,
that lack-of-substance Franceschini foam.
So, why did Paolo run? What made him roam?
Perhaps he was investigated, vetted?
Could be his conscience kicked him, pricked him, fretted.
Or did he know, before that solstice dawn,
he'd need to be beyond the Pincian Hill?
The plan his brother threatened to fulfil,
The blood they were committed now to spill,
as soon besmirched a bishop as a pawn.

The Comparini

(Pro-Guido)

The *fons et origo* of all this strife,
the breakers-down of all fiduciary fences,
were Pietro and Violante, man and wife.
Above all else, two things drove them in life:
to foment mischief – and recoup expenses!
Money and mayhem addled both their senses!
Count Guido was a model of restraint,
and opened up his home without complaint:
endured the scandal, ignominy, taint
with all the Christian patience of a saint.

(Against Guido)

It's quite the polar opposite. He treated
the Comparini worse than animals, depleted
their wealth, denied them food and warmth, and viewed
their daughter as his chattel. He was cheap.
A coarse, malignant bully who was rude
to women, Guido didn't pay his bills,
ignored his marriage contract (indeed, cheated
the woman who first helped him take the leap
by bringing him the Comparini). Feud
and faction, classic Franceschini ills,
pursue him everywhere. When he's defeated
(he always is, because he lacks the skills
to manage litigation), when he's sued,
he bleats his lawyers' fees were far too steep:
refusing payment, hurries for the hills,
and everything collapses in a heap
of acrimony. With his attitude,
he'll always be the victim, always screwed.

The Franceschini

(Pro-Guido)

Left helpless by these Comparini tricks,
the Franceschini saw their hopes' miscarriage:
what could they do? Soliciting to sever
the ill-conceived and ill-portented marriage
would probably not prove a facile fix.
So far, they knew, they hadn't played it clever.
They'd fixed the family future on a whore,
and suffered much derision on that score.
They couldn't sue the Comparini – ever –
despite the animus they rightly bore.
You litigate? You open up the sore,
invite the idle gossips to disparage.
(That thing of Shakespeare's – wading through the gore).
In certain cases, when to sue is … never.
Another thought was thrusting to the fore:
annulment might be Acheron, not Styx.
The only way to show the bitch the door
might turn into the nastiest of kicks:
you lose, you're stuck with her for ever more.

(Against Guido)

If this was helplessness, what counts as might?
The Franceschini curs unleashed their spite
(to start with) on the parents, hurling threats
and tightening the life-restricting chain.
Aggression feeds the passion that it whets,
the hand is stimulated by the cane:
the punisher, emboldened to complain,
expands his jurisdiction, casts new nets.
The Comparini could no longer dwell
in such an atmosphere, but now it gets

considerably more ugly, more insane:
Pompilia descended into hell.
As property, she had no right to flight,
no angel-light to brighten up her cell,
no hope that any saviour might dispel
her misery. Before her, endless night.
The Franceschini gave their rancour rein,
their victim tangled in a hopeless plight,
and friendless. It's the way of martinets
to savage anything they cannot quell.
An enemy who can no longer fight
provokes (in most of us) a kind of pain:
confronted by a terror we can smell
(wild animals or humans, even pets),
we can't help but relent. Fierce passions wane.
But with the Franceschini, scrub all bets!
We look to them for clemency in vain.
As pre-ordained as adders are to bite,
the *dénouement* is easy to foretell.
But what of Canon Conti's pirouettes?
His vacillations haven't served him well.
Such fables as we're able to obtain
suggest his life has been extinguished, quite!

What Happened at Castelnuovo

(Pro-Guido)

Confronted with his wife's dishonest scheme
in circumstances hurtful and appalling,
the noble Guido wisely stayed his hand.
It was not he who'd clandestinely planned
this escapade. He found her whoredom galling,
a world of hurt beyond one's darkest dream.
Confederates? He had none to command:
here, in this strange and unaccustomed land,

he faced the prospect of a violent mauling.
He did what any decent man would deem
the proper thing to do. He sought the law.
Whenever tempers boil and feelings teem,
when indignation stings and nerves are raw,
the law is where a good man takes his stand.
Though human conduct has its warps and woofs,
some felonies are palpable and solid.
The Castelnuovo crime, so vile, so squalid,
provided Guido's pain with perfect proofs!
Was Guido, then, prevaricating? Stalling?
We readily concede, it could so seem.
But soft. Although exasperations gnaw,
and flames of shameless infamy are fanned,
the well-bred man, confronting the extreme,
holds back – for he is conscious of his calling.
Redress was sought and violence abjured,
the provocation of the pimp ignored.
Besides, which side resorted to the sword?
Who stood in jeopardy of life and limb?
Who, in this incident, was almost gored?
Unbalanced by the cravings of her quim,
the harlot-wife it was who lunged at *him*!

(Against Guido)

A man of honour faced with mortal strife
knows what to do. He stands up to malignity.
He'll fight Goliath to protect his wife.
But Guido is devoid of basic dignity,
and that's why those who know him all abhor him.
He bade the *sbirri* do his fighting for him.
The only time that sex was ever raised
was by Pompilia's husband. For his part,
for her he saved his muse's finest dart:
he saw to it that blatant falsehoods blazed:

his blameless wife he touted as a tart.
Pompilia's a rose, a sword's a cross,
while Guido represents an albatross.
Suppose that he had functioned as protector:
would she have hurried to the papal sector?
At every turn he's anxious to impugn
the sixteen-year-old, emphasise her vices.
Confronted with his life's defining crisis,
he acted like a snivelling poltroon.

Internecine Differences

(Pro-Guido)

The other side's asides are simply wrong.
At Castelnuovo, Guido faced a storm:
He felt some fairly equitable qualms.
He'd brought a blade, and nothing else, along,
and had a calculation to perform.
Were paramour and boyfriend bearing arms?
For thieves and runaways, that is the norm.
What if they brandished pistols in their palms?
And last September's judgment was a farce!
Adultress and abductor went scot-free!
A real court would have thrown away the key.
What ailed the bench? The French would brand her '*garce*'
(far better still, to brand it on her arse!),
and he should now be swinging from a tree!
You call it punishment? We call it petty.
Was ever such fiasco seen in Rome?
He's in Civita, eating his spaghetti,
while she was lodging free in *Le Scalette*,
until the fraudster parents took her home!
The Procurator – who will pay his fee?
Perhaps he works for love. And who's Tighetti?

(Against Guido)

How cowardly, this Guido-pamphleteer!
The nameless wonder slanders learned men
in safety, knowing that his poison pen
can stab at leisure, mostly from the rear,
aware that judge and counsel (by the bond
of legal protocol) cannot respond.
Count Guido says his spur was injured honour:
if that were so, he surely would have acted.
He didn't, so his motive must be fear.
The only person in this sorry tale
who wielded firearms was the Coward Count:
he clapped a pistol to a young girl's ear.

The Court's decision *vis-à-vis* Pompilia
was wise, well-reasoned and (what's best) humane.
What's Guido's problem? Is the man insane?
He's got a blood-lust addling his brain
(as long as he's not fighting!), haemophilia,
aversion to the prospect of agreeing,
and more so when the subject, *Le Scalette*,
is dedicated to the child's well-being.
And why throw in that mention of Tighetti,
a private citizen, not charged with any crimes?
We've guessed the answer, seen it many times.
He slights the Procurator of the Poor
and tries to tar Tighetti with a smear:
the lawyer's doing his job, and nothing more.
The other is both blameless and sincere.
But Guido's not for goodness, he's for gain.
That he's been swindled is his one refrain.
His wife is pregnant, vulnerable, frail?
So much the better: thus might he prevail!
Count Franceschini bears the mark of Cain.

The Guilt of Guido

(Pro-Guido)

That Guido killed his wife is not denied.
A long humiliation – sly affair –
elopement – constant injury to pride –
to be a cuckold in the public glare –
is more than any honest man can bear.
So, Guido must concede uxoricide,
but argues that the act was justified,
for who would kill her if he didn't care?

Three years or more together: not one child.
What happens when she turns to Caponsacchi?
She suddenly gets fertile (or defiled).
The story's sordid and the turn-out tacky.
'Contessa' (it's absurd, but so she's styled)
is nothing but a cleric's sexual lackey.

(Against Guido)

What Guido did was worse than simple murder.
A violent tunnel-vision Polypheme,
he brought a brood of brigands into Rome
(assassins native to his Tuscan loam),
in furtherance of such a heinous scheme
as Rome has never witnessed heretofore.
If that be frightful, Guido fetched it further:
he fed and lodged and armed his evil team,
devised to violate Pompilia's purdah,
to slaughter daughter, parents in their home.
Abate Paolo, too, is splashed by gore.
The Maltese mainstay, Odescalchi's girder,
he knew the basic outline – maybe more.
There's much in brother Guido to deplore,

but Paolo's going, knowing, is absurder.
A jumped-up, jawless, Jansenist Jerome,
The well-born wench his ministry's one theme,
his well-worn saw the Babylonian whore,
erotic sonnets in a calf-bound tome –
while claiming Caponsacchi is extreme!

The weakness in his case is simply stated:
the man's not mad by any normal measure.
He planned it all, and knew what he was doing.
(Or why the litigation, all the suing,
the jealous eye, pursuing Pietro's treasure?
Why all the observation, slily viewing
the Comparini household?) Guido waited
full fifteen days, then murdered at his leisure!
A homicide so deftly orchestrated,
with entry ruses, lookouts on the corner,
the villa out at Milvio, mandated
to lodge the killers, needed some construing
(to hang around the centre might just warn her!)

If Guido claims his sanity, ungluing,
resulted in her death, then why escape?
The murder plot, all autumn in the brewing,
was taking on its long-expected shape.
No, Guido wasn't some demented ape,
entangled in some unintended scrape.
Solicitor, corruptor and suborner,
He homed-in on the family he hated,
and slaughtered them because it gave him pleasure,
then ran because he felt his guilt, vacated
the scene he knew might lead to his undoing.

He tried to use the sacrament of marriage
to steal a scudo, pilfer someone's penny.
And when the treasure proved too hard to trouser,

His fallback was to denigrate, disparage.
A con-man can't rely on *honoris causa*,
for that needs honour. Guido hasn't any.

The Innocence of Pompilia

(Pro-Guido)

The proofs are plenty of Pompilia's guilt.
Apologists will struggle, in dismissing
the evidence of Caponsacchi-kissing.
Ability to write? The beans are spilt!
Her signature is proven to the hilt
and, though detractors persevere in hissing,
Contenti's even-handed reminiscing
was fatal to the stack of lies she's built.
The bed they shared? Both answered with distortions.
Her wedding-contract proves her lies. She signed!
With Caponsacchi forcibly confined,
she finds another sack of corn to grind,
to whom the cost of lawsuits she apportions:
but did he also fund her failed abortions?

(Against Guido)

The Countess suffered years at Guido's hands.
Her husband is a bully. And the house
(remember, Guido signed away his lands:
the house is not, and never will be, his)
was shaping up to be her death-trap, so
she had to flee from brother-in-law and spouse.
Relentless inquisition, query, quiz,
had taken their toll. She simply had to go,
to save her life. No motive more (or less!)
No evidence, not even weak, desultory,
exists that proves Pompilia's adultery.

Confronting death, and willing to confess,
she spoke of no concupiscence. What's more,
whatever stricture, limitation, norm
the court imposed on her, she sweetly bore.
Do guilty people readily conform?

No letters laced with love have come to light,
for one straightforward reason. None exist.
The tawdry forgeries in Guido's fist
would not convince a novice anchorite.
Why would two people, fleeing hell for leather,
concern themselves to take their letters along?
And doesn't it seem curious – nay, wrong –
that both sets, his and hers, were mixed together?

A point is taken that Pompilia signed
a contract document. So goes the claim,
it's obvious she could write. The point's declined!
The poorest peasants, people who are blind,
know how to make their mark. Of all the lame
attempts at proof, this one deserves more shame
than Guido's other arguments combined!
A young and virile man could save your life.
Suppose you write, soliciting his aid:
perhaps you hint you'd like to be his wife –
what impropriety have you displayed?
The bible and apocrypha are rife
with tales of moral matron, modest maid
who helps things happen, evil might evade,

by application of a little guile:
what would a woman be, without a wile?
It's understood that feminine allurement
has always been a method of procurement.
Composers base their operas (cacophonies!)

on legends such as Judith and Holofernes,
the ways of God and Man to reconcile!

The fairer sex, the sybilline sorority,
(so Guido says?) submits to marital fetters,
is clapped in wedlock, conquered by authority.
He really does believe it? Thinks that wives
are subjects of their husbands (that is, 'betters')?
And if they write what he deems suspect letters,
they answer for it, forfeiting their lives,
their bodies torn by hooked and jagged knives?

The driver of the diligence, 'Venerino',
has stated that the refugees were lovers.
But when one asks the question, 'What does *he* know?',
his statement falls apart, since one discovers
his back was to his charges. With no moon,
a rutted roadway, perilously strewn
with rocks and pitfalls, horses in full flight,
one doubts he saw his own rough hand that night.
His words remain his words, but words can fail,
and wiser counsels oftentimes prevail,
when context is considered. They just might
have bought his words, by freeing him from jail.

The screed in Guido's favour makes great play
of Castelnuovo, and the junior groom
Jacopo, whom it celebrates, and whom
it honours with the *sobriquet* of 'host'.
It claims the said assistant seems to say
(it's quoting from his evidence-in-chief)
that Caponsacchi, in Pompilia's room,
was cuddled up beside her where she lay.
Is this an issue, or an idle boast?
That morning, in that now far-distant May,
Jacopo, in attendance at his post,

saw sword-hilts grasped, a burgeoning affray.
A lawyer's adage: 'Counsel comes to grief
when praying witness statements in relief
unless he reads the page which follows.'
When cross-examined, the selfsame witness said
he saw nobody sharing any bed.

Here, within the papal jurisdiction,
adultery's a capital offence.
So, what of Caponsacchi? His conviction
brought just a change of parish. That's immense!
The court discerned a minor dereliction
of priestly etiquette, a lack of sense.
To hint at more is fiction and pretence!

Topsheet Teaser

At Caponsacchi's trial, no guilt was found.
My evidence? No punishment accrued.
No proof was proffered – not one single ground.
How should the 'Fugae' topsheet be construed?

The topsheet, slightly tattered, lightly browned,
displays the word 'adultery'. When viewed
by one atop the Areopagotic mound,
who knows the courts, I'm driven to conclude

it's simply wrong. Law clerks reduce to writing
the judgments that they've recently (mis)heard,
while advocates and litigants are fighting
to buttonhole those clerks, contend, consult.
Some harrassed Clerk has copied, word for word,
the allegation, not the case result.

THE TOPSHEET OF THE PRESENT PLAINT, today,
the Guido murder trial – a case in point!
What might the dateline in the corner say?
Some sloppy scribe decided to anoint
the document with month and year, conjoint –
the problem is, it's sixteen ninety-eight,
but March has yet to happen. Said in play,
for sure, but errors can – and do – occur.
The case we may re-open, as it were,
and Caponsacchi's innocence infer.

Adultery must happen in a place.
It's not a chimera, it leaves a trace.
They didn't do it on the road to Rome:
Thrown back and forth in thundering calesse,
by Venerino viewed, invigilated,
beset by botheration and distress,
(it wasn't quite the night for playing chess!)
it's fairly sure that no-one fornicated.
Nor could the thing occur in Guido's home:
Pompilia was under house arrest.
Their scrutiny outmatches 'fine tooth comb'.
Forbidden to approach the windows, lest
she got her just deserts, the family, stressed,
(our readers will forgive the palindrome)
observed her without respite, without rest.
In Castelnuovo, neither: riding hard,
the couple barely slept and barely ate.
When Guido came upon him in the yard,
the Canon, fully-clothed, serene, sedate,
was seeing to the horses, standing guard.

And if we grant the premise? Cede the sex?
What was the Comparini's mortal sin?
Their corpses left as mutilated wrecks,

With heads attached to bodies by mere skin,
they'd been defaced by barbs, from crown to chin.

Four days they held her in a squatting pose
because she couldn't sit and couldn't lie,
tormented by her wounds. She did not try
to criticise, calumniate or curse
her killer. As the testimony shows,
she bore no rancour – really, the reverse.
The whispered words she fought to interpose
through gasps of pain serve only to disclose
the deepest decency a human knows:
to grant forgiveness to her mortal foes,
as life was bleeding out. What could be worse?
This modest little fawn, retiring, shy,
had only men to bathe her, change her, nurse
her through those long last hours, those final throes,
her daylight narrowed by the waiting hearse.

So, who could be so callous in that strait,
to disregard the peril to her soul?
Who'd choose to meet her Maker, less than whole?
Misrepresent the truth, prevaricate,
when balanced on the brink of heaven's gate?

Canon Conti

(Against Guido)

The keystone of it all is little-known
to Romans. Canon Conti was a priest,
averse to friction, fond of comfort grown,
some say the archetypal aretine.
He loved good jokes, good company, good wine,
and from the evidence that has been pieced
painstakingly together, it appears

that nothing in his nature was malign.
An easy-going reveller, one hears
(perhaps a trifle squeamish, lacking spine),
but liked by all, from greatest down to least.
Arezzo politics are byzantine,
but ever since *confetti* sweets were thrown,
the Canon had been seeking to align
with Franceschini *and* Pieve spheres:
but, isolated in the battle zone,
at bay between his in-laws and his peers,
he couldn't seem to function on his own.
The seeds of his destruction had been sown:
he saw the leading families combine.
Hostility towards him had increased
(his warmth towards Pompilia, the yeast),
and then last month the Canon's darkest fears
were realised. The Canon is deceased.

Who Is the Malign Spirit?

(Against Guido)

The Franceschini have a boss – but who?
Whose is the brain that's steering all they do?
It can't be Guido. (Note: we said, a 'brain'.)
There's someone thinking all their actions through.
You'd postulate it's Guido? Too much strain!
It's not Abate Paolo, precious prelate:
an eminence for sure, but purely grey:
the man to hatch the plan, but not to sell it:
and when the gloves came off, he ran away.
It's never Beatrice. Hate her only fuel,
she certainly possessed the motivation.
But though she was unquestionably cruel,
great age had withered her imagination.
Who, then, is left? Gave Canon Conti poison?

Had learned enough to forge romantic letters?
Possessed the character to goad the boys on?
Believed the Franceschini had no betters?
We bow before the laws of defamation.

PRIMUS STUDIORUM DUX

THERE'S ALWAYS SOMEONE OUT TO BOWL A BEAMER,
enslave us or deprave us, even 'Circe' us:
the prey can only pray for a Redeemer,
a selfless Guelph, a personable Perseus.

Life will, of course, defeat us in the end,
but still we thrill, instilled in shrill belief
that rescue's near. Our superhuman friend
is on his way (right now!) to our relief.

In vain cocaine was leant on by DeLorean,
and Shelley's skylark didn't stop him drowning,
but Lizzie Barrett merited a saviour.
Her hero was an eminent Victorian,
the rescuer of spinsters – Robert Browning!
A Belisarius bestrode Belgravia!

IMAGINE YOU'RE A WOMAN, with a mind
as trained, acute and fertile as exists.
Imagine that your erudite, refined
creations top each year's best-seller lists.

You write in English, French and Portuguese.
Translating ancient classics from the Greek,
(for you, no bigger deal than shelling peas)
you thrill the world, to hear Orestes speak!

But this is eighteen forty. There's a catch.
You're middle-aged and single. 'On the shelf'.
Your father keeps you housebound, unattached:
he wants you as a frill, not for yourself.

The man's a monster. You're not free to act.
He holds you here, unnoticed, bored, unwed.
Your only means of protest at the fact
of kidnap is, you've taken to your bed.

Like many women, both before and since,
you're 'delicate'. It's how you take a stand.
But what of that long-dreamed of, handsome prince,
your rescuer? Don't worry. He's at hand!

Elizabeth M. Barrett is your name.
A gentleman comes calling, loves your work.
He's Robert Browning, of 'Sordello' fame,
and suddenly there's light amid the murk!

He shows up every day at Wimpole Street,
and soon you loosen the paternal tether:
with Mister Browning, you've re-found your feet!
You'll marry him, then run away together!

The banns were read discreetly, days ago:
the journey's booked. No vacillating now!
The father's out on business: down below,
in Wimpole Street, a hansom waits: but how

to saunter past the servants? What a fright!
My trusty Wilson – glad I could suborn her:
Well, here we go – I'll sleep in France tonight!
Brave Robert's waiting, just around the corner!

The thing was carried off without a hitch.
They wed, they fled. So farewell, Wimpole Street!
And far from wish undone her Dunmow Flitch,
Elizabeth's contentment was complete.

One's fate can turn upon a single act.
Two poets lived as one – idyllic bliss!
They now had what they previously had lacked –
each other. Fiction can't improve on this!

I DREAMT I DWELT IN MARBLE HALLS,
Being a Tale related by Cristina Paperozzi

IN A LITTLE *CITTADINA*
not so many years ago,
'twixt the Arno and the Po
there occurred a misdemeanour
which upset the status quo.

Mi ricordo tanto quando
all the people lived at ease,
close to Parma (lots of cheese!)
and our handsome Duke Bertrando
even liked the Piedmontese!

With his consort Isabella,
lucky man, this Duke Bertrando,
riding in the open landau
(*anche lei è molto bella*),
like a youngish Marlon Brando.

Every bower has its bug,
every paradise its devil:
someone ugly and dishevelled

was about to pull the plug:
Ormondo wasn't on the level.

Who is this Ormondo guy?
Placeman at the ducal court,
wants a girl in every port:
thinks the Duchess worth a try,
thinks he might 'besiege the fort'.

Isabella, young in years,
doesn't wait to contemplate him.
She won't even tolerate him.
Insults stinging in his ears,
he must hear the girl berate him!

Now Ormondo wants to hurt her.
Why not truss her like a goat?
Maroon her in an open boat?
Cut her adrift, desert her,
abandon her to climes remote?

'I'll explain she's got a man.
Adding relish to the platter,
furnishing dishonest data,
furthering my evil plan,
leave her name in tawdry tatters.'

Since Ormondo had a crony,
this accomplice lent a hand.
Grabbing Isabella, and
abducting her, this same Batone
took her to La Spezia strand,

placed her in a ruined boat
and towed her to Livorno Sound
(that's where poet Shelley drowned):

barely did it stay afloat
until, at last, it ran aground

on a lonely, rustic beach
in a place that's named Corniglia
(bit like Yorkshire, only hillier).
Isabella tried to reach
rocks adorned with bougainvillea,

where a road wove through the wood.
Someone praying at a grotto
in a *tono molto sotto*
said, 'Your dress is far too good
(by the way, I'm Tarabotto)

to snag it on these thorns and brambles.
Why are you alone out here?'
The man exuded wholesome cheer.
'Never, in my countless rambles
have I met a child so dear!'

(In our hour of stress and danger,
how it helps to have a friend!
Here comes one who will defend
our heroine – a kindly stranger,
loyal and watchful to the end!)

Tarabotto left off praying,
took his staff and shoulder-bag.
'Just beyond that limestone crag
where those mountain goats are playing,
lies my home. We mustn't lag:

my *signora*'s cooking lunch!
She can furnish clean attire,
and we've got a roaring fire.

Could be wrong, but I've a hunch
you're no cowgirl from the byre!'

Far too weary to demur,
Isabella followed on.
Happiness, it seemed, was gone
and most unlikely to recur.
What would be the *dénouement*?

    * * * *

What could Isabella do?
Clearly it was politic
(instead of roaming, weak and sick,
sleeping in the morning dew)
to perpetrate this happy trick.

Tarabotto and his wife,
rooted in the Tuscan loam,
offered her a loving home.
She resolved to live the life,
though it be in monochrome.

Forest folk were fended off,
told she was Dolores' niece, a
girl who'd lived thus far in Pisa.
Scrubbing floor and filling trough,
she took the name (and role) of 'Nisa'.

Nisa never told the truth,
never bragged of marble halls.
Wooden cabin, logs for walls
must suffice our rural Ruth,
marchioness of milking stalls.

On occasion, she recalls
the heavy velvet of her dress,
emblem of lost happiness.
In this world of clogs and shawls,
Nisa knows she once was blest.

Lying in its wooden chest,
perfume folded in its furls,
darkness drowning gems and pearls,
Nisa's gown is laid to rest,
taffeta and satin swirls

shut away, as if she'd hid
all prospect of return, and shrunk
from hope, illusions sunk
beneath the weighty wooden lid
which capped that rough and rustic trunk.

Placing her aboard that barque
on that cold, abandoned strand,
brute Batone never planned
a crumb of comfort. In the dark,
something must have stayed his hand:

a portrait of her husband-duke,
undervalued, cast away,
looked up at him from where it lay,
an unignorable rebuke.
He threw it in, then cast away.

* * * *

Now she's looking at the picture:
in the cabin, weeps alone.
Feelings she has never shown,

thanks to self-denying strictures,
force her silence. Unbeknown,

on a little block of wood
Isabella writes some verses
setting out the love she nurses,
but believes is gone for good.
With her love, she intersperses

reasons why she's held her tongue.
Evil men traduced her honour.
Never was a *bella donna*
visited with greater wrong.
Leggere la sua buona …

In her solitude, she said:
'Bad men claimed I'd lost my virtue.
Being powerless to alert you
(I was kidnapped, never fled),
I'll stay silent, never hurt you.'

Isabella to Bertrando

There never was a love more taintless, chaste
than this I feel for you. I did not slight
the trust that you reposed in me, despite
the slurs you've heard. And now I'm faced
(though faultless) with a life of needless waste,
I'm striving still to occupy the height
of self-denial. By this sacred light
which guides me, I will not see you disgraced.
My fate it is to find myself encased
in misery, but cannot let my plight
besmirch your honour, which must blazon white
for all humanity. In you I placed

my selfhood when I wed you. Others' haste
to slander me will not extinguish Right.

Decency can't help but shine,
no matter how it's drowned in gloom.
Dolores never would presume
to peer inside that chest of pine
but one day, cleaning Nisa's room,

found the portrait, then the block
which contained the sonnet, and
recognising Nisa's hand,
felt she should undo the lock,
and quickly came to understand:

the child was married to a duke.
Somehow she had been maligned,
somehow to the sea consigned.
'Choice or chance or fate or fluke
brought her here. Why were we blind?'

Now the gown made perfect sense.
Little Duchess Isabella
wasn't some obscure *zitella*.
No use sitting on the fence –
Tarabotto has to tell her …

That's when Tarabotto came
across the threshold, grinning wide,
swollen with domestic pride.
'I've been chosen, I've been named
to be Bertrando's local guide!'

This could not be simple chance.
(Nisa absent, gone to town
to barter eggs and eider down),

and this latest circumstance:
Duke Bertrando, whose renown

spread through Tuscany, was due,
with impressive entourage:
Tarabotto placed in charge
of helping with the passing-through:
this was Destiny, writ large!

'Don't be taken in, Your Grace!
That one's gone! Admit, you lost her!
This is clearly an impostor!
Don't you recognise the face?
(I suspect it's Jody Foster!)'

What a tangled web we weave
when we practise to deceive!

THE BROWNING VERSION

Why even would you make this crude incursion?
At best, you're going to end up vilified.
The lady's not for burning – *you'll* be fried!
Depiction of The Prophet would be safer!
You read about Pompilia Francesca,
and suddenly you think you're Arnold Wesker!
You claim it's true, your story, like you're Lucian:
Well, all you're going to get is retribution!

I didn't want to slight The Browning Version,
or settle, in my overweening pride,
on swimming stubbornly against the tide.
Instead, I tried to be a triplet Shaffer,
a chortling Orton to his formal Rattigan,
play up the couple and play down the Vatican.

I always knew my slew was Lilliputian,
as much in concept as in execution.

You see me as a Mede, though I'm a Persian.
I'm trying to see legality applied,
not seeking socio-cultural suicide.
You'd think I'd mocked the eucharistic wafer!
Like arteries, opinions tend to harden:
prepare your mightiest bolt for fools in Arden.
Dilution, diminution, prostitution?
Thank goodness none of us is Rosicrucian!

TO A MOLINIST

You'd hand us, then, the hottest of potatoes?
It doesn't need a twenty-tome tractatus.
Some ships are meant for people, some are freighters:
a telescope will show the moon has craters.
Molinos, grinding blind, can only grate us:
Your meaning-middens merely enervate us.
God's not the statement (rather, the hiatus!),
goes undisclosed to logic-operators.
'Supreme'? A glacier's dream, on which we're skaters,
and not some scheme of syllogism-staters.
The Find's defined by nature's indicators,
and never by meridians, equators,
or man-contrived, unwieldy apparatus:
unless The Simplest, cannot be The Greatest.

IL PASTOR FIDO, Being a tale told by Giacinto Arcangeli, Procurator of the Poor)

THE LIFE AND SOUL OF PANTOMIME OR PARTY
(with footprint from Spoleto down to Spain),
Arcangeli the Advocate is fain
to celebrate commedia dell'arte
(or anything remotely D'Oyly-Carty)
– we ought to add, he has a first-rate brain
(on which account he's pardonably vain).
At memorising mounds of stuff by heart, he
is number one. He's learnt a play verbatim –
the drama, Amaryllis and her swain –
with sharp recall that's anything but hazy!
As sybarite we'd surely have to rate him,
since self-denial goes against his grain.
His Parma playhouse palco – il Farnese!

STRAY LEAVES: 'Our human curse …'

Our human curse (or blessing)? To explain!
The Old Pretendor, or the Younger Pitt,
a destiny that's manifest (True Grit?
The Shootist? Which encapsulates John Wayne?
Some sapphic subtext stalks Calamity Jane?)
We pull apart, dismantle, sever, split
and seek what's close to kosher, most legit:
to leave it peaceful goes against the grain.

Accounting for an outbreak of malaria,
we leap upon the sacred, not profane.
It falls on Man to expiate some stain.
The gods inflict a Blokhin or a Beria
according to a consequential chain,
to punish us for Burgess and Maclean.

STRAY LEAVES: 'The cause, we later find …'

The cause, we later find, was more mundane
(a parasite that likes mosquito-spit).
Our 'wait-a-minute,-that-thing-wasn't-it)
is what we do when germs prove more germane.
We want Andromeda to take the strain,
but often, 'it was magic' doesn't fit,
and Hillandale's the villain – biter, bit –
for, after all, the yankees sank the Maine.

The self-abusers sometimes turn up hairier:
could Courtly Love not salvage Kurt Cobain?
(Or was it Courtney Love? Please ascertain.)
Perhaps, as one explains, one should be warier:
a shotgun blast can incommode the brain:
'the gods are thirsty' – feeblest refrain!

ARCADIA, the magic land
of hooting owls and chirping crickets!
Summers long, and winters bland:
the girls make love, the bees make wax,
and no-one's heard of parking tickets
or paying Value-Added Tax.

Babbling brook, romantic crag!
Sturdy oak, and verdant green!
Happiness? It's in the bag!
Daisies decorate the sward
as pigeons coo, and peacocks preen:
nothing harsh or untoward

could ever stop our crops from springing.
Sparkling wine and frothing beer,
nightingale and throstle singing!
Economy, classed as 'emerging':

things are cool – but, once a year,
we have to sacrifice a virgin.

Nor nematodes nor arthropods
would be enough – she must be human.
To mollify our gloomy gods,
to death a maid we must consign,
and this we do – always presuming
her ancestry is part-divine.

We're bothered by an ancient curse.
To expiate an age-old wrong
(or even put it in reverse)
two young people must get wed
who, like the virgins, must belong
to dynasties divinely-bred.

There's Silvio. It's widely known
that he would rather slaughter deer
than offer any girl a bone.
He loves the forest and the chase
and always acts a little queer
when there are birds about the place.

Amaryllis (foxy chick)
also claims Olympian blood.
Of local totty, she's the pick:
with a forebear such as Pan
Amaryllis really could
win the heart of any man.

Arcadians are fearful that
should these two become estranged
there's no-one else to put in bat.
With end in mind of ending doubt,

nuptials have been arranged
(country folk don't hang about!)

Plot Complications

But Silvio cares nothing for love or romance,
gives no thought to kissing, has not learned to dance:

completely phlegmatic to poems and music,
in matters of courtship, a stone-cold refusenik.

If Silvio's sluggish at stirring the lymph,
the same can't be said for Dorinda the Nymph!

Dorinda's besotted with lover-boy Silvio:
she'd padlock herself to that *Ponte* named *Milvio*

or cut off her curls for one cosy caress,
but Nimrod the Hunter just couldn't care less!

Another young lover we're keeping our eye on –
Myrtillo the Shepherd, an ardent Achaian –

is so overcome with romantic afflatus,
it might interfere with his refugee status.

He doesn't love Flora, Fiona or Phyllis –
he's head over heels with our own Amaryllis!

Though Rilly the Filly returns his affection,
she's leaving him grieving. Abject, his dejection!

She's told him to keep it like sister and brother:
the reason is clear – she's betrothed to another!

You find it confusing? The going gets brisker!
Myrtillo is loved by a nymph named Corisca!

(To follow this plot calls for copious computers):
Corisca herself is pursued by two suitors!

And who are the suitors? Well, *satyrus primus*:
her four-legged friend bears the name Polyphemus.

Please pardon the poet if by pastors you're peppered!
The other who's hopeful? One Corydon, shepherd.

I:1 SILVIO, LINCO

Sylvan Silvio

How I love the break of dawn
      beneath the stately trees!
The curly fern, the timid fawn –
      and summer's lavish ease.

The spreading spurge, the furtive fox –
      delightful to the senses!
And Linco, of the greying locks,
      my prized amanuensis!

Linco's Lament

Had I but such a ruddy cheek
      as you, young friend,
then I would be the Greekest Greek!
      I see my end

approaching, as the ebb of life
      goes on, apace:

but you are due to take a wife –
>   so, run the race!

I love your cheek (I love them, both!)
>   That youthful curve
becomes you, and I, on my oath,
>   live just to serve.

Between your cheeks I'd interpose
>   some honeyed words:
for love is verse, while hunt is prose.
>   Observe the birds!

My age commands me leave the field
>   to younger bloods,
reluctant though I be to yield:
>   farewell to woods!

The sage has spoken heretofore
>   *of loving misdemeanour:*
and now he tells a yarn of yore –
>   *Amintas and Lucrina.*

Amintas and Lucrina

The blackbird in the myrtle-tree
>   who sings at evensong
is telling of a tragedy,
>   lamenting ancient wrong.

Amintas and Lucrina loved,
>   but not in equal part:
Lucrina, prinked and painted, gloved,
>   had fortified her heart.

Her man Amintas, loyal, true,
        was faithful and devout.
But what did vain Lucrina do?
        She gave her favours out!

Amintas' love grew deeper, while
        Lucrina waxed more flighty –
comportment which was sure to rile
        Love's goddess, Aphrodite.

The goddess' forehead wore a frown,
        her lovely eyes were narrow
as, from Olympus aiming down,
        she loosed a golden arrow.

The missile's hit was mighty hard,
        the suffering immense:
our fruit lay rotting in the yard,
        for all was pestilence!

'We must our rulers have displeased,
        some deity insulted:
the heavens have to be appeased,
        the Oracle consulted!'

(An oracle's a sort of god
        that lives in rocky cracks.
On things to come it gives the nod,
        so humans might relax.)

The voice wailed out like Marley's Ghost –
        what else to sing a dirge in?
'Lucrina's toast, but uppermost,
        each year, one trembling virgin.'

'How may we pray the curse away,
        or put the thing on ice?'
'Your prayers don't work. Don't be a jerk.
        Just make the sacrifice.'

'Our teeny-boppers, yearly topped,
        will more than likely strain us.
Is there some sop we might adopt?'
        (This from the priest Montanus.)

'Oh, very well,' the Voice from Hell
        from out its crevice drifted.
'If we hear tell of wedding bells,
        the sanction will be lifted.'

'But bear in mind, we want the kind
        of candidates that matter.
So, be inclined to only find
        Saul Bellow or Sepp Blatter.'

'It's all been aired,' The Voice declared:
        'You've had your forecast fun.
Two people paired, Arcadia spared.
        Go on, then. Get it done.'

They took as read what Voice-Hole said.
        Why not a dancing pigeon?
Believe your bread's a dude long dead?
        How wacky is religion?

Lucrina had to lose her life:
        Amintas upped and said,
'I ask that I should wield the knife.
        Why not kill me instead?'

Amintas paid his lover's price
        without a second thought:
Lucrina saw the sacrifice
        and cried aloud, distraught:

Lucrina's Lament

O faithful love, O valiant love!
        You have offered me
        devotion, blemish-free,
the ardour of the mating dove!

O guiding light, O northern star!
        Now I have it clear:
        my fate is, to adhere:
I come to you, wherever you are!

And, taking up the sacred blade,
        she plunged it in her breast:
thus, uncomplaining, undismayed,
        a higher love expressed.

I:4 MONTANUS, solo

A Funny Thing Happened on the Way to the Amphitheatre

Though now a man you'd trust to cash your gyro,
in youth the High Priest's practices were heinous
(it's not by accident he's called 'Mont-Anus').
Today he wouldn't steal a bookie's biro,
far less frequent the dodgy parts of Cairo.
Not marching now with Scipio Africanus
nor undertaking former go-both-wayness,
he meets by chance his lifelong friend, Tityro.
(We'd liken Monty to the deity Janus
– the go-both-ways thing – but what would it gain us?)

They've come here to the theatre to assuage
preoccupations brought on them by age.
Where better than the ring of Orchomenos,
to sit and think before the sacred stage?

MONTANUS:
I love to tread upon this hallowed ground
              and look around
              and feel the power
that wells up from the earth. This is the hour,

when Aphrodite ushers in the dawn,
              not so forlorn
              as evening guise,
when she, the only light to fire the skies –

ENTER TITYRO

TITYRO:
My friend! Twice fortunate am I this morning,
              as heaven's awning
              discloses you
here in the theatre, beneath the blue,

my purpose is to ponder parenthood.
              So wise, so good,
              what brings you here,
companion of my youth, revered and dear?

MONTANUS:
I, too, am here because I am a father:
              I'd put it, rather,
              in terms of pain:
I lost my son, but feelings still remain.

A dream has troubled me this very night
                without respite:
                and once again
I come to shun the company of men.

TITYRO:
My daughter, as you know, will marry soon:
                far from a boon,
                this coupling
besets me as an unauthentic thing.

A marriage is a union of two hearts,
                but this one starts …
                I pause, my friend:
relate your dream. I'd hear it to the end.

Montanus' Dream

What is this grief that follows me?
What is this inner lethargy?
Must I forever bear this guilt?
And cry, for milk that's long since spilt?
A kind of curse it often seems
that follows me through all my dreams.

If this, my office, has a use
(the high priest of Arcadian Zeus)
then I will learn, before I die,
what these dreams must signify.
Be it early, be it late,
dreams are all I contemplate.

In my youth it all seemed sport,
and action skipped ahead of thought:
thus, wastefully, is wisdom won!
I altered when I lost my son.

Twenty winters came and went,
twenty autumns to repent.

I wove his cot of river reeds,
unequalled for a baby's needs,
a covered coracle in form:
but then there came that sudden storm
and Alfeo's alluvion
rose up, and child and cot were gone.

A dream of triumph and regret
(whose curious humour's with me yet)
kept on recurring though the night
has left me devastated, quite:
it spoke of love and loss, of nation,
of heartbreak and of consolation.

Seated, I, on Alfeo's flanks
(I find I'm drawn to river banks),
I saw an old man with a boy.
'This one you must not destroy,'
he told me, as he left the child.
At this, the clouds churned black and wild.

The river had been, up to this,
the bluest badge of summer bliss,
with glassy depths and frothing narrows –
but instantly to bows and arrows
its waters turned, yet kept on flowing.
The child beside me, somehow knowing

that comfort was my pressing need,
tugged at my hand, to bid me heed.
He pointed to the myrtle bush
where sat a songbird (blackbird? thrush?)

and once again the sun burst through,
and colour fired the land anew.

'Before there's joy, there must be woe,'
the creature sang. 'This must you know.
He who accepts, and pays the cost –
his happiness shall not be lost.
The storm will spend itself, and then
Arcadia will be fair again.'

The Complaint of Polyphemus

I:5 POLYPHEMUS, solo

I swear I'll get revenge on you, Corisca!
Olympus damn you, and all heartless schemers!
What's good enough for ram, will serve for ewe:
I'm not the sort of satyr to be crossed,
and I will be to you as frost to grass!

What kind of useless losers do you deem us?
What makes you think that you can, with us, screw?
Do you suppose we like it, being tossed?
You'll know it when my hammer hits your glass!
You'll royally regret your role as risker!

Complacent! I will pierce you, through and through!
The hard of heart will live to count the cost.
The prick, and not the trick, quickens the ass.
A fraudster-broad like you must needs be brisker
to put one over on old Polyphemus!

You think to fling me out to face the frost?
Acerbic-souled, you're cold, and bold, as brass!
Your arrogance is hanging by a whisker.

You're not the first who's tried to bowl me seamers:
you're just the latest case of *déjà vu*.

You use me and abuse me, then you pass:
a shallow and a shameless trivial frisker!
You deem us imbeciles, and then you cream us!
But I will punish, persecute, pursue!
We'll see, before I'm through, who's won, who's lost!

II:1 MYRTILLO, with Shepherds

Myrtillo Recalls an Agreeable Experience

Myrtillo is an immigrant. As such,
he enters on the lowest social rung
and, being able-bodied, fit and young,
is put to shepherding. He can't earn much,
but high-born ladies haven't slipped his clutch.
In some forsaken field, amid the dung,
uncelebrated, unobserved, unsung,
he tells of Amaryllis, she whose touch
abides with him and animates his soul.
And as he tells his tale of love among
the shepherds, leaning on his crozier pole,
and every ounce of sympathy is wrung
from simple hearts, one sees that, on the whole,
Myrtillo is apparently well-hung.

WHEN FIRST I CAME, the maidens thought it novel
(Achaian accent, and my slender form:
I hadn't yet the aspect of a man).
Since then, I've had to bow and scrape and grovel,
accepting as my lot my shepherd's hovel.
I know not if they had subversive aims,
but I was welcome in their teenage dorm
– and take my word for it, their welcome's warm!

We played all sorts of pretty parlour games.
Which one was I? Persephone, or Pan?
And that's exactly where the fun began:
that not-quite-knowing seemed to fan the flames!

The rite one night was, depilate my thighs
and slip a kirtle on my slender hips
(they baited me, to see if I would rise!)
Then, not content adorning me in gauze,
They kneaded rouge into my needy lips.
My forehead was enhanced with latticed lace
and colour painted on my hairless face:
my hair, unspared, got alice-band and grips.
As per the universal law of squaws,
they flayed irregularities and flaws,
erasing any trace of out-of-place,
and somehow gave me sexy, soulful eyes!

Diaphanous and dainty like the rest,
I felt, for once, how they feel all the time,
though Amaryllis was by far the best,
acknowledged by the others as sublime
(I couldn't help but note her tiny thong).
And then they said there had to be a mime,
called 'Dido and Aeneas Share a Kiss'.
I found myself inexorably pressed
towards participation's precipice
(you guessed – with Amaryllis). What a tongue!
I'd never known intensity like this.
Our kiss was louche, lascivious ... and long.

Since Rilly was the sleeping-quarter queen,
she offered me the kissing-cousin prize.
She'd clearly found a thing she could enjoy.
I thought I heard her mention 'overflow'.
Was I a girl to her? Was I a boy?

Or did I hover somewhere in between?
And does it even matter? Who's to know?
I'm not sure if she's innocent, or wise,
and though I'm basking in the afterglow,
she's not as keen as maybe might have been,
indifferent her glances and replies.
I feel inept with girls (the word is 'coy').

II:2 DORINDA, SILVIO

Ill Met by Moonlight

In desperation, dryad doll Dorinda
is chasing Silvio. Both are on the hunt.
In baseball parlance, Silvio opts to bunt,
but Dorrie is as dangerous as tinder.
As someone said (perhaps the poet Pindar),
the only way to make the piglet grunt
is, stick it thoroughly. A little blunt,
you think? No, florid phrases hinder!
'You bagged one baby goat? That's all you did?
Is there no female fox you'd rather find?'
He totes the goat between them (tertium quid?)
as if it hid him. Clearly, love is blind.
His thoughts to infant ungulates confined,
he asks her lamely, 'Do you want a kid?'

As HOMER TELLS, Arcadia's filled with flocks.
If Silvio is somewhat slow to rise,
Dorinda disses crap Achaian cocks.

With men, it doesn't help to criticise:
'cajoled' works better, 'chidden, softly chaffed'.
Go frontal, and it falls contrariwise.

Dorinda has her faults, but she's not daft!
'She wins,' she knows, 'who never knocks, but mocks.'
A man is manageable, once he's laughed.

She closes in on Silvio the Ox
and, gazing at him with those doe-like eyes,
as well as flicking back her curly locks,

Route One (direct approach) the dryad tries.
'When will you pierce me with that hunter's shaft?'
Rebuffed again! It's time to weaponise.

Since he won't board her, neither fore nor aft,
what sinks a sailor swiftly? Hidden rocks!
This calls for cunning, and some womancraft:
Dorinda will adopt a deft disguise!

II:3 AMARYLLIS, *sola*

Hymn to Arcadia

O, happiest the shepherdess
who, with companions gay
and innocent of ugliness,
just whiles away the day.

No need to labour in this land:
we sway from play to sleep,
since Nature, prodigal and bland,
provides abundant sheep.

Who notices the years flit by?
We're never pressed or put on.
On lower pastures as on high,
lamb slowly grows to mutton.

ENTER CORISCA

CORISCA
O Amaryllis! Sight for my sore eyes!
(Save that I herded you ...) What a surprise!

AMARYLLIS
Acclaimed as constant, nymph of wide renown,
Corisca! My, your skin is very brown.

CORISCA
You flatter me, I think. You, more than me,
are here to celebrate the myrtle tree.

Ode to the Myrtle Tree (Duet)

There's many wish for bushes lush as ours,
but we alone can claim the fertile myrtle:
we sculpt its boughs to grace our shady bowers.

Athenians can keep their golden showers.
As pretty as a girl's embroidered kirtle,
our myrtle, like the chest of Austin Powers,

invokes San Gimignano's phallic towers.
Our land requires the voice of not one turtle:
we spurn your Lydgates, as we shun your Gowers.

Berlin can keep its Moabits and Mauers.
We're in no haste to be displaced, or hurtle
towards a fate which sooner, later, sours.

CORISCA:
What do you want in life?

AMARYLLIS:
> Happiness.

CORISCA:
> One?

But why not two, or three?

AMARYLLIS:
> Contentment!

CORISCA:
Oh, I see. Your marriage is approaching:
just let me know if you require some coaching.

AMARYLLIS:
I'll tell you frankly …

CORISCA:
> What?

AMARYLLIS:
> … I'm reconciled,

but wretchedly unhappy. He's a child.

CORISCA:
His pedigree's unequalled, I am told.

AMARYLLIS:
So? Silvio has no standing, leaves me cold.
Our wedding night will be a rite of rape.

CORISCA:
You don't have any method of escape?

AMARYLLIS:
A woman is a chattel, bought and sold.

IN TRUTH, I'm not at all disposed to marry.
Though not too hot on ratiocination,
or all the pros and cons of vitiation,
I mean to end this thing, and will not tarry.
The forest! What's it got, but carbonari?
I'm using every ruse – equivocation,
or faggot-failure of consideration.
I know myself. I'm not inclined to carry
an overgrown (and under-weaponed) child.
I want this nest of nematodes annulled.
Is there a synonym for, 'I've been gulled'?
'Benighted, unrequited or beguiled'?
There's that in me which wants to be defiled:
I long to be, not traded-off, but pulled.

CORISCA: (BISBIGLIA, a parte)
How easy, when one's rival is so dim!
She loves Myrtillo: feelings to the fore:
it's she who blocks my avenue to him:
small force I'll need, to batter down this door!
I'm niggled by a gnat named Corydon,
but nothing that a double-play won't save:
if he's with her, I'll say they got it on:
it now remains to lure them to my cave!

AMARYLLIS, with friends.

AMARYLLIS:
Happiest that shepherdess
who never feels the barb
of jealousy or guiltiness,
who never needs a better dress
than Mother Nature's garb.
Unlettered in impiety,
       what use have we

      for paints or pearls?
Girls love to play with girls!

Who can doubt that happiness
from innocence is born?
Fierce animals cause no distress,
nor menace us, and even less
impale us on the horn.
Indifferent to gain or loss,
      content to toss
      our comely curls,
girls love to play with girls!

Far from strain, away from stress,
we know no males, save elves:
with none to flatter or impress,
our own concerns can we address,
and satisfy ourselves.
We know no cautions or restraints:
      with swirling feints
      and dainty whirls,
girls love to play with girls!

CORISCA
Our Nature comes from somewhere up above,
but Law is only human, therefore mutable.
One thing I know for sure is irrefutable:
this life's too short for just a single love –
so let's manipulate the marriage-mart!

You'd like to see your marriage contract torn
in fragments? Don't you want to be confined
within a loveless union? What's been signed
and sealed is man-made, therefore can be shorn
of legal force. But Nature needs a shove!

'Your' Silvio loves Lisetta. He's a knave!
You'd like to free yourself from sordid Silvio?
Then you are Constantine, at *Ponte Milvio*!
You'd rather be the mistress than the slave?
Show Silvio you're 'to the manner born'!

A forest nymph she is, this fair Lisetta.
He hunts her fervently: she is his hart
(I'm sure that more than once she's felt his dart!),
but on another pedestal we'll set her.
The plan is, we will trap them in my cave!

This plan is eminently executable.
My fragrant cave is called 'the bearded well',
festooned with aromatic asphodel:
for secret lovers, saliently suitable –
and, as a trollop-trap, what could be better?

A hollow stone by Art or Nature made,
the cave (remote, secluded, hidden, blind)
is not a site that snoopers tend to find,
but we'll surprise them in th
eir secret glade:
indignant we, imperious, inscrutable.

Each tranquil morn I'm troubled by his horn
as Silvio assaults my sylvan cell.
I hate to see his *amour-propre* swell
intemperately. All I feel is scorn,
and that is why I'm coming to your aid.

Think! Once his treachery has been displayed,
the marriage-promise can't but cease to bind,
and you can put the wanton from your mind.
Just catch him *in flagrante* with his jade:
you'll make him rue the day that he was born!

Another Ode to the Myrtle

Rose of the wide Sahara!
Pole of masculinity!
Acclaimed as a divinity
in Mishna and Gemara!

Beloved herb of Horus,
The fragrance of the dawn,
whose braided leaves adorn
the grave of Polydorus!

Sacred salve of Socrates,
precious bloom of Tunis!
Myrtus Communis,
Sceptre of Hippocrates!

O Crown of Aphrodite,
O Garland of Demeter!
No fruit was ever sweeter,
no modesty so mighty!

II:4 Enter POLYPHEMUS, to CORISCA

Triumphant in the chase,
he grapples her and squeezes her,
yet senses his embrace
affronts and merely freezes her.

He knows his lack of grace
discomfits and displeases her:
however, face to face,
he pinions her, he seizes her.

POLYPHEMUS
Will you indulge your satyr?

Will you not hold me dear?
If once you'd only flatter,
you'd have me rise and rear!

CORISCA
Is this some vulgar satire?
Am I a hunted deer?
Affront was never flatter:
if free, I'd turn my rear!

POLYPHEMUS
This coldness makes me smart:
I'd rather have you kind:
I feel your fluttering heart,
my longed-for golden hind!

CORISCA
Why won't you play it smart?
You are the backward kind:
release your captive hart,
and leave your lust behind!

The raptor is persuaded
to let his quarry turn,
but once his grip's evaded,
Corisca's first concern –

escape! In this, she's aided
by absence of all robes:
by ferns enfolded, faded,
goes a glorious pair of globes!

IN THE GLADE THE NYMPHS HAVE GATHERED:
dancing hard, they're getting lathered:
below the cave, down by the pond,
eightsome reels – that kind of thing

highland fling – that kind of deal
on y danse, tous en ronde!

Nymphs of Licoris, Corisca
(former prettier, latter frisker)
Amaryllis in the middle –
games like this are forest sport
when you're caught, bestow a kiss!
Rilly's trapped – this game's a fiddle!

Fingertips (blindfolded, she)
Rilly's grabbed a myrtle tree!
She thinks she's holding Licoris –
central trunk, with jointed limbs –
hers or hims? She's snared a hunk –
this *albero*, Myrtillo is!

The rule? The captive gets a kiss:
but something's gone a bit amiss.
He's telling Rilly he's in love!
Was this a scheme for falsehood's sake?
How did a dick-brain make the team?
She spurns him. Push has come to shove!

MYRTILLO
Unhappy me,
who yearns to be
more lustily embraced:
I'd pay a fee,
to lazily
in Rilly's juices baste.

AMARYLLIS
Unhappy me,
whose front must be
a woman, straitly-laced:
ironically,
the world would see
us, innocent and chaste.

MYRTILLO, leaving
Oh! This was not expected.
My hart, love's dart denies.
I'm totally rejected -

I see it in her eyes.
I'm adversely affected:
it can't be otherwise.

AMARYLLIS'S LAMENT
as she retires towards the Temple.

The pain I feel – ah, this, my cruel grief!
Ambitious fathers promise us abroad,
and we abandon those whom we've adored.
Myrtillo is my evidence-in-chief:
I'd take his hand, and furnish hand-relief,
if we were in some bosky bower immured.
I'd give him all that flesh and blood afford,
were those decisions mine. But we're the fief
of power-greedy men, who would as lief
ignore a daughter's grievances, uncured
as, should she wander, put her to the sword!
We women thank the gods that life is brief,
curtailing this, our wan recitatif!
Life is not lived by women, but endured!

AMARYLLIS MEETS CORISCA, along the way

CORISCA
What can ail you, little dove,
to make your pretty face so sad?

AMARYLLIS
I've shunned Myrtillo, whom I love,
and that is why I'm feeling bad.

CORISCA (bisbiglia, a parte)
We all have men we need to dump
(I'm shedding Corydon).

Here's a chance at which I'll jump
for mayhem – bring it on!

(to AMARYLLIS)
But why eschew a lover, when
you clearly think he matters?
They're rare enough, those special men:
why leave the thing in tatters?

AMARYLLIS
One is loved and one is loathed,
one worshipped, one derided.
To Silvio I am betrothed:
my fate has been decided.

CORISCA'S COUNSEL
This life's too short for just one single love:
regard fidelity adjust a fetter,
as Silvio does. He's here to meet LISETTA,
the forest nymph who is, in truth, his hart.
As he bestrides the dew-bejewelled lawn
each tranquil morn, he wakes me with his horn.

To him, you are a bridle or a glove:
an agent of restraint, and little better:
so don't be a Griselda, be a Cheta!
What Nature grants, we optimise through art.
To be a rook has agency: a pawn
has had itself of options wholly shorn.

You need to be an eagle, not a dove.
A woman should not live as Nature's debtor,
but push against the forces which beset her,
and wield a tool to match the hunter's dart.
The path that's easiest is badly-worn,
eliciting from travellers only scorn.

Today's the day when push must come to shove.
He's in that cave, and just about to pet her:
it's man-behaviour, right down to the letter.
They're in there now. It's all about to start.
Let's hurry down and trap him with his fawn:
this done, the marriage contract is stillborn.

A HOLLOW SPACE, by Art or Nature made,
whose taut caresses every man must crave
(and often used our menfolk to enslave),
will prove its worth again. The ivy braid
around its fringe may promise soothing shade,
but sisters frequently elect to shave
the undergrowth which might conceal the cave,
since some prefer the structure unarrayed.

A CAVE IS NOTHING BUT AN APERTURE.
So tucked away, unthreatening, demure,
it bides its time: unmarked by human eye,
awaits the unsuspecting passer-by.
Impaling is the purpose of the lure,
as lethal as the fly-trap to the fly!

ENTER CORYDON

CORISCA bisbiglia a parte
So Corydon appears appears on cue,
in answer to my summons:
he'll do whatever i say do
such dominance is woman's!

CORISCA a voce alta
You think, like Bernardino in Cisterna,
that you have gained the prize:
but I've beguiled your eyes:
Pompilia, entranced by her lucerna

is closer to your size.
Manipulating guys
does not require disguise:
la donna cambia, alterna,
and all your hopes defies.
Entra, ragazzo, laggiù caverna!

CORYDON GOES INTO THE CAVE

MYRTILLO APPROACHES CORISCA, on the track

CORISCA
Myrtillo comes! So slender, loose of limb!
He's even more attractive, out of doors:
I'll try my hand, attempt a little earth.
Love often makes its move in friendship's guise.

If this one only knew my lust for him!
The outline of Myrtillo, on all fours!
How rare to find you on this forest turf –
a welcome, since unwaited-for, surprise!

MYRTILLO
Forgive me if my countenance is grim:
a taste corrupted, pleasant things abhors.
To Amaryllis, I have little worth:
desire for death with preservation vies.

CORISCA
One great restorative, my twitching quim:
just say the word, Myrtillo, and I'm yours!
The antidote to misery is mirth:
a nubile nymph can cool your scalding eyes.

MYRTILLO
I'll run the risk of seeming somewhat prim,

but I've no taste for salty carnivores.
Denied the one I want, I welcome dearth.
Mere sex for pleasure's something I despise.

CORISCA
The cave interior is rather dim,
since Rilly likes the lights off when she scores!
It's there she sins with some unworthy serf.
And you're the one who wants to moralise?

STRAY LEAVES: 'What is there to be feared of …?'

What is there to be feared of, Amaryllis?
You know that you're in love with your Myrtillo,
and love will find its way to Amarillo!
You're Sybil Shepard and you've nailed Bruce Willis,
or he's Tom Cruise and you are Kelly Gillis:
like Donald Trump, enamoured of MyPillow,
you've spent a winter weeping like a willow,
but now you're feeling feisty, like Thom Tillis!

If Silvio is in there with Lisetta,
He's in flagrante, trapped with his abettor!
It's not a thing the gods can overlook!
The die we roll can sometimes end our debtor:
For you, events could not have worked out better!
Just catch them at it, and you're off the hook!

AMARYLLIS, sola

I WENT INTO THE TEMPLE OVER THERE
with heavy heart, to make an intercession:
and now that I have offered up confession,
I'm whole again, and come out light as air!

I marvel at the potency of prayer.
It has the skill to energise, to freshen!
The gods may liberate at their discretion:
young corn again, I went in as a tare!

And thou, dear cave, until I've done my work,
exposing Silvio's decency veneer,
permit this slave of love in thee to lurk!
Myrtillo makes me feel a little queer:
it must be love. I seek your welcome murk,
to shed true light. I think the coast is clear.

ENTER POLYPHEMUS

POLYPHEMUS
I still don't understand why I'm alone.
Corsica's in the cave with Corydon,
and not with me. Severely put upon,
I'm slighted and abandoned, on my own.

For what she's done, Corisca must atone:
I look for hints of interest, see none.
The eyes are mocking which with love once shone.
I'll block her passage. Here's a handy stone.

HE ROLLS A LARGE STONE AGAINST
THE ENTRANCE, AND GOES AWAY

CORISCA, AT THE CAVE

THIS ISN'T AS I LEFT IT – WHAT OCCURS?
Athwart the entrance lies a massive rock!
Did Amaryllis budge the bulky block?
The strength required is surely more than hers.
I note great hoofprints in the ambient furze:
far larger than are made by grazing flock.

And who is near, who may the cave unlock?
Who seals herself without due egress, errs.
If she's inside, that means Myrtillo's free.
If he's the eglantine, I am the bee!
I sucked him once, and haven't had my fill,
for in my nightly dreams, I suck him still!
This all falls pat – let's open up the cave;
when she's condemned, I get the lad I crave!

LINCO, WITH DORINDA

4.2
I've brought you here, Dorinda dear,
your sorrow to beguile.
And when I see you from the rear,
I cannot help but smile.

Your love for Silvio brings no cheer,
Though you have loved the while:
But love will always hover near,
and lovers reconcile.

The loving stratagem that we're
about to put on trial
will (if you trust, and let me steer)
prove quite a worthwhile wile.

A hunter's prey you must appear
albeit pelts are vile.
Adopt this deerskin outer gear,
and linger, cervo-style,

with all the hints of forest-fear
invention can compile,
Hippolytus you'll domineer,
as sure as there's a Nile.

LINCO:
Yes, I am Linco, wise man to the Prince.
You knew me years ago, my little mouse:
I was a servant in your father's house.
My standing has augmented somewhat since,
but I do not forget my little quince.

DORINDA:
I'd have you help me vanquish Silvio's heart.
I well remember how you nurtured me
– the signs are there for anyone to see.
What can I do to take the lodestone's part,
and draw him to me? How attract his dart?

LINCO: (bisbiglia, aparte)
No question, Silvio adores the hunt.
She used to be, as some would say, a babe:
but looks are fodder of the astrolabe.
She needs to learn (one hopes, without affront)
the tragedy of *ante nos fuerunt.*

DORINDA:

Since Silvio's devoted to the hunt,
I need to make my feelings manifest.
That we're their prey is known, but unexpressed.
This costume is not constant in the front:
if only, Silvio, you could see my breast!
I'd show you things that I have long suppressed.
Is this a stratagem, or just a stunt?
Will my preoccupations be addressed?
Will dressing as a deer advance my quest?
No more prevarication: I'll be blunt:
by being here, so animally dressed,
I'll draw my lover, put him to the test.

And, by this act, two wills have coalesced.
Thus what is love, if not self-interest?

4.3 CHORUS OF ARCADIAN MEN

With blackening the homeland we are tasked.
The ruin of Arcadia we moan,
out here, before the audience, alone,
while others work their fingers to the bone,
adjusting scenery.   That's why we're masked;
we'll later move among you, quite unknown:
for anything we said that made you groan,
we neither have to pay for, nor atone.
Before we have in approbation basked,
we'll do the thing to which all men are prone,
and denigrate our women: slight, disown:
they're whores, from adolescent up to crone.
No man, who sought a favour, went unblown:
no woman chaste, save she who wasn't asked.

STICHOMYTHIA
TITYRUS:
It's time, I think, to get my daughter married.

MONTANUS:
Or even past the time. Some say you've tarried.

TITYRUS:
Such offers as I had were bad – I parried.

MONTANUS:
The man who owns an asset's often harried.

TITYRUS:
Imagine if your son had but survived.

MONTANUS:
Oh, what a union had we then contrived!

TITYRUS:
Our long-discussed alliance had arrived!

MONTANUS:
But when I lost him, we were both deprived.

TITYRUS:
Ay! What a pain it is, to have a daughter!

MONTANUS:
We've heard, before today, of lambs and slaughter.

TITYRUS:
Montanus! Blood is thicker, still, than water!

MONTANUS:
I'm not the one who says that Silvio bought her!

TITYRUS:
The gods, inscrutable, destroyed your son.

MONTANUS:
The game, I sometimes think, has just begun.

TITYRUS:
We can't say whom they favour, whom they shun.

MONTANUS:
I lost, but have the feeling that I won!

MONTANUS, TITYRO, CORISCA, before the Cave.

ENTER POLYPHEMUS

POLYPHEMUS
The same old faces as before!
Arcadia has nothing new!
Though I had not expected more,
I feel no pleasure, seeing you!

CORISCA
And who are you, abhorrent beast,
to slight descendants of the gods?
Delightful is Arcadia's least:
While you are uglily at odds.

POLYPHEMUS
Handsome is as handsome does,
and you are just a wanton.
The world will know you, not like us,
depicted by Imelda Staunton.

CORISCA
There is no good, there is no bad,
the god I follow is desire:
that you've been passed on makes you mad,
but you no longer light my fire.

MONTANUS
Your passion, by your very stance,

TITYRUS
is moving you extremely,

MONTANUS
but foreigners might look askance,

TITYRUS
and find this fight unseemly.

POLYPHEMUS
Unseemly. Am I? That's my lot!
Hypocrisy, you'll see, homegrown:
what scandals has Arcadia got?
I'll push aside the blocking stone.

HE DOES SO, TO REVEAL AMARYLLIS AND CORYDON

Two Composite Arcadian Sonnets

MONTANUS
There's nothing to be said. Adultery.

TITYRO
Adultery's a capital offence!

CORISCA
In sentencing, Arcadia's not desultory.

POLYPHEMUS
It can't be trolled for sitting on the fence!

MONTANUS
Concealed. And with a man. I'd say we've sussed her!

TITYRO
We have to exercise due diligence!

CORISCA
What arguments could anybody muster?

POLYPHEMUS
There's little to be said against events.

MONTANUS
Since facts are facts, and all are inculpatory,

TITYRO
Her wedding prospects now appear lacklustre.

CORISCA
We don't mind if you sin, but be discreet

POLYPHEMUS
We're hardly hearing anything hortatory.

MONTANUS
Proceed to sentence. Nothing could be juster.
It's quite condign to bind her hands and feet.

TITYRO
Will anybody speak in her defence?

MONTANUS
We want no words of false equivalence.

CORISCA
Defending her would be impertinence.

POLYPHEMUS
It needs a master orator. Mike Pence?

TITYRO
The state can't kill its citizens. It's wrong.
Our task is to augment, and not deplete.

MONTANUS
I knew you were a Leftie all along!

CORISCA
You must admit the chick was indiscreet!

MONTANUS
The sin that she's committed is immense:
to me, Tityro's honour's uppermost:
away with reason, and grandiloquence:
I'll get my butcher's knife. That girl is toast.
The way it ends is really rather meet:
Her wedding-gown becomes her winding-sheet!

ENTER DORINDA, sola, dressed in a deerskin

DORINDA
If this be madness, it is of the heart.
Emotion took me, bore me as it rose
(as autumn leaves are borne upon a wave),
until I seem a clown. The motley Linco made
will serve me in this forest, since its scent
belongs as much here as the morning dew.

ENTER LINCO, unseen
The hour is apposite, and Silvio's due:
he has a hankering to take a hart,
and thus am I, his true retainer sent
to scare the wildlife from the silent rows.
If once my master hit upon a maid,
all could relax, and early mornings waive.

ENTER SILVIO
I love it when the morning branches wave
and Nature pays Arcadia its due!
Here is a track – I'm not mistaken – made
by some benighted and abandoned hart.
And here's my quarry. Hard to miss the rose,
which offers so spectacular a scent!

He fires an arrow, which strikes DORINDA.

DORINDA
Sweet prick! The noisome dart was heaven-sent!
I spotted Silvio to Linco wave,
and, though I'm injured, something in me rose:
now pity stirs the sluggish residue
that lies immobile in that frozen heart:
by piercing me, his shaft has inroads made!

SILVIO
The prey is not a doe! A human maid
have I impaled! My hardened head I sent
into her thorax. Did I get her heart?
Dorinda! All my coyness I now waive,
and offer you my hand, as is your due.
I'll marry you today, my forest rose.

LINCO
The oarsman, when he sees his error, rows
the harder, to make good the gaffe he made.
Your gesture, Silvio, will blame subdue.
And if Dorinda signals her assent,
I'll seal you man and wife. My rector's wave
will hereby unify you, as one heart.

DORINDA
How wonderful the wound! How brave the wave!

SILVIO
How grave the shaft! How resolute the hart!

LINCO
Let's to the cave, and have a rescue made.

ACT FIVE, Prologue

'The time has come,' the author said,
'to introduce a talking head.'
Such personages do no wrong,
and boy! they move the plot along.

They have no life, they do no work:
Armenians, they, to the Turk.
The fruit of Logic's bland behest,
they'll bore the tits clean off your chest!

V:1 CARINO, solo

CARINO
'Nor shall you laugh, save in Arcadia.'
No matter where we roam, we love the nest:
no sun or shade is sunnier or shadier:
initial bedding has to be the best.

The homeland beckons me, now that I'm old:
the Patria pulls me, like I were a lode:
much have I travelled in the realms of gold:
Myrtillo urges me, as if a goad.

I settled in Achaia (coastal zone):
the floods were on, in Alfeo's estuary;
I found a foundling, raised him as my own:
Myrtillo washed up in a myrtle tree.

The Oracle must be consulted, no?
The cliff-crack god: 'Yes, raise Myrtillo, but
you have to guard the secret, hide it, so
my strong advice to you is, keep it shut!'

Myrtillo grew to be a handsome youth:
I honoured what the Oracle forbade:
I never told a single soul the truth.
A merchant seaman I, I plied my trade.

I saw the world and kept an even keel:
I had adventures (leave that as a teaser):
imprisoned in Mycene (no big deal),
I published poems in the town of Pisa.

Myrtillo chose Arcadia, my old home,
entirely of his own unswayed volition.
An old man now, I tread my native loam,
and thus conclude this tedious exposition.

STRAY LEAVES: PISA SONNET

The *campo dei miracoli* from the air:
the little restaurant I call my own:
the bar where you can charge your mobile phone,
and no-one's ever heard of Tony Blair.
The baptistery – I climbed this very stair!
Decay to which our flesh is all too prone –
Benozzo showed us, working all alone!
Vasari's elegance, in this, 'his' square,
and everything in lovely, pink-white stone,
and that includes the Chapel of the Spines.
It's Galileo's town, let's not forget.
The wall defines the fine Cathedral zone,
and mention should be made of pink-white wines:
no need to even name The Minaret!

V:2 TITYRO, alone

TITYRO
Which one is better, when you have a daughter,
to know that she is sexually loose,
or see that well-loved neck inside a noose?
What may a father hope for? Slag, or slaughter?

It's really all a question of my honour:
if I could save her, would I take her back?
Of course I wouldn't. Think of all the flak!
The girl's a guttersnipe – ergo, a goner!

For Amaryllis, then, this means the vault.
They dominate, because they own the womb,
And we can't win, though we control the tomb!
I want my daughter's death – and it's her fault!

ENTER A MESSENGER

MESSENGER
My Lord Tityro! Tidings from the cave!

TITYRO
Your name, churl? By your fathers set no store?

MESSENGER
Whoever names me, has to pay me more.
You'd learn how Amaryllis 'scaped the grave?

TITYRO
I don't see how that sort of thing can happen.
She has ability, true, like her mother.

MESSENGER
No, this was intervention by another.
She's just a girl, you know – not Max Verstappen.

TITYRO
I'm reconciled to see my daughter dead.

MESSENGER
She's very much alive, and off the hook.

TITYRO
Montanus always does things by the book.

MESSENGER
Just so. A youth will perish in her stead.

TITYRO
A guy must die? That seems a tad severe.

MESSENGER
The model is Amyntas. Undismayed,
Lucrina's partner chose to take the blade,
though innocent.

TITYRO
                     We do such horrors here!
I'll hie me to the cave. But tell me, sir,
exciting things are happening, but we
must learn of them through knaves on bended knee?

MESSENGER
Greek drama, mate. That's how it must occur.

FINAL SCENE: OUTSIDE CORISCA'S CAVE

MYRTILLO, trussed, is kneeling on a makeshift altar.
MONTANUS isstanding over him, wielding a large knife.
Onlookers include CORISCA, POLYPHEMUS, chorus members,
shepherds, shepherdesses, nymphs, &c.

MONTANUS
How fortunate you are, to die so young!
When bitterness invades the human heart,
we find ourselves depressed or highly-strung,
on beta-blockers (and that's just the start!)
manoeuvred into marriage by some tart,
you would have found that life is full of shit.
Before the body starts to fall apart,
Idealistic, undiminished, fit –
believe me, son, you're better out of it.

MYRTILLO
I like your use of 'son'. May I say 'father'?
It's intimate. Since I'm about to die,
it helps me. But reject it, if you'd rather.
I'm not a push-the-limits kind of guy.
I'm just a heifer, lowing at the sky.
No inkling, when I came here from Achaia,
(I make the sacrifice, and don't ask why)
that Fate would float down straits so wholly dire,
and put me on my lover's funeral pyre.

ENTER CARINO & TITYRO, severally.

TITYRO
I'd hate to see Montanus cut his throat –

CARINO
Arcadia has not moved on from this?
The boy is tethered tighter than a goat –

TITYRO
– I'd so much rather him than Amaryllis!

CORISCA
It seems to me that lad could use a kiss.

CARINO
I'll watch the early phases, and then go:
the ending of a life, I'd rather miss.

MONTANUS
You want to make a (short) oration?

MYRTILLO
                                    No.

MONTANUS
Are no objections offered up? Just so.

MONTANUS prepares to make the sacrifice.

CARINO, moving close to the altar.
Objection! If I'm wrong, I will repent me!

MONTANUS
Why, stranger, will you aggravate the gods?

CARINO
Me? Aggravate? The gods it was that sent me!
And I arrived in time – against the odds!

POLYPHEMUS
One hears of spoiling children, sparing rods –

CARINO
Observe the birthmark on the young man's shoulder!

CHORUS
The plot up-ended! Who said Homer nods?
Before she is another minute older,
produce the girl indicted by the boulder!

TITYRUS
You think the blemish bears importance, friend?

CARINO
As true as I'm Arcadian, it does!

CHORUS
The story's getting hard to comprehend:
The stranger's claiming now he's one of us!

CARINO
My name's Carino, and my father was
the counter of the state's communal coins.
(I think I'm hearing recognition's buzz.)

MONTANUS
You know this youth? Say how, the law enjoins.

CARINO
He is my son.

MONTANUS
              The offspring of your loins?

CARINO
Not that, exactly. But I brought him up.

MONTANUS
How so?

CHORUS
        The girl has not yet been produced.
We want to see our Daisy, Buttercup.
Is there some reason why she can't be loosed?

MONTANUS
To give my popularity a boost
(election year) I'll have the suspect brought.

CORISCA
This is more layered than a plot by Proust!

CARINO
I found him in a myrtle bush, in short.
It was the year when Marathon was fought.

ENTER AMARYLLIS

AMARYLLIS
I feel like Constantine at Ponte Milvio.

TITYRO
Congratulations, daughter. You survived.

ENTER SILVIO, WITH DORINDA

AMARYLLIS
But yet in chains. I have to marry Silvio.

SILVIO
Release is hereby easily contrived.
How timely have my bride and I arrived!

TITYRO
'My bride', he says. We ought to raise a cup.

DORINDA
Of celebrations knowingly deprived,
we've opted of the forest dew to sup,
and you can tear the marriage contract up.

MONTANUS
The baby in the myrtle bush – tell more.

CARINO
Remember how the Alfeo was in flood
the year of Marathon? The tidal bore
deposited a cradle made of wood
and curiously fashioned – for the hood,
some loving hand had fashioned, as of lace,
in workmanship exceptionally good,
in finest raffia from Samothrace …

MONTANUS
… a sun-protector for the baby's face.

CARINO
How could you know this detail? How behave
as if you wove that hood yourself … unless …

TITYRO
… you launched that vessel on the angry wave!

MONTANUS
For twenty years, I've lived with my distress.

It ends today. This was no lucky guess,
for all is ordered by the gods above.
You are my son. I openly profess
my parenthood, and thus a father's love.

HE THROWS DOWN THE KNIFE.

MYRTILLO
The gods are great – but sometimes need a shove.

MONTANUS
If only there were two of noble line
disposed to marry, they could lift the curse
that haunts our almost-perfect realm.

TITYRO
                              In fine,
the message of the Oracle is terse:
to put the bane that blights us in reverse,
two half-divines must marry with dispatch.

AMARYLLIS
If I should wed Myrtillo …

MYRTILLO
                          … I've heard worse!

TITYRO
Myrtillo-Amaryllis! What a match!

CARINO
You've played a blinder, son – she's quite a catch!

STRAY LEAVES: ON TWO JUXTAPOSED COLUMNS IN THE CHURCH OF SANTA MARIA IN COSMEDIN, ROME

They don't quite correspond – and never will.
One's porphyry, and one's albino white.
Corinthian, alongside composite.
Like Tristram Shandy, paired with Stuart Mill,
or Iwo Jima, tacked on Bunker Hill.
With neither plumb-line nor theodolite
they're fairly similar, in terms of height.
Both capitals bear pock-marks from the drill.
Why can't we co-exist? For good or ill,
we view existence as some kind of fight:
our will to win, that sleepless eremite,
has lumbered us with guilt like Emmet Till.
Our choice is binary: a Buffet shill,
or rage against the dying of the light?

Nature Versus Law

Should Nature lay down axioms? Should law?
It all depends what axioms are for.
Can lizards live by Nature? 'Course they can.
That doesn't mean the same is true of Man.
A stained-glass window is composed of gules:
a social network needs its social rules,
and isn't that what Law is? Simple forms
get by on more or less untrammeled norms,
and that means Nature. Dolphin, just as daw,
they all rely on instinct. There's no plan
as true for Cromagnon as true for corm),
so aren't we, too, still red in tooth and claw?
Nine-tenths of us look down on working mules,
because they don't attend the better schools.

That Obscure Object of Desire

Man's instinct drives him on to enter caves,
those fissures which, although by Nature made,
pray human intervention in their aid.
This owner trains the ivy, that one shaves:
some seem like cradles, some resemble graves.
Though many sport elaborate brocade,
the vast majority cleave to the shade:
the wishing-wells of heroes, as of knaves.
As pigeons chase the lodestone in their nose,
so men pursue the urging in the hips
(the more so when the knowing hosts expose
Brazilians, depilation, landing-strips).
The whole world has one word upon its lips –
the end of the unending hunt – the rose.

Small Latin and Less Greek

A playwright tries to write a playful scene. He
resorts to thoughts in Catalan or Slav.
What other option does the poet have?
He has to rhyme, at times, with 'Paganini',
or chooses to refuse (eschews 'blue meanie').
He steels himself to steal from Pag'n'Cav,
or nab vocab from Chatterton or chav,
is never narrow (marrow mates zucchini).
So if he lards his lines with *objets trouvés,*
be generous towards him, Gentle Reader.
Je vous en prie, ne faites-pas ce que vous pouvez:
el hace su mejor, y enseguida:
the dog days don't require December's *duvet,*
so let him coin (purloin?) *Zigeunerlieder.*

Peace Ho! Count the Clock

Are things supposed to happen when they do,
or may the poet take a different view?
Fidelity becomes A.J.P. Taylor,
but maybe looks amiss on Norman Mailer.
I'm sitting in Marconi's on the Hill:
Maria la Maggiore means to fill
the canvas as I feed a handsome sparrow,
as if the Eclogues of a certain Varro
were still in print. (Oh, print came *after* that:
you have to be a chrono-acrobat!)
I'm working on a bottle (*Pinot Grigio*)
and, if I'm right, the *ultimo vestigio*
will see me through the sonnet that's to be.
The chop house dates from nineteen twenty-three:
could Raphael have got drunk here? Possibly!

WRITTEN STATEMENT OF DONNA COSTANZA DONATO, PREPARED FOR THE *PROCESSUS FUGAE*

There's very little I can tell the court.
   I will, of course, tell what I can.
I took the view it was a bit of sport:
   the Canon is a typical man.
It wasn't hard to recognise his shape:

The girl appeared familiar to me.
   I couldn't see her very clearly,
but gossip animates the 'quality'
   in towns like ours. Sincerely,
it struck me as illicit – an escape.

I crave forgiveness. I should set the scene.
   (My counsel tells me not to write
opinion. He suggests I keep it clean
   of anything that smacks of spite.)
The road is very narrow, really stony

at one point on the route from Castiglion.
   The scent of vine leaves and mimosa
hung in the darkness and the stars that shone
   picked out a carriage, coming closer
(we, passing through the hamlet of Gragnone,

were heading for Arezzo). I think the hour
   was after midnight. Wooden wheels
were rumbling in our direction ('our'
   is wrong – say 'my'). Of all ordeals,
passing in the darkness on a track

so *stretta*'s quite the worst. We slowed right down
   to inch along. The other, too,
crept slowly. Though the risk that we might drown
   was hardly probable, we knew
the stream was on our left, and getting back

without an accident oppressed our minds
   (I mean, 'my mind'). Wheels boss to boss,
we edged one past the other. Window blinds
   were open. As I looked across,
the woman closed the curtain in a rush,

but not quite fast enough. I recognised
   the Canon. (Counsel at my side
is urging me – and I am well advised) –
   the man was Caponsacchi. I'd
prefer to pause a moment. If I blush,

it's just because this room is very close.
   I'm ready now. I'll say politely,
and try not to be prolix or verbose:
   I know her too, albeit slightly,
for she's the wife of Guido Franceschini.

My lawyer asks if I allege a 'tryst'.
   Why else would they be out at night
together? Can I say they fondled, kissed?
   I can't. But hiding from my sight
suggests they were (we say) *sotto i pini*.

This Caponsacchi is a dangerous man:
   seduces women, uses girls.
His manner's smooth, and sedulous his plan:
   you hardly know, as it unfurls,
the spider's trapped you in his web of silk.

He uses, then discards, his conquered prey.
   Insists he really loves you, then
discards you, disregards you, throws away
   the love you've given. That's why men
(especially those of Caponsacchi's ilk)

must not be trusted. Women may not own
   nor house nor horse: can't even go
to see their mothers, travelling alone
   from Ca' Petrarca to Pretorio,
the kind of bind the Canon's kind exploit.

(At counsel's urging, I should now point out
   I wasn't on my own that night.
That all was well, the court need have no doubt.
   No hot hegira, febrile flight.
There with me was Antonio, my steward.)

The girl was *la romana*, as we call her
   (the one in Caponsacchi's arms).
She's dark, like *la Contenti,* only smaller.
   She sealed it with her curtain-qualms.
She knew that I had seen her. She was skewered.

I grant she was as lovely as the rose,
as noble as the lonely albatross.
That winter when the Trasimeno froze
is when she came to us. Who ever knows
what lies before us? In my mangled prose
you may, if you are sympathetic, gloss
(amid the hesitant but heartfelt dross)
how I fell, also. When Pompilia chose
her Clotho, she took on her Atropos.
The opening must pre-ordain the close:
What witnesses set down, the Fates emboss.
Though Time may trick us, Circumstance impose,
the heart is not deceived. I here depose
that I, too, trod the Stations of the Cross.

THE CONGRESS OF THE WITS: (3) Madama Lucrezia

We women have two feet (one face!) of clay,
with wigs we wave away our alopecia.
The trick is, painting over our decay:
'deception' is the feminine of 'vices'.
With corset-bones we cozen drones. Display
is all. Our mating-call? 'How green was my *valet!*'

We won't give way, or ever fade to grey.
We'll file and fill, finagle every feature.
A simple pimple predicates dismay,
a sag's a drag, a wrinkle is a crisis!

With hoola-hoop, we keep the droop at bay,
and usher-in the darling buds of May,

and heaven help the hair that dares to stray!
We gouge and scrape, and rape anew Lucretia!
To try the tape, and speculate on spray,
preoccupies us, unperturbed by prices.
We trample on the truth? We'd rather say
our craft is not to 'con', but to 'convey'.

Long hours I've spent, constructing this array,
creating an attractive siren-creature:
as centre-piece of my *décolleté*
I've got (I'm sure you'll spot) the Knot of Isis.
So, calm my nerves: uneasiness allay:
What do you say? Am I in face today?

THE HISTORY OF THE TRUE CROSS:
(4) Burying the Wood

Like every fool, King Solomon believes he's won.
He'll bury all three crosses. But, *piuttosto*,
he should have, if he could have, read Ariosto:
you're up on top? The wheel has just begun.

In American, to 'get wood''s something good
if this had only been an American poem
(a few among them write, and sometimes show 'em)
then wood would stand, just as the True Cross stood.

To 'hide the wood''s as good as it can get,
tumescent penis hidden to the hilt,
in places once synonymous with guilt
but Solomon is not about to let

a new and better magic thrive, will show
the crosses of the King and His two thieves
must be interred, as if they were stray leaves
and out of sight (thus out of mind) must go.

The dangling jacket sleeve? Superbly wrought!
That cheeky glimpse inside his underwear
assures us of his manhood. It's all there!
Their struts are straining, concentrating, taut,
they're burying three crosses, as they ought:
they can't afford an anti-jewish scare.
And so the relics, bulky, wooden, square,
must go to ground, where they will not be sought.

The timber's neat diagonal divide
leaves Heaven empty, featureless, serene,
while we, in our sublunary demesne,
face toil and tumult on the human side.
But symbols can be difficult to hide:
disposal sometimes leaves a legal lien.

ROSINA IN THE OVEN, Being a Tale related by Agnese Santa Olivieri

How sisters spit and mothers might misgovern,
will form the fabric of the coming tale.
Domestic life's not always cakes and ale,
especially if the home's a witches' coven!
Rosina was a preciosa joven,
whose semi-sister fought her, tooth and nail.
We'll hear of hemp and hindrance by the bale,
and of the final triumph of the oven.

Since heroines are never meant to fail
(Rosina's queen, Assunta slutty sloven),

we'll follow her up hill, and then down dale:
her hemp will be exemplary when woven
(you can't weave hemp: pro-temp, the rhyme's a shove-in)
and when Rosina's tested, she'll prevail!

I SING OF FIRE (AND AIR AND EARTH,
   and latterly of water).
A woman died while giving birth
   to a delightful daughter.

Rosina's father didn't waste
   a moment, didn't tarry:
he seemed in some unholy haste
   to rapidly re-marry.

In time was born an irksome thorn
   who'd make a churchman chunter:
a churlish child, a spiteful spawn,
   half-sibling named Assunta.

Rosina's unassuming grace
   (Assunta was much fatter)
and well-proportioned, pretty face
   antagonised the latter.

'What can we do?' asked Mother, who
   was wholly *parti-pris*:
'She'll spin, and herd the cattle, too,
   and how she does, we'll see.'

(This from Assunta.) If she hemped
   and also watched the cows,
Rosina wouldn't be exempt
   from rancour or from rows,

if once her always-perfect work
   was faulty (let's get blunter:
they'd think that she'd begun to shirk,
   resembling Assunta.)

They gave Rosina hemp to spin
   while tending to the cattle.
Assunta wore her grimmest grin,
   a cut-price Quetzelcoatl.

Rosina asked the cows for help.
   'I don't know where to start!
No matter if it's hemp or kelp,
   I just don't have the art!'

A wise old cow said, 'Listen now:
   I have the very thing.
Just have a word with every cow,
   and here's what you should sing.'

Cow, cow, little cow,
take my distaff, spin it now:
wind the skein around your horn,
work for me this very morn.

The cows, contented, came back home
   beneath the setting sun:
Rosina carried on her head
   the hemp, superbly spun!

Assunta spat and shook her fist.
   'We'll better her next time,
so give her twice as much to twist
   before the church bells chime!'

Assunta's plans once more went wrong
   when cattle went to browse:
at evensong, who came along?
   Rosina, hemp and cows!

The spiteful sister flared and stared.
   Said Rosie, to her face:
'All grace is shared, if you're prepared
   To offer others grace.'

Assunta told her mother, 'So:
   we need a change of plan.
Rosina stays, and I will go.
   If she can do it, I can!'

The morning, came, Assunta went
   the cows and hemp to tend.
Despite the stress she underwent,
   she reached a messy end.

She jabbed the cattle with a prod
   but all she had to show
was one almighty ugly wad
   of unimpressive tow.

Assunta tried another tack,
   but this time fairly drastic:
she said, 'Rosina won't come back,
   which I will find fantastic!'

By now the mother, feeble soul,
   no longer filled the bill.
She let the daughter take control,
   surrendered to her will.

'I want a lettuce from the field:
    to fetch it, that's your job.'
Rosina said she wouldn't yield:
    'I'll never stoop to rob!'

'If I command it, you must go,
    comply with what may suit me!'
'The farmer has a powerful bow,
    and probably will shoot me!'

That's what Assunta hoped to see:
    would brook no more entreating:
'Bring a lettuce back for me,
    or undergo a beating!'

So, after dark, Rosina crawled
    across the farmer's field.
At lettuces she tugged and hauled,
    but none of them would yield.

At last, she saw a turnip there,
    so big and firm and round:
she gripped its leaves with cautious care
    and yanked it from the ground!

She's done her best to wrench and wrest:
    a peal of squeals explodes!
Inside the hole, inside their nest –
    a family of toads!

Rosina scooped the babies up
    and held them to her breast:
she used her hands to try to cup
    them gently to her, lest

they come to harm – but lackaday!
   It's harrowing to tell!
Protect them as Rosina may,
   one tiny toadlet fell!

'My leg is broken! You're to blame!'
   the little fellow cried:
'Because of you, I'll grow up lame!'
   'I'm sorry,' she replied:

'I'd never cause a moment's pain
   to any living thing!'
The other babies, in refrain,
   were energised to sing:

'You're beautiful and very kind,
   and we're inclined to love you.
There's no-one you need hide behind,
   nor anyone above you!'

The injured one, less positive,
   came out with something worse.
'The harm you've done, I won't forgive:
   you'll live beneath my curse!'

'The sun will bake you into a snake,
   to slither in the mire.
My malediction won't unmake
   until the Trial of Fire!'

Rosina went home, terrified,
   remaining in the shade.
Her every instinct was to hide,
   affrighted and afraid.

Anxiety won't always smother
the radiance of a cutie.
Even Assunta and her mother
　admired Rosina's beauty.

Henceforth she huddled safe indoors,
　avoiding solar blast:
could only wander lonely moors
　when sky was overcast.

But, not the type to groan and grouse,
　unlimitedly loyal,
content to cook, and clean the house,
　she turned to cheerful toil.

A handsome man rode by one day
　– a lord he seemed: nay, grander –
and saw Rosina, broom at play,
　a-sweeping the veranda.

'How strange is this! How can it be?'
　he wondered, by degrees:
'Why is a beauty such as she
　in trappings such as these?'

Her grace and her surroundings, how
　distinct – as cheese and chalk! –
provided him the grounding, now,
　to move right in and talk.

Assunta saw the couple locked
　in earnest conversation:
alarmed, annoyed, disgruntled, shocked,
　she boiled with indignation!

Her face was greener than her gown,
   although her gown was green!
She sent her mother rushing down
   to try to intervene!

'God save your grace,' the mother said,
   'You'll find no profit here.
This wretched girl's as good as dead –
   vexed by a hex, I fear!

We have to keep her from the light,
   seclude her, for her sake:
should sunshine hit her, what a fright!
   She'll turn into a snake!'

'I hear your comments. I'm afraid
   they're (on their face) distressing.
Whom might I have,' the young man bade,
   'the honour of addressing?'

'Her father's wife,' the beldam blushed,
   'but not such as begets her.
Your servant, sir,' the mother gushed.
   'My name is Amarezza.'

'It seems to me,' the youth opined,
   'Rosina's wasted here.
This girl's not foremost in your mind.
   There's none here holds her dear.'

He said, 'I think I should reveal
   That I'm a wealthy knight.
I'll send a carriage which can seal
   her from all harmful light.

Rosina, if you'll just say yes,
   I'll take you for my lady,
and you can live in happiness:
   we'll shack up somewhere shady.'

Replying in affirmative
   without the least 'perhaps',
the wench was whisked away to live
   in riches, under wraps.

Each sun came up, the frost to melt,
   and sank each eve, vermillion,
but couldn't touch Rosina's pelt
   or turn her ass reptilian.

The young knight's name was Ettore.
   The two fell deep in love.
And she, on strolls et cetery,
   bore parasol and glove.

Such sentiments could but increase,
   and soon the troth was plighted.
Extended was the hand of peace:
   the family, invited.

But only Amarezza came:
   Assunta shunned the marriage.
The mother said, 'Since I'm the dame,
   my gift shall be the carriage.'

The plump one had a perfect plan,
   a plot she'd put to proof:
she trowed to try what treachery can –
   a trapdoor in the roof!

Her carriage was constructed well,
   its secret subtly hid:
no well-intentioned wight would tell –
   a light-admitting lid!

Their wedding-day got under way:
   bright sunlight, right from dawn
enhanced the banquet's flower display
   (reception on the lawn).

Grease is the word the servants heard
   throughout the summer lovin':
one hundred scrubbed and scoured and stirred,
   two hundred fed the oven.

The husband had a fabulous feast
   elaborately planned:
his oven, a voracious beast,
   the grandest in the land.

For brushwood, branches, bracken, boughs
   the *sganarelli* scoured:
whatever faggots folks could browse
   that yawning mouth devoured.

The sun beat down. Complexions, tanned,
   absorbed it – how superb!
Rosina wore a wedding band!
   Déjeuner sur l'herbe!

Each happy guest, demurely dressed,
   applauded the approach
of knight and bride, now bishop-blest,
   in Amarezza's coach.

At this point, Amarezza struck.
   The trap door felt her fist!
So newly-wed, so out of luck!
   Strong, slanting sunlight kissed

Rosina's face, through opened hatch.
   The cabin, once opaque,
because of that clandestine latch,
   now held a bright green snake!

The serpent slithered through the door
   and off into the brake.
Her 'mother' slid down to the floor:
   'How grievous my mistake!'

To Amarezza's fresh distress
   Rosina, virgin martyr,
had left an empty bridal dress
   – and one abandoned garter!

The wedding seemed a ruin now,
   but still the oven roared:
when one has guests, one must allow
   sufficient bed – and board!

Retainers toiled, the faggots flowed,
   Tahona blazed, the keener:
but where now was the nematode
   that once had been Rosina?

That fire may be a force for good
   has often been recorded,
and Virtue gets (as Virtue should)
   quite frequently rewarded.

A cook took up a pile of wood
   from off the mound of kindling
that waiting near the oven stood,
   replenishing, not dwindling.

He tossed it through those moiling maws:
   insatiable inferno!
but something wriggling gave him pause:
   a worm did he discern? Oh!

For goodness' sake! he's hurled a snake!
   The poor thing would be toasted!
Forget the hake he's sought to bake –
   he'd have a reptile, roasted!

But poetry eclipses prose.
   The latter, flat, forlorn,
can tell us only what it knows,
   unable to adorn.

As fresh and white as any rose,
   and naked as a fawn,
escaping from those thermal throes,
   Rosina sprang, newborn!

LO SPOSO DELUSO, Being a Tale told by Giovanni-Battista Mucha

IN PIAZZA SAN FELICE (THAT'S IN FLORENCE),
events went down a fair few years ago
(we have three witnesses to tell us so)
that fill the faithful with a fierce abhorrence.
Unhealthy longings always lead to woe!
Anselmo was a merchant in the city,
and married to the beautiful Camilla.

A *Schauspiel* (better Sheridan, or Schiller?)
to tell their tale should grace *Palazzo Pitti*
(on second thoughts, it should be Arthur Miller).

The moral of the tale won't break your brain:
the error never ceases to amaze!
Perhaps some men pass through an awkward phase,
and need to test their wives (example? 'Shane'!)
Why risk it all? What do you stand to gain?
She's pretty and she loves you. Happy days!

Camilla was, of course, a *bella donna*
 (how could Anselmo opt for something less?)
But beauty oft engenders real distress:
he wondered, could he trust her with his honour?
The way to prove the wine is in the press,
so this is where we meet his friend Lothario,
accustomed to the kiss and the caress,
renowned in town, but not for playing chess
(the outcome of this sorriest scenario
the sharper readers readily can guess).

'If I am Mammon's cur, you're Cupid's whelp,'
said merchant to philanderer, one day.
'I want these doubts of mine to go away.
Can I conclude she's faithful? Won't you help?'
Lothario, uncertain what to say,
cried 'I will do my damnedest, by San Telmo!
You'd have me wear a mask? I'll play my part,
accomplish all that can be done by art!'
This answer gratified his friend Anselmo:
the lover knew just what to do by heart.

It often happens, in this life of ours,
that friendships blossom, time with place concurs,
we launch out on *liaisons dangéreuses*,

but find ourselves immersed beyond our powers,
for we are innocents, they *connoisseurs*.
Desire is like a plant that looks for light.
You close it in a casket for a change,
more easily to manage it, arrange:
its runners prise the case agape, despite
the padlock ... but what surfaces is strange!

Anselmo would leave suddenly for Rome,
and give Lothario leave to use the house.
The friend would have full access to the spouse,
who'd thus become a prisoner in her home,
as innocent and helpless as a mouse.
The two men talked of projects, plans and pacts,
which all revolved around Camilla's shame.
They never doubted where to pin the blame.
No matter how detestable their acts,
the woman got the stigma all the same!

Her servant, Leonella, was her friend
from childhood, and the two were very close.
The servant was flamboyant and verbose,
whereas Camilla, fearing to offend
by words or gestures gross or grandiose,
was by her nature quiet and demure.
Lothario attended every day,
and though she hadn't very much to say,
he sought to woo her. Dangling the lure,
he worked away at leading her astray.

A wife-to-husband letter so abrupt
was rarely ever penned. She dished the dirt!
Anselmo's so-called 'friend' fetched up to flirt,
she put (as though both hands were cupped
around her shouting mouth). She wrote of hurt,
of feeling isolated as she fought

to guard her husband's honour, and her own.
How *could* Anselmo leave her here, alone?
He'd hurry back to Florence, as he ought?
Protect her from the 'friend', so shameless grown?

So far from being minded to return
was Ser Anselmo, he devised another ploy
to amplify his absence. What a joy!
Lothario might assail, Camilla spurn:
could foolish curiosity annoy
a man as blessed as he? His wife was true,
his friend dependable. What could go wrong?
(he'd have his antiphon before too long!)
Anselmo's strange enthusiasm grew:
His urge to test his wife continued strong.

Is there a rampart that can not be breached?
A castle is there, that can never fall?
The wildest-eyed of zealots, even Saul,
can be converted, conquered, carried, reached.
Camilla's only human, after all.
Lothario has seen her, close at hand.
He loves the way those braids of hair enmesh,
that scent of hers, unchanging, yet so fresh:
delights in all her mannerisms, and
adores that satin, taut against her flesh.

It came to pass. Lothario digs saps.
He undermines her walls, he storms her gates.
As Miguel de Cervantes intimates,
no fortitude is proof against a lapse.
Camillas, Katherines, Corinnas, Kates,
they're all in thrall to Nature. In the end,
however high or halcyon the cause,
our universe has two immortal laws:

assedi are pure bastards to defend,
and pumping blood drowns out the parsons' saws.

Anselmo's back in Florence. Don't you think
'I've seen the thing I hankered most to see,
so don't let's push things,' ought to be
his stance from this point forward? On the brink
is not the place to dice with jeopardy.
Of course, he chooses badly. He's delighted
to hear Lothario's self-regarding lies.
The latter claims he's driven to despise
philanderers and liars. So near-sighted
has he become, his self-deluding eyes

see nothing. He says, 'Keep on as before.
Besiege her, press her hard. I need to know
how much she can endure, how far she'll go.
Don't think of backing off her. Give her more!'
Lothario looked at him, long and slow.
'This is the fool,' he thought, 'that I'm betraying.
Can he be serious? He eggs me on!
This honour that he vaunts is dead and gone,
although he doesn't know it. I'll keep playing:
we'll see who's standing at the *dénouement*.'

'Adopt the posture of a rustic swain,'
Anselmo says, 'and send her sonnets, please.
This works with women. Conquer by degrees!'
'I'll storm her with *strambotto* and *quatrain*,'
replies Lothario, 'show for sure that she's
inviolable: panegyric pome
will never lift her – she'll remain unleaven,
as certain as her berth awaits in heaven,
unravishable as Renaissance Rome.
Let's raise a glass to 1527!'

The husband chooses 'Chloris' as her name,
the lover writes the lines. A fortnight later,
all three are eating: *Ode to Chloris' Crater,*
Where Galilean Gadgets Gladly Came
(he might have kept his face a little straighter).
Camilla knows Lothario hails from Pisa –
that's why she purrs. Anselmo, so myopic,
rejoices at 'erections telescopic':
our tawdry Tasso trails another teaser –
'I'll train my tool on transiting her tropic!'

Lothario's bamboozling his friend:
His 'Chloris' sits before him, *parti-pris*,
already conquered. Similarly she,
so ready to dissemble and pretend,
affects an air of equanimity:
she knows the words are hers, straight from her lover.
Anselmo thinks his clever stratagem
is working like a dream. Dissembling phlegm,
internally he's crowing. He'll discover
that *he's* the one who's being duped by *them*.

(Two observations, with permission: first,
the ones who look to us will take their cue,
for good or ill, from what they see us do:
our moral turpitude brings out the worst
in pupils, children, household retinue.
And second, there is no-one quite as zealous
for punishing deception as the traitor.
Discern your doxy, winking at the waiter,
and you, the backdoor-man, insanely jealous,
can't wait to denigrate and castigate her.)

The lovely Leonella caught on fast:
her mistress, then, was sexually lax?
Why mightn't she fall, also, through the cracks?

She brought a boy home, and they had a blast
(and didn't bother covering their tracks!)
One night Lothario, lurking in the street,
observed the love of Leonella, leaving.
Predictably, his thoughts were not on thieving –
his doubts about Camilla were complete.
Suspicions now were settled, past retrieving.

How might a charlatan exact revenge?
He'll roll her over, like an alligator,
induce the ones who cherish her to hate her.
He'll build a quarantine, a fence, a henge:
the surest way to hurt her – isolate her.
He tells Anselmo how the bet is lost.
Camilla has surrendered willingly.
The matrimony now consists of three.
The Rubicon has certainly been crossed.
Camilla has a lover: namely, he.

Anselmo's devastation is entire.
He has no words beyond, 'It isn't true'.
Lothario suggests the thing to do –
effectively, he says they should conspire –
and spy on false Camilla, to accrue
sufficient evidence to close the case.
The tapestries Anselmo bought from Paris!
Secluded there, he'll listen, and embarrass
his faithless wife, confront her face to face:
a broken man, he hides behind the arras.

Lothario regrets what he has done.
He sees the anguish of his grieving friend,
and wonders where this thing is going to end.
Dismantling the web that he has spun
will surely help alleviate, amend.
What better course of action could exist

than tell Camilla that her husband knows?
Together they can ponder, in repose,
what steps to take. He asks her for a tryst,
and turns his thoughts from poetry to prose.

Surprisingly, Camilla speaks up first.
'My handmaid, Leonella, is a vandal!
She's brought on me – I don't know how to handle
the shame of it – I'm utterly immersed –
she brings her lover here – a public scandal!'
Lothario is wholly unconvinced.
He thinks Camilla's story is a trick
to talk away her 'visitor', a slick
self-serving subterfuge. Unminced,
his words come out, cascading fast and thick.

'Anselmo knows what you and I are doing.
He's hiding in your room, to overhear
whatever we might say when we appear.'
Her fury, now she's faced with trouble brewing,
emerges cold and disciplined. 'I fear,'
she says, 'you've done irreparable harm.
When in my husband's presence, do not speak,
except to answer questions. Keep it meek.
The best that you can do,' (her voice was calm)
'is help undo the havoc that you wreak.'

Lothario is left outside the room
and told to wait. Within, there is no doubt
of where Anselmo's hiding. Being stout,
he makes the arras bulge. Its folds entomb
the cuckold, but his feet are sticking out.
Camilla (with exaggerated wink
and stage-articulation) cries, 'Alas,
that things have come to such a sorry pass!

Take heart, my Leonella. Do not shrink:
for, like the sacrifice of Holy Mass,

you plunge Anselmo's dagger in this breast,
and are ennobled! Free me from this pain.
(Before you do, enlighten me, explain:
how did I – I, who strove to be the best,
provoke Lothario, prod him to profane
my continence? Like Leda and the swan,
did I arouse him? Stimulate, entice?
You think me baby, scary, sporty spice?
Am I a teaser? Did I lead him on?
Then find me guilty. I will pay the price.'

Since women have much nimbler wits than men
('emotional intelligence', the name),
the lovely Leonella guessed the game.
She took the plaints and doubled them again.
'We women always seem to get the blame!'
(Not bad, for starters!) 'Why are we so weak?'
(Hmm, getting better.) 'When they draw their knives,
we women pay the balance, with our lives.'
(She's on a roll! She's on a winning streak!)
'I save my keenest pity for the wives!'

(Savonarola seldom spoke so well.)
'How many matrons patronise the vault?
A wife stands vulnerable to assault,
denied the refuge of the virgin's cell.
Men get the pleasure, women get the fault!
And woe to Ser Anselmo!' (Leonella
struck hard and true – but wasn't finished yet.)
'I lack the brains to work out why he let
another foul his house. Mere *zitadella*,
I saw so much to lose – and naught to get!'

The man behind the curtain is uneasy.
Stay where he is, perhaps? Should he emerge?
Conflicting feelings, swirling, now converge:
indignant, anxious, grateful – even queasy!
He can't decide – seclude himself, or surge?
A swoon! He sees Camilla's coy collapse
on Leonella's lap. They're breast to breast,
one heaving bosom to the other pressed
(another of those wily women's traps?)
Recovering, Camilla (still distressed)

instructs her maid to fetch the waiting 'guest',
Lothario. Anselmo, through the gaps,
is watching, listening. Camilla wraps
her shawl (not very tightly) round her chest
and starts a loud soliloquy. 'Perhaps
I'll kill myself, or maybe stab the 'friend'.
To be, or not to be, that is the question,
but who should die? I'm open to suggestion!
The letter I astutely chose to send
is sure to give Anselmo indigestion.'

The husband wasn't keen on dagger-play
and wanted to avert an accident.
He'd got the gist of what Camilla meant
(and even what she might go on to say).
Besides, it now seemed fairly evident
Lothario would shortly be at hand,
and curtain-lurking definitely lacked
the comfort factor … No time to react!
Camilla drew a limit in the sand
(she scratched it on the parquet floor, in fact.)

And suddenly, Lothario was there,
with Leonella smiling at his side.
Anselmo felt he might as well abide

behind the arras (best to have a care:
Timidity has grandsons, unlike Pride!)
'When, Traitor, were your try-ons not repelled?'
(This from Camilla.) 'What emboldened you?
To what are your impertinences due?
For what am I in such *disprezzo* held,
that you feel free to run me through and through?'

She leapt on her alleged *innamorato*
and grabbed his collar, brandishing her blade:
Lothario was dumbfounded and dismayed:
this kind of thing could not occur in Prato:
an ambidextrous distaff ambuscade!
By gestures and by touches she conveys
that nothing here is seriously wrong.
Lothario is quick to play along,
since fraudsters are the quickest to appraise
the scams of others. Whether weak or strong,

he tacitly surrendered her the lead.
'Some lightness in me, lack of moral fibre,
unlike Lucrece who, beside the Tiber,
accomplished that which decency decreed.'
(this was, of course, before the age of cyber)
communicated cleverly Camilla,
to benefit the dolt behind the drapes.
Pomona chose her succulentest grapes
to add some passion to the thriller-chiller:
the greatest, this, of famous great escapes!

So, playing to the Gobelin-swathed gallery,
she howled out, 'That is why I need to die!'
The knife, within the blinking of an eye,
was plunging like a social worker's salary:
'My mistress' blood!' came Leonella's cry.
There was in fact some blood, but they'd been tricked.

Camilla had the acumen to guide
the weapon: lethal force was not applied.
Her naked shoulder had been slightly nicked:
the blow of vital organs landed wide.

Her lover takes the lesion on the lam.
Distraction is an action he holds dear,
just as a Bengal Lancer loves his spear.
Presented opportunity to scram,
Lothario is simply 'outta here'.
To give Anselmo pretext for egress,
the womenfolk announce they will 'retire':
Camilla's wound will urgently require
a change into a freshly-laundered dress
(her lack of treatment seems not half so dire!)

Anselmo! What possesses you, you fool?
You are the author of your own disgrace,
and yet you hurry from your hiding-place
excited as a child released from school,
to fold Lothario in a warm embrace!
Dishonour's on you! You, its architect,
confuse the worst of all worlds with the best.
Have you forgotten that your 'friend' confessed?
By tempting trouble, what did you expect?
Why were you malcontent when you were blessed?

'My dear Lothario, the whole thing worked!'
Anselmo seems to think the pantomime
he's just observed disposes of the crime.
Lothario, embarrassed, sorely irked,
regards it as the obverse of sublime.
The cuckold, thrilled, is harping on it still:
his cozener has conjured up a phrase
to nail Anselmo's self-deceiving haze:

'deliciously deluded' fills the bill.
And still the gull is gushing endless praise!

Again he offers access to his home,
but now Lothario is somewhat loath
and says he is expected – on his oath –
to deal with certain matters down in Rome.
Unfruitfully they pass the evening, both.
But meanwhile, Leonella's having fun.
(The cat's away and mice are wont to play!)
Her gentleman is calling every day,
and no-one would describe her as a nun.
She's making something – not just making hay!

Returning to the house in San Felice
Anselmo, feeling out of sorts and aimless,
detects a sound – that little hussy's shameless!
His penchant for pontification-preachy
possesses him – 'But Master – we are blameless!'
The servant knows she's in the hottest water.
Anselmo's in the room. 'So that's your game!'
(The pity is, we can't quite say the same
for Leonella's man (let's put it shorter:
he's now three-quarters through the window-frame!)

The blow that's coming, somehow must be parried.
'He's now my husband – almost – nearly – sort of:
the licence is the only thing we're short of.
He's promised me that next month, we'll be married!'
(She shrugs towards the lad: *first thing I thought of!*'
Allowed to leave, the lover's in the wind,
but Leonella's pickle just got worse.
Anselmo's angry, and he's not averse
to daggers. Fearing that she'll soon be skinned,
she ventures, 'Women! Tainted by The Curse!'

Don't kill me, Ser Anselmo! Hold off. Wait!'
She tried her hand at auto-intercession.
'Though some might criticize my indiscretion,
I have important matters to relate,
such fractious fare as may your frenzy freshen!'
His knife-point, still, is pressing on her neck:
his blood is circulating, fast and furious:
but Leonella's winning. Now he's curious.
He holds his homicidal hand in check.
'A harlot's promise oftentimes is spurious …'

He scans her face and tells her, as he scours,
' … but I'll afford you finite clemency.
Keep to your quarters, under lock and key,
and I, returning with the daylight hours,
will hear you and assess your probity.'
And this is where the author intervenes.
Anselmo's angry – ludicrously limp!
His maid has proved a sexy little imp –
preposterous reactions, silly scenes!
Is not the point that he's Camilla's pimp?

With motive, opportunity and means,
what kind of moron wouldn't simply kill her?
They always do this in the so-called 'thriller'.
We adults tell our children, 'eat your greens',
envisioning voluptuous vanilla,
but for ourselves. What does the villain gain
by shutting up Sean Connery in a cell?
He'll overcome his guardians – can't you tell?
Where did you learn your craft? Don't traitors train?
So kiss your secret missile base farewell.

The story seems to pivot at this point.
We have divergent versions, many endings.
You'd sooner have reunions than rendings?

New limbs have sprouted from this severed joint:
perhaps we'll ponder them as patent-pendings.
The first, the maid. At dawn, Anselmo meets …
sweet nothing. Leonella is long gone.
There's little in the room to dwell upon:
an open window, rope of knotted sheets.
The Happy Harlot's with her Jolly John!

'Republican', we note, concludes with 'can'.
Though Leonella took her share of flak,
initiative's a thing she didn't lack.
In Florence, as a famous courtesan,
she flourished: made a fortune on her back.
The second one, Camilla's, ends with schemes
to hide her in a nunnery. For once,
Lothario's was a full and frank response
(those convents were convenient, it seems,
for dumping women one no longer wants).

Reluctantly, I am the spoiler-spiller:
this version is confused, if not conflated,
with truth. Grand Duke Francisco coldly hated
his father's consort, also called Camilla,
within a convent's walls incarcerated.
They say the night her servant was enclosed,
Camilla took her sapphires, clothes, and fled.
Her fear of revelations is what sped
her exit. Even though that be supposed,
we don't know what was later done or said.

What seems the Via Crucis, proves the Crown.
It's from our doubts that rich conjecture springs.
Not knowing gives our thought its golden wings.
We're never going to pin what happened down:
but isn't that the beauty of these things?
We like to know the story is well-built:

offended by an ending trite, capricious,
we stay away from stuff that's meretricious,
assembled like a crazy patchwork quilt –
but we are wrong. Not knowing is delicious!

Which leaves Anselmo, hero of our saga.
One rumour has him friends with Perugino,
another that he wound up in Urbino,
a court official serving the Gonzaga:
a third, he worked alongside Cesalpino.
Forgive Camilla, live with her again?
Or slit her throat, to satisfy his honour?
Could all the blame be neatly heaped upon her?
Is this a thing that's prevalent with men?
Then every grown-up woman is a goner!

Some speculation spread as far as Spain
(the home of the Invincible Armada):
It held Anselmo stopped at a *posada*
fatigued by fulminations of the brain
(an organ which had never yet worked harder).
He sat alone in silent melancholy,
unable to emit a single word:
and as he pondered all that had occurred,
his eyes were opened to his former folly.
How self-awareness renders us absurd!

So, seated at a table just outside
the tavern door, imbibing *manzanilla*,
Anselmo gratified his enophilia.
The landlord came out frequently and plied
the Tuscan's cup. A rider, unfamiliar,
(our host informs us) just then happened by.
'The two men spoke in Latin. No-one can
discern such matters, here in Benaoján,'

el dueño commented. 'We all must die,
the law of life. And yet – who was the man?'

They found Anselmo's body in his room
the morning after. He had left a note
which, fortunately, we can briefly quote.
'This tavern now must serve me as my tomb,
where I will expiate my sins,' he wrote.
'I bear no bitterness towards my bride:
indeed, it's I who should be tarred and
feathered.' Thus, his consciousness had hardened.
And there it ends, with no hint how he died.
We hope he left us feeling, somehow, pardoned.

THE SLEEP OF SORROW AND THE DREAM OF JOY, Being various Scraps of Verse discovered among the Papers of Massimo Taparelli, Count d'Azeglio, after his Death

D'Azeglio had read of our Pompilia.
It pained his gentle soul that those with knives
were all too apt to butcher sisters, wives
or anyone unarmed. Was Guido silly, or
was what he practised proper paedophilia?
When Man's ascendancy at last arrives,
the selfish apes will leave off taking lives.
Our toils, to date, are just our juvenilia.

He would have wanted Gambi over Spreti,
have swapped a Scarpia for a Donizetti.
He put our problem powerfully, prettily:
imprisoned in her home, denied expression,
unable to be more than a possession,
that girl is us. Pompilia is Italy.

Va, Pensiero

Go, my thoughts, on golden wings
to where my feet would love to tread,
to where the blackbird of the twilight sings
as day subsides and shadows spread,
to where the gentle murmurings
of languid streams console the dead.
Oh my land, so fair, so lost!
All our troubles come from men.
Can the sunlight crack the frost?
Will I see my home again?

Carry me across the waves
to where my soul will sleep at peace,
to where the ageless architraves
disdain our turbulent caprice:
where none are owners, none are slaves,
and winter yields to summer's lease.

Com'è Gentil

How perfect, and how right,
this sweet mid-April night!
The moon is fresh and frail,
for once without her veil!
The breeze is all tranquility,
but whispering a mystery:
the stars are bright above –
why don't you come, my love?

Turn to me and say that you love me,
and I will tell you that you are divine.
Promise me that you are part of me,
give me assurances that you are mine.

La Cisterna

The women bicker at the parish pump.
Because they're ignorant of French or Spanish,
They blame each other. Economic slump?
That's in the ether. Rancour's far more clannish.

A life that's lived within severe constraints
is no existence: *ma lei lo tollera.*
When cholera is raging, all complaints
degenerate to squabbles over cholera.

This life is vacant, hollow, unfulfilled:
to be herself, she'll have to break away.
Though prisoners may toil, they never build:
Italia, sebbene sola, farà da sè.

Since marriage seems another form of rape,
she needs to overturn the *status quo.*
She'll never grow, unless she can escape:
in order to escape, she has to grow.

SAN CLEMENTE GATE

The curfew tolls the knell of parting day
as dying sunlight struggles up the wall
and shadows in the alley, waxing tall,
crowd out the feeble warmth of fading ray.

Whoever's in the town, perforce must stay.
The doors are chained to comers, goers, all:
We here abide, denied by night's thick shawl:
those bound for San Sepulcro, under way.

A housecat blinks. His food is guaranteed.
In here, he feels no need to forage, fight,
refine the lethal team of reach and sight:
the closing of the gate has been decreed.
As honest burghers settle for the night,
There's something, still, that hankers to be freed.

DOCTOR ANTONIO LAMPARELLI, PROCURATOR OF THE POOR, DEFENDS CANON GIUSEPPE CAPONSACCHI AT THE *PROCESSUS FUGAE*

Is nothing good or decent left?
We bandy accusations such as these –
adultery, abduction, theft –
with irresponsibility and ease.
   We take a man
     (because we can)
and drain his reputation to the lees.

My learned friend is (granted!) deft
and doesn't wait or hesitate to seize
lacunae in the warp and weft
of evidence, compiling by degrees
   a pretty plan
    more subtle than
a Palestrina *contrappunto*. He's

debasing his undoubted skill
to posture as intemperate aggressor,
to put this youngster through the mill,
for being what? A priestly snappy dresser?
   But worse by far
    (in my view) are
the insults that he hurls at the *Contessa* !

The venom flowing from his quill
can have no object, other than distress her.
The Court admires his learning still,
but deems his leaning to extremes the lesser.
   His repertoire,
     believes the Bar,
non dovrebbe essere permessa.

I own, it differs from the norm
for wives to run away with handsome men,
but 'any port in any storm'!
And who can such a woman turn to, when
   the one she wed
     is so ill-bred,
he violates her time and time again?

Since fish and fowl aren't uniform,
who blames recalcitrance in one poor hen
who tries, but who can never warm
to yielding under blows, or wielding pen,
   or ending dead?
     Not me. Instead,
she needs to flee the foul domestic den.

If Caponsacchi took a risk,
he did it as a selfless, generous favour.
I'm taking issue with the Fisc:
this hero helped a girl without a quaver,
   did all he did
     as *tertium quid*
whose only motivation was to save her.

The road was straight, their pace was brisk,
and Canon Caponsacchi didn't waver:
the fountain and the obelisk
of Popolo were gifts he almost gave her.

The Count undid
　　　his noble bid,
but who could want a saviour any braver?

When governor and bishop fail
to offer their protection to a child
(and child she was, beyond the pale)
'community' means nothing. Spurned, reviled,
　　the *estranea*
　　　sought dragon-slayer,
and found him. Guido, who was really riled,

gave out commands, to no avail:
declared her insubordinate – nay, wild.
(Authority will not prevail
where needs and deeds have not been reconciled.)
　　At each new layer,
　　　he sought to stay her,
but merely Pelion on Ossa piled.

The marriage had been built on fraud,
and Guido hardly tried to hide the cock-up.
What was the Canon's one reward
for stepping in? All summer in the lock-up!
　　And who could say
　　　that running away
had failed to push Pompilia's stock up?

It dawned on Guido, feeble-jawed,
the thickened waist was likely not a mock-up:
the thought oppressed him, niggled, gnawed:
a pregnancy! (More vulgarly, a knock-up!)
　　The family way,
　　　or passion play?
What cuckold ever cares to count the clock up?

Authorities like Decian say
mens rea can't survive a good intention:
abduction charges fall away
where what was done was furthering prevention
   of worse offence
   like murder, hence
I offer Decian for the Court's attention.

We'll let the chips fall where they may.
Relying on a long-revered convention,
defendants have the right to pray
(I'm certain of the Bench's condescension)
   in their defence
   benevolence:
and in their aid I've made abundant mention.

And John agrees. The Pharisees
set out to trap The Saviour, force His hand,
but Jesus beat them off with ease.
The letter of the law was their demand
   but, ashen-faced
   as Jesus traced,
they read their own shortcomings in the sand.

Authorities as apt as these
all advocates can easily command:
as cedar trees are Lebanese,
they're common as a desert's grains of sand,
   or footsteps traced
   in Asian waste,
from Ctesiphon to ancient Samarkhand.

The 'Castelnuovo Letters', mined
(allegedly) from toilets at the scene,
so non-specific, vague, unsigned:
what may they, in forensic language, mean?

Soiled goods at best,
   which we suggest
were found in, are best left in, the latrine.

They were, indeed, a lucky find:
for escapees will hardly, as routine,
bear damning cargo of this kind:
they hope to make the break completely clean:
   will have suppressed,
   emptied the chest,
'fore dangers unforeseen and ill-defined.

These letters seem Bellini-based,
a middle-brow cowgirl-and-shepherdfest.
Their lymph is nymphs-by-satyrs-chased,
the sort of piffle Poussin once professed.
   With terms like 'troth'
   and 'quoth' and 'loth'
these literary languishings are dressed.

They manifest a type of taste,
conventional and dullard, but expressed
in learned words, not urgent haste
(directed to no person, unaddressed).
   Here, on their oath,
   these prisoners both
(when called on by my colleague to attest)

denied all fault. As with the kiss
described by Venerino, I invite
this congregation to dismiss
all charges. Since the girl can't read or write,
   in honesty
   it's hard to see
what led the Prosecutor to indict.

Who wrote those letters? This
has exercised my wits, as well it might.
A party who was prejudiced
against Pompilia, and out of spite
  aspired to be
  maliciously
a perjured serpent, half-afraid to bite.

THE COUNTESS OF CELLANT, Being a Tale told by Fra Angelo Celestino

A woman knows by instinct where to touch
her man: his frailties, completely understands
(in certain cases, comprehends too much!)
He thinks he rules? He wriggles in her hands:
he acts upon the world, but she commands.
The rose stays seemly, seemingly just waiting,
but all the while, her scent's intoxicating.
To make a stir on earth – that's why we're here!
Does God exact day-labour, light denied?
The valued worker is the volunteer.
Within this narrow crack where we abide,
We yearn for motion, seek to set aside
outmoded notions of what's good or ill:
there's making progress, or there's standing still.

BIANCA WAS A WOMAN OF LOW BIRTH.
Her father made his millions in a way
that rendered unto Caesar silver's worth:
he kept his talents toiling, night and day,
declined to 'delve like Adam', as they say.
Bianca was the toast of Monferrato,
her fortune, far from merited, *donato*.

The most-sought-after maiden in the city,
as spoiled as milk that's boiled, the woman-child
reached adolescence limber, spritely, pretty.
She sauntered, simpered, smouldered, sidled, smiled,
and those she looked on, brazenly beguiled,
and (as it's always been with fine-limbed girls)
began collecting men like stringing pearls.

Since Monferrato had a marchioness,
this lady saw herself as matriarch,
with power to ban, authority to bless.
How brave the couple, minded to embark
on marriage, lacking her approval mark!
Bianca having two ennobled suitors,
alerted this regina of recruiters.

(Discerning students of this sorry saga
will pay attention to the lovers' names,
for they are legion) Gismond of Gonzaga
was one potential husband. In all games,
one needs antagonists to fan the flames:
the suitor now attempting to supplant
Gonzaga was Count Cesare of Cellant.

The marchioness promoted Gismond's cause,
but secretly Bianca wed the Count.
On learning this, the older woman's claws
remained retracted. 'Character's the fount
of all our fortunes. Given the amount
of defects that the little slut displays,
I'll bide my time and wait for better days.'

Whatever moves the heavens, sends us signs.
The warnings swarm around us. If we heed,
not just some constellation which aligns,
but omens – a Madonna's seen to bleed,

an inability to sing the Creed –
we'll steer our lives the better. Wisdom brings
a gift for seeing patterns in these things.

The Empire, or the Papacy? You choose!
Since Europe (that's the planet) first began,
by way of battles, revolutions, coups,
two titans have been fighting. Fault lines ran
(not for the last time!) right across Milan.
When Habsburg Carlos gathered up Castile,
the portents for a wedding weren't ideal!

That meteorite in China – seen by whom?
Columbus' cousin – what more do you want?
The Genoese was speaking from the tomb!
Bianca, headstrong, wilful *nonchalante*,
insensitive to tip-off as to taunt,
contracted marriage that was bound to fail,
like hoisting mainsail in an arctic gale.

Bianca fought her husband, as she must.
The thing she needed now? A second home,
some leagues from Monferrato, shake the dust
of Asti from her shoes. If not quite Rome,
at least in Pavia she could preen and comb,
and bathe four times a morning, free from stress.
Who offered her the house? The marchioness!

And who was then in Pavia? Had she known
(perhaps she did!) the marchioness could scarce
have lit a bigger blaze. Bored and alone,
Bianca went in search of love affairs,
and in the process stumbled unawares
on Ardizzino, Viscount of Veneria,
who had Imperial business in the area.

No matter if he's handsome: steeped in shame,
a man is vulnerable if deformed –
and Ardizzino, conscious he was lame,
was easy prey. Bianca's ardour warmed:
the citadel surrendered, scarcely stormed.
Though men suppose they conquer, women choose
to leave the drawbridge down. They never lose.

If this was love, it wasn't quite the kind
we read about in poems. Disrepute
polluted all their actions. Love is blind
and, stubbornly intent on Love's pursuit,
they carried on a life so dissolute
that Pavia was quickly sliding down
in reputation. It was scandal-town.

But nothing lasts for ever. Woman's taste
(at least *this* kind of woman!) turns out frail.
Soon, Ardizzino finds himself displaced.
The reason that he's now beyond the pale
is, now another well-connected male
has come to Pavia. Ardizzino's through.
Bianca's moving on to pastures new.

Roberto held the County of Gaiazzo.
(The story I'm attempting to relate
requires an Ariosto, or a Tasso!)
Bianca's fierce libido was in spate.
Remembering that 'character is fate',
we know why she committed the enormity
of laughing at her former love's deformity.

Surprised and wounded by this spiteful trait,
Count Ardizzino, knowing he'd been trounced,
allowed what had been love to turn to hate.
The woman he'd adored, he now denounced:

abandoned Pavia before the vixen pounced
a second time. Resolved at last to sever,
he parted for Milan (he thought) for ever.

Bianca urged Gaiazzo, now 'her' man,
to murder Ardizzino right away.
Gaiazzo lent agreement to this plan,
but something bade him privately to stay
his hand. A nobleman does not betray
a fellow and a friend without demur:
and never for a harlot such as her.

The word got back to Bianca in a trice.
For all her faults, one triumph stood out proud:
she owned a secret service beyond price.
Her gathering of intelligence allowed
immediate reaction. Her avowed
enforcer, majordomo, right-hand man
was Don Pietro, 'Phantom of Milan'.

(Another lover? You were warned before
to notch a tally!) Swarthy and morose,
Don Pietro the Sicilian (keeping score?)
was Bianca's chief of staff. She kept him close,
and kept him hoping. Far from being verbose,
Pietro was a sullen, silent presence
in contrast to his mistress' effervescence.

Gaiazzo, coming back to Pavia, found
Bianca's interest had taken wing:
she'd dropped him for her husband. This was crowned
by rumours she was pregnant. Wondering
if she was feigning (who'd do such a thing?),
he kept his distance, and his dignity.
Milan would welcome him. And he'd be free.

She's narcissistic, craving men's attention:
stability's a trait she doesn't own:
it pleases her to trample on convention.
That Ardizzino's still in love is known:
contention is her fascination zone!
The husband doesn't get a second glance,
for Ardizzino's welcomed to the dance!

But murder still obsessed her. Day by day
she worked on Ardizzino, sapped his will.
Gaiazzo was her target – that's to say
she urged her recent victim now to kill
her ex-assassin, with the codicil
that this was Ardizzino's own best course:
to claim his lover through the use of force.

But this young man is not a naive fool.
He knows Bianca seeks her selfish ends.
Remaining self-contained, remaining cool,
he travels to Milan. He still pretends
(though he and Count Gaiazzo are good friends)
the murder plot is active. Face to face,
the two young men unburden, and embrace.

Gaiazzo crossed himself. 'The damnedest whore!
I'm mortified I ever called her mine.
Still, you and I are friends, were friends before.'
Bianca's 'network', sinister, malign,
was watching this *rapprochement*. In fine,
her *protégé* Pietro, privily placed,
sent message back to Pavia, post-haste.

Bianca knew she had to kill the two.
She had (she thought) a reasonable plan,
but scarcely had a hope of seeing it through,
unless two things should happen: get a man,

and move her operation to Milan.
They both fell pat! She travelled under cover,
promoting Pietro (finally!) to lover.

The bastard of the Count of Collisano,
Pietro lived under a surly star.
Cashiered for cowardice back in Locarno,
he'd lusted after Bianca from afar.
Astute enough to leave the door ajar,
Bianca chose this night to open wide
and, blind to signs, Pietro pushed inside.

That very day, another Lombard plain
(the end of April, fifteen twenty-two)
saw war in all its horror. There was slain
Pietro's father – not that Pietro knew.
One thing a man is ill-advised to do
is enter on an enterprise the day
that he who gave him life, threw life away.

However they dissemble or conceal,
there's never been a man who wasn't frail:
the sturdiest Achilles has a heel.
The female is more deadly than the male
and, all things being equal, must prevail.
Bianca understood this all too well:
She conquered most completely when she fell.

Pietro was besotted. This was love!
She needed him (weak woman!) to protect her
(she worked him like her fingers worked a glove!)
She wrought him as a Roland, hewed a Hector,
and hoped he wouldn't (blinking eyes) reject her.
Two mortal enemies deserved to die.
Was he the man to let the chance go by?

Pietro and his bravoes stalked their prey:
assassination plans were quickly laid.
Since theirs was not an art of smiling day,
they lay in ambush in a colonnade:
poor Ardizzino never saw the blade
that, slicing darkness, hacked his life away.
His brother, too, was slaughtered in the fray.

The Duke of Bourbon's soldiers, lodged close by,
arrested Pietro's bravoes on the spot.
They'd seen events unfold, seen two men die.
Don Pietro and accomplices, the lot,
had bloody hands – and still the blood was hot!
For Pietro, every lingering hope was gone:
would he betray the one who'd egged him on?

A letter from Vienna – Bourbon's raised
to Civil Governor. With this, he's seised
of Pietro's process. Pietro was amazed
to learn that torture was an option! Teased
by hopes of mitigation, if he pleased
the court, and named his (as he'd thought her) wife,
he'd rot in prison ... but preserve his life.

They led Bianca to the courtyard block
(since nobles are decapitated, for,
in social terms, to hang would be a shock
from which the line would not recover), nor
acceded to her final '*por favor*'.
The thing that commentators dwell upon,
she begged to see 'her lover'. But which one?

MEN MAY DIE OF IMAGINATION

The medieval point of view?
The coolest thing a scribe could do
was write a well-worn tale anew:
the Holy Grail, the Wandering Jew:
something borrowed, something blue.

Decameron, Magnificat:
you camp on someone's ziggurat:
the top cat is the copycat.
Invention? Dreaming up New Hat?
Oh, has it really come to that?

LA SALTA DE LA CONTESSA, Being a Tale told by Gregorio Guillichini

The story's recounted again and again,
but still it's a tale people tell:
when very young girls marry jealous old men,
the matter can never end well.

Our lass was a beauty, her clan Tolomei,
Siena the city that made her,
and Nello the falcon who savaged his prey,
Maremma the mire that betrayed her.

While some who are given to thinking the worst
or are intellectually lazy
will never resile from the rancour they've nursed
for the *gentile donna senese*,

there are those who propose that humanity grows
by turning its face to the sun:

canaries are never as common as crows,
but which would you welcome, which shun?

Siena, which Nello avoided for shame,
despised him as 'Ghibelline vassal'.
He dropped Pannochiechi, his family name,
and called himself after his castle.

Maremma owns nothing as solid as stone,
and apt was the new nomenclature:
de Pietra, the name by which Nello was known,
uncannily captured his nature.

Maremma Amara

Maremma's a mother who murders her young,
and nothing of substance survives.
Boundless and soundless, where no songs are sung
and only the ivy-vine thrives.

A bird that flies over Maremma
and loses her way in the night
Will never return or remember
she's taken her very last flight.

Maremma's a venom to tarnish the tongue
from which all that's bitter derives.
When horseflies have bitten, and leeches have clung,
you'll question why you are alive.

There's nothing to drink in Maremma
and nothing that's wholesome to eat:
the water will give you distemper:
it's acid, polluted by peat.

Dead foxes have rotted on stakes where they're strung,
and bees have abandoned their hives.
A land from which goodness was long ago wrung,
of all expectation deprived.

Mere living is hard in Maremma,
the marsh pulling everything down:
one yearling in ten takes the tether,
the others foredestined to drown.

Maremma begins by corrupting your lungs
albeit you've lately arrived:
the bogs are not wholesome for living among,
especially not for young wives.

The Character of Nello

I see no point in sitting on the fence.
A bully is a certain individual
(I wouldn't, for the world, attempt to kid you all)
whose slant on ranking, pecking-order sense,
is out of all proportion. So immense
is this distortion, grasp of scale so scant,
he'd just as soon be seen a sycophant.
The two sides of the coin are Trump and Pence.
There's none who crows so keenly of his candour as
the bare-faced liar: nobody believes
that property is sacred, quite like thieves:
no self-regard's so brittle as the slanderer's,
uniquely piqued, the fraudster who deceives.
The most possessive lovers? The philanderers.

Nonentities like Nello, in the city,
molested by their meagre self-esteem,
once back in native marshes, reign supreme,
oppressing others without pause or pity.

But bullies are a breed apart (God love them!)
Although they'll happily apply brute strength,
they're toadies, too. They'll go to any length
to kiss the orifice of those above them.
The man who hurts his woman in his home
behind jalousies is a form of life
beneath the reptile. He's a moral gnome.
And yet, we find the cruelty chromosome
is not uncommon. Some would say it's rife.
Il cazzo doesn't serve? Insert the knife!

It's time now to know Margharita,
who stands at the heart of our tale.
(You may not be happy to meet her,
but narrative needs to prevail.)

Her family seat was Sovana,
Pitigliano her other estate:
the spawn of *Maremma toscana*,
in her, causing harm was innate.

Five husbands she'd taken and broken,
five spouses she'd treated as slaves.
What might, then, a marriage betoken?
Five grooms who were now in their graves.

A woman is like a phantasma,
enticing us into the fen:
concoction of placket and plasma,
but wholly effective on men.

Affairs are affairs – not disputed,
but this one was more than a romp.
'Sovana' and Nello were suited –
two reptiles, at home in the swamp.

Five Reasons Why Pia Had to Die

It's frequently the case, when men do wrong,
that consciences are salved by casting blame.
We look to string the human race along:
project-our-sins-on-others is the game
(at least for those impervious to shame).
When Nello cited Pia's improper love,
he knew that he was guilty of the same,
and she was spotless. When push comes to shove,
self-interest is all we're ever mindful of.

The majordomo was another source
of baseless bile, of vile malevolence.
Unable to impose on her by force,
he found a spigot for concupiscence
in spite that was unseemly and immense.
To punish Pia was his one objective,
obsession with revenge that made no sense,
but channeled through a talent for invective,
a cruel aptitude which proved all too effective.

Did Pia love her brother? No surprise.
Rodrigo was a Guelph? And what of that?
But Nello looked on love with jaundiced eyes,
in jealousy was quite the acrobat,
contorting and contriving. Crush a gnat?
This was the man to summon up artillery:
should Pia kiss her sibling, smell a rat:
he'd fret and fume from Francis Day to Hilary,
and once more, innocence was sentenced to the pillory.

A wife, to some, is just a breeding-mare,
and Nello's aspirations were dynastic.
The time was passing, still there was no heir:
solutions surfaced which were somewhat drastic.

It strikes us as a tad iconoclastic,
but murder was the settled-on recourse.
If Margherita waxed enthusiastic,
nor she nor Nello truckled with remorse,
for homicide was less a nuisance than divorce.

Ser Nello wanted Monna Margherita
and, truth be known, they made a perfect match.
It's hard to picture any juncture neater:
a pair of brigands (cudgel he, she snatch).
Just one thing now was needed to detach,
to seal her off, obliterate, to smother,
to isolate her, ready for despatch,
then Margherita might bewife (and mother):
the two assassins certainly deserved each other.

THE RACCONTINO — WHAT A SPLENDID FORM!
A story meets a poem — two in one:
you cut your cloth in couplets, save some lines
are static, like a rhyming antiphon,
while others whisk the narrative along!
Sad songs there are which, wasted, woebegone,
consist of only bleached-out horizontals,
as if the ribcage of some mastodon
could sit in sterile impotence to make
a puffed-up, puerile, pointless Parthenon —
(I trust that you're still following my sense,
that freshness, fervour, all that carry-on,
depends on ends cascading vertically
towards a pre-determined denouement.)

UBALDO! SHOULD YOU CROSS HIS PATH, beware!
The malformed majordomo's buckled spine
was like his character. Surpassing small,
this midget managed somehow to combine
a menace never found in stouter men

with slyness which was almost serpentine.
Ubaldo ran affairs for Nello, who
had, unawares (or maybe by design),
devolved authority. Place-holders are
some three parts craven, seven parts malign
and keen to wield their master's power: also,
with sharper weapons than the porcupine,
they prove to be inordinately spiteful.
Ascendancy can be a heady wine.

THERE'S SOMETHING DARK WITH MEN AND DOMINANCE:
authority's an aphrodisiac.
Ubaldo could, he felt, impose his will
on Pia, and in turn she'd love him back.
The man's monstrosity was manifest.
That this remiss, malodorous macaque
might sleep with Pia? Absurdity itself!
When she rebuffed the odious attack
instead of, as expected, giving in,
Ubaldo started on the vengeance track.
That powerlust and matters sexual
are intertwined, this mean-souled maniac
makes obvious. In no uncertain terms,
a wedge was now inserted in the crack.

Thus Pia's tender years, her innocence,
her wearing of her heart upon her sleeve,
encumbered her as only virtues can:
her fatal flaw was being too naive.
Begrudgers like Ubaldo never, never
allow their victims refuge or reprieve
and, confidently waiting-out his triumph,
the midget planned *progetti* to deceive,
respecting which the Monster gloated over
his master Nello's failure to perceive.
Without repose Ubaldo lingered spiteful,

knew perfectly the outcome to achieve,
deploying his considerable cunning,
his *amour-propre* on permanent *qui-vive*.

       * * * *

BOTH CHURCH AND HOUSE, still face-to-face today
across the tiny square which bears her name,
Palazzo and *Piazza* Tolomei,

become the setting, form the Gothic frame
of Pia's tragedy. Our scene now shifts
to Guelph Siena, town which overcame

the strength of Florence in those endless rifts
which scar Italian history. A home
in recent centuries to nesting swifts,

the fine old palace rivals even Rome.
Beneath these eaves a selfish, jealous man
(incited by a vicious, vengeful gnome)

denied his wife her life's allotted span.
The fine-spun fabric is the first to fray:
Here's where hope ended, and the end began.

       * * * *

A MARSHMAN'S NO RESPECTER OF FRONTIERS.
As winds and currents wander where they please,
he has no lines to which his mind adheres,
no clutching of the solid, as do trees.
To him, no separation into spheres,
no binding Nature's hands with boundaries
makes any sense at all. He comes and goes,
and never thinks 'encumber', or 'enclose'.

WHEN NELLO FOUND HE FACED A LEGAL SUIT,
he understood, at least, he had to fight.
The fine points of fee simple absolute
bemused him, found no purchase, didn't bite:
refute, rebut it, counterclaim, dispute
was all he knew. There is no black and white:
the rabbit knows his enemy, the stoat,
before it ever takes him by the throat.

The legal case might last perhaps a year:
he'd needs be in Siena, have to stay,
and maybe out of foresight, maybe fear,
while lodging in Palazzo Tolomei
he had to have his majordomo near.
Ubaldo got the transfer under way,
despatching cooks and candles, load by load,
as de Pietra's household hit the road.

It's clear that Pia was likely to rejoice
to see her home once more. Amid the cattle,
the bedding and the clothes, her modest voice
was lost. An army lurching into battle,
the household lumbered on. She had no choice,
for – well she knew – she was her husband's chattel.
She crossed her Siena threshold once again,
but under supervision of two men.

Was Nello nervous of the poisoner's arts?
It's certain that he didn't place much trust
in local foodstuffs. From Grosseto, carts
plied back and forth as frantic factors fussed
and sacks and saddles, wheels and oxbow parts
clogged up the courtyard, much to the disgust
of neighbours. Nello even sent to Spain
for plain, untainted Andalucian grain.

A year's supply of ears bulks rather large.
It filled the cloister like a desert dune,
transported from the coast by cart and barge.
The lack of labour proved inopportune,
but one young man who seemed to be in charge
appeared to have been sumptuously hewn
from flawless marble. Nervousness belied
his studied languor. Turmoil churned inside.

The new arrival toiled as hard as any,
indifferent to mockery or malice.
He filled his barrow up, like Salimbeni,
and paid regard to neither cut nor callus,
his one behaviour (not observed by many),
too-frequent glances up towards the palace.
If Pia, at some moment, happened by
an open window, and she caught his eye,

emotions surged within him, plain to see.
Of some strong passion Pia was the source,
and what he bore, he bore unhappily.
Fierce feelings manifest themselves perforce,
exacerbated by proximity,
yet nothing in this youth was crude or coarse:
appearing more a poet or a priest,
he didn't look a labourer in the least.

That's when the opportunity arose.
Installing grain in the *palazzo* loft,
the young man found himself alone. He froze.
The coast was clear. His leather apron doffed,
He glided down the ladder on his toes
and eased into the passage. Treading soft,
he made his way to Pia's bedroom door
(he'd been here oh, how many times before!)

Embraces, kisses, even happy tears,
expressions of the greatest tenderness –
then Pia whispers anguishes and fears.
Reluctant, but to lessen her distress,
he disengages, draws back, disappears,
although he'd rather die than acquiesce.
Her secret visitor? It's Pia's brother,
the exiled Guelph Rodrigo, and none other.

But someone's watching. Everything's been seen.
The looker-on is laughing under cover,
amusement seasoned by the meanest spleen.
To say Rodrigo came as Pia's lover?
It's more attractive when it's more obscene.
He knows how Nello thinks. Let him discover
the hunted Guelph was intimate with Pia …
Ubaldo is convulsed with that idea.

The order was peremptory. 'We go.'
So Nello's household had to pack their things
and head back to Maremma. In one blow,
his lordship gathered up his underlings
and set at naught the legal status quo,
but bitterest of all these sunderings
was that of Pia, severed from her city,
aware that she could now expect no pity.

To modern eyes it's just a castle shell,
a lonely ruin, sinking year on year
by incremental inches down to hell
in cheerless silence. One can almost hear
the marshland's liquid innards churn and swell.
One single tree, long dead, aslant, austere,
survives the mire. Beneath the Countess' cell,
it marks the fatal place where Pia fell.

Pᴀ ᴡᴀs ᴍᴜʀᴅᴇʀᴇᴅ. Wʜᴏ ᴡᴀs ᴛʜᴇ ᴀɢɢʀᴇssᴏʀ?
The emperor of the swamp? Misshapen praetor?
The paramour, so eager to unseat her?
Or were all three conspiring to oppress her?
Who played the leading role, and who the lesser?
Ubaldo, Nello, maybe Margherita.
Before her death, her husband thought it meeter
she make her peace with God. Which sad confessor
was summoned to her cell? All hope deferred,
she tumbled to her death. And her successor?
The word most oft averred is that she purred,
as might a female tiger, when she heard.
This tale is told, Otranto to Odessa,
of Pia's fall – La Salta de la Contessa.

THE LUCKLESS GIRL

She wasn't a tall one (Contenti was shorter!),
an amorous girlfriend, affectionate daughter.
Her long hair was thick, and looked grand in a plait:
I'd term her voluptuous (foes called her fat).
Her air was as rare as the moon in a well,
her pelt was the colour of crème caramel.
Could I point to a talent that set her apart?
No I couldn't, except for her wonderful heart.

But one thing I'd point to, I'd call it her essence.
I don't have the words, but she had incandescence.
We're born in this world and we have to go on,
and yet something continues here, after we're gone.
It could be as simple as lives we've affected,
but something about us continues, connected.

A STRANGE DISDAIN, Being a Tale told by Donna Costanza Donato of Arezzo

A sorry tale to dwell upon
   I offer you:
the story of Giovanna d'Aragon,
   as tragic as it's true.

She wanted happiness for others,
   but lost her own:
her fiercest enemies, her own two brothers,
   for eagles fly alone.

What is this life? A prison pen,
   a ship of fools?
A game without a name, where none but men
   dictate and state the rules?

They married her, while still a child
   (you know this tale?):
she worked to be contented, reconciled,
   but all to no avail.

Italian youth admires the blade,
   and loves to fight.
Thus young Giovanna was a widow made,
   beneath the eaves of night.

She bore a son, though past the time
   her husband bled,
and she (an able woman, in her prime)
   ruled in his stead.

Then Beccadelli chanced along,
   to take the role
of steward. She decided, right or wrong,
   to delegate control.

If two young people share a space
   and share regard,
to move from empathy to embrace
   is never very hard.

Her cardinal brother set the rules
   (as menfolk can):
'Do not misjudge us, think us fools.
   You've known a man:

you therefore know the itch of lust,
   and so beware:
do only what is decent, what is just:
   you're in your brothers' care.'

Luigi was the cardinal's name.
   This proud divine
was not himself entirely free from shame:
   he kept a concubine.

The Duchess and the steward grew
   still closer yet.
And everything they did, the brothers knew:
   the tragic scene was set.

Luigi told his chambermaid
   (his paramour)
of how the family honour, thus betrayed,
   would be redeemed in gore.

When Beccadelli specified
    a secret marriage,
he kept his word. Of course he kissed the bride,
    but rode behind her carriage.

A daughter came who took her name,
    but broke her heart:
the child was raised in silent shame,
    sequestered and apart.

In 1510, with child again,
    Giovanna chose
to beard the brother lions in their den
    and stultify her foes.

Loreto was her destiny
    and, as she said,
'My children are the best in me:
    I'll love them, if I'm dead.'

She rode out to the Virgin's Shrine
    quite openly,
and meant the world to view it as a sign
    of non-complicity

in all her brothers' strictures. When
    she started out
she signalled to her two oppressing men
    that she was not about

to sacrifice her liberty.
    Unhappy lover,
The husband Beccadelli – where was he?
    Waiting in Ancona,

beyond the reach of Naples' arm
   (or so he thought).
But when Giovanna, with accustomed charm,
   spelt out to her cohort

of noblewomen what she'd done,
   to her dismay
they turned their horses, almost every one,
   and simply rode away.

Men's loyalty is slow to flame
   and quickly cools.
Loreto earned a shameful name:
   the Pilgrimage of Fools.

Giovanna had transgressed the norm
   ordained by men.
She tried, but could not hide, her form:
   was pregnant once again.

Luigi had her seized and chained
   and shut away.
She'd draw no comfort from what life remained,
   Nor see the light of day.

And what could Beccadelli do,
   now tragic loner?
Luigi later sent assassins, who
   attacked him in Ancona.

They strangled her in some damp cell.
   Amalfi shore
she'd never tread again, this side of Hell,
   or nurse her children more.

Who crafted this barbaric yoke?
   Sudan to Spain,
why must men massacre their womenfolk
   with such a strange disdain?

THREE SONNETS IN WHICH ARE ENCAPSULATED THE 366 POEMS OF PETRARCH'S 'CANZONE'

It's my misfortune that I fell in love,
and not her fault – though, if I tell the truth,
an utter paucity of human ruth
personified her playlist in the push-and-shove
of passion. Marble hand in velvet glove
might best describe it. 'Nature, red in tooth
and claw' is better. Factor-in her youth,
and I'm outgunned in all of the above.

The hawk knows, when presented with a dove,
especially one as guileless and uncouth
as I was, what to do. And so it goes.
Each lackey gravitates towards a boss.
The law's immutable: you plucked the rose?
Va bene. Now you're shouldering the cross.

You who hear the sound, in scattered rhymes,
of my complainings, born again as art,
will find the sweet commingled with the tart.
I readily confess to youthful crimes
when I was 'other', in those other times:
what then I was, now seems a thing apart:
I'm closer to the end than to the start
and more with dread than joy I've heard the chimes
at midnight. My old soul, as dry as tinder,
no longer heeds the summons to the chase.

We all have memories we can't efface:
embarrassment, ineffable as debt,
crawls into passion's shell. I, burnt-out cinder,
am left with just one legacy: regret.

An innocent was martyred on the cross
this very day: appropriately, I
was destined, in a certain sense, to die:
'Good Friday' is a term I want to gloss.
At mid-point in his journey, Helios
(in transit from the nether to the high)
exults, which means, is able to defy
the power of night – Anubis, Thanatos.
No matter who appropriates this day,
it cannot be diminished by defeat:
as waves of faith rinse over and retreat,
its pith remains sufficient and complete.
When love condemns the heart to disarray,
salvation is a cycle. We repeat.

THE CONGRESS OF THE WITS: (4) Il Babuino

You say the Romans laugh at me. So what?
You think that I'm embarrassed, or afraid?
You picture me discountenanced? Dismayed?
My body's covered in ungainly hair:
do you suppose a snigger on the stair
will enervate my *modus operandi*?
To you, I'm just a starry chelovek,
engrossed in woodbines and the football pools:
a human with the urges of a goat:
inordinately hungry, stupid, randy,
the straight street's unacceptable buffoon.
Since fifteen eighty-one I've seen a lot.

Since irony has been my stock-in-trade
(the witty placard and the pasquinade),
I've often smelt the sulphur in the air:
some despot's Hundred Days are my *Brumaire*
(though Sammy Cahn is hardly Napper Tandy,
and Garibaldi ain't no Gregory Peck!)
Do I alone remember 'Ship of Fools',
a restaurant on the Tiber? Yes, a boat,
where Audrey Hepburn sipped that virgin shandy,
the other having jettisoned *High Noon*.

Including Xenophon augments the plot.
'We go to war with Doria.' What's conveyed?
Do we get Death or Dearth from Fortune's jade?
The public has an answer to its prayer,
you're granted what you coveted. Beware!
I got *my* slot from one Patrizio Grandi.
The public wants what's hung around its neck,
and can't distinguish excrement from jewels.
I like to think that I'm the antidote,
the Che Guevara, Bernie Sanders, Gandhi,
your ever-present neighbourhood baboon!

You think it's over? You know diddly-squat.
Even these un-warlike people strayed,
persuaded that their fate turned on the blade.
I saw them in their thousands pour down there,
to listen to him in Venezia Square:
the metaphor is something-babies-candy.
The Abyssinian, just like the Czech,
acquired a working knowledge of the rules:
forget your fantasies, like 'fair' and 'vote':
we sell a more intoxicating brandy!
The sad part is, it's all so opportune!

Er war, einmal, eine leichteglaubige Volk,
das glaubte an den wahren Weihnnachtsmann.
But Mussolini wasn't Grant or Polk:
you're in uncharted waters with a mass-man:
in Wirklichkeit, il Duce war der Gassmann!

THE VANITY OF HUMAN WISHES

Siena's neat cathedral has a wall
which dwarfs its parent. Visitors will find
it wrong in scale, contrarily-aligned.
Devoid of ornament, ungainly, tall,
it hardly holds our interest at all
until we learn how arrogance designed
an overreaching duomo. We are blind,
our dreams and schemes predestined for The Fall.
The Sienese colossus came to grief
because the workers perished in the Plague.
Our plans are grandiose, our future vague,
the dangers undetected, unaddressed.
Siena learned, calamity trumps belief:
yes, Petrarch lost his Laura to La Peste.

THE HISTORY OF THE TRUE CROSS: (5)
The Recognition and Testing of the True Cross

It looks like 'Adelaide', an opera stage
elaborate and colourful, quite wide;
two scenes in one, divided by the hill
with changes both connective and abrupt.
Its earthiness denotes the left side's quiddity,
its mood less Cimarosa than Karl Orff;
Jerusalem? Arezzo? Gimignano?
So Burlington, black bomber-jacket Bertie,

the key of Helena's working-class collective!
Three crosses undergo their resurrection,
which carries us into the right-hand section,
with changes both contrasting and connective.
The church facade, of course, is pure Alberti.
We might have had the Jordan or the Arno,
no wider than the Rhine at Dusseldorf,
to lend it topographical validity,
but Helena must not be slighted, 'upped'.
She kneels her entourage, for good or ill,
the dark embodiment of ruthless pride,
and does her sleight-of-hand, her *sortilege*.

She battens on some funeral cortege
although she doesn't know the boy who died:
the tact of Helena being next to nil,
she feels entitled, free to interrupt.
The Left has physical solidity,
personified in Helena's dwarf.
Ubiquitous as keyboards decked with QWERTY,
the regular, right-living aretino
(foreshortened here in nicely-done perspective)
enjoys the church's, state's and art's protection,
a sort of rank unnatural selection.
To date, our evolution is defective.
The future's free (they learned this at Locarno,
and couldn't bind the world as far as thirty),
but she will tell the world she watched him morph,
her miracle timber mating his morbidity,
to make a mortal human incorrupt.
She didn't ask his leave to ply her skill
and swore his resurrection bona fide
whose skin-tone still remains unhealthy beige.

ATTESTATION OF FRA CELESTINO ANGELO DI SANTA ANNA, BAREFOOT AUGUSTINIAN PRIEST, TO BE ACCEPTED WITHOUT DEMUR, INASMUCH AS HE GAVE CORPOREAL AND SPIRITUAL SUCCOUR TO THE CONTESSA FRANCESCA POMPILIA FRANCESCHINI, EVEN TO HER DEATH: WHEREIN HE SPEAKS OF HER GOODNESS, AND HER DECLARATION THAT SHE NEVER ONCE VIOLATED HER CONJUGAL FAITH

I stayed there. I was present at the end,
and God will judge me if I tell it wrong.
I held her in these arms, and will defend
her memory. The suffering was long
and pitiful to watch. A fragile child,
her open wounds continually draining,
unable to find comfort or repose,
took everything God sent her, reconciled
to coming death. Serene and uncomplaining,
took up her cross as if it were a rose.

Francesca Comparini was her name.
I give my oath, as Augustinian priest,
she never once apportioned fault or blame.
When finally I saw the child released
from all her agonies, to my confusion
I understood I'd worshipped with a saint,
whose heart already kept some other time.
My sinful presence felt like an intrusion:
I saw that preternatural restraint
and knew that I was touching the Sublime.

Four days, she lasted. No-one thought of sleep.
Not one offensive or impatient word

fell from her lips, though knife-wounds' ceaseless weep
annoyed her, and she trembled like a bird.
And had she cursed us men, or even God,
we would have understood. Nine men we were,
and she alone with us, a modest child:
we cleaned her, dressed her: no-one thought it odd,
and let alone indecent. We somehow learnt from her,
and all emerged ennobled, undefiled.

'Inter me in the habit of a nun,
I've just a little longer now to wait,'
she lisped. The final crisis had begun.
'I'll see my parents at the Beautiful Gate.'
I started on the penitential rite.
'Forgive the perpetrator of this deed,'
said I, 'please strive as you have never striven.'
Her features shone, as if with inner light:
'No, Padre,' she replied, 'there is no need.
Already we're at peace, and he's forgiven.'

An evil tree cannot bring forth sound fruit,
as is averred in Matthew, chapter seven.
Francesca breathed her last. Without dispute,
she's in Our Saviour's arms right now, in heaven.
Before she slipped away, I asked *the* question.
I asked her if she'd ever, by some act,
her marriage-promise happened to offend.
She seemed a little puzzled. The suggestion
was strange to her. 'Oh no, I die intact!'
Augustine: *as the life, so is the end.*

PRIVATE LETTER FROM GIOVANNI BATTISTA MUCHA, SOMETIME APPRENTICE TO THE APOTHECARY G.B. GUITENS, WRITTEN IN HIS OLD AGE, CONCERNING HIS ATTENDANCE ON THE COUNTESS POMPILIA FRANCESCHINI DURING HER FINAL AGONY

Affection is the feeling will abide.
I see her still, with men arranged around her:
that's how she was, when Master and I found her,
inclining forward, sort of on her side.

She wasn't irritable, never cried,
although her suffering so nearly drowned her.
it came in waves: at times she seemed to founder,
but then the tide of torment would subside.

My sense of her? A very lucid brain.
I had a better chance than most to view it.
One wonders how she drew the strength to do it –
refuse to be defeated by the pain.

She wasn't self-regarding, wasn't vain
(*quod bene vixit, bene qui latuit*).
Her life was all but over, and she knew it,
and narcissism went against the grain.

Your father, G.B. Guitens of Brabant,
practitioner and Master of his craft
('*das Blut ist ein ganz besonderer Saft*'),
cared nothing that emolument was scant.

I see him now, that broad-brimmed hat aslant,
felicitating patients as he laughed,
'De goede mannen worden nu gestraft!',
with *graag gedaan* his universal chant.

Enough. Your father matters, but my theme
remains Pompilia. We are trained to be
consistent, thoughtful. Not disorderly.
The Countess was a saint. I'll not blaspheme,

exaggerate or build a head of steam
with tainted claims that lack validity
or adequate restraint. My test is *me*.
Our hard-earned yardsticks guard against extreme

assertions. Moderation is our way.
We deal with feelings, but rely on facts:
don't judge a man by words, but by his acts.
There is a voice we never disobey,

and that's the rite of law, the light of day.
The faulty man who injures and detracts
has failed to meet the standard he exacts
of others. So we stay above the fray

The second day, her wounds were weeping plasma.
Her loss of blood had taken grievous toll.
I heard her words: 'Giovanni, there's a shoal
of artless souls around us, a miasma

of those who just exist…' Then surged a spasm, a
paroxysm of pain. 'What is your goal?'
'To make Your Worship – and all others –whole.'
'I knew you'd say it,' lisped the frail *fantasma*,

her skin transparent from her suffering.
She was the noblest girl I'd ever known,
and this my finest hour. We were alone.
She pressed into my hand some little thing,

metallic, cold. It was her garnet ring.
I sensed it wasn't something to be shown,
but rather treasured. My fingers felt the stone,
so silky smooth from endless burnishing:

it wasn't difficult to understand.
The mounted ruby glistened fresh as blood.
She'd handed me a thing completely good:
instinctively accepting her command,

I knew I'd have to guard the golden band
against that future day when Fortune should
appoint my own successor. What a flood
of feelings overran me! In my hand

it nestles now. The graven C and R
(I run my finger over them to feel
those emblems which, to recondites, reveal
as proudly as a hoplite's battle scar

what we have been, may be, and who we are),
are both our symbol and our sacred seal,
adopted when we took on power to heal,
when passing through the realm of Hamilcar.

WE, THE UNDERSIGNED, BEING INTERROGATED FOR THE TRUTH, HAVE MADE FULL AND UNQUESTIONED STATEMENT ON OUR OATH, THAT WE WERE PRESENT AND ASSISTED AT THE LAST ILLNESS FROM WHICH FRANCESCA POMPILIA, WIFE OF GUIDO FRANCESCHINI, DIED.

She died a saint. We know, for we were there.
We washed her many wounds, and brushed her hair.
Eight men we were, and three of us are priests,
convinced that human beings are more than beasts,
each with a sliver in us that's divine.
No word came from her which was not benign,
although her body suffered exceedingly.
The gossips speculate misleadingly,
but we know how it was, for we were there.
When lucid, she was quite prepared to swear
in holy sacrament, and did it more than once.
we will not publish details for the nonce,
since reconciliation under seal
is sacrosanct, but feel we can reveal
what *wasn't* said. Confessors asked if she
had ever once befouled the sanctity
of wedlock, and she answered, no, not ever.
She'd hoped for harmony, had had to sever
the physical bond which should oblige a wife,
but only *in extremis*. Saving life
is, too, a scriptural imperative.
Her fears bore fruit. He did not let her live.
'May God forgive him,' quoting her direct,
she offered, unsolicited, unchecked
(and noted down by us, for what it's worth),
'as I have pardoned him, down here on earth.'

Four days she lingered, then crept off to rest,
and in our eyes she stands forever blest.

STATEMENT OF DONNA ALLEGRA BORRI, SWORN PURSUANT TO A LAWSUIT IN THE EPISCOPAL COURT OF AREZZO, AN ACTION WHICH WAS SUBSEQUENTLY DISCONTINUED

It seemed a silly thing to me
        to bring them here from Rome,
to live in perpetuity,
        so distant from their home.

For what will Romans make of us?
        Arezzo's unrenowned
beyond its narrow *finibus*.
        That's why we're walled around.

The plan was mad. It couldn't work,
        was neither sane nor just.
A pact between the Greek and Turk?
        There has to be some trust.

Since I'd known Beatrice all my life,
        I ridiculed the scheme.
Her tongue is sharper than a knife:
        they thought they'd forge a team?

It's Beatrice' kitchen, Beatrice' wine,
        it's Beatrice' son they'd married:
what influence, what clout, in fine,
        did they suppose they carried?

The husband kept away from me
        (or rather, I from him):
I like the aristocracy,
        men elegant and slim,

who know about *sans-réseau* ruffs,
        and ride out with the hunt:
who sport those new *point-duchesse* cuffs
        (forgive me if I'm blunt):

Pietro, grossly overweight,
        did nothing – that's *niente* –
unless you say he drank and ate,
        in which case, he did plenty!

Arezzo men of quality
        (the ones that I know are!)
participate in polity
        (not propping up the bar).

If every hour that heaven sends
        is spent in dissipation
and vulgar workmen are your friends,
        you've gone beyond salvation!

He told me of those pewter pots,
        as after one he hankered:
said I, 'Of crystal, I own lots:
        but tell me, what's a tankard?'

And Violante – quite as gross,
        in quite another way,
was unendurably verbose,
        with nothing much to say.

In Rome, I reckon, she'd been used
        to playing bossy wife
– but rule the Franceschini roost?
        not on Beatrice' life!

Besides, for all of Beatrice' airs,
        she'd bide her time for days,
then scrounge the Friday scrag-end spares
        that butchers throw to strays

Tomaso – Guido's father – died.
        Encumbrances were many.
It's awkward when you've all that pride,
        yet don't possess a penny.

The in-laws, moving in? Let's say
        it wasn't quite the norm,
and I would lay a pontiff's pay
        the welcome wasn't warm.

The Comparini thought they'd booked
        fine wines and groaning larders
– but no such luck! They'd hardly hooked
        the Chigis or the Spadas.

Like some sleek snake that seeks out slime
        in dirty, murky caverns,
Pietro wasted little time
        in checking out the taverns.

One evening, having highly dined,
        and copiously boozed,
Pietro heard his knock declined!
        Insulted and abused,

he lingered in the street, resigned.
        He tripped. His hip contused,
he passed a month in bed confined,
        his body badly bruised.

And that began the lock-out phase
        whenever he went drinking.
And Violante, several days –
        what was the woman thinking? –

I'd hear commotion in the street
        (observed by *La Pallina*):
locked out again, no food to eat –
        I knew what this would mean. A

timid knocking at my door.
        'I wonder – could I stay?'
And all she had was what she wore.
        What could a Christian say?

I blame the daughter for it all.
        There's really no excuse.
The man would even come and call!
        Pompilia was 'loose'.

I never saw an act of sin,
        if that is what is meant,
but hold a monkey by its chin –
        you'll fathom its intent.

It's just a phrase the people use.
        It means, there's no pretence
can fool us all. The cutest ruse
        can't baffle common sense.

Good question – why Pompilia did it.
        Your guess, as good as mine.
The moral compass *lassit, cidit*.
        Degraded, down to swine.

The bitch's itch to seed her eggs,
        the yen of every hen:
the niche's twitch between the legs:
        dominion over men?

Such things have happened in the past,
        in coffeehouse or carriage.
She's not the first, won't be the last
        to defecate on marriage.

They paint their jowls in *putta* pink
        and flaunt their naked necks:
they stick their arses out, and think
        that they've invented sex.

You ask me day and time and place,
        the things I don't retain.
I know it by her smirking face,
        I know her partner's pain.

Just learn from Nature, just be wise.
        The unassuming doe
when wildcat first assails her eyes
        can recognize her foe.

There was a winter, long ago,
        when Trasimeno froze:
I walked a league in knee-deep snow.
        A woman always knows.

THE TORTURED TIMBERS OF THE GOLDEN HIND
now constitute the table in our hall,
where Spanish armour decorates the wall.
Here, thought and eloquence are intertwined
and esoteric learning is enshrined.
Our sacred symbols spur us to recall
presumptive heirs of Amadis de Gaul,
the patrilinear paladins of Mind.
Three Temples on the hill, the Middle best,
we lettered men, a cut above the rest,
the precious few who heed the subtle Call,
in snow-white surplices the Brothers dressed,
the Rosy Cross emblazoned on each chest,
are hoplites of humility withal.

THE LAD WHO LOVES WILL LIKELY MEET WITH PAIN.
We've oft observed that character is fate
and no-one, while the river's still in spate,
learns anything. Your woman's on the wane?
She's passed from adoration to disdain?
Congratulations. Now you'll change your state.
You'll navigate beyond the narrow gate.
There's not a rose that grows, except with rain.

So, go compose that querulous quatrain.
Berate your fate in rancorous refrain.
The day will dawn when passion must abate:
what happened, happened – but was not in vain.
Love elevates you to another plane.
What ends unhappily may make you great.

THE SPANISH HARPSICHORD TEACHER

It's January, fifteen fifty-nine,
and we're in Rome again, to judge behaviour
which seems unseemly – first we'll hear Ottavia,
who'll sketch for us the basic storyline –
of how self interest can intertwine
with lust. This lass ain't quite the modern Flavia,
which makes her human. Choosing for her saviour
her music teacher may seem asinine,
as does a scheme to pin one's hopes on Naples.
But adolescents don't know how to plan –
their fantasies still constitute their staples.
She wanted free of purgatree and papals,
and, had she known of it, might pick Japan!
Who was at fault? The culture, or the man?

On 24 January, 1559, in the house of Captain Ventura, The Bargello, before the Magnificent Lord Salamonio, OTTAVIA ROSSIGNOL gives evidence against BERNARDINO PEDROSA, her harpsichord teacher

They call me Ottavia.
As Christ is my Saviour,
   I'll murder my mother.
Won't let me wear lipstick;
One characteristic,
  a penchant to smother.

Thinks sixteen's a child,
but I'm not reconciled
   to lickrish, or hairplaits, or dolls.
Insists I wear vests:
her term for these breasts?
   'Beelzebub's Knolls'!

When I met Bernardino
(he's called, 'El Latino'
   the barrio was buzzing.
His friend Agostino
(or is it Martino?)
   had married my cousin.

His job to instruct me
(my mum hoped he'd fucked me)
   in *clavicembalo*:
but she was afraid he
would see I'm no lady
   and beeswax ain't tallow.

We moved onto song
and I didn't take long
   to end in his arms,
for we practised alone
and my titties had grown,
   and music hath charms.

I loved him, I guess,
though I have to confess
   that I needed an ally.
Since I had to escape
and I'd heard about rape,
   I looked and thought, 'Shall I?'

I had reached the last ditch
'cos my mother's a bitch,
   and I'm sexually active:
he could whisk me to Spain.
It infected my brain,
   and it seemed so attractive.

We could live in Pamplona
or perhaps Barcelona
 —   he favoured the seaboard.
Surviving or sinning
I knew I was winning:
   We kissed at the keyboard.

My mother enabled
his presence at table:
   he started to hate her.
He seemed less than keen:
He said, 'this will mean
   I'm considered a traitor.'

But I won in the end;
he agreed to attend
   and to squire me away.
'My mother's a loser,'
I averred, 'and a boozer,
   unable to pay,

you've taught me for nothing:
enough of her bluffing,
   let's build a new life.
Let's get to Gaeta,
to exasperate her —
   what news of your wife?'

All doubts were confounded;
his castanets sounded
   on Saturday night.
It was a no-brainer:
we made for Catena
   where muleteers might

foregather for drinking.
Bernardo was thinking
　of travelling cheap;
since we're travelling south,
we can live hand-to-mouth,
　regardless of sleep.

Now that Naples is Spain
it's the Inn of the Chain
　where you step in and order
a room for the night,
and the muleteers might
　take you down to the border.

I'll answer you nicely,
but can't say precisely:
　the Arch of Ottavia
on one side. The other
reminds me of Mother:
　the *Rupe Tarpea*.

I guess he's confessed
that we slept fully-dressed
　but had sex in the morning.
He brooked no delay:
took the Appian Way
　through Sebastian's awning.

I'd hoped to explore
Santa Croce, and more –
　the great tomb of Gaius:
but he'd turned imperious
(all Spanish and serious):
　Quo Vadis slipped by us.

'We're not on an outing,'
(he'd noticed me pouting)
  'and husbands must rule,
or it ends in divorce,'
but he gave me the horse,
   and he mounted the mule.

Of course there was doubt –
I was sussing him out –
  piastra de Petri.
At Castelgandolfo
our muleteer Rolfo
   said, 'Next stop, Velletri.'

'Est mihi libertas'
the locals assert as
  'imperialis':
but I was aware of
being under the glare of
   the Pope's summer palace.

And then onward we ploughed,
winter daylight allowed,
  e l'uomo governa,
to the only inn free
(for they only have three)
   in the town of Cisterna.

He offered me marriage.
Not slow to disparage,
  'You're bonkers,' I said.
We found ourselves nicked,
by the landlady tricked:
   arrested in bed!

I'll censure no other
than my bloody mother,
　who drove us to this:
now nagging, now bragging,
and then finger-wagging,
　then taking the piss.

'He can't hardly soil you,
but let him despoil you,
　and then comes the sting:
your brother bursts in
and, observing the sin,
　insists on a ring.'

Life shows us the seams
and it's not like in dreams
　or romantic mind's-eye:
I was stood, in *buricchia* –
it couldn't be ickier –
　with spunk down my thigh.

Some officers held me
while others compelled me
　to put something on:
but with what lay around
sbirri instantly found
　that something was wrong.

As I'll answer to God,
Bernardino is odd,
　and the thing he most loved,
was to whisper, 'You're Otto,'
have me dress in panciotto,
　all trousered and gloved,

and suppose he says 'no,
it's just safer to go
   as a young muleteer,'
why did he measure me
when I asked him to pleasure me,
   and then pay for the gear?

Yes, I knew he was married,
but his wife (he said) tarried
   on her deathbed in Spain,
but soon as she's dead,
he and I could get wed,
   and we'd toast with champagne.

He called me his houri
who could not bring a dowry,
   but what did it matter?
On his farm in Urturi
he'd grow wine like a fury,
   and get richer and fatter.

'El Latino' Pedroso Touches the Scriptures and is Examined, 25 January 1559

You torture me, I'll say who set
The Great Fire of Chicago.
It was Alanis Morisette,
that hairy-lipped virago!
I'd kill, to liquidate my debt?
Go check out Mar-a-Lago!
Rosanna and the clan Arquette
are grifters, *sin embargo*
the one you really need to get?
The woman-cop in 'Fargo'.
She doped a pony during Tet –
its name, I think, *L'Escargot*.

BERNARDO IS MY NAME, surname Pedroso:
Logroño on the Ebro was my town
before I made for Rome.   I'm here today
because Ottavia tempted me astray.
Her mother has a house in *Via Giulia*,
that long, straight street of popular renown.
The way Camilla rode her got her down.
Ottavia is full of 'ifs' and 'coulds',
but has no understanding of Apulia:
without a dowry, she is damaged goods –
or as we say in Spanish, 'in the woods'.
Camilla thought me suitable, *hermoso*,
and hinted strongly that we 'mingle bloods'.
I wouldn't say I *think* so, sir: I *know* so.
Be careful with those folks – they're out to fool ya.
Ottavia saw me whisking her away,
In fact, the more inclined I seemed to stay,
the worse she grew, aggressiver, unrulier.
She told me to abscond her, with a frown,
and I said 'not a chance – it's *peligroso*.'

Sanguini, who's from Naples, also met her
and, more than just some Tom or Dick or Harry,
both loved her and was predisposed to marry.
Or was he simply stringing her along?
She told me that they'd fooled about and kissed,
and though she'd hesitate to term it rape,
he'd felt inside her cotton camicetta
and even more. She told me in a letter,
that they'd gone all the way. It wasn't wrong,
because he'd said he'd marry her. The twist?
The plans of mice and men oftimes miscarry,
and what had been true love now seemed a scrape.
She turned to me for help. and came on strong.
A selfless man, I thought I could assist
a child to get her love life back in shape.

She said her only option was escape
to Naples, and implored me not to tarry:
I let her feel the sharpness of my tongue
for having failed to handle matters better,
but hardly thought the youngster would persist.

'Il punto non ritorno', no return,
she claimed she'd reached: whatever lay ahead,
she wanted. It meant drowning in the Tiber
if forced to go back home. She paid me money
to dress her as a boy. My main concern,
although the day was beautifully sunny,
and we had seemed to pass the watershed,
was Otti's secret illness. She had said
that sometimes she would start to feel 'real funny'
and, even though she was no great imbiber,
she acted like a drunk. Her muscles pained,
and what she needed was a day in bed.
Cisterna's where we'd chosen to adjourn:
and though the bedroom's where we both remained,
there was no hint of sex. I spooned her honey!
The truth is, I've a rash. It tends to burn
when I don't change my tights. The woollen fibre
had grown quite soiled, malodorous and stained.
I never was a full onboard subscriber
but, thanks to her mad scheme, I'm now detained.

Ottavia is questioned again, this time at the Corte Savelli. It is 4 February.

Bernardo paid to dress me as a boy.
He said they suited me, those corduroy shorts
(I couldn't help but notice he was sweating).
I thought it a disguise, a scapegrace ploy,
but look how we have landed in the courts!

I've often felt that sex is just my fate
When I was eight years old, I wound up shagged
(and strange to say, it didn't seem upsetting).
I wasn't new to this. I told him straight.
My state was unambiguously flagged.

My brother Silvio sold me to his mate,
his fee, a ring with amethyst or quartz
(an incident that only wants forgetting).
My only memory is of his weight,
and feeling ill at ease, or out of sorts.

My mother has a talent to annoy:
Bernardo in my bed? I'd term it 'dragged'!
(I think the current term is 'heavy petting').
Camilla knows the tactics to employ:
abduct me? He surrendered! He was nagged!

Ottavia is now Confronted, Faccia a Faccia, by the Presence of Bernardo Pedrosa

What did I know of Spain? It was Bithynia
to me. A foreign chap they called 'albino'
who came from there was marrying Lavinia,

my cousin, and his buddy, Il Latino,
discovered me as if I were Virginia.
(The husband of my cousin was Martino.)

We stopped our music lessons months ago,
but I'd been begging him to bear me off
for quite a year. He wasn't quite gung-ho.

My mother, crueller than a Romanov,
was now unbearable. He knew it, though
his snout was firmly in Camilla's trough.

I loved him like a fifteen-year-old loves,
and know he wasn't unaware of me.
My mother paid him with a pair of gloves!

I pleaded for escape on bended knee:
He said we weren't exactly turtle-doves,
and child-abduction was iniquity.

But bit by bit, I won him to the scheme
(the night I got in bed with him sure helped!)
Bernardo kept returning to the theme

that we'd be caught. He hated if I yelped
at frozen hands. These Spaniards, and esteem!
He said he'd drop me if I ever whelped,

at least before the wedding. All I knew
was, I'd be dressing as a teenage lad,
and little towns that we'd be passing through.

It seemed important that I thus be clad,
and he was in control. And kismet, too –
that Naples was now Spanish made him glad.

The signal to depart? His castanets.
He'd click them in the street. What did I wear?
My normal stuff. 'As boring as it gets,'

was what he wanted. 'Cause no kind of scare,
no turmoil. Nothing promised, no regrets.'
My head uncovered, and my shoulders bare,

I launched into the *Via Giulia* night.
'We're heading for the Tavern of the Chain,'
and there I first became his catamite.

(I think they call it Lovatelli Lane.)
To Bernardino's obvious delight,
I donned the outfit of a rustic swain.

We ate a meal downstairs, then went to bed.
That's when he shagged me for the only time.
(His groin appeared all pustulent and red.)

He's now in trouble, and he claims that I'm
the one who caused it all, and want him dead.
But I'm a child, incapable of crime.

Our guide is waiting in the vestibule:
before the sun is up, we're out the door.
A horse for me, Bernardo on a mule.

Velletri's reached at breakfast: I deplore
the toilet, which is just an open pool.
Cisterna's next, we get there right on four.

The thrill has gone before it can begin.
I'd hoped to live in Spain, but now I shan't.
'They'll send me home, arrested at an inn:

they'll try to trace me: to ensure they can't,
I'll tell them I'm a prostitute: for spin,
my only living relative's an aunt.'

* * * *

BERNARDINO
She's lying to you, lying through her teeth!
No intimacy happened in Cisterna.
Did you get pregnant? Did I wear a sheath?
Come on then, tell us, since you're now so clever:

I could have had my way with you whenever:
why wait to take you in some cheap taverna?

I slept one night under your mother's roof:
Who came to whom? You crept under my covers.
Let's call your mother if we need the proof!
I didn't have to take you out of Rome,
I could have fucked you in your mother's home!
If I had snapped my fingers, we'd be lovers.

OTTAVIA
I got in bed beside you, that is true.
And in my mother's home, you never shagged me.
I never loved another, only you:
I would have let you do it, there and then:
not something I would offer other men.
But yes, it was Cisterna where you tagged me.

BERNARDINO
Have you forgot the time you went berserk
and ran upstairs to hide away and cry,
and all because I said I'd found new work?
If I could pay to rid myself of this,
I'd do installments, count myself in bliss:
without a sigh I'd put the money by.

I GUARANTEE THE COURT, I've barely kissed her.
I helped her when her mother wanted rid:
I chaperoned her as I would my sister:
by all her lies and scheming set no store:
no gentleman could possibly do more.
I can't remember half the things I did.

I asked two convents, all to no avail.
She's sleeping with some guy from Vallicella:
the nuns pronounced her quite beyond the pale.

I don't think I can put it any blunter:
she's nothing but a feral dowry-hunter,
who paints herself as bland as mozzarella.

7 February 1559: The Witness Giovanni Battista Fossaro is Examined

My name is Giambattista di Fossaro,
I live in the Piazza Lancelotti.
My knowledge of the Spanish guy is spotty,
but as for what he said to me, *lo daro*.

I've heard he's now imprisoned in the *Nona*,
the rumours say for sex that's out of order,
then trying to get across the southern border.
But I'm not privy to the facts, Your Honour.

Two weeks before Ottavia ran away
I, on a beer-and-cheap-cigars foray,
was in the doorway of San Salvatore,
avoiding heavy rainfall. What a day!

I noticed Bernardino in the square.
He called me to him, said he had to know
about a punishment. How would it go –
and this is what he asked me, then and there –

for any man who, hauled before the beaks,
had carried off a virgin and had fucked her,
given that she'd asked him to abduct her?
(Forgive me saying 'beaks' – that's how he speaks).

I said, 'I'm no-one's Doctor of the Fisc,
but should they catch such ne'er-do-wells and scallies,
it has to be the gallows or the galleys:
is any bit of totty worth the risk?'

He didn't like my answer. 'But the flight
is her idea,...' A good friend came along,
that's Curzio, and he asked me what was wrong.
He heard it all, and said, 'Gianni's right!'

Bernardino is Questioned Again (11 March)

The money? Where I got it? Let me see ...
the *sbirri* said it wasn't looking good,
and if my aim was to remain at large ...
(I think I'm saying more than suspects should!)
Ottavia gave ten scudi straight to me
(no doubt this will provoke another charge),
and so I paid the officers their 'fee'.

Invited me to sleep there, in their home?
No, they insisted. Actually, Silvio,
who came with me to Mozarabic masses:
I knew him from his job at Ponte Milvio.
Camilla's house is near Eligio's dome
(she paid me nothing for a year of classes,
the meanest patron in the whole of Rome!)

You *think* I was a fixture there? I *know* so!
Ottavia, and Fulvia, and Danira
(in other words, Camilla's precious girls)
adored my stories, drawing ever nearer,
(their favourite, *Orlando Furioso*).
No matter what Ottavia now hurls,
she loved me as an artist, virtuoso.

You need to ask who else was in the queue:
Sanguini and Guardino were her lovers.
I'm singled out, incarcerated wrongly.
Whoever checks her history discovers
that she was easy pickings for a screw.

Domenico pursued her very strongly.
Of course we know Alfonso got there, too.

One night, Camilla wouldn't let me in.
She said, 'I'm sorry, Silvio is out.'
Said I, 'He's not the reason why I'm here,
as well you know. Ottavia's about?'
I heard Guardino's scratchy violin.
'She's entertaining company, I fear.'
Her mother was abetting her in sin.

At Santangelo, where are beheaded
the toffs, I found him. 'Women need a spouse,'
was his approach. I hated his frivolity.
'She spends the day at Domenico's house.'
This was the news that, most of all, I'd dreaded.
He said it with an air of jollity.
'It's one less headache, once we've got her wedded.'

But that fell through, and I was better fed
than ever, when our lessons were resumed:
they fussed around me, like I was a king!
The pasta, and the oysters I consumed!
And why? What change of metaphysics led
to this epiphany, awakening?
They'd somehow heard my wife in Spain was dead!

Bernardino Undergoes the Strappado

What does it matter if I banged the tart?
She turned up at my flat in Panic Street –
She asked, 'The Naples thing – when do we start?'
I was in mourning. This was indiscreet.
I said I'd let her know when we could meet.
Although I knew it wasn't very wise,
the trattoria has a window seat –

it's on the corner, and it's called 'Brassai's' –
I simply slipped my thing between her thighs.

It wasn't full-on sex – she said it hurt –
You're right. I've never mentioned this before.
She said I'd soaked it through – her underskirt –
It wasn't making love. I set no store
by heavy petting with a randy whore.
(They let Bernardo down.) Let me explain.
I lost the seed inside 'the tradesman's door' –
we did it once – a term we use in Spain –
and that was at the inn they call 'the Chain'.

The plan was hers – no, mine – there *was* no plan –
Her mother had devised some hare-brained ploy
to palm her off on some Frascati man –
it was a trick – the wooden horse of Troy,
to make her look as if she were a boy.
I could have earned a living teaching Song –
she said that I could use her as my toy –
in Naples. I believe there's nothing wrong
if easy girls are somehow strung along.

    * * * *

AND THAT IS WHERE THE LEGAL RECORD ENDS.
We don't know what became of either party.
Did Bernardino manage, hale and hearty,
to reach a grand old age? Or, for amends,
went off to join the papal fleet? Depends.
What of our lively, pocket-size Astarte,
Ottavia? Yes, precocious (some say tarty),
did she and Bernardino part as friends?
She's neither (a) a virgin, nor (b) passive.
Her mother hardly triumphed in instilling
in her awareness that, to make a killing

when walking down the aisle is something massive.
To tell the truth, she seems a tad too willing,
as was apparent in her legal grilling.

The dowry is the villain of the piece.
A girl who's poor must take appalling chances,
in spite of Douglas Sirks and Abel Gances.
A woman's world is governed by caprice,
with matrimony as the golden fleece.
No matter how society advances,
how up-to-date our concept of romance is,
the problems for the female never cease.
A man who enters into a liaison
must promise marriage, or must proffer cash:
but indiscretions are a badge to blazon,
resulting in a swelling diapason.
A man's rewarded when the cymbals clash:
a woman's finished on the day she's rash.

The brother Silvio – is he not Guido?
Ambivolent towards his sister's wooer,
he then becomes the runaways' pursuer.
Accommodates his Spanish friend's libido:
his attitude is patently podrido
but, with sis's wedding options growing fewer,
the one who's been the obvious wrong-doer
turns mega-decent in his marriage credo.
If stuprum is illicit defloration
abductio illegal sequestration,
Bernardo doesn't seem enthusiastic.
But neither can we label him monastic –
his tendency is clearly pederastic,
despite the solemnest asseveration.

Camilla lacks the art of Violante:
She doesn't know the killing things to say,

the things that blow the enemy away:
Pietro Aretino isn't Dante,
Vasari's good, but couldn't be Bramante.
Both daughters' education went astray:
les filles, we all concede, are mal gardées
(which shows what Romans know about Chianti),
but every mother is a social climber
(we can't forget the yellow harpsichord).
Camilla is the one who can't afford
to throw away the Cunning Mother Primer.
It's not too hard to understand that I'm a
fan of guile, albeit untoward.

The family's the villain in the end.
The actus reus of the charged offences
(let's set aside uncalled-for consequences)
is not appropriate. What's there to mend?
(Apart, that is, from Silvio and his friend).
You've taken leave, I take it, of your senses?
A daughter's not a ledger of expenses,
a burden that you're hankering to send
to die shut in some convent, or to wed
some chump who'll take her off your hard-pressed hands.
You talk of vineyards, bonds and rolling lands,
but never mention loving her. That said,
you'll see her bedded, that you may get fed.
Am I the only one who understands?

Mettle

The bricks were sweating, nervous. Icy slime
had soaked his coat-sleeve, much to his disgust.
Tall baulks of formless timber seemed to climb
towards the bulbous shadows. Guido, trussed
and pinioned, tried to scratch the saline rime
that nagged his upper lip (for scratch he must),

using his shoulder. Someone's hand-held lamp
was scouring crazy patterns on the damp.
As Fisc officials fidgeted and fussed,
Count Guido, motionless, gouged free of Time,
stared at the torture implements. Nonplussed,
unravelled, unaware of glare or grime,
he saw steel jaws, unsoftened by stale dust.
The hanging chains, once brushed, gave up a chime
as sinister as that serrated clamp
which dominated all the waiting ramp.
The irony was utterly sublime.
They'll 'put him to the question', as discussed.
As fitted the prevailing paradigm,
They'd tear his vitals, gouge him, drill him, thrust
their white-hot spikes quite through him, till his crime
was suitably admitted, as was 'just'.
Some may withstand the pincers' chew and champ,
but Guido knew he wasn't of that stamp.
His eyes had hardly started to adjust.
Prolonging this perverted pantomime
would only satisfy the sadists' lust.
If necessary, he'd recant in rhyme.
His knuckles scraped the carapace of rust
of some utensil, turning to decamp.
He felt no pain, beyond necrotic cramp.
as when he gives his wife the right to rule.
His only daughter's wedding was concealed:
He should have known the cart had lost a wheel!

THE CARDINAL POINTS (1)

Spring Equinox

I loved on Saturdays in March, at dawn
(back then, each day was Saturday) to root
in pond and hedgerow. Light was pale, dilute,
and buds clung tight and hard around the thorn.
This season, with the world so freshly born,
enchanted me. Each flicking, wedge-faced newt,
sedge on his face, unconscionably cute,
each ink-black eye from thousands in the spawn,
each clear cold pool, each acid-green young shoot,
each minnow which acknowledged my pursuit
and twitched my hand-held line (no hope of rod!),
each copse, so self-contained and absolute,
with nascent blossom dusted, bluebell-shod,
appeared to me a pledge of life from God.

Summer Solstice

This is the Life!

What better than a summer afternoon?
Where else, but on the trail to La Toscana?
Who is it mounts a mens that's not more sana,
devouring a voluptuous Verdi tune?
Which month might one elect, that wasn't June?
I'll pass on Sassafrass and Lisdoonvarna,
and binge on bars, basilicas and Barna.
I like my treasures liberally-strewn.
You're cynical? Think pinnacles don't serve?
I can't agree. A twelvemonth of frustrations,
quotidian imposthumes, humiliations
are answered now. We've (finally!) capped the curve.

The clouds will come again, of course, but verve
must also have its vestals. A libation!

Autumn Equinox

We always knew the night was closing in.
We lizards know our basking days are done.
The sun can touch, at best, only the skin:
our period of mourning has begun.
Our valley's in the shadow of the hill.
A blackbird, tugging berries busily,
bemoans the lack of cover. So do we.
And winter takes the weak ones. Always will.

When loved-ones take their leave, we know the pain
is necessary, if there's going to be
the joy of future greeting, and the rain
which damps October spirits is the key

which sets the coming resurrection free,
when bluebells blaze beneath the darkest tree.

Winter Solstice

Sol Invictus

December rains have dragged last, lingering leaves
down into litter. Sodden almond-casks
that once bore kernels, strewn discarded masks,
repose redundant. Thoughts are threadbare sleeves
devoid of comfort. Like a lonely cello,
the wind whips fitfully about its tasks.
A chaffinch flicks a fruitless shell, and asks:
the year must disappear to sere, to yellow?
Expecting legible patterns in dispersal,
she wishes worldwide winter worked for her,

have secret feelings yield the universal.
The nutshell, now inert, helps her infer
that life must die, but strangely, must prevail.
Arezzo's just the belly of the whale.

TESTIMONY OF JACOPO DI CESANO IN THE PROCESSUS FUGAE, SUMMER 1697

The Handyman Jacopo's what they call me,
or the other one's 'Jacopo di Cesano',
my village near Merluza. Didn't get far,
but I know life. I know how people are.
So why are popes and priests all called 'Urbano'?
You don't suppose the girl who wipes the shelves,
the lad at 3am who hammers, helves
and gets your wheel to work, are more than elves,
bit-players in the epic where you star?
I know it, and it never fails to gall me,
but yes, it's true, it happened to befall me;
I saw two gentlemen go *mano-a-mano*,
ma tutto era moltissimo piano
(it's rare for latins to do more than spar).
We're all the same. These clashes can't enthrall me.
There's nothing lovers do that can appall me.
What honour is at stake? It's all *in vano*.
I've watched them in the bedroom and the bar.
We know his type because we know ourselves,
since Eve's foredoomed to sin, and Adam delves.

The tall one was the hero type. I saw
that, though well-bred, he was a decent man.
He needed me to change his coach's team:
the work on which I willingly began,
and would in twenty minutes at a pinch
complete. My final task was just to cinch

the horses' belly-straps. One final inch
and they'd be good to go. He knew he'd clinch
his goal. The *vetturino* said the scheme
was, get to Rome, before The Husband can
affect the outcome. That's when, through the steam,
we saw him riding up – none other than
The Husband. When emotion is this raw,
observe the man. The tall one didn't flinch.
The only hero is the one that's 'ready for',
who understands the moment is extreme;
I saw determination in his jaw:
the other one, unequal to his theme,
whatever may have been his master-plan,
he lost his nerve and took his gripe to law.

The village idiot can help us out.
While all the others make their feelings known,
what did he fondly think could come of this?
Has he no knowledge of the female mind?
What *denouement* could following bring about?
Did he not see that once the bird has flown
there can be no more healing the abyss?
As those who will not see, there's none so blind.
Here was the boy who'd never gone without.
Was Guido ardent, adamant, or stone?
This could not have been settled with a kiss.
To me, his personality combined
beyond the overlaid filial-devout
two elements – male arrogance, full-blown –
and that which pushed him to the precipice –
the rich-boy-balked-entitlement behind.
The sons of nobles sup not from the spout:
whatever they dislike, they may disown:
they think they're scoring hits with every Miss,
to take responsibility, disinclined.

Nihil difficile amanti, sed ...
from this there is a truth we may distil:
our lovers loll where angels fear to tread.
We men don't realise. How plain it shows!
These girls arouse us, that's just how it goes,
and some of us are pushed by this to kill.
A kind, perhaps, of natural selection
which centres on the bedroom – nay, the bed –
convinces us that we deploy our will.
The things that pass between us go unsaid,
and that not wholly out of circumspection,
our natural reluctance to disclose.
We hope our arc will tend towards perfection
est Deus in nobis, agitante calescimus illo:
or were we put here just to be misled?
Are we best shaped to garner, or to spill?
De te fabula, narratur – no direction
will help you when you reach your point of flexion.
The crueller the thorns, so goes the prose,
the tenderer, more lovely blows the rose!

You ask me if it strikes me as bizarre
to see young men and women share a room:
the answer's no. These units are for hire,
and whether folks sport civvies, night attire –
it's not my business if they wear a shred.
Who cares if novice nuns sleep toe to head,
or cardinals and choirboys share a bed?
I have no inkling who these people are.
We don't care if you're Hus or Hamilcar,
divorcé, lover, or a nervous groom,
you're dressed in a *buricchia*, clad in red,
you're welcome to a balcony and fire.
I'll never disrespect you and assume
I know to what you're hooked (still less, to whom):
a tired voluptuary, or newly-wed:

what gives you pleasure, what provokes your ire:
the people you despise, perhaps admire.
Suppose you pass the evening in the bar,
your door left inadvertently ajar:
I will remain as silent as the tomb.

The girl had all she needed – that's allure.
She's Gilgamesh, the other's Enkidu.
She's no-one's heroine, she's just a fly:
she's journeyed, had adventures, built a nest;
go, climb the Servian Wall, its stones well-dressed:
you'll see where temples, claypits, houses lie:
though Nineveh is clad in marble, sure,
the cedar which has always been its glue
seems suddenly to be in short supply.
Should Gilgamesh remain a cedar-hewer
or should she now abandon this, her quest?
She'll go to Rome, and see the drama through.
What else is there, in life, for her to do?
We'll each of us sons, lovers, wives abjure:
there's nothing to forgive or justify,
no potent force beyond self-interest.
Bequests are just a messy residue.
Most things are obvious, and yet obscure:
what's written here is only half in jest:
if you can read it, she will never die.

MARRIAGE ON EARTH, Being a Tale told by Allegra Borri

Astraea Redux

How will it help, rehearse the harm again?
Does evidence grow stronger, when repeated?
We've read our fill: ferocity is meted

to certain women, by some types of men.
There's Artemisia and Aphra Behn:
of how those two unfortunates were treated
we're lacking no exemplars: you've depleted
the impact of your poem. Show one, not ten!
But oh, the shallowness of human minds!
How soon the shock that recently impressed
returns in ripples of irreverent jest!
Each man begins forgetting what he finds
before he's finished gasping. What we'd wrest
exceeds our grasp (I can't recall the rest).

Holy Conversation

Il seicento – what a time to live!
The christian crisis reaching critical mass –
astride the stages, Faust and Fortinbras –
a taste of honey, through a silken sieve!
Bestow our favour, here withhold, there give
(it's taken as read, we'll be the ruling class) –
the morning levée, after lunch la chasse –
and 'mountebank''s a nicer word than 'spiv'!
The past is like the future. Both are pleasant
(a reverie comes free of frost or cost!):
their beauty is, that neither is the present.
We fancy we would dance and feast on pheasant,
but soft – the here-and-now, correctly glossed,
connotes our paradise, so lazily lost.

Erasmus writes, Copernicus confirms,
that life will not afford you farthingales.
Too soon, your tapis-Gobelin fades and pales,
replaced (familiar taste!) by diet of worms.
For most of us, Herodotus and herms
are idle dreams. Imagination fails.
This race is run on rigid iron rails.

Reality is genocide and germs.
We take the past to be a golden age
of sunny villages (Belle-Rive? Bethphage?),
but Pisan pictures painted by Benozzo
can show convincingly that things were not so.
We lived with gozzo in the gargarozzo
and always will, as far as we can gauge.

THOSE FLORENCE ART REPOSITORIES CAN VARY
(as can the art within). Just amble out
and scout the suburbs: batten on Butteri –

(an unexciting mannerist, no doubt,
yet find his Holy Family With Saints,
tucked in a convent near a roundabout) –

astonishment will stifle your complaints!
Can these be likenesses of our Medici,
posterity-preserved? Butteri paints

four generations. Sensitive to each, he
consigns their characters to changeless oil.
There's Ferdinando (sacerdotal, preachy)

with earthy Cosimo, paternal foil.
Anaemic Isabella, nervous, knowing,
her body turned from Paolo in recoil,

and Paolo *il paffuto* plainly showing
what comes of self-indulgence. To his right,
sleek F-16 beside a bulbous Boeing,

Francesco oozes something of the night.
The vertical's a kind of prophylaxis
to separate the black sheep from the white.

Grandmother, mother, son and brother axis –
we're taking Isabella's point of view –
suggests a plan beyond pragmatic praxis.

How might the clued-up connoisseur construe
this baby-Baptist and that Jesus-child?
No problems of decipherment ensue

concerning infant Jesus, meek and mild.
Virginio is Isabella's boy –
in this are all the experts reconciled –

but why include the Baptist? Why deploy
another swathe of symbolism still?
Is Isabella cutely playing coy,

or is this an expression of her will?
Giovanni was the brother that she lost,
whose place no other man could ever fill.

Giovanni as Battista, haloed, crossed,
contains and seals-off Paolo's forward thrust.
The Word has won (the banner, being tossed

by baby's hand), defeating force and lust
(we're not forgetting Isabella's Wheel).
The story, then? Betrayal of her trust.

There's plenty that a painting may reveal.
And if we study childhood, might we not
acquire a new perspective – break the seal?

When Cosimo was Arthur, Camelot
received a new Medici ('forty-two –
the Siege of Perpignan, and who knows what),

arriving just as August's fire was through.
Young Isabel, before she got to twelve,
was raffled-off in marriage (rival crew,

same racket, name Orsini). Let's not delve
into the whys and wherefores. That was then,
when maids were merchandise, perhaps to shelve,

or liquidate for cash. You have a hen,
you'll never want for cocks. Beside the Arno
a father dealt away a girl of ten:

the lucky husband, Paolo (that's Giordano)
would prove her nemesis. They don't end well,
these kiss-and-tells: remember Sadi Carnot?

An Introduction to Isabella

Eleven years of age and married off!
   (This theme will start to bore you!)
The tale of Isabella de' Medici,
a dame of ruched-up robe and costly coiff,
   is set out here before you.
   The stanza I've invented
(and modestly baptised) is the *tredici*.

Of *déjà-vu*, of *veni, vidi, vici,*
   I have not yet relented.
Another woman tortured. 'Oh, you're preachy,'
   I seem to hear you scoff,
but not a word of this has been invented.
   It happened, I assure you!

Her life began in fifteen forty-one.
   The city of the boar
(or of the lily, if you're so inclined)

was Isabella's homeland. Florence shone
   with culture, learning, lore.
    Her meagre time away
was spent unwillingly. She paid no mind

to Venice, Rome. That others were unkind
   would sting her with dismay.
Aesthetic, intellectual, refined,
   inferior to none –
and yet her bloated corpse was on display
   at the age of thirty-four.

Betrothed to an Orsini as a child,
   habitually abused
by men around her (father, husband, brother),
she lived, apart from others domiciled:
   effectively refused
    to play her menfolk's game.
Malaria deprived her of her mother

and took away the one beloved brother,
   and nothing was the same
ever again. Although she loved another,
   was never reconciled
to sacrificing liberty or name.
The men were not amused.

Isabella's Youth

The child, they say, is father to the man.
     Our salad days
      in many ways
recalibrate (or obfuscate) the plan.
No-one continues as he first began.

Giovanni was the one who owned her heart.
>	That gentle mind,
>	uncritical, kind,
companion, brother, equal, counterpart,
established standards from the very start

that later comers could not hope to reach.
>	What man indeed
>	could ever feed
her hunger for the Beautiful? Who teach
as *he* taught? When he died, who fill the breach?

Not Paolo the Orsini, that's for sure.
>	A man achieves
>	(like padded sleeves)
accoutrements which push him to the fore.
A pathway to her father, nothing more.

The pestilence plagued Isabella's life.
>	One brother dead,
>	the doctors bled
her mother, too (the Grand Duke's Spanish wife).
Then brother Garzia received the knife,

but all were dead within a dozen days.
What must this do
to someone who
observes a sudden *coup de foudre* raze
her loved ones? Are there words for this *malaise*?

Another difficulty must be aired.
>	The scholars know
>	Great Cosimo
insisted on 'prerogative of laird'.
It seems that Isabella wasn't spared.

Vasari says he saw the sceptre bared,
        and Isabella
        (claims the teller)
was in the frame. The gamebird thus ensnared,
could all this damage ever be repaired?

Events, events! A life is always shaped
        by what's around.
        You're saved? You drowned?
What matters isn't how the walls are draped,
but how you managed when your knees were scraped.

The death of Michelangelo – in fine,
        there was a cost:
        a rudder lost,
she learned that lives can't help but intertwine.
But how to live without the aretine?

Embracing risk is one of life's key skills,
        but luck is all –
        and when you fall,
susceptibility to ambient ills
will make its mark. She suffered serious spills

when on the hunt, on horseback. One is struck,
        when one reviews
        the latent clues,
by Isabella's fortitude and pluck?
No, by her total paucity of luck.

A leaden pipe, of all things, proved the spectre
        which ruined all.
        One fluky fall
eliminated Cosimo – a vector
depriving Isabel of her protector.

Benvenuto Cellini Ends His Memoirs Abruptly

The Duke did what no father ever should
(I think you understand me). In his pride,
he led his party (lacking local guide)
across the wide Maremma, then in flood.
Young Cardinal Giovanni, handsome, good,
contracted tertian fever, promptly died.
Some things are made of marble, and abide,
but humans, even princes, are like wood,
predestined to corruption. Paolo's bride
seemed worst affected. What begins, must end.
Aut nullus was the watchword, then, for Caesar.
I waited until palace tears had dried.
Aware that lutto pays a dividend,
I, nonchalant, betook myself to Pisa.

Bracciano and Baroncelli

You'll cross this land from Fiesole to Fano
and land on nowhere so devoid of cheer.
No easy laughter laps the rafters here.
Between Arezzo and the tranquil Arno,
you're seeking vileness? Cercherai invano:
but if to Lazio you persevere,
the sottobosco stings, the slopes are sheer.
Be warned. Attenzione, buon toscano!
So why forsake Siena, Signorelli,
the papacy of grape and chandelier,
the sphere of balcony and belvedere?
Where Browning, Byron, Chaucer – even Shelley –
Masaccio as well as Machiavelli,
once trod, who wouldn't hold the cobbles dear?

FRANCESCO IS THE BROTHER WHO, alone,
though younger, being male, assumed the throne.

A sinister young man,
no friend to Isabella,
Bianca's willing pawn,
as friendly as a stone.
The polity he ran
meant nothing, just his standing.
Grand Duke by name, he reigned but didn't lead:
he lacked the ruling-skill his dad had had.

In fifteen seventy-two, Florence was prone
to big events, a virtual battle-zone.
A palace fire began,
but also something stellar:
Virginio was born –
an heir, now, of her own!
The Princess' fallback plan
ensured a happy landing.
She'd Baroncelli, perfect for her need,
her out-of-town (thus independent) pad.

The Ricci Conspiracy

There's Pazzi, Pucci – shall we now add Ricci?
You love the hugger mugger – ah, go on!
Their plots are more far-out than Q-Anon.
A woman who likes sex is labelled 'itchy',
while one who speaks her mind is known as bitchy!
Bianca's consort sought his own black swan:
('Buonaventura' – name to dwell upon!)
He chose a Ricci wife: the odds were titchy
that this would work out well. The Ricci men
awaited him on Trinità Bridge. (Again,
it's *maschi* who decide the woman's fate.)
The bridge's walls with Pietro's brain were splashed,
they left his corpse in such a gruesome state.
The faithless wife? Next night, her throat was slashed.

So how does this touch Isabella? Well,
she bent her brother's ear, to intercede:
more damning yet, assassins often bleed
and need a hiding-place, a citadel.
The knaves were Baroncelli personnel,
and knew where they could hide away. Indeed,
that surgeons should attend was pre-agreed.
Who, then, could be the guiding machiavel?

The question is, why get involved at all?
Why court the taint of murder, like a canker?
Buonaventura, unimportant, small,
was hardly worth the risk of rumour, rancour:
but Isabella hoped the squalid brawl
would weaken the position of Bianca.

IT'S STRANGE HOW LITTLE THINGS BETOKEN BIG.
Has France just fallen? Hitler does a jig,
>	A water-pipe fell down,
>	and right on Cosimo's head:
>	the trauma caused a stroke
>	(remember Guido's wig?)
>	Our weak point is our crown.
>	From there, he just got iller,
could not recover from the pipe affair.
Who'd think a scrap of lead could kill a duke?

That's how Francesco got the ruler-gig.
The fig-tree blighted, Florence took the sprig.
>	The so-called 'human frown',
>	before his dad was dead,
>	assumed the ducal yolk,
>	the etiolated twig.
>	The princeling of renown
>	lingered with Cammilla,

borne everywhere inside a sedan chair.
Thus destiny can turn upon a fluke.

Vasari's death in fifteen seventy-four
wrapped up an era. Tuscan troubadour,
> Cosimo's Albert Speer,
> had finally quit the stage.
> Arditi (Bastiano)
> said now, and ever more,
> the world must live in fear.
> A ruler with no rules
would not resist the rise of evil men.
This was the noon of Bianca trionfante.

And Isabella's cousin, Leonor,
has plenty of unpleasantness in store.
> Francesco was sincere:
> despite her tender age
> she'd never see the Arno,
> considered her a whore,
> but not so hard to steer
> (since women are mere mules).
He'd murder her in some Medici glen,
a sixteenth-century Sam Trafficante.

So why was Leonor so harshly-viewed?
What prompted this Medici attitude?
> Her husband Pietro's honour
> had now been compromised –
> the worse for Leonor!
> Caught in the Pucci feud,
> the youngster was a goner.
> Two swords on cobbled stones,
both Isabella's lovers (old, old story),
and one was Troilo. Torello had to die.

In June of seventy-six, the very food
was poisoned. Leonor, for being lewd,
        had hatred thrust upon her,
        was heartily despised.
        What could they not endure?
        So sweet of voice and mood,
        the beautiful Madonna
        called Isabella's clone
was, once they'd offed her lover, Antinori,
dispatched at Caffagiolo in July.

Why own so many villas in the trees?
The Poggio a Caianos, Cerreto Guidis?
        Patricians need a place
        when policy's concerned
        to analyse their stance
        regarding enemies.
        A problem to efface?
        Two out-of-order wives.
They shipped them back to Florence, packed in crates.
It's obvious. They'd paved the way for it.

So Leonor and Isabella (not just these)
were 'punished' and were 'disappeared' with ease.
        But once they'd bagged their brace,
        to Troilo scrutiny turned.
        What if he's fled to France?
        Assassins work for fees.
        Just name your coup-de-grace:
        with arquebuses? Knives?
That's why they keep up countryside estates.
Upset rich men, you're going to pay for it.

La Modista Raggiratrice

The husband spends a lot of time in Rome,
while she holds court alone at Baroncelli.
The lover Troilo makes himself at home,
but how can Isabella hide her belly?

So Nora came along in 'seventy-one:
Virginio emerged in 'seventy-two.
Medici pedigree, or pious con?
There is no birth-control. What can she do?

The crisis comes in fifteen seventy-six.
She spends a month or two at Caffagiolo.
Though Paolo's not averse to Roman chicks,
it's clear his wife has not been flying solo.

Whoever said this life had to be fair?
But who said women didn't get their equal share?

An Extract from Venetian Ambassador Paolo Tiepolo's Report to the Doge on Florentine Affairs, Concerning the Character of Paolo Giordano Orsini

(a)

The worst voluptuary
       Your Highness ever saw:
he's Wisdom's adversary –
       on every side, a flaw.

A salon sanguinary,
       a cat without a claw,
he makes observers wary
       without inspiring awe.

Where Prudence might be chary,
        he's only neither-nor:
what kind of condottieri
        has never been to war?

The Grand Duke's tutelary
        when duns and bailiffs gnaw
preserves him proudly airy –
        or what's a marriage for?

        * * *

(b)

When pressed to sell more parcels of his land,
  he's careful to conceal from Isabella
each tawdry trade-off, lest she understand
how fast her dowry ran into the sand.

The Duke has almost ostracised him, and
  he knows nor Porcellino nor Novella:
he woos his wife at Cosimo's command,
so Florence might as well be Samarkhand.

While healthy empires burgeon and expand,
  Giordano is a severer, a seller,
impulsive policies, ineptly planned,
the heat he feels, by foreign forces fanned.

Although his name and station may be grand,
  the individual's a bottom-dweller.
La Serenissima trust him? By this hand,
not half as far as Arno can be spanned!

Two Gentlemen of Ferrara

Cortile (are their names) and Conegrano.
Ridolfo first, with Ercole successor,
ambassadors to Florence (from Ferrara).
They form a sort of tag-team (more a relay),
Cortile being second in to bat.

Ridolfo, both effeminate and *vano*,
a socialite, a flesh (of all kinds!) presser,
he's jester, jackass, janissary, jarrer,
attached to Isabella (lay where *she* lay),
reporting back to Este backstairs chat.

Replacement (or opponent, *mano-a-mano?*)
is Ercole, the classic second-guesser.
As cold as Kronstadt, *sec* as the Sahara,
the cobra of the court is Cortile,
communications coded, affect flat.

If Florence isn't Rome, nor is it Fano:
the drama queen, hard-drinking dandy dresser
may be an *avis*, but is hardly *rara*.
Ridolfo's shirts are redder than *le mille*,
but not with blood. The boudoir's where he's at.

Who wouldn't look for fun along the Arno?
Cortile is (by most) adjudged the lesser
(to Conegrano's Francis, Santa Clara),
his profile narrower than that of Chile:
but what is looked for in a diplomat?

Women Beware Women

1. Camilla, or How the Game Goes

As Grand Duke Cosimo was growing old,
his Spanish consort Leonora died.
   Libido which belied
   his sixty years all told
   could hardly be denied.
He took a second wife before the first was cold.

The substitute was (*plus ça change*) Camilla,
one far from favoured in Medici lore.
   We've met her type before:
   of style, not one scintilla:
   a vulgar painted whore:
the Vicky Hodge of hunting lodge and country villa.

Hyenas find a corpse on which to feast.
The father of Camilla placed his arms
   without the faintest qualms
   (a true-born *arriviste*)
   like Denning's drooping palms
      above his lintel. Doubtless, someone's palms were greased.

This marriage was a secretive affair,
since Cosimo well knew how florentines
   would read between the lines.
   Your common people care
   if someone undermines
beloved blood-lines. *Sans-culottes* are doctrinaire.

Francesco was the duke's acknowledged heir
and married to Johanna (*really* royal!)
   Ensconced on Tuscan soil
   but painfully aware

that commoners despoil
blue blood, she hates Camilla with a passion rare.

Johanna placed a boycott on the *Pitti*.
In sympathy with Florence *hoi palloi*
   determined to destroy
   Camilla, turned the city
   against her, but the ploy
could come to nothing. Sex remained the nitty-gritty —

and sex was what Camilla could bestow.
She never loved the duke, that much was clear,
   or even held him dear;
   however, Cosimo
   was utterly sincere
in needing her proximity in bed, although

she made no bones about it — she was bored
and had no use for mopping fevered brows.
   Who cares for wedding vows?
   Her husband she ignored,
   preferring to carouse,
returning just to copulate. (She could afford

this little kindness.) All that this achieved
was, hastening the death of Cosimo.
   In all the to-and-fro
   as wider Florence grieved,
   she shrugged her shoulders. 'So?'
But what awaited was a payback preconceived.

The brutal battle fought at Mookenheyde
this very month of April, seventy-four
   is never mentioned more:
   but when the old duke died,

the new one (this before
he mourned his father) swept the concubine aside.

Francesco knew that concubines contrive,
so sealed her in a convent, far from friends.
   That's where her story ends.
   Though fated to survive
   three decades more, she spends
her wretched life enclosed in cloisters, buried alive.

2. Johanna, or A Qualm of Honour

A Habsburg princess counts as Europe's cream,
but points are lost by being plain and thin,
and not Italian. Hating carnal sin
and failing on the son front turns the team
against you. If you're armed with only prayers,
and heedless whom your preachiness offends,
the chances are you'll end bereft of friends,
and stumble into all the deadly snares
that women set for women. There arise
more earthy girls, adept at spawning heirs,
with better buttocks and more shapely thighs.
Aghast to learn (at last!) of love affairs,
you'll rue that you've (through ruses you despise)
become The Fool of Florence, unawares.

THE DEAD OF WINTER NEVER SEEMS PROPITIOUS
and Florence might not suit a *Prinzessin*,
but when Medici greyhounds grip on hares,
whatever else may happen, they get theirs.
Johanna was a tender seventeen;
December weddings may not feel auspicious,
but what are wives? They're merely foaling mares,
and Cosimo was horribly ambitious.
The Habsburgs couldn't possibly object;

Francesco was inscrutable, serene,
a duke-in-waiting, eligible, *echt*!
By 'sixty-five, who still was superstitious?
When Isabel beheld the streets bedecked
with arches, she was prompted to reflect
on shapes that gaped. Vaginas! 'This must mean
my little brother's set his heart on heirs!'
What later happened could have been foreseen.
A juncture so ungracious, injudicious,
between the most improbable of pairs –
what other end could anyone expect?

What was a wife? A child conveyor belt?
Johanna, notwithstanding Habsburg *hauteur*,
was well aware of this. Francesco's bride
existed to produce Medici heirs.
Her first six efforts failed – each one a daughter –
and half of them, as infants, merely died.
Seen not so much as mother, more aborter,
the foreign felon, sowing female tares,
she soon perceived her reputation slide.
Not quite the type to take things in her stride,
and sternly certain *hat die geistige Welt
Verdienst*, she went Loreto-wards. She felt
through mother-power, all obstacles would melt.
In fact, if anything, affairs grew fraughter.
Compare her to Bianca – splitting hairs?
The latter led a cavalcade. Her airs
were regal, and (it cannot be denied)
she bore a boy-child. As Johanna knelt
in prayer before *Madonna of the Stairs*,
The Whore had won. She felt it in her water,
and kept from Florence squares and thoroughfares.

Her husband was consistent. 'Permafrost'
might best describe his feelings for Johanna.

From Michaelmas to next year's Pentecost
he kept himself aloof, uncoupled, distant.
His first concern was always La Toscana,
and when a young Venetian took his fancy,
his wife was one *persona* quickly tossed
aside – not just *non grata* – non-existent.
Who was this sexy northern *Monna Vanna*?
Her name, Bianca. By some doukomancy
she battened on Francesco, belled him, bossed;
Johanna, far from mounting a riposte,
saw nothing. In her haughty German manner
and sketchy Tuscan, she remained persistent
in fierce *naiveté*. Suppose by chance he
transferred the ducal court from *Loggia dei Lanzi*
(on such a change, Bianca was insistent)
across the Arno, setting up his banner
in openly connubial occupancy,
who wouldn't (save Johanna) prove resistant?

Great Cosimo, Johanna's father-in-law,
swept up Camilla, garbage from the gutter,
and married her. Johanna castigated
the fall from dignity which must ensue.
'Untouchables, are we? Is this Calcutta?'
Her words would have more impact than she knew.
In days to come, deserted, isolated,
she'd seek his help (as Cosimo foresaw).
Revenge is sweet, albeit when belated,
and so he told her, 'nothing I can do'.
Johanna's sun had set. The fast crowd feted
Francesco's paramour, who caused a flutter
by taking on the Carnival Revue
(her comedy, *The Shaming of the True*).
The blow above all else that devastated
the woeful wife, what was the final straw,
was seeing the virtuous Isabella draw

the curtain, close her coach's shutter,
while giggling with Bianca. That guffaw
summed up the plight in which her spite had put her.

3. *Bianca, or the Little Pretty Deft and Tidy Thing*

We all know someone very like Bianca.
How high to rate her? Let me count the ways.
Though blindfold, she finds gallants in the maze.
The Helen after whom the helots hanker,
devoid of pity, undefiled by rancour,
she – redolent of fragrant salad days –
so born to scorn Europa's hopeless craze,
will end, not with a whim, but with a banker.

There's something to be said for winning ways,
that art of knowing whom to throw it to.
Girls, greener than the euchre table's baize,
wait helplessly and watch her points accrue.
Accordingly, she wins both prick and praise;
without reserve, I tender her to you.

The Ferrarese Ambassador, Ridolfo Conegrano, Writes to Adolfo d'Este, 13 October, 1573

Such throaty timbres – oboes and bassoons –
such gowns! My Lady, apricot and plum,
her sleeves ablaze with blue October moons –
for one short night, her villa had become
the very essence of elysium!

To 'fortify' us, as My Lady said,
against the winter tedium to come,
to banish melancholy, drive out dread,
she threw an Autumn Ball. Delirium!
We met the equinox with pipe and drum.

The quality of Florence all attended,
and never were Their Graces better fed!
The sun was up before our revels ended –
and Isabella?   Still no thought of bed!
Three further galliards she'd yet to tread.

It seems I hear those trumpets even yet,
and taste the sweetmeats of that epic spread
(she'd plied us with light moscatel to whet
the palate) – I believe my mortal head
will throb for ever more, autumnal red!

22 May, 1572

It's fascinating. Here, the duke-to-be
is making love quite blatantly behind
his German consort's back. Why can't she see?
He hadn't seemed the fornicating kind
until this new one. And she's quite a find!

By courier, tomorrow, I'll be sending
some affidavits, rubricated, signed.
I don't think this will have a happy ending.
Her name's Bianca. Is the uxor blind?
Venetian cheeses have the toughest rind.

The family's Cappello from Murano
(they're not exactly what you'd call refined).
She ran away (with lover) to the Arno,
but now the loved-ones that she left behind
are out for vengeance, and they're of one mind.

Decorum is, these days, in short supply.
This busty bitch is blatantly befriending
the woman she's betraying on the sly.

It also seems Francesco is defending
(and paying for!) Bianca's reckless spending.

The lizard-king Francesco, misanthrope
without a saving grace has never shown
affection of this magnitude or scope.
Bianca proves he isn't carved of stone!
But how could she ensnare him on her own?

There clearly had to be some deep-felt need
subsisting in his heart of hearts, unknown,
but don't forget – the wife had failed to breed!
(The Habsburgs, too, are only flesh and bone,
and to familiar frailties all too prone.)

Bianca headed south with Buonaventura,
escaping Venice with unseemly speed.
Pietro was her partner-pimp-procurer,
and put her to Francesco, fee agreed
(succession must be – somehow – guaranteed).

What's in it for Bianca? First, protection!
Her family is keen to see her bleed.
Pietro can't personify perfection,
and *she* thinks *she* can be the tallest reed.
Who knows to what this 'love' may one day lead?

Pietro Buonaventura sure had luck.
To rise so rapidly, he must be blessed!
The Minder of the Wardrobe, pleat and tuck,
ensured the duke-to-be was deftly dressed,
in all his little whimsies acquiesced.

Remarkable how rich he soon became!
He bought a townhouse, started to invest.
A ducal intimate in all but name,

He ruched the ruffles on his master's chest
and guaranteed the pantaloons were pressed.

You rise in your profession? It's a fact:
some folks will try to denigrate and blame.
Ventura turns out *buona*? They'll detract.
They'll claim your gorgeous wife is on the game
and you are benefitting from her shame!

Pietro now had influence, it's true,
and wasn't slow to utilise the same.
He granted boon or cancelled interview,
dispensing ducal largesse to the lame
and chose who went (and certainly who came!)

Bianca's star was rocketing, not rising,
a fact that Isabella chanced to spot:
she knew Bianca needed neutralising:
but how to beat the bushfire, stop the rot?
She came up with a rather clever plot.

There was a Florence woman named Cassandra,
related to that querulous Ricci lot.
The rumour was that Pietro, pimp and panderer,
was rutting there. Since Ricci blood was hot,
provoke the menfolk: just imagine what

might happen if their dagger-hands get itchy!
The world won't miss one fast-and-loose philanderer,
and this could happen, since the clan with which he
was messing was the quick-to-anger Ricci.
(Alleging Isabella's lack of candour, or
suggesting she's a self-regarding slanderer
would go too far. Let's say she can be bitchy!)

The Trinitá Bridge

One single bridge (and not the better-known),
in nineteen forty-four largely destroyed
(a vain attempt on their part to avoid
the Schwerpunkt of the Allies) on its own
has witnessed many marvels. This mute stone
saw Dante both distraught and overjoyed
at Beatrice' passing. Browning, here, was buoyed
to find the narrative which he could hone
into his masterpiece. This urban space,
depicted (there) with masterly restraint,
so splendidly endowed with Tuscan grace,
is tarnished, too, by turn: Italian taint!
They butchered Buonaventura in this place
so sanctified by Ghirlandaio's paint.

Cassandra's nephew is by now incensed.
Pietro's warned by friends, but he disdains
to live in shadows, sealed off, guarded, fenced.
They found him on the bridge. You see these stains?
They smashed his skull. You're looking at his brains.

Should Isabella bear her share of guilt?
You know she should. She took enormous pains
to plan the thing and, in it to the hilt,
her need to knock Bianca down explains
her acts. Just ask yourself, which party gains?

Did Isabella want Cassandra dead?
You'd even doubt her hand was on the tiller?
The latter's throat was severed in her bed,
while in the gilt-and-marble of her villa
the former gathered close Pietro's killer.

Bianca will survive what here befell her,
but now the case is altered. Blood's been spilt.
Here starts the downward slide of Isabella,
an ever-steeper, ever-deepening tilt.
They lose their footing, who on blood have built.

Without Pietro, Bianca surely now
would be more pliable: was she not caught
bereft of income? Might she not allow
a *rapprochement*, alliance of some sort?
Such is, at least, what Isabella thought.

A serious Medici palace fire
brought Isabella's strategy to nought.
She had a son at last (who was the sire
was anybody's guess!) She was, in short,
distracted. Still, a type of truce was sought

and patched together. This provisional pact
asked little of the 'sisters', save require
prior warning, should the one or other act.
The pact proved Isabella's political pyre:
Bianca was already reaching higher.

The handsome Troilo, Isabella's lover,
the object of her sexual desire,
could flourish here in Florence under cover
of someone like Bianca, wife-for-hire –
a project all can ponder and admire!

For Isabella, Bianca would be better
attached to Troilo, rather than apart,
but fatally, she failed to fit the fetter.
She wanted Bianca wed but a-la-carte,
removing Troilo from the marriage mart.

In no sense was the one the other's debtor.
Bianca, independent from the start,
was bigger than the bounds that life had set her.
Though oceans still remained for her to chart,
Bianca knew to trust her innate art.

When Grand Duke Cosimo's illustrious life
concluded (April, fifteen seventy-four)
the heir Francesco briskly ditched his wife,
escorting Bianca to the brazen boar
to rub its nose for luck. Who could ignore

the symbolism? It was plain to see –
nay, fully in your face. More than before,
the grandest man in northern Italy
escorts his mistress on the ballroom floor:
The rumour has become an open roar.

A cocktail of astuteness, luck and stealth
has brought Bianca to the heights, whence she
(securing Pietro's sequestrated wealth)
enjoys Francesco's generosity
and lives in independent luxury.

She welcomes Isabella in her coach.
The one whom the Venetian refugee
would not have dared, at one time, to approach
now fawns on her with fulsome flattery.
The garter's firmly on the other knee!

Pucci and Pazzi

One window in the corner's always sealed,
and has been so since fifteen fifty-eight.
A monument to undiminished hate,
right on the vertex where the Pucci shield

still glowers, down on Servi, cracked and peeled,
the blindest eye in Florence marks the date.
They moved, not merely to eliminate,
or drive defeated foemen from the field,
but with a nasty need to extirpate.
Though powerless pontiffs might pontificate,
Medici vengeance, pitiless, entire,
as cruel and pagan as the crucifix,
unyielding as the window-blocking bricks,
pursued the plotters to their funeral pyre.

Pazzi and Pucci

Salviati failed again – condemned to lose
the Baroncelli, Isabella's pile
(conspiracy seems hardly worth their while).
If Pucci bankers promised to refuse
to help buy Imola, how then excuse
their subsequent behaviour? Latin guile?
The winners have no need to reconcile
their glaring inconsistencies. You choose
the other side, your faults will be on show:
no matter that at Nineveh you waved
the Pucci flag, or how well you behaved:
there's one thing that the planet cares to know.
One brother died, Lorenzo, though, was saved:
Medici vengeance is the afterglow?

No United Front

A desolate Johanna, Leonor,
an Isabella driven to despair,
Fernando absent, Pietro unaware,
Francesco thinking his Venetian whore
was world enough. The rest he could ignore.
Orazio Pucci was the man to dare,

but secrecy is not Italian fare.
Francesco loved revenge and, on that score,
before his father Cosimo was cold
he'd locked Cammilla up. Orazio died
in August. Of the plotters, none denied
that Leonora numbered in their fold,
but she was 'of Toledo' (which was gold).
Francesco, though, could wait for time and tide.

The Symbolic Importance of Paintings Associated with the Baroncelli Mansion of Isabella Medici

In Italy, they think it 'playfulness'
when nothing ever makes the slightest sense.
You hunt for Platform Two with diligence,
but Three comes after One. You have to guess
where Locker Twelve might be. Like playing chess,
potential options overwhelm, immense;
and that is why I'm sitting on the fence.
The Palatina Gallery, no less!
Andrea's Assumption might divulge some truth
regarding Isabella, and her youth:
(late fifteen twenties, nothing else will do!)
Attribute it to this researcher's sloth,
but I can hardly analyse them both -
same time, same place – del Sarto painted two!

The New Ferrarese Ambassador, Ercole Cortile, Writes to Adolfo d'Este by Cryptogram: 31 October, 1575

First and Last (1)

Paolo's in Bracciano. Isabella
has not been seen in Florence since Twelfth Night.
The Duke strides openly with his *zitella*.
Though counsel counsels pride as counsel might,

Francesco isn't listening. Despite
his wise men having wrestled, wrung and wrangled,
Bianca leaves tomorrow at first light
on pilgrimage, tiara'd and bespangled,
Loreto-bound. She's crowned, all opposition strangled.

Her retinue is richer than a queen's,
more in-your-face than was the cast-off German's.
It isn't hard to see what all this means.
She won't be going there to hear the sermons.
We'll see a swelling bigger than Mount Hermon's
before the year is out. It's quite amusing.
The only thing she's found Francesco firm on's
restricted diet. Bianca's banned from boozing,
in case she's pregnant. Having thus refrained from using

a glutton's charter, every other way
of self-indulgence lies at her command.
Her townhouse has been painted, to convey
a sense of her importance. It was planned
and executed by one artist's hand –
that's Buontalento. Florence is agog!
Court architect – the new Vasari – and
inordinately modish, now must slog
(like all of us) to Poggio. 'Florence on a dog

leash', that is what the wits are whispering (gently).
Bianca's villa opens, Martinmas –
and everyone must be there, evidently.
One hears that, etched on every pane of glass,
we'll find the hat-motif. Baked salted bass
and madrigals! We'll none the less endeavour
to bear it with aplomb. The rich (alas!)
are seldom clever. Had you bid me sever
all contact, I'd have spent All Souls in peace. However,

she wants us at her villa. I'll attend.
One other thing has happened – small enough,
but illustrative of the recent trend.
Bianca, *boule de suif* or bit of fluff,
went riding in her carriage, off the cuff.
She blocked another coach, which also needed
to cross the Trinitá. Bianca's tough,
felt no-one had more right-of-way than *she* did,
insisted that the other cede – and she succeeded!

In fact, the lady in the other coach,
bizarrely, was Francesco's wife Johanna.
(Does precedence depend on first approach?)
The latter-day Venetian Monna Vanna
despatched her footman in patrician manner
to hoik the Habsburg back, without alighting.
One wonders if the Austrian's *mens sana*
will hold much longer. At the time of writing,
she keeps to German only – but her words are biting.

His Highness Don Francesco has begun
to style Bianca openly, 'Grand Duchess'.
The word is, she will soon produce a son.
We're witnessing the perfectest of Putsches!
A viable boy-child stamps her card as much as
Medici blood. The forest fire was fanned
by Isabella's fawning gestures, such as
riding in the carriage, acting grand
and holding (ostentatiously) Bianca's hand,

before these strange events had run their course.
The news is dripping out in tiny doses
that husbands have gone further than divorce.
Through asking questions, one arrives at gnosis,
but people in power are parrying the process.
Smooth courtiers are shamelessly denying

what is, in fact, a tart's apotheosis.
The fledgling cuckoo-chick is finally flying,
once having supervised the other siblings' dying.

La Trama della Morte

1. Letter from Cardinal Savelli to Paolo Giordino Orsini, February 1575

I thank you for your letter, urging me
to look into the matter of Lorenzo,
whose wife insists, from blind obstinacy,
she will not live with him. He's *innocenzo!*

As well you know, she's citing foul abuses,
but I have done exactly as requested:
despite their allegations and excuses,
both wife and mother have now been arrested.

They're obdurate at first, but then they trim;
in case Lorenzo's still in any doubt,
until she swears she's going back to him,
nor Marta nor her mother's getting out.

Whomever I imprison, Heaven binds:
whom I release, the Lord above us looses.
Whenever we with *donne* get entwined,
we put our necks in unforgiving nooses.

2. Diplomatic Despatch from Ercole Cortile to Alfonso d'Este, on 22 January, 1575

Last night, a strange thing happened to your servant;
at Baroncelli, as Your Highness knows,
the Lady Isabella held a jig.
She's famous for her cellar and her larder:

in Florence, though the very puddles froze,
to not attend would rank as being unmannish,
so who was there? Your very own Cortile!

The Nuncio grew altogether fervent,
undignified demeanour, abject pose,
(he even cast aside his silver wig!)
and tried to dance the modish *gagliarda:*
Your Highness can imagine how that goes!
We diplomats are classified as clannish,
but this was just too mortifying, really!

I pride myself in being quite observant
and, as the thing was drawing to its close,
who sidled up? The one we call 'The Fig':
she clung to me with unbecoming ardour.
I felt her as we talked metamorphose
into a thing emotional and Spanish
and honestly, quite sexy, touchy-feely.

She wept. And what emerged? *En conservant*
the secrets of the bedroom, I'll compose
a coded message. I was feeling big:
to keep control felt harder, so much harder
with every revelation that arose;
her sense of seemliness just seemed to vanish,
and she was kissing, openly and freely!

3. *First and Last (2)*

Pietro has that crazy inbred taint,
disturbed Medici inner self. How quaint!
So when it comes to sexing her, he ain't

fucking interested. It's such a bore!
He's into kinky stuff, with whip and whore:
in other words, ignoring Leonor.

She's well aware what all these things betoken.
I've heard her words, to me directly spoken:
the Spanish girl is cut adrift, heartbroken.

4. Florentine Diarist Bastiano Arditi Records Details of an Audience (21st September, 1575) Between Martino Corbolo (Secretary to the 'Eight') and Troilo Orsini

Ser Troilo knows how courts work: so he said,
'I'm delighted that Your Honour has made time
to hear me. Judex est lex loquens, is my motto.
You'd beard the snake? You must address its head.
I feel myself suspected of a crime:
I've come to see the marrow of Gli Otto.'

'Your Excellency merely needs to say,'
replied the August Other, with a bow,
'what ails you. I'll for sure consider it,
and if I can assist in any way,
you know that I will do it here and now.'
Undying friend, or dirty hypocrite?

'The Grand Duke has arrested all my men,
on charges, if existent, all too scanty:
I want them freed today.' 'No human force
can interrupt the legal process, when
we have a death like that of Agnolanti:
with charges laid, the law must run its course.'

'What evidence is furnished? Let me hear.'
'My dearest Troilo, why are you so touchy?
I cannot analyse our case with you.'

'My influence has waned more than I feared:
I've been ambassador – I've helped the Duchy –
Bavaria and Paris, Poland too –

my house is broken into, brother seized.
It is unconscionable! You'll not shift?
Return to me my harpsichord and cello –
they've done no wrong.' 'I gather you're not pleased.
To intervene is not within my gift.
And then there is the matter of Torello.'

'Such perfidy's not easy to believe.
I ask for help, and get sarcastic laughter.
This conversation makes the whole thing clear.
If Florence isn't safe for me, I'll leave:
I am the one Francesco's really after.
I'll trouble you no more: I'm out of here!'

5.

And so he left our city. Where to go?
The obvious direction, heading home,
the family redoubt – Orsini Rome.
But Troilo was, as people in the know
were well aware, still Isabella's beau.
Far better, seek some other honeycomb
to be anonymous in monochrome.
Would Paris serve him best for lying low?
Like Michael Corleone on the lake,
Francesco's arm was long. The urge to strafe,
or castigare, means all smiles are fake:
bonomia starts the hart from out the brake.
Were Troilo's Travels progress of the rake?
Was there a place on earth he could be safe?

6. Did Francesco Try to Poison Leonor?

We all have sicknesses from time to time.
But when you're young and hearty, twenty-three,
you have an expectation to be free
of vomit-buckets, diarrhoeia, slime
(the inescapables, the paradigm
of illness). What if, fairly frequently,
the symptoms, noticed first in February,
can cut you down, a woman in your prime?
Today, we'd take some snips of Leonor's hair,
and test for arsenic. Then, 'happenstance'
was best forensic practice: that, and prayer.
Who'd poison a Medici? Who would dare?
How did a kid, condemned for an affair,
survive it all? She built up tolerance.

¿Y cómo explicar la Leonor, y
su infelicidad? There is a story.
Vespasian: decet imperatorem stantem mori.
Francesco told del Oddi, 'Antinori
must die on Elba. hoc tibi est honori.'
We men deserve domus et placens uxori,
but good ones are margarita e stercore.
A man without a woman is corpus sin pectore.
To say that we're imbued with virtutis amore
is obvious and redundant, mere nugae canorae.
We have to dominate: vincere aut mori.
It's hard, but nil sin magno labore.
They're tarts – fructo congniscitur arbori:
and yet, we love them – cedamus amori.

If you were Leonor, you'd take the lure?
Your Spanish folks are trying to get you out:
Medici norms that you have dared to flout
include adultery and treason pure:

you helped the Pucci, nor did you abjure
your role in it. You don't feel any doubt
about a hunting-trip, where family clout
is total? Confidence is premature!

You'll feel about as snug as if you played
away from home, let's say at Widzew Lodz.
Is Caffagiolo somewhere that you've stayed
before? Are you not just a bit afraid?
Why might they want you in a country lodge?
Can't you see through this crude Medici dodge?

7. *Letter from Pietro de 'Medici to His Brother, Grand Duke Francisco, 11 July, 1576*

I'm writing to Your Highness to advise
of yesterday's unfortunate event.
(The tragedy was just an accident,
as I am writing now to emphasise.)
It's always sad when someone noted dies:
My Lady Leonor, I must lament,
was overwhelmed by death, in bedroom pent.
I hereby notify of her demise.
The melancholy news of her release
from mortal torment of which You now learn
is sure to bring Your Highness mental peace.
My bounden duty is Your mere caprice:
you'd have me come to Florence, with the urn?
To stay at Caffagiolo, or return?

8. *Should Isabella Have Been Suspicious of Her Husband's Instructions to Accompany Him on a Hunting Expedition to Cerreto Guidi?*

She had some reasons to believe that 'no'.
These hunting-trips were normal for the clan,
and Isabella, better than a man,

could ride and shoot. In comfort at Cerreto,
her sense of augury would be quite low:
to bring her entourage was in the plan,
her reassuring human caravan.
At least this wasn't Rome, or – worse – Bracciano.

But, on the face of it, one must say, 'yes'.
Her friend and cousin, three short days before,
had died at Caffagiolo. What is more,
she knew her brothers. Able to assess
what might occur behind Cerreto's door,
could Isabella not imagine? Guess?

9. Disposing of Isabella's Possessions: Cortile Sends News to Ferrara

Francesco names Bianca as her heir!
She also gets Virginio, Eleanora,
(that's Isabella's darling girl and boy,
the pair of whom, as yet, are under six,
and both of whom the father has rejected,
as someone else's offspring, damaged goods).

Her mansion, Baroncelli, now stands bare.
Without her things, it's infinitely poorer
(a month ago, it was her pride and joy).
Now Paolo passes nights there, just for kicks,
which no-one had envisioned or expected,
and former friends all stay away in floods.

Bianca's even claimed her underwear:
the absent Troilo, Isabel's adorer,
they also have intentions to destroy.
It's tragic that these footpads had to mix,
that robber-baron hierarchs intersected:
Medici and Orsini mingled bloods.

10. First and Last (3)

It's Baroncello, just beyond the square
where once reigned Isabella, Paolo's 'ex'
and, since her downfall, Paolo holds the key.
He, having nought to occupy him, sits
and counts the income from his dividends:
and Baroncello's where he does the 'biz'.
(You want to know the tree? Regard its fruits!)
It's where he plays his games of ducks and drakes,
the venue used for vice, the mansion where

he seeks his pleasure, where he moves and shakes.
He sees himself, still, striding warship decks
(Lepanto looms in perpetuity),
regales us with his tales of Greatest Hits,
and uses women for his selfish ends.
When evening comes, he 'gets his gear on', viz,
he loves to wear his thigh-length leather boots
and has his servants tinker with his hair,
in Altr'Arno drinks, then later takes

his predilection, pleasure, and recruits
professionals, impersonal, for sex
(no lover of true intimacy, he).
He knows no poets, raconteurs or wits.
He has no inner life, no thoughts, no friends:
his conversation has no fun, no fizz:
his only purpose, staving-off despair.
His only opera, the noise he makes
with six or seven Prato prostitutes.

Finally

'Orlando Furioso' by Vivaldi,
the Sicily Campaign of Garibaldi,

lasagna eaten fresh in tavole calde,
commedia dell'arte with Grimaldi,
Italian institutions that we love,
but not the sonnet sequence of Tedaldi.

Why want a rival woman's underwear?
Why commandeer her poet? Why go there?
You own her children, own her sedan chair.
You've won her city – would you own the air?
If only we had Bianca here before us,
we'd hit her with a deadly questionnaire!

Why is Francesco guilty, in our eyes?
Why see him in the orchestrator's guise?
Each person who, we're driven to surmise,
displeases him, eventually dies.
Receiving news of murders, day by day,
the Grand Duke shows no vestige of surprise.

THE CONGRESS OF THE WITS:

(5) *Marforio*

Lapels are narrow
then they're wide:
what is left
that's not been tried?

You'll find them in the Flavian,
all over Angkor Wat,
their badge a bottle of Evian.
Girl-garment starts a top,
but then becomes culottes,
a fashion one-stop shop
which totty counts as hot.

The guy in baseball cap
(too often back-to-front)
and singlet which says GAP
(he's NAFNAF down below) –
a look which (let's be blunt)
worked forty years ago …
the silly Roger Hunt!

The boys have names like 'Piers',
the girls are always 'Lisa':
snowboarders they, and skiers:
they've 'done' the Parthenon,
and pyramids at Giza,
but get the basics wrong:
Octavius was Caesar?

They've all been up the Eiffel,
they've all 'supported' Pisa:
best frisbee park? The Güell!
Testaccio's just a mound,
and food comes from a freezer.
No *trattorias* found:
lunch is a wedge of pizza!

Those who've seen the scene
from 'Roman Holiday'
are consequently keen
to head for Cosmedin.
I ask you in dismay,
what can a visit mean,
with turnstiles in the way?

They're in the Pantheon line,
and gossiping of kids
left back at Columbine
as if the change of air

was Aitken to Duluth:
who'd be so unaware?
Alas, the sins of youth!

THE HISTORY OF THE TRUE CROSS:

(6) The Dream of Constantine

Light Admitted (2)

In tents, at Milvian Bridge, this summer night?
The background story's rapidly narrated.
You make them tetrarchs, they are going to fight.
Young Constantine is by Maxentius hated,
pitched battle on the morn anticipated.
An angel brings the latest from the boss.
'It's effortless for you, because you're fated:
for Christendom, you couldn't give a toss.
You want to win? Just ride in with The Cross.'

Piero knows, a painter has to flatter.
What's Beauty? Symmetry that's stimulated.
Though paint defines the darkness born in matter,
in Piero's hands, it's light – not fabricated,
but true-to-life. The moment is awaited.
As Constantine snores on, Maxentius' men,
unfed, unrested, semi-etiolated,
foresee their immolation. Yet again,
the awkward stance of Piero's Madeleine.

LA GAZZA LADRA, Being a Tale told by Angelica Battista

A princess once had gorgeous hair
and no-one was allowed to touch it.
Herself alone could comb and care,
and only she caress and clutch it.
So long and thick and slick and lush,
an hour a day in morning hush
she combed it with a silver brush.
One day, amid the songbirds' trill,
she set her comb down on the sill.
A magpie happened to alight,
resplendent in his black and white:
in bare an instant, back in flight,
he'd stolen with uncanny skill
the comb now clamped inside his bill!

(This princess' name was, by the way,
Luisa-Maria, or 'Smarrita'.)
She lunged at it. To her dismay,
the mishievous magpie was much fleeter.
It just so happed, the very next day,
a silver hairgrip, on display
on selfsame sill, soon went stray:
Smarrita saw, through window-frame,
the mugger magpie was to blame!
He beamed from branch of nearby beech,
invulnerably out of reach,
emitting something like a screech,
his beak unable to proclaim
his triumph (hairgrip held in same).

The third day, when a brush was taken,
and right before Smarrita's face,
all royal decorum was forsaken

in the cause of giving chase!
Down a ladder made of silk
(or some fine fabric of that ilk)
the colour of a marmot's milk,
across the front lawn's dips and hollows
Smarrita teeters, totters, follows
into Woebegotten Wood
(where nothing comes to any good!)
Has Smarrita understood?
No Adonises, Apollos:
this is where the warthog wallows!

The magpie bounced from bough to bough
with spritely nimble nonchalance,
while poor Smarrita had to plough
through bush and shrub. However, once
a rustic cabin came in sight,
the thief decided to alight
(to the chasing girl's delight)
high on the cabin's roof. The lass,
flopping down on open grass,
had never breathed so hard before!
Flitting to the forest floor
and skipping through the open door,
the thieving magpie, bold as brass,
hopped out of sight. A pretty pass!

Smarrita stayed a little while
swooned on the sward, immobile, resting,
but thought again of magpie guile,
and said, 'the beast at least needs testing!'
The piebald bird kept out of sight,
no hint or squint of black or white:
the thing was missing, vanished quite!
That door still yawned – why not go in?
Smarrita's patience, wearing thin,

impelled her onward, through the door.
She thought she'd grab her brush, no more,
and hardly guessed what lay in store.
A man sat there – tall, handsome, thin –
to greet Smarrita with a grin!

STRAY LEAVES: PADDY STOPPED AT EMPOLI

In Ireland, wellies sell, and wells are holy:
our names are legion in the roll of honour.
We have a singing priest (Sinead O'Connor),
and though we didn't think of ravioli,
we have produced an extra-special goalie,
the legendary hero, Packie Bonner,
renowned as Glasgow Celtic's Number Oner.
We're not restricted to our frontiers, solely:
the land of Stradivarius and Stromboli
embraced one of the lads, and did so wholly!
(The place is EM-poli, and not Em-PO-li.
You'll find it easy if you say it slowly.)
The Church of Rome, today, would be a midget
if not for San Donato, our boy Donagh.

STRAY LEAVES: BRIDGET THE FIDGET

There's many fallen women in Kildare,
and most of them beyond the help of prayer:
but when a bird named Bridget took the veil,
we gained our saint – the Mary of the Gael.
Now here's a girl all Irishmen revere,
for she converted water into beer.
She did not want too sexy to appear,
so Bridget's digit poked out her own eye.

The girl did miracle on miracle,
quite unimpaired by anything empirical
and, lest you think my tone somewhat satirical,
the day she heard that Donagh was a goner,
she flew to Fiesole (all saints can fly)
and hung her cloak on sunbeams, for to dry.

'I WONDER IF,' the Princess asked,
'you've seen a silver-filching bird?'
The youth replied, 'That's me unmasked!
Before you shriek, or say a word,
I'm subject to a fairy's curse,
the terms of which I can't reverse:
I have to steal. What's even worse,
compelled to take a magpie's form
outside this shack, come sun or storm,
I must await a virgin – but
to break the spell (unkindest cut!)
she must agree to being shut
within these walls, and must perform
the rites decreed in fairy norm.

Smarrita, being a virgin still,
(remarkably!) thus qualified:
and furthermore, for good or ill,
felt something for the lad she eyed –
new feelings, hard to comprehend.
Said she, 'I hope your luck may mend
and, incidentally, to that end,
I'm keen to do what goodwill can.
You seem to me a decent man
who labours under grave affliction.
May I remove this malediction,
and free you from your fraught constriction?'
Since this was how her thinking ran,
the youngster thanked her, and began:

'Specific actions that I need
may sound eccentric to relate
but, should you do them, I'd be freed
from this intolerable fate.
The girl must watch yon mountain chain
unstinting, through this window-pane.
She mustn't fidget, or complain.
I warn you now, it won't be fun!'
The Princess cried, 'Let's get it done!'
She settled, staring at the range.
The young man left. A subtle change
came over her, exceeding strange.
She persevered, though. Once begun,
she wouldn't quit until she'd won.

The days went by, and then the weeks.
Her hair felt coarser, thicker, fuller.
And as she watched the distant peaks,
she sensed her hair was changing colour.
One sunny day, the lad returned.
'Your dreary vigil stands adjourned!
My spell's dispelled!' The girl discerned
an alteration in his face:
some kind of shift had taken place.
He brought no thanks, no praise, no present:
his tone was haughty, more than pleasant:
'Your hair! You look just like a peasant!'
The mirror showed (his lack of grace
aside) it was indeed the case.

The Princess' hair, once silken gold,
was tough as wire, and black as coal.
It was appalling to behold!
Instead of seeking to console
the one who'd rescued him, the youth
berated her. 'You're so uncouth!

I cannot stand you. That's the truth!'
Then, without a comment more,
the lad (so charming, heretofore)
turned on his heels and strode away.
His silhouette, in shadow-play,
stood out against the light of day.
Expectorating on the floor,
the youngster sauntered through the door.

Smarrita was, of course, distraught.
She wept a while, but then at length
it dawned on her. She really ought
to head for home. She summoned strength
to leave the cabin's dismal scene:
how bright the grass seemed – and how green!
That's when something unforeseen
unfolded. In a forest clearing,
easily within her hearing,
she saw and heard three fairies dancing!
And knowing this was not mere chancing,
Smarrita, cautiously advancing,
was jubilating more than fearing.
The fairies stopped and watched her nearing.

'What's the thing that ails you, Miss?'
Smarrita told her sorry tale.
'You mustn't worry over this.
We three will see that you prevail.'
The crushing burden of distress
was instantly dispelled – and yes,
at Fairy Number One's caress,
Smarrita's hair turned blonde again!
Amazement was compounded when
the second fairy touched her gown.
What had been stiff and listless brown
was heaven-blue, with seed-pearls down

the satin seams. The third one then
produced some gems unknown to men

and conjured up a necklace. She
adorned Smarrita's snow-white throat
while saying, 'We would like to be
your lady-courtiers, to promote
your interests, protect your rights,
and settle scores for suffered slights.
Anyone who stands and fights
against injustice should command
a faithful friend, a helping hand.'
What followed next was just a blur.
Princess and fairies swiftly were
in a city that was new to her.
'Where is this place? What is this land?
Whose soil is this on which we stand?'

'The place's name is not worth stating.
You see the palace, with its banners?'
(This from Second Lady-in-Waiting):
'Your magpie-man must mind his manners!
That's your mansion, over there,
confronting him, across the square.
Which is plusher? You compare!'
'We are in his monarchy,'
offered Lady Number Three,
'and though he's now a mighty king,
he's due for Fortune's downward swing,
and you will be his reckoning.'
Smarrita took them in for tea,
on her new mansion's balcony.

They had a rather splendid view –
palatial pomp, to look upon!
'Here's the thing that you must do.'

(It came from Fairy Number One.)
'Since the rascal has no shame,
He's sure to flirt. Just play the game.
Whatever *he* does, do the same.'
The Second Lady said, 'In sum,
he'll see you're pretty, and he'll come.
Let him flatter, let him flirt.
Just be passive. Be inert.
Don't do anything overt.'
Said the Third One, 'Just stay mum.
You win this game by playing dumb.'

STRAY LEAVES: HATE-PLOUGH

an equinocturne

You'll know, if you're a polymath,
the perils of the sylvan path
where lurks the dreaded Gynopath:
of Freud and Grimm, of Joy and Wrath,
of Horrid Hughes and Primrose Plath.

Just as Winter swallows Summer,
so Harlequin, deceptive mummer,
proves the queller, overcomer.
He's the Other, Different Drummer,
lust's disgust (oh what a bummer!)

Caperuça pert and prim
deep in forest, out on limb,
falling victim to a whim
stalked by universal Him
grimly out to plough her quim.

Show incisors, get out claws,
ready salivating jaws,
eyes like serpents', teeth like saws,
innocents walk into maws:
ruddy lips from hips and haws.

When all's done and all's been said
(the Wolf has got you into bed),
and Sex and Death the only laws,
there's still Inanna's get-out clause:
exhume the bride (Who died? The groom!)
The woman steps out from the womb.

* * * *

They told her she should tell the king
that, to be truly wooed, in fairness,
she needed someone who could bring
the Golden Rose of Self-Awareness.
It all unfolded as foreseen.
He saw her, liked her. His demesne
was hers, if she would be his queen.
She said, 'If I might interpose,
Your Majesty's impressive prose
has made me feel the cynosure.
What modest maid could hope for more –
how come we've never met before?
But who would have me, Heaven knows,
must bring to me the Golden Rose.'

The King was utterly in love.
He led his minions from the front,
for when push came to frantic shove,
he himself took up the hunt.
At last, the rose was finally found!
But royal hopes were swiftly drowned:

Smarrita (Lady Fortune) frowned.
'Before I'll walk from mine to yours,
from mansion step to palace doors,
I must insist on one more boon:
the rose's petals must be strewn
in carpet manner, to festoon
my every footfall. One abhors
the feel of soil or naked floors!'

The king did as Smarrita asked.
A path was laid from door to door
of golden petals, as was tasked:
what woman, wooed, could hope for more?
She quizzed her aides, 'What happens hence?'
The First One said, 'It makes most sense
to dress in utmost opulence.'
'But even so, let's be discreet,'
(this from the Second), 'in bare feet.'
'If treachery constructed traps,'
the Third opined, 'why then, perhaps
one thorn could pierce, provoke collapse?
To prank a prick, that's our conceit.
so swoon, and we'll complete the cheat!'

In unison the threesome chanted,
'We'll fill the fool with fulsome dread!
Niente è concesso, nothing's granted:
on the path he may not tread!'
A silence on observers settles:
the Princess steps onto the petals,
as gingerly as if on nettles.
The king is watching as she goes,
so delicately on her toes,
but halfway over – such dismay!
A shriek! The Princess faints away!
Both king and court in disarray!

All rush to help, to diagnose.
Oh wretched thorn! Oh bloody rose!

The first upon the scene, the king,
beside himself, asks 'Is she dead?'
Unable to do anything,
upon the path he dare not tread.
All hats are doffed, no eye is dry:
her suitor sniffles, sigh on sigh
as 'Ladies' bear her shoulder-high
back to her mansion. Thrice an hour
the king does all that's in his power
through counsellors and trusted minions
to scour his duchies and dominions
for oracles or wise opinions.
What use are treasure, troops or tower?
By thorn we're thwarted, felled by flower!

'Why should the rose,' exclaimed the king,
'the finest thing in all creation,
put forth a thorn to pierce and sting
and cause such perturbation?
To further her recovery,
it's at her side I need to be:
I'll plead with her to marry me!'
Smarrita's answer, curt, concise
(conveyed on Ladies' loyal advice):
'To one condition, please adhere:
I must insist that you appear
reclining on a funeral bier.
Beneath your butt, a bed of ice
is not required, but would be nice.'

From palace throne to mansion hall
(the atrium, to lie in state)
the king was carried on his pall,

midst trappings tragic and ornate.
His face was solemn, yet composed,
the royal eyes serenely closed:
pomp and pathos, juxtaposed.
To mark the monarch's mock demise
the great and good, to say goodbyes,
now gathered round the catafalque
(the like of which, since James K. Polk,
had not been seen). Nor bar nor balk
deterred Smarrita, discourse-wise:
'It's time for you to use your eyes.'

(At this, the noble eyelids rose.)
'You moral midget, ethical elf!
I'm just a woman, yet you chose
to utterly debase yourself!'
Without a word or gesture more
(save spitting smartly on the floor),
she turned and walked out through the door.
Taken totally aback,
recoiling from the fierce attack,
the king can only watch her go.
'So how was I supposed to know?
My own shortcomings worked this woe,
the self-awareness which I lack.
Yes, that's the virgin from the shack!'

In the Grip of Superstition

A world without the safety net called Thought,
where people strive to do the thing they ought,
absorb the puerile precepts that they're taught:
their dread is, death will snatch them falling short –
eternity of agony, if caught!
The final thread they hang by's pulled too taut.
Already sinners when they're born, distraught

to hear the Levites' interim report
which sets their singularity at naught
and, facing fire unending for a tort,
(unless they're rich – salvation can be bought)
resort to exhortation of a sort.
Whenever hopes are dashed or plans abort,
their answer is, 'appease the Juggernaut!'

EL VIOLINCELLO DEL CARDENAL, IN WHICH BOTTINI'S INVESTIGATORS REACH OUT TO CARDINAL PIETRO OTTOBONI, CURRENT CURATE OF THE CHURCH WHERE POMPILIA WAS CHRISTENED, MARRIED AND IS BURIED

Lorenzo in Lucina – what a church!
So 'bijou' – perfectly Pompilia's scale:
it's here she was baptised, wore wedding-veil.
But what we touch, we humans must besmirch:
just here, her tiny coffin had its perch,
within the collar of the altar-rail.
The crime egregiously beyond the pale,
the place idyllic for a day's research.
You wear your leather down when you're a staffer:
the bread-and-butter aspects of the case
are not as entertaining as the chase,
but when the great Bottini is your gaffer,
you just get on with it. A charming host
is one who entertains with every boast.

You're welcome! I've expected you the while:
Bottini wrote to tell me of your mission.
The Chancellery is my humble pile
(You like the *Maddalena*? It's a Titian.)
I have to take the sobriquet, 'patrician':

this one, *Aureliano in Palmyra*:
are we the products of our own volition?
Here, breathing underneath the bust of Hera,
our newly-opened bottle of madeira.

So how's Bottini? Driving you, no doubt,
too hard. We're more or less the selfsame age:
I have an inkling what it's all about
(please take it easy: time to disengage:
you've got to see my self-constructed stage!
Next week, *Il Matrimonio Segreto*.)
It never generates a living wage:
I'd make more money grafting in the ghetto.
I've signed a copy of (my own) libretto.

I see you note the figures in grisaille.
All painted by Arezzo's *charivari*:
Saint Andrew, there, deceives the human eye.
And bearded, there, Saint Nicholas of Bari:
you think that Tuscan sky unduly starry?
Perhaps perspective strikes you rough and ready?
A hundred days – that's all it took Vasari.
Said Michelangelo, who thought unsteady
the basis of the project, '*sì, se vede*'.

Yes, all the best musicians end up here.
You'll often hear me called an epicure.
Are you a cello fan? It has no peer
and, though its origins remain obscure,
the four-string is the form which will endure,
more melancholy than its *gamba* fellow,
and infinitely sexy. Its allure
is strong, like Kremzer White or Primrose Yellow
and, like a fine madeira, brown and mellow.

I love the opera because it's silly!
Some arbitrary (white and wealthy) man,
well past his best, decides to wed some filly,
for no compelling reason, save he can,
the hunter sizing-up the *ortolan*.
Lei? Dovrebbe sentirse obbligata
(check out the varied versions of Tristan):
thus every woman is at heart a martyr
(I'd have you read *Andromeda Liberata*).

The moonpath on the dark lagoon,
the soaring dome of the *Salute*,
Columbine and Pantaloon
Timor mortis conturbat me.

Alexander? True, my uncle.
His monument? It was my duty
(Ottoboni shun carbuncles!)
Timor mortis conturbat me.

These Roman statues, bravely hewn …
I've always had an eye for beauty –
Apollo Belevedere, Baboon –
Timor mortis conturbat me.

Rustication – rug cartoon –
putti buttocks, fairly fruity!
Masonry, so thickly-strewn …
Timor mortis contrbat me.

Pietro Ottoboni. Curate of San Lorenzo in Lucina, digs into the Parish Archives, February 1698

Such fragments as I know of him, I'll share.
His name Bartolomeo, surname Mini:
you'll find his kind of curate everywhere:

they don't bear names like Chigi, Arnolfini.
They pray for forty years and then they're dead,
and leave a trunk of volumes in the shed.

I was a child and living then in Venice
when Mini ruled the roost at San Lorenzo.
My plan? To beat the world at Real Tennis,
be more admired than Cola di Rienzo,
but Family put paid to all of that;
it fell to me to wear the scarlet hat.

His entry bears the date, the twenty-third,
the month July, the year was sixteen-eighty;
the ceremony six whole days deferred –
six days is nothing ponderous or weighty:
you're seeing if they live before you pay
the christening costs (who throws good cash away?)

Francesca Angela Maria Gloria
(a feast of names for such a tiny girl)
Pompilia Camilla Ann Victoria,
the names unspool, the epithets unfurl:
she's beautiful, bewitching, graceful, grand,
and all in Mini's unmistakeable hand.

Parish Outhouses

Wherever there's a church, you'll find the sheds
where studded trunks of long-dead curates go
(who wants old books of bachelors on show?)
Their sermons, bundled up in balding threads,
the offspring of their ripened eunuch heads!
Those lonely men knew things we'll never know
of Polycarp, Tertullian and co.,
those brainy, unacknowledged thoroughbreds!
For you, I am uncorking such a genie.

No record now exists of when he died.
And if you ask why bring him up, then I'd
explain that I am pretty good at listening:
you're here to get the proofs of one girl's christening.
So I present Bartolomeo Mini.

Some Notes in the Autograph of Bartolomeo Mini,
Presented by His Successor as Curate of San Lorenzo,
Cardinal Pietro Ottoboni

The twenty-fourth of August – it's my feast!
Bartolomeo Mini is my name.
There's something inchoate for which you're yearning?

Lorenzo in Lucina – I'm the priest!
Officiating hourly as the same.
You'd hardly call it work – at least I'm earning!

Just don't forget to face towards the East
(that vague direction whence Salvation came
and whence, they say, the Big Yin is returning).

Three meals a day are guaranteed – at least
there's something justifies the pious game.
Just put aside your studies and your learning.

They see a crucifixion altarpiece:
'How Guido Reni loved the Lord,' they claim,
and then to Sansovino sagely turning.

'see how his Christianity released
his inextinguishable inner flame!'
More likely, it was hunger that was burning!

The painter, like the public, has been fleeced!
The Church controls commissions – that's its aim –
the only work available concerning

the miracles of Francis has increased!
'Yes, I can do it – put me in the frame!'
It's work, for cash: who's Church cisterces spurning?

But my *bête-noir*'s the Beauty and the Beast,
how men molest their women – murder, maim.
We see it all around without discerning
our Christian duty to apportion blame.

'Mit Brenender Sorge', a sermon written by Bartolomeo Mini, and Preserved by Cardinal Pietro Ottoboni

You meet humiliation in the street:
some guy insults you, steals your parking-space.
Can you recover from this loss of face?
Or is your way of dealing with defeat
to hurry home and take it out on them?

The instant that you show your wife your fist
you cease to be a man. The day you slap
a woman, you're no longer on the map.
You've now become a sad somnambulist,
a thing that even criminals condemn.

A woman shouldn't be her husband's slave.
We men are bigger, stronger. That's a fact.
Does that mean mothers ought to be attacked?
Is that the way we Christians behave?
From such does all our self-assurance stem?

Yet every day we hear the same thing said:
'Don't come between a husband and his wife,

not even if it costs the woman's life:
we must respect the matrimonial bed.'
The husband's choler trumps the neighbour's phlegm.

And how effective is our Mother Church?
This is a pressing problem. This is pain.
To tolerate it goes against the grain.
By doing nothing, brethren, we besmirch
our womenfolk, the human race's gem.

Why have a caste of curates? Why anoint?
We can't cure ills. I question what we're for.
You have no sword? Pick up an ass's jaw.
Yet all we seem to do is disappoint.
Now isn't that a damning apothegm?

I, Pietro Ottoboni, undersigned,
of San Lorenzo curate for the nonce,
am asked to check my records and I find
(the vellum volumes) page one fifty-two
the year of our salvation sixteen-eighty,
July the twenty-third, there was baptised
Francesca Ruth Pompilia Elaine
Camilla Angela and all the rest,
performed by one Bartolomeo Mini.
The child was six days old, as was the norm,
and all conventional and true to form.
The father's name was Pietro, Comparini,
and to the facts herein he gives his pledge,
the mother's moniker alongside his.

The other side, no matter how inclined,
can never dent your leader's nonchalance,
so forge ahead: you've got them in a bind.
Your arguments feel trivial to you,
but, to the neutral ear, they're fresh and weighty:

Pompilia will be immortalised.
You'll hear about the Tavern of the Chain.
What's stated's fine, but what's unmentioned's best:
I love a church with poche immagini.
The afternoon was stiflingly warm,
although an hour before we'd had a storm.
I like the paucity of serafini.
No matter what the others might allege,
Saint Thomas couldn't doubt it. There he is.

CELLINI'S CRUCIFIX

Escorial and Angelo

Simplicity is stamped on its construction,
severity delineates its whole.
Its majesty requires no introduction,
Nobility, not arrogance, the goal.

The griddle of Saint Lawrence' reproduction,
or temple of King Solomon its role?
Begun on virgin soil without obstruction,
it reeks of one man's singular control.

They always want a city of the dead
to stand against (outfox) the drip of Time,
but nothing can remove the taste of lead,
or make your case to those who lie ahead,
except perhaps a ditty or a rhyme,
our only hope of touching The Sublime.

Returning home, Saint Gregory the Great,
the Scourge of Sceptics, saw an angel sheathe
his sword, a gesture meant to celebrate
the deaths of all schismatics, as I breathe!

The ghosts of Tosca, lefty apostate,
and Hadrian and Clement, writhe and seethe.
'Haphazard' in Italians is innate,
where popes and caesars blend and interwreathe.

Sant'Angelo could never be Hispanic:
its blacks and whites, its layers, twist and flex.
It's situated near the Street of Panic,
its growth has been disorderly, organic:
subjected to Time's balances and checks,
as quirky as each murky Pontifex.

White on Black

The universe consists of *contrapposto*,
no matter what the *locus*, or the era:
Ayn Rand will do, as well as Ariosto,
and Camberwell as well, as will Carrera.

Some colours have the power to excite,
to stimulate, eviscerate, attack:
there's something in that warped, organic white
when set against the flat, unyielding black.

A man's a latin cross (Da Vinci knows)
but, as he flourishes, becomes a rose.
We look for meaning to the female pole:
we call it consciousness, we call it soul,
and find it in our paintings and our prose,
in other words, the part of us that grows.

The Story of a Masterpiece

The bowels of Sant'Angelo is where
the project started. Eating diamond dust –

creation metaphor – constrained to dare –
incarcerated, dare the sculptor must.

He wants the crucifix to mark his tomb.
Saint Mary, which he contemplates with relish,
is not the church his statue will embellish:
a funeral can thus become a womb.

It took him twenty years to carve the stone.
In fifteen thirty-nine he had a dream
in papal jail, the crucifix its theme.
In fifty-six he needed to postpone

the work again, locked up in Tor di Nona.
By fifteen sixty-five, his native city
possessed the figure (sitting in the Pitti),
this time a gift to Cosimo. The honour

had passed, now, from Novella (isn't life funny?)
to grace the future tomb in San Lorenzo
of Cosimo, that latter-day Rienzo,
for no more reason than he had the money!

Cellini was imprisoned (what? You guessed?)
His sentence was, for five-year crimes of passion,
(he used a boy 'after the Italian fashion')
commuted down to simple house-arrest.

A string of deaths (Cellini was the first)
ensued. He died in fifteen seventy-one.
Just three years later, Cosimo was gone.
Vasari (Mannerism's Damien Hirst)

was lost that summer. Suffering rebuke,
Francisco needed Philip on his side:

the Spanish king could halt the downward slide
by honouring Francisco as Grand Duke.

But this is now the summer of seventy-six:
Two women, who are Spanish and half-Spanish
are ordered on Francisco's whim to 'vanish'.
To heal the rift, he needs dictator-tricks.

And there it hangs today. One man's memorial,
so far from home or expectation, graces
(its gorgeous curves abutting hard, flat faces)
the sombre, un-Italian Escorial.

Benvenuto Cellini Sees a Salamander

It was not here, but in the Otherwhere,
where chimed another time. I, free of care,
was kneeling at some game, as if in prayer,
my back towards the fire. The wooden chair,

the altar of my game, in plain paroles
engrossed me. As my mother carried coals
to seed another hotbed, no controls
seemed necessary. This, a day of wholes,

in womb-like warmth, unwittingly aware
of fire, oblivious of colder poles
like all-enfolding water, earth or air,
was safe from harm. For future goals

the salamander saved me. Truculent trolls
dislodged the coals – but never harmed a hair.

A TRAVELLER ARRIVES IN AREZZO

The sun on this September afternoon
is not quite what it might have been in June,
but hot enough. My barman's chatting on,
while somewhere, some lopsided carillon
is clanging tunelessly. I'm in the square
of San Francesco in Arezzo, where
I've longed to be for years. Rome's far behind
(in fact it's hard to summon Rome to mind,
albeit I was there not long ago.)
Tranquility! I almost feel as though
I've plunged in freezing water. And the sight
of fiesta flags, inflamed by evening light
can make the heart start pumping. It's too late
(for me) to learn to free-associate,
but what feels right, is right. I'm in a groove,
and who can say if I will ever move
from this precise position? Favourite pen,
a fine coarse notebook and 'remember when' …
can life improve on this? When things combine,
we feel we've touched the hem of The Divine:
perhaps I'm heading for a nuclear fall,
but sunlight slanting on that craggy wall
is just as good as (better than, perhaps)
a coffee in that place from 'Google Maps'.
Until I found Palazzo Guillichini
Gregorio, life's classic 'in-betweeny'
was lost to me: but I, 'traquer le lièvre',
can get the story from the cause célèbre.

GREGORY THE GREAT

STRAY LEAVES: 'Bit-players lard the layers ...'

Bit-players lard the layers of the drama.
If Hamlet's detonation is atomic,
there's always one whose role is almost comic.
Horatio is, to Helsingor's self-harmer,
like Fuzzy Zoeller, facing Arnold Palmer.
Meet Guillichini! (almost gastronomic,
as if a type of pasta!) Nearly gnomic –
not Jack the Ripper, charmless Jeffrey Dahmer.
He's holed up in San Vito e Modesto
(The church that's near the Via Sacra? Questo!)
For helping Caponsacchi mount the 'fuga',
he's fearing retribution – loaded Luger,
left on the table – waiting, praying, bracing –
his tragedy is, nobody is chasing!

IT STRIKES YOU AS ECCENTRIC (I CONCEDE!)
at I stay here alone as summer climbs
towards its zenith. Guilty of no crimes,
why should a local noble feel the need
(while others of his age are out and roaming)
to sit immured in church, this glorious gloaming?

I'd love to be there, now the streets are sandy,
to give the horses traction. My own faction
is sure to win this year! I'll miss the action.
I hear the roaring in *Piazza Grande*
and weep a little, knowing I'm enclosed
(albeit my detention's self-imposed).

I take you for a traveller, sir (your clothes:
besides, Arezzo's not so vast that local faces
can pass unknown). You'll see some lovely places

(and just as likely hear some ugly oaths).
The enmities that rend us never tire:
division thrives, when driven by desire.

My enemies in town (and they are plenty),
and many of my friends, say I'm contrary.
I'd argue Jesus wasn't born of Mary.
It irks me that I'm known as *'il stridente'*,
but there it is. Perhaps if I translate?
I'm 'Gregory the Grind' – no, wait – 'the Grate'.

I think the problem is, I have a brain.
Arezzo's not a lousy place to live,
but brilliance is a sin they can't forgive:
it goes against the grubbing burgher grain.
It's perilous to see among the blind:
Giordano Bruno's outcome comes to mind.

We had an incident a month ago.
I mention it because you're bound to hear,
and best to meet it free of snark or sneer.
A pretty woman struck a mortal blow
against our stale complacency. At last!
My *locus standi*? Member of the cast!

She loved to pray alone in the *Giuseppino*
(they finished it the very year she came),
the plainest, squattest box-like little frame:
it's halfway up the via Saracino.
'Like waking up inside a tomb,' she'd say,
but that is how her life was, every day.

You know the kind of girl who peddles sex.
It's never mentioned, but it's always there.
She has the art. She keeps it in the air,
and doesn't give a damn whose life she wrecks!

It's all about her ego, and the boys
can go to hell. It's 'pulling' she enjoys!

What made it all so crazy yet so true
is, something passed between us – that I swear!
The best is, when you think there's something there.
It seemed to me there might be, but I knew
she'd opt for Caponsacchi any day.
It's all anticipation, anyway.

STRAY LEAVES: BLOTS IN THE 'SCUTCHEON

You're going to write your epic? Vary the pace!
Pentameter (iambic) jogs just fine,
but come at it as if the human race
had no idea of syllables-per-line

(which, of course, it doesn't). Switch it round.
Your modern readers, miffed, will not immerse
themselves in something where they might get drowned.
They'll follow hearses sooner than blank verse.

And humour is a minefield (don't we know?),
but no-one needs to set himself to fail.
The only jokes that work are jokes-to-go:
don't hang your humour on a single nail.

Defending lawyers is a thankless task,
but I will now attempt it. What you've done
is, set some straw men up, and all I ask
is, stay away from stereotypes like 'nun'

or 'barrister' or 'bowler-hatted gent'.
The gags fall flat. The shots are cheap and petty.
Four gifted men who'd think you'd lost the scent?
Arcangeli, Bottini, Gambi, Spreti.

Choose exile? Be a Petrarch, or a Dante?
I know I wouldn't thrive on foreign soil.
I need pale golden wine and olive oil.
How would I live? The classic dilettante,
I've Tuscan goods I'd never want to trade,
like Maytime sun, aslant a colonnade.

* * * *

STRAY LEAVES: A STRIDENT PHILOSOPHY

Both Dante and Boccaccio would say,
conventional consent is quite enough.
Why would you want to strain for other stuff?
For Juan de Díos, there's no other way:
Fernando, Isabella? Santa Fé.
Why wander from the highway, risk the rough,
inventing Weltanschauung off the cuff?
Because it's our imperative today.
To tell me God has plans for me won't do.
Your system needs a manual? Then it's wrong.
I won't be told you have the gold that's true,
or pitched to, proselytized, or strung along!
When Beauty finds me, just the way I feel
convinces me directly that it's real.

Is reproduction perfect? No, Thank God!
(or Thank the Trackless Void). You read the code
and replicate it. Nothing paid or owed.
But life's not like that. Go through on the nod?
A lot of times, perhaps. But something odd,
a lucky accident, an episode,
a hitch – a glitch – occurs. Now we're a node
where nothing known, no clone, has ever trod.
Our errors are the engines of our fate,

the portals where potential gets to act.
Byzantium was humbled, Rome was sacked?
The way to view a grave is as a gate.
A mirror tells the truth until it's cracked:
mistakes are things to seize on, to create.

You've never heard of our 'Arezzo Boys' –
how could you have? You're still arriving, just.
Ten families, Arezzo's Upper Crust,
can furnish fifteen gallants. Joy of joys!
We, scions of the wealthy, raising dust?
You bet we are. Our parents are nonplussed,
but what of that? We like to make a noise:
our dual diversions, violence and lust –
puttanas, puch-ups: (pardon puns) our thrust
is thus pursued in perfect equipoise!

And Caponsacchi's been our leading light.
Reliable as Roland in a rumble,
he charms the *chochos,* never lacks a tumble.
Despite the Rites, he's out there every night,
and (though Gibraltar's rock may one day crumble)
Giuseppe never will so much as stumble.
For fun, we christened him 'The Acolyte',
but he's the one who makes us all feel humble,
as fit for fisticuffs as for a fumble,
as predisposed to fornicate as fight.

Young noblemen with nothing else to do
embrace whatever mischief you'll devise,
particularly wench-and-weapon-wise:
no roguery's too low. Our rowdy crew
have one debauchery that they despise,
and one alone: they'll never patronise
a lowly tap-room. Beer and rabbit stew
are not befitting. Gentlemen tell lies

(it's automatic, if you womanise),
but sins exist that we're not party to.

And if the civil Governor approves
or disapproves, why should we even care?
The magistrates do nothing. Wouldn't dare.
Poor creatures run in predetermined grooves
(we even have a parent who's the Chair!)
A certain kind of citizen (we say 'square')
regards us as regaled with horns and hooves,
and they of course are easiest to scare.
They close the blinds and stick to solitaire
while we go shagging anything that moves.

* * * *

THE GREAT ELOPEMENT! HOW DID IT BEGIN?
With Caponsacchi marshalling resources.
We crossed the Borgo to Canale Inn
(and what I say, the man himself endorses,
for I was at his side). A detail – dressed
in cassock still, he took our wine and 'blessed'
the bottle. Venerino was within,
doing something with the lunchtime sauces,
but Agostino of the easy grin
was right there with us, and enjoyed the jest.
Giuseppe, ostentatious oligarch,
explained the disposition of his forces.
He'd need Chimato's carriage and two horses,
which Venerino was required to park
outside the San Clemente portal, lest
the watchmen pass the vehicle, and mark
this strange anomaly. Should they arrest
the driver – this he strove to underpin –
the game was up. His plan was to embark
at midnight, with the benefit of dark.

On Venerino and his pony-tail
turned boundless banter. 'What if I should fail,'
Giuseppe asked, 'to recognise the cony?
In total darkness, accidentally nail
the one with sexy hair?' 'Why, dye it pink,'
suggested Agostino. 'I'm a male,'
said Venerino, adding fuel to fire.
I laughed so hard, I thought I might expire.
But this was not a day for cakes and ale.
Said Caponsacchi, with a subtle wink,
'I have to make my way to Patrignone
to put on more appropriate attire,
and then return – and all on Shanks's Pony.'
The Canon was concerting with his crony,
to square what snoopers should be made to think:
Canale calls it, 'preaching to the choir'.
The coach sets off in darkness, black as ink –
I had to change my clothes – there's nothing phony –
if anyone were minded to inquire,
in Caponsacchi's cask, they'd find no chink.

You want a seminar on social class?
A kind of balcony we call 'the deck'
outside the Pieve on a Sunday morn
will do it for you. Here, the better-born
foregather on their way to Midday Mass.
The next day, sitting on the balustrade,
I saw Pompilia and Porzia pass,
arm in arm, the first a nervous wreck:
the other wore her trademark mask of scorn.
Pompilia seemed to fear some ambuscade:
she smiled on small-talk-social-masquerade,
but looked as though her bonnet bore a thorn:
a vein was twitching in her silky neck.
Why would Cathedral-types turn up on spec
here at the Pieve? Had she come to warn?

She fought to keep anxiety in check,
but I could see that she was so afraid,
she looked about to enter a morass,
aware that she was unprepared to wade
while carrying a burden of pure brass.

And there was Caponsacchi at the door,
berobed and smiling. When he made his bow,
the 'better people' started to advance.
As orchestrator of the pyx and plate,
the Canon's role was to officiate:
each *Galantuomo*, every *Gnädige Frau*
(the peasants he could easily ignore)
evinced a *bonhomie*, a warm rapport.
Pompilia had seemed afraid before,
but would this be the fiercest test to date?
And which of us, confronted by this fate,
would pull it off? The one that we adore,
in greeting us, regards us half-askance?
She held herself together, I'll allow.
But as she left the deck to navigate
the *Pieve*'s grey and unadorned expanse,
she might have benefitted from a glance
directly upwards, where the seasons dance:
while March puffs on his pipe, prepares to plough,
December slits the gullet of his sow.

* * * *

That afternoon, we went to loll and brood.
Our house beside San Vito worked out right,
because we watched the watchmen on their beat.
With Caponsacchi in unsettled mood
(an actor, hours before his opening night,
might wish that he were somewhere else instead),
we had the window open on the street.

(When women passed, we shouted something crude!)
My brother Pietro Paolo loves a fight,
and he was on our team. As Pietro said,
to watch the lazy changing of the light
from white to amber, then to obsolete,
worked wonders on the Canon's attitude.
Pompilia, meanwhile, was fetching food.
She took a tray to Beatrice (still in bed
with some vague palsy, disinclined to eat).
Suocera wouldn't have the cloudy red
(the *nuora*'s sleeping-draught was indiscreet),
so Guido drank it down and poured fresh white.
(The fish was also fouled, on which he fed.)

Thus Guido, drugged, was eager to retire.
Pompilia went to bed, but clearly she
was nervous, and excited as could be.
(The Canon shared, contemporaneously,
Pompilia's version of events with me).
She listened to the snoring. When the coast
was clear, she donned her pre-prepared attire.
The property next door (it's called 'The Birches')
was empty, so we wouldn't need a key.
Eleven struck, and like a hungry ghost
my brother slunk towards his lookout post,
along the *Via Sacra*. All the 'perches'
(the points where watchmen park themselves the most)
were known to us. We knew that we were toast
if ever we were swept up in their searches.
That's why we chose to choose the Street of Churches,
the *Via Sacra*. Nothing could transpire
once on that route (we hoped). The truth besmirches
the legend, all too often. We require
a part of us that's purer, nobler, higher.

We armed ourselves and sworded, arquebussed,
we sallied down the Coppersmiths together.
The night was close. The falling of a feather
would quite have caused alarm. Arezzo's spine,
il Borgo Maestro, normally a 'must',
we shunned, because the *capotari* comb
the street all night. The Franceschini home
loomed high above us, menacing us dully.
We slipped into the vacant '*Le Betulle*'
and clambered through the scullery, as discussed.
Was Guido there? (We knew him as 'The Gnome'.)
If so, we'd have to kill, or die. My utter trust
in Caponsacchi fortified me fully.
The scuffing of a footfall, creak of leather,
informed me where Giuseppe was. A mine
could not be darker. Then I caught the shine
of lining: Caponsacchi's silver-chrome
expensive hat. I couldn't work out whether
another person stirred – we crossed a gully –
Pompilia was there! She'd won, then, with the wine!

Pietro Paolo, meanwhile, had been stopped
and questioned (quite severely) by the *sbirri*.
He told them he was walking off the beer he
had taken in a bar, which proved too gassy.
He knew the cool demeanour to adopt:
bastante sycophantic, charming, cheery,
as boneless as a bowl of semolina.
He told them of a tyke who should be shopped,
if they could find a rat. Gaspari Massi!
They'd find him with the daughter of Lanvina
(you have to grant, this subterfuge was classy:
San Spirito's as far away as Passy
to Les Lilas, from where the coach was propped
and waiting.) Though the constables were leery,
the questioning grew noticeably keener.

The *capotari* veered, appeared to opt
for Arlecchino and his Columbina,
of Pietro Paolo promptly growing weary.
My brother asked them, 'Have you seen her *chassis*?
Just like her mother, only younger, leaner.'

On either side, oppressive convent walls,
and high above, a strip of starry sky
to orient our steps. I brushed her cape
– not meaning to – discerned her compact shape
and thought of how her handsome almost-priest
had changed her. No more off-the-shoulder shawls:
the cleavage-feasts had definitely ceased!
My touch touched off an *I-don't-want-this* sigh,
so different from before. Who can say why
the prank that once enchanted, now appalls?
Perhaps her apse aligned on her escape.
That bodice which was often apt to gape,
those breasts, against constraint disposed to vie,
would not (at least for me) now be released.
Surrounding sisters, in their cistern-auls,
who'll never wear blue crepe or gold-fringed drape,
could hardly be more hostile to The Beast.
Our last left-turn! The night had turned out dry,
and that was something positive, at least:
my slow ascent, the painfullest of crawls.

The San Clemente Gate was locked and barred
of course, but Caponsacchi was a guarantee
that things would work out well. He'd thought about
such obstacles. There was no human guard,
and that was something. One terse 'follow me'
was whispered, clearer than most people shout.
I saw him in the moonlight, resolute,
advancing on the city wall's redoubt
which locals call the '*torrione*'. Mute,

we scrambled up the crumbling fort, all three,
our steps uncertain in unstable scree.
Our climb was treacherous, and rather hard,
manhandling as we were Pompilia's 'loot',
including as it did a man's serge suit.
A downhill element – and we were out!
It felt exhilarating to be free.
We'd faced the kinfolk, with the sbirri sparred,
and Caponsacchi's plan had now borne fruit.
We didn't even need to scour or scout:
we heard the coach roll from the tavern yard.

It made no sense to dawdle or delay.
A whispered word of thanks, a brisk embrace:
the coach was mounted, baggage thrown on top.
I pressed my lips against her little face:
she murmured, 'grace to him who offers grace'.
A creak of axle, and they were away.
I turned to go, but felt diminished, weaker.
The carriage, I could hear, was gathering pace.
Before I slept, there was one final stop
I'd need to make, to check if Borgo Cenci may
be up in arms, sounding alarms. Why chase
the chance of trouble? Be a problem-seeker?
Permit the plods to catch me on the hop?
(My brother was unique, but I, uniquer:
with weapons on me, guilty of affray!)
They caught me as I crossed by *La Chiavica*
(a curious place to put a coffee shop!)
It came to nothing. Speaker after speaker
dismissed me as a harmless, feckless fop.
And Guido's house stood silent. Not a trace
of anything amiss, so I could drop
my guard at last. It had been quite a day!

NO HEAVIER SIN, Being a Tale told by Half-Rome

STRAY LEAVES: 'The tumbrils trundled …'

The tumbrils trundled past the Chiesa Nueva
where I myself will lie when stilled by death
(but, unlike Adam, I will have no Seth
to seed me). Resurrection's out of favour.
I've stared into the tomb: there's nothing graver:
love's labours suit me better than Macbeth.
The power of prayer, the shaman's shibboleth,
won't save me. None but cretins never quaver.

Appointed Pontiff's Priest of Santa Prassede,
increasingly I mull my own mortality.
That day must dawn, no matter if I'm ready,
of whimpering for mercy. Whether steady
or wretched in my cowardice, reality
will wrap me in the hearse's hospitality.

STRAY LEAVES: 'I'm drugged by death …'

I'm drugged by death's undithering banality.
As callous as a Carolina slaver,
it doesn't celebrate, nor does it waver:
who baked oblivion into physicality?
The facts of life are fatal to vitality.
The first who go (undoubtedly the braver)
are ground to nothing by the Great Depraver,
since nothing living might evade fatality.

I learned my Tuscan in the town of Lucca.
The locals never took to me, 'the Roman'.
I mastered Spanish, so they called me 'Frenchy'
(took vows of chastity: they termed me 'Fucker').

In irony, you'll usually find an omen.
My tawdry tragedy is named, 'The Cenci'.

Parents always harm their charges
    (some without intent).
Uncontrolled control enlarges
    felt entitlement:
    John O'Groats to Kent,
    as from Aix to Ghent.

Power always prompts abuses
    (parents, prelates, popes).
Nurture nurtures necks in nooses:
    Priapus interlopes,
    gravitas means gropes,
    helplessness kills hopes.

Fathers often feign laments,
    claim they've drained the sluices,
mended every fence:
    exculpations, lame excuses,
    tawdry time-outs, trivial truces,
    while innocents tread via crucis.

STRAY LEAVES: THE TRUMP OF DOOM

He's big and blonde and ugly and vulgarian,
and sure that he's entitled (being rich),
expects his whims to swim without a hitch.
He's hardly First World – comes across Bulgarian,
with instincts that are pure authoritarian.
Preferring proclamation over pitch,
he deems his daughter 'one voluptuous bitch'.
A sexually sordid septuagenarian,
libido high, IQ acutely low,

his only mode of interaction? Force.
*Cruel, mendacious, narcissistic, coarse,
he doesn't know the things he doesn't know.
Despicability wells from one source:
you wreck the person if you never say 'no'.

It's painful to relate a sorry tale
of parenthood abused, a father sunk
below the point where heaven might avail,
his sense of shame so shrivelled down, so shrunk,
that basic human fellowship had ceased.
This man could pray no merit in his aid,
nor claim the cold inertia of a stone.
   No belly-crawling beast
has ever so malignantly betrayed,
or wrought depraved pollution of, its own.

Francesco Cenci, nobleman of sorts,
had reached the final decade of his life
ungarlanded. No frequenter of courts,
he'd rather terrorise son, daughter, wife
and scour Abruzzi for whatever prey
presented opportunity for gain –
or better, might engender wide disgust.
   There never passed a day
when Cenci's crazed and pleasure-addled brain
was not convulsed in schemes of sickly lust.

He disregarded judgments, paid no fines,
provoked affrays, was physically ferocious:
from infancy, displayed disturbing signs:
his wards declared him 'sexually precocious'.
You'll find a person's essence if you delve
into his boyhood. Arrogance, aggression
and reckless wealth were what defined this child.
   He, married-off at twelve,

pursued a course of wilful indiscretion,
and all who came in contact were defiled.

Some sins cry out to heaven, so they say.
Francesco fathered twelve, but only five
(in terms of adulthood) saw light of day.
The lucky ones, methinks, did not survive.
If Providence was punishing the father,
it hardly proved effective. He, depraved,
despised his sons. The dead he didn't miss.
      He liked his daughters: rather,
it was their genitalia he craved.
One special caught his fancy – Beatrice.

In and out of jail for 'nameless vices'
(what could they be? We hesitate to guess),
he brought upon himself the final crisis.
Not even he could hide the girls' distress.
Emerging from confinement keener, meaner,
he raped the daughters. Word reached, by and by,
the Roman representative of God,
      who rescued Antonina
(the very pope who didn't blink an eye
at burning Bruno, just for being odd).

The sons, as males, were free to leave the home:
it's hard to blame them when they took this course.
So Giaccomo and Paolo ran to Rome
and, given Antonina's forced 'divorce',
poor Beatrice, now left alone with him,
was taken to a place he could defend.
Francesco, with his victim thus secured,
      indulged his every whim.
To ponder pain with no foreseeable end
gives us a glimpse of what the girl endured.

Above the village of Petrella Salto
the castle squats, a harpy on a hill.
The locals merely murmur '*quello alto*',
as if it held some evil portent still.
Here Beatrice was imprisoned like a sow,
an orifice for rutting on, no more:
secondo il suo scopio empio.
        But if we once allow
that fate may open any prison door,
we meet her rescuer, Olimpio.

Olimpio Calvetti, his full name:
custodian of the castle, and a man
whose Christian conscience quickly overcame
his dread of Cenci. He conceived a plan:
'where systems of protection don't exist,
then natural justice hands us all the right
to act alone, eradicate the threat.
        A man who won't be missed
can be eliminated, swept from sight,
so we live on without the least regret.'

Olimpio was a young and virile man,
and strikingly good-looking. There are those
who claim a carnal confluence began
between the *gamine* and her rescuer. Who knows?
We know only the *mores* of the age.
A woman had no fallback, no enjoyment
of legal remedies. She dared to put
        the matter right? Engage
an agent? When Olimpio lost employment,
the stage was set, the plan was now afoot:

to check Francesco, they would need to slaughter
their oppressor. Could they call on others?
Olimpio went to Rome, leaving the daughter

to bide her time. He called on Beatrice' brothers,
and soon convinced all three to come aboard.
Francesco was bedridden with the gout,
and thus defenceless. Things were falling pat!
      To put him to the sword
would not be difficult to carry out,
a simple thing, to snap one's fingers at!

The seventh of September was the day,
the year in question, fifteen ninety-eight,
a hundred years before the dagger-play
in *Via Vittoria* – melancholy date!
Olimpio entered with a butcher's knife
and hid himself within the castle keep
to wait for darkness, and the hour of blood.
He aimed to take Francesco's life,
attacking while his victim was asleep,
then desecrate the body if he could.

And so it passed. Olimpio had in mind
the need to feign an accident: he flung
the corpse out of the window. Thickly-tined,
a dead tree stood below. Francesco hung,
a dismal Dysmas, awkwardly impaled,
a wretched spectacle for passers-by.
The corpse was skewered like a sucking goat,
      inelegantly nailed
by lifeless branches – one had pierced an eye,
another passing wholly through his throat.

The Cenci argued, this was suicide:
their father owned a conscience, after all.
When overwhelmed with guilt, the sinner died
intentionally. Apt that he should fall!
You'd change your story, once you've given out
your version of what happened? Big mistake!

'The balcony was rotten,' so they said:
         'there can't be any doubt.
He had a heavy frame, enough to break
those termite-tortured timbers, should he tread

on just that beam. An accident, you see?'
Do balconies, with reckless ease, collapse?
Do owners of the same, imprudently,
entrust their bulks to rotten hulks? Perhaps.
But now there had to be a full inspection.
The Cenci brought about their own demise.
Francesco was a giant, big of bone,
         The balcony's weak section
contained an aperture of no great size.
He hadn't jumped, or stumbled. He'd been thrown!

The conduct of the siblings made it worse.
The brothers came, from Rome, but didn't pay
for obsequies or prayers around the hearse.
The priests, deprived of stipends, in dismay
began to preach against 'unruly youth'.
The swooning Beatrice claimed to have the 'humours':
she was, in fact, about to be a mother.
         They couldn't hide the truth:
they whisked her back to Rome, but still the rumours
gave out that she had borne a son (and brother!)

The Roman populace was on their side
(at least for now). The wistful Cenci whelps
had suffered greatly, which was not denied,
and Beatrice was a babe (which always helps).
The father's nastiness was known in Rome,
and people had no sympathy for 'pervs'.
To have *mens rea*, first you must have *mens*:
         and in the Cenci home

Bernardo (that's the youngest) had 'bad nerves'.
And was this not a case of self-defence?

Today we think of torture as an evil,
since we've become more human, more humane.
We've undergone a sociable upheaval
and (most of us) dislike inflicting pain.
It wasn't always quite so cut and dried
(well, cut at least). There was a school of thought
which held that agony served justice best.
       It was a point of pride
that litigants-in-person really ought
to test their claims with flames: proof's pure when pressed.

Do torturers pursue objective truth?
I have my doubts. If someone tortured me,
I'd readily admit that John Wilkes Booth
taught Sonny Bono (badly) how to ski.
When Giacomo was tested, he confessed
and inculpated all his siblings, too.
Then Beatrice and Bernardo did the same.
But no-one could have guessed
that Beatrice' mitigation would fall through:
she won no credit for her father's shame.

Pope Clement wasn't clement. How could he,
the father of all Christendom, abide
a sin which struck against paternity?
It fell to him to parry parricide.
Bernardo, being retarded, would be 'saved'.
He'd have to watch his family members die
and then, by way of further expiation,
       the boy would be enslaved
in papal galleys. Meanwhile, on the sly,
the pope would gain, by 'punitive taxation',

the Cenci fortune. Almost to the day,
a year on from the fall of Cenci *père*,
the tumbrils trundled. All along the way,
the hapless Giacomo was forced to share
his cart with blazing brazier and pincers,
there to tear and torture him before
he reached Castel Sant'Angelo, and death.
      The red-hot steel 'convincers',
if anything, oppressed Bernardo more:
required to watch his brother's final breath,

he first endured the sight, the sound and stench
of Giacomo's agony. He pulled his cape
across his face, but guards moved in to wrench
it free. Today, there could be no escape.
Just where the bridge of Hadrian meets the shore,
before the papal castle's joyless gate,
is where they were beheaded, Beatrice last.
      The Cenci are no more.
The child of Beatrice? No-one knows its fate.
Thus all are drowned and swallowed by The Past.

An Obelisk Opines

Augustus ordered them to bring me here.
By then I was already middle-aged.
I've witnessed things I wouldn't want to dwell on:
decapitations, thousands here to jeer.
You'd think that I could stand here, disengaged,
but granite slabs are things to cast a spell on,
or so it seems to me. The child came near,
Pompilia, before the war was waged,
before the husband made himself a felon.
He passed this Gate, the night of rage and fear:
they brought him back next morning, trussed and caged.
No further than a man can throw a melon,

Just there, they struck his head off. My two cents?
Why seven weeks between the two events?

Epic Pulsa

The grandiose is frozen in no time.
It offers no development, no motion.
A painted ship upon a painted ocean,
an epic is a tapestry in rhyme
(Longinus said it best, *On the Sublime*):
grand thoughts, fine epithets and strong emotion:
Athenian no, but philosophically Phocian:
a height to which we humans rarely climb.
The upper register does not persuade,
it does not treat or truckle, traffic, trade.
It condescends to nothing but depiction,
and all accomplished in the finest diction,
and stands alone, unaltered, undismayed,
rejoicing in its glorious dereliction.

Peptic Ulcer

If wind and rain rinse boulders smooth in time
(no matter that stone's matter's hard and dense),
then solids have no claim to permanence,
and form is just a passing pantomime.
Bulk rises, then subsides, into the slime,
but fluids have accrued omnipotence,
have drenched the universe (dew diligence?)
Suppose what flows to be the paradigm.

What's interesting? Partings and conjunctions.
What makes your digit fidget is the knuckle.
A belt has but one business-end: the buckle.
We love what works, accommodates, what functions.

We move, we prove, we interact, we truckle:
a breast is best employed when babies suckle.

THE MAGNANIMITY OF SCIPIO, Being A Tale told by Antonio Lamparelli

When seeking out a tale to entertain us,
we're torn between the tasteful and the tacky.
This schism 'twixt the worthy and the wacky
makes every one of us a kind of Janus,
pursuing both what's hortatory and heinous.
Here's something from the brief of Caponsacchi,
the legend of a Celtiberian lackey
(he details of his tribe need not detain us)
who met a proud descendant of the Gracchi.
It bears no trace of what would, in the rest of us,
amount to moral turpitude or greyness.
This is a noble story. It's the best of us.
Let's hear (though little credit it may gain us!)

AT LAST, he saw the Roman camp, below
in the man-made clearing. Allucius lingered
on the forest fringe, safe among trees
weeping with late summer rain.
It would soon be dusk. Bonfires twinkled
down where their sentries were standing guard.
The unmistakeable tang of musk
was now in his nostrils. Damp earth
offered its fragrance freely here,
where tomorrow *boletos* in strings
would sprinkle the loam in creamy profusion.
Pallisades made of once-healthy trees,
felled in full youth, formed a harsh ring
on the artificial flatness below.
He had to go down. This he knew,

though it offended every sense. 'Go,'
he told himself. 'Duty demands it.'
That masculine circle, alien space,
offended both him and the gods of the forest.
In that strange place shaved of trees
Stena was waiting. How would she be?
Future queen of his people she had been,
but what now? What becomes
of a woman whose freedom is taken away?
Like a forest sheared of trees, she will be
broken, soulless, now. The fragile thread
of honour sustains the spider's work
but, swept aside so easily,
it is gone for ever. What would he find?
What faced him in that Roman camp?
A man with a future brutally uprooted,
he hesitated in the comforting damp.
Ushered in by the soldiers, he asks
to speak with the man in charge. They bring
the general, no less, Scipio Africanus –
imperious, tall and surprisingly young.
Allucius explains. His betrothed, name of Stena,
was recently seized. By custom and law
he must escort her back to her home,
no matter if sullied, or even dead.
he understands, it's the way of armies
who take women. But he needs to mourn.
Scipio regards him long and searchingly.
'The girl's parents – can they bring gold?'
'Then she's alive still? You want treasure?
In order to ransom her, certainly yes.'
'Then let it happen,' orders Scipio.
'And the girl …?' Smiling, the Roman asks
'What do you suppose has taken place
while she's been in our hands, young man?'
'An indelicate question,' returns the other.

'I'll press you.' (This from the tall patrician.)
'She may still draw breath, but is surely ruined.
I dread to know the truth of her condition.'
Great Scipio smiled. 'You are quite mistaken.
We've been as elder brothers to your loved one.
With us, she's been cherished, as she should be
as if in her own parents' house.
Do you imagine that, having such beauty,
A fine young woman of such spirit, such grace
in our charge, we would be negligent of our duty?
Allucius commingled confusion and delight.
Protocol forgotten, he clasped the hand
of the general. Then Scipio spoke again.
'We give her back to you freely, as a gift.
And when her parents furnish the treasure,
we offer it as the dowry. Be content.'

Why seek excursions and alarms?
Why can't Krupp and Thyssen see?
You merely cow your foe with arms:
You vanquish him with decency.

Evening Star

Throughout the lilac light, sailing serene,
the dying Phoebus' silent acolyte,
unwavering you watch the waves excite
our claybound glories, glinting damascene.
You float above, part unapproachable queen,
part courtesan, a Juno-catamite,
noli me tangere, who may invite,
or might ignore. Your uncorrupted sheen
reminds us when we draw the sword, we sheathe
it at our peril. Shine on us, to teach:
abundance is the concubine of dearth.
Appear to us at sunset to bequeath

a dictum that no mortal may impeach:
our death is pre-recorded in our birth.

Morning Star

The scatterer of hope-suppressing night
who summons up the dawn in tangerine
and ochre, firing life where death has been,
restorer of the sun-king's lawful rite,
quotidian overarching stately flight,
horizon to horizon: all between,
sidereal superlunary demesne,
the realm of that untroubled eremite
who soars above the surly clouds which wreathe
around us: you've enabled us to reach
beyond our matter-patrimony, earth:
your gift to humankind was to bequeath
ability to master thought and speech,
and know that death is but another birth.

FORTUNE'S FROWNING FACE, Being a Tale told by Caterina Fiori

STRAY LEAVES: 'What are we after …?'

at are we after in the tales we tell?
A young and decent woman is coerced
(think Stockholm Syndrome, Fritzl, Patty Hearst):
There should be dirty secrets, kiss-and-tell
(the film should have a theme song by Adele).
The odds were stacked against her from the first:
She lived for love (until the bubble burst),
but now she is a Citizen of Hell.

How many messed-up marriages, escapes
and penis-substitutes! (We call them knives.)
How many stunted, unaccomplished lives!
A man resorts to force? We say he rapes.
Can we aspire to cease to 'sire' our wives,
or is this still the Planet of the Apes?

A TALE TO MAKE THE NERVOUS WINCE
       will painfully unfurl
with secrets of a Scottish prince
       who bagged a Belgian girl.

'A prince? That's not so bad. Why gripe?
       Let's not be too pedantic.
According to the stereotype,
       these princes are romantic!'

Well, this one doesn't fill the bill.
       His gallant days are through.
He's flabby, flaccid, drunken, ill
– and almost fifty-two.

She's unaware of purple cheeks.
       A proxy takes his place.
She's been his wife for several weeks
       before she sees his face.

Her uncle deems the Scottish Crown
       facilely bought and sold:
Louise, as light as thistle-down,
       is nineteen summers old.

She's beautiful and very bright,
       loves poetry and art:
to hold a salon, her delight.
       Her husband dines apart.

He's disappointed on two counts.
>   The first is, no male heir.
With time, recrimination mounts:
>   why brook a barren mare?

His second grouse is, he had thought
>   a wife would boost his name.
by touting her around, he sought
>   to shore a shaky claim.

Charisma, looks – she's got the lot.
>   She catches every eye,
but Charles's bolt is long since shot:
>   the world has passed him by.

Louise is disillusioned, too.
>   Her dreams of royal splendour
are wasted on a loser who
>   is only a pretendor.

Disclosures of a painful nature
>   cause ructions, as they should:
no matter what its nomenclature,
>   this thing is never good.

Red scratches on Her Highness' throat?
>   A playful cat, no more.
And what might swollen eye connote?
>   She walked into a door.

No matter how the boiler's stoked,
>   plain decency insists
the man, no matter how provoked,
>   must never use his fists.

So, blame the woman. Blame the drink.
>   Go, blame your downward slide.
We don't care what you say, or think:
>   your problem lies inside.

It first imparts a buzz to you?
>   Then wormwood leads to gall?
If that's what absinthe does to you,
>   Don't touch the stuff at all.

How much does duck accept from drake
>   before she flies the nest?
She's taken all that she can take:
>   the outcome can be guessed!

Attractive-passive, sex-on-legs,
>   (one thinks of Greta Scacchi),
she's drained this marriage to the dregs:
>   whence comes her Caponsacchi?

STRAY LEAVES: TURNING-POINT

Daraa changed everything for T. E. Lawrence.
For Charles, one day, the planet's axis stirred:
he grasped, at last: he hadn't been preferred:
the Pope would never name him Charles the Third.
For Rome, he now conceived a fierce abhorrence,
as vehement as patently absurd.
Louise was not consulted. Had she heard,
could it have mattered, whether she concurred?
The 'prince' transferred his 'queen' and 'court' to Florence.
Malodorous, possessive, angry, gross,
the prince rejected Tuscan invitations
(since 'royalty' should not hold nobles close),

refused to form parochial relations,
alone, aloof and brandy-comatose.

* * * *

HEROIC COUPLETS! THAT'S THE ONLY WAY
to eulogise Vittorio. Tragic Play!
It's very much his vehicle: *Galatea,*
Merope, Agamemnon, Don García!
Vittorio's mighty line – how does it go?
'Oh, Sophonisba! Sophonisba, oh!'
'Unbalanced life' – that's him – *Koyaanisqatsi:*
the author of the line, 'I'm just the Pazzi'.
Éclat comes far more often than *élan:*
no better way to classify him than
'Sardinia's McGonagall'. Oft-times,
he'll use outmoded language, facile rhymes.
Astute, but not as cute, as Violante,
Vittorio is the true *Asti spumante.*
His narcissistic heroes, just like him,
are joyless, friendless: plots are endless, grim.
A title for his style was settled on,
but 'Titanism' has a cast of one.
Disorganised, impetuous, ill-bred,
he claims an 'anti-geometric' head.
Whatever else he may be guilty of,
the first words in his *memoir* are, 'self-love'.
A mix of apprehension and attraction
besets his feelings for the female faction.
At six years old, he lost his sister Julia:
a convent took her. Furiouser, unrulier,
his adult life is one long repetition
of fusion, fission, pillage and perdition.
Vittorio is always 'ultra', 'other',
exacting vengeance on his distant mother,
offending *ersatz* uncles (we'd say, patrons).

His paramours *sans cesse* are married matrons.
Incapable of levity or lark,
he paid the lover's levy in Green Park.
Two keys to understanding this strange man
are first, before his love affairs began,
he gorged on hemlock and was violently ill.
He'd eaten more than was required to kill
himself, but vomited profusely. Second,
his frantic voyages: he must be reckoned
the widest-travelled youth on Planet Earth,
but utterly devoid of joy or mirth,
derives no satisfaction from his toils.
It's quite as if some melancholy coils
around his heart, a chill which seems to merge
into a violent, self-destructive urge.
There's nothing in his life that's sound or solid,
his loves, which should be noble, have been squalid.
Prince Charles is sinking lower by the day.
To try to keep his regal claims in play,
He's now renounced the faith of Rome, which means
he's smashing into smoking smithereens
the basis of his welcome, here in Rome.
Dependable as any metronome,
the Pope pays out a pension. Were it known
that Charles is now a traitor to his own,
he'd be a homeless mendicant – same day.
What makes a man throw everything away?
He's trashing every oath he's ever sworn,
because his god is now John Barleycorn.

STRAY LEAVES: LOCHABER NO MORE

My heart was captured by that lonely glen,
its shroud of summer mist like bridal white:
a solitary granite Jacobite

still peering out to sea. Devoted men,
romantic cause! A boy I was, back then,
as willing as all innocents to fight
for what was handed down to me by right:
we lost him. Will he not come back again?
A stifling August, traffic-throttled Strand:
abandoning an errand, quite unplanned,
I stepped into a narrow island-church.
'Charles Edward Stuart swore here, underhand,
to change his faith, and thereby to besmirch
his people's cause, and leave them in the lurch.'

* * * *

Is CHARLES A JEALOUS MAN, or just possessive?
The question has importance, though a tease:
why is he so restrictive, so aggressive?
What is his real opinion of Louise?
It's said he'd dread to see his love rejected –
or she's a trinket-toy, to be protected.

Although he fends society from his wife,
he can't avoid the opera. His box
is private, and to shut out human life,
he's had a bed brought in, which blocks
all access (and all egress!) He can snore
contented, with his bulk against the door.

All physical affection long since faded,
they sleep in separate bedrooms, yet it's known
that hers is bolted, barred and barricaded:
she comes and goes by passing through his own.
One rumour is, he doesn't really care,
but can't risk doubt (should she produce an heir).

Vittorio has come to Florence, too:
among the 'quality', cuts quite a dash
in tailored uniform of Piedmont blue.
Apart from this successful social splash,
He's here to break some horses, write some plays
and set Italian sentiment ablaze.

Louise is now an adult. She's matured.
She's still a bookish youngster, a *savant*,
but far more confident and self-assured.
And wisdom means, 'I know what I *don't* want'.
Repulsive husband, stimulating friend:
small doubt whom she would cleave to, in the end.

And suddenly, the rupture is a fact.
Saint Andrew's Day is passed in heavy drinking,
a beating preludes an 'unnatural act':
Louise flees to a convent, quick as blinking.
What boots it if the Pope forbids divorce?
This marriage just dissolved itself, perforce.

A *cicisbeo* is a lady's man,
a captive cavalier, a courtly lover:
refresh the lady's winecup, proffer fan,
attend her assignations, undercover:
Vittorio adopts the role with ease,
the servant and protector of Louise.

Critical Mass

For love to happen, circumstances must
align and coincide. For Queen Louise,
revulsion and impatience, by degrees,
have drained away her reservoir of trust.
Her one unspent emotion is disgust.
Vittorio is seeking guarantees,

and here's the balm to quiet his unease:
a woman who can raise him from the dust.
Like Italy herself, Vittorio is rubble,
immense potential, feeling for a form.
Louise is drowning in a sea of trouble,
but here's a man, unthreatening and warm.
She'll guide his growth, correct him and redouble:
and he will be her shelter from the storm.

A WOMAN ON THE RUN IS NOT A NUN,
not even when in convent domiciled.
She needs her change of linen, finely spun,
her gowns, her bracelets, *coiff*, divinely styled.
Louise despatches servants for her things,
but Charles rebuffs them. When the underlings

return with empty hands, Louise composes
a note, to bring it to the Pope's attention.
His Holiness replies that he proposes
to look again at Charles's papal pension.
Pretendor caves to Pope in abject failure,
and Duchess is supplied with said regalia.

The man of scarlet hat and sable sleeve,
so derelict of action, strong on talk,
in terms of men and women, so naive:
meet Charles's brother, Cardinal of York.
(A word to cassocked virgins: arrogant fools,
if you don't play the game, don't make the rules!)

He can't condemn the violence. 'To Rome!'
There, there's a convent named the Ursuline
where battered women make a home from home
(to save Louise, or dress the Stuart vine?)
With Catholics, no truth is ever found.
The malefactors just get moved around.

From Tuscany to Rome, by horse-drawn carriage!
(One feels one's heard this kind of thing before.)
Vittorio comes, too. Let none disparage
his presence as Louise's paramour:
as ever, he's observant – even fervent –
but dressed – to save appearance – as her servant.

And here's the confluence. Two stories meet.
The convent where Louise is now confined
lies on the *Via Vittoria* – very street
which housed Pompilia. (As if designed
to bloat the irony, a torso-adorner
named Franceschini has the Corso corner.)

Let's leave the lovers at the window-grille
(she on the inside, he out on the street).
We almost feel that we can see them still,
lips working hard, but not disposed to meet.
Let's think of love as comic masquerade
(but not forget the entrails-searching blade.)

Vittoria's a very modest street,
an arrow's flight from one end to the other.
Here, Corso and Paulina almost meet,
a narrow gorge where someone tried to smother
three women's lives in the space of ninety years.
Pompilia was hacked to death, of course,
but two more (that we know of!) mutineers
found refuge in the Ursuline, perforce:
both cases (not discreet, but not discrete)
concern the Young Pretender and his brother,
for history is fated to repeat.
If Charles is farce, what happened to his mother
is tragedy. Maria also knew
Vittoria, and died at thirty-two.

THE HISTORY OF THE TRUE CROSS:

(7) The Battle of the Milvian Bridge

As conflicts go, it isn't ultra-fierce.
The Christians show, the others bugger off:
the river isn't ruffled in its trough.
About as threatening as Ambrose Bierce.
They must have got their banners from a Sears
and Roebuck catalogue (forgive the scoff):
the Christians are a horse-hoof Stroganoff,
less Jesus Militant than Mildred Pierce.

But Constantine will show them all who's boss.
(Is that Maxentius, sinking in the mud?)
He's coming at them with his puny Cross.
We're missing so much of the right-side limning:
Cascina-like, he caught the pagans swimming!
A funny kind of battle, with no blood!

ADELAIDE, Being a Tale told by Francesco Gambi

In German, Adelaide's name is '*Adelheid*',
   in simple terms, nobility,
a concept not conferring right or might,
   and signalling fragility.
Through cycles of imprisonment and flight,
   she finally found tranquility.

You're young and beautiful? That means,
   'by men manipulated'.
A princess born? For all your broad demesnes,
   'by lower orders hated'.

Aspire to higher than Guelphs or Ghibellines?
   You're unsophisticated,

and prey to fiercer wolves. Fifteen years old,
   and traded-off in marriage.
We've heard this tale before. It's often told,
   and easy to disparage.
A clueless daughter bartered, bought and sold,
   likes riding in a carriage.

Today you feel entitled, but tomorrow
   the suffering begins.
You're strolling down the staircase in *Ca d'Oro*
   festooned in furs and skins,
but all you own is temporary, borrowed
   (that's why your mink's head grins).

When Adelaide became Italian queen,
   her husband was Lothair.
With Berengar the Second on the scene
   (who thought the deal unfair),
One rival made the other (so we glean)
   drink poison, unaware.

Now Berengar was in the driving-seat,
   his wish-list was overt:
dynastic plans would never be complete
   unless the royal 'skirt'
contracted one more marriage, *tout de suite*,
   with offspring Adalbert.

However, Adalbert was no great catch.
   Like many a noble child,
he had a handicap (which wasn't scratch!),
   'debility', so-styled.

Had Adelaide consented to the match,
  she would have felt defiled.

Was Berengar prepared to let it go?
  As sure as pigs might fly!
He'd taken all those pains to overthrow
  the government, so why
would anyone make trouble, *à propos*
  the strictures he'd apply?

In modern times, a woman in distress
  has things that she can do:
(that's not to minimise or second-guess
  the pain she's going through):
approach a women's group, enlist the press,
  or file a suit or two,

but options, way back when, were precious few.
  One choice was, kneel and pray …
yet from a realistic point of view,
  she had no cards to play.
For Adelaide, the only thing to do
  was simply run away.

An outlaw, in the marshes! Mud and fog,
  where now raw fish sufficed,
in place of partridge pie! The Queen of Quag
  still had a *Sumpfesgeist*:
the loyal priest Warinus braved the bog,
  her eunuch-who's-for-Christ.

Warinus' work? Whatever Adelaide wished:
  companion, minion, aide,
he counselled, gathered firewood, hunted, fished,
  and all of this unpaid.

Thus day by day, *im ganze Land Ansicht,*
   he laboured, undismayed.

But Berengar the Bloodhound had her scent
   and wouldn't let it go.
Vindictive adversaries don't relent.
   His packhounds tracked her, so
She found herself 'in pestilent prison pent',
   the plaything of her foe!

Since Berengar is burning with an ardour
   that winning cannot slake,
he feels the need to twist the halter harder,
   for motives quite opaque,
her *carcere* a castle on the Garda,
   a long and lonely lake.

The wife of Berengar was known as Willa.
   She flew at Adelaide
so viciously, she seemed about to kill her
   with teeth and nails and blade:
if capture was Charybdis, she was Scylla!
   The victim's face was flayed.

To Scaliger her castellan compelled her,
   as chronicles allege,
where Adelaide, as patient as Griselda,
   poised on the water's edge,
beheld the bars and battlements that held her,
   as still as stagnant sedge.

One comfort, in her misery, remained her.
   Warinus, faithful priest,
detained on trumped-up letters of attainder,
   served with her. As her yeast,

he helped her rise, advised her and sustained her.
   Her fortitude increased.

If only Adelaide could find it in her
   to sensibly relent,
the wedding could be finalised by dinner.
   Insistent notes were sent
but Adelaide, attenuated, thinner,
   stood firm against consent.

The Fortress Scaliger abuts the lake
   though one side touches land.
A tunnel dug admitted no mistake,
   would need to be well-planned,
and this Warinus, for his mistress' sake,
   assumed the work in hand.

He toiled with water streaming through the gaps,
   with bleeding hands he slaved,
in constant fear of imminent collapse,
   both heat and cold he braved,
extending out exploratory saps,
   unaired, unlit, unpaved.

A year or more had passed (how count the days?)
   She'll hazard the escape:
She'll plunge into the labyrinthine maze
   where blackness drowns all shape:
she'll trust her fate to subterranean ways,
   like broken mouths agape.

Eternities of crawling in the dark,
   inhaling soil and slime,
once overcome reluctance to embark,
   she's lost all sense of time –

then suddenly, there's daylight, strident, stark,
   and turbulence sublime!

If once again she's wallowing in dirt,
   subsisting in a *fossa*,
at least she's free, adrift, alive, alert
   (Heredotus' Atossa).
It`s time to meet another Adalbert,
   l'eminenza rossa.

The princeling of another lakeside fort
   (the Castle of Canossa),
Count Adalbert maintained a cut-price court,
   a bargain Barbarossa,
was struck by Adelaide when, out for sport,
   the hunter came across her.

This second Adalbert offered protection
   within Canossa's keep.
It seemed to Adelaide a resurrection,
   but fate's relentless sweep
delivered (yet again) utter dejection,
   in one ungainly heap.

Though Adalbert, that Carolingian Joffre,
   believed the war was won,
opposing tropos filled every trench and trough
   which under turrets run,
extending out to cut Canossa off:
   l'assedio had begun

For Adelaide, so recently confined
   in cells beneath the ground,
the prospect of a siege oppressed her mind.
   Warinus quickly found

a bold solution. Not at all resigned
   to being castlebound,

he came up with a scheme to wriggle through
   the enemy's blockade.
Investment lines are porous, as he knew,
   guards easy to evade:
his plan was sound and, in his mistress' view,
   most adequately laid.

With effortless aplomb, he passed between
   the castle keep and Parma,
immune from molestation, mild, serene,
   the quintessential charmer
adopting for his mask a drab routine,
   insouciance for his armour.

Apart from being a master of escape,
   Warinus was the best
at diplomatic horse-trade. He could scrape
   or wrangle, wring or wrest
a purchase-hold of any size or shape
   from princes. He impressed

the grandees and the landgraves of the west.
   This polymorphous priest,
pragmatic yet precipitate, professed
   connections in the east:
at bishops', beys' and baronets' behest,
   his influence increased.

Observed in this *parterre* or in that grotto,
   conversing with the great,
like something from a *fête-galante* of Watteau
   (but slightly more sedate),

he might, if asked, compose the odd *strambotto*
   or dine off silver plate.

Depicted posing on the *ponte rotto,*
   beneath the Ostian Gate,
conversing with some cardinal (*ma sotto*),
   of high affairs of state,
assessing portraits by Lorenzo Lotto
   (or something more ornate),

he chanced one day upon the Emperor Otto
   and put it to him straight:
'The saving of my mistress is my motto,
   and I believe in Fate.
Let's leave these frescoes: rescue versus Giotto?
   Which carries greater weight?'

Great Otto turned out uninclined to tarry
   — in fact, he proved quite keen:
with Adelaide available to marry
   (her portrait had been seen!),
how might a fight to rescue her miscarry?
   She'd soon be Otto's queen!

On sighting fast-approaching northern forces,
   Berengar's bullies ran,
and Adelaide (according to the sources)
   (excepting The Koran)
had everything she'd hoped for, local lore says,
   decided by a man.

The Holy Roman Empire, then, was hers,
   commencing from that day:
but to Warinus, not one document refers:
   he melted quite away.
To Berengar befell the fate of curs,

abandoned like a stray …
   a tale to be unfurled some other day.

THE GATHERER OF SOLES, Being a Tale told by Desiderio Spreti

A lusty young fellow looked up at the sky
and at little white clouds that were scurrying by,
   and said, 'Why must we always be facing
   the fate to which, daily, we're racing?
I'll never, not ever, accept I must die!'

He asked all the people who lived in his town,
and when they responded, their words got him down.
   'It would seem that they're all fatalistic,
   and offer no hope to the mystic.
I need new horizons,' he said with a frown.

'One sees in this region, fatality's rife,
as much in the mind as one finds with the knife,
   whereas I hold the settled opinion
   that death doesn't deserve such dominion!'
He would look for a land where they guaranteed life.

They say for the brave, opportunity knocks,
and a heart that is hopeful will open all locks.
   Not one day of his search was concluded
   when the youngster to whom we've alluded
encountered a man with a handcart of rocks.

'I hope you can tell me the thing I would know,'
said the eager young man. 'There's a place I must go,
   where the people are not cursed with dying.'
   'Stay with me,' said the other, replying.
'I must break down this mountain, rebuild it below;

so work here beside me, and for all that long while
as we tear down the mound and the boulders repile,
   there's a spell will continue to charm you;
   not a force on this earth that can harm you.'
A miss, as they say, is as good as a mile,

and that's why the young one demanded out flat –
'When we've lifted Olympus, what comes after that?'
   Said the other, 'you're no ignoramus.
   I believe, then, that Death may reclaim us.
But a century's more than the span of a gnat.'

'A hundred short summers? To me, it's the same
as to fall in the thrall of our all-too-small frame.
   I've no liking for trucking and trading.
   It's the Finite I'm bent on evading.
I will bid you farewell. Please get on with your game.'

The youngster continued a couple of days
till a forest emerged, vast and green through the haze:
   he saw timbers so truly immense,
   and a canopy gloomy and dense,
he with caution its mighty proportions appraised.

He noticed a man who was chopping a tree.
'Indicate to me, friend, on which path I must be
   for the land where the people don't die?'
   'Here's a forest you shouldn't pass by,'
said the woodsman. 'You can stay here with me.'

'My goal is a place where mortality's hold
has been broken.' 'But here, as the years may unfold,
   you can live in the absence of fear.
   We are safe. There's a forest to clear.
When it's done, you'll be more than 200 years old.

They say that we woodsmen are coarse-grained and gruff,
and the language we use is ungainly and rough,
   but life is uncertain and short:
   we don't live as long as we ought:
yet you think two hundred not nearly enough?'

The perambulant youngster took leave of his host,
since reluctant to argue from pillar to post,
   for he knew what he wanted to find.
   And, forsaking the forest behind,
he directed his steps to the littoral (coast).

A man and his duck were alone on the beach.
'Gentle sir, there's a place that I'm anxious to reach.
   It's a land where death doesn't exist,
   where they need neither coffin nor cyst,
and no sadness is felt (so philosophers teach).'

The man stared him out, without blinking.
'You'll have noticed, my mallard is drinking.
   If you'd care to remain here with me,
   once my pet has ingested the sea,
you'll have lived long enough, I am thinking.'

'Forgive me for asking – how long will it take?
He delights me as being a diligent drake,
   and although I am no Chester Nimitz,
   I'm aware that an ocean has limits:
what's your timescale for lapping the lake?'

'It's a quality question, and a pertinent puzzle.
I'd say fifteen score years. His magnificent muzzle
   on which all my ambitions depend
   is quite certain to win in the end.
So the sea's a three-century guzzle.'

'And when it's all finished, I still have to die?'
'That's a truth I embrace and won't try to deny.
   I can't fathom what else you'd expect.
   Take a moment to think and reflect:
the end-point (consumption)'s baked into the pie.'

The young man abandoned that desolate shore,
striking out on his quest of inquiry once more.
   When a palace loomed large up ahead,
   he decided to ask for a bed,
but before he could knock, someone opened the door.

Since the youngster was clearly expected to speak,
he began with 'My task is entirely unique:
   to extinction I'll not be a slave:
   I refuse to be groomed for the grave …'
'That will do,' said the man, 'you have found what you seek.'

And the palace proved perfect, with nothing to pay,
and the fellow remained there for many a day.
   He reposed in *terraza* and hall,
   where he wanted for nothing at all.
Thus he idled uncountable summers away.

One morning, the youth told a truth to his host.
'Of the yearnings I feel, one oppresses me most:
   I left all of my loved-ones behind,
   and I've finally made up my mind –
I'll return to them.' 'Fool! You will find only ghosts!'

The lord of the palace went on, with a frown:
'There's a scythe known as Time, which has snicked them all down.
   Did you think you'd got something for free?
   'I accept. What you say may well be,'
said the youth, 'but at least I can see my home town.'

'I can see from your face you're determined to go,'
said the lord. 'Very well, if it really is so,
   I will aid you. You don't need to ask.
   And to help you accomplish your task,
take my filly named Sisi, as white as new snow.'

In a tone like a moan, all forbidding and low,
he remarked 'there's a thing that you really should know.
   In the saddle you will have to remain,
   crossing mountain or river or plain.
If you step down, you'll die in an instant. Just so.'

But the lad only lay back and lazily laughed.
'Give me credit, dear Master, for having some craft!
   To the hearse I am always averse:
   deep in danger I will never immerse
us – but easy! Little Sisi will serve as my raft!'

He rode by the beach of the man and his duck
and he saw human bones: 'Oh well, he had no luck!'
   The forest was treeless and bare,
   the mountain was no longer there.
He was pleased that he hadn't got stuck

in tasks which were futile and offered no boon.
He headed along a small pathway, and soon
   a cart which was blocking the way
   prevented all progress. He halted to say,
'You can see by the rise of the moon

that darkness is falling, and I need to pass.
So, carter, permit me my way, or alas!
   You'll keep me out here, and benighted!'
   'Young horseman, suppose you alighted:
you could help me in moving this mass.'

'I'm sorry to tell you I'll never step down.
My succour is something,' he said with a frown,
   'you're going to have to discount.'
   'Young fellow, you need to dismount.
How else will I manage to get to the town?

You see that my cargo is old leather soles.
The people must burn them, in absence of coals.
   The natural forest has died,
   and leather I might have supplied,
but my wheels have got trapped in these holes.

These people are facing a total defeat.
No mountain, no goats – so they can't feed on meat.
   The sea doesn't offer up fish,
   so they're also deprived of this dish.
My leather, at least, is a weak source of heat

for cooking their turnips and similar crops.
They don't have the option of markets or shops.
   The shoe soles are fuel for their fire:
   what else could these people acquire?
If I don't supply them, their livelihood stops!'

'The things that you've told me cannot be ignored,'
said the rider, 'my feelings must go by the board.
   I'll help you. What else can I do?
   These people's resources are few:
The lend of a hand I'm prepared to afford.'

As soon as the youngster stepped down from his horse,
the carter approached him and seized him by force:
   'I tricked you. My true name is Death.
   It's time for your very last breath.
Your life, I'm afraid, has completed its course.

For aeons I've laboured in endless pursuit.
Those soles are from shoes I've worn out on the route.
   I notice you're helplessly mute,
   for now there can be no dispute,
since Death is the one absolute.'

BELLINDA AND THE MONSTER, Being a Tale told by Urbano Romano

There was a wealthy merchant of Livorno.
Antonio (the merchant) had three daughters.
Like all such cities, this one had four 'quarters',
with flags and favours (not the *Mezzogiorno,*
but *La Toscana*). Each was *molto bella*
(the chicks, that is – not neighbourhoods). Assunta
and Carolina (bitches, to be blunter!),
like something from a Cinthio *novella,*

betrayed the young Bellinda. *Nel suo turno,*
Bellinda just forgave them, never fought, as
they went on dates with masculine escorters,
abandoning Bellinda to the *forno.*
(It sounds like something out of Cinderella!)
The heart, they say, can be a lonely hunter,
and shamelessly might older sisters shunt her;
Bellinda, though, would prove the true *zitella.*

The sisters, known in town as 'Shrimp' and 'Shorty',
were famous for their arrogance and spite.
Bellinda, on the contrary, was quite
respected for her sweetness. On a sortie
(a rare event!) Bellinda, ever zealous
to show politeness, angered Carolina
and mortified Assunta. They were meaner,
and thought her weak (but really, they were jealous!)

Their way with marriage offers? Call it naughty.
They countered each proposal with a slight
(while young Bellinda always said 'I might,
but not just yet,' and 'thank you'. They were haughty,
and scoffed, 'We'll never marry carpet-sellers!'
In truth, each passing day would find them keener
to trap a man. (The pen of Malespina
could not do justice to these cottage-dwellers!)

Antonio, the father, lost his ships.
They foundered in some far-off ocean storm.
(Antonios and ship-loss were the norm
in these Italian stories.) 'Let the chips
fall where they may,' said he. Now, facing ruin,
he planned to move his daughters to a fen
where still he owned a rustic rural den.
For Shrimp and Shorty, this was not a shoo-in!

'Forget it!' squealed the sisters, hands on hips.
'We need Livorno, where it's clean and warm.
To cottage life we can't – and won't – conform:
We won't go play the peasant – read our lips!'
Bellinda loved her father. His undoing
now made her love him twice as much again.
Her selfish sisters might go chasing men,
but she would be content with firewood-hewing.

But, sadly for the sisters, local folk
were well aware affairs were dry as tinder
(extend the metaphor!) burnt to a cinder:
the suitors spurn a *sposa* if she's broke!
The youngest sibling, cheerful at her churn,
was still attracting men. By Saint Ignatius!
So beautiful, so modest and so gracious,
she made them beat a pathway through the fern!

Petitioners could pester, prod and poke,
but no-one got the better of Bellinda.
She knew some winsome ways to hedge and hinder,
deflecting suitors with a gentle joke.
Her reason wasn't Delphic to discern.
The would-be husbands, tediously tenacious,
appeared to Belli vapidly vexatious:
her father was her principal concern.

In country ways, Bellinda proved adept.
The sisters, hating this bucolic state,
ignoring irksome housework, sleeping late,
begrudged and bickered as Bellinda swept,
serenely scrubbing threshold, darning cuff.
They called her '*zoticona*', '*contadina*',
and as she slaved and smiled, the names got meaner –
'*cafona*', '*puttarella*', 'bit of rough'.

A battered, storm-torn vessel slowly crept
along Livorno's sea-wall. Blessed Fate!
One ship had made it home. To celebrate,
Antonio, elated, said 'Accept!
I'll treat you to a mantle, or a muff!'
Two sisters yelled for perfume, or pashmina:
Bellinda, though, that comely Colombina,
said, 'Bring a rose, and that will be enough.'

But when Antonio reached Livorno beach,
his luck was lacking and his fortunes festered.
His cargo wasn't large, and creditors pestered.
A lender is an unrelenting leech,
and soon the ship was shucked, the boards were bare:
Antonio, tired of paying through the nose,
took what remained, went shopping. First he chose
Assunta's gift, 'a shawl the colour of air'.

For Carolina, next, a gown of peach.
The money went. The sun, exhausted, westered.
Our footsore merchant found himself sequestered,
benighted, walking home. Each oak, each beech,
surrounding him, oppressed him. Such a scare!
A storm whipped up. To multiply his woes,
It dawned on him he hadn't bought a rose!
He trudged on, cold and wet, beset by care.

He heard the cries of hungry wolves begin.
The icy wind had chilled him to the core,
and rain was lashing, fiercer than before.
The merchant quivered, sodden to the skin.
Then, just as things were growing truly grim,
Antonio saw a hanging lantern light.
A house, and hope of shelter! Through the night
it shone, his chance of saving life and limb.

Against the blinding rain and tempest din
he fought his way towards the mansion door.
'A haven such as this, who could ignore?
I'll ask these people if they'll take me in.
My chances of surviving this were slim
until this moment. What a welcome sight!
He pounded on the door with all his might,
but no-one answered. Antonio, on a whim,

depressed the handle – and it opened slowly.
Candles burning warmly on the wall
illuminated paintings. Down the hall
the merchant edged, in awe. 'By all that's holy!
Such opulence! How happy is my fate.
What house could I have found that's cleaner, drier?
And look – this room contains a blazing fire!
He settled down before the glowing grate.

Surveying all, Antonio whistled lowly.
Forgotten now were thunderstorm and squall.
Some unseen hand had troubled to install
a luscious feast! Antonio was wholly
amazed at crystal cup and silver plate.
The meal itself was something to admire,
with grape and grouse a glutton might desire.
Who owned this place? Who managed this estate?

He shouted, but the house was empty, mute.
A spell before the fire, absorbing heat,
and then Antonio thought, 'It's time to eat',
and helped himself to turkey, turbot, fruit.
Demolishing the whole delicious heap,
he polished off the wine, and now felt weary.
Locating bedrooms on the upper tier, he
selected one, and promptly fell asleep.

Awakened by the sun, he can't compute
what's happening. Last night – the wine, the meat –
and now this feather pillow, cotton sheet –
and, laid out on a chair, a clean new suit!
Who put it there? The mystery is deep
and, up to now, there's nobody to query.
The garden beckons. Still a little bleary,
he spots a little thing that he can keep.

Before Antonio's eyes, a glorious rose
adorned the garden's marble-statue quarter
(the other parts were labyrinths and water).
This rose topped off a shrubbery, enclosed
by gravel paths more regular and neater
than anything he'd ever seen. No flaws
or blemishes gave contemplation pause
in this, the sacred Sanctum of Demeter.

The merchant plucked the flower. 'I suppose
there's no objection…' 'Vandal! This means slaughter!'
A monster, snarling at him! 'For my daughter!'
The Monster flared. 'So, this is how it goes!
I offer you my home …' He seemed to teeter
from anger to acceptance. Next, his claws
retracted. Finally, he licked his jaws.
'You clearly love your daughter. May I meet her?'

Antonio, astounded and amazed,
could barely comprehend this new atrocity.
The Creature seemed to change with such velocity!
One moment he was calm, the next one, crazed!
The Monster, meet Bellinda? He agreed,
for, after all, he'd been the Monster's guest.
He'd here been warmed and rested, fed and dressed.
And if Bellinda knew, he knew that she'd

comply with swift alacrity. Still dazed,
he took another look at this monstrosity,
so capable of kindness and ferocity!
The Man of Commerce rapidly appraised
his present situation: yes, concede,
and bring Bellinda, at the Beast's behest.
A merchant must be minded to invest:
One never knew where such a ruse might lead!

But now another obstacle was raised,
the Monster moved once more by animosity:
'You've chosen to abuse my generosity,
your house and family will all be razed!'
The merchant answered, 'If I'm ever freed, …'
'Enough!' the Monster cried. 'I am impressed.
Please take the gems and fabrics in this chest
And give them to your girls. My very best!
You've heard my words, which surely you will heed.'

'I have to cross, on foot, ravine and river.
It won't be easy, carrying the chest.'
'The chest will go before you. Haven't you guessed?
Whatever thing I promise, I deliver.'
The Shrimp and Shorty, babbling empty blather,
attacked the chest, removing bolts and bows,
to pounce on presents, like two cawing crows.
Bellinda was just glad to see her father.

Antonio had something good to give her,
and while the sisters, selfishly obsessed
with maximising profit, keen to wrest
the slightest benefit, the shiniest sliver,
Bellinda sought no part in pillage. Rather,
she laboured in the yard, with back door closed.
Antonio presented, and she took, her rose,
though still up to her elbow-ends in lather.

The father must assail the daughter's ears:
he tells her of the Monster, and explains
the terrible commitment that remains,
and of the Monster's menace: how he fears
an adversary with a reach so long.
The risks of non-compliance must be weighed
against Bellinda's peril: if betrayed,
the Monster might inflict appalling wrong.

With superhuman wisdom for her years,
Bellinda speaks. 'Who loses, and who gains?
I won't expose my family.' She deigns
to visit with the Monster. Through her tears,
she bids Antonio not to come along.
'The debt of family honour must be paid.
This is an interview I can't evade.
I'll meet the Fiend alone, and I'll be strong.'

Antonio insisted, emphasised
his duty as a parent. Since he made
the point so forcefully, he swayed
his daughter, and Bellinda compromised.
And thus they headed for the Monster's lair.
The merchant tried the mansion door anew,
depressed the handle – it allowed them through.
The house was empty. Nobody was there.

The courtesy could not be criticised.
A breakfast table stood there, fully-laid
with knives and forks of silver, plates of jade,
the napkin for Bellinda, daughter-sized.
Such food, so beautiful! At last, the pair
were finished. That's when father – daughter, too –
began to bristle: nothing marred the view,
but both could sense a presence, were aware

of something menacing that might be near –
and in a flash, he came. To her distress,
Bellinda saw the Monster's ugliness,
and saw that it was worse than she had feared.
His skin was slimy and it glistened black.
The face was wrinkled, inelastic, old,
with bloodshot eyes, protruding as they rolled:
his tattered talons overgrown and cracked.

'There's something I must ask, Bellinda dear,'
the Monster started. 'Answer me. Confess.
You came here freely?' Belli answered, 'Yes.
I stand before you as a volunteer.'
He then addressed the merchant. 'Here's a sack.
Inside you'll find a fortune, coins of gold.
Consider your Bellinda bought and sold.
Return to where you came from. Don't come back.'

Antonio's Anguish

He left his daughter there. That makes him weak?
Abandoning his very flesh and blood
because the Monster said so? That's not good.
But in his turpitude, he's not unique
(and after all, he has a venal streak,
and gold's a compensation) – but what should
a father do, apart from knock on wood?
One can't help but recall a gruesome Greek
who lopped his daughter's head off, for a breeze.
Your girl is your casino chip, but she's
a wasting asset, useless usufruct,
of value only while she's getting fucked:
think Marie Antoinette, Mary of Guise.
So why do fathers feel this faint unease?

THE MERCHANT TOOK THE MONEY: WORDLESS, went.
Bellinda felt a growing sense of dread:
Important things the Monster left unsaid
were things Bellinda hoped to circumvent,
but how to do it? Vulnerable, prone,
without the possibility of flight,
she pondered on her now-exquisite plight.
What could she parry, or at least postpone?

The fall of night would be the main event.
What had the Beast in mind, regarding bed?
At present unmolested and well-fed,
she wondered if the Monster might resent
a show of maiden-modesty. Unknown
to her, the Monster was already out of sight:
Bellinda found a note which read, 'goodnight'.
Relieved, she went to bed. She was alone.

Next morning, when she woke, she took a look
around the premises. Along one side
of what she called the 'hall', immense and wide,
she found a fireplace with an ingle nook.
It seemed to her ideal to settle here,
and use it as her haven, set apart
from vaster public spaces. She could start
to get her bearings, overcome her fear.

The first thing that she found there was a book,
a sort of introduction, or a guide
explaining all the mansion. And inside,
when once she had undone the clasp-and-hook,
she found a message, palpably sincere:
'Bellinda, all this opulence, this art,
is yours. You are the ruler of my heart.
I hold you precious and forever dear.'

The girl remained alone the livelong day.
At sunset he appeared, outside the doors.
'May I come in?' 'It's your house.' 'No. It's yours.'
He clearly had important things to say.
'Bellinda, do you truly find me hideous?'
'I do. The truth should never be denied.
But some of us are beautiful inside,
and that's what matters. No-one's so fastidious

that others who are kindly may not sway
her feelings. 'Sight Dismisses, Love Restores',
and I am not a person who abjures
November, just because it isn't May.'
'Please marry me, Bellinda. Love, insidious,
might steal upon you …' 'No,' the girl replied.
'To wed or not, I must not yet decide.
To answer otherwise would be perfidious.'

The Monster bade goodnight. His words were curt.
Bellinda found herself alone again.
Retiring briefly to her private den,
She mused on how the Monster had seemed hurt.
Taking the guidebook from its secret place,
she saw new entries where the old had been,
of beauty unexpected, unforeseen:
'all grace to her who offers others grace'.

The season changed. The summer's floral skirt
gave way to ochre ruffles in the glen.
Bellinda loved these mist-wreathed mornings, when
she'd find new words to thrill and disconcert:
'Although we have to die, yet we can trace
our permanence upon the flimsy screen:
our deeds are not ephemeral. They mean
that who we are can never be effaced.'

She grew to cherish supper-hour each dusk.
(The Monster was punctilious at keeping
this dinner-date.) Across the lawn came sweeping
the rich aroma of the roses' musk.
Bellinda loved to watch the darkness steal
by increments across the garden floor
and listen to him talking. 'I would feel so poor,'
she said, 'if ever you forwent our twilight meal.'

One dusk, as by the ballustrade they strolled,
beneath the ballroom's overhanging eaves,
the Monster pointed out some lovely leaves,
beginning now to blush with autumn gold.
'This is the famous Laughing-Weeping Tree,
a warning-sign, intelligence resource,
for when the leaves are drooping, losing force,
disaster menaces your family.'

'However, if the leaves are upright, bold,
the tidings which the magic tree receives
are wholly positive. There, no-one grieves:
Livorno's mourning-bell need not be tolled.'
One week went by. Bellinda chanced to see
The leaves all pointing skyward. 'Look! The source!
You'd let me … ?' 'Shh …,' the Monster said. 'Of course.
Attend Assunta's wedding? I agree.'

'Return within one week, or find me dead.'
This was another of the Monster's shocks,
more evidence his style was heterodox,
designed to make Bellinda watch her tread.
'This ring is yours. Please take it. Should the gem
cloud over, you will know that I am sick.
No matter if you think it politic
to linger there, return – or stand condemned!'

She thought of all the things the Beast had said,
the now-familiar mix of tricks and knocks
(he'd filled with frills a giant travel-box,
so she might shine, when seeing her sister wed).
'No sapphires are required, no lacy hem:
suppose he needs me – I'll return as quick
as possible. It's not through bribe or trick
that my commitment may or may not stem.'

Bellinda's sisters, far from being curious
about her strange new friend, raised sneers and snags,
like calling him her 'Mister Moneybags'.
In fact, they weren't just jealous, they were furious.
Assunta, soon to be the *sposa nuova*,
was marrying a local boy, a joiner –
a working lad, but not a money-coiner.
She saw Bellinda as a pig-in-clover.

These insults may have been entirely spurious,
but taking trash-talk from obnoxious hags
is never nice. From riches down to rags
they'd dropped, and thought they'd opt to be injurious.
They'd never seen their sister's 'friend'. Moreover,
assuming he must be a rich *Zigeuner*,
they called Bellinda *'putta'* and 'purloiner',
a wealthy gypsy's jade, a 'kitchen-stover'.

Assunta stole (and hid) the Monster's ring!
But little was her gain. Bellinda knew.
Demanding what was hers, she raised a hue
and cry so clamorous, the household King,
Antonio, took notice. (Chance to shine!)
Quite forcefully, the father intervened:
which sister was amiss, was quickly gleaned:
the case was closed (and he had grown a spine!)

(In speaking of the minxes' meddling,
let's jettison the Gypsy and the Jew.
There's gristle (and galore!) for us to chew
without us taking on that toxic thing.
The Rio Grande? You'd prefer the Rhine?
Depending on the pap on which you're weaned,
you won't have thought about it – merely leaned.
Your line is on the Tajo, or the Tyne?)

Alas for them, the gem (*lattiginosa*,
or milky, cloudy), unambivalent,
demanded action – so Bellinda went.
(It's like a storyline from Vargas Llosa!)
She ran into the mansion. No-one there!
She coursed the lower level, then the upper:
no sign of him. No silver covers, cup or
table laid. She started to despair.

Along the garden path *la ponderosa*
cried wildly for him. Open sentiment,
more palpably than words, proves eloquent.
Indifferent to her Monster, was she? No, sir!
He couldn't be located anywhere.
But just when rescue plans seemed to be scuppered,
The Monster took his place at sunset supper!
(As Mrs. Beaton said, first catch your hare!)

'I've really been unconscionably ill,'
began the Beast. 'In such a circumstance,
I'd hoped there might be more than just a chance
of your support, but you have batted nil.'
'I hurried here, as soon as things were steady.'
'I look for something more than cabin crew.
It's clear that you don't love me.' 'Yes, I do!'
They sat in silence, letting those words eddy.

'I'd like us to get married. Say you will.'
Bellinda hesitated, looked askance.
(She was no diplomat, no Cyrus Vance.)
'I can't expostulate. I lack the skill.
Destroy the dollar, melt the maravedi –
I feel like Docteur Rieu (and Miou-Miou, too):
detached, but waiting. Let the points accrue!
I'll know. And you will, too. I will be ready!'

The Monster wasn't stupid. He decided
to play Bellinda like she was a fish
(the dish that's colder is the better dish).
The Beast, betimes, leant backwards and abided.
(Is dithering compatible with love?
Some wise-ass says, all comes to he who waits,
another warns that 'he who hesitates…'
What happens, then, when push must come to shove?

More months went by, and winter turned to spring.
The leaves were pointing up. Bellinda used
the Carolina news to be excused,
with promise of returning on the wing,
should she be needed. She was not his nurse,
but swore to help him. What this latter vow did
Bellinda didn't see, her heart enshrouded
with happy thoughts. The Monster was immersed

in misery. Deciding not to cling,
he waved her off as if he were amused.
Her sister, it appeared, was being abused
(the married one). Bad tidings in a string
accompanied her visit. From her purse
she took the gemstone ring, and dark thoughts crowded
around her, for the stone was dull and clouded,
just like the last time, only this was worse.

She left Livorno and her sister's wedding
without a thought, her only aim to streak
towards her loved-one. Though the news was bleak,
her consolation was, he'd sense her heading
towards him. Rushing through the evening chill,
intent on getting to him, by and by,
her thoughts ran thus: 'If only I could fly!
I have a sacred promise to fulfil!'

Arriving at the house as night was spreading
across the lawn and bats began to squeak,
she longed to hear familiar floorboards creak,
but no-one came. She kissed the gemstone, dreading
she might have come too late. The house was still.
Retiring to the bedroom with a sigh,
she knew, the coming morn, she'd have to try
to face the day – but did she have the skill?

Bright morning, and laburnum fronds were shedding
their yellow petals when she heard him speak!
And there he was! Attenuated, weak,
but still alive! He had some trouble threading
his words together. 'Darling, I've been ill.
In fact, this time I was resigned to die.
You didn't come.' He struggled not to cry.
'Should this occur again, then die I will.'

The garden was a sombre scene. Leaves, drooping,
did not bode well. 'Your father, dear, is dying,'
the Monster told her. Lacking time for crying,
Bellinda started gathering and scooping
her things together. 'I had better pack.
I'm going to Livorno, can't ignore
the evidence. I must arrive before
the worst occurs. How troubles seem to stack

against us!' Since Bellinda had to go,
the Monster helped to speed her on the wing.
It's always a mistake when lovers cling,
and as he waved her off, he told her so.
Antonio, though feverish and swollen,
revived on seeing his favourite arrive.
Bellinda understood: she must contrive
to cleanse his innards, irrigate his colon.

She offered words of comfort, sweet and low,
while gently easing-off the Monster's ring.
The sisters didn't help with anything,
expecting her to nurse him, even though
so young a girl could not be wise as Solon.
Determined she would keep the man alive,
Bellinda worked with energy and drive –
but saw her ring had once again been stolen!

'I'm leaving now. I have to hurry back,'
Bellinda said. 'It's clear that Father's healing.'
(He'd pressured Carolina to revealing
that she had robbed the ring.) The stone was black!
The mansion, when she reached it, seemed so strange!
The iron gates were gnarled by years of rust,
and window sills were carpeted in dust.
She looked with horror on the dreadful change.

'Is this the outcome of some weird attack?'
she wondered. Walls were cracking, paint was peeling,
enormous cobwebs hanging from the ceiling.
She took her book down from the dusty stack.
Emotions rushed upon her in a range
which ran from brief elation to disgust.
A painting of *her rose* had now been thrust
between the pages! Rushing to arrange

another rescue, heading for the yard,
she found the Monster stretched out on the ground,
beneath the rose bush. Listening for a sound,
she heard him rasping. He was breathing hard.
She knelt beside him, watched the ebbing life,
beheld the ruined mansion. Then she said,
'I couldn't bear, my love, to see you dead.
I watch the marks of suffering, signs of strife,

I look upon this face, so drawn, so scarred,
and know I must revive you, bring you round.
Please live, my Darling, and we'll both be crowned.'
His eyes blinked open, met her mild regard,
emotions in both faces running rife:
she smiled, and placed both hands around his head:
'Unless you rally, how can we be wed?
I kiss you, and I'll gladly be your wife.'

It seemed that music filled the perfumed air.
The house, transformed, was shining, clean and new,
and where the Tree of Tears and Laughter grew,
the leaves were pointing upwards, everywhere.
A young man at her side was handsome, bright,
and didn't offer threat of any kind.
Bellinda didn't pay him any mind,
but shouted, 'Where's my Monster?' (She was quite

distracted by the change, the sudden scare.)
'But I'm your Monster,' said the young man, who
remained beside her. Now her interest grew.
'You have an explanation you can share?'
'I was under a spell, a magic blight,
but now my Monster days are far behind.
You freed me when you kissed me,' he opined.
Bellinda was astonished. 'Is that right?'

To answer her he kissed her, and she knew.
Down from the mansion stepped Antonio,
his illness gone, his face all healthy glow.
'Oh, Father! You are here! Recovered, too!
I've never in my life felt such content!
Where are my saucy sisters, callous kids?'
They, turned to marble, chunky caryatids,
were holding up the mansion's pediment!

A BUNDLE OF LOVE LETTERS, ALLEGED TO HAVE PASSED BETWEEN THE COUNTESS POMPILIA AND THE CANON CAPONSACCHI

Lacunae tease, inadequacies loom:
oppressed by dark presentiments of doom,
attenuated, taunted by the tomb,

it's Youth we turn to, to dispel our gloom!
Pompilia's amusing in her mien.
She's angry, abject, all things in between:
We watch her pout and postulate and preen
(if girls can't do it when they're seventeen,
when *can* they do it? So, we'll let her off).
It's not confined to curling-tongs or coif,
since Guido 'found' these letters in a trough:
coincidence to make a con-man cough!
Such detail – like the handkerchief, the broom!
So passionately written ... but by whom?

I.

My Dearest Sir,

       I will not speak again.
I fear that I've already said too much.
You are the most appealingest of men,
and what's more, recognise yourself as such.
The things I want to say would make you vain,
and I would blush to speak them to your face.
My heart no longer answers to the rein.
I offer grace to him who offers grace.

II.

My Own Signor,

       I hope you weren't alarmed:
the Old One wasn't thinking of the street.
Her mind was on the sofa. I repeat,
you brooked the Cyclops, and emerged unharmed.
We've moved the sofa, on the Old One's whim,
to underneath the window. As you passed,
her one concern was loudly to lambaste

the servants. She's not fond of crimson trim!
The coast is clear, go where you want to go.
(She's ga-ga, and the penny hasn't dropped:
besides, you'd devastate me if you stopped!)
It makes my day to watch you pass below.
As soon as I have any news to share,
I'll be in touch. And when I get some leisure,
I want to spend it all on wanton pleasure,
and tell you things of which you're unaware!

III.

Myrtillo, My Adored! My Very Life!
Forgive me for not looking, yesterday.
The short one – she is Conti's brother's wife –

(Oh, I forget. Of course you know.) Dismay!
Attached to both *suocera* and *cognata*,
I didn't have a chance to break away,

Or even glance at you. I am a martyr!
The Capuchins is not exactly fun,
but I was under strict anathemata.

I wanted so to gaze up at my sun!
My heart took in your every move, however
(you know – the one your name's engraved upon).

Your Amaryllis, always and forever,
with feelings unallayed, and passions rife:
deserving you, my ferventest endeavour.

IV.

My Well-Beloved,
                    Who always brings me pain!
            Ignore that man.
He wants to take your place, but never can.
            He likes to lurk.
When you're at odds with me, you do his work.
I'm yours, and will forever yours remain.

But yes, the letters are a real concern.
            The Jealous One
had not an inkling what he'd hit upon.
            He put them by.
I know they're perilous to keep, but I
can't bring myself to hide them, far less burn!

He didn't read them. In his way, he's trusting.
            He doesn't think.
But let's not push our fortune to the brink!
            Am I resigned,
you ask, or have I changed my fickle mind?
I'm solid. There's no tacking or adjusting.

Now for you. Are you having second thoughts?
            I need to know.
If something's made you nervous, tell me so!
            As for red wine,
it seems that Nature's thwarting our design:
the Old One says she's feeling out of sorts.

V.

You didn't pass my window yesterday.
Signor, I feel constrained to ask you why.
I watched and watched and watched, to no avail:

I wanted so to see you, down below!
At length I simply had to move away,
since Canon Girolamo (dirty spy)
was watching me. I feel like I'm in jail.
I moved, so that my watcher wouldn't know
my purpose, but I kept myself in play
by drifting past the farther window. I
was fortunate enough to scent your trail:
you reached the doorway where you love to go!
Your sweetheart greeted you. I have to say,
you have a thing for sluts. (I mustn't pry!)
Perhaps if you're aware you're going to fail
to keep your date with me, you'll tell me so?

Now, Conti tells me he would love to see
your octaves. What am I supposed to do?
They're intimate. I feel a kind of dread,
because – let's call it, 'language of the street'.
The Old One is improving, by degree.
It seems her fever's slowly working through.
Tomorrow, she'll be rising from her bed.
Angelica's preparing stuff to eat
again. There goes my short-lived liberty!
We're turning back to lamb-and-lentil stew,
but *meno male*, now the wine is red:
so what about the plan? Revise? Repeat?
Enjoy your doorway darling. Surely she
knows how to please a man. I've seen the queue!
It's not my place to censure you. Instead,
I ask you, sweet *Signor*, to be discreet.

VI.

My sweet Narcissus,
                     Yes, I have your letter!
I read it with enchantment – and relief,

because you're not annoyed. I am your debtor.
I'll curb my more-than-tedious *recitatif*:
my co-conspirator, aider, abettor
(no, that's not fair – my champion-in-chief!),
I'm learning from you. Shorter, sparer, better:
you've taught me less is more, so I'll be brief.

Since others, to our peril, might construe
our meaning, I will be oblique in lieu
of obvious: I know you'll take my cue,
and comprehend. The 'other one' came through!
So, once it's in my hands, I will pursue
our plan of action. Yes, it's overdue:
but I'll receive it soon and, when I do,
I'll pass it (through our 'channels') straight to you.

The Jealous One (thank heaven!) is away.
Their total failure to engage a maid
has meant the Old One is obliged to stay.
No balcony encounters, I'm afraid!
The cat is absent, but the mice can't play.
My comfort is, our ecstasy's delayed,
but not abolished. April melts to May.
We'll have our moment at the ballustrade!

I trust my heart's sincerity: in short,
my love is not a chimera. It's real.
Perhaps you sometimes think me overwrought:
believe me, I maintain an even keel!
Emotion is more violent than thought,
so to the god of love I make appeal.
I know that I'm behaving as I ought:
I'm guided, not by norms, but what I feel.

I hope my letter-storm is not vexatious.
I want to be your boon, and not your bane.

Forgive me if I'm overly loquacious:
I'd die before incurring your disdain.
Serene in your superbity, sagacious,
you'll never have to study how to reign.
And I, devoted, vehement, voracious,
your servant and your sweetheart shall remain.

VII.

Signor, my most beloved,
                            best-embraced,
you can't imagine how it's going here.
We're all in tumult and my 'lines', I fear,
show all the signs of amateurish haste:
but criticism, stoically faced,
improves us. (Faint, but hope-sustaining, cheer!)

To a False One

I am not versed in lovers' ways
  and (some would say) naïve:
I'm prone to be impressed by praise,
  the glibbest lies believe.
I have not lived sufficient days
  to stand on the qui-vive
and, fooled by insincere displays,
  proud peacocks I perceive

as purest when their fiercest blaze
  the worst imposture weaves.
Sequestered in this Cynics' Maze
  where hearts are worn on sleeves,
I've learnt that love brings forth dismays
  as thick as summer leaves.
The lesson, then, (to paraphrase)
  is, she who enters, grieves.

I've had a brush with *Il Signor Dottore*,
on Borgo Maestro. 'Oh! Where are you going?'
(He'd obviously been lurking, somehow knowing
I'd have some errands.) 'I'll come with you, *Cuore*!'
Since fortunately, as I hope for glory,
I had Maria with me, to-ing, fro-ing,

the Other had perforce to speak in snatches.
I sent Maria in to order fuel
from Manzi's, and he started: 'Why so cruel?'
(I loathe the kind of coward who detaches
a lady from her maid, to talk in patches!)
And thus unfolded our hiatic duel.

At Canto Bacci for some cumin seeds:
in went the maid. 'You called me false, in verse!'
I told him I regret not saying worse.
His handsome words preceded ugly deeds:
the 'Lovers' Bower''s now a patch of weeds.
I used those very words, incisive, terse.

We'd reached Canale Tavern's open casement,
and I was anxiously inclined to smother
all compromising talk. 'You have another!
Please give my best regards to my replacement.
Sovara weeps with me.' This self-abasement
was more than I could take. Then, Conti's brother

approached me from the Borgo Seteria.
He made the most exaggerated bow,
(the Conti like to joke – you well know how!)
and called me Aphrodite, Galatea,
and other nonsense. He had no idea ...
I didn't have a thing to disavow!

VIII.

Revered Signor, Beloved and Adored,
accept this letter as my most profuse
apologies. Downhearted, listless, bored,
I opted not to leave the papers loose
and mail the thing to Rome. I cede the field.

They haven't found a single thing of mine.
No revelations, poring over names:
you think I'd cast your pearls before the swine?
All letters are committed to the flames!
(I'm sorry that the Roman one was sealed:

I know that you were keen to introduce
yourself, but I grew restless – and, in fine,
I felt my neck within a tightening noose,
so sent it. All *your* letters I enshrine
inside my bosom, carefully concealed,

until I've read my fill. No threats or claims
could tease them out. (A project quite divine!
We might, some day, by way of secret games,
play 'hunt the letter' – and, should you combine
your trawl with tickles, I might even yield!)

I fear that some may hide behind the arras,
So when you pass below, don't make a sign.
They have no proof. Their purpose is to harass,
and we should not toward their goal incline.
We should remember, prudence is our shield!

The Jealous One is eager to embarrass.
Just yesterday, he buckled on his sword
to do worse than Aeneas – maybe Paris:

more mayhem than the Iliad can afford.
If nothing's risked, then nothing need be healed!

IX.

Is this some kind of ludicrous mistake?
You think me stupid, or (worse) insincere?
Your manner is offensive, cavalier.
You're qualified, you think, to find me fake?
Is this a call you're competent to make?
I wish I could confront you, have you hear
that if you met my eyes, in every tear
you'd see your own reflection, and would ache!
The Graces guide your movements. More than they,
should Venus your exquisite limbs assay,
she'd think how you have wronged me and, aghast,
would see your beauty, like the Milky Way,
mysterious, interminable, vast,
and understand a heart that beats so fast.

X.

Revered Signor,
                I have to give it up.
Your pet, who slavers when her Lord is due,
can not endure your absence. Bitter cup!

I'm forced, by all I've come to feel for you,
to contradict myself. And so I sup.
In plainest terms, let's do our window-view:

please come to me at our accustomed hour,
delicious in its fixed uncertainty.
I had not thought you'd undermine my tower

with saps as subtle as you've used on me.
So be it: I surrender to your power.
Return, and celebrate your victory.

Of course, you mustn't visit if it means
you have to let some doe-eyed doxy down!
I've seen the over-painted beauty queens

you go for. There's a thousand in this town
(like one across from me who prinks and preens!)
Please come. I'll wear the salmon satin gown!

I'd hate to be the cause of someone's pain
(and hate myself for begging for a crumb!),
but here I am, with fever on the brain!

Enough. I've said too much again. In sum,
you've other interests than my little lane,
it's just a fact. But if you *want* to … come.

XI.

My Well-Beloved,
                your poems are so deft,
I'll make no comment: more than I deserve!
To be their subject, seems a sort of theft:
your muse lacks merit, but she loves your *oeuvre*!

You want to know what's happening in the house:
well, no-one's talking to me here – not one!
A relatively gentle-mannered spouse
is all I boast – a rare phenomenon!

You Tuscans! When I find you well-disposed,
I tremble. I have seen civility

which all too often, when it's diagnosed,
is there to camouflage hostility.

Cognato Girolamo couldn't be gruffer.
When I am in my room, he locks my door.
But he is just an addle-brain, a duffer,
while you know how to hurt me much, much more.

The Franceschini feed me salted hake,
but you have made me love you, as your slave:
their surliness and cheapness I can take,
but you deny the only thing I crave.

They say the test of fire enhances gold,
and steel that's hammered leaves the anvil tougher.
I should accept the pain, and be consoled:
you elevate me when you make me suffer.

On Thursday I 'retired' at half-past eight,
in order to avoid your social call.
(Where ice is thin, it's prudent not to skate!)
Dissembling is the hardest part of all.

I should have said – I'm back in my old room.
Maria knows the signs we used to make,
so check the balcony: if there's a broom,
you'll know the coast is clear, and no mistake.

XII.

My Well-Beloved,
                  I have received your letter.
It pleases me – much more so than the others!
I want you to regard me as your debtor,
because this latest missive duly smothers

anxieties which plagued me. *Pastor Fido!*
I'm thrilled you like it. *Sleepless in Siena*
is coming next. (They're from the shelf of Guido,
who'll never notice.) I'll be your Vienna,

and you Myrtillo. *À propos* 'Drusilla',
I've heard some welcome news, concerning you.
She said you're coming to the summer villa!
It all seems too fantastic to be true.

A thing that – if I could – I'd bring about
is, kiss and fondle you my entire life.
(I might as well – I'm blushing! – spit it out):
if I could rule the world, I'd be your wife.

So, Conti has declared himself unwilling
to serve us further as our go-between!
Leave him to me. That soil is easy tilling.
I'll bring him round. I'll show you what I mean.

I'll make big eyes and, fluttering my lashes,
I'll tell him what he wants to hear the most.
Ten minutes, and resistance will be ashes,
and once again we'll have our pigeon-post!

You tell me, 'let a note down on a string',
but haven't stipulated hour or day:
we need to coincide on such a thing.
Imagine if the letter went astray!

The Jealous One is three days in Sovara!
The soil has not enough (or too much) chalk,
and then another problem in Cerbara:
at least a week for us to meet and talk!

I've hit another snag with the Confessor:
he says he's 'absolutely disinclined'.
He told me, 'find some other intercessor.'
What's caused this all-too-sudden change of mind?

Another thing – the street-door has been closed:
it's difficult, but if you persevere,
we'll manage our encounters unopposed.
I'm half-inclined to let you in the rear.

STRAY LEAVES: URBANO ROMANO

A sophist tends to be sophisticated,
and this holds true from Oslo to Odessa.
When garlanding a charlatan confessor,
we often leave his sex-drive underrated.
Arezzo had a curate, antiquated,
who wasn't local. Urban he, and Roman
(as may be gathered from his clear cognomen).
His lust for life (think, 'wife') was unabated.
Urban il Romano was a bold one
whose sacerdotal famine proved a feast:
for when, in penance, some signora 'told one',
his masculinity (so termed) increased.
Though no-one's certain if he ever 'rolled' one,
a man's a man, though sacerdotal dotard priest.

Pompilia confessed to him, as stated.
Like Polly Peachum faced with Mackie Messer,
She played it passive, parried her oppressor,
and limited the dirt she intimated.
The sacristan, extremely stimulated,
discerned her accent: 'She's no Tuscan yeoman!'
He shaped up as a shrewd shamanic showman:
indulged, ingratiated, infiltrated.

He felt he'd won the jackpot, and a gold one,
with penitential preying not policed:
he'd never yet effectively cajoled one,
but here was opportunity, at least.
They say there is no sucker like an old one,
or, scratch a beadle and disclose a beast.

XIII.

Beloved Idol,
             whom I count as mine,
I know about your various embroilments!
The Old One isn't drinking any wine.
(I'm sorry thus to add to your entoilments.)
I love it when you call me Trantaphyllis
(she's sick, and off the wine, and doesn't sleep).
Rodamne is my favourite – or Lillis!
We'll have to wait before we take the leap:
you can't conceive how hard her being ill is!
Since I'm the one who takes her tonic to her,
I'm admirably placed, and can divine
the course of her recovery. In fine,
I'll tell you when I'm ready to subdue her.
Your loving sweetheart – and your Amaryllis!

XIV.

Adored, Beloved and Thrice-Worshipped Heart!
I'm ravished but confused by all this praise:
the latest notes arrived here in a clutch,
and honestly, I don't know where to start!
Sciocchezza on my part – don't take it badly,
for I'm not used to this. It's all too much!
(Ignore this tripe – I *crave* communiqués!
I study each and every little phrase –
virility, concision, manly art!)

I need to put the horse before the cart,
and not contrariwise: I love you madly!
Forget the Doctor – he, to me, is dead.
Confine him to my foolish girly phase,
and think of what the future holds, instead.
He proved himself a *poseur:* therefore, sadly,
he's bobbing in my wake. No need to tread
upon his grave. The Old One's out of bed!
She's got 'our' broom, to serve her as a crutch,
and slurs her words (she might be talking Dutch!),
but wants her wine again! I serve her gladly!

The Doctor is a foppish languid toff
and I'm your Ariadne, as you know:
he never was, nor could have been, my 'beau'.
He was a stage I had to pass (don't scoff!),
a silliness I needed to outgrow.
Let's leave him now. We Romans say, 'less said,
more rapidly are aspirations sped.'
I want to lead you through the Cretan maze,
transport you to Arcadia, to show
a paradise 'where sheep may safely graze'.
Yes, I'm a girl who dreams and reminisces,
but now's the time for action – no delays!
We've dealt with Donna Beatrice's malaise:
there'll never be another chance like this is!
I send a thousand million tender kisses
(a pet-name purge, perhaps? I favour 'Missus'!)
The *Angelus* is when the Old One's fed.
I'll hover by the shutters, on and off,
while pouring out her wine (don't you love 'red'?)
and when you are beneath my window, cough!

XV.

You tell me she is burning, and I'm glad.
She cannot say you're swarthier than I,
and I am fair enough. So let her cry!
Another comment that I'd like to add
is, look at how the hussy's always clad –
disgusting. She's a Franceschini spy,
so let her stew, like them, and pass her by.
The good deserve the good, the bad the bad.
You should have told her that you're carved from ivory.
Or let it drop, you like to lap my milk!
Her dirty game is one-night would-be wivery,
but fustian doesn't feel the same as silk.
I want to leave. No more of her connivery!
I'm done with La Contenti and her ilk!

Be careful, then, tonight, that you see me:
don't wave unless you know there's no mistake.
These days, the Jealous One is wide awake:
as near to bliss as we shall ever be,
let's not destroy it inadvertently.
I do not chide: remember what's at stake,
and use a little caution, for my sake!
It's worth it for our future, you'll agree.
I'll watch for you, my darling, after seven.
Don't be discouraged if the blinds are down.
I've you for joy, anxiety for leaven
(while you are free to range around the town).
Long hours to wait, before I glimpse my heaven!
(Don't loiter near that house of ill-renown!)

XVI.

My Dearest, Most Deserving, Well-Beloved,
I send you Rosalinda's boundless thanks.

The Gadfly, I must tell you, stung my flanks
last evening. On the Poggio, scented, gloved,
he called to me imperiously and shoved
a sonnet in my hand. His conduct ranks
with Girolamo's. Thankfully, the banks
of il torrente were unpeopled. Loved
as dearly as you are, you'll not construe
this news as any kind of test:
for me, you are the handsomest, the best,
and other men's attentions I eschew.
Of loyalty to Guido I divest
myself: all that I am, I rest in you.

XVII.

Adored Signora:
                   Sunday – can we go?
Tomorrow, that is – time is tight. Decide.
We go now, or I fear we never will.
I understand: you're daunted – terrified:
I hate to press you, but I have to know.
Let's grasp the moment, while we have it still.

The town is short of horses, as of broughams
(the Bishop leaves on Wednesday, taking three):
I'm sure I can secure a coach-and-four.
Just put all the arrangements down to me.
Then, not withstanding hurricanes and storms,
by Wednesday we'll reach Rome (if not before!)

Tomorrow morning, if I've bagged our ride,
I'll pass along, beneath your window-sill,
so watch in case my handkerchief should fall.
I'll drop it once – repeat – a single spill,
and that means everything's solidified,
and we are going over Clement's wall.

The plan, then. San Michele striking eight
will find me in the Borgo (other side,
where shadow's denser). Now, your final chore:
you must ensure the family is plied
– that's every person – with the opiate.
Then you can tell Arezzo, 'Never more!'

(Remember not to touch the wine yourself!)
When all are snoring soundly, let me in,
and I will help you carry off your 'haul'.
Our coach is small – don't load us to the chin!
Don't empty every cabinet and shelf.
The night may well be chilly – bring a shawl.

If all goes fatally, throw ope the door!
I'll rush inside and free you from their hands,
or what befalls you, I will, too, abide:
expect of me what chivalry demands.
we'll either wade to safety through their gore,
or I'll be proud to perish with my bride!

LIVISTROS AND RODAMNE, Being an Attempt at a Novella, but Clearly no More than a Fragment, Composed by The Other Half-Rome

STRAY LEAVES: MAN PROPOSES, GOD DISPOSES

Ours is an endless yearning to construe,
convert some track into an avenue,
make totem poles from firewood, hack and hew
pampooties from a pelt of caribou,
but rarely do we ever follow through!
We are a flaccid, not-so-solid crew!
Our plans prodigious, acts accomplished, few!
So why does everything we do, unglue?

Why are we left with rancid residue
in place of pyramids? Do we accrue
an all-too-social fear of peer review?
To halt our hubris, did some god imbue
a failure-function in us? One thing's true:
we always bite off more than we can chew!

From the castles of Killarney
to the pastures of the Po
or wherever young folk gather,
there's a thing they're keen to know.
Is our noble nature blarney?
Are we nothing more than dust?
Is our talk of love mere blather?
Is it nothing more than lust?

At the court of Queen Myrtane
in Armenia, long ago,
came a servant, in a lather:
'There's a minstrel, waits below:
his accent's yerevani,
and his tale is *Love's Unjust*:
will you hear him? Would you rather?'
And she answered, 'Yes, I must!'

In the courtyard of the palace,
on the Patio of the Dove,
stood a young man, bearded, tanned,
free of gorget, garter, glove.
Like some hero drawn from Sallust,
eyes illumined by the fire,
Rapsodos raised up his hand
for silence. 'What's Desire?'

'Are we beasts? Is Nature callous?
Or are we guided from above?

Can sheer sincerity command?
Might eloquence engender love?
I have triumphed over malice,'
(at this point he touched the lyre)
'I have been a lover, and
I need to know if something higher

can inspire or quicken us.'
Looking closely at the Queen,
Rapsodos began to sing.
In the Cyclades, between
Mitylene and Mykonos,
Lay an island known as Cos.
Livistros, its youthful king,
considered Love as outright loss.

'Why let Venus pick on us?
I prefer to stay serene;
not for me, the Pierian Spring.'
Stavros sought to intervene:
'Sire, though grief may sicken us,
each of us must bear our cross.
Love has benefits to bring.'
'Thank you for the thoughtful gloss,'

said the King, with recognition
of his wise man's point of view.
'You've often told me how divine
this Love can be. Can that be true?'
'Love is passion, not perdition,'
Stavros tremblingly replied:
'I have seen the stars align.'
That very night, the wise man died.

On the Patio of the Dove,
Queen and courtiers sit enthralled –

from her seat Myrtane starts –
'Klivoton – that's what you're called!
Now I know the power of Love!
Far from suffering an ousting,
words have force to conquer hearts.
Eloquence outmatches jousting!'

Upright by the courtyard brazier,
Rapsodos, whose eyes are wild,
says 'Yes, my Queen – you thought me gone!
Can it be, we're reconciled?'
Now the coals are redder, lazier,
have undergone a change of mood.
Myrtane and Klitovon
regard each other, Love renewed.

ALWAYS ENDING, always starting,
    love affairs are like the seasons.
Lovers meeting, lovers parting,
    know the heart retains its reasons.

Klitovon once loved and lost her:
    might his passion now prevail?
She saw through 'Rapsodos', impostor,
    and listens to the lover's tale.

* * * *

HAS ANYONE EMERGED FROM LOVE UNSCATHED?
Although I know the world, although I'm strong,
albeit in the Lethe I have bathed,
I bear my scars, and I have borne them long.
So gather close, and feels the embers' glow:
we find a kind of comfort in a throng.
The stars are far off, and the moon is low:
come listen to a careworn lover's song.

A meadow in the Cappadocian hills
in April, in the early morning hours –
how heavenly! The songbirds' dainty trills,
the multi-coloured carpeting of flowers!
Gnarled, timeworn trees were bursting into leaf:
Constantinople never boasted towers
so brave, so beautiful! It's my belief
that earthly Nature draws on Heaven's powers.

I sat and watched, and breathed the morning calm,
a statue in my saddle. Chattering rills
sang antiphons to ferns of timeless charm,
whose leaves had final curls, like osprey bills.
And then I saw him, farther down the slope.
Oppressed (my guess was) by imagined ills,
he moved as if devoid of human hope.
The tulip fills with raindrops, bows, and spills.

His posture was not alien to me.
I've been a lover. Now, I roam the earth
pursuing something that can never be,
my innocence, my peace, a second birth.
A need to speak with him rose in my breast
and, easing spurs into my stallion's girth,
I started forward. Opulently dressed,
the stranger clearly was a man of worth.

* * * *

In Which Livistros is Chided over his Sense of Entitlement, Embodied in His Slaying of a Dove

Livistros! Pampered prince, sad solepsist
who butchers baby goats to make his gloves!
You, in your insolence, your reckless pride,
assuage each whim with a wafting of the wrist,

and take it on yourself to slaughter doves.
Oh, isn't this existence hard enough?
You, endlessly-indulged somnambulist,
egregiously exploiting all that moves,
is this – the light that's in us – yours to snuff?
Have we to hope Lord Livistros approves,
petition his permission to exist?
I chose to die because my lover died –
a sensibility you've clearly missed!
I knew, the day you slayed her at my side,
that *sentit* is a higher realm than *ist*.
Oh, how unfortunate, the heart that loves!
Livistros' path is smooth, where ours is rough.
Remain within your luxury's fixed grooves:
we lesser things are made of sterner stuff.
You know where vengeance dwells? Beyond the cyst.

THE CONGRESS OF THE WITS:

6. *Il Facchino*

Conservative – a defect in the genes
(it's scientific). Theirs, a tuneless carol,
a sea that's waterless – a sort of Aral,
and though we Spartakists are not machines
(still less are we Ted Bundys, Edward Giens),
you wonder why I have to tote this barrel.
It's what is known as working-class apparel
(all toffs are elegant: we're testudines).
Was Michelangelo, as some have claimed,
my father? There's no doubt I've got his nose!
Or was il naso mio thusly maimed
by some right-winger's brickbat, deftly aimed?
Opponents are not axiomatic foes:
why do our disagreements come to blows?

AND NOW THE LAWYERS. FIRST UPON THE STAGE
will be Arcangeli, for the defence.
His reasoning can be a little dense,
as though he knows the battle he must wage
to be beyond him. Fighting to assuage
the doubts he cannot shake, his inner sense
of falling short, his failing confidence
will prompt him to succumb to fits of rage,
a petulance unworthy of his rank.
Effectiveness is difficult to gauge
in this our subtle art but, as each plank
is pulled from under him and each pretense
engulfed by enfilading fire, his age
will tell, and seem (to him) incompetence.

OPENING SUBMISSION OF DOCTOR GIACINTO ARCANGELI, PROCURATOR OF THE POOR, IN DEFENCE OF GUIDO FRANCESCHINI AND CONFEDERATES AT THEIR TRIAL FOR HOMICIDE

Illustrious and Reverend My Lord,
Count Guido Franceschini's noble blood
is what this matter turns on. May one kill
to vindicate one's honour, and yet not

be put to death? *Concedo io* he should
be punished. Giurba says, 'If blood you spill,
the law will always take it untoward.'
But are we talking guilloutine, garotte?

I hardly think so. Marriage boded ill
for Guido. Victim of his in-laws' plot,
he ended with a wife whom he deplored,
but cured the harm, as any good man would.

Pompilia? Francesca? As you will.
Whatever name the papers may record.
Deception never comes to any good,
and what we call her matters not a jot.

The pseudo-parents, grabbing what they could,
attached themselves to quality. With skill
that's preternatural, they sought – and got –
a heretofore unheard-of 'sweet' accord,

transferred themselves to Guido's neighbourhood,
and in his very house proposed to squat,
no term determined, eat and drink their fill.
And then they wondered why they were abhorred!

* * * *

Francesca was failing to furnish an heir,
   but wanted to live unrestrained.
Aware of the grudge that the family bore,
   her feelings of loyalty waned.
The putative parents purported to yearn
   for release, which they duly obtained.

They headed for Rome, where their urgent concern
   was their daughter's disgrace to declare:
they haled her the spawn of some ha'penny whore,
   a slur they were eager to share.
The aretine bishop was badgered and pained,
   with the girl camping out on his stair.

With orders to poison and pillage and burn
   and repay Guido's goodness in gore,
and then to escape to the Latium lair,
   Francesca required an 'amour':

corrupted a man who'd been fully ordained,
   a crime all believers deplore.

Her hatred for Guido now wholly ingrained,
   she plotted her plans to return.
Her paramour parson was prompt to prepare,
   canonical calling to spurn:
he furtively furnished a carriage-and-four,
   and the butter was out of the churn!

* * * *

Francesca and her lover-priest
   made a dash for Rome,
but *fille de joie* and *arriviste*
   didn't make it home,

for Guido caught them on the road
   and had them both detained:
but why no consequences flowed
   has never been explained.

The priest deserved the scaffold, but
   was banished to the coast:
why nothing happened to the slut –
   that baffles me the most!

Francesca, for her mortal sin,
   was convented at first,
but promptly wound up living in
   the place she should have cursed!

* * * *

The pseudo-parents owned her once again!
She spawned her bastard there. We think it rather

fitting how she, in 'Deceivers' Den',
transliterated 'padre' into 'father'!

It's difficult for someone as well-born
as Guido is, to wear the shroud of shame,
subjected to the ridicule and scorn
of all Arezzo. How to clear his name?

He found four feudals from his family farm.
To use the modern parlance, he was 'triggered'.
He meant to do his wife no mortal harm,
but just to leave her suitably disfigured.

Five Tuscans rode to Rome at Christmastime,
the listless, lifeless season of the year,
the realm of swede and sorgum, rooks and rime,
nor did they bring or meet with any cheer.

A ruse was used: 'a message from the priest!'
At this, the pseudo-parents dropped their guard:
the deadbolt, agitated and released,
let retribution, pitiless and hard,

engulf the Comparini. Rightly so! –
reprisal gushing from lascivious acts.
It neatly starts and ends in Popolo.
And there, My Lord, you have the sordid facts.

* * * *

STRAY LEAVES: DULCIA VENENA

We know who Learned Counsel's vulgar vicar is:
the clergyman is none but Caponsacchi.
Arcangeli's exhibiting *aboulia*.

Uncorking *Lex Cornelia de Sicariis*,
and even reaching back to grab the Gracchi,
he's flexing every *Lex,* including *Julia.*

Ill-starred inquisitor, Italian Icarus,
a bungler with the bluster of Bourbaki
(admittedly, the latter was unrulier),

Arcangeli is like a lump of liquorice:
what's sweet is toxic, smooth is often tacky.
The *genus* is renowned: it's called *sterculia*

(but is it *foetida,* or is it *urens?*)
Bourbaki's floundering (or is he Flourens?)

     * * * *

A MAN MAY KILL HIS ERRANT WIFE, and not
bring down upon himself the loss of life.
This is the popular – nay, catchy – gloss
arrived at by the experts. Farinacci
appears, when first perused, to hedge and tarry
on Beatrice Cenci: when you clear the sedge,
however, Farinacci's going nuclear.
She merited the sword, but rather owing
to failure on her part. The daughter-father
nexus held up sound: approve the slaughter,
but only if the slaughter's water-course can move
that injured honour was the driving force.
Rainaldi opts to pass the matter by:
thus we distinguish him, *quod indicat*
that honour, unestablished since brought in,
saves none. You need the mercy of the Prince.

     * * * *

YOUR WIFE COMMITS A SEXUAL TRANSGRESSION?
In any jurisdiction where divorce
is unavailable, you've no recourse
by which you may remove the blemish, freshen
your noble name, save righteous aggression.

You catch her *in flagrante?* By confession?
You have no choice! You cut her throat, perforce
(and later, show appropriate remorse).
When all is said and done, she's your possession:
don't mention murder – merely indiscretion.

    * * * *

MENOCHIO, of course, 'On Arbitration',
is pertinent. And Gomez, to be sure:
the latter, followed cleverly by Claro.
The line's continued by the great Guazzini,
and capped by both the spirited Sperello
and Sacred Rota's Recentest Decisions.

Since Gomez argues, where there is conflation,
(in other words, admissions are not pure),
construction should be anything but narrow,
and benefit must go to Franceschini.
Guazzini would acquit even Othello!
Confessions should be whole, without excisions.

Admit admissions, but with trepidation:
accused who qualify, supply the cure.
A man who adds 'because', gets to the marrow!
The bottle, opened, lets escape the genie.
On this is Claro Farinacci's fellow,
both prudent jurors. Theirs are sound provisions,

applicable to this, our situation.
The Sacred Rota is our cynosure,
as straight and certain as an archer's arrow
(if time were not so tight, I'd cite Guarini!)
The law is at its best when clement, mellow:
and though it handles conflicts and collisions,
serenity is what the law envisions.

    * * *

Forestall the Fisc and spike his gun –
to such do my instructions run.
Suborning helpers – that's just prudent,
as counsels any first-year student.
Conventicle's its fancy name:
it's hiring helpers, just the same.
A young opponent, hardy, armed:
in Guido's shoes, who would have qualmed
to bring some back-up, four in all,
to meet whatever might befall?
Who pays his men, offends no law:
what's privity of contract for?
A plaint in action (they will state)
is guaranteed to aggravate
such misdemeanour as occurred.
(They know the argument's absurd!)
You kill the shill that's suing you
(as some defendants tend to do):
his grievance grounds out, due to want
of prosecution: nonchalant,
just wait, and propagate the drought:
then, straight-faced, hasten, strike it out.
The dead man had a cogent case,
but both are gone, without a trace.
No man can let a wanton live,
still less (in the alternative)

endure pollution longer than
the chance to kill her when he can.
In court and convent, well-protected,
she fell as soon as she defected.
They opened to the lover's lackey:
'I bear a note from Caponsacchi.'
A clever ruse, not poisoned fruit –
too tragic if it doesn't suit!

* * * *

FRANCESCA BROKE HER MARRIAGE VOWS – NO DOUBT.
The wonder is, she didn't end in fetters.
She left her husband for a lusty man,
abandoning her family (her betters),
pursuant to a calculated plan.

Fidelity, the bond she chose to flout,
was not her only crime. The night she ran,
she and her priest, dishonest debtors,
took cash and jewellery. And this began,
we must remember, with romantic letters.

It's all too clear what those two were about.
She let the priest into her husband's home,
to steal his property. She and her 'shriver'
took diamond necklace, lifted silver comb,
and took the booty to their coach-and-fiver.

And they were kissing as their coach set out.
We have the legal statement of their driver!
Thank Providence, they never got to Rome:
for Guido caught the ducker and her diver,
within a bowshot of Saint Peter's dome!

Francesca, disinclined to go without,
was sleeping in her Castelnuovo room,
indulging her adulterous addiction.
(Was this the night he fertilised her womb?)
But now, within the Pontiff's jurisdiction,

Count Guido had the felons by the snout.
Her faithless flight was founded on a fiction.
No need to postulate, or to presume:
this very court decided on conviction
and, in so doing, sealed the sinner's doom.

* * * *

THE BAD ONES, like the good ones, by their acts
reveal themselves. Her letters say it all.
                All of us recall
the Paolo letter's litany of facts,
by which the Comparini gang contracts
a scheme to slay their in-laws. What a gall!

She stated, in that letter, how content
she was to have a husband, kind and wise,
                to lovingly chastise
her childish flaws. It's obvious she meant
those handsome words: malevolent
the hands that gripped her, in parental guise!

Love-letters, as they're called, prove her a trull.
At best, she led the lover by his nose:
                we're driven to suppose
that Caponsacchi was her guilty gull –
or worse, they both surrendered to the pull
of lewd indulgence. Her very words expose

her lack of honesty. Inviting scorn,
committing Castelnuovo perjury,
                      she claimed what could not be:
that she and Caponsacchi came at dawn:
but several other witnesses have sworn
it was a night arrival. Infamy!

She lied. She said, on oath, she couldn't write.
She lied about the Franceschini wealth.
                      With disconcerting stealth,
she robbed her family, the selfsame night
she shamed her husband's name. Illicit flight,
she claimed, was undertaken for her health!

A person on her deathbed, one presumes,
is mindful of the saving of her soul:
                      the one enormous goal
as daylight fades, eternal judgment looms,
to keep from hell. What sort of person dooms
herself by telling lies as black as coal,

to help her paramour, who faces jail?
What kind of wife assails the bishop's palace
                      with tales of spite and malice,
to cause her husband chagrin and travail?
Who trails the Governor, trying to prevail
with filth and scandal? Who could be so callous?

September last, she stood her trial for Flight.
The Fisc, back then, set out to reprehend her.
                      He asked this court to send her
to prison, but today he says she's right.
How strange, now that he has a second bite,
he's straining every sinew to defend her!

Processus Fugae: don't you find it strange
that, if she'd suffered threats of blood,
              she didn't when she could –
in other words, why didn't she arrange
(here, in a court of law) to ring a change?
Why not denounce abuses, as she should?

Because there *were* none. What, then, of her son?
A mother's love is all-embracing, no?
              Apparently, not so.
We know Francesca wasn't quite a nun.
Her latest lover tempted her to shun
the baby. Her estate went to the *beau.*

              * * * *

WHOSE BABY MIGHT SHE BE? HER CHILD IS WHOSE?
She's either Comparini, or she's not.
Enough of shady ambiguity:
pass water, or (they say) get off the pot:
a bourgeoise brat, or run-off from the stews?
Suppose the first – what's then the consequence?
Well, Comparini malice is immense.
They exercised enormous ingenuity
(and not for gain) to denigrate, abuse
and sully Guido's name in perpetuity.
Francesca's not their progeny? Then what?
Why then, there's no more sitting on the fence:
the product of untrammelled promiscuity,
she married Guido by a dirty ruse.
The Comparini, when she tied the knot,
contested every tittle, every jot:
and all the time they practised vile pretence,
to Franceschini detriment, expense!
At least we can applaud their perpiscuity.
One wouldn't be surprised if they were jews.

And who had caused her delicate condition?
It had to be the husband or the priest.
(Her intercourse with Guillichini ceased
before the previous March.) She didn't dare
inform Arezzo (though increasing weight
and girth provoked across-the-board suspicion.
As waistline (and anxiety) increased,
Francesca chose to flee. And who to bear
the burden of so delicate a mission?
The Canon Conti? Gregory the Great?
It had to be her partner in perdition,
the priest who'd placed her in this parlous state.
Alternatively, counter-intuition
suggests the boy was Guido's: did she care?
Elopement meant that, at the very least,
she'd robbed the Franceschini of their heir.
The third concern concerns the girl's estate:
such scraps of evidence as can be pieced
together could be squared to indicate
a *tertium quid* who also got his share!

* * * *

I TURN TO CAPONSACCHI'S BALEFUL ROLE.
A man in holy orders having sex
with someone else's wife is bad enough,
but Caponsacchi sank so deep in sin,
we have to class him as a misanthrope.

The handsome rascal only had to flex
his ample muscles, strum his mandolin,
and she became his eager 'bit of fluff'.
He taught his conquest how to rob and dope
her family, and prejudice her soul.

Before the vile decision to elope,
the priest began to exercise control:
at night, convinced the girl to let him in,
outrageously to pick through Guido's stuff:
de minimis, withal, *non curat lex.*

Preferring silk against his sinning skin,
the runaway sloughed off his holy stole.
When rabat and biretta start to vex,
the gallant goes for gold, rebuffs the ruff:
his codpiece is the cassock's allotrope.

But Guido called the randy dandy's bluff.
(They hang themselves, bequeathed sufficient rope.)
The husband found them, huddled in their hole!
The sordidest and squalidest of wrecks,
they foundered in the bedroom of an inn.

    * * * *

THE COUNT HAD FOUR COMPANIONS IN THE SLAYING:
that all five were involved, there's no gainsaying:
there's evidence which ties them to the slaughter,
but justice does not predicate 'no quarter':
  to say the gang
  should have to hang
is not appropriate, and holds no water.

Accomplices take orders, as required.
Is any crime revealed by being hired?
Look, rather, to the officer commanding.
And further, if the purpose of the banding
  is anodyne,
  the banding's fine,
and Guido acted to restore his standing.

It matters that the principal's involved.
In such a case, the hirelings are absolved.
The master's acts exonerate his aides,
and they, subservient by several grades,
    not mandatories,
     auxiliaries,
are blameless of the brandishing of blades.

If helpers guard the killer, and no more,
protect him as he welters in the gore,
Caballo says they're innocent, perforce.
Caballo is against me, and of course
    I seek what's just,
     as counsel must:
I say Caballo's backing the wrong horse.

Had time allowed, I would have made the case.
The Fisc's avowals, faulty on their face,
are contradicted by the total weight
of learned jurists' writings. They dilate
    (Parisius, Marsilius:
     de Castro's quite punctilious)
on what, for flunkies, makes a fitting fate.

They all opine that death would be too hard.
It follows, if the court must disregard
the gallows, then the vigil and the rack
were not appropriate. We must go back.
    Fair-minded men
     should think again:
what cards are left, take torture from the stack?

Strapado stalls, we're left with no confession
(my learned friend, I'm sure, makes that concession):
in crudest layman's terms, a brutal shivving
should not remove my clients from the living:

                    you use a knife,
                    you lose your life –
a formula too fierce and unforgiving!

                * * * *

FRANCESCA WAS ILLITERATE, they claim.
She couldn't write those letters to her lover,
because she couldn't write. She swore it blind!
So how did she compose her *billets-doux,*
or read the answers from her errant knight?
How daub the characters on every sheet?
How bend her lover's will? How thrill? Excite?

She says she couldn't even sign her name,
that jotting yes or no was far above her,
but this assertion's clearly undermined
by Caponsacchi: he contends she threw
her written letters from her window-height
by pre-arrangement, to him in the street.
We have the evidence, in black and white!

Francesca's letters play a clever game,
as anyone who reads them may discover:
the language languid, learned and refined,
cemented by a literary glue,
with references truly recondite.
The educated style, demure, discreet,
was never scribbled by a neophyte!

                * * * *

YOU WANT TO KNOW WHY SHE ABSCONDED?
You don't need to look very far.
When motives are multiply-fronded,

decisions are often bizarre:
this was plain as a two-cent cigar!

The story's as old as Lot's daughters,
as common as copper for coin:
the easy part, parting the waters:
far sooner we'd sever than join,
when led by the twitch in the groin.

Why she didn't retire to a cloister
is not very easy to see:
it's not like the world was her oyster!
A woman she happened to be:
it wasn't her business to flee.

If running to Rome was a mission
that couldn't be stayed or deferred,
it should have been brought to fruition
by having an intimate word
in ears where she would have been heard,

for example, with Marzi-Medici,
a model of manly discretion.
As eager to learn as to teach, he
was certain to view her transgression
as something that prudence could freshen,

and rinse of its sexual stigma.
He knew all the people of quality:
and here lies the central enigma.
Companions who, free of frivolity,
not given to japing or jollity,

as mellow and cool as October,
could well have escorted the lass.
So, citizens seemly and sober

selected for standing and class
might thus have resolved the *impasse.*

A sort of informal adoption,
some elderly widow, perhaps?
An adequate aretine option
was better than aventine scraps:
Francesca chose moral collapse.

STRAY LEAVES: PLUMA AGGRAVANTES

If I elect the tango as my dance,
do things look blacker if I am a preacher?
Will it go worse for me if, as a teacher,
I turn to pre-teen pupils for romance?
Should all right-minded burghers look askance
when, classifying Khas as 'lesser creatures',
I draw authority from reading Nietszche?
Or will they hardly cast a second glance?
For here we meet the sharp end of the lance.
A detail which may deepen or enhance
my criminality (says my impeacher),
which draws a dreadful punishment perchance,
is termed an aggravating circumstance –
or, equally, an aggravating feature.

* * * *

FOUR AGGRAVATING FEATURES, says the Fisc:
conventicle, the first. But what is that?
Great Sixtus, by his famous bull, *'Immensa',*
proclaimed a law which states (I'll say it flat)
when four men socialise, they run the risk
of death beneath some papal obelisk
by hanging or beheading. Oh, the time!

The morals! Now it counts as kompromat
for men to come together, chew the fat!
In modern Rome, the Pope is now the censor
and men must mind their company, their chat.
Today, association is a crime.
With papal ukase, brusque as it is brisk,
the Governor's Banns, or local statutes, chime.
So I (extended metaphor), a fencer,
must call on my dexterity to whisk
the rapier from my foeman's hand, and I'm
aware that argument will wax intenser.
My thrust will be as just intelligencer,
while they use aggravation to begrime.

The second is the carrying of arms.
We owe it to the recent Constitution
bequeathed to us by blessed Alexander,
Venetian pontiff, Pietro Ottoboni.
Some ancient worthy said (I think it's Lucian)
that if you have to beard a salamander,
best take an arquebus. I must, in candour,
confess that what I've said is sheer baloney.
His Worship smiles. I crave his absolution!
The arquebus is modern. Counsel's qualms
extend to any argument that's phony.
I hope the Fisc is hearing these alarms!
What's *salsa* for the *oca* binds the gander.
When Guido, like a latter-day Lysander,
recruited volunteers from Tuscan farms,
was he incurring legal retribution?
To say, 'You're now my son', as in the Psalms,
to call on claybound clod or cross-grained crony,
is 'help me in my strife', as per *canzone*,
sufficient pretext for an execution?

To kill *ex causa litis* is the third.
One thing above the rest, the courts abhor:
when some disgruntled litigant decides
to substitute his anger for the law,
and murder his opponent in the suit.
This kind of conduct has to be deterred!
It's utterly unseemly and, besides,
how can we ever settle a dispute
when parties fall like flies to homicides?
The Fisc avers that this is what occurred
in this our instant case, but at its root
(we say) such ambiguity abides
that who has cheated whom is more than moot.
Unravelling is what the courts are for,
and where the boundaries are badly blurred,
we have our able judges as our guides.
There is an old and venerable saw,
'give justice only when both sides are heard':
to kill three litigants, we own a flaw,
but aggravation? That's forbidden fruit.

And finally, a homicide in jail –
the weakest of my learned friend's positions.
The case law's clear: a person, once confined
in lawful, court-accredited detention,
is safe from all unwarranted attention.
We can't let private grievances prevail.
Permitting angry parties to assail
a prisoner offends our fine traditions
– a detainee in proper prison, mind!
So much in law depends on definitions.
So, notwithstanding eloquent submissions,
the prohibition can't extend to bail.
as many legal scholars have opined,
asserting 'liberty-with-some-conditions
amounts to custody' is bound to fail.

What one might term domestic intervention
(albeit armed with daggers, barbed and spined)
does not offend our sanctuary convention.
The Comparini home, in our contention,
was not a papal prison, so-defined.

STRAY LEAVES: DE RAPTU HELENAE

We know what Paris did, and why he did it.
She wasn't just your neighbour's cousin Janet –
he'd snatched the hottest totty on the planet!
An old and cranky husband can't forbid it,
but if she was concupiscent, she hid it.
So exit Helen, Menelaus manet,
and Paris pulled his pretty pomegranate!
And as for Helen – timet mulier, or fidit?
Content to be abducted? Would she rather
be left in peace, or looted in a lather?
We'd like to know her feelings, when he caught her.
Some ambiguity about her father
makes matters worse, by muddying the water.
A flighty floozy, or a wife and daughter?

These aggravating factors can indeed
(potentially!) augment a punishment.
The problem that the Fisc must now confront
(supposing that he can in fact succeed)
is, how to make these scrapings supersede
the statutory tariff. I'll be blunt:
these prejudicial features – *ubi sunt?*
The Fisc's about to take a pointless punt.
We ask ourselves, why does he feel the need?
Because he wants to see my client bleed!

The Pincian is not the Palatine,
the Ponte Rotto's not the Pantheon,
and though the Fisc sings like a dying swan,
he can't turn stagnant water into wine.
So, let him polish pointlets till they shine!
The web he wants to weave is woebegone,
a Saturnalian Satyricon
or, as the French would say, *roman roman*.
His circumstances don't with law align:
they aggravate, but do not redefine.

* * * *

Recovering his honour was the urge
which spurred him to recruit his group of men.
Remember, Guido took his time! He waited.

(Of course, the Prosecution seeks to scourge
the Count because he didn't, there and then,
dispatch the woman who had fornicated.)

They settled on the city's frowzy verge,
sequestered in their *Ponte Milvio* den.
Collectively, what was anticipated?

We know how, all too often, motives merge.
They stalled their action nine days, maybe ten:
by this is thoughtless violence negated.

The purpose was undoubtedly to purge
his shame, and make for Tuscany again.
The killing was in no wise aggravated.

* * * *

WE GO TO MUTA FOR A CASE IN POINT.
A man admittedly employed deceit
in order to confront his wife (estranged,
alas!) and, for her shamelessness, to mete
out punishment emphatic and complete.

The husband was still willing to anoint
her, should she undertake to be discreet.
He found her unrepentant and unchanged,
and took her life. He left her in the street,
a carcass for the feral dogs to eat.

In sentencing, the issues were conjoint:
a killing, with deception – how to treat
the husband? Things were fittingly arranged.
His punishment was adequate and meet:
to row the galleys of the papal fleet.

A GLANCE, now, through the lens of Sanfelicius,
who tells us of a sharp domestic schism:
the wife's transgression, worse than Molinism,
was something infinitely meretricious.
From early on, the signs were inauspicious.
The marriage fell apart by fits and starts,
until the wife, despite the Lex Cornelia,
ended quite as dead as Saint Cecilia.
The husband felt sufficiently capricious
to mutilate his partner's private parts.
Yet, viewed through Sanfelicious' primmest prism
(the husband had offended Rome's decorum
by carrying armorum igneorum),
the penalty, just four years' ostracism.

* * * *

A COUPLE OF CATALAN CASES
reported on similar bases
may help us decide
on the precepts applied
in the sentence my client now faces.

Offences concerning the Banns
are addressed by Matteos de Sanz:
wives were killed or abused,
noting firearms were used,
in pursuit of elaborate plans.

The culprits eventually vanished –
in other words, both men were banished –
we should keep in mind
they were fearsomely fined:
we can all learn a lot from the Spanish!

* * * *

A LAWFUL PURPOSE HAS THE STRONG EFFECT
of making meetings legal. This applies
to Guido, who was salvaging his honour.
This is a ruling of the Sacred Rota,
our highest court of law, correctly rendered.

I think my learned friend hopes to deflect
the point by citing cases thick as flies
around Lucrezia Borgia's *sottogonna*:
but are they probative? Not one iota!
His argument is dead before it's tendered.

A man is injured when a ship is wrecked:
a chip of marble blinds a mason's eyes:
my body's not my honour, by Madonna!

they'll hardly keep conventicle afloat, or
support the other nonsense he's engendered.

* * * *

I STAND UPON THE WORDING OF THE BANNS.
The scholars Serafini and Blanchetti
(both cardinals) say, laws are meant to mend
the rips and fissures which at times occur.

THE TEXT SUGGESTS A PENALTY WHICH SPANS
all gatherings which fail (to Doctor Spreti
I offer thanks for such superbly-penned
research: to such a talent, I defer!)

However, on the point of those with plans
which reach fruition (lest you think this petty,
pray hear me out), the Banns to silence tend.
Qui tacet consentire videtur!

* * * *

AND ON, then, to the carrying of arms.
The same is not a stand-alone offence:
it merges with the crime for which they're carried.

A man must answer for the one he harms:
to say as much is merely common sense.
What if he harms the one to whom he's married?

Guazzini gives the arquebus example:
The husband feels his honour is impugned,
and takes his weapon, bent on satisfaction.

The powers of the court are more than ample:
he's punished, not for weapons, but the wound –
by far the less condemnable infraction.

And verily, who clambers up the wall
by city ordnance courts the pain of death,
but lawyers can be dexterously deft:

if taken in the precinct with his haul,
is he about to draw his final breath?
No. Castigate him only for the theft.

    * * * *

Vexatious Litigation

The moment she says 'nunc dimittis',
She's showing she knows where the slit is:
a female philanderer's charter
now comes into play,
and I'm sorry to say
you're reduced to a masculine martyr.

She's suing you vexatiously,
and you can't raise a finger:
she's acting contumaceously,
to slap you with a stinger:
she's holding on tenaciously,
in case some traces linger,
and doing it audaciously
to put you through the wringer!

She's arguing *ex causa litis:*
you're now going to learn what 'submit' is:
she's got a garotte called a garter.
To your utter dismay,

you are bound to obey.
It would never have happened in Sparta!

      * * * *

THE CONSTITUTION OF THE BORGIA POPE
declares it ultra-criminal to kill
a man (or woman) if you're tangled still
in litigation. It's the slippery slope
if plaintiff or defendant's free to spill
his adversary's blood. Our only hope
is, let all parties know we take it ill.
You'd go against the Holy Father's will?
You'd push the waste-my-rival envelope?
Fine. Welcome to our 'aggravation drill':
your neck will feel our retribution rope.

But aggravation finds no purchase here.
To raise the matter (we say) is fallacious:
the Comparini lawsuit was vexatious,
intended as a barb, a spiteful smear.
Malevolence so stark, so ostentatious,
abuse of process clangorously clear,
can not be left to thrive. The court is gracious,
and will be (we are certain) perspicacious
in acting as a skilful scrutineer.
Your Lordship, so straight-shooting, so sagacious,
will make *ex causa litis* disappear.

      * * * *

TO KILL A PERSON WHILST ON PRISON PREMISES
is not a poison chalice (merely mustard-y):
the charge, as laid, is hardly Guido's nemesis:
one's parents' home is never 'custody'.
And furthermore, we have another layer.

His wounded honour rendered Guido blind:
he didn't form the requisite *mens rea:*
in other words, there was no guilty mind.

* * * *

Unfortunately, blood has now been spilt:
let's not spill any more. Need Guido die?
Or should our common decency apply?
This aggravation shambles has been built
on insubstantial spite, on shifting silt.
Justiciers, My Lord, like you and I
are here to track the truth, expose the lie:
our purpose, not to titillate or tilt.
It's not our place to grandstand, gratify
our crueller instincts, or to stitch a quilt
of patchwork pedantry, to vilify.
The Fisc is out to stymie, stultify.
He'd love to plunge the sentence to the hilt,
but provocation takes the edge off guilt.

We say that Guido stabbed his wife, at worst:
at best, he ordered it, and saw it through.
But when the court considers why he slew,
who can forget the umbrage that he nursed?
We might say, morally, he was coerced:
a factor which no lawcourt can eschew.
With time, the sharp resentment only grew,
unquenchable as any mortal thirst.
It climaxed in the fatal rendez-vous.
Should Guido have relented, or reversed
his dark trajectory? We misconstrue
humanity, to think he'd change his hue.
Don't label him iniquitous, accursed:
he did what any decent man would do.

SUBMISSION OF DOCTOR DESIDERIO SPRETI, ADVOCATE OF THE POOR, IN DEFENCE OF GUIDO FRANCESCHINI AND HIS ASSOCIATES DURING THEIR TRIAL FOR HOMICIDE, JANUARY 1698

Is my meticulous perhaps your petty?
Is your resilient another's drudge?
Do we admire an arguer who will not budge?
A bridge is far more useful than a jetty,
a rapier needs more skill than a machete.
The man who's standing now before the judge
evinces clarity, despises fudge.
He's Desiderio, and he's surnamed Spreti.

The Advocate of All the Roman Poor,
his thankless task is speaking up for Guido.
However disagreeable the chore,
this is a man of conscience, as of credo:
no point he'll pass, authority ignore:
at last has Guido found his pastor fido!

I PRAY IT PLEASE OUR PONTIFF: I APPEAR
              to open the defence.
The homicides alleged against these men –
those four are farmyard workers, this a peer –
              make scanty legal sense.
              Count Guido Franceschini
has answered to your summons once again,
indicted by my eminent learned friend,
              the feted Fisc, Bottini,
sustained by Master Gambi's able pen.
              My learned leader here
(I now unstop the bottle, loose the genie!),
the great Arcangeli, whose eloquence

and diligence are prized from Prague to Prato,
              will shortly have his say.
Three Comparini people lost their lives.
(Concessions in my paltry *pizzicato*
              will merely pave the way
                  for full and frank admissions.)
I hold that men are right to murder wives,
provided that the climax of the knives
              meets certain preconditions.
My Lord, when Ser Giacinto once contrives
              his clinching *obbligato*,
the prosecutors, competent tacticians,
will find themselves with clumsy feet of clay.

A Roman woman weds a Tuscan count.
              The duties of a wife
displease her, so she takes a local priest
as lover. As the scandal starts to mount,
              the rumours which are rife,
              the *mores* she's disdained,
embolden her. She wants to be released.
Thus lust to scandal is as bread to yeast:
              irrevocably stained,
descended to the level of a beast,
              (how painful to recount!)
she runs away. Audacious, unconstrained,
she and her lover flout our Christian life.

The husband tracks them down, has them detained.
              They're punished by the court.
Effrontery on impropriety piled!
A baby is delivered, unexplained.
              Its provenance, in short,
              is hardly esoteric.
The husband, denigrated and reviled,
is now confronted with a bastard child,

                    the offspring of the cleric!
A man must to his worth be reconciled,
                    respect, once lost, regained.
He killed her at the story's climacteric,
as all good husbands and good chritians ought.

'I killed her. Honour is the principal thing.'
                    Ambiguous? Obscure?
Impossible to addle or mistake.
Count Guido's words are clearly uttering
                    in verbal cynosure,
                    spontaneous and brisk,
the best confession that a man can make.
No cause or reason to divide the cake.
                    'One moment,' says the Fisc,
'let's cut the part which says, 'for honour's sake' '.
                    But Guido's reasons ring
as monolithic as the obelisk
of Axum, and as likely to endure.

So, as I tilt my lance at honour's cause,
                    I mention off the cuff
(this to Your Lordship), Justice is not blind.
Enlightened judges, yes, apply the laws,
                    and yet are better stuff:
                    the decency they bring
converts them to defenders of a kind.
Should this man to the scaffold be consigned?
                    To Ulpian I cling!
A cuckold is disordered in his mind
                    – and there I wish to pause:
get home on honour, death must lose its sting.
And don't forget – suspicion is enough.

Yes, four of five defendants have confessed,
                    but torturers extracted

admissions in conditions far from just,
suspicious circumstances which, at best,
        adversely have impacted
        proceedings. Here's the gist
of Paolo's Constitution: torture must
be kept for crimes which fill us with disgust.
        The Bible has been kissed?
        Or should we take those witness' words on trust?
In summary, the test:
        for 'most atrocious', torture is enacted –
but only where the strongest proofs exist.

Of aggravating factors, there are none.
        I've nothing to pre-empt.
The lesser is subsumed within the greater,
and Policardo, not to be forgone,
        has nothing but contempt
        for part-time pulpit preachers
whose prosecuting passion tries to cater
for what is, mildly-put, extraneous data.
        The aggravating features
        are nullified, should any surface later,
for we can blame them on
        'disordered mind', as legal scholars teach us.
In any case, all nobles are exempt!

The doctrine which we've named *ex intervalo*'s
        agreed and settled law,
and so the Sacred Council has decreed.
The man who waits, then kills, need fear no gallows:
        if Samson's ass's jaw,
        relying on Marsilius,
were wielded in revenge for some dark deed
which went before, what if the doer bleed?
        (You think me supercilious?
        Then so, too, are the authors whom I plead.

Stay stranded in the shallows!
                Some advocates are prudently punctilious,
while others, half-hermetic, hem and haw.)

Like haemophiliacs, all men of noble blood
                appear encumbered debtors:
they're victims of their honour, in a sense.
Their good name matters (emphasis on 'good').
                Count Guido knows no letters:
                but when he killed his wife
it was a sort of noble self-defence.
There's no *mens rea* where you lack the *mens*,
                although you hold the knife.
                You'd hang his minions for the same offence?
I can't see how you could.
                A noble's honour is his very life.
But if he lives, then so must his abettors!

Her deathbed declaration has no worth.
                It wasn't made on oath.
Those men who tended her were all suborned,
the greatest money-grab on planet Earth,
                transacted by them both:
                he, heir to her estate,
she, the bed-polluter unadorned
who husband, home and hearth so coldly scorned.
                Hers was a fitting fate,
                  felled by the very husband she had horned:
with Cayetano's birth,
                Tighetti's opportunity for growth
put coppers on the friars' begging-plate.

The parents of That Woman also died:
                they got what they deserved!
As Guido tells, at every turn they stalled him,
insulted him, equivocated, lied,

      deceived, deflected, swerved.
      The ice on which they skated
proved thinner than they'd thought. The names they called him,
the rumours that they mongered so appalled him,
      that in the end he hated
        his proxy parents. What especially galled him,
it cannot be denied,
        was trumpeting her bastardy. Unnerved,
he took revenge. They were exterminated.

Confessions are unsafe, and vitiated.
       I've said as much, and clearly,
and Blasio has not confessed at all.
The case against the co-accused, as stated,
       asserted cavalierly,
       is unsupported fiction.
These men are Tuscans, we should all recall,
not subject to our laws. We strike the wall!
      In abject dereliction
      of moral law, the Fisc remains in thrall
to theories unrelated
       to law or fact. We punish less severely
accomplices, says Baldo, on conviction.

Our laws forbid, within the walls of Rome,
      the carrying of arms.
If men cohere in groups of more than three,
it's called 'conventicle' (illegal on our loam),
      while other social harms
      such as the use of guile
may aggravate, or worsen by degree,
crimes perpetrated in the Holy See.
      It's hard to reconcile
       the fourth – 'domestic breach'. Why should it be?
Invading someone's home

                    makes murder worse? The Fisc rings these alarms
from Cosmedin's cloud-cleaving campanile!

The learned Policardo: 'knives and guns
                    shall merit no reproof'.
Thus weapons are disposed of. Now the rest.
The small infraction, so the doctrine runs,
                    does not bring down the roof:
                        within the greater charge
it finds itself subsumed. I might suggest
conventicle is thoroughly addressed
                    by homicide. The large
                        offence includes the lesser in its ample breast.
Guile! My submission shuns
                    this flawed assertion. The villain's warp and woof
has always been deception. If you barge

across the threshold of my Caelian house
                    and cut my wretched throat:
suppose you find me sleeping in my bed
and there you slay me and my doting spouse:
                    do I end up more dead
                    than if I were attacked
inside the Rospigliosi, say, instead?
I'd care where I was hacked, and where I bled?
                    The law bites on the fact,
                        not on unknowables, like sense of dread.
Transgression trumps a grouse!
                    The prosecution's not allowed to float
emotion for the evidence it lacked.

The Canon Caponsacchi stood right there,
                    in this, Your Lordship's dock,
convicted of adultery. He, a priest!
Your Lordship is most certainly aware
                    that young, vainglorious cock

                    just twenty weeks ago
was sentenced with his lover, since deceased.
The lover was, effectively, released.
                    My learned friends will know
                            the sentencing remarks which sent the beast
to ostracism, where
                    he's lucky to escape the chopping-block.
For one last damning shaft I bend my bow.

Three days, two nights, they passed in that caleche,
                    That Woman and her suitor,
en voyage from Arezzo to this city.
We know about temptations of the flesh.
                    The priest was not a neuter.
                    Why did he go along?
His work was in Arezzo. Out of pity?
Of course it wasn't! Now the nitty-gritty:
                    it was the same old song,
                            and she sang descant in the curate's ditty.
They halted to refresh?
                    A man and girl alone means sex, says Muta,
and more so if she's pretty. Is Muta wrong?

My reverence for the Fisc has, since my youth,
                    been utter and immense.
My jibes are never meant *ad hominem*.
Imperfect mortals, striving for the truth,
                    will tend to offend, incense,
                            produce more heat than light.
The logic of our job is to condemn,
detract, create a tribal 'us and them'.
                    But rancour's never right:
                            our mission is to build Jerusalem.
If I have seemed uncouth,
                    I tried (but failed) to match his eloquence.
I've learnt some law. The Fisc is erudite.

SUBMISSION OF DOCTOR FRANCESCO GAMBI, PROCURATOR OF THE FISC, IN THE PROSECUTION OF COUNT GUIDO FRANCESCHINI AND HIS ASSOCIATES

This man and his accomplices, we say,
    committed homicide.
No subtle arguments remain in play.
There's nowhere left for them to hide
    in open light of day.

Count Guido Franceschini, aretine,
    a minor nobleman,
contracted marriage to preserve his line:
he, thirty-six years old, an also-ran,
    was seeking to combine

his fortunes with the wealth (as he supposed)
    inheritable soon,
of one young Roman girl. The deal was closed,
but Guido wound up baying at the moon,
    his penury exposed.

The girl he'd wed was thirteen years of age,
    Pompilia of Rome.
He sought to clap his in-laws in a cage
by bringing them to his Arezzo home,
    and there to wage

relentless mental war of dour attrition
    on the parents of the bride.
He held their worldly goods. His simple mission?
Impose conditions no-one could abide,
    provoking nuclear fission,

and drive the Comparini out. The child,
        now part of Guido's goods,
would have to stay. Humiliations piled,
ferocious lawsuits flowed like Florence floods,
        with affidavits filed

in Tuscany, as in the Papal States.
        The Comparini left
(December until Easter were the dates).
The mother, preternaturally deft
        at vengeances and hates,

devised a spike to trouble Guido's tripes.
        She cut her daughter loose.
A changeling child! A million guttersnipes
of Roman slums, the offspring of abuse –
        such were Pompilia's types!

So fragile, Guido's feelings for his name,
        so ominous his dread
of living in Arezzo mired in shame,
that those responsible must end up dead.
        He knew just who to blame.

That's when the greatest hammer-blow came down.
        His pretty wife eloped,
together with the gallant of the town
while Guido snored, so sweetly duped and doped,
        a comic cuckold clown.

Recovering, he set off in pursuit
        and caught them at an inn:
but Guido was too timid (or astute)
to start a swordfight that he couldn't win.
        He chose to prosecute.

He thought the fugitives would meet their death,
   but nothing of the kind
occurred. Defendants, claimant held their breath:
'One minor indiscretion's all we find.'
   And, just like scriptural Seth,

Count Franceschini set to planting seed,
   but these were dragon's teeth.
A will to vengeance, fanned by abject greed
(with knowledge of ineptness underneath.)
   The wish invokes the deed.

Instead of death, the Canon got three years'
   professional relegation.
Count Franceschini can't believe his ears:
his faithless wife Pompilia's destination,
   amid applause and cheers,

a lodging in the convent *Le Scalette*,
   protecting life and limb.
As mentioned by the learned Doctor Spreti,
the court was trying to shield his wife from *him*.
   A man as small and petty

as Franceschini cavilled to defray
   his wife's routine expenses.
In consequence, the court said she could stay
at home again – and Guido lost his senses.
   Someone would have to pay!

Pompilia was pregnant. No-one knows
   who sired her baby boy
(not even the father), Franceschini chose
a makeshift team to track down and destroy
   imaginary foes.

The five assassins came on Christmas Eve
        (the one that's just gone by).
They had one single object to achieve:
the Comparini family had to die.
        Their plan was then to leave

for Tuscany, and safety. They would use
        a trick to breach the home,
a Caponsacchi message as a ruse.
They'd stab the adults, then get out of Rome:
        how could they possibly lose?

The family was subsequently killed.
        Pompilia held out
for four long days, since Providence had willed
that she alone eliminate all doubt
        before her voice was stilled.

The murderers were captured in Merluzza,
        within the Papal Lands.
Each blood-encrusted, horseless Tuscan loser
was taken with his dagger in his hands,
        endorsing his accuser.

DURING A LUNCHEON ADJOURNMENT, GIOVANNI BATTISTA BOTTINI, ADVOCATE OF THE FISC, FINALISES HIS FORENSIC STRATEGY

I did it, Cecco! Bagged the table corner.
The staff suppose us humble papal scribes,
which I quite like. I won't be a suborner,
a 'look at me, I'm distributing bribes!'

The alcove's for the *Nuncio* and friends.
I far prefer to dine with *capotari*
and ledger clerks on tavern table-ends.
How good is this? Saint Nicholas of Bari!

I love the bustle, seek the cheek-by-jowl,
and won't eat in the Vatican. Calf's liver!
How splendid! (These poor things we disembowel!)
My one strict stricture – get across the river!

The gravy's good today. You have to try it.
You've brought your notes? Arcangeli's submission?
That's excellent. I love the Roman diet.
The *gnocchi,* won't you, Cecco? *Nur ein Bischen!*

They've saved a pale Venetian table-wine
that might delight you. Startlingly strong,
it's clean and clear and quietly divine,
and feels like gold leaf wrapping round your tongue.

Arcangeli's a good and decent man.
His knowledge of authorities? Unique.
But playing hard-faced cards? He never can.
He comes across as vacillating, weak,

but really he's just honest. Won't you share?
He has no guile. You see it in his face.
The *saltimbocca*? That's ours. Put it there.
He knows his client hasn't got a case.

His opening remarks were by-the-by.
You're right – he wasn't sitting on the fence!
But I caught Guvnor Venturini's eye:
what counsel says is never evidence.

* * * *

There's something at play here
that must be addressed,
and 'case-law distraction'
expresses it best.

They read something at us
at only a skim:
we panic, and think that
we're out on a limb.

There's naught so misleading
as belching out cases:
you've got the decision,
but what was the basis?

The facts and the figures,
at best, are elided:
we struggle to know
how the thing was decided.

They're tight with the truth
when they set out their stall:
suppose he went guilty?
That changes it all!

Arcangeli's crafty:
I know him of old.
I know how his openings
always unfold.

They're pucker authorities?
Nah, it's a cheat!
He's reading the headnotes,
ignoring the meat.

He wants to upset us –
it's one of his talents,
to make us feel nervous
and throw us off balance.

Each case is a planet,
with oceans and land,
with shallows and seaweed,
expanses of sand.

It needs to be pondered
and savoured and studied,
not used as a ruse,
so that waters are muddied.

Arcangeli's putting us
under the lash,
but if he keeps spouting,
I'll settle his hash.

He knows he can't linger:
he's got other courts.
Let's seek an adjournment,
to read the reports!

* * * *

They've got to prove adultery to win it;
it's not enough to claim it – they must show it!
And how might they do that?
Don't let the thing become a zoo;
ask yourself what does the other side
least of all want us to do?

So, sing the legal doctors like a linnet,
their names are sonorous, so be a poet!

Just reel the names off pat;
Pomponius is with us, Labeo,
Gomez, Gaillard (how the names elide!) –
throw Solon in, and Draco, too!

Revenge must be immediate, or bin it.
If it was really sex, we have to know it:
they must do more than chat.
Why dawdle months, then see it through?
Why was it January, the mother died?
He let 'his' baby's birth fall due!

* * * *

ARCANGELI RELIES UPON THE LETTERS
to say she was dishonest. The Eloping
will constitute his second limb. These 'metas',
he hopes, will get him home to a decision.
He'll cite the husband's surreptitious doping,
but we can meet his surmise with derision!

Arcangeli and Spreti are go-getters,
you know the type – bad haircuts, shoulders sloping –
who liberate their brains from real-life fetters,
confounding common-sense with baseless 'vision'.
Incontinently speculating, groping,
one thing they never offer – that's precision.

The Castelnuovo judges are our betters:
an outcome gentler than the wildest hoping
leaves Caponsacchi and the girl their debtors:
Arcangeli's dark factual collision
is thus impossible. There is no coping
when 'should' and 'is' are in such hard division.

The law says, who asserts is he who proves.
Your honour is the thing on which you dote?
You're then estopped from saying it behooves
the government to wield a mighty chopper:
control your own affairs? That's how you'd vote?
Then if you come to law, you'll come a cropper.

To witnesses, reactions run in grooves:
Contenti's pretty, says they passed a note:
but pretty girls have often horns and hooves:
and though the judges love a Happy Shopper,
she has no clue what anybody wrote.
What else, save black, was Caponsacchi's topper?

A winning point is one that heartens, moves;
you know it, for you feel the urge to gloat,
and I'm inclined to shout from Roman roofs:
'You think you've got a runner? We've a stopper!'
Arcangeli can't show, merely showboat:
Pompilia did nothing that's improper!

* * * *

Necessity is not hemmed-in by law,
nor should it be. This was no student jape,
no throwing-on a cape, yet pause to thieve
the husband's jewels, then fade into the night.

The child was in a very ugly scrape.
We'd all do what we could, just to relieve
the strain. She wasn't one to fly a kite.
It's not a case of What The Butler Saw:

She'd lost her parents, with no chance to grieve.
The girl was bullied, broken – flattened, quite –

the babe that was to be was sure to gnaw
at her, provoking pictures of escape.

Say, 'love affair.'. It's maddeningly trite:
a gutter-press and media gew-gaw:
too facile, just a cloak with which to drape
a thing so vast and painful to achieve:

so hard to carry off without a flaw.
She did it, and she kept her moral shape.
Imagine what it took for her to leave:
imagine how she suffered in that flight!

* * * *

Her note to Paolo strikes me as the key.
He's justifying to his bully brother
the thing he is, the way he has to be.
 As Miller said, there'll never be another.

A woman has to look out for herself
and this holds true, whether she's weak or strong;
she plans to not be 'by-passed', 'on the shelf' –
your bodyguards might kill you – Huey Long.

Imagine you're Pompilia, and you meet
The Perfect Man (albeit sacerdote).
Can life without him ever be complete?
Is every man some type of Don Quijote?

If you were ever in that situation,
You'd want a man like him to be your lackey;
he's perfect for your age, your sex, your station;
who wouldn't want Giuseppe Caponsacchi?

* * * *

Arcangeli loves La Contenti.
He thinks her his Witness of Plenty:
      we bring up her shame
      and blacken her name
in the eyes of the Court's Cognoscenti.

Some Bronte broad (Emily, Charlotte)
might merit a letter that's scarlet:
      she can spin out a tale
      but to little avail –
for you can't trust the word of a harlot!

And what did the coach-driver face?
Malodorous, pestilent place!
      Shut up in a cell
      – simulacrum of hell –
you're poor – no-one champions your case!

Who knows when imprisonment ends?
(You're locked up by Guido's good friends.)
      But a word at a trial
      with a wink and a smile,
may magically pay dividends!

'Just say that you spotted some kissing.
Unreadable novels, like Gissing:
      just spin out a yarn
      and go twice round the barn,
just like when your dad's reminiscing.'

Five years, lots of days will go by:
two thousand, not seeing the sky.
      But he got unbarred:
      it wasn't so hard:
he had two thousand reasons to lie!

* * * *

MOSCARDO AND MARSILIUS OPINE:
we must respect a dying declaration.
And you may think that's only common sense,
a natural and obvious assumption.
This doctrine has the merit to combine
the best of all that's Grecian (some say 'Thracian')
with Europe's other current that's immense,
Teutonic wisdom, better known as 'gumption'.

To claim it has no worth is asinine:
it's Western Logic's total abnegation.
You want to overturn it? Evidence
is what you have to offer. A presumption
though underlying, hidden, clandestine,
which still enjoys a virulent gestation:
(a creed, they say, which favours the Defence
and rules the world, as widespread as consumption).

STRAY LEAVES: IN A SPANISH CLOISTER

You're on your deathbed, staring at the void:
why damn the soul that's now to be released?
Elation isn't centred in the priest,
but you, the masochistic paranoid
(I'm still a doughty advocate of Freud)
are looking at a famine or a feast.
Undisciplined remarks, thoughts unpoliced
and you will find all future joy destroyed.

It's hard for protestants to ponder hell
as do the papist toilers in the quarry.
That moment when the gaudy carousel
comes off its axis, and the whole thing stops,

you mustn't die without first saying 'sorry':
confession is the handiest of props!

THE SACRAMENT OF RECONCILIATION –
can you buy into it, or can you not?
Is it a thing, or is it diddly-squat?
A vapid papal anal syncopation?
Just Blatty and the Jesuit population
of Georgetown stay the ones to give a jot?
or is Confession real, effective, *hot*?
Or is it purely arid abnegation?

You're dying, and you're focused on salvation –
all good ideas are plain (harmonious fists):
and this is where you fail, you Molinists –
Augustine and Boethius, and Pelagian –
to make a cast-iron case, *contra Pelagius,*
the worst thing you can do is seem outrageous.

* * * *

WHAT NEED HAVE WE OF STATUTE, legal tome?
We lean upon the common law: insist.
Don't lose your bearings in the case-law mist:
illegal knives, unauthorised assembly –
who cares if they turned Pópolo into Wembley?
Yes, wear the glove, but wear it on a fist:
we'll let Arcangeli and Spreti twist:
just let the library lie: no need to comb
the antecedents of the Courts of Rome.
It's all too easy to get edgy, trembly:
what boots it, they were murdered in their home?
He killed the parents – we don't need a list,
or aggravating factors for more grist:
we just need proofs – and proofs enough exist!

* * * *

THEY'LL SAY IT'S WRONG
that torture was allowed:
that, all along,
a nobleman so proud
should get by on his word.

But he's the worst
of cowardly wincers,
coughed up when first
he glimpsed (not felt) the pincers,
and sang out like a bird.
That's what throws it.

There is no doubt
they'll want the call reversed,
it's turning out:
since then the bubble's burst,
and out goes his confession.

But Venturini
was not born on a farm,
like Franceschini.
This judge – no vestige of alarm –
enjoys a wide discretion.
And he knows it.

* * * *

AFFIDAVITS OF PRIESTS WHO ATTENDED
the girl, in her ultimate throes,
they will argue, should now be suspended –
procedure is sorely offended –
by testaments hollow as those.

Our evidence should be up-ended,
their argument seemingly goes:
the decent young man who befriended
and spent well, and stoutly defended
his Cross (though disguised as a Rose),

the one whom we know as Tighetti,
the lover who stayed at her side,
will find himself slandered by Spreti.
The theory appears somewhat petty –
since, after all, somebody died!

Like Guido was sure the *confetti*
(a thing husbands take in their stride)
were aimed, and his child-wife complied,
the zealots (increasingly sweaty)
are saying that seven priests lied!

* * * *

THE LETTERS WHICH WERE 'FOUND' IN THE LATRINE
(oh, wasn't that a rather fortunate find!),
conveniently light on names and dates,
created to impress the reader's mind,
unrealistic, fact-free and opaque.
What is this letter-novel meant to mean?
Someone has used a recipe to bake
this strange confection, whose inherent traits
suggest one author, one unbroken fake.
The moods expressed, the passions and the hates,
stuff biographical from which we glean
bald facts of what I'd term the gossip kind.
As evidence, it's worthless – undermined
by lack of detail, such as enervates
concocted testimony – as is seen
when some third party deigns to undertake

a forgery. No living person signed
these documents, a fact which indicates
a fabrication. Propaganda's sake?
Or aimed at Caponsacchi, out of spleen?

It's crap, that Amaryllis and Myrtillo,
the kind of guff on which young virgins dote:
a fantasy (which is to say, fool's charter),
composed for those who cry into their pillow.
But someone, somewhere, capable of guile
devised these letters, thought them through, and wrote,
and laced them with Guarinian crank and quote:
this someone listed every pecadillo
and clearly knew the two enamorata.
To say they're genuine is a non-starter:
Pompilia couldn't write, and her denial
is now a matter of judicial note.
The plan, no doubt, was at some roadside willow
to tackle Caponsacchi by the throat,
confront him with this bundle's poison phiall
and watch the chemicals which therefrom billow.
It's soft on Guido, well-known saint and martyr.
It's women's stuff, emotional and vile,
all written in a cloyed romantic style,
the work of Canon Conti's cold *cognata*.

* * * *

THEIR THEORY OF THE LETTERS GOES LIKE THIS:
they hold that Caponsacchi got off light.
Inordinately humble and polite,
without confessing, eager to confess,
ineffably retiring and contrite
(demeanour which can't help but have effect),
as inoffensive as if he were Swiss,

he underlined his titre de noblesse,
and worked his magic: able to deflect

as charmingly as later, Alger Hiss
was apt to do, and show he was upright.
Nothing was done within Saint Peter's sight
and, to his real and unallayed distress,
in civitatem, just a neophyte,
he was not Roman, accordingly not echt:
tis trip had been a youth's anabasis.
He was by this preposterous finesse
judicial harshness able to deflect.

But this account is easy to dismiss:
at Castelnuovo on the final night,
immured with her and quite prepared to fight,
he was within our borders. Authors stress
(read Cyrill, Farinacci) no priest might
slough off his Romanness, nor reject
(if he would wish to enter into Bliss)
the Holy Father's infinite caress,
to whom he always has to genuflect.

STRAY LEAVES: A GAME AT CHESS

A love affair is like a game of chess,
and so it was with her. To her dismay,
she had to serve herself, she had to play.
Suppose it Courtly Love: she must address
the power of sex – nay, sexual excess –
but life is rarely black or white. It's grey.
She'd have to be the fawn, the Hart at Bay.
Arezzo would provide her grave, unless.

The Canon did it all because he could;
it seemed a chance for fun, from where he stood
(with Courtly Love, it's someone else's wife).
Is Love the same as Sex, or is it not?
Is Easyjet the same as Aeroflot?
She played the game to try to save her life.

    * * * *

Don't we all know the status of a lawyer's top-sheet?
A court heard the witnesses, back in September:
it made, as it must, its determination.
but a top-sheet proves nothing, it's a deception.

For Pompilia, the ruling was not a defeat:
no sentence was passed then, we have to remember:
no finding of guilt, case termination:
though that's contrary to the widespread perception.

She said she was blameless, a point to repeat:
It's not our intention to re-stir the ember:
but everyone knows that a dying declaration
is the best that there is, as a hearsay exception.

    * * * *

'So why is Caponsacchi, then, excused?'
the cry goes up. 'Let's get the Canon here!'
'We won't have talk of quality or breeding:
let's jail the crooks, the innocent are cleared.'

But Caponsacchi isn't the Accused.
No court has force to drag him by the ear:
he needn't post for bail or enter pleadings:
or answer to a jury of his peers.

My Learned Friend appears a mite confused:
nonplussed, where recently so cavalier.
The Canon plays no part in these proceedings –
defendants are the ones to be cashiered.

THE HISTORY OF THE TRUE CROSS: (8)
The Battle of Nineveh

A static battle, when all's said and done.
Is that Chosroes, kneeling, on the right?
His captors seem excessively polite.
A bearded man is joining in the fun
and doesn't seem to know the Greeks have won
by such a feeble neck-stab, flimsy, light,
(his victim isn't putting up a fight)
we'd hardly think the warring had begun.

The foreground figure, pleading for his life,
is just not realistic: William Blatty
the one who's coming for him with the knife,
whose breastplate is inordinately natty,
is balancing a soup-plate on his head:
and thus does Piero fill our hearts with dread.

STRAY LEAVES: THE BATTLE OF BENEVENTO

Historians love battles. They're so neat!
They sort the issues, like a balance-sheet.
Reality's too ragged.   Nothing squares,
and expertise? That's merely splitting hairs.

So how did Manfred manage his defeat?
How pass his time on Purgatory Street?

For Dante, it would seem, 'who loses, dares'.
The Church of Rome can kick a loss upstairs.

'The Last Chance' is the name of this saloon:
you're playing, but the dealer's Richard Boone:
each Roman holds the best card in his paws:
the universal, wipe-all, get-out clause.
Thus, no-one born a Teague would ever lie
if there is half a risk that he might die.

FEDERIGO'S FALCON, Being a Tale found among the Posthumous Papers of Massimo d'Azeglio

That look of fierce disdain, nobility!
That regal plume of chestnut ruddy-brown
with speckled breast! No hint of weak servility
besmirched the falcon's fine, imperious frown.
He loved the way it sat in proud tranquility
above his desk. He gazed down on the town
which spread below his window with an air
of brittle hope (or thinly-veiled despair).

Ser Federigo was of noble stock.
His patrimony took in twenty farms,
with crops of chestnuts, olives, pullets, cocks,
but penury now ruffed the millpond's calm.
The poplar copse and barn were now in hock,
low pastures sold. The nephews were alarmed!
So, piecemeal, parcels, paddocks mortgaged off
provided funds for gifts. We mustn't scoff

to learn that Federigo was in love,
and sadly, wholly, profitlessly so.
Fair Monna was the delicate white dove

to Federigo's clumsy clawless crow.
You've met her kind. Serene, aloof, 'above',
while Federigo worshipped from below.
She took the necklaces, which she construed
(as Beauty will) as nothing but her due.

Estates and tithes were frittering away,
but little Federigo cared. His two delights
were Monna, and the falcon. Come what may,
he fantasized on lonely, frugal nights
of riding into Fiesole one day,
attended by a dozen sybarites,
(and though she's someone's wife, and someone's mother)
the bird on one arm, Monna on the other.

And now to Monna. When her child fell sick,
she watched in anguish as the boy declined.
The fever burned. He hung between the quick
and the departed, in his crisis pined
for one thing only – could this be the trick
to save him? What was on his raving mind
was Federigo's falcon. All's not lost.
She'd get the bird, no matter what the cost.

Imagine Federigo's sudden joy
to see her, dressed divinely, walking up
from Fiesole! The few he still employed
were summoned. 'We must drink from pewter cups,
no stint of treasure!' Pleasure unalloyed
was in his grasp. 'She's sure to stay and sup!
So plunder pantry, bring forth soup and fish!
Damn! Is there nothing for a special dish?'

For once, she was approachable, it seemed.
They talked and drank, and flirted with their eyes.
This was better than he could have dreamed!

Her thin silk dress defined her shapely thighs.
The moment came. The pewter platter gleamed
as it was carried in. 'Here's a surprise!'
The lid was lifted off, at his behest.
There, trussed and roasted, lay the falcon's breast.

THE CASTLE OF OTRANTO, Being a Tale told by Giovanni Battista Bottini

Some may knock
Hilaire Belloc
or pound a
Pisan Canto,
but humble, great,
all venerate
The Castle
of Otranto.

Pearl Buck sang
of Kuomintang,
and Chesterton
Lepanto,
but naught compares
for frights and scares
with the Castle
of Otranto.

Frisco has
its Alcatraz,
and Pisa
Camposanto,
but none exude
the nightmare mood
of The Castle
of Otranto.

Farewell to Arms,
collective farms,
or Lorca's
lovely *Llanto*
are barely sensed
when set against
The Castle
of Otranto.

WHAT IS A CASTLE, but a vain attempt
to keep at bay a horror, dark, adverse,
that sniffs its way towards our flesh and bone?
It seeps through portals, leering with contempt
at battlements and barriers. The Curse
can find us, where we sleep, alone.
Rank weeds creep up, malodorous, unkempt:
a moaning wind weaves through them, to disperse
their evil seeds, unstoppable once sown.
Our crude carnality can fool us, tempt
a sense of something 'out there'. This perverse
conception causes castles. Walls are thrown
around us. Though we toil on soil and stone,
the menace is internal – and our own.

THE RUMOUR HOLDS, an ancient malediction
besets the castle. In the murky past
some species of a spell, they say, was cast.
With physical, comes moral, dereliction:
usurpers squirm beneath the bleak conviction
that what they've grasped is soiled, and cannot last
(in fiction, one might ponder Gormenghast).
The present despot, Manfred, has amassed
a fortune as corrupt as it is vast:
accordingly, his throne is his affliction,
his opulence-addiction, crucifixion.
Authority (hence cruelty) unsurpassed

Is leading to a wretched valediction.
As to the others, so unto this last.

When Good Alfonso 'seemingly' returns,
the coarse incumbent cannot help but fall.
The tyrant knows the writing's on the wall.
Yea, gems which line his throat shall turn to querns.
For all his gallowglasses, all his kerns,
regardless of the chieftains in his hall,
this is the destiny he can't forestall.
His wine will turn to wormwood, gold to gall.
His progeny will perish, one and all.
Whoever studies past endeavours, learns
from reading faint inscriptions on quaint urns
that whom the goddess loves, she always spurns
and autocrats, from Saladin to Saul,
once lifted up, more certainly may fall.

A wedding was awaited. This was May,
and battlements were draped with nonchalance.
The servants, idle, smiling for the nonce,
adjusting bunting, primping each display,
wore coronets of eglantine and bay.
A puckish patio breeze provoked response
from ribbons decked around each polished sconce,
enticing helmet-plumes to prance and play.
The word came down – the bride was on her way!
Prince Manfred (*honi soit qui mal y pense*)
escorted Isabel. His perfect day
was suddenly occluded in dismay –
'Your son, my lord. You need to come at once.'
The servant's face was agitated, grey.

Across the cloister, redolent with quince,
Don Manfred hastened. In the presence room
what seemed a black, gigantic helmet-plume

completely filled what had been, moments since,
a laughing space. Loud cries – 'The prince! The prince!' –
were ringing out from chambermaid and groom.
An unmistakeable *tableau* of doom
met Manfred's eyes. What father would not wince?
But there it was. It could not but evince
the fact of what had happened. Through the gloom,
he marked a massive helmet. Striking hints
of recent death abounded. Keen to rinse
the tiles of blood, men doused the steely tomb,
but Manfred's son lay crushed. He was convinced.

What happened here? The helm of giant size
had fallen (from the ceiling? from the skies?)
and now the wedding-groom lay bloody, crushed.
The runnels where his lifeblood late had gushed
were clotting now. A hundred startled eyes
regarded Manfred with a wild surmise:
the company was motionless and hushed.
The prince's temples twitched as anger rushed
upon him. For this horrible surprise,
he cast about for someone to chastise:
as men looked at their boots and women blushed,
a tall young peasant took his cue, and pushed
towards the front. To servants' stifled cries,
he spoke. 'I've seen this helmet in the guise

of Don Alfonso, often called 'the Good',
or rather, as his headpiece, where he stood
as soldier-hero statue, in yon church.
There's not a man alive who dares besmirch
our great Alfonso in this neighbourhood.
He will return, because he said he would.'
'Arrest that man!' cried Manfred. 'Let him perch
beneath the helmet, till he feels the birch.
Once other foes are fought, he'll pay with blood

for being a necromancer, as he should!'
He left the pounced-on peasant in the lurch
of helmet-prison, and commenced a search
of castle precincts. Manfred understood
the present danger: 'After me, the flood!'

The laird let out, 'I've lost my wedding,'
which words occurred to hearers as bizarre:
more natural to say, 'I've lost my son'!
Towards the bridal quarters briskly heading,
apparently to no-one, near or far,
he cried, 'the dynasty is not yet done!'
Along the passage, resolutely treading,
he burst in through the portal, left ajar:
and there was Isabella. 'Pretty one!'
The adolescent bride, already dreading
disastrous news from some malignant star,
could sense the cataclysm had begun.
'Still undefiled,' said Manfred, 'as you are,
ci saranno nozze – there's no bar!'

A wolf will trigger terror in the hart,
although she's never seen the thing before:
and Manfred's unexpected ambuscade
occasioned an involuntary start,
he filling as he did the open door,
his face and upper body in the shade.
'I have unwelcome tidings to impart,
but still there's comfort,' said the carnivore.
'Our wedding is not voided – merely stayed!'
'Your words confuse me, but I fear a dart
with poison barbs.' The child could not ignore
the prince's animation, which betrayed
the face of false solemnity he wore,
a predator detected by his spoor.

For Isabella, Manfred was too near:
she sensed that he was on the point of kissing.
At just this moment, messengers arrived:
they told the prince his prisoner was missing.
The news which filled the prince with far more fear
concerned Saint Nicholas' Chapel. Scowling, hissing,
Don Manfred strode away. She had survived!
Young Isabella fell to reminiscing
about the statue in the chapel apse,
the Good Alfonso, of enormous height,
decked in the armour of a red-cross knight.
Alfonso had been vandalised, perhaps?
Recovered, almost, from her recent fright,
she turned to pondering her present plight.

Indeed, the statue-knight was altered now.
Within the chapel, in restricted light,
as if a hero from the *Iliad*
Alfonso stood. His superhuman height,
his fine physique and magisterial brow
(the surplice, rosy cross on flawless white)
recalled the tall young peasant Manfred had
so recently imprisoned, out of spite.
He differed from before in one respect:
the head which had been helmeted was bare.
The beadsman knelt in lisping whispered prayer
could not but mark the contrast, and reflect:
what force could lift the helmet out of there,
and waft it, unsupported, through the air?

For Isabella, this had been a morning
of horrors unforeseen and wild extremes.
That Conrad had been killed was, clearly, weird
but not in truth unwelcome. She had feared
the prospect of this marriage: in her dreams,
she'd seen a deep and ugly chasm yawning.

Her usefulness to Manfred lay in spawning
a further generation. Now his schemes
had come to nothing, Isabel was cheered:
for Conrad's lolling tongue and feeble beard
had quite disgusted her. Otranto teems
with perils, and she'd taken as a warning
the interest the prince had seemed to take.
Was Manfred, then, some vile incestuous rake?

At just that moment, footfalls sounded loud
along the passageway. It had to be.
The self-assurance of the stride could leave
no doubt. This must be Manfred. No reprieve,
no open-handed magnanimity
could ever be requested, less allowed.
He clung about her like a funeral shroud,
sweating, petting forearm, patting knee,
insistent fingers on her silken sleeve,
annoying and unravelling the weave.
The penetration of the prince's key
within her lock oppressed her, but she vowed
however Manfred badgered her or bullied,
she'd keep her own integrity unsullied.

So, in he comes. He lacks the lover's ease.
'I'm yours, my Isabella, to command.'
But she recoils. 'The Christian degrees
of consanguinity forbid it, and
I'm promised to your son, as you well know!'
She saw that she had clearly struck a nerve.
 'And this the boy who died an hour ago!'
'He wasn't worthy of you … didn't deserve … '
One hand of Manfred's took his daughter's hand,
the other lighted on her pelvic curve,
but Isabella struggled free. 'No, no!'
With decency offended, anger fanned,

she reached the passage in one nimble swerve
and vanished in the shadows, skirts aflow.

Now night had fallen, torches on the walls
cast shifting flickers from inconstant flames,
and threw weird shadows down the narrow halls,
exposing ancestors in portrait frames.
And suddenly, blue moonlight flooded in
through open windows, as the stormclouds' sable
was rent apart. He heard a sound begin,
an eerie rustling, the stuff of fable,
a noise not of this earth. Those helmet feathers!
Had Manfred wished to never see them more,
his hopes were dashed. Exactly as before,
the giant helmet plumes, like mountain heathers,
convulsed and trembled. Shaken to the core,
Don Manfred hurried through the chamber door.

But in the corridor, his progress stalls:
a portrait-figure speaks out – 'Shame of shames!'
Its anger punctuated by the squalls,
the ghastly ancestor steps down, and blames
Don Manfred: 'You are mired in sin,
and now our line, inherently unstable,
is at an end: for you have soiled your kin
with lust and incest. You have proved unable
to free yourself from egotism's tethers.
You've opted from the outset to ignore
the Right, despite prerogatives galore!
A hero is a human soul who weathers
the tempests of adversity that roar
through every life, and makes it to the shore.

Authority is loaned to those who lead
by those who are entitled to protection,
but you have cast away the sacred creed

to follow every sinful predilection.
A leader needs to lead a blameless life,
and menacing your son's prospective wife
has brought down on your unrepentant head
the very dereliction that you dread.'
And what of Isabella? She well knew,
Saint Nicholas of Bari was the friend
of virgins under menace. To this end,
expecting Manfred presently to pursue,
she'd heard a secret tunnel might extend
towards the chapel. Might she hurry through?

Down, down she fled. The staircase of cold stone
bore neither sign nor symbol. On she went,
impelled by terror, utterly alone,
committed to this dubious descent.
At last, a door! Gargantuan, antique,
its rusty, bulky hinges grind and shriek
as Isabella tugs, and passes by.
A subterranean air-surge seemed to sigh
before her, through the tunnel. Up ahead
was felt or sensed, much more than heard or seen
a denizen of this despised demesne,
some living thing, alerted to her tread.
More welcome has a greeting never been
than this, the 'thing' ingenuously said:

'I will not injure you – don't be alarmed.'
He blew, a match-rope glowed: and then, anew,
his torch took flame. Young Isabella, charmed,
beheld the sturdy man who filled her view.
'Whoever you may be, I hope you're kind.
I must beseech your help, to flee from here.
Of all the terrors which oppress my mind,
the wrath of Manfred is my pressing fear.'
The stranger's torch gave light so bright, immense,

it filled the tunnel. Tones sincere and warm
came from the man. 'I'd die in your defence!
In me, you've found your refuge from the storm.'
A trapdoor to the chapel must be traced:
The chase was on. There was no time to waste!

'We'll find your trapdoor. Would you know my name?
I freely give it. I am Theodore,
but what my story is, or whence I came,
must bide. A time and place more apposite
awaits us. Ah, your trapdoor! This is it!'
It wasn't, as expected, in the floor,
but in the ceiling. Peering at the same,
so high above her head, so tight a fit …
'It must be her – she can't have travelled far!'
This voice was Manfred's – in the catacomb!
'The chapel lies above. The Church of Rome
will shield me!' With the metal plate ajar,
the fellow helped her through. She said, 'You are
an honest man. Seek you the priest, Jerome!'

The plate in place again, young Theodore
prepared to bear the brunt of Manfred's wrath.
Internally, he resolutely swore
to purchase time for Isabella by
directing any search for her awry.
Here came the pack of hounds! The tunnel path
was thronged with hunters, Manfred to the fore:
he viewed the youth with cold, imperious eye.
'You!' yelled the prince, 'why are you here?'
'The helmet which imprisoned me was so
absurdly heavy that the beams below
collapsed. The headpiece cut a swathe so sheer
through flooring timbers, that I felt in fear
of falling hellward, but it proved not so.'

With verbal barbs the older man assaults
his prisoner, but shows his own malaise:
the younger meets him with an even gaze
and Manfred, mindful of his myriad faults,
instead of pressing onward, pauses, halts.
Adept of epigram and deft of phrase,
inimical to menaces or praise,
young Theodore (the Theseus of these vaults)
achieves ascendancy. With clear relief,
Don Manfred turns to servants, new-arrived,
with pasty, frightened faces, hose down-gyved,
with cries of 'Ghost! A ghost!' This leitmotiv
is something Manfred recently survived:
his attitude is carefully contrived

to show no weakness to his underlings,
though what he feels inside, none yet has guessed.
The two retainers, palpably distressed,
amid their muddled words and mutterings,
describe an armoured knight (says one, with wings)
of giant size. His helmet bore a crest
with sable plumes: the red cross on his chest
shone out, the most refulgent of all things.
Oh, what a perturbation in the soul!
The phantom forebear Manfred had just seen
had not resembled this one. Could this mean
that human agency had lost control?
Were ghosts the norm now? Outwardly serene,
the prince maintained a mild, majestic mein.

Ironically, the sidelines are the spot
to see more of the game than any player.
A priest now pushes through the pressing knot
of courtier and ghastly-tale-conveyor.
Jerome his name, imperious his air,
incumbent of Saint Nicholas's chapel,

a man of learning, poverty and prayer,
uncompromising, unafraid to grapple
iniquity, whatever its complexion,
yet also capable of deep affection,
he stood before the prince. 'Now, at my altar,
the Lady Isabella asks protection.
My oath to heaven as a Knight of Malta
requires I grant it – and I shall not falter.

As Conrad's bride, the lady is your daughter.
A marriage contract cannot be undone –
on this, the Church will never grant you quarter.
I know the parent's part. I had a son.
My wife and boy meant everything to me
(yes, I was married, many years ago)
and when my family was lost at sea,
I took the tonsure. I would have you know
I swear by Theo's birthmark (arrowhead
in aspect, on this shoulder, purple-red)
that Isabella's now my spiritual child.
My duty to the living and the dead
will be discharged – to that, be reconciled.
She shall not be molested or defiled.'

'I want her brought to me. That's a command,'
said Manfred. 'I am still the sovereign here.
Who thwarts the prince's wishes courts disaster.'
'Your words are water, running into sand,'
replied the curate. Manfred, with a sneer,
said 'Openly defy me, would you, pastor?
My will, you'll find, is peril to withstand.'
Jerome's response was patently sincere:
'Then do your worst. I serve a greater Master.'
If Manfred quailed at this, he hid it well.
'No other realm, as far as I can tell,
awaits us. Not a man for hex or spell,

I look for proof, which can alone compel.
Perhaps the Castle is already Hell?'

Jerome exploited Manfred's self-esteem,
his weakest point. 'This handsome lad you flaunt –
a lucky shipwreck on Otranto's shore?
If Isabella were inclined to dream,'
(the priest continued, warming to the taunt)
'he's just the kind she's minded to adore.'
The prank provoked the prince to his extreme.
'A sorcerer, with fakery to flaunt:
but I know how to deal with Theodore.'
A surge of strange emotion swept the priest:
his rate of respiration had increased.
Might famine finally give way to feast?
A curious coincidence, at least –
'The name of my poor son, so long deceased!'

Like anyone enjoying his success,
the priest is disinclined to break it off.
'No matter how you may vituperate,'
(this comes from Theodore) 'I nonetheless
refuse to guzzle at the selfsame trough!'
Jerome can see that Manfred is irate,
and relishes a little verbal chess.
'At which Pierian Spring did this boy quaff?'
(And Manfred, as expected, takes the bait:
but where to stop?) One nuance turns finesse
to flaccid failure. Still disposed to scoff,
the curate banters, 'Who will educate
our old dictators?' Manfred's eyes flash hate.
But soft! A clanking bell. The postern gate!

Who could this new arrival possibly be?
It has to wait. The prince has formed the view
that Theodore's life is forfeit. He must die

(the prince announces) instantaneously:
decapitation, with no more ado.
But in the name of heaven, Manfred, why?
The trapdoor, says the tyrant, is the key:
its recent use is easy to construe,
and necromancy futile to deny.
He aided Isabella to be free,
was apprehended here, beneath the clue.
The capital disposal must apply,
the fate of traitor, renegade and spy.
The trapdoor glowers down, like Heaven's eye.

'The fault is mine!' The priest Jerome, abashed
that jokes of his could furnish this result,
approaches Theodore. 'The Manfred cult',
begins the pastor, 'really should trashed.
Forgive me if your future hopes are dashed.'
'It's nothing, Father. I am an adult,
and neither curse my fortune nor exult.
The prince gave orders. Theodore must be lashed,
his hands behind him, with his neck laid bare.
'Will you submit, then, to Our Saviour's will?'
Oh, what a word is *voglia*! With a chill
of recognition, and a silent prayer,
Jerome observed the birthmark! Could he dare
believe his son was living, breathing still?

Down here below, estranged from air or sun,
dank tunnel walls play tricks with space and sound:
some frights are amplified, some comforts drowned.
what harsh metallic scraping has begun
above our heads, that makes the vermin run
for cover? Something dragged along the ground?
That bell again – who'd ominously pound
so hard against the gate? The Fates have spun
a knotty fabric. Manfred turns to ask

Jerome to go and see what can be done,
confront the visitor, admit or shun.
'You know, beleaguered prince, the giant cask
is moving. I will undertake your task.
Before I take one step, release my son!'

What choice does Manfred have? 'Your son is free.
But who will now restore a son to me?'
'You cause your own misfortunes, choose to live
with sins that are not easy to forgive,'
replies the priest. 'Halt, insolent divine!'
(this comes from Manfred). 'Perpetuate my line –
a noble cause, you'll grant? Tomorrow's bride
is Isabella, priest. And you'll preside!'
Jerome, incensed, with arms around his boy,
unleashes thunder. 'Why must you betray
those things that other people seek to cherish?
Is there no innocence you won't destroy?
Your claim's pure perfidy, and sure to perish.
Seek you the crown will never pass away.'

'It seems, Jerome, you fail to understand.'
The prince's manner, suddenly so bland,
reveals a change of tactic. 'Heaven's curse
is thwarting all my policies, and worse –
my son is taken from me, as was yours.
My sins are one thing, but a fool ignores
the signs he's given. Help me to annul
my present marriage. She, the shameless trull,
is daughter to my mother. This is why
I'm punished. Won't you help me start again?
Let Isabella furnish me an heir.'
'Is there no calumny you will not try?
Your blameless wife of thirty years must bear
invented insults? Abjectest of men!'

A new, insistent ringing of the bell
disrupts this intercourse. Jerome ascends
the tunnel stairs. As if to make amends,
the tyrant turns to Theodore. 'So, tell.
What prompted you to succour Isabel,
and risk my wrath?' 'My courtesy depends,'
retorted Theodore, 'far less on ends,
than present miseries I may dispel.
I asked the lady whom she fled pell-mell,
and she replied, 'a tyrant'. Very well.
She's just the sort to whom my arm extends,
regardless of whom else such help offends.'
The prince's retinue erupts in cheers:
'A new Alfonso, after all these years!'

Accompanied by servants bearing flames,
the curate climbs the crumbling 'caracol' stair.
Astonished when he gains the castle square,
surprised that night has fallen. Window frames
with bulky mullions, turrets with no names,
seem live with malice. Through rain-laden air
he spots the giant helmet. 'Have a care,
my boys – it's moving!' Gingerly, he aims
his steps towards the postern gate
and throws it open. There, beyond the grate,
a warrior (in place of pilgrim's gourd
he bears a blade before him, upright, straight)
stands waiting. From within the armour plate:
'The Knight, they call me, of the Mighty Sword.'

'You bear us' asked the curate, 'good or ill?
And if the latter, may we know your *pianto*?'
'I'm seeking the Usurper of Otranto!'
Jerome approved the raising of the grille.
'Is Isabella held against her will?
(This from the Knight.) I swear, *dal mio santo*,

Saint Nicholas of Bari, *così tanto*,
the man who harms her, be he breathing still,
shall not live long!' The curate is impressed,
but plays his cards, for now, close to his chest:
a righteous knight, imperiously encroaching
upon the tyrant Manfred's fetid nest
cannot but augur progress. 'Enter, guest!'
The longed-for climacteric is approaching.

The Story of the Knight of the Mighty Sword

The Marquis of Vicenza is my lord,
      one Frederic by name,
and he commands my conscience and my sword,
      in truth one and the same.

The life of Great Alfonso, called 'the Good',
      was drawing to its close.
Alfonso made provision, as he should,
      intending to repose

the lordship of Otranto in a man
      (Alfonso had no sons)
of flawless virtue. This, then, was the plan,
      but human fortune runs

in channels that no mortal may predict,
      and Good Alfonso's choice
was thwarted, and a family was tricked
      left without a voice,

when Manfred's father tampered with the will.
      But thieves don't sleep anight:
usurpers' nerves are tortured, ever still:
      Wrong's not as strong as Right.

The decent man, thus ousted from Otranto,
        made Tuscany his home,
bewailed his fate in many a Pisan canto
        and sent his son to Rome.

The lad grew tall and manly, and in time
        he found a special girl.
A happiness unblemished and sublime
        was destined to unfurl

in tragedy. Though child birth is a blessing,
        too frequently the wife
(I find the telling terribly distressing!)
        must sacrifice her life.

The young man, as do many such exemplars
        of Christian probity,
put on the red-cross tunic of the Templars
        and sailed from Italy.

At Jaffa, hurled against the Ottoman,
        the novice fought and bled
and, captured in the month of Ramadan,
        was classed as 'left for dead'.

His infant daughter, back on Pisan shores,
        was raised as an *orfana*.
Her beauty was the kind the world adores:
        they named her, '*la Toscana*'.

The girl's real name, in truth, was Isabella,
        intelligent and good,
and far from being a status-less *zitella*,
        she was of noble blood.

She prized a letter, in her father's hand,
       which none could steal or burn:
he'd written, 'I am in a far-off land,
       but one day I'll return.

We own a castle, daughter. You and I
       are masters of the same.
Together, we will storm its walls, thereby
       establishing our claim.'

THE KNIGHT REMOVED HIS HELMET. THOSE AROUND
who knew Otranto's legend, bent the knee.
'Our sufferings are ended. It is he!'
'The face of Don Alfonso, I'll be bound!'
'What brings you,' asked the prelate, 'to this ground?'
'A fatal interview with tyranny.
So bring Usurper Manfred here, to me.'
A throat was cleared. All turned toward the sound.
There Manfred stood. 'Sir Frederic, I think.
Too tough, I see, for Suleiman to slaughter.
But I forget my manners! Come, let's drink
before my hearth. I've something more than water
to cheer you – Copertino, thick as ink!
You'll soon be reunited with your daughter.'

Around the courtyard, not a feather stirred.
A tyrant and a knight stood face to face.
In Manfred's calm expression, not a trace
of fear could be detected. Undeterred,
he spurred the Knight to take him at his word.
Unquestionably manifesting grace,
the prince projects emotional embrace,
which Frederic accepts. Has he concurred,
or is this move strategic? What to make
of naming Isabella Frederic's child?
The Knight is Frederic? and here to shake

the tyrant's empire? Manfred seems too mild:
his equanimity belies no quake.
How can these counterclaims be reconciled?

Before the fire, supposed source of cheer,
the tyrant Manfred still seems at a loss:
'Wass denkst du über dieses alte Schloss?'
initiates no thaw. August, austere,
the Knight declines the wine, ignores the beer.
His giant sword before him, like a cross,
he sits as motionless as mountain moss,
but Manfred feels the need to persevere.
'The sword is quite unnecessary here.
You'll set it down?' The other shakes his head.
'I wish to say what you don't wish to hear,'
says Manfred, 'but I mean to be sincere …'
'Then keep your silence,' snaps the Knight. 'Instead,
abandon this, my castle. Disappear!'

'Allow me to rehearse my point of view.
This is *my* castle, which my father Don Manuel
bequeathed me. It's my home and citadel.
You ask me to surrender it to *you*?
Collapse at hint of insurrection, *coup*?
You know me not! The Lady Isabel,
upon her own volition, chose to dwell
within my walls. When Conrad died, she grew
to venerate my virtues, to pursue
a union of two houses, epipheme…'
'Dishonest lecher, not a word is true!
My meeting with my child is overdue.
I'll hear no more of your perverted scheme.
Produce her now, or take what may ensue!'

A moment of high drama, to be sure.
Would Manfred opt for combat, take the lure?

A *novus actus interveniens*
provides the prince with just enough defence
to save the situation: brash as drunks,
a breathless cluster (cloister?) of brown monks,
Jerome the foremost, burst into the room!
'Another vision at Alfonso's tomb?'
The tyrant isn't pleased to see the friar:
once free of frying-pan, perceives the fire.
This wild incursion of distracted brothers,
contrived or not, inevitably smothers
the *contretemps* emerging with the Knight,
but Manfred dreads the words the curate might

divulge unwittingly: that Isabella
is shut away, a kind of Cinderella,
and seeking sanctuary, not free to act.
And this Jerome accomplishes, in fact.
Alarm! She's disappeared! The girl's escaped!
A brother saw her leaving, hooded, caped,
along the landward concourse. 'How is this?'
The Knight speaks out. 'Someone has been remiss.
Why was my daughter's freedom thus restricted?'
The tyrant says, 'It's not as you've depicted:
I, anxious for her safety, …' 'This can wait!'
The Knight's already striding for the gate,
his sword unsheathed, expression passing grim,
as Manfred urges servants – 'Follow him!'

* * *

Remember Theodore, the handsome youth?
Released by Manfred (pardoned? No, forgotten!),
he's roaming through the forest on the slope
below the castle, having found a gate
which lacked a sentry. What has just transpired
is only now bedevilling his soul.

The curate is his father, it would seem!
'Was I so nigh beheading? Did I dream?'
Though drifting through the trees without a goal,
he finds himself elated – nay, inspired!
'What happened in the tunnel – was it Fate?
To love? To struggle? Some of each, I hope!
I'm to the purple born – or misbegotten!
The truth is always, stubbornly, the truth.'

Then, suddenly, a movement in the brake –
some savage predator, or Manfred's spy?
'Who's there?' he calls. A woman, in response,
cried 'Do not hurt me!' Curious circumstance!
Emerging from the undergrowth she came:
'Fair Isabella! How can you be here?
I had not hoped to see your face again.
Alone, I roamed the castle's bowels, and then,
improbably, you happened to appear –
you stand before me now, one and the same!
Two such encounters cannot be by chance:
a miracle, it seemed, to meet you once!
To keep you safe, I'm quite prepared to die.
This is no accident, no blind mistake!'

At cries of 'Isabella!' in the air,
the couple started. 'Wait – it's just one man,'
said Theodore, 'and Manfred needs a clan.
It can't be him. He simply wouldn't care
to foray in the forest. Chase a hare?
He'd take a pack of hounds!' With this, he ran
toward the noise. Not quite a moment's span –
the youth was lost to sight. She didn't dare
pursue him. But the stranger knew her name!
How could this be? She was no jewelled dame –
a lady, yes, but not of public note.
And instantly her bosom was aflame:

She mulled this new emotion, whence it came,
and touched the letter that her father wrote.

When Isabella came upon the fight,
It wasn't clear to her what she had found.
Sir Frederic, the knight, lay on the ground.
but once she understood the baleful sight,
far from feeling chastened or contrite,
she was elated. Fortune had not frowned
on her protector. Theodore had downed
the older man, whose lifeblood, hot and bright,
was spilling on the bracken, overcame
his dolour and confusion. 'Just the same!
The way the curls are clustered at your throat:
the image of your mother! Might I claim
the honour to embrace you, Daughter? Blame
your tardy father, far too long remote!'

All caution gone, she fell upon the neck
of this, her longed-for father. Tears of joy
commingled with compassion for the wreck
whose life was ebbing. Anchises at Troy
could not have seemed more tragic. Held in check
were tears of grief (for oft these two alloy!)
'I have your letter with me – always do –
for I have never doubted you'd appear,'
sobbed Isabella, 'and, at last, it's true!
One thing alone I'd have you volunteer:
Otranto is remote, concealed from view:
I have to ask – how did you find me here?'
As if new-liberated from some spell,
Sir Frederic began his tale to tell.

The Dream of the Knight of the Mighty Sword

As I lay shackled in my Jaffa cell,
        oppressed by thoughts of home,
one arrow-slit admitted light which played
upon the facing wall, and thus relayed
        into my gloomy hell
        a glimpse of heaven's dome.

Who knew when waking faded, sleep crept in?
        We drowsed the livelong day.
So stultified with boredom had we grown
that we inhabited a twilight zone.
        Our gaolers – were they *djinn*?
        No man could rightly say.

It felt as if I dreamt – perhaps I saw –
        my daughter, come of age.
She wandered through a castle, dark and dank:
from every squeak or skittering, she shrank:
        she seemed afraid, in awe
        of this, her stony cage.

The vision faded. Now there came a man
        I'd never met before.
He told me Jaffa Forest was the key
to finding Isabella. Who was he?
        'My name is Christian.
        I trod this very shore

in times long past. Select a wild-grown rose
        which thrives in Jaffa Wood,
and he who represents both gain and loss
will counsel you on how to win your cross.
        Then, armed with each of those,
        your blood once more finds blood.'

'But here I'm held, a captive of the Moors!'
        in anguish I replied,
'How scour the forest if I am not free?'
'If you are honest, you'll have liberty.
        They'll open wide all doors.
        Just trust me, and abide.'

Some time elapsed – an hour? Perchance a day?
        I watched the shadows grow
across the facing wall. My captors came
to tell me I enjoyed a certain fame,
        and they were here to say
        that I was free to go.

Apparently, a man of noble blood
        attracts extreme cachet
among the heathens. 'What befalls these others?',
I asked about my coarse, unlettered brothers,
        as field commanders should.
        They answered, 'They must stay.'

The arrow-slit which signified the sky
        let fall a drop of rain.
My heart was yearning for that open beauty,
but heart must be subordinate to duty:
        'If these men must remain,
        Then, plainly, so must I.'

The vizier's face erupted in a smile.
        'That answer is the best!
We've learnt your social rank. An honest mind
could not take freedom, with his men confined
        to endless durance vile.
        You've passed our moral test!'

I gained my freedom when I turned it down:
        it's strange how things unfold!
My destination was a wooded glen:
and in the meantime, I was told my men
        could march to Jaffa town,
        where all would be paroled.

Such heaven, moving through a forest glade!
        In place of cell door's clang,
I heard the gentle music of the wild,
and wandered quite alone, and quite beguiled,
        as dappled roebucks played
        and forest finches sang.

Then, chancing on a cave deep in the trees,
        I heard a human groan.
On entering, I found a holy man.
He lay there sweating on his rough divan,
        beset by some disease,
        expiring, all alone.

'I ask your Christian pity! Bring me water.
        I am from Syracuse,
but here I'll die. My life is near its end.
Please grant me this small favour, friend!'
        My purpose was my daughter,
        but how could I refuse?

I scooped up water from the nearby stream
        and brought it to his bed.
According to this dying eremite,
he'd been oppressed by visions in the night:
        he told me of his dream,
        and this is what he said:

The Hermit's Dream

Saint Nicholas appeared to me
        from out a stormy sky
He said, 'My son, I set you free.
        Your time has come to die.'

The turbulence of churning clouds
        betokened threat of rain:
I saw a dance of burning shrouds,
        and cried, 'Where is my gain?'

'The very fact that you should ask,'
        replied the stately saint,
'is proof that you've performed your task
        without the faintest taint.

Your place in Paradise awaits.
        Your work on earth is done.
Before you stand the shining gates,
        the Portal of the Sun!

Until this hour I've held my peace,
        My secrets under seal,
but now your life's about to cease,
        I've something to reveal.

A man will come to eat and rest,
        and slake his journey's dust.
You need to help him in his quest,
        for what he seeks is just.

Direct him to the clearing's edge,
        where stands the tallest tree,
beneath its roots to delve and dredge –
        and what will be, will be.'

I fed on simple rustic forest fare,
        God-given nuts and fruits.
The hermit sighed, and closed his eyes to life.
My only implement the good man's knife,
        I buried him in prayer,
          then set about the roots.

What lay interred, once freed, emerged a sword
        (I'd thought it was a cross).
(Two 'graves' I'd dug, conjoined by rare connection:
one made for death, and one for resurrection.)
        The hilt bore verses scored,
          which spoke of gain and loss.

The helmet which accompanies this blade
        awaits you in the place
where Wrong now reigns: none save Alfonso's blood
can help a soul repose, as princes should.
the menace to the maid
        must fade when faced by Grace.

A focus, then, of evil must be found.
        Soft! In some unseen church,
a bell was tolling for *venerdi santo*.
Some spirit lisped, 'The Castle of Otranto'.
Where lay this troubled ground?
        I set about my search.

A thousand guides in soil and air and water
enabled me to reach
Apulian shores. The night-occluded fence
of forest lay before me. I could sense
        the presence of my daughter
          beyond that lonely beach.

And now I have her, though my time is short.
          And this, my worthy foe,
I heartily forgive. It's understood
that he and Isabella ... well, all's good.
Your task, now, is to thwart
          a tyrant. Go now, go!

STRAY LEAVES: IN DREAMS

Five kinds of dream our distant forebears knew,
and here we will rehearse the retinue.
Arcane are some, while others are abstruse,
But let's begin with those which have no use.

(Adherents of Fromm-Reichmann, Jung or Freud
on reading this, perchance, will get annoyed:
sententious comments verging on opprobrious
are not for us – your target is Macrobius.)

'Ne do no fors of dremes,' the poet sings,
but doesn't mean our rich imaginings.
He talks of *visum*, *swevene* in vernacular,
a type of dream that's wholly unspectacular.

Mere shapes and flickerings that make no sense,
and quite within a greyhound's competence:
don't take our word for it – the phrase is his:
'Nothyng but vanity in swevene is'.

The next is called *insomnium* and serves
to print your daily routine on your nerves.
The carter doesn't dream of distant suns.
He pictures how his new four-wheeler runs.

And now we meet a handy kind of dream,
which has the 'heads-up' as its central theme.
The ancients knew it as *oraculum:*
It means, 'the dude is dead, not deaf and dumb'.

'Don't fly tomorrow', warns your sainted mother:
you thus avoid some plane crash or another.
So, timely warning is the rule of thumb,
and all are thankful for *oraculum.*

There's one that is a literal prediction,
devoid of ambiguity or fiction.
It's like a trailer of what's coming soon,
and *visio* it's called (*avisioun*).

When truth-disguised-as-metaphor prevails,
and allegory wears her seven veils,
the dream is *somnium*, and it's the best,
because it's more 'artistic' than the rest.

* * *

The Castle has its fissures and its faults
where exhalations of the earth escape,
as if our concrete world were just a veil,
a front, concealing something quite alive.
Colossal slabs of igneous basalts,
crude colonnades of metamorphic shape
ubiquitously charcoaled in grisaille,
provide the fractured fabric of the hive.
Uncouth accretion-mounds of crystal salts,
like froth collecting where the granites gape,
seem most like mosses, able to prevail
where nothing born of Nature should survive.
Don Manfred, striding through his ugly vaults,
enshrouded by a long, ill-fitting cape,

has seen his machinations falter, fail,
and, forced to try what cunning can contrive,
he gains the open gallery, and halts:
below, the pewter tempest-waters drape
their ragged kirtles over jagged shale,
as if there they some profit may derive
from futile and repetitive assaults.
'A penitent, perhaps? I'll don the crepe
and ask forgiveness, spin a poignant tale.
Jerome would give his benefice to shrive
my rotten soul. The Vatican exalts
returning sinners!' Timbers grind and scrape.
His fortress, like a rusting coat of mail,
can not now save him. 'May my project thrive!'

The castle courtyard makes a sombre sight
as Frederic is borne in on his litter.
Could anything be seemlier or fitter
than Isabella's presence at the rite?
That Theodore had slain the older knight
did not prevent her tears from falling, bitter.
Otranto, then, the seat – what of the sitter?
Observing from the balcony's lone height,
intent on wounding, yet afraid to bite,
he watches Theodore as if Macbeth
were studying Macduff. 'May I invite,'
asks Manfred, 'our handsome neophyte,
the author, as I hear, of recent death,
upon his provenance to shed some light?'

Theodore's Tale

Some feign divine afflatus
   to sanctify their boasts,
and some inflate their status
   by gabbling of ghosts,

but I require no fiction
   or harrowing of hell
to state in simple diction
   what factually befell.

My father stands beside me
   and hears the words I say:
he's welcome to deride me
   if from the truth I stray.

At five years old I travelled
   (my mother at my side):
our fortunes came unravelled
   upon the Barbary tide.

We lived to rue our bravery
   in sailing for Algiers,
when taken into slavery
   by berber buccaneers.

My mother neatly listed
   my details down, by hand,
meticulously twisted
   into a tiny band

the hide on which she'd written.
   I wore it on my arm.
In Bucharest or Britain,
   I'll always keep the charm.

We lived in stark privation
   as captives of the Moors:
severe our isolation
   on lonely Afric shores.

My mother's health diminished:
   her usefulness had ceased
and, when her life was finished,
   they ditched her like a beast.

Her death, although distressing,
   unfettered me to shape
my fate – it was a blessing,
   for now I could escape.

The saint I chose was Eunice,
   as fitting for a son:
she eased my path to Tunis –
   and life had now begun!

To Sicily I worked my way
   and sought my native town,
only to learn, to my dismay,
   our walls had tumbled down!

The peasants raked a waste land, baked
   by unrelenting sun,
where plaster flaked and muscles ached
   for sustenance, hard-won.

I asked them of their former lord,
   and where he might be found.
They told me had gone abroad.
   His wife and child had drowned.

He, devastated by this blow,
   had taken Holy Orders,
all ease and comfort to forgo,
   beyond the Bourbons' borders.

But some had heard, by word of mouth
   (infallible *discanto*!)
my father had regained the South –
   which brought me to Otranto.

This tale affected Manfred. His demeanour
continued, outwardly, supremely calm,
but twitching temple and perspiring palm
suggested he's had episodes serener.
This impudent, illicit intervenor,
this Theodore, was causing him alarm.
So plain his language, powerful his arm!
But there were irritants yet keener.
A young Alfonso – it was quite bizarre,
the strong resemblance! Locals were impressed,
and locals should be Manfred's. Worse by far,
comportment! (Isabella's might suggest
she favoured Theodore.) Alfonso's atavar
was causing agony in Manfred's breast.

'Conduct the knight to Nicholas of Bari,'
instructs the prince. 'I'll pay him my respects.'
Alone, he takes the passage which connects
the courtyard with the church. He does not tarry.
'I daren't allow my project to miscarry,'
he ponders. Although Manfred genuflects,
he gives no thought to rituals or sects.
'Without delay,' he ponders, 'I must marry.'
The word goes out: the prince will pray alone.
Jerome, he knows, regards him with contempt.
While Isabella's feelings are unknown,
they hardly matter. Better to pre-empt
the seeds of opposition, not yet sown.
'Secure my throne, or die in the attempt!'

The chapel door burst open. This surprise
so startled Manfred that he drew a blade:
the new arrival was a chambermaid
who, hair unravelled, stared with bulging eyes:
'A giant hand!' As if to emphasise
the vastness of the vision, she portrayed
with milling arms and frantic masquerade
a ghastly thing of overwhelming size.
No tyrant can, no matter how he tries,
forget the deadly threat of ambuscade:
but Manfred's dagger-hand was (briefly) stayed.
'What is this nonsense, blockhead? Wild surmise!
You'd blight this place with frightful, baseless cries?
Give thought to him, whose death-watch you invade!'

Bianca stared, as if she hadn't heard.
'It moved toward me – metal-mantled, mailed!
So massive, like a monster, shiny-scaled!'
'Silence, blockhead! Not another word!
Your imbecilic rantings are absurd!'
His habit of authority prevailed,
though only superficially. He quailed,
but inwardly. Bianca had averred
that supernatural events occurred,
and Manfred knew it for the truth. Assailed
by force which dwarfed his own, his courage failed.
The chapel door, left open, slightly stirred:
a frightened Manfred whimpered. Fact now blurred
with fiction. Dynasty? That ship had sailed.

STRAY LEAVES: THE STATESMAN AND THE PLACEMAN

The statesman is distinguished by his mien.
He pays no heed to caucuses or clans

and has no truck with sharks or charlatans.
He never acts from spitefulness or spleen,
is never ambushed by the unforeseen.
One common theme illumines all his plans
(the very thing that grubby partisans
can never grasp): the wise man is serene.
His opposite, the placeman, never learns.
Unable to create, he just reacts,
is borne along by currents, twist and turns:
events crowd in, his envelope contracts,
he can't manoeuvre. Pinioned by the facts!
For this are voting-vessels known as urns.

THE TRAGEDY WITH WHICH THE STORY ENDS
is rapidly related. To the altar
comes Isabella, veiled in black, with psalter,
to pray for the deceased. Her 'beau' extends
(now she and Theodore are more than friends)
an arm to steady her. *In una volta,*
Don Manfred strikes, and earns himself the halter.
To crass assassination he descends,
defrauding Isabella of her life.
They overwhelm him, confiscate the knife.
A lightning flash – and Theodore is framed
with arms around his dying would-be wife.
Thus Manfred's tenancy is duly shamed,
and thus the New Alfonso is proclaimed.

FRANCESCO ROSSI, *DETTO* 'VENERINO', RELATES HIS STORY TO THE REGULARS OF AREZZO'S CANALE INN

STRAY LEAVES: IAMBICS

Catullus, Ovid, Horace, Juvenal
– and Martial, from Calatayud, not least!
Their poetry had humour as its yeast.
Francesco Rossi, busboy, tal y cual,
is sitting in the Inn of the Canal,
recounting how he came to be released.
Though fare on which true satirists would feast,
his version lacks acerbic rationale:
oh for a captious pen to give it shape!
Unlettered sailor, teamster (later, waiter),
he's turned debater, auto-vindicator:
and I shall be his lodestone and equator!
Go, navigate some sound, or round some cape,
but my iambics you shall not escape!

In Porto Venere, where I was born,
the young and lusty men went off to sea,
and I was no exception. As a lad

I hankered for adventures like Cape Horn,
but pain and mutilation? Not for me!
The merchantman, and not the ironclad,

provides the uniform that I have worn.
But when I settled here in Tuscany,
I met more perils than I'd ever had!

Ten years I furled the sail and sang the shanty,
and drank in every harbour bar there is,
Torino all the way to Taormino.

I picked up Spanish, plying the Levante
from Barcelona almost to Cadiz:
I've loved in Pisa, lost in Piombino,

and left a gypsy girl in Alicante.
My life is like this beer – it's kept its fizz!
So, listen to the tale of Venerino.

GIUSEPPE CAPONSACCHI. CALL HIM FRIEND?
I can't claim that. I'm just a working man,
and he was 'quality', much better than
the likes of me. He'd often condescend
to share a cup, to fraternise, to 'blend',
but he was of Arezzo's foremost clan.
I never would presume. The thing began
at Christmas: I was present at the end,
Whit Sunday. By our ancient feudal laws,
I could have claimed the worker's week of rest,
but I'd got wind of Caponsacchi's cause.
Had I been ignorant, his mere request
would have recruited me. There'd be no pause.
For me, he was the bravest, and the best.

* * * *

He neither was, nor claimed to be, a priest.
It wasn't an affair (far less, a rape!)
He loved his silver trim, his velvet cape,
but that is where his egotism ceased.
They'd have you think him some voracious beast.
Don't get me wrong – no man enjoyed a jape
as much as he. No stranger to the grape,
he had a love of mischief. Unpoliced,
the scrapes would have continued – nay, increased,
if 1698's an indicator!
I've never known a *compañero* straighter,

and she was no mere Roman *arriviste*.
Their friendship, none more innocent, none greater:
now one is ostracised, and one deceased.

Complain? Protest? I'm of another school.
I'll tell my story in immortal prose,
and change the world through artful ridicule –
for who's not eloquent when liquor flows?
We know our rights, but no-one knows his duty:
the thing today is, no-one's ever wrong.
I like a drink, but I'm obsessed with beauty,
and no absteemer ever wrote a song.
Don't sneak a nip at home, go own the bar!
Small flaws, concealed, the world will take as great:
the greatest good is, being what you are.
swill down a noisy beer, then get up late!
So, with your wisdom mix a little folly:
life doesn't need to be so melancholy.

Venerino's Drinking Song

I sailed the seas and took my ease
and spent my share of silver:
embraced the breeze and drank the lees,
from Malta to Manilva.

Audaciously I might opine
that silver has no worth:
for feckless metal cannot shine
when buried in the earth.

A drunkard's words are juvenile,
a hymn to heathen Horus:
what's past's too vast to reconcile:
our chorus lies before us.

You'd use a knife to cut a knot?
You'll also need a whetter.
Just slip some humour in the slot:
you'll find it slices better!

Some sprinkled daisies may disarm
as well as mighty cedars:
The humble poet yet may charm
his few discerning readers.

I'm glad I'm poorer than a monk,
and not a millionaire:
No hemlock brew was ever drunk
from cups of earthenware.

They all go off to college, yeah,
like countless grains of rice.
They think to get some knowledge there,
but bridle at the price.

'Why sing with irony?', you ask:
See where mankind has got to!
I deem it, when I mull my task,
beyond my powers *not* to!

I find no lack of living-room
beneath the spreading sky:
the best of me escapes the tomb:
I shall not wholly die.

THAT FRANCESCHINI LIST OF CONTRABAND
they say the girl took with her – let's get real!
Begrudgers think in terms of 'cheat' and 'steal':
Pompilia did nothing underhand.
The loot they claim she lifted would have spanned,
nay filled, the Spanish gorge of Seteníl.

I watched her with these eyes, saw her ordeal
in clambering the city wall. She'd planned
so poorly, she forgot to bring a shawl.
The theme of theft is Franceschini-think.
She knew by now she had to be a mother,
and aimed to save her baby, and that's all.
I'll grant she put an opiate in their drink:
the motive, safe escape. There was no other.

All in this bar are close Arezzo friends.
We know that Franceschini nest of eels,
and how they are with property and deals.
They find irregularities and bends,
and chances to pervert things to their ends.
For once, I've glimpsed beneath official seals
and seen what sheer skulduggery reveals.
It all towards *Madonna Porzia* tends!
No man would ever cook up such a list,
with hues that would confuse astute chameleons!
mauve anchor-patterns, taffeta and twill,
cerise chemise, a misty amethyst,
and coronets be-clustered in carnelians!
It reeks of vixen, and I smell her still!

And this the household where a sucking lamb
must serve a week, as meagre sustenance!
Should we not, then, regard their 'wealth' askance?
The claim of theft was obviously a sham.
I'm hazarding a Latin epigram:
when blind leads blind, what hope of brisk advance?
When Guido lets his sister lead the dance,
they're sure to end *ambo in foveam*.
Our town is paralysed by surly faction.
You're either of the *Duomo* or the *Pieve*.
While we're espousing openness, attraction,
the other is prohibitive and heavy.

We'll stand our ground. The Franceschini levy
is ditch-bound, since it's founded on reaction.

STRAY LEAVES: THE ELUSIVE CANON

What are we, then, to make of Canon Conti?
A Knight, less of the Temple, more the Garter:
 though in the race, he's clearly a non-starter:
between the town's two tribes a makeshift ponte,
a minor character (think Branwell Brontë):
we see him as a meddler or a martyr,
no Andrew Jackson (more a Jimmy Carter),
as proud of protegées as Carlo Ponti,
more neo-realistic than Visconti.
Let women rule the roost? A poisoner's charter!
Perhaps if he'd not been so needy-wanty?
Our faults of character cost us, pro-rata.
He, brittle as a briar in Capodimonte,
was putty in the hands of his *cognata*.

My orders from Canale were direct:
to take the waggon to Clemente Gate
at sundown, and then – basically – to wait.
'There's someone Caponsacchi would protect,
so take them to Camoscia. Once you've checked
that they can travel on, although it's late,
and all is well, then I anticípate
you'll head for home whenever you elect.'
My passengers would meet me after dark,
which meant the gate would long be locked, of course
(impossible, and dangerous, to force).
I'd have to wait outside. I chose to park
beside that little tavern, named The Horse,
a newborn Noah, in his artless ark!

A pastel lavender infused the sky
as afternoon morphed gently into night.
The sparrows left off chipping as the light
diminished, and the bats began to vie
for mastery, so soundless and so shy.
The *Ave* tolled at San Domenico, the rite
which marks the death of day, and must excite
the *birruarri*, who arrived to ply
the bar which nightly shuts the city's eye.
Slow, sluggish minutes shuffled by.
Before me, San Clemente, blindly brown:
 off to my left, the bastion, broken-down,
we call the *torrione*. Time to sleep
a while, as stars emerge and shadows creep.

What roused me was a very gentle noise,
the clack of rocks and pebbles as they fall.
There was no moon. I peered towards the wall,
and spotted Caponsacchi, by his poise.
And with him was Pompilia, joy of joys!
She tottered down the broken turret's sprawl,
more beautiful than ever I recall –
but wait – there's one of Caponsacchi's boys!
Gregorio Guillichini, with a gun.
For fun, they call him 'Gregory the Great'.
I edged the horses forward, whistled low.
The firearm seemed a little overdone.
It weren't the moment to equivocate:
'I'm taking two, no more,' I said. 'Let's go!'

If Guillichini had some other plan,
he didn't voice it. In the others got.
The horses took my signal for the trot,
and we were moving. Guillichini's clan
would tear their hair out: what worse scandal, than
to have a son detained? A tighter spot,

Pompilia's: by throwing in her lot
with this one, she'd acquired a fearless man.
Why was she hated by the aretines?
The child was, at the oldest, seventeen.
I pondered what the reason might have been
that such a sweetheart raised so many spines:
and as I thought of spitefulness and spleen,
there came to mind some half-forgotten lines:

IF YOU SHOULD FIND A BLUSHING ROSE
replete with satin petals,
for sure it will be fast-enclosed
by throngs of stinging-nettles.

It's you men write the poems to?
The fairest face in town?
Then Envy will come after you:
it never punches down.

WE SKIRTED ROUND AREZZO'S FROWNING WALLS.
I kept the masonry close, on my right
and steered by memory, not sense of sight,
as far as where Torrente Castro falls
ad rus ex urbe, whence it lizard-crawls
towards Peneto, to deplete its might
on vineyards saturated in black night.
We turned the corner. Silence-shrouded stalls
informed us that we'd reached San Spirito,
the handsome gate, Arezzo's Popolo.
A wicket there, uncomfortably tight,
permits the stragglers to come and go.
Might some stray reveller observe us? No.
The grille was lifeless and deserted, quite.

Relieved, we started down the Consular Road.
I drove the team as fiercely as I could,

because I somehow sort of understood
this was combustible, and might explode
in violence, and fear's a forceful goad.
We passed one carriage. This side, brook in flood,
that side, touching axles, wood on wood.
And that's the only moment that we slowed.
I knew the lady – well, I knew her coach.
Her name's Donato, like our Irish saint,
but saintly's something that she surely ain't.
Not unequivocally beyond reproach.
And even if the lady showed restraint,
her steward, Manzo, has been known to poach.

The road was frightful on a moonless night,
at points a track, indifferently built,
but Caponsacchi bade me go full tilt.
The journey that he'd have me expedite
should take five hours – but we three halved it, quite!
Just rock and rut the surface, black as guilt,
uneven as your mother's patchwork quilt:
my constant fight to keep the horses tight
took (though I say it) superhuman might.
When, finally, the team began to wilt,
the posthouse at Camoscia hailed in sight.
We'd broken zero bones. No blood was spilt.
We'd hurtled like an albatross in flight,
and I'd discharged my duty to the hilt.

Five leagues, until we washed up in Camoscia.
Above all else, I needed to refresh
the horses. With regard to the caleche,
would they require it more? He'd found one posher.
Giuseppe let me go. Like bolt-and-washer,
I would have gone to Rome with him. We mesh!
He lifted her, and almost seemed to squash her,
so flimsy and so fragile was her flesh.

I gave him all I had – my silver comb –
then hitched a pair, and turned the team for home.
One final glimpse. I saw the phaeton vanish,
engulfed in blackness, resolute for Rome.
He'd grown, somehow. Not laddish now, but mannish.
'¡*Vaya con Díos!*', my clumsy prayer in Spanish.

I used the evening star to navigate
my way back home. I carefully adhered
to straight-and-narrow. Oddly, as I neared
Arezzo's walls, I saw that wicket-gate
fly open. 'Bless Your Worship, out this late!'
He gave no answer. Guido, by his beard!
I reined my horses in, just as he cleared
the obstacle. He looked ahead, dead straight,
his face the true embodiment of hate.
Remounting, for the Consul's Road he steered.
His mission? Not so hard to formulate.
The glitter of his eye was fierce and weird
and, as he passed the coach, he volunteered
'I'll catch and kill them as they copulate!'

That governor Medici – what a swine!
All silken hose and artificial stammer.
'I sport a rapier, but I wield a hammer.'
He travelled out to spike me, by design –
Maria delle Grazie, rustic shrine –
he smells of lavender and latin grammar.
'*Nessun fumo*,' says he, '*senza fiamma*.'
'Your Worship's words will wither on the vine,'
says I, 'addressed to dullard brains like mine.'
'Then let us drop,' says he, 'all glozing glamour:
you'll pay for midnight masquerades. In fine,
your wretched arse is headed for the slammer.'
Medici (though Canale raised a clamour)
to prison did, in fact, my arse consign.

I spent the summer in that stinking cell.
Medici came to see me. 'Oh, such bliss!
What lodging could be wholesomer than this?'
He nosed the tuberose pinned to his lapel.
'You've known the argosy, the caravelle,'
he grinned. 'I'm sure you sometimes reminisce!
But galley-slave?' His voice dropped to a hiss,
and still he smiled. 'I think that might be hell!'
'It's not my place to bully, or compel,'
the guvnor told me, 'but I'd be remiss
if I did not inform you. There's a spell,
a charm, to yank you back from the abyss,
and even check you out of this hotel.
Just tell us that you saw them pet and kiss.'

I knew that they would haul me into court
and ask me what, if anything, I'd seen:
I knew precisely what this move would mean.
I'd have to lie my nuts off. That, in short,
was my dilemma. As a witness ought,
I sought to tell the truth. To keep it clean,
however, meant a drastic change of scene.
I'd have to take up rowing – not as sport –
but in the papal galleys. 'Yes,' I said,
'I kept an eye upon them as we fled.
I saw them kissing, like they were in bed.'
I wish the court had viewed the coach, instead.
My place and posture made me look ahead,
to steer the horses' footfalls as we sped.

I lied on oath, and don't feel bad at all.
I did it so that justice might prevail.
I sang – and better than a nightingale!
Arezzo's lock-up – stolid, squalid, small –
had lost (let's say) its power to enthrall.
Four months in prison isn't cakes and ale:

Giuseppe got a pass, the bird made bail.
My state of mind was, 'Why not scale the wall?'
When everybody knows you, beck-and-call
has meaning, so escape's beyond the pale.
(I've had it with these clichés.) Calm or squall,
avoiding galleys was my holy grail.
You catch the bottom-feeders when you trawl:
should I remain the only one in jail?

I want to mention what are called 'young blades'.
The street-brawl is the amber that they're set in.
If Girolamo's now a brutal cretin,
it's down to that. Gang violence pervades
Arezzo's very fabric. Ambuscades
are normal. Once, the rival factions met in
a vast affray. The Franceschini ate in
a restaurant they call 'The Pallisades'.
You'll know the story from the pasquinades:
Pier Paolo Caponsacchi (older sibling
of our Giuseppe), captain of such raids,
so smote the Canon, there can be no quibbling:
the spastic's only 'ask' is, bullying maids.
You doubt his brain is broken? Watch him dribbling.

Venerino Remembers the Countess

If you've been shipwrecked, it's a certainty –
you'll tremble on the mildest-mannered sea.
But now, in place of exploits, I like sleeping.
There's even pleasure, of a sort, in weeping.
Love and friendship? They're not quite the same,
but love may enter, cloaked in friendship's name.
Old books, old wine, old opera, old cheese:
I'm for old times, but glad to live in these!

Pompilia, they called her. Fair of face,
and very quiet. My experience
of women is, the ones who have true grace
have learnt to hold their tongues. Without pretence,
she had real beauty. Eyes, so dark, immense!
Her motto should be pricked in cambric lace:

Ignore me, I'll embrace you!
Adore me, and I'll flee!
Suppose you run – I'll chase you:
get fresh, you're history!

* * * *

'Offending Octaves'? Bawdy rhymes,
a bit of vulgar verse.
We live in topsy-turvy times.
What banker ain't done worse?

Just two young folks who did no harm,
an eagle and a Dove,
disarming in their guileless charm,
and all they did was love.

But things don't die, they merely change –
a thought for us to cherish.
Constituents just rearrange:
they never, ever perish.

No matter what abuse they'd hurl,
he didn't weigh the cost.
He wasn't wrong to help the girl,
but look at what he lost –

hence, wrong in terms of what's at stake.
He did it for her sake.

What does a spell in exile take?
One poem, one mistake.

LA MONTEJAQUEÑA, Being a Tale told by Venerino

A country once endured a civil war
(if folks can't fight, then what are countries for?)
The ugly part is brother *contra* brother,
father *contra* son, and daughter-mother.
For in a civil war, some things occur
one wishes hadn't happened, never were.
The Civil Governor (from Setenil)
had lost the urge to empathise, to *feel*,
and when hostilities got under way
the murderers were promptly making hay:
denounce this man because his accent's funny,
condemn that man because you owe him money.
And who decides who lives, and which one dies?
The Civil Governor with the lifeless eyes.
His name? Donato Ruíz Dominguez Gil.
He'd grown so much accustomed to the kill,
he signed the forms emotionless, unthinking.
Tall and gaunt (result of heavy drinking),
he sent a thousand men to meet eternity
and called them 'the unfortunate fraternity'.
One morning he just happened to be sober
(it was the twenty-second of October)
and heard his wife excitedly proclaim,
'today the saint who granted you his name
is honoured. We must celebrate his feast!
The poor are fed. A prisoner released?'
An echo in the cavern of his soul
reminded him of when he'd once been whole.
A childhood glimmer, long-lost blamelessness,

produced a feeling almost like distress:
and thus Donato Ruíz Dominguez Gil
discovered that his heart was human still.
A prisoner on the palace esplanade
stood waiting for the final fusillade:
the Governor stood the firing-party down,
and spoke. 'If there's a woman in this town
who'll make herself this wretch's lawful wife,
and teach him how to live, I'll spare his life.'
The poor man heard, with chagrín and dismay,
the offer stood for just Donatus' Day!
If no-one could be found to marry him
before the midnight hour, then things looked grim!
Today it's hard enough to spread the news,
but back in those days, people didn't use
to travel much. They ploughed a narrow furrow.
Their only mode of transport was the *burro*!
By afternoon, no woman had been found:
the search now spread to villages around.
Now time was short, but as the deadline neared,
in Montejaque a *salvatrix* appeared!
A woman of the village said she'd wed
without coercion, influence or dread,
to save a life. They married, and it's told
they lived in harmony till, very old,
the woman passed. Unwilling to abide
without her, and inclined to coincide,
that very day the husband also died!

THE HISTORY OF THE TRUE CROSS: (9)
The Exhaltation of the Cross

This lump of wood is who we are.
It nails our *Kulturgeist*.

Samantha Fox to samovar,
our brand is Jesus Christ.

And what if He did not exist?
The question's not germane:
The Man Himself has not been missed
from Saskatoon to Spain.

We need a hook, a selling-point
as simple as can be,
a shape that we can all anoint –
a fish, a moon ... a tree!

NAY, GUILTINESS WILL SPEAK, Being a Tale told by Alessandro Baldeschi

STRAY LEAVES: THE MOOR OF VENICE

*En la ciudad que se llama Sevilla
se encuentra el callejón Gago.
Es donde el Don Santiago
tenía su sede (o silla).
Su elegantísima villa
(aquí es el mito muy vago)
construido de piedras del lago
en cuya hermosa orilla
(y donde el sol siempre brilla)
pasó Jesucristo, El Mago
(perdone si yo me rezago):
compuesta de planta sencilla
(la casa) que es maravilla
dejada por falta de pago
allí yo ni regreso ni trago
con Iago la clara manzanilla.*

Cornaro Cornered

This all occurred in 1489.
Upheaval from the Rhine down to the Rhone,
with Cyprus centre of a combat zone,
and empires rising, others in decline:
Queen Catherine, Venetian concubine,
was ousted from her husband's cypriot throne
and ostracised, abandoned and alone,
as Europe was convulsed from Rhone to Rhine
(another baby-bride, abused and spurned).
Columbus, meanwhile, scrutinized Japan
(as he believed it) as a preacher burned
in Florence, and a painter in Milan
packed up his brushes, one more supper earned,
and Portugal reached out for Hindustan.

OTHELLO WAS A MAN OF SABLE SKIN,
        adopted son of Venice:
physically graceful, slender, tall,
        whenever foreign menace
        or treason from within,
        'our fearless cannonball'
Othello was the hero to forestall
        the danger. Born to win,
Othello was admired and loved by all.

Among the city's virtuous *signore,*
        the beauty, Desdemona,
for modest goodness stood alone:
        a native of Verona,
        hers is a tragic story.
As history has shown,
shortcomings, be they hidden, known,
        della mente o del cuore,
decide the outcome, once the dice are thrown.

If only we could see what lies ahead!
    (Alternatively, no:
the path is strewn with pain and grief.
     It's better not to know!)
     The couple planned to wed:
     a loving *leitmotif*
(their courtship was as beautiful as brief),
     enlaced with golden thread,
his gift to her, a bridal handkerchief.

It happened that Venetian dispositions
    on Cyprus needed change:
the perfect choice as field commander
      was eager to arrange
      this urgentest of missions.
      Othello, in all candour
regarded as a modern Alexander,
      held brilliant ambitions:
but one within his number had plans grander.

Iago Ballesta

To paint him short in stature says it all.
He talks of love, but brutish physicality
is what he means: concretion and carnality.
Strong limbs there are which please, but some appall:
enormous thighs look ill on someone small.
The ugliest is not corporeality,
but Iago's utter absence of morality,
his sneering self-aggrandizement withal.

A weapon for a name, and so the man:
the grace is lethal, sinister the charm.
And while the brain is fierce, the front is calm:
There's something alien in him, 'other than':

He'd twist a knife in tripes without a qualm.
He wants to wound you, just because he can.

OTHELLO FELT UNEASINESS OF MIND.
        He loved his wife so dearly,
He didn't want to part from her,
        and told her so sincerely.
        She said she was inclined
        (could such a thing occur)
to voyage with him. 'I assure you, sir,
        I'm utterly resigned,'
said Desdemona, 'humbly to defer

to your, my master's, wishes. But believe
        that what my heart desires
is to be with you. I can bear
        tornados, earthquakes, fires
        in order to achieve
        (effectively, to share)
whatever goal my husband's soul may dare!'
        She caught him by the sleeve:
'Your noblest gift to me, let me be there.'

They sailed to Cyprus. To the Moor's delight,
        it passed without event.
A modern Jason steered his Argo
        without impediment
        to Famagusta Bight.
        Amongst the human cargo,
an army ensign by the name of Iago.
        This discontented knight
enjoyed Othello's ear, without embargo.

The Spaniard gave no thought to others' skins:
        seljuk or sephardim,
Don Iago held no animus.

It made no odds to him.
His favoured deadly sins
were Lust and Envy. Thus,
when women knelt to sing the Angelus,
the pinch of inner djinns
provoked in him a lunge lascivious.

On Desdemona centred his obsession
(though she was unaware).
All lechers seek the blameless. She,
bespoken, decent, fair,
engendered his aggression.
Inveterate jealousy
of him who held command of land and sea
plus yearning for possession
of her, his wife – O, double perfidy!

* * * *

ANOTHER CAPTAIN IN OTHELLO'S FORCE
was handsome Cassio. This gentleman,
a soldier since Othello's rule began,
did nothing which was ignorant or coarse.

Othello's consort, like some doting matron,
bestowed on him disinterested favour:
she did it for the pleasure that it gave her
to recognise young promise as its patron.

The Moor himself was fond of Cassio, too.
The art of soldiering his true devotion,
He joyed in ensigns worthy of promotion:
he looked for heroes in his retinue.

When La Cornara found herself expulsed,
the able Cassio won a colonel's sword:

the Spaniard earned no furtherment. Ignored,
with jealousy and bitterness convulsed,

he swore that Desdemona had to die.
To chosen soldiers, Iago laid it bare:
'She's being toped by Cassio. An affair!'
He spread the lie with vehemence – but why?

He may well have believed it. His type do.
They never hesitate to light a fire
precisely at the seat of *their* desire.
But there's another explanation, too.

When sheep meet wolves, it never turns out well.
To void Venetian trust was his design:
in this, evinced great artifice. In fine,
Iago was the matchless Machiavel.

The army is the bulwark of the nation:
If discipline is lax, the thing collapses.
So, how to minimise our moral lapses?
How should we punish insubordination?

Is violence appropriate, or rash?
'The only thing they understand is strength.'
Can castigation run to any length?
Are hapless hoplites asking for the lash?

You use your sword to hit a man: that's that.
He needs to show respect for your commission.
This isn't torture, this is admonition.
You didn't use the blade, you used the flat!

It's not the thing itself, but what transpires.
They all chip in, they all express a view:

it gathers up resentment's residue:
thus ingle nooks result in forest fires.

'You stand accused of conduct unbecoming,'
Othello said to Cassio. 'Will you make
an answer?' Ventured Cassio, 'This mistake –
I cannot think the depths that you are plumbing

could be the offspring of a rational mind –
is grievous, and I ask you to relent.
I am a soldier, and not eloquent,
but what is here alleged is less than kind.'

It happened that the Moor's attractive wife
was present for this *fracas* (as were others).
She told Othello, 'I had thought you brothers!
For such a thing, you'd ruin Cassio's life?'

But Iago knows precisely where the nerve is
that needs a tweak. 'An officer of standing
–   as Cassio is – defers to those commanding.
That's how we function. 'Tis the curse of service!'

And to Othello, then: 'A word apart,
My Lord?' He takes Othello to one side:
'It gives me dolor, Highness, to confide.
Perhaps she has a reason. Of the heart.'

Iago to Othello

You'd sacrifice your honour to a thief?
Rely upon a woman, not a knife?
How often has that blade preserved your life?
How frequently have females brought you grief?
Will you persist in this obscene belief,
though lust's abroad, and fornication's rife?

Are you a man? Then look you to your wife!
How long since last you saw the handkerchief?
The Devil stalks your chamber, forked and hooved:
are you the only one who doesn't know?
I have both watched him come and seen him go.
His passing will be heartily approved:
impediment most usefully removed!
You think him loyal? By Janus, I say no!

I wonder if My Lady has the pox:
she who receives, may give it, just as well.
Though Cassio's lode attracts, it can repel:
his vice is to his virtue equinox.
Gallinas ven bien, but blind are cocks
and tumble clumsily in every well,
nor ever know the reason why they fell.
Renounce the Valley of the Thousand Shocks!

The sow accepts one seeder, spurns another,
and she herself could never tell you why.
The spasm that results may make her mother,
but might not crown you sire. Put pesos by!
Your dagger is the coin will reimburse:
¡Pavilate! Put money in your purse!

THEY ASKED THE ENSIGN FOR HIS POINT OF VIEW.
He said he didn't feel at all aggrieved,
while praising Cassio for what he'd achieved.
The plaint was archived, with no more ado.

A public-facing matter reached its end,
but other things now threatened to collide:
Othello had been scalded, mortified
by promptings of (as he supposed) his friend.

* * * *

WAITING IN AN ANTE-ROOM,
        Iago hears raised voices.
Dissent! A mare that he can groom!
        In this his heart rejoices.

'But Cassio's your friend!' he hears,
        in Desdemona's tones.
The conversation seems to end
        with, 'Men are more than stones!'

Indeed they are. They can be swayed.
        But men are also less:
for where's the boulder, can be played?
        The pebble you'd finesse?

The consort closed the argument
        by opening the doors.
A final parting barb was sent –
        she shouted, 'Oh, you Moors!'

A word is uttered in a trice,
        but what it may betoken
is rarely weighed, though choice is nice:
        once spoken, it is spoken.

'Her handkerchief, I have. I'll say
        she gave it to Cassio, flat.
Now racial rancour comes my way –
        the thing is falling pat!'

Othello and his man are face-to-face,
        with Desdemona gone.
Reluctantly, 'It's not my place …
        but have you pondered on…?'

A hestitant yet honest friend
        is how he comes across,
who won't conceal, yet cannot mend,
        the magnitude of loss.

Iago fights to find the word,
        but then the truth escapes:
'She said to Cassio – this I heard –
        she's had her fill of apes.'

Rejones is the sport of princes
        which the Spanish love:
the death-stroke – how *el toro* winces,
        when run-through from above!

Long moments pass. No words emerge.
        The thread of life is broken.
Then, ruins of a sentence surge:
        'Some evidence? … Some token?'

'Your wedding-gift. The handkerchief,'
        he started, *ojos vacíos*.
'a rose, embroidered in relief –
        the trinket now is Cassio's.'

A stricken bull, life gushing out,
        will oftimes seek the fence
and stumble, bleeding from the snout,
        with neither sight nor sense.

Othello lunged around the room,
        unfathoming, unseeing:
as if some private phantom-tomb
        engulfed his very being.

        * * * *

STRAY LEAVES; OF WIVES AND KNIVES

In complex narratives, some words recur
(a better term would be, 'cling like a burr').
You lust for 'life'? You're threatened with a 'knife',
and 'death' perforce brings on a final 'breath'.
One's reservoir of rhymes sometimes runs dry:
What wayward word's preferred to wed with 'wife'?
Recherché lexicon like 'stipe', or 'knipe'?
When strife is rife, what can you do? Contort
your lines? Resort to haughty clichés? Fie!
Of 'Arthur', what's important? Only 'Morte'.
As Piero pondered, when he painted Seth,
when palette's poor, depict the stereotype.
Thus, shortfall ushers in the shibboleth.
One rule is sacrosanct. (Just ask a Slav!)
The pool is puny? Go with what you have.

IF IAGO HAS A PLAN TO 'HELP OTHELLO',
we know whom it will help in point of fact,
to whose advantage all the odds are stacked.
He plays his master like a violincello.

His tone is sympathetic, gentle, mellow.
You'd take him for a paragon of tact.
He has a cold capacity to act
the role of a responsive, caring fellow.

To talk with Cassio (while the Moor observed)
might coax the former into rash admissions:
since Cassio had the best of dispositions,
he would be open, not the least reserved.

Othello acquiesced. At first unnerved,
he came to welcome Iago's propositions:

unmindful of his ensign's dark ambitions,
he gave assent, and never after swerved.

As Iago talked with Cassio he laughed,
as if in disbelief at what he heard.
'You've never toped her? Really? That's absurd!'
The Moor learnt nothing. Voices didn't waft

across to where he hid. Iago's craft
obliged the Moor to judge by deed, not word:
he saw the gestures, gauging what occurred
by eye alone, as Iago quipped and chaffed.

The ensign comes to where Othello waits.
He plays the part of helper to the hilt:
he pauses, even trembles, seems to wilt:
and then the dam gives way. He intimates

his scornful laughter's meaning. He relates
the fiction he so skilfully has built:
how brazenly has Cassio owned his guilt:
feigns fellow-feeling for the fool he hates.

Iago hands two items to his master:
the handkerchief is finally restored,
and with it comes a fine Toledo sword.
Othello holds the tokens of disaster,

his face as motionless as alabaster:
'And was the handing-over not deplored?'
'I asked, and my request was not ignored.'
'My grief was infinite. But now it's vaster.'

STRAY LEAVES: THE FAVOUR AND THE BLADE

A handkerchief, adorned with cambric lace,
Toledo sword, with careful patterns chased,
by being placed together are debased.
Exquisite artefacts: a fall from grace,

a human tragedy, is here disclosed.
The fabric shows a finely-fashioned rose,
a seeming cross, the weapon. Hateful foes
debauch them of their meaning, juxtaposed.

As one, the wedded handiwork is tendered,
the linen and the pommel both embossed.
How readily the rapier was surrendered!
how languidly the handkerchief was lost!
How easily is enmity engendered!
How frequently is friendship turned to frost!

* * * *

OTHELLO:

Republics may not contemplate a king,
But here in Cyprus, far from the Lagoon,
the Commandant is much the nearest thing.
Since vessels are arriving very soon,
you stand to benefit from news they bring.

Suppose you grant me just one simple boon,
and murder Cassio, slit his throat or wring
his sinning neck, you'll find it opportune.
You'll govern Cyprus, then the Doge's ring
awaits you. Move before the next full moon!

IAGO:

The ímpetus to act is surely yours!
A husband has to honour honour's cause.
It falls on him who's wronged to settle scores.
And so it is, according to the laws
of Christendom, from Asolo to Azores.

Your talk of my ambitions gives me pause.
I know not how it is among the Moors,
but Destiny has unforgiving jaws:
I dare not do an act on Cyprus shores
That may impugn me. I must have no flaws.

OTHELLO:

La Serenissima will stand me down.
They've heard my strength is failing, cannot mend:
I know not how they know. Before I drown,
I still retain the right to recommend.
Fulfill my wish, and you can have the crown.

Comply. Commit. Converge. Come, condescend.
Lose nothing by it, yet acquire renown.
On you all Fate's contingencies depend:
I see you comprehend it by your frown.
So, act. I see your thoughts are tending to this end.

STRAY LEAVES: HONI SOIT QUI MAL Y PENSE

The strongest-ever answer? 'I don't know'.
You've given nothing to the other side,
and hollowed-out a hole where you can hide:
your questioner has nowhere else to go.

And so, the stratagem of many beaux,
to trap their lover, setting up 'you lied',
unravels (even when she's caught astride
a subway grate). The doctrine of Monroe

ring-fenced a continent, is proof against
interrogators, even of North Korea.
So, 'Where's the handkerchief?' he asks, incensed,
and Desdemona answers, 'No idea':
has something hit a wall, or just commenced?
The answer, in a word, is 'Cytherea'.

* * * *

THE FAMOUS CEDAR TREES OF LEBANON
form Desdemona's boudoir's ceiling-beams:
her rafters, as a kind of antiphon,
are made of northern Europe's finest fir.
The ensign, by the scurviest of schemes,
has entered her preserve to bludgeon her
to death. With this achieved, the saboteur

will compromise the structure of the roof.
His hope is that the subsequent collapse
obliterates the crime, removes all proof.
Unhouse a mortice, prise a cedar stilt:
the weight of slate and terracotta caps
will crush her corpse. 'The thing was jerrybuilt,'
can then be said, eradicating guilt.

He knows that Desdemona is not here.
It pleases him to breach her private space.
Aroused by mixed malevolence and fear,
he gathers up a linen underdress
and presses it obscenely to his face.

His crisis past, he squats in a recess
to cover both her access and egress.

Then comes the rattle of the fatal door.
She cannot know it, but the clock has chimed
the limit of her life. She'll never more
hear Monteverdi's Vespers in Saint Mark's,
or laugh through Cinthio's stories, ribald-rhymed,
or share a sunlit meadow with the larks,
or love beneath Verona's soaring arcs.

The Schism

The letters patent in italic hand
(in words the Doge himself had plainly penned)
informed Othello bluntly of the end
of this, his first – and clearly last – command.
On top of this, here came his Spanish 'friend',
to tell him of the stocking filled with sand,
and how the roof-collapse had gone as planned,
and now he'd come to claim his dividend.
When conscience and concupiscence contend,
ferocious flames may oftentimes be fanned.
The Moor is changed. Can Iago understand?
Of course not. Claybound souls cannot transcend.
Her honour, compromised? Why, yes – with pride:
and both before and after she had died!

* * * *

IAGO WAS SUMMARILY DISMISSED.
He felt that he'd been promised the succession
and now, by some unconscionable twist,
the prize was being swept from his possession.
To him, the only course was to persist –
the answer to all problems was aggression.

How best to gain again Othello's eye?
It seemed quite simple – Cassio had to die.

        * * * *

THE ENSIGN DOES NOT THINK AS OTHERS THINK.
He doesn't think, 'Othello is offended:
His own shortcomings drove him to this brink –
He instigated more than ne intended.'
Once calm, the soul from further harm will shrink
(though what has happened cannot now be mended).

One hopes that conscience opens up a chink,
and animosity can be suspended:
no matter how we sin, how low we sink,
we reach a point where perfidy is ended.
Whatever bitter draught we chose to drink,
It's notwithstanding with redemption blended.

But Iago wasn't made like you or me:
by reconciliation sets no store.
In him exists no human sympathy:
If wrong brings poor results, he'll wrong some more.
Submersed in blood with equanimity,
he'll wade through blood to reach the distant shore.

What some do highly, others holily,
for Iago is one long unsettled score.
'I'll kill again: the Moor will fawn on me.'
Morality is nonsense to ignore.
The only thing that matters is utility:
'While Cassio lives, I'm rowing with one oar!'

        * * * *

AT THE FAMAGUSTA GATE
there's a tunnel, long and strait,
foul-aired and fungus-ridden.
Cassio's here to meet 'a friend',
unaware how this will end:
a cloak-and-dagger virgin.

At the Famagusta Gate
menace hovers, inchoate:
a shudder comes unbidden.
Someone's moving in the square:
glints of metal, here and there:
pools of blackness burgeon.

At the Famagusta Gate
interlopers navigate
a medieval midden.
A sudden surge, a savage cry:
hot blood spurting from a thigh:
'Convey him to a surgeon!'

Gangrene

The dry one has a positive prognosis.
(Though neither type's a windfall, all in all,
we'd all prefer a pustule to a pall,
accept a little localised necrosis).

The wet one forms around traumatic lesion:
completely lethal, rapid in formation:
the only hope, immediate amputation.
One's logic doesn't need to be Cartesian.

When Iago learned that Cassio had survived,
his need was to proliferate infection:
not only would this shield him from detection:

corrupting Cassio, carefully contrived,
could steer his fortunes in the right direction.
The plan, as improvised, approached perfection!

        * * * *

Does Iago come to see the amputee?
    Why, certainly.
What cause is served, by talking to the same?
    He'll shift the blame!
They fight: suppose a shift, by Fortune's Whore,
    onto the Moor:
then Iago rolls in gratitude galore!
But if Othello dies by Cassio's hand,
then Iago's better-placed to take command!
Why, certainly he'll shift the blame onto the Moor.

Who murdered Desdemona? *Tertium quid?*
    Othello did!
Which word describes the slaughter of a bride?
    Uxoricide!
(What's offered here is sheer mendacity,
    it's plain to see.)
For Iago's plan to reach its apogee,
he needs to steel the colonel to redress:
his lies are gambits, in a game of chess.
Othello did uxoricide, it's plain to see.

        * * * *

It never would occur to malefactors,
the other side could ever play it straight:
that anyone might simply commentate,
unmoved by reciprocity of hate,
defeats the understanding of detractors,
and predators presume we all predate.

Plans laid by what we now must call 'bad actors'
suppose that every sucker takes the bait.

It's obvious to Iago, clear as day,
that Cassio will do what Iago would,
assassinate Othello, blood for blood:
he's overlooked that Cassio is good.
He sees the world in quite a different way.
The envious ensign has misunderstood
that some of us might put the law in play,
oblivious to such a likelihood.

Instead of dead, Othello is arrested,
the euphemistic 'question' is now put:
the Moor is mute, his mouth stays firmly shut
through *sibille, strapado,* crush and cut.
He's comprehensively been torture-tested,
and not let slip a word of what's afoot:
his torturers admit that they've been bested.
Enough's enough, but this has been a glut.

Non grata in Venetia, this *persona*:
better move him to Adige's shore,
where he'll have other pleasantries in store,
for they have known Othello heretofore.
Resolved: an ostracism to Verona
sees Venice disembarrassed of the Moor.
The kinsfolk of a certain Desdemona
are keen to settle one outstanding score.

* * * *

AND THIS IS WHERE OTHELLO LEAVES OUR STORY.
Unnoticed, silent, uncomplaining, stoic,
he roamed the alleys of Verona's ghetto,
each day a life-in-death, *memento mori*.

His death was not delayed, and not heroic:
they knifed him in the *Pigna* vicoletto.

* * * *

THE ONLY THING THAT MAY REMAIN
      unmentioned, unresolved,
is what befell Othello's thane,
      and what his fate involved.

Don Santiago Churriguer
      Ballesta Alarcón
had vanished into thinnest air:
      when justice struck, was gone.

From Cyprus, Iago crossed the waves.
      For thirty years, no news:
one legend claims he traded slaves
      in Spanish Vera Cruz.

By fifteen-twenty, there he is,
      established in Seville,
with thriving vineyards in Jeréz,
      beneath Lebrija hill.

We hear again of sordid plots
      and mention of the devil:
the leopard cannot lose its spots,
      and water finds its level.

Don Iago brought a suit of law
      against Duke Luis' son:
by this, his greed, his fatal flaw,
      was finally undone.

Don Fadrique remained aloof
    (for he controlled the claque):
He had the plaintiff put to proof,
    which signified the rack.

When tortured, Iago's body burst.
    He, universally scorned,
was left in agony, unnursed,
    to die unloved, unmourned.

TRIAL AND DEATH OF COUNT GUIDO FRANCESCHINI AND HIS COMPANIONS FOR THE IMPIOUS MURDER OF PIETRO COMPARINI, HIS WIFE, AND DAUGHTER: WHICH LAMENTABLE SLAUGHTER OCCURRED DURING THE PONTIFICATE OF INNOCENT XII.

The years have rushed to dust, as years will do.
Today another, taking up his pen,
would burn through this, our tragedy, again.
Our author writes of folk he never knew:
can skill-at-narrative invoke a hue,
a vantage-point, which supplements our ken?
Our judgment is adjusted. Well? What then?
A thousand facets constitute what's 'true'.
Count Guido lacked the intellect, we know,
to ponder consequence. Some grasp at grudges,
are weaned, are lean, on spleen. This being so,
is guilt 'up to the hilt'? Are we his judges?
Concede his world's not ours, the needle nudges.
But soft! The blade descended, long ago.

A tiny archive close to Sant' Ignazio,
    Dominican depository of tomes,

sequestered sightless in its silent rooms
a thing composed (supposedly) in Lazio,

but lost for centuries. No author's name.
From time to time a library exhumes,
regurgitates, the pulp that it consumes,
and old controversies burst into flame.

Who knows what prose has yet to come to light?
Neglected journal, documentary gem?
What composition, apt of apothegm,
may still emerge to vindicate, indict?
Though not quite kosher, might an ammonite
break surface to corroborate, condemn?

A WEDDING WAS REQUIRED. THE HOUR WAS LATE.
Four children, middle-aged, without an heir,
and ruin looming. Insecure the stair,
and cracked the window where the wind's lament
lugubriously echoes their despair:
'How can we come by money?' In this strait,
although they know that cash is excrement,
at least it fertilizes the estate.
A poor protagonist to circumvent
the all-too-brooding, imminent descent,
Count Guido was unlikely to ensnare
a Chigi but, the coffers being bare,
the caitiff could two catalysts conflate:
he might grab gold, and – who knows? – procreate!

Abate Paolo, brother with a brain,
took on the task. His brand of priestly chic
contrasted with the other's frail physique
and lack of savvy. Unimpressive sentry
to Paolo's Roman general, gloomy, weak,
his beard a thick and unrestricted mane,

with knowledge of the world so elementary
he even lacked the wherewithal to feign
the superficial poise that rural gentry
can sometimes carry off. His point of entry?
Assertive surliness. That too-big beak,
his hawkish nose, declared his sullen streak.
Like Sisyphus condemned to fruitless strain,
the fool despises heights he can't attain.

And so began the matrimony trawl.
They battened on the Comparini child,
Pompilia. A schedule was compiled,
inflating Guido's wealth. 'They can't refuse us!
The mother's such a snob. 'Contessa' styled,
decked out tin tiara for the ball –
she's gagging for it. Laughable. They're losers!
Signed over bonds, in setting out their stall:
it's easy, mugging alcohol-abusers.
They've made themselves the beggars, us the choosers.
The power of attorney's duly filed,
the fussy father (finally!) reconciled.
The chance of other claims? Minutely small.
They're old, and she's a girl. We bagged it all!'

The questions which arose (and still arise)
are, why displace wholesale to Guido's home?
Abandon all they'd ever known in Rome?
And why persist, when facts were coming out,
in falling for that Franceschini foam?
Had wool been pulled across the father's eyes
so utterly as to extinguish doubt?
Was he oblivious to Paolo's lies?
He'd previously tried to nose about,
but only Violante carried clout.
She felt her future lay on Tuscan loam
and, caring nothing for the pontiff's dome,

she rolled a reckless die. It wasn't wise.
She'd be (quite literally) cut down to size.

Arezzo now, and Guido's haughty mother.
Aloof, unfriendly, unforgiving, dour,
she had (within her world) a lust for power.
Madonna Beatrice threw unseemly fits
or withered opposition with a glower,
while Girolamo, Guido's damaged brother,
exuded menace. Such domestic blitz!
With woeful winds continuing to wuther
through wintry windows, wearying their wits,
sustained by nothing more than gruel and grits,
what could the Comparini do, but cower
inside their icy bedroom, worsted, sour?
To shield Pompilia, they had to smother
their rancour, while protecting one another.

Pietro feels his way along the alley,
head bent against the slanting Tuscan sleet,
anticipating something warm to eat,
his breeches sagging badly at the crotch:
but no-one's there to take his coat, or greet
the homebound hero, sated by his sally.
His fingers fumble for the doorlock notch,
but voices from within, aggressive, snarly,
erupt at him. 'Piss off! We'll call the watch!
You reek of Morellino, stink of scotch!
You're causing a commotion in the street!
This decent household, Christian, discreet,
wants none of you, you drunken Roman scally!
You've made your bed – go sleep at *Il Canale*!'

He doesn't beg a chance to say he's sorry.
There's no use crying: too much milk's been spilt.
The downpour's caused his tricorn hat to wilt.

It's disagreeable, but not a shock.
So much for toasted sausage, feather quilt!
When Violante tries a rescue foray,
unravels chain and disengages lock,
then scurries out, she's soon the second quarry!
The door is slammed behind her – hear them mock!
We're needy neighbours, hesitant to knock.
Let's walk the twenty yards, admit our guilt,
play prodigals, repentant to the hilt,
and try the patience of *Memento Mori*
(Pietro's name for morbid Doctor Borri).

It had to come. The Romans chose to go.
Pompilia's position, always bleak,
began to show a far more sinister streak:
humiliated, spurned with cuff or curse,
a dagger jammed against her teenage cheek,
she saw her parents' footprints in the snow
and wondered, 'Can this thing get any worse?'
She could not guess what yet she'd undergo.
To us, in kinder times, it seems perverse
that husbands could command, control, coerce,
but Guido (though extreme) was not unique:
there *was* no help a married girl could seek.
Alone, disowned, she viewed the status quo:
it was the best that she would ever know.

A papal jubilee! A Roman spring!
How Innocent the Twelfth has made his mark!
How May was made for strolling in the park!
We sample simples, quaff the chalybeate,
as Phoebus strides across his widest arc.
It's time for cleansing, time for freshening:
confess, and sins are stricken from the sheet,
for heaven wants to hear canaries sing.
Violante? She's the type you'll never beat.

Her words are claymores, though her tone is sweet.
Adventurers are eager to embark,
and pyromaniacs to light the spark:
the scorpion convulses for the sting ...
'she's not our daughter – not our anything!'

What nagged at her to nuke the nuptial *nido*?
Concede, indeed, a pseudo-parturition?
Was she a fool to drool this cruel admission?
Or did she have some other goal in mind?
Why run the risk of nuclear family fission?
Why pummel Pietro? Pain her *pastor fido*?
Well, hatred – unlike love – is far from blind.
Our Violante lived by just one credo:
to pay you back in kind (that is, *un*kind!)
You cross her, and her cross-hairs are aligned.
Was this an act of innocent contrition?
Of course not. She was on a secret mission.
The target of her tungsten-tipped torpedo?
None other than the good-for-nothing Guido!

Again Arezzo. Guido needs to hide
the things he's done behind his own front door.
It's full-blown summer, sixteen ninety-four:
Pompilia is fourteen years of age.
'Suppose she writes a letter, routine chore,
to Paolo down in Rome? Suppose I guide
her writing, steer her hand across the page?
She tells him she's a happy, grateful bride.
Concerns he may have formed she can assuage:
she now despises Comparini rage.
Her husband chides her, lovingly, for sure,
but stories of abuse, he can ignore.'
At first he blustered, bullied, badgered, lied,
becoming by degrees uxoricide.

The fact remains, a child was being abused.
Intimidation, menaces and force –
to what tribunal could she have recourse?
A woman is the plaything of her man.
No women's refuges, and no divorce.
She agitated, slated and accused,
But closed no safer than when she began.
At every turn, she found her pleas refused.
She did as much as any victim can.
To those with clout, she literally ran.
Of course they knew. Pompilia, the source,
gave dates and details until she was hoarse.
It's not as if they justified, excused.
They didn't care. In fact, they were amused.

Since every door was closed, she turned for succour
to Canon Conti, known to Guido's sister
(the one who, at the opera, had kissed her),
frequenter of the Franceschini house.
For sure, he found it painful to resist her
when lovely lower lip began to pucker,
but ardour for escape? He had to douse
her recklessness: a diver and a ducker,
Gian Conti didn't dare to flout her spouse
(with some unfairness, some have named him 'mouse'):
In some capacity, he could assist her,
and mentioned Caponsacchi ('*il gaudista*').
For, after all, Pompilia was a looker
(and many claim that Conti tried to fuck her).

But Caponsacchi wasn't keen at first.
Reluctance was his posture, largely owing
to internecine friction, still ongoing:
grave injuries, inflicted on the brain
of Girolamo, limiting and slowing
his mental functions which, ineptly nursed,

had left the Franceschini less than sane.
'In this, my brother Piero was immersed.
Although this gambit goes against the grain,
you sense your hopes are not entirely vain'.
Pompilia frowned, then smiled demurely, knowing
the seeds were burgeoning that she'd been sowing.
At this young Caponsacchi softly cursed
and said, 'he'd do as much as any durst'.

'Myrtillo''s motivation? Noble cause?
An aretine to set beside Petrarca?
Or did his daemons well from somewhere darker?
What reason could he have to run this risk?
His mind was in the clouds, or the cloaca?
We'll grant that every human has his flaws,
but Caponsacchi was an obelisk,
a beacon, warrior-priest who wins applause.
He braved the husband, as he braved the Fisc
– or was his impetus this chance to whisk
(as might a bus boy or a Broadway barker,
a *spiaggia* pimp or fairground fakhir)
a beauty from the safety of the laws?
Why else take maiden in his man-beast maws?

So, Porzia – that is, Conti's brother's wife,
as well as Guido's sister – lost the plot.
To her, her family circle, 'Camelot',
was something sacrosanct. Tall tales suggest
that Conti got his entrails in a knot.
You can't imagine *il veleno*'s rife?
I doubt Lucrezia Borgia could have guessed!
It's called, by ministers, 'In Place of Strife'!
If of a double-crosser you'd divest,
dice chicory and chives with chicken-breast.
Pugnale's less pernicious than the pot.
Thus Guinevere put paid to Lancelot.

Nux vomica with nutmeg, not the knife,
is how they brought an end to Conti's life.

The couple ran away. Guido gave chase.
The two would say, this wasn't dereliction:
their bid to get to Roman jurisdiction
made perfect sense. Adultery and rape
were not involved. The wife's sincere conviction
was, had she failed to hurtle from that place,
the husband would have crushed her like a grape.
She'd now be dead, and this a murder case.
This was a rescue, not a jig-jig jape:
a logical, methodical escape.
If Guido's weakness reeks of seedy fiction,
the climax showed his central contradiction:
his monologue was honour. Face-to-face,
he *had* none. He provoked his own disgrace.

Was Caponsacchi man, or charlatan?
Was Guido the aggrieved, or merely peeved?
By speculation, nothing is achieved.
Still, Guido had a chance to stake the claim.
The way to win the day and be believed
was, kill the lovers outright, rather than
to call the cops, and thereby take the blame.
You run them through, or you're the also-ran.
To seize the moment is to break the frame:
you make the running, and you make your name.
When out of tavern courtyard Guido heaved,
the lost momentum couldn't be retrieved.
According to the cosmic master-plan,
that's where the journey to the block began.

Another thing occurred of consequence.
Abate Paolo upped and disappeared.
His poetry was burned, his desk was cleared.

Surprised to lose his buttresses and shorings,
(let's mix the metaphor) Count Guido veered.
No circumspection, sitting on the fence,
no back-up plans or careful underscorings:
now all was impulse, reflex, present-tense.
In lieu of glue, emotional outpourings:
the Count's canoe, untended, slipped its moorings.
What else could be expected? Rudder sheered,
the good ship Guido could not now be steered.
No sense of purpose, where there is no sense:
and no *mens sana*, where there is no *mens*.

The solstice is the dead time. Branches, sticks,
the life-sustaining wood, even the vines
are shrunken down and useless. No-one dines,
since sunset halts all life. The hearthside cricket
throbs his long lament in end-stopped lines
in solitude, behind cold chimney bricks.
In Milvio, we've found no copse or thicket
to give us warmth or comfort. Candle wicks,
like horses, can't be had. Our outer picket,
the winter sun, is feeble and the ticket,
which would have got us rides? His Lordship whines
of Rome's antipathy, but his designs
may be the shortfall. Oh for harvest ricks!
We've even burnt the kitchen crucifix.

The mood is ugly as the hungry jackals
slink through the portal, closing for the kill.
Limbs are a-tremble: January chill?
Anticipation of defenceless blood?
Determination substitutes for skill –
a voice is answering – erecting hackles –
a chain unfastening, complaining wood –
and then it's done. We've slipped fear's shackles.
The sterile icy air feels clean and good –

exhilaration where foreboding stood –
the square stands empty and the air hangs still –
a fountain, silent in its frozen spill –
hard breathing in the darkness – Santi cackles –
beneath our feet, a Popolo puddle crackles.

There are occasions witnessed by us all
when normal people do outstanding things,
as if quotidian torpor sprouted wings
and wafted us above the thing we are.
The poet's task? To take these blossomings
and cause us to collectively recall
(to ease the gate called consciousness ajar)
that what is done heroically, can enthrall.
Directed by some undetected star
(like Joseph and the wife of Potiphar)
our heroes, though of common blood, are kings
who mark our joinings and our sunderings.
No human is excluded from The Call:
thus Everyman is Amadis de Gaul.

The killers run out through the Popolo Gate
sans horses, planned withdrawal, compass, map,
the stern Aurelian Wall's reluctant gap
permitting egress, narrowly. What then?
First, Guido comprehends he's lost his cap.
Each act of thinking seems to enervate:
for these are damaged, self-disgusted men
who've just destroyed three humans. Now, too late,
a sense of balance, surging back again,
appals them. Starting for their Milvian den
(where else to scurry?), fearful of a trap
in every wayside fountain's rhythmic slap,
they wonder how they'd summoned so much hate
while feeling at their backs Pursuant Fate.

In Via Vittoria, neighbours mill about
in stunned confusion, shaking, weeping, talking.
But calmer minds are quietly uncorking
the wine of justice: present on the scene,
oblivious to gossiping and gawking,
Patrizi's busy, figuring it out.
From what the Captain manages to glean,
the husband is involved, without a doubt.
No time to lose: he chooses to convene
his company of *sbirri*. *'This must mean
they left on foot, for Milvio. They're walking.
With luck, we'll overtake them at the forking
(Flaminian and Consular). Let's scout
the posts and coaching inns, within, without.'*

Attenuated, sick at heart, dejected,
the slaughterers slunk from another inn.
Their deference to Guido, wearing thin,
was close to snapping. Horseless they remained.
(Baldeschi speaking.) 'Take it on the chin?
So which among us was it, who neglected
to buy the permits? Worse than addle-brained!'
The Count kept mute. *If Santi's disaffected,
it's dangerous. There's nothing to be gained
by waking sleeping landlords, plainly stained
with gory evidence of recent sin.
Cold-calling is a game we'll never win.*
Exhaustion and Merluzza intersected.
And here, the snoring butchers were detected.

Guido's Telling Answer

Patrizi asked him why he'd killed his wife.
And what did Guido say? 'It wasn't me.'
A master-stroke of imbecility.
He should have said, 'My honour is my life,

and female infidelity is rife!'
His wife lived long enough for 'it was he'.
His cap was found in close proximity.
No question, but he put her to the knife.

It's best to catch them while the tears are fresh,
we lawyers say. Don't let them think ahead.
They'll weave a tapestry, they'll make a mesh.
If honour was what stung him, as he said,
then surely, on the very night she bled,
he'd say so, not deny it all instead.

So, Guido and his bravos are in jail,
the very prison where the others were
(the Canon and the Wife, the him-and-her) –
Carceri nuove, in the *Via Giulia*.
The lawyers come to Guido to confer.
'Not Guilty', as a strategy, will fail.
The problem, as we see it, sir, is *mulier
interfectae*. You can not prevail.
Throughout the world, from Asti to Apulia,
the people (though admittedly unrulier)
agree with us. You have to argue, sir,
'I killed her, and my honour was the spur.'
You'll do some time – it won't be cakes and ale –
are we *consensu*? Hang it on that nail?

Honoris causa isn't an excuse.
The court case was the talk of all the town.
Inevitably, 'death' was handed down.
His advocates had ably, bravely striven
but, like that thing with Canio the Clown,
the puncturing of innards is abuse.
The golden rule, the universal 'given':
with others' lives, we don't play fast and loose.
What boots it if the man says he was driven?

It cannot be, and should not be, forgiven.
The common folk, the people of renown –
you sin together? Then together drown.
The gander gets the sauce he served the goose:
the nobleman the axe, the rest the noose.

The Holy Father is the last appeal
– petition, rather. Little comfort there!
Pope Innocent is witty, debonair,
but no-one's liberal. His one concern
is public order. Terrorists, beware!
To keep his kingdom on an even keel?
No firearms, free assembly. Overturn
convictions with these features? Let's get real.
He took one evening to review (and spurn)
the stay of execution. Why adjourn?
Though kind, closed mind. Fair, but doctrinaire.
The Fisc's true friend, the detainee's despair.
A friendly little pontiff, made of steel,
confirms and orders Guido's last ordeal.

Awoken in the middle of the night
by members of the Vigilance Committee
(a February night, forlorn and gritty),
Count Guido learned the worst. He was to die.
When men confront their end, it's never pretty:
when Franceschini, shivering with fright,
received a cross on which to fix his eye,
he started kissing it with all his might.
At times he'd jabber prayers, but did not try
to leave his crucifix, or put it by.
The fearsome Brotherhood of Death and Pity,
the sight most terrible in all the city,
arrived before the early morning light
could usher comfort in, however slight.

A mention of Patrizi now falls due.
The Captain had specific orders: catch
the killers. This he did, and got a scratch
along his forearm. No-one noticed then,
or bothered with an antiseptic patch,
preoccupied with prisoners: made do,
until they reached the *Carcere* again,
with rags for bandage. What was to ensue?
Pompilia, her parents, Guido's men,
then Conti, Guido – now Patrizi – ten
gave up their lives, but few of them could match
the Captain. Here's a coda to attach:
one feels that, even if Patrizi knew
the quest could kill, he would have seen it through.

The five condemned, kept purposely apart
before this point, were able now to meet,
if only to be taken to the street
(we have a sketch of Guido's wretched face,
defining this, his ruinous defeat).
Each man was thrust into a waiting cart.
The *cortege* trundled at a crawling pace,
encumbered by spectators from the start,
come out to see the Tuscan count's disgrace
despite the narrow alleys' lack of space.
The nonsense chanted with insistent beat
(the intercession of the Paraclete)
droned on and on through Rome's congested heart,
epitome of sacerdotal art.

They reached the Corner of the Pasquinade
beneath the talking statue's tart regard
to take Communion, shackled to their guard.
Inside the chapel (called '*Agonizzanti*')
where those who are unfortunately-starred
and facing execution may pray aid,

like something from the lower rings of Dante,
the five *abbandonati* knelt and prayed.
Our evidence of heaven's fairly scanty,
and therefore to be doubted. *No obstante*,
the supernatural is very hard
for those with necks in halters to discard.
Among the damaged, desperate, dismayed,
The presbyterian pointmen ply their trade.

And meanwhile, in the normally quiet square
of Popolo, there is frenetic bustle:
exerting vast amounts of brain and muscle,
authorities are building gallows here.
Yes, here, where years ago with satin rustle
the child Pompilia would take the evening air,
her hand clasped in her father's. Look what's near!
That bald Babuino – ugly body hair!
The square is now a place of little cheer,
whose balconies, so flowerless and austere,
will do a roaring trade when hucksters hustle
this very afternoon, when touts will tussle
before the double churches, everywhere,
and for which the whistling workers now prepare.

Eight weeks ago, five desperados came
full-tilt through here, to pass the city gate:
same square today, just slightly later date,
but every pocket-dipper, every fop
and all the in-betweens anticipate
the fun of seeing five men die in shame.
For one-stop shopping, Popolo pops up top:
enjoy the spectacle, apportion blame.
His four accomplices are for the drop,
while Guido, being noble, gets the chop:
well, lucky him. They say he married late:
some students never learn to conjugate.

As carpenters complete the wooden frame,
it's bread and circuses – the same old game.

Forever onward the procession pressed,
around Navona wound, as Rome observed.
Had Guido known, he would have been unnerved
to see Minerva, called, 'The Fall of Reason',
the very spot where Galileo swerved,
recanted, threw his hand in and confessed:
the Aretine was nothing like the Pisan,
but had the same *vergogna* in his breast:
not quite the height of scientific treason,
but each capitulation has its season.
The Pantheon, so perfectly preserved,
this hallowed ground, immaculately curved,
containing the remains of Italy's best,
was left behind. To Popolo's palimpsest!

By now it's afternoon. The light won't last.
No matter how they torture, tar-and-feather,
they can't intimidate the winter weather.
The tumbrils gain the Square of the Colonna,
where Guido and his wife were brought together.
Aurelius' Column, Corso's mizzenmast,
looks different now. He met his *belladonna*
in summer sunshine, not this overcast.
The fault for what was done must lie upon her,
for what was done, was done to salve his honour.
Her house! The harpsichord of yellow leather …
the songbird, with the dainty ankle-tether …
No profit, reminiscing on the past.
Here's Popolo, approaching all too fast.

A dream arrived, disturbing Guido's sleep.
When darkness falls and water barrels freeze,
a troubled man has nowhere he can hide.

Preoccupations cramp him by degrees
(what was that talk of Care's unravelled sleeve?)
Unpleasant visions, like a cloud of bees,
oppressed his head. He'd feel the pallet heave,
then find himself on surly slopes so steep,
he had to scramble up on hands and knees.
No place to shelter on this mountainside.
No goats, no sheep – and, notably, no trees.
The hilltop took forever to achieve,
to meet a sight no devil could conceive –
Pompilia was hanging, crucified!
He saw two drops of blood and water seep
reluctantly from lesions in her side.
He watched her spirit leave her as she died –
she'd proved a bride impossible to keep –
the seemly thing, it seemed, would be to weep –
but though he cried inside, he couldn't grieve.

With Christmas passed, they're handing out the spikes,
with savage barbs which suit the brutes' dysphoria.
(Pascuale said he'd never seen the likes.)
There'd be no horses, ornamental brasses,
nor any kind of ride – not even asses!
This latter had emerged as quite a shock:
what's not quite normal (nay, completely crass) is,
the Master hadn't known to purchase passes
for hiring Roman horses. *Santa gloria!*
The in-and-out would be laborious hikes.
The plan was, once they'd found the *Via Vittoria*,
for Santi and the Count to go and knock
and, when they heard the turning of the lock,
unveil upon the victims vicious strikes,
each driving home his dagger to the stock
(*il grande capitano*, Frenchy pikes!
As glorious as Lepanto, only gorier!)
and leave the wife *de benedetta memoria*.

The getaway? They'd run around the block,
then find an inn, for raising of the glasses!

Black night has crept in on the empty square:
Babuino fountain – so, we're almost there!
With hoods and caps pulled low against the sleet,
the younger thugs stand lookout in the street:
a bang on Pietro's door – now for the cheat!
The enemy are close now, unaware,
about to be confronted in their lair!
'Who knocks?' 'It's Caponsacchi!' And the snare
works perfectly! Violante, first to greet,
is first to die. The overture's complete!
In febrile satisfaction, flay her face,
repay those strong resentments, so long nursed!
Pietro now, and wants to pray for grace –
afraid of Hell – fell him – so much the worse!
You always ran to judgment: run there cursed!
The garden door – of course! The bitch has burst
out through it. There's the kitchen – give her chase!
We might have guarded it, if we'd been versed
in half the subterfuge this tribe embraced.
So get her. Let's exterminate the race!

Pompilia paid no heed to where she fled.
In just a nightdress, through the starless black,
she heard the *Greci*'s unmistakeable chimes:
her bare feet felt the sandy path which led
to where the locksmith lived, but there the track
confused her. Better gain the house, instead!
She turned, and heard blood-curdling Tuscan calls:
'She's got behind us! Come on – double back!'
The kitchen candle, through the backdoor crack,
conducted her to where the lattice climbs.
She scurried past pure horror in sheer dread,
the corpses of her parents in the hall,

half-slipping on her mother's blood-soaked shawl,
then up the narrow staircase: there to crawl
in desperation underneath her bed.
Her blood and hair, today, still stain the wall:
unwarranted, the ugliest of crimes:
they'd breached her abdomen some twenty times.
'We're finished now,' the husband Guido said:
'To Ponte Milvio!', leaving her for dead.

And yet she wasn't dead – at least, not yet.
And, even as her life-force ebbed away,
she managed, fitfully, to think and talk.
She told investigators of the crew
that Guido'd brought to aid him, and abet
the murders. More: she knew where they would stay
and – even more – she said they'd have to walk:
they'd argued bitterly as they withdrew.
Patrizi and his *sbirri* retinue,
as keen and clear-eyed as the kestrel hawk,
apprised of Paolo's *finca*, drew their net
around the Ponte Milvio. Disarray
and bloodstains, and a slew of damning clues
they found, but not the felons. 'Neighbours say
they left an hour ago. On foot. That way!'
We owe Patrizi an enormous debt.
He and his *sbirri* took the consular fork
and came upon the killers. Blood was let.
The Captain's arm was cut, nor did he balk,
but fell to the infection which accrued.

The party stopped at Milvio, riding back.
There, Guido underwent an inquisition,
with full notes taken, in his brother's shack.
When Guido asked, 'What makes you think that I've
got anything to do with murder missions?',
they said, 'Pompilia told us.' 'She's alive?'

The Count had not imagined this. Amazed,
he proved to be the first of all the five
to make admissions. How could she survive?
Santi sneered, and Blasio's blushes blazed.
They trussed each prisoner like a saddlepack,
both peer and peasant, in the prone position,
with Guido gibbering like a man half-crazed,
and on Patrizi's word the Romeward drive
began. In Rome, the riff-raff's bloodlust raised,
the church of San Lorenzo, decked in black,
received poor Pietro (cheated of contrition)
and Violante (robbed of recognition
by every plunging thrust and slashing hack).
Pompilia would linger four more days.

THE CARDINAL POINTS (2)

Remember Don Fabrizio, *detto* Spada?
The Cardinal who wrote our first account?
We drink again from this, the purest fount!
His theme has turned, this time, a little harder:
he offers us a villain, *sin embargo*
it's not the one sequestered in Seville:
invites us to imagine, if we will,
how Guido's head was turned by Santiago.

Historians must stay away from fiction?
We sense you, Gentle Reader, looking odd at us:
before you yell 'Scholastic dereliction!',
we ask you to remember your Herodotus.
We have a duty, granted, to explain,
but can't we (on occasion) entertain?

Express a thing that happens to be true?
We speak our minds, they clap us in the galleys.

They'll build us up? I doubt it, Buttercup!
It's spoken? Is it written? Both, sedition!
We keep it quiet? It's the Inquisition.
We write our feelings down? They string us up.
There's no escape for one who shilly-shallies:
so what's a citizen supposed to do?

Si parliamo, in galere.
Esitare è perdere.
Si scrivammo, impiccatti:
chi scrive, è spazzati.
Stiamo in quiete,
siamo foraggio di prete.

THE FIRST DRAFT OF WHAT APPEARS TO BE A PROPOSED NOVELLA, FOUND AMONG THE PAPERS OF CARDINAL FABRIZIO SPADA

What do we mean by saying, 'speculation'?
We're saying, in effect, that it's a guess.
But when the 'facts' present us with a mess,
conjecture can resolve the situation:
it fills in gaps, elucidates causation:
so, sometimes, fiction fashions a finesse.
Then should we, from established fact, digress,
to shed some light on listless litigation?

Did Guido always contemplate her death?
We don't know what went down on Paolo's farm,
when solstice iciness condensed the breath:
was Guido always set on mortal harm,
or was he, to Baldeschi, a Macbeth,
susceptible to evil-tending charm?

* * * *

I deprecate perverters of the facts,
the kind of crap you'll stumble on in Acts,
and yet I may investigate in verse
(intelligent, imaginative tracts,

the sort a skilful artist might rehearse):
a failing marriage, poverty (or worse)
as causes of some mystifying crime.
Explore the facts and logically nurse

the cause-célèbre's half-digested chyme:
with luck, with perpescuity, with time,
you might uncover motivations which
(investigated through a love of rhyme)

might offer new solutions, rare and rich,
that sing to us, as if with perfect pitch:
the sphere of possibility contracts
once we determine what provoked the itch.

* * * *

What can a little fiction, therefore, do?
Imagine Guido skulking on the farm
at Ponte Milvio: beyond all harm,
all five are dead: I mean the Tuscan crew.
We'll never separate what's false from true,
but knives with barbs are not the kind of arm
you carry, if you don't intend alarm.
What sort of scare would Guido carry through?
Baldeschi was, we know, the killer type:
enjoyed, we also know, his master's ear.
Since Guido was an easy ship to steer,
Baldeschi battened on the cuckold's gripe.

Malevolently, Guido's puppeteer
provoked a vengeance of a sterner stripe.

* * * *

Alessandro Baldeschi Counsels Guido at Ponte Milvio

I'll say my piece and take the pain I'm due.
Fie, 'tis the curse of service. Impolite
I am, but villeins might dueñas indict.
Did she deceive her father, marrying you?
You have, it seems, but one course to pursue.
To assay gold, there's none relies on sight:
the test of virtue turns upon the bite.
If you're a man, do what a man must do.
The art is not to suffer, but pre-empt.
You'd stay your hand? Then 'pimp' is not a slight.
He hath, and is again, to cope your wife:
dare do yourself a profit and a right:
I will be near to second the attempt.
Here's your redress. Behold your Genoa knife.

STRAY LEAVES: VERANILLO DE MEMBRILLO

Somehow, the silver birches simply know.
This splendid heaven, pure refulgent blue
can not abide. The grass fronds, stiff as glue,
like swifts and grillos, uninclined to go,
are troubled by the carking of the crow.
It's autumn, and the rains are overdue.
A corpse whose hair improvidently grew,
September is deceptive afterglow.
At dusk, a silence falls across the close:
the trees stand tall and motionless, morose:

now unobtrusive, heretofore verbose:
tart evergreens like laurel, tamarind,
immortal olives, silver in the wind,
sing 'adios verano, adios!'

SAINT MARTIN'S SUMMER

(Caponsacchi in Civitavecchia)

November! When the auburn autumn leaves
retard the tinkling brooks of Vallombrosa,
and kitchen chimneys draw the old ones closer:
when timid fieldmice nestle in the eaves
and oaken chests give up our longer sleeves,
and finer fabrics cede the game to grosser:
we close John Grisham, open Vargas LLosa:
Orion rises, and Arcturus grieves.
But sometimes there's a gracious interlude.
Though winter waits offstage with all its lines
word-perfect, still a kind of summer shines.
The breeze feels older now, of muted mood,
not so disposed to boast its vital signs,
inclined to amble through the golden vines.

'THE SLAIN ARE NOT UNDONE,' she always said.
The boy I was could not have understood!
(All new arrivals have to pass this arch,
So dark, so low. Be thankful it's not March,
but Martinmas, with scent of fragrant wood.
The spring brings wind from Africa, instead!
It screams through here. Our Easter banners shred
and, in the hinterland, the pastures parch.
But this, the calm, we call our 'adulthood').

You'll notice that the oak is still in leaf,
the symbol of the city. (Mind that nail!
To rip your habit! So inopportune!)
These seaward stones, so bulky, crudely-hewn
(like me!) constructed on the giant scale,
have snags and defects. Not quite *Chateau d'If!*
She called me Dysmas, the Repentant Thief,
to mark the good in me, not to impugn
my honesty. And thereby hangs a tale,

the yarn of Ariadne, and the thread
she offered to her hero. Her belief
(so far from golden fleece or holy grail)
supposed that gratitude could hardly fail.
Ill-founded suppositions come to grief!
The other, through the labyrinth once led,
gave not a moment's thought to getting wed.
We always set our spinnaker to fail,
and ever does our keel feel for the reef.

How fitting that you chose this time of year,
the season of disposal and dispersal,
to seek me here. The thing of which I'd speak,
a love quite unrepeatable, unique,
can somehow by a curious reversal
(as bonfires scour away the brittle, sere)
become the property of all who hear:
your life is mine and, by the same mystique,
 my intimate contains your universal.

(Turn left here, at the fountain.) From the fief
of selfish indolence, she set me free.
Civitavecchia's a kind of jail,
I know, and you are here to talk of bail:
Arezzo, though, for her could never be
a place of ease. She looked for no relief.

(I'll speak her name!) Pompilia's motif
was, she was in the belly of the whale:
'I'll grow, I know, and gain my liberty!'

She ushered life to what in me was dead.
Acedia – indifference to sloth –
embroiled me in warm toils I could not shirk.
With her, I learned to live, not just to lurk.
My faults were bared, and she provided both
the hand that mocked them and the heart that fed,
my *fons et origo*, my fountainhead.
Awaiting miracles just does not work!
Our defects are the seedbeds of our growth.

And this is where I am now – Prayer and Death!
(It took some time, but now I have the key.)
One moment – it's reluctant, this new door.
'Returning were as tedious as go o'er'.
(The only thing I have is memory:
Civita has no books.) It's from Macbeth.
The image I retain of Piero's Seth
is, like the Thane of Cawdor on the shore,
a man who feels the beat of Destiny.

Amintas and Lucrina – is that us?
Though one is still alive and one is dead,
I felt we were bedevilled from the first.
No matter how you struggle, if you're cursed,
there's only ever tragedy ahead.
I threw away my future (just like Hus!),
a thing that you and I may well discuss,
but certainly my fate was not the worst:
I was sequestered, but Pompilia bled.

When all is said and done, ten people died:
Pompilia, of course; her father, mother:

five executed – Guido, four abettors:
ignoring innocents arraigned in fetters,
the captain named Patrizi was another –
and one the Franceschini brush aside,
but, while I live, I'll never let them hide –
the carrier of messages and letters,
Giovanni Conti. He was like a brother.

You bring the latest from the Holy See?
This papal interregnum offers hope:
two years of famine – could this be my feast?
(A soothing of severity, at least?)
Between ourselves, in jockeying for pope,
Albani has the better strategy.
Become a cardinal, it seems to me,
then as a sort of afterthought, a priest.
That's how the lawyers do it. Interlope!

Nostalgic for my hometown? Certainly.
Where two streets cross – we say, *Canto de' Bacci* –
is where I'll head, as soon as I'm released.
This life of mine has somehow to be pieced
together. If the future's looking patchy,
well, *meno male*, I've a family.
The consolation of philosophy!
I know my understanding has increased.
I'll salvage something from the *calcinacci*.

Our ease of mind, at best, is merely leased,
suspended over catacombs of care.
I've visited Assisi once or twice:
a lot of Giotto frescoes – very nice!
Embedded in a cliff, all light and air,
the worst of wolves appears as sheep be-fleeced!
We're living in the belly of the beast,

a gloomy clutch of caverns, cold as ice.
I don't suppose that you were ever there.

The city bustles, orderly, benign:
commercial and canonical can thrive.
You cannot speak of reason to the Dane
and lose your voice. We gaze down on the plain
with satisfaction, glad to be alive.
There beats another heart beneath the shrine.
Inimical, it seeks to undermine
the flimsy norms which (we believe) obtain,
but we are just a suburb of The Hive.

You'd pass from childhood to a man's estate?
There has to be a challenge, an ordeal.
The adversary manifests as elves
or dragons, but is really just ourselves.
That serpent which you crush beneath your heel
is in your psyche born, and quite innate.
You dream that you are passing through a gate?
It means you've won. The Victor-Spirit delves
beneath, the hidden symbols to unseal.

Between us, we named Guido, 'Sticky-Hair'.
His was the sin of Minos. You'll recall
The King who could not grow into his role.
A monarch must not have a petty soul.
The patriarch should govern for us all,
not for his narrow self: should be aware
that all who look to him deserve his care.
But Sticky-Hair fixated on control:
this lack of magnanimity marred all.

The forces acting on her were immense.
She never understood them, this I know.
She found herself assailed on every side.

As I beheld her with unbridled pride,
I saw her find the wherewithal to grow.
With no superbity, grandiloquence,
her personality her sole defence,
she sailed on, undefeated, till she died.
They killed her, but they could not bring her low.

Mistake, to marry Guido? Yes indeed.
An error, Violante feigning girth? In quartals!
But would we wish undone the bogus birth?
I tell you, no. Misjudgments have their worth.
They open new dimensions to us mortals.
Mutations function as the future's seed.
Who knows where our miscalculations lead?
But rest assured, we need them here on earth.
Our blunders are not accidents. They're portals.

It started in a downpour on the day
she married in a rainstorm. Waters broke,
Pompilia was launched upon the flood.
She opened all the windows (air is good!)
before the Franceschini hounds awoke,
then we embraced the night, that fateful May.
Abate Paolo, when he ran away,
Destroyed his diaries, as delinquents should,
burnt all his books and poems at a stroke.

The judgement (made on wood) brought vindication.
A humble whittled gavel, ringing down
in Santa Croce, gave her back her name.
It came too late to save her. All the same,
it caused a great commotion in the town.
Arezzo's best, arrested! Perturbation!
Ereshkigal the sister's implication
in Conti's death escaped official blame,
but people know. In obloquy she'll drown.

One question still intrigues me. Was she great?
Or just a normal girl? She had a way –
she *made* you love her. By a conscious act?
No, not at all. She definitely lacked
the self-awareness, ego, self-display.
Hers was a soul incapable of hate.
She modestly accorded greater weight
to others' views, stayed passive when attacked.
She often termed herself, 'The Hart at Bay'.

You'd find it hard to fabricate a myth?
But isn't it the thing you do each night,
unconsciously? Invention's acolyte
is sleep, experience the dreamer's pith,
abundant as riparian regolith.
Each failed affair and every stinging slight
you've ever undergone could well ignite
the furnace where you'll labour as a smith,
creating novelties which, never new,
repeat the pattern that we somehow need.
A dream's a monomyth, a private rite,
and yet we recognise the reverie breed.
Enough of them will finally accrue
to constitute a Stygian stalactite.

The legend of Leandro must be told.
Civita (beaten by the Saracens)
was on the point of ceasing to exist.
The city sacked, survivors set a tryst
at safe remove from naval guns or garrisons,
beneath an oak, where open country rolled.
Leandro was a sailor. Now grown old,
he'd lost no vigour. Brandishing his fist,
he told the meeting, 'Save your lame comparisons!

I am no Priam, and my town's not Troy!
My home is here, and I for one insist
that what we have, we have the guts to hold.
So what, if strangers rob us of our gold?
We earned it, lost it – it will not be missed.
They may despoil us, but they can't destroy!'
At this each adult, every girl and boy,
took heart anew, and once again grew bold.
The cry went up – 'Return! Rebuild! Resist!'

Pompilia was of that very mould.
A saviour, yes, but in a greater scheme.
I saved her from her husband – some crusade!
It's she who ought to have the accolade.
She saved me from myself. They all blaspheme
who say she cozened, captured me, cajoled.
As long as there are men, she'll be extolled.
She made the sacrifice that must be made,
to give us back our great communal dream.

DOCTOR ANTONIO LAMPARELLI, PROCURATOR OF THE POOR, PETITIONS THE COURT TO RESTORE THE GOOD NAME OF COUNTESS FRANCESCA POMPILIA FRENCESCHINI, DECEASED

I ask a declaration from the court.
The well-known Convent of the Convertites
asserts what it would claim are 'ancient rights'
against my client. What it wants, in short,

is seizure of Pompilia's estate.
By dint of dicta found in papal banns,
'dishonest girls' and other also-rans
on death must forfeit property ... but wait!

I thwart the Convertites in this, their sport.
The court has knowledge of the tragic fate
my client underwent. The tempting bait
of her inheritance, though keenly sought,

is not a lure for ghetto dogs to chase.
I seek a ruling that Pompilia's name
be free forever of all blight or blame
as of today. No future plaint or case

may ever gain a hearing in this city
or in the world. And I will not descend
into the pit to draggle, dodge, defend,
or treat of her, save through my silent pity.

Even the lowest felon may efface
his guilt by dying. This may not be pretty,
but it's a fact: the Curia Committee
has ruled upon it. None may now debase

departed burglar, petty thief or fence.
Caballus writes, and Pelligrini shares
his view, that it is open to the heirs
to seek a legal deed of innocence,

where such a thing is meet. She was assailed
(I hardly think what follows is disputed),
and Guido was condemned and executed.
The argument he mounted, therefore, failed.

If *honoris causa* represents the sense
of what he offered, his defence entailed
a clear *non-sequitur*, and was derailed.
This court found no adultery. Immense!

If there was no adultery, why then
there was no wrong. The reason why she fled?
To save her life, or share a sinful bed?
As Bossius argues, it is better, when

we're faced with two elections, to select
the motivation free of stain or guilt
before the option wherein blood gets spilt,
the lawful cause above the less correct.

On this arm there's a vulture, that a wren:
the law is cautious, careful, circumspect,
but really, it behoves us to reflect
on what's vouchsafed us by Pompilia's pen.

Her letters are unevidenced, unsworn,
and clearly written under some duress:
her husband had a reason to profess
his lack of guilt of bullying, to fawn

upon his brother Paolo, play down tales
of misbehaviour. Who composed those letters?
A girl of fourteen, bullied by her betters,
or sentient strumpet? Weigh it in the scales.

Where can a woman go, if she is shorn
of masculine protection? She needs males
if she's to move. A ship which has no sails,
a single woman, flaccid and forlorn,

can hardly leave her house. Where would she go?
She has no refuge, friendly port of call,
no agency to shelter, help forestall
the torrent of abuse the world will throw.

A woman facing peril needs to know
some decent man who's open, well-disposed,
whose view's not *machilista,* blinkered, closed:
if only half our men were minded so!

When summoned, Caponsacchi wasn't slow
to take the tortured youngster under tow.
And what he gave her wasn't just for show –
he risked his life. What more can one bestow?

A couple on a frolic of their own
would wander willy-nilly, nowhere-bound,
more confident when on untrodden ground,
a sward to hunting husbands quite unknown.

Our fugitives made patently for Rome,
along a public highway. On the ride
they didn't dawdle, dally, halt or hide.
He strove to guide his *protegée* safe home.

Their feet were planted firm on Latium's loam
when evil overtook them. Peter's Throne
was in their reach, if only they had known,
three hours away from Sant' Andrea's dome.

Pompilia has often been maligned
because of letters evidencing sin
allegedly discovered at the inn –
Mirtillo, Amaryllis – all unsigned!

These documents were never analysed.
We cannot say who wrote them. It may be
that somebody in Guido's family
has faked them, in a hand deftly disguised!

Examine them, and you will surely find
they're vague and wholly unparticularised:
they're unacknowledged, and unrecognised,
generically constructed and designed.

* * * *

IF EVER YOU PUT SOMEONE 'IN THE FRAME',
this is the perfect model of the set-up:
timeless, placeless, factless and impersonal.

DON'T OFFER DETAILS, like your victim's name,
just give them innuendo without let-up:
you don't want solids, which you'll then rehearse, and all.

Yes, this is how to play the dirty game:
Pretend that you're indignant, angry, het-up:
The trick's in giving nothing, while you're cursing all.

* * * *

ONE THING WITH WHICH I SIMPLY HAVE TO DEAL,
since I'm Pompilia's advocate, is this:
a claim that something serious amiss
transpired, a thing from which there's no appeal,

according to Pompilia's detractors:
that Caponsacchi left Pompilia's house,
at dead of night came secretly *heraus*.
Of all the many aggravating factors,

this one might seem to set the damning seal.
The witness has no doubt there were two actors,
Pompilia implicated – *reus actus*!
But not so fast. Assertions oft conceal

a labyrinth of compromising dross.
Take no-one's word at surface value. Look
inside, not at the cover, of the book.
Explore the tree-trunk, and ignore the moss.

The witness has three weak points to her claims.
To start with, she's the only one who places
the Canon in that home. In many cases
the prosecution stumbles in its aims

because it can't corroborate its point.
And secondly, the woman is a whore.
I've never used such vulgar terms before,
but I am here to vanquish, not anoint.

She's guilty of the very thing she blames
Pompilia of being. Let's disjoint
her reasoning, and thereby disappoint
the Convertites. The woman she defames

was younger, more attractive, better-clad.
(And now we reach my third point.) What is more,
the man she claims was creeping through that door
turns out to be the love she almost had.

I have the court's attention, that is clear!
The woman named Contenti loved and lost
the Canon. If her evidence is glossed,
her love for Caponsacchi was sincere.

His visits fell away, which made her sad.
It's bad enough when lovers disappear,
but what she later chanced to overhear
went close to driving Margharita mad!

A tart develop feelings for a client?
(In certain quarters, lawyers count as tarts!)
Both concubines and counsellors have hearts,
and in her world, the Canon was a giant.

He was the nicest man she'd ever had
and by degrees becoming passive, pliant,
a poco a poco, growing more reliant
– but no-one's hopes are ever ironclad.

Imagine how she felt the day she learned
the younger, prettier neighbour was his goal!
Imagine the commotion in her soul,
how feelings of resentment must have churned!

And so she gave her evidence on oath.
Can we be sure she kept an even keel?
Can any of us shed the things we feel?
Was vengeance lurking in the undergrowth?

STRAY LEAVES: COUP DE FOUDRE

They told me, if you're camping and it's raining,
to never touch the fabric of the tent
inside: they said it breaks the seal, explaining
that any person so improvident

as to commit the camper's cardinal sin
and not to worry where his digit went
would link the liquids: rain would trickle in.
A lawyer now, I know just what they meant.

You have a client, and you feel, you care.
She trusts you with her secrets, which you share.
At first you're formal: gradually, you warm.

Today you notice how she wears her hair:
you take her hand, to help her on the stair:
you've touched the canvas – now endure the storm.

Enough of La Contenti, malcontent.
My argument is coming to its close.
I have three shorter matters to propose,
and then all words are windborne, tears are spent.

They say Pompilia drugged the family wine.
It never was established by the Fisc,
but what of that? What kind of fool would risk
discovery by those Franceschini swine?

The driver of the carriage says he went
flat-out towards Camoscia, which is fine.
The road was rough, there was no moon to shine,
and yet he saw 'the lady and the gent'

with lips on lips, in love's embraces. This,
while steering through the blackness hell-for-leather,
though they were sat behind him, locked together.
Who were the perpetrators of this kiss?

He says he didn't know her at the time,
or didn't realise that it was her.
so what, then, are we likely to infer
about his powers of observation? Prime!

In prison, staring into the abyss,
no end in sight (though guilty of no crime),
up to his scruples in insight and slime,
he told them what they wanted. Couldn't miss!

And last, corroboration – where I started.
My client said she needed to escape

to save her life. This wasn't just some jape,
some dalliance, romantic and light-hearted.

The Canon Caponsacchi uttered words
when challenged by the husband at the inn:
he didn't try to run, or save his skin.
Sometimes, a little thing that's overheard's

the strongest evidence. It's logged and charted.
Jacopo, yardman, up before the birds
to harness horses, feed the flocks and herds,
heard everything. The Convertites, outsmarted!

'I am a man, and what I did was done …' –
he testified before this very court
(you'll find it in the printed-up report):
and thus this humble Castelnuovo son

gives something we can anchor as a fact.
He doesn't have a terrier in this fight:
he's neither Tuscan, nor a Convertite:
no matter how he's slighted or attacked,

his words support Pompilia. As a nun
they buried her, with most exquisite tact:
we mustn't let our avarice distract
us: gold may glitter, but it's not the sun.

And now my work is finished. I have toiled
these nineteen months for one whom, I avow,
I truly loved. I give her over now
to justice, undiminished and unspoiled.

ON FRIDAY 18 DECEMBER 1772, BEING THE 25TH BIRTHDAY OF GAETANO FRANCESCHINI (UNDER ROMAN LAW THE DATE OF HIS ADULTHOOD), THE AFOREMENTIONED RECEIVES THIS LETTER FROM DOMENICO TIGHETTI (OF SACRED MEMORY)

Ten died, Gaetano. You and I survived.
Your mother and grandparents on the floor –
no legal expiation can efface
the way they chose to kill them. Worse than sad.
the Franceschini posse numbered five –
Agostinelli, Gambassini, add
Pasquini, Baldeschini, Guido more.
They could have got away without a trace,
had Guido ordered horses. By God's grace
the also-rans were hanged, and Guido knived.
One Canon Conti was a tragic case –
an asset to Arezzo – tonsured, wived –
but hardly safe from poisons on that score.
A female relative judged passing bad
his pandar role – and thus his death – contrived.
But Gregory the Great had gone before.
He lost his life at only twenty-four –
not yet full-formed, not yet more than a lad.
A fever took him, in his exile-place
which, if he'd stayed at home, he hadn't had.

I'm told now, by my lawyer, it's eleven.
Apparently, the captain of the sbirri,
when apprehending them, received a scratch:
blood-poisoning resulted. Knock on wood!
For every soldier-hero, I'd say seven
are killed by dirty water. Hara-kiri!
It seems the aretine bucolic batch

were trying to walk to Tuscany. Who could?
As sure as Shakespeare came from Dartmouth, Devon,
our killers, twelve miles on, footsore and weary,
decided on some dry, unguarded patch:
there, in Merluzza, where the barnyard stood!
The fragrant hay must then have felt like heaven,
the January rain so cold and dreary:
to sleep, perchance to dream, perhaps detach
themselves from what they'd done. It felt so good!
But evil works with punishment for leaven,
and when Patrizzi comes, who needs a theory?
Pietro's glasses-case, a perfect match,
is lying there, inside Pasquini's hood!

Today at twenty-five you are a man
by Roman law. How swiftly things transpire!
It seems like yesterday that life began:
and, as I promised you, I'll touch my lyre
say 'How I Met Your Mother' – there's a phrase!
The wealth you now inherit lit the fire.
I visited Paolina as a buyer,
the sweeper-up of Pietro's papal bonds
(your mother's standing, frankly, was no higher
than that of Rome's acknowledged demi-mondes,
and for her keep the Comparini clan
sought cash.) I loved her. Need I count the ways?
'The Pregnant Roman and the Parmesan' –
it sounds like, does it not, those fairground plays
in which the rich remainderman absconds?
To keep the tale as centred as I can,
the coin that I was ready then to raise
prevented them from turning vagabond.
Although a waver of no magic wand,
I certainly incurred Pompilia's praise.

We're ultimately each one on his own,
no matter how our friends and neighbours rally:
one person wide, the entrance to the Valley,
where each of us must walk the walk alone.
To have one other who completely cares
is more than we can hope for, less expect.
No matter how your cortilège is decked,
the ride is one no other creature shares.
Like L'Enfant et les Sortilèges, nightmares
are hovering around us, quite unchecked.
I'm not your father: that, you've always known.
(That's badly-put, and isn't quite correct:
by some illogical, vicarious love-tally,
I've never ceased to hold myself erect
and count myself your parent where I dared.
I'm flattered that I set a certain tone:
the child was far from spoilt, the rod was spared
(your mother's name for me was, 'Shilly-Shally'),
but she would be delighted, al finale,
to see how you, bellisimo, have grown.

So why did Guido stab them? Who can say?
I never knew the man. I have no answers.
Some men are simply made a different way
from us. For them, aggression's an enhancer,
a furnisher of options. Indignation
is what he would have said. Your mother died
since violence by men is justified
against unfaithful wives. It's speculation,
for he to me is strange as night to day.
Some think there was another force at play:
the humble origins of Guido's bride
(her mother was, I hear, a barroom dancer:
a lethal blow to Guido's cherished station!)
But I think this is all exaggeration,
and something else was pricking Guido's pride.

Though none would label me a great romancer,
I think that teasing was the deadly cancer –
it's why his brother Paolo ran away.
The ribbing was the real humiliation,
the torture Guido just could not abide.

An ageing yob is all, a Don Pasquale.
An influence more baleful and malign,
Pompilia's true nemesis, in fine,
was Caponsacchi. Perspicacity
his middle name, in all that stinks immersed:
he knew what he was doing, naive she:
she wouldn't be his last, nor was his first!
If you'd seek out this lecherous Svengali
(I don't see why you would. He has to be
long dead when you read this – as dead as me!)
But if for facts on him you have a thirst
consult Arezzo's *atti criminali*.
The phrase goes, flown with insolence and wine,
and that was him. We once arranged a parley
(his sort can be bought off) which proved the worst:
he was completely drunk when in he burst.
He must have sampled vine and malt and barley
in outlets from the Arno to the Rhine,
and sat your sainted mother on his knee –
regardless of the fact that she was mine!

ROSA TROVATELLA, OR THE GIRL WHO FED JESUS, Being a Tale told by Bishop Marchetti of Arezzo

There was a kind old man who lived alone.
His name, Pierino, gives no indication
of origin, or even avocation.

We read the sole word 'merchant' on his stone,
but what he bought and sold is not now known.

On opening his door one sunny morning,
he found a little baby in a cot
(abandoned by some trollop, like as not)
protected by the shadow of his awning,
contented, blowing bubbles, sometimes yawning.

He saw she was alert, a girl '*è bella*'.
The old man, fascinated and beguiled,
decided there and then to keep the child,
the issue of some Pincian *favela*,
and chose the name of 'Rosa Trovatella'.

Though not religious in the normal way,
Pierino was a decent man, and good,
and did the things a valued neighbour should,
but never taught the little girl to pray,
and Rosa never knew Communion Day.

It happened, when the child was eight or nine,
that Pierino had some work to do
across the city, and he took the view
that Rosa should come with him, and combine
his business dealings on the Esquiline

with pleasure. While he parleyed with his cronies,
let Rosa Trovatella look about
(she'd find some things of interest, no doubt)
and then they'd luncheon grandly at Marconi's,
and giggle at those frightful foreign phoneys!

Alone for once, the nine-year-old had fun!
She found a Roman arch, 'of Gallienus':
perhaps a friend of Scipio Africanus,

of whom she'd read. The lovely morning sun
delighted her. With just a skip and run

she came upon a 'chapel', as she thought it:
plain ochre walls, a modest wooden door
intrigued her, and she wanted to explore.
She felt a little nervous, but she fought it:
'It oughtn't to be wrong to visit, ought it?'

From street to church was diving in a pool
of dark tranquility. So silent, green,
so undisturbed and blissfully serene!
Adjusted to the gloomy vestibule,
she ventured gingerly into the cool

oasis of the spacious ancient nave.
The child had never seen mosaic before,
so what a fine surprise she had in store!
She gazed in wonder at the architrave,
the portal to the apse's magic cave!

She marvelled at the shimmering blues and golds,
the haloes, wings of angels, slender towers,
the gorgeous deep blue sky, the crimson flowers:
she loved the glistening robes, arranged in folds,
the sparkling arches, glass-encrusted moulds.

All painted plaster, porphyry and pyx,
the place enthralled her. Quietly, she said:
'I wonder, do I live, or am I dead?'
And, taking to her knees on tufa bricks,
she found herself before a crucifix.

'What happened, friend?' she asked the jasper figure.
'You must have met some ruffians, I fear.
It seems unseemly, they should nail you here.'

And Trovatella's eyes, surprised, grew bigger:
she saw the carving nod its head with vigour!

'Those people hurt you badly, didn't they?'
The graven image nodded once again.
'That's so unfair! Where was your father, then?'
A swishing cassock passed, as if to say,
'your time is up, come back another day.'

The sacristan (for he it was) returned.
'I'm sorry to dislodge you from your perch,
Young Missie, but it's time to close the church.'
While snuffing out such candles as still burned,
the orderly (belatedly) discerned

that something wonderful was taking place.
Young Rosa seemed a princess on her throne:
'Poor soul! I will not leave him on his own!'
The light of decency lit up her face.
'The way you've treated him is a disgrace!'

The sacristan suggested, 'Dear, you're wrong.
For us it was that Jesus paid this price.
We often celebrate his sacrifice
with incantations, incense, prayer and song –
for here, God's made and eaten all day long.'

Now Rosa Trovatella was aroused.
'You pinion him with nails through hands and feet,
then you abandon him. You think it meet?
And as for all this hokum you've espoused –
just look at how you've hurt him, how he's housed!'

She turned towards the figurine to ask,
'You'd like it, Dear One, if I stayed with you?'
The statue nodded. 'Then that's what I'll do!'

The baffled sacristan dreamt up a task:
he'd raid both kitchen shelf and cellar cask,

and bring a plate of pasta, aptly dressed
in olive oil. These doings seemed divine:
what else to do, but bring a cup of wine?
The self-assurance of his little guest
had left him unreservedly impressed.

Returning with the goblet and the plate,
he gave them to the child. 'Ah, *maccaroni*!
I'll soon be with my father (*chez* Marconi).'
And then to Jesus: 'If you drank and ate,
You'd help me greatly – or I might be late!'

She fed the figure and she helped him drink.
The pasta (which in those parts serves as bread)
was golden, and the wine was ruby-red,
the blood of long-lost summer, dark as ink.
'It's time, Dear Friend, to take you down, I think,'

and Rosa started working on a nail
then, of a sudden, pulled her hand away.
The sacristan observed, to his dismay,
that (far from being able to prevail)
she'd pricked her finger. Calm, but very pale,

she said, 'It always happens as decreed.'
The blood was oozing, steadily and fast,
and Trovatella mused, 'my life has passed.
It's quite alright, there's nothing that I need.
I've always known that I was born to bleed.'

And as she died, so must we die ourselves.
Does anything remain of us? Who knows?
Perhaps we lurk in poetry and prose,

awaiting liberation, rows on rows,
against the day when someone comes and delves
among those musty tomes on dusty shelves.

LOS ENAMORADOS DE ANTEQUERA,
Being a Poem that Giovanna Boba learned as a Child, and now recites

Not seeming to belong to the tierra,
a brooding shadow stains the smiling plain.
The haggard outcrop fills our souls with dread.

In discord with the distant blue sierra,
its face-recalling form, curled in disdain,
has earned the sobriquet, 'the Indian's Head'.

A relic of a dead and distant era,
the crag is cursed and destined to remain,
lone monolith where no-one dares to tread.

The standard is the problem, not the bearer,
unless, that is, in medieval Spain
the norms are broken. Someone ends up dead.

There never was a love intenser, rarer,
a love at once both sacred and profane.
Unable to abide, the lovers fled

from Archidona down to Antequera
in search of an hospitable domain,
encountering their tragedy, instead.

Awake! The purple harbingers of day
are in the cloudless heavens, and the play
   of light aslant the pueblo walls ensures
that night and silence have been chased away.

Though humans live and die, the land endures.
The morning calm consoles us, and obscures
   the scar which marks this place as '*la frontera*',
the rift between the Christians and the Moors.

The city of the plain is Antequera
(which continent can boast a city fairer?)
   and Tello is a youth who took up arms,
and whom the Muslims captured. Will they spare a

Christian boy, too young to know his psalms?
Will Tello meet with callousness or qualms?
   He's lived so little time, he hardly shaves!
But we live with incursions and alarms,

and, be they Prussian Uhlans, papal zouaves,
invasions lap the shore like ocean waves,
   relentlessly – and pointlessly, it seems.
We happen frequently on common graves

where skulls grin up at us, a femur gleams,
and ask ourselves – how came we to extremes?
   One life is granted us – why strike it down?
And why must peasants perish for regimes?

A humble lad must die to save a Crown?
Not far from Antequera lies a town
   where flies the crescent flag, named Archidona.
A clean white saddle on sierra brown,

it perches on a ridge. The muslim owner,
one Jubril Pasha, self-important loner,
   had room within his heart for just one creature:
his adolescent daughter, named Tazgona.

The father was an ineffective teacher.
He meant to move his daughter, couldn't reach her.
   Impelled to grip too tight, you kill the bird.
He tried to master her, beseech her,

but nothing worked. Their boundaries grew blurred.
A love too fierce? What failing is inferred?
   Unfortunately, precedents exist:
Tancredi and Ghismonda, in a word.

Of what, then, does society consist?
Subservience is offered, rings are kissed?
   Some mortals dress some others in prestige?
Some mortals stamp their status by the fist?

That *noblesse*, to continue, must *oblige*
Tazgona understood. Her father-liege
   was not the philosophic kind of king.
Could Archidona's walls withstand a siege?

How best construct an aqueduct to bring
sweet water from that all-too-distant spring?
   Our Christian prisoners? Do we treat them well?
Could she not cherish them, beneath her wing?

An almost-regal visit, cell to cell,
was organised. The thing that then befell
   Tazgona, when presented to young Tello,
was nothing more (or less) than Cupid's spell.

And likewise, love engulfed the brave young fellow.
He knew he wasn't at his utmost *bello*
   (a month inside a dungeon takes its toll,
and even Tello's skin had turned dull yellow),

but just a glimpse of her, and he was whole.
The two communicated, soul to soul,
   and love, reciprocal and heartfelt, flowered.
As fast as thought, Tazgona knew her goal

must be to free him. Passing on, she showered
the jailer with her praise, and meanwhile scoured
   the dungeon for its weak-point, which she found.
One lonely jailer could be overpowered

(but no wise injured). Deftly gagged and bound,
he'd raise no hue and cry, his gutturals drowned
   by sturdy walls and slapping fountain spouts:
until relieved at dawn, emit no sound.

About the scheme, she entertained no doubts.
There'd be no future for them hereabouts:
   this love meant exile. Christian and Moor
could never form a union. He who flouts

religious prohibitions must endure
a universal odium. Abjure
   the tenets of your father at your peril:
and live in infamy for ever more.

Religious rubric suddenly seemed sterile.
The rapture of release had wrought her feral,
   and canyons of conventional belief,
once amethyst, now seemed like fractured beryl.

She crept down to the dungeon like a thief.
The sun was down, and darkness brought relief.
   This danger that she courted might prove utter,
but as Tazgona knew, she would as lief

cease living as lose Tello. In the sputter
of feeble candle light, her heart a-flutter,
   she finds young Tello's cell. He is awake.
Around her, sleeping inmates sigh and mutter,

The key is in the lock, and no mistake!
The fortress of her father to forsake,
   as deft as Porphyro and Madeleine
they shift through shadows welcoming, opaque.

The knightly caste of medieval Spain
lacked property or wealth, could not sustain
   a stable marriage, even if allowed:
Tazgona had her motive. Plainly, gain

was not the god to which Tazgona bowed.
They picked a pathway through the sightless crowd
   of sleeping muslim warriors in the halls
to reach the castle yard. A single cloud

reveals – it frees the moonlight, as it crawls
across the firmament – the fortress walls
   and here, a small unguarded postern gate.
Now Tello acts. His whistle promptly calls

his horse, Fiel, who comes. They mount him straight,
and off they go. But, tragic to relate,
   the whistle has aroused the drowsing hordes,
and Jubril is alerted. He, irate,

demands pursuit. Boots thunder on the boards,
and moonlight glints on scimitars and swords,
　as men ride out, like flies in summer flock
to chase with all the haste that time affords.

For Tello, Antequera proves a shock.
A million tents and sentries closely block
　all access. Foes are following. What remains?
Tazgona points. It's obvious. The Rock.

As Fiel can feel a slacking of the reins,
he knows a thing is ending. For his pains,
　he's now without a master, who's en route
towards the summit. Treading goatherd lanes

go Tello and his love. In hot pursuit
come Jubril's men. Their crossbows cannot shoot
　in this restricted space. They have to scramble
up mountain gradients, ever more acute,

where none but *ibex musimon* may ramble,
where nothing grows but *prunus* and the bramble,
　this high above the *carex* and the sedge.
But this, on Tello's part, has been no gamble:

Tazgona, too, unspeaking, makes her pledge.
They come, at last, upon a windswept ledge.
　Without a common language they can share,
they're shifting resolutely to the edge.

as if one person. Creatures of the air,
they launched themselves into the dark. Thus their
　predicament became the best of cures:
escaped a fate for which they didn't care.

IL MULINELLO, Being the Story of Rimini, as related by Doctor Bartolomeo Albergotti

It smites you from a blue, untroubled sky.
At first, you thrill to feel its eddies play
and, quickened by exhilarating spray,
you feel a fierce necessity to fly.
It isn't always easy to descry
the gulf between protagonist and prey,
delight too often morphing to dismay:
the only time you fall is when you're high.
There's more to vortices than meets the eye:
illusions fade, and plans gang aft agley.
The varnish tarnishes and, by and by,
you'll find that brazen thighs have feet of clay.
You live for love, but love begins to die
the day the whirlwind wrenches you away.

STRAY LEAVES: MY MASTERY OF HISTORY

My mastery of history is spotty:
I know that Cleopatra was a queenie
in Africa (some kind of Hot 'n' Totty),
but did Muhammad sing, 'I Dream of Jeanie'?
A feud between two clans strikes me as dotty
(the Albergotti and the Guillichini)
like Leonardo versus Buonarotti,
or Susan Hayward contra Sonja Henie.

From Hakenkreuz to Horus hieroglyphic,
attachments are notoriously knotty.
Suppose we condescend to the specific:
some cleave to Plácido, some Pavarotti.
Pre-eminently, parties prove Pol-potty,
polemically, parochially prolific.

TWO FAMILIES IN CONFLICT IN RAVENNA
>	were looking for a truce.
As always happens, both sides chose to enter
(to extricate themselves from their Gehenna)
>	in marital abuse.
>	A fraud in all but name,
affectionless, a facile feud-preventor,
a Malatesta married a Polenta –
>	a diplomatic game.
To pull their radicals into the centre,
>	to change the mood, the tenor,
was each establishment's official aim:
but obviously this was an excuse.

The Malatesta factor had two brothers.
>	The elder, Giovanni,
was martial, yet his party's *ponte rotto*
(it's almost like these sons had different mothers!),
>	though logical and canny,
>	retained a secret shame.
A fitting sitter for Lorenzo Lotto,
Giovanni held the nickname of 'Gianciotto'
>	(in other words, 'the lame'):
Aut cessio aut ense was his motto.
>	Though courteous to others,
he rued his mutilation all the same,
and saw contempt in every nook and cranny.

But if we term Giovanni knave of hearts,
>	not made for sportive tricks,
we own his brother Paolo was the king.
This youth enjoyed in Adriatic parts
>	among Veneto chicks
>	a modicum of fame.
Of Paolo's handsome face the poets sing:
no stranger he to dalliance and 'fling'.

             And scarce a hatted dame
had he not courted on some garden swing,
             since Cupid's toxic darts
enabled him, upon a whim, to tame
both messroom-maid and modish meretrix.

The plan to catch a cute uxorial Esther
             appeared a tad outlandish,
the cripple being brutal and obtuse,
and not exactly Robert, Earl of Leicester.
             So, being underhand-ish,
             the Malatesta came
to this conclusion: 'why not put to use
young Paolo's charms? Let's play it fast and loose!'
             The victim in the frame,
the trussed and trusting juicy insouciant goose,
             wed *Paolo* Malatesta.
Such proxy orthodoxy, who can blame?
What girl would want to marry Captain Standish?

Francesca da Polenta was the bride.
             Disaster unalloyed
lay waiting for this unassuming child
whose fortunes underwent a fatal slide.
             Unable to avoid
the machinations of unscrupled men,
to doing others' bidding reconciled,
she found a love unbridled, violent, wild.
             This fragile little wren
Bestrode the vortex, rode the stormclouds piled.
             Exhilarating ride!
The whirlwind has to end, but only when
whoever's caught up in it is destroyed.

To pack the cripple off to Rimini
             to woo, would never do.

'Expose our failings to the public glare?
Reveal our defects to the bride-to-be?
       Don't ever say what's true –
       it goes against the grain.
Send Paolo as his proxy – have a care
to show ourselves as handsome, debonair.'
       (But fever in the brain
destroys all ploys. They started an affair,
       defied diplomacy:
Francesca was a milkmaid, and her swain
returned her love. Predictable, but new!

The wedding went ahead, as first conceived.
       Francesca understood
her obligations as Gianciotto's wife,
but still – against reality – believed
       that her *cognato* could
       (and this would need some tact)
continue to bring beauty to her life.
Giovanni, though, resorted to the knife
       and mercilessly hacked
his wife and brother, calling 'Lust is rife!'
       And so the sin was shrieved,
unravelling a misbegotten pact,
a love that could not come to any good.

ON 9 SEPTEMBER, 1698, IN THE EIGHTH YEAR OF THE PONTIFICATE ON INNOCENT XII, IN ADMINISTRATIVE BUILDINGS ATTACHED TO THE BASILICA OF SANTA CROCE IN GERUSALEMME, THE MOST ILLUSTRIOUS AND REVEREND MARCANTONIO VENTURINI, DEPUTY GOVERNOR OF ROME WHO HOLDS THE CRIMINAL BENCH, GIVES JUDGMENT IN THE MATTER OF TIGHETTI VERSUS THE CONVERTITES

STRAY LEAVES: 'A THING THAT'S ALWAYS COOL'

A thing that's always cool about an altar:
it has some worthy's shoulder-blade or knuckle
(I'm daring you to satirise, or chuckle)
within its fabric. Catholics don't falter:
so, whether it's in Yorkshire or in Yalta,
the sacred praying-bay with any luck'll
contain a relic, mega-holy, muckle,
with which our Enemy won't dare to palter.
Did anything of use survive the Flood?
Salt-water fish could breathe, as well as fresh?
And when it dried, 'this bit is Bangladesh' –
which dude decided that? And from the creche
of God's creation, salvage something Good
and put it in a table – Adam's wood!

The story of Pompilia ends today.
No further affidavit, plaint or suit
will linger like a winter haemorrhoid.
Just here, against the great Aurelian Wall,
we quash all claims, extinguish legal rites
which could arise, and say it from The Chair.

Recourse to Law will settle your dispute,
but you may see your fondest hopes destroyed:
one party loses, winner takes it all.
We judges say, you'd best avoid these fights,
and find a way to compromise, to share,
unless you are addicted to the fray.

This altarpiece of Reubens is devoid
of scriptural support: no word of Paul
adjures us, seek among the Israelites
these relics of Our Saviour, pure and rare,
this table of our office to inlay.
It's nowhere written down, but we've grown cute:

the letter of the law won't solve your brawl?
Well, human ingenuity invites
a class of bold interpreters to dare
to tease the truth out, balance, weigh, assay.
At last, someone must divvy up the loot:
for that, impartial judges are employed.

Defendants, then. The Corso Convertites.
Tighetti sues them as Pompilia's heir.
One argument, perforce, must fall away,
the other point of view must pluck the fruit.
So who the Court's concordance has enjoyed,
and who is thus consigned to caterwaul?

I'm looking out across our little square,
but feel somehow that Heaven's holding sway:
these trimmings of the judge's bench, though mute,
are with my thoughts, in some strange way, alloyed.
Of all the spots across this urban sprawl,
we've landed in the magickest of sites!

AN ANCIENT TEMPLE FLOURISHED ON THIS SPOT
(of Sol Invictus, so the experts say),
and Santa Croce keeps it up today:
the soil beneath your sandal soles is not
of Italy, and (lest it be forgot)
this wood, recovered in a distant May,
was brought to Rome, is proof against delay.
We humans dance our purposeless gavotte,
but Heaven is conducting al cembalo.
We won't get far without our holy lumber.
You'd plough a field? Far better, leave it fallow.
We think we'll change the world, but we encumber,
and what we judge profound is always shallow:
your lapis lazuli is mere burnt umber.

DEFENDANTS TO THIS SUIT, the Convertites,
ask me to hand to them the wherewithal
of someone else. Are they just flying kites,
or is their chose-in-action on the ball?
Do they have legal claim, or shameless gall?
The plaintiff says (although he's largely mute)
the nuns are wrong. The sisters stake their all
on statute: they may plunder ill repute,
and that's the law Tighetti must refute.

The Corso convent, sinister, ochroid,
is leaning on its customary rights
which, in the past, have often been deployed.
to seize estates of female sodomites,
and fallen women, who have spent their nights
obliging menfolk in return for pay.
Tighetti says this nastiest of slights
is groundless, and the nuns are making hay:
such defamation never should hold sway.

Of she who died, I'm certainly aware.
A year ago, and almost to the day,
I sat in judgment on a strange affair
fresh out of Castelnuovo. (By the way,
adultery was charged. To his dismay,
the husband – who was clearly paranoid –
was angry when I granted her a stay
for want of proof). Apparently annoyed,
he schemed her death. And thus she was destroyed.

How do we fall in love? The question's moot.
(Yes, even judges can be overjoyed
by golden hair, the tinkling of a lute.)
Pompilia knew her worth and surely toyed
with others' hearts. The pleasure hadn't cloyed!
She'd seen her parents die. And she, their heir,
(I say without a hint of schadenfreude)
possessed a minor fortune, and to spare!
It was pure luck to have Tighetti there.

So, do the Convertites have feet of clay,
or are they right to claim Pompilia's loot?
Can nuns conduct an erudite ballet?
Rapacious they, or legally astute?
(I've cocked the hammer: I'm about to shoot!)
I've done my best, according to my lights,
my ratio, all-embracing and minute:
and if my ruling never quite excites,
perhaps you'll grant the verdict hits the heights.

The whole thing renders down to one man's call.
One party weeps, the other punches air.
One judge holds many destinies in thrall,
but what alternative could e'er compare?
There must be judgment, even if we scare
young Lamparelli there, whose Parman drawl

we've grown to know. Should anybody care,
I'm giving up my offices this Fall:
this case, my border with Cisalpine Gaul.

We say, pronounce, dispose of and adjudge
adultery unproven, as between
Pompilia, and anyone at all.
It follows, if Pompilia's pristine,
No matter how you filibuster, stall,
this is a finding that you cannot fudge.
We thus restore Pompilia's reputation,
unfettered by the slightest perturbation.
All suits are rubricated null and void,
all claims against her, cancelled and destroyed.
She's free from menace, long-term and diurnal,
Reposing in a silence that's eternal.

The Call to Adventure

No blunder ever is the merest chance:
they happen for a reason. She was born
in circumstances which invited scorn.
The honest burghers looked at her askance,
but she was at the point of Shiva's lance:
a Ruth reliant on another's corn,
her future to an older man forsworn,
she passed four summers in a Tuscan trance.

Our sense of self is dangling on a string,
and patent certainties to which we cling
are not the boat: in fact they are the holes.
We see the surface ripples, not the spring
and, unaware that Destiny's a thing,
suppose ourselves the captains of our souls.

The Tomb of the Womb

We're dealt a hand at birth, and that's our lot.
You render sonnets from the Portuguese,
and all the while, you're dying by degrees.
The arc curves to the coffin from the cot:
our seven-score-and-ten is all we've got.
The high-wire act is framed by the trapeze,
our vaunted Liberty is that of bees:
a bailey circumscribes the proudest motte.
The birth-canal is just a nascent grave,
each breath a debt: one drawn, one less to pay.
The arc of justice is, at best, concave:
our deities, at best, have feet of clay.
No matter how we rave or misbehave,
we're sepulchred within our DNA.

The Womb of the Tomb

The earth which nourished you will eat you now.
How satisfying, not to be awake!
No boss's glare, no cut-off point to make!
No conscience-stinging furrow left to plough!
No medieval chancel to endow!
No hunger now to assuage, thirst to slake!
No hart annoys us, whimpering in the brake.
No sweat can blind us – no more fevered brow!
And *dolce far niente* here – what bliss!
Like mistletoe, the coffin's architrave
appeals to us, with promise of a kiss:
is anywhere as promising as this?
And though it's not exactly what we crave,
there's lots to say in favour of the grave.

Voiced and Unvoiced

Bring in the wings, abandon this position!
I'll take the melancholiest decision,
condemn myself to History's derision.
So much for Carthage's boundless ambition.
There will be time enough for inquisition
when none who took the field for this collision
reproach us with 'ineptitude' and 'vision'
in speeches redolent with erudition.
We know it isn't going to be nice.
Those banqueters, so effortlessly wise,
will never know Iberians are mice,
nor will they care. Who needs to analyse?
They'll never find their knackers in a vice,
or ever clasp a brother as he dies.

Brief Endorsement – handwritten, but unsigned, on the Backsheet of Giacinto Arcangeli's Trial Brief, dated 22 February, 1698

You'll understand the darkness drowning me
once you've perused this paper, which confirms
that now we name our principal in terms
of 'Guido, he of blessed memory'.
What use is ardent argument, rehearsed
so lavishly, loquaciously and laced
with learning? What's the point of wit or taste?
Of all my heartaches, this one is the worst.
The sentence in its strange severity
was carried out this morning. Someone raced
with what appears to me unholy haste
to judgment. And your own celerity
in culling proofs went, finally, to waste.
I know to whom this horror should be traced.

Ave, Atque Vale

Pompilia's dead, but lives as an idea.
A single line encapsulates the *oeuvre*.
The ones who are suppressed may also serve:
the model of the unloved wife (like Leah),
or those assassinated (think of Pia),
Pompilia played it straight (or did she swerve?)
Did Guido, too, his wedding vows observe?
(The rhyme's a little ropey? *Culpa mea*!)

Perhaps, because of her, some girls are freer:
Perhaps our modern women have more nerve.
Pygmalion commends his Galatea,
whose beauty shines from each unconscious curve –
the only immortality (it's clear)
that anyone can hope for … or deserve.

TO THE READER

They're playing God, they're re-inventing wheels.
The plaintiffs have exhausted their appeals,
and Time, as Thetis' son said, wounds all heels:
Maggiore lives on *neve al agosto*.
We're navigating (some) on even keels:
If Weisselberg goes federal, and squeals,
then Trump will understand how Gotti feels.
Art is not contraband, it's *contrapposto*.
You like your haikus? Not the biggest deals!
There's nothing square in Rome, except the meals.
The false one follows, but the real one steals!
You think you know your wine? You don't know *mosto*!
Who writes a word, his inmost self reveals:
I'm not of Arden, I'm of Ariosto!

Glossary of Foreign-Language Terms

PAGE	TERM	LANGUAGE	MEANING
30	Malevolenza, ipocresia	Italian	malevolence, hypocrisy
30	nonni	Italian	grandmothers
30	excisia	Italian	things excised
31	abbastanza abbagliante	Italian	fairly dazzling
31	ersatz	German	false
32	dorso	Italian	back
33	prodigi	Italian	prodigies
34	Barolo, bisi	Italian	red wine, peas in garlic
34	putta	Italian	woman of low standing
34	non il pane, ma il sorgo	Italian	not bread but sorghum
34	Smorto, sporgo	Italian	dull, sagging
35	sebbene si accorgo	Italian	even though I can see
36	cavatina	Italian	simple song, implying regret
39	impasto	Italian	dough
40	settine	Italian	theatrical scenery
42	Il faut avoir bonnes	French	You've got to have servants
43	tenuta	Italian	property
46	il fare lo gnorri	Italian	playing dumb
46	Il duomo per pieve	Italian	swapped the cathedral for the Pieve church
46	ma no secondo	Italian	but not according to
47	codino	Italian	pony-tail
48	atenti I gigli	Italian	beware the lilies
50	sbirri	Italian	amateur police
50	qui vive	French	on the alert
50	braccialetti	Italian	bracelets
50	fazzoletti	Italian	handkerchiefs
50	fanciulla	Italian	girl, young woman
51	distretti	Italian	neighbourhoods
51	torrion	Italian	bastion in a castle wall
51	condottiere	Italian	medieval warlord
52	poco fa	Italian	a short time ago
53	palle	Italian	balls (courage)
53	procesus fugae	Latin	elopement trial

PAGE	TERM	LANGUAGE	MEANING
57	pugnale genovese	Italian	dagger of Genoa
58	Lei di santa memoria	Italian	She of sacred memory
59	La vie, la morte, sont guidées par les noces chymiques	French	Life and death are guided by the Chemical Wedding
61	donnaccia / nonna	Italian	slut / grandmother
61	fallo	Italian	fault, error
61	sciacallo	Italian	jackal
61	ex intervallo	Latin	after a delay
61	É nella sua casa	Italian	He's where he belongs.
63	arguti	Italian	'the witty ones'
64	Veni et comedi, ergo vici	Latin	I came and ate, and therefore conquered
64	fuori le mura	Italian	outside the city wall
65	vermutti scuri	Italian	dark vermouths
66	la batalla delle chiese	Italian	the battle of the churches
66	senza sapienza	Italian	without intelligence
67	sottogonna, sottoveste	Italian	petticoat
67	Chè Vittoria, chè Colonna	Italian	What a victory, what a column!
68	Non me interessa peste!	Italian	Smells don't bother me!
69	tertium quid	Latin	third party
71	abusano	Italian	abuse
71	persona non plus grata	Latin	a person who is no longer welcome
71	cognato	Italian	brother-in-law
71	dis aliter visum	Latin	the gods saw it differently
74	traversar' il ponte	Italian	cross the bridge
75	indigeni	Italian	indigenous people
83	Adorata mia Signora, vorrei sapere ...	Italian	My adored Signora, I wish to know ...
83	Amatissima mia, Signora, io ricevo ...	Italian	My beloved Signora, I am in receipt of ...
83	raccogleticcia	Italian	badly-organised
83	burattini	Italian	puppets
83	ricatto	Italian	blackmail
85	amor es alegría	Spanish	love is happiness
86	cosí	Italian	thus

PAGE	TERM	LANGUAGE	MEANING
87	sempre	Italian	always
90	spassolo	Italian	hilarious
90	comme une ange	French	like an angel
90	rotrouenge	French	troubadour song
91	Je suis Marie, je suis de France. J'en ai besoin, je recommence: l'air est doux, le jour est bon, et je retourne d'Avignon: je me sens triste, je dis pourquoi. Je suis une femme (c'est mon envoi) si amoureuse mon oriflamme ma bannière autrefois fougeuse, n'est plus chère. Mon âme est las: si tu as aimé tu comprendras.	French	I am Marie, I am from France. I need it, I start again: the air is soft, the day is good, and I return from Avignon: I feel sad, I will say why. I am a woman (this is my chorus) so in love. My banner, my once fiery banner, is no longer dear. My soul is weary: if you have loved you will understand.
93	Frauendienst	German	duty towards women
95	Vous dites l'amour, je vois la chasse	French	You say love, I see the hunt
98	droits pour son seigneur	French	rights for her master
100	ispiratrice	Italian	inspirer
103	Dixit uxor, filia non est!	Latin	The wife said, she's not my daughter!
104	Nemo me lacessit ex Etruria	Latin	No-one from Tuscany bothers me!
108	camisa	Italian	chemise
108	Gl'Ingannati	Italian	The Tricked Ones
109	quartiere	Italian	neighbourhood
110	i zanni	Italian	the crazy ones
113	strada	Italian	street
113	nostromo	Italian	butler
113	Signora Majordomo	Italian	the butler's wife
113	marquese	Italian	marquess
113	genitore	Italian	parent
114	L'astuzia della donna è notoria.	Italian	Women's cunning is well known.
114	Avanti!	Italian	Forward!
114	boccheggiante	Italian	the gasping
115	coloratura	Italian	artificial adornment

PAGE	TERM	LANGUAGE	MEANING
116	La Bracchiera –buona gente!	Italian	"The Brazier" – a good sort!
117	Gli Innocente	Italian	The Innocents
117	scapoli	Italian	unmarried men
118	Orti di Napoli	Italian	The Gardens of Naples
118	Quindic'estati fa	Italian	fifteen summers ago
119	il miracolo	Italian	the miracle
120	comare	Italian	co-mother
120	sofista	Italian	sophist
125	altri bambini	Italian	other children
126	Rex Judaeorum, Res Judicata	Latin	King of the Jews, A Thing Already Adjudicated
133	Quello che impenna	Italian	the one that rears up
134	habito	Spanish	(nun's) habit
140	cap-a-pe	French	armed for action
145	favela	Spanish	slum neighbourhood
147	Terre-Sainte	French	The Holy Land
147	no digamos nada	Spanish	we're not saying anything
149	deformis et obscoenus	Latin	ugly and obscene
153	mea anima magnificat	Latin	my soul magnifies
153	le roi des raconteurs	French	the king of storytellers
153	uxoricide	Latin	wife-murder
154	ma irrilevante	Italian	but irrelevant
154	tutti santi	Italian	all saints
154	cognate	Italian	sister-in-law
158	le scalette	Italian	the steps
164	spendereccia	Italian	spendthrift
165	parruchiera	Italian	hairdresser
167	vita nuova	Italian	new life
169	cosí fan tutti	Italian	thus do they all
170	iscritto	Italian	signed-up member
170	spada	Italian	sword
179	carcele	Italian	prison
180	pozzo di Tofano	Italian	the well of Tofano
180	roman-à-clef	French	novel featuring real people
180	rimani cheto sul tuo pozzo	Italian	remain tranquil on your well

PAGE	TERM	LANGUAGE	MEANING
188	che la storia non sia scherzosa	Italian	let's hope it's not a funny story
188	sposa	Italian	wife
189	chi pesca	Italian	who fishes
190	Wirklichkeit	German	reality
191	quis custodiet ipsos custodes?	Latin	Who guards the guards?
194	spina	Latin	spine, central divide of the chariot-racing course
196	vernice fresca	Italian	wet paint
197	dell'isola della sardina	Italian	of the island of the sardine
203	L'Annonce Fait à Marie	French	The Announcement Made to Mary
203	galant'huomo	Italian	gentleman
203	le cognoscente, tutti, impiegano il dolce nuovo stile albertiano	Italian	all the people in the know are employing the sweet new Albertian style
207	rematore	Italian	rower
208	parenti acquisiti	Italian	In-laws
209	zitella	Italian	young maiden
209	ragazzina	Italian	young maiden
217	Soccorri!	Italian	Help!
220	loro trucchino	Italian	their schemes
221	menzognas	Italian	lies
221	faggioli	Italian	beans
222	aprendido de repente	Spanish	quickly learnt
222	irredente	Italian	unredeemed
227	spaccone	Italian	braggart
229	genero	Italian	son-in-law
231	cuento chino	Spanish	shaggy dog story
232	figlio di putto	Italian	son of a bitch
233	mazzo	Italian	bunch of flowers
234	senese	Italian	of Siena
240	pallina	Italian	little ball of fluff
240	vicina	Italian	neighbour
241	da ... fino	Italian	from ... to the end
248	obbligato	Italian	obligation imposed
249	che spavaldo	Italian	what a swaggart

PAGE	TERM	LANGUAGE	MEANING
250	fueros	Spanish	laws born of custom
250	pratese	Italian	of Prato
251	sangue caldo	Italian	hot blood
251	tuo fratello	Italian	your brother
251	podestá	Italian	magistrate
253	jabroni	various	fool
254	le gratin	French	the upper crust
257	samizdat	Russian	clandestine meaning
259	shiksa	Yiddish	non-jewish girl
259	hijo de puta	Spanish	son of a bitch
260	una orden	Spanish	a command
261	enthymeme	Greek	incomplete syllogism
263	Quelle Stesse Parole!	Italian	The Very Same Words!
263	Basta! Fuori!	Italian	Enough! Out!
263	Non mi regale con i tuoi fiori	Italian	Don't regale me with your flowers
263	Si puó?	Italian	Can you?
263	nido di memorie	Italian	nest of memories
263	sono ventitre le ore	Italian	it's at eleven o'clock
264	seguiriya, sarabande	Spanish	arcane dance rhythms
264	palco	Italian	theatrical stage
268	per sempre tua io sarò	Italian	I will always be yours
270	ragazze o pagliacci?	Italian	girls or clowns?
271	mente	Italian	mind
271	suaveté	French	smoothness
277	senza pausa	Italian	without pause
280	fons et origo	Latin	fount and origin
284	garce	French	whore
297	cittadina	Italian	small town
297	Mi ricordo tanto quando	Italian	I remember so well when
297	anche lei è molto bella	Italian	she is also very beautiful
299	tono molto sotto	Italian	a very low tone
302	leggere la sua buona	Italian	read how good she was
325	bisbiglia, a parte	Italian	whispers, aside
330	on y danse, tous en ronde	French	there they dance, all in a circle
330	albero	Italian	tree

PAGE	TERM	LANGUAGE	MEANING
333	a voce alta	Italian	aloud
333	lucerna	Italian	lamp
334	la donna cambia, alterna	Italian	the female changes, alternates
334	Entra, ragazzo, laggiù caverna	Italian	Enter, lad, this cave
337	cervo	Italian	deer
338	ante nos fuerunt	Latin	who went before us
339	stichomythia	Greek	short-line dialogue
347	campo dei miracoli	Italian	field of miracles
357	objets trouvés	French	found objects
357	Je vous en prie, ne faites-pas ce que vous pouvez	French	I beg of you, don't do what you can do
357	el hace su mejor, y enseguida	Spanish	he's doing his best, and soon
357	Zigeunerlieder	German	gypsy songs
358	ùltimo vestiggio	Italian	last drop
359	stretta	Italian	narrow
360	sotto I pini	Italian	under the pines (wooing)
362	piuttosto	Italian	rather
363	preciosa joven	Spanish	beautiful youngster
372	sganarelli	Italian	servants
372	déjeuner sur l'herbe	French	lunch on the lawn
373	tahona	Spanish	oven
374	Lo Sposo Deluso	Italian	The Disappointed Husband
375	Schauspiel	German	theatrical play
378	assedi	Italian	sieges
378	strambotto	Italian	a traditional verse-form
384	disprezzo	Italian	contempt
389	posada, manzanilla, dueño	Spanish	inn, a type of wine, landlord
391	Va, pensiero	Italian	Go, my thoughts
391	Com'è gentil	Italian	How gentle it is
392	La Cisterna	Italian	The Well
392	ma lei lo tollera	Italian	but they put up with it
392	Italia, sebbene sola, farà de sè	Italian	Italy, albeit alone, will do it for herself
393	lacunae	Latin	things that are missing

PAGE	TERM	LANGUAGE	MEANING
393	contrappunto	Italian	counterpoint
394	non dovrebbe essere permessa	Italian	it shouldn't be allowed
395	estranea	Italian	foreign girl
396	mens rea	Latin	guilty mind
398	donato	Italian	inherited
406	la salta de la contessa	Italian	the leap of the Countess
406	gentile donna senese	Italian	elegant Sienese lady
407	de Pietra	Italian	of stone
407	Maremma Amara	Italian	Bitter Maremma
409	il cazzo	Italian	the dick
423	starry chelovek	Russian	old man
425	Er war, einmal, eine leichteglaublige Volk, das glaubte an den wahren Weihnnachatsmann.	German	There was once a gullible people, who really believed in Santa Claus.
425	In Wirklichkeit, il Duce war der Gassmann!	German	In reality, il Duce was the gasman!
425	la peste	French	the plague
426	sortilège	French	magic spell
429	quod bene vixit, bene qui latuit	Latin	he who is unknown lives well
429	Das Blut ist ein ganz besonderer Saft	German	blood is a very special juice
430	die goede mannen warden nu gestraft	Dutch	it's good men who get punished now
430	graag gedaan	Dutch	my pleasure
433	finibus	Latin	borders
434	sans-réseau, pointe-duchesse	French	fashion terms (lace)
434	niente	Italian	nothing
437	lassit, cidit	Latin	gets tired, collapses
440	clavicembalo	Italian	harpsichord
442	Rupe Tarpea	Italian	Tarpean Rock
443	piastra de Petri	Italian	Petri dish
443	est mihi libertas	Latin	it's my freedom
443	imperialis	Latin	imperial
443	e l'uomo governa	Italian	and the man is boss
444	buricchia	Italian	undergarment
444	panciotto	Italian	waistcoat

PAGE	TERM	LANGUAGE	MEANING
445	sin embargo	Spanish	however
445	L'Escargot	French	The Snail
446	hermoso: peligroso	Spanish	noble, handsome: dangerous
452	lo daro	Italian	I'll give it
460	sol invictus	Latin	the undefeated sun
461	ma tutto era moltissimo piano	Italian	but everything was very flat
462	vetturino	Italian	coachman
463	nihil difficile amanti, sed	Latin	nothing is difficult for the lover, but
463	est deus en nobis, agitante calescimus illo	Latin	there is a god within us and his stirrings keep us warm
463	de te fabula, narratur	Latin	It is you that is spoken of in this fable
464	Astraea redux	Latin	the good times are back
465	il seicento	Italian	the 1600's
466	gozzo, gargarozzo	Italian	goiter, gullet
466	il paffuto	Italian	plumpness
468	tredici	Italian	thirteen (thirteen-liner)
470	coup de foudre	French	lightning strike
472	lutto	Italian	mourning
472	Cercherai invano	Italian	You will search in vain
472	sottobosco	Italian	undergrowth
477	La Modista Raggiratrice	Italian	the deceitful milliner
479	vano	Italian	vain
479	mano-a-mano	Spanish	hand-to-hand
479	le mille	Italian	the thousand
482	Prinzessin	German	little princess
483	echt	German	real
483	hat die geistige Welt verdienst	German	she deserved the spiritual world
489	Schwerpunkt	German	main thrust
495	mens sana	Latin	healthy mind
497	gagliarda	Italian	galliard
498	Judex est lex loquens	Latin	the judge is the law, speaking
498	gli otto	Italian	the eight

PAGE	TERM	LANGUAGE	MEANING
499	castigare, bonomia	Italian	punish, bonhomie
500	¿Y como explicar la Leonor, y su infelicidad?	Spanish	And how to explain Leonor, and her unhappiness?
500	Vespasian: decet imperatorem stantem mori.	Latin	Vespasian: an emperor ought to die on his feet.
500	hoc tibi est honori	Latin	this is your honour
500	domus et placens uxori	Latin	home and a pleasing wife
500	margarita e stercore	Latin	pearls amidst excrement
500	corpus sin pectore	Latin	a body without a chest
500	virtutis amore	Latin	the virtue of love
500	nugae canori	Latin	melodious nonsense
500	vincere aut mori	Latin	win or die
500	nil sin magno labore	Latin	nothing without huge effort
500	fructo cogniscitur arbori	Latin	the tree is known by its fruit
500	cedamus amori	Latin	yield to love
504	tavole calde	Italian	hot tables, street cafes
507	smarrita	Italian	Luisa-Maria, but also "lost"
514	Caperuça	Spanish	Little Red Riding-Hood
519	Il violincello del cardenale	Italian	The cardinal's cello
519	maddalena	Italian	Mary Magdalen
520	Il Matrimonio Segreto	Italian	The Clandestine Marriage
520	charivari	Italian	
520	si, se vede	Italian	yes, and it looks like it
520	gamba	Italian	viol da gamba, six-stringed cello
521	ortolan	Italian	victim
521	Lei? Dovrebbe sentirse obbligata.	Italian	Her? She should feel obliged.
521	Andromeda Liberata	Italian	Andromeda Set Free
521	Salute	Italian	Health (a church in Venice)

PAGE	TERM	LANGUAGE	MEANING
521	Timor mortis conturbat me.	Latin	Fear of death disturbs me.
524	Mit Brennender Sorge	German	With burning concern
526	poche immagini	Italian	not many images
526	serafini	Italian	seraphim
527	contrapposto	Italian	opposing positions
530	traquer le lièvre	French	hunting down the hare
531	questo, fuga	Italian	that one, elopement
532	il stridente	Italian	the jarring one
532	locus standi	Latin	reason for being included
534	Weltanschauung	German	world view
535	puttanas, chochos	Spanish	whores, vaginas
538	Gnädige Frau	German	gracious lady
539	suocera	Italian	mother-in-law
539	nuora	Italian	daughter-in-law
540	il borgo maestro	Italian	main street
540	capotari	Italian	men of the watch
540	le betulle	Italian	the birches
540	bastante	Italian	enough, quite
542	secondo il suo scopio empio	Italian	according to his wicked aim
553	boletos	Spanish	wild mushrooms
555	noli me tangere	Latin	none may touch me
560	éclat, élan	French	impact, high spirits
567	Ca'd'Oro	Italian	a palace in Venice
568	Sumpfesgeist	German	spirit of the swamp
569	im ganze Land ansicht	German	seen throughout the land
571	l'eminenza rossa	Italian	the red eminence
571	l'assedio	Italian	the siege
573	ponte rotto	Italian	a monument in Rome
573	ma sotto	Italian	but softly
580	mezzogiorno	Italian	Italy south of Naples
580	La Toscana	Italian	Tuscany
580	molto bella	Italian	very beautiful
580	novella	Italian	novel
580	nel suo turno	Italian	in her turn
580	forno	Italian	oven
581	sposa	Italian	wife

PAGE	TERM	LANGUAGE	MEANING
582	zoticona	Italian	female lout
582	contadina	Italian	peasant
582	cafona	Italian	low-class girl
582	puttarella	Italian	strumpet
591	sposa nuova	Italian	new bride
593	la ponderosa	Spanish	the marvellous one
601	meno male	Italian	things aren't so bad
603	qui-vive	French	on guard
604	cuore	Italian	heart, sweetheart
611	sciochezza	Italian	nonsense
614	poggio	Italian	hillock
620	sentit, ist	Latin	feels, is (nobler to be a feeling creature than merely to exist)
620	il facchino	Italian	porter, workman
620	il naso mio	Italian	my nose
621	concedo io	Italian	I concede
623	fille de joie, arriviste	French	pleasure-girl, chancer
624	dulcia venena	Latin	sweet poisons
624	aboulia	Greek	lack of will
625	Lex Cornelia de Sicariis	Latin	Cornelius' Law Against Assassins
625	Lex Julia	Latin	Julius' Law
625	sterculia	Latin	rubbish
625	foetida, urens	Latin	from faeces, or urine
625	quod indicat	Latin	which indicates
633	de minimis non curat lex	Latin	the law does not extend to trivialities
637	pluma aggravantes	Latin	aggravating feature
638	salsa, oca	Italian	sauce, goose
638	canzone	Italian	songs, poems of Petrarch
639	ex causa litis	Latin	to help yourself in your legal dispute
640	de raptu helenae	Latin	concerning the rape of Helen
640	manet	Latin	remains
640	timet, fidet mulier	Latin	the woman fears, trusts
640	Ubi sunt?	Latin	Where are they?
642	armorum igneorum	Latin	firearms

PAGE	TERM	LANGUAGE	MEANING
644	qui tacet consentire videtur	Latin	he who remains silent apparently agrees
645	nunc dimittis	Latin	you are now released
649	pizzicato	Italian	subdued style
649	obbligato	Italian	virtuoso style
651	ex intervallo	Latin	after an interval
660	Nur ein Bisschen!	German	Just a bit!
678	llanto	Spanish	lament
681	ci saranno nozze	Italian	there will be a wedding
690	voglia	Italian	will
692	pianto, dal mio santo, così tanto	Italian	cry, by my saint, so much
696	Wass denkst du über dieses alte Schloss?	German	What do you think of this old castle?
697	novus actus interveniens	Latin	new intervening act
697	contretemps	French	disagreement
704	venerdi santo	Italian	Good Friday
705	visum	Latin	very simple dream
705	insomnium	Latin	routine dream
706	oraculum	Latin	a dream containing a warning
706	visio	Latin	a dream predicting the future
706	somnium	Latin	a complex metaphorical dream
710	discanto	Italian	descant
712	in una volta	Italian	in one go
713	detto	Italian	called, known as
713	tal y cual	Spanish	so and so
717	ambo in foveam	Latin	both in the ditch
719	birruarri	Italian	men who shut the gate
720	ad rus ex urbe	Latin	from the city to the countryside
722	Vaya con Dios	Spanish	Go with God
722	nessun fumo senza fiamma	Italian	no smoke without fire
727	salvatrix	Latin	(female) saviour

PAGE	TERM	LANGUAGE	MEANING
727	Kulturgeist	Spanish	In the city named Seville the Gago alley can be found. It is where Don Santiago had his seat (or chair). His most elegant villa (here the myth is very vague), constructed with stones from the lake on whose beautiful shore (and where the sun always shines) passed Jesus Christ, The Master (forgive me if I'm taking too long): composed of a single floor (the house) which is a marvel, abandoned for lack of payments: there I will never go again, nor drink the bright manzanilla with Iago.
728	della mente o del cuore	Italian	of the head or the heart
729	rejones	Spanish	bullfighting on horseback
737	ojos vacios	Spanish	empty eyes
737	sibille, strappado	Italian	two legal forms of torture
747	memento mori	Latin	reminder of death
747	nido, pastor fido	Italian	nest, faithful shepherd
754	il gaudista	Italian	the fun-seeker
755	spiaggia	Italian	beach
756	il veleno	Italian	poison
756	pugnale	Italian	knife
756	nux vomica	Latin	a poisonous plant
757	Carceri Nuove	Italian	New Prison
761	mulier interfectae, consensu	Latin	murdered woman, agreed

PAGE	TERM	LANGUAGE	MEANING
761	no obstante	Spanish	nevertheless
764	vergogna	Italian	shame
765	de benedetta memoria	Italian	of blessed memory (dead)
766	sin embargo	Spanish	however
769	Si parliamo, in galere.	Italian	If we talk, it's in prison.
770	Esitare è perderé.	Italian	He who hesitates is lost.
770	Si scriviamo, impiccate	Italian	If we write, we hang.
770	chi scrive è spazzati	Italian	whoever writes is swept away
770	stiamo in quiete	Italian	we're at rest
770	siamo foraggio di prete	Italian	we are priests' fodder
770	Kulturgeist	German	spirit of our culture
776	calcinacci	Italian	rubble
783	maschilista	Italian	sexist
784	heraus	German	from indoors, outdoors
784	reus actus	Latin	guilty act
786	a poco a poco	Spanish	bit by bit
786	coup de foudre	French	lightning-strike (love at first sight)
793	favela	Spanish	slum
802	ibex musimon, prunus, carex	Latin	tough animals and plants
803	il mulinello	Italian	the whirlwind
803	Hakenkreuz	German	swastika
804	aut cessio aut ense	Latin	surrender or it's the sword
812	dolce far niente	Italian	it's sweet to do nothing
814	mosto	Spanish	crude, strong, first-press wine